Expositions of Ho

Second Kings Chapters VIII to End and Chronicles, Ezra, and Nehemiah. Esther, Job, Proverbs, and Ecclesiastes

Alexander Maclaren

Alpha Editions

This edition published in 2021

ISBN : 9789355341464

Design and Setting By
Alpha Editions
www.alphaedis.com
Email - info@alphaedis.com

Contents

THE SECOND BOOK OF KINGS

THE STORY OF HAZAEL

'So Hazael went to meet him, and took a present with him, even of every good thing of Damascus, forty camels' burden, and came and stood before him, and said, Thy son Ben-hadad king of Syria hath sent me to thee, saying, Shall I recover of this disease? 10. And Elisha said unto him, Go, say unto him, Thou mayest certainly recover: howbeit the Lord hath shewed me that he shall surely die. 11. And he settled his countenance stedfastly, until he was ashamed: and the man of God wept. 12. And Hazael said, Why weepeth my lord? And he answered, Because I know the evil that thou wilt do unto the children of Israel: their strong holds wilt thou set on fire, and their young men wilt thou slay with the sword, and wilt dash their children, and rip up their women with child. 13. And Hazael said. But what, is thy servant a dog, that he should do this great thing? And Elisha answered, The Lord hath shewed me that thou shalt be king over Syria. 14. So he departed from Elisha, and came to his master; who said to him, What said Elisha to thee? and he answered, He told me that thou shouldest surely recover. 15. And it came to pass on the morrow, that he took a thick cloth, and dipped it in water, and spread it on his face, so that he died: and Hazael reigned in his stead.'—2 KINGS viii. 9-15.

This is a strange, wild story. That Damascene monarchy burst into sudden power, warlike and commercial—for the two things went together in those days. As is usually the case, Hazael the successful soldier becomes ambitious. His sword seems to be the real sceptre, and he will have the dominion. Many years before this Elijah had anointed him to be king over Syria. That had wrought upon him and stirred ambition in him. Elijah's other appointments, coeval with his own, had already taken effect, Jehu was king of Israel, Elisha was prophet, and he only had not attained the dignity to which he had been designated.

He comes now with his message from the king of Damascus to Elisha. No doubt he had been often contrasting his own vigour with the decrepit, nominal king, and many a time had thought of the anointing, and had nursed ambitious hopes, which gradually turned to dark resolves.

He hoped, no doubt, that Ben-hadad was mortally sick, and it must have been a cruel, crushing disappointment when he heard that there was nothing deadly in the illness. Another hope was gone from him. The throne seemed further off than ever. I suppose that, at that instant, there sprang in his heart the resolve that he would kill Ben-hadad. The recoil of disappointment spurred Hazael to the resolution which he then and there took. It had been gathering form, no doubt, through some years, but now it became definite and settled. While his face glowed with the new determination, and his lips clenched themselves in the firmness of his purpose, the even voice of the prophet went on, 'howbeit he shall certainly die,' and the eye of the man of God searched him till he turned away ashamed because aware that his inmost heart was read.

Then there followed the prophet's weeping, and the solemn announcement of what Hazael would do when he had climbed to the throne. He shrank in real horror from the thought of such enormity of sin. 'Is thy servant a dog that he should do such a thing?' Elisha sternly answers: 'The Lord hath shewed me that thou shalt be king over Syria.' The certainty is that in his character occasion will develop evil. The certainty is that a course begun by such crime will be of a piece, and consistent with itself.

This conversation with Elisha seems to have accelerated Hazael's purpose, as if the prediction were to his mind a justification of his means of fulfilling it.

How like Macbeth he is!—the successful soldier, stirred by supernatural monitions of a greatness which he should achieve, and at last a murderer.

This narrative opens to us some of the solemn, dark places of human life, of men's hearts, of God's ways. Let us look at some of the lessons which lie here.

I. Man's responsibility for the sin which God foresees.

It seems as if the prophet's words had much to do in exciting the ambitious desires which led to the crime. Hazael's purpose of executing the deed is clearly known to the prophet. His ascending the throne is part of the divine purpose. He could find excuses for his guilt, and fling the responsibility for firing his ambition on the divine messenger. It may be asked—What sort of God is this who works on the mind of a man by exciting promises, and having done so, and having it fixed in His purposes that the man is to do the crime, yet treats it when done as guilt?

But now, whatever you may say, or whatever excuses Hazael might have found for himself, here is just in its most naked form that which is true about all sin. God foresees it all. God puts men into circumstances where they will fall, God presents to them things which they will make temptations. God takes the consequences of their wrongdoing and works them into His great scheme. That is undeniable on one side, and on the other it is as undeniable that God's foreseeing leaves men free. God's putting men into circumstances where they fall is not His tempting them. God's non-prevention of sin is not permission to sin. God's overruling the consequences of sin is not His condoning of sin as part of the scheme of His providence.

Man is free. Man is responsible. God hates sin. God foresees and permits sin.

It is all a terrible mystery, but the facts are as undeniable as the mystery of their co-existence is inscrutable.

II. The slumbering possibilities of sin.

Hazael indignantly protests against the thought that he should do such a thing. There is conscience left in him yet. His example suggests how little any of us know what it is in us to be or to do. We are all of us a mystery to ourselves. Slumbering powers lie in us. We are like quiescent volcanoes.

So much in us lies dormant, needing occasion for its development, like seeds that may sleep for centuries. That is true in regard to both the good and the bad in us. Life reveals us to ourselves. We learn to know ourselves by our actions, better than by mental self-inspection.

All sin is one in essence, and may pass into diverse forms according to circumstances. Of course characters differ, but the root of sin is in us all. We are largely good because not tempted, as a house may well stand firm when there are no floods. By the nature of the case, thorough self-knowledge is impossible.

Sin has the power of blinding us to its presence. It comes in a cloud as the old gods were fabled to do. The lungs get accustomed to a vitiated atmosphere, and scarcely are conscious of oppression till they cease to play.

All this should teach us—

Lessons of wary walking and humility. We are good because we have not been tried.

Lessons of charity and brotherly kindness. Every thief in the hulks, every prostitute on the streets, is our brother and sister, and they prove their fraternity by their sin. 'Whatever man has done man may do.' '*Nihil humanum alienum a me puto.*' 'Let him that is without sin cast the first stone.'

III. The fatal necessity by which sin repeats itself in aggravated forms.

See how Hazael is drifted into his worst crimes. His first one leads on by fell necessity to others. A man who has done no sin is conceivable, but a man who has done only one is impossible. Did you ever see a dam bursting or breaking down? Through a little crack comes one drop: will it stop there— the gap or the trickle? No! The drop has widened the crack, it has softened the earth around, it has cleared away some impediments. So another and another follow ever more rapidly, until the water pours out in a flood and the retaining embankment is swept away.

No sin 'is dead, being alone.' The demon brings seven other devils worse than himself. The reason for that aggravation is plain.

There is, first, habit.

There is, second, growing inclination.

There is, third, weakened restraint.

There is, fourth, a craving for excitement to still conscience.

There is, fifth, the necessity of the man's position.

There is, sixth, the strange love of consistency which tones all life down or up to one tint, as near as may be. There comes at last despair.

But not merely does every sin tend to repeat itself and to draw others after it. It tends to repeat itself in aggravated forms. There is growth, the law of increase as well as of perpetuity. The seed produces 'some sixty and some an hundredfold.'

And so the slaughtered soldiers and desolated homesteads of Israel were the sequel of the cloth on Ben-hadad's face. The secret of much enormous crime is the kind of relief from conscience which is found in committing a yet greater sin. The Furies drive with whips of scorpions, and the poor wretch goes plunging and kicking deeper and deeper in the mire, further and farther from the path. So you can never say: 'I will only do this one wrong thing.'

We see here how powerless against sin are all restraints. The prophecy did not prevent Hazael from his sins. The clear sense that they were sins did not prevent him. The horror-struck shudder of conscience did not prevent him. It was soon gagged.

Hear, then, the conclusion of the whole matter. Christ reveals us to ourselves. Christ breaks the chain of sin, makes a new beginning, cuts off the entail, reverses the irreversible, erases the indelible, cancels the irrevocable, forgives all the faultful past, and by the power of His love in the soul, works a mightier miracle than changing the Ethiopian's skin; teaches them that are accustomed to evil to do well, and though sins be as scarlet, makes them white as snow. He gives us a cleansed past and a bright future, and out of all our sins and wasted years makes pardoned sinners and glorified, perfected saints.

IMPURE ZEAL

'And Jehu gathered all the people together, and said unto them, Ahab served Baal a little; but Jehu shall serve him much. 19. Now therefore call unto me all the prophets of Baal, all his servants, and all his priests; let none be wanting: for I have a great sacrifice to do to Baal; whosoever shall be wanting, he shall not live. But Jehu did it in subtilty, to the intent that he might destroy the worshippers of Baal. 20. And Jehu said, Proclaim a solemn assembly for Baal. And they proclaimed it. 21. And Jehu sent through all Israel: and all the worshippers of Baal came, so that there was not a man left that came not. And they came into the house of Baal; and the house of Baal was full from one end to another. 22. And he said unto him that was over the vestry, Bring forth vestments for all the worshippers of Baal. And he brought them forth vestments. 23. And Jehu went, and Jehonadab the son of Rechab, into the house of Baal, and said unto the worshippers of Baal, Search, and look that there be here with you none of the servants of the Lord, but the worshippers of Baal only. 24. And when they went in to offer sacrifices and burnt offerings, Jehu appointed fourscore men without, and said, If any of the men whom I have brought into your hands escape, he that letteth him go, his life shall be for the life of him. 25. And it came to pass, as soon as he had made an end of offering the burnt offering, that Jehu said to the guard and to the captains, Go in, and slay them; let none come forth. And they smote them with the edge of the sword; and the guard and the captains cast them out, and went to the city of the house of Baal. 26. And they brought forth the images out of the house of Baal, and burned them. 27. And they brake down the image of Baal, and brake down the house of Baal, and made it a draught house unto this day. 28. Thus Jehu destroyed Baal out of Israel. 29. Howbeit from the sins of Jeroboam the son of Nebat, who made Israel to sin, Jehu departed not from after them, to wit, the golden calves that were in Beth-el, and that were in Dan. 30. And the Lord said unto Jehu, Because thou hast done well in executing that which is right in Mine eyes, and hast done unto the house of Ahab according to all that was in Mine heart, thy children of the fourth generation shall sit on the throne of Israel. 31. But Jehu took no heed to walk in the law of the Lord God of Israel with all his heart: for he departed not from the sins of Jeroboam, which made Israel to sin.'—2 KINGS x. 18-31.

The details of this story of bloodshed need little elucidation. Jehu had 'driven furiously' to some purpose. Secrecy and swiftness joined to unhesitating severity had crushed the dynasty of Ahab, which fell unlamented and unsupported, as if lightning-struck. The nobler elements had gathered to Jehu, as represented by the Rechabite, Jehonadab, evidently a Jehovah worshipper, and closely associated with the fierce soldier in this chapter. Jehu first secured his position, and then smote the Baal worship as heavily and conclusively as he had done the royal family. He struck once, and struck no more; for the single blow pulverised.

The audacious pretext of an intention to outdo the fallen dynasty in Baal worship must have sounded strange to those who knew how his massacre of Ahab's house had been represented by him as fulfilling Jehovah's purpose, but it was not too gross to be believed. So we can fancy the joyous revival of hope with which from every corner of the land the Baal priests, prophets, and worshippers, recovered from their fright, came flocking to the great temple in Samaria, till it was like a cup filled with wine from brim to brim. The worship cannot have numbered many adherents if one temple could hold the bulk of them. Probably it had never been more than a court fashion, and, now that Jezebel was dead, had lost ground. A token of royal favour was given to each of the crowd, in the gift of a vestment from the royal wardrobe. Then Jehu himself, accompanied by the ascetic Jehonadab, entered the court of the temple, a strangely assorted pair, and a couple of very 'distinguished' converts. The Baal priests would thrill with gratified pride when these two came to worship. The usual precautions against the intrusion of non-worshippers were taken at Jehu's command, but with a sinister meaning, undreamed of by the eager searchers. That was a sifting for destruction, not for preservation. So they all passed into the inner court to offer sacrifice.

The story gives a double picture in verse 24. Within are the jubilant worshippers; without, the grim company of their executioners, waiting the signal to draw their swords and burst in on the unarmed mob. Jehu carried his deception so far that he himself offered the burnt offering, with Jehonadab standing by, and then withdrew, followed, no doubt, by grateful acclamations. A step or two brought him to the 'eighty men without.' Two stern words, 'Go, smite them,' are enough. They storm in, and 'the songs of the temple' are turned to 'howlings in that day.' The defenceless, surprised crowd, huddled together in the dimly lighted shrine, were massacred to a man. The innermost sanctuary was then wrecked, corpses and statues thrown pell-mell into the outer courts or beyond the precincts, fires lit to burn the abominations, and busy hands, always more ready for pillage and destruction than for good work, pulled down the temple, the ruins of which were turned to base uses. The writer, picturing the wild scene, sums up with a touch of exultation: 'Thus Jehu destroyed Baal out of Israel'—where note the emphatic prominence of the three names of the king, the god, and the nation. That is the vindication of the terrible deed.

Now the main interest of this passage lies in its disclosure of the strangely mingled character of Jehu, and in the fact that his bloody severity was approved by God, and rewarded by the continuance of his dynasty for a longer time than any other on the throne of Israel.

Jehu was influenced by 'zeal for the Lord,' however much smoke mingled with the flame. He acted under the conviction that he was God's instrument, and at each new deed of blood asserted his fulfilment of prophecy. His profession to Jehonadab (ver. 16) was not hypocrisy nor ostentation. The Rechabite sheikh was evidently a man of mark, and apparently one of the leaders of those who had not 'bowed the knee to Baal'; and Jehu's disclosure of his animating motive was meant to secure the alliance of that party through one of its chiefs. No doubt many elements of selfishness and many stains mingled with Jehu's zeal. It was much on the same level as the fanaticism of the immediate successors of Mohammed; but, low as it was, look at its power. Jehu swept like a whirlwind, or like leaping fire among stubble, from Ramoth to Jezreel, from Jezreel to Samaria, and nothing stood before his fierce onset. Promptitude, decision, secrecy,—the qualities which carry enterprises to success—marked his character; partly, no doubt, from natural temperament, for God chooses right instruments, but from temperament heightened and invigorated by the conviction of being the instrument whom God had chosen. We may learn how even a very imperfect form of this conviction gives irresistible force to a man, annihilates fear, draws the teeth of danger, and gathers up all one's faculties to a point which can pierce any opposition. We may all recognise that God has sent us on His errands; and if we cherish that conviction, we shall put away from us slothfulness and fear, and out of weakness shall be made strong.

But Jehu sets forth the possible imperfections of 'zeal for the Lord.' We may defer for a moment the consideration of the morality of his slaughter of the royal house and the Baal worshippers, and point to the taint of selfishness and to the leaven of deceit in his enthusiasm. We have not to analyse it. That is God's work. But clearly the object which he had in view was not merely fulfilment of prophecy, but securing the throne; and there was more passion, as well as selfish policy, in his massacres, than befitted a minister of the divine justice, who should let no anger disturb the solemnity of his terrible task. Such dangers ever attend the path of the great men who feel themselves to be sent by God. In our humbler lives they dog our steps, and religious fervour needs ever to keep careful watch on itself, lest it should degenerate unconsciously into self-will, and should allow the muddy stream of earth-born passion to darken its crystal waters.

Many a great name in the annals of the Church has fallen before that temptation. We all need to remember that 'the wrath of man worketh not the righteousness of God,' and to take heed lest we should be guided by our own stormy impatience of contradiction, and by a determination to have our own way, while we think ourselves the humble instruments of a divine purpose. There was a 'Zelotes' in the Apostolate; but the coarse, sanguinary 'zeal' of his party must have needed much purifying before it learned what manner of spirit the zeal of a true disciple was of.

Another point of interest is the divine emphatic approval of Jehu's bloody acts (ver. 30). The massacre of the Baal worshippers is not included in the acts which God declares to have been 'according to all that was in Mine heart,' and it may be argued that it was not part of Jehu's commission. Certainly the accompanying deceit was not 'right in God's eyes,' but the slaughter in Baal's temple was the natural sequel of the civil revolution, and is most probably included in the deeds approved.

Perhaps Elisha brought Jehu the message in verse 30. If so, what a contrast between the two instruments of God's purposes! At all events, Jehovah's approval was distinctly given. What then? There need be no hesitation in recognising the progressive character of Scripture morality, as well as the growth of the revelation of the divine character, of which the morality of each epoch is the reflection. The full revelation of the God of love had to be preceded by the clear revelation of the God of righteousness; and whilst the Old Testament does make known the love of God in many a gracious act and word, it especially teaches His righteous condemnation of sin, without which His love were mere facile indulgence and impunity. The slaughter of that wicked house of Ahab and of the Baal priests was the act of divine justice, and the question is simply whether that justice was entitled to slay them. To that question believers in a divine providence can give but one answer. The destruction of Baal worship and the annihilation of its stronghold in Ahab's family were sufficient reasons, as even we can see, for such a deed. To bring in Jehu into the problem is unnecessary. He was the sword, but God's was the hand that struck. It is not for men to arraign the Lord of life and death for His methods and times of sending death to evil-doers. Granted that the 'long-suffering' which is 'not willing that any should perish' speaks more powerfully to our hearts than the justice which smites with death, the later and more blessed revelation is possible and precious only on the foundation of the former. Nor will a loose-braced generation like ours, which affects to be horrified at the thought of the 'wrath of God,' and recoils from the contemplation of His judgments, ever reach the innermost secrets of the tenderness of His love.

From the merely human point of view, we may say that revolutions are not made with rose-water, and that, at all crises in a nation's history, when some ancient evil is to be thrown off, and some powerful system is to be crushed, there will be violence, at which easy-going people, who have never passed through like times, will hold up their hands in horror and with cheap censure. No doubt we have a higher law than Jehu knew, and Christ has put His own gentle commandment of love in the place of what was 'said to them of old time.' But let us, while we obey it for ourselves, and abjure violence and blood, judge the men of old 'according to that which they had, and not according to that which they had not.' Jehu's bloody deeds are not held up for admiration. His obedience is what is praised and rewarded. Well for us if we obey our better law as faithfully!

The last point in the story is the imperfection of the obedience of Jehu. He contented himself with rooting out Baal, but left the calves. That shows the impurity of his 'zeal,' which flamed only against what it was for his advantage to destroy, and left the more popular and older idolatry undisturbed. Obedience has to be 'all in all, or not at all.' We may not 'compound for sins we are inclined to, by' zeal against those 'we have no mind to.' Our consciences are apt to have insensitive spots in them, like witch-marks. We often think it enough to remove the grosser evils, and leave the less, but white ants will eat up a carcass faster than a lion. Putting away Baal is of little use if we keep the calves at Dan and Beth-el. Nothing but walking in the law of the Lord 'with all the heart' will secure our walking safely. 'Unite my heart to fear Thy name' needs to be our daily prayer. 'One foot on sea and one on shore' is not the attitude in which steadfastness or progress is possible.

JEHOIADA AND JOASH

'And when Athaliah the mother of Ahaziah saw that her son was dead, she arose and destroyed all the seed royal. 2. But Jehosheba, the daughter of king Joram, sister of Ahaziah, took Joash the son of Ahaziah, and stole him from among the king's sons which were slain; and they hid him, even him and his nurse, in the bedchamber from Athaliah, so that he was not slain. 3. And he was with her hid in the house of the Lord six years. And Athaliah did reign over the land. 4. And the seventh year Jehoiada sent and fetched the rulers over hundreds, with the captains and the guard, and brought them to him into the house of the Lord, and made a covenant with them, and took an oath of them in the house of the Lord, and shewed them the king's son. 5. And he commanded them, saying, This is the thing that ye shall do; A third part of you that enter in on the sabbath shall even be keepers of the watch of the king's house; 6. And a third part shall be at the gate of Sur; and a third part at the gate behind the guard: so shall ye keep the watch of the house, that it be not broken down. 7. And two parts of all you that go forth on the sabbath, even they shall keep the watch of the house of the Lord about the king. 8. And ye shall compass the king round about, every man with his weapons in his hand: and he that cometh within the ranges, let him be slain: and be ye with the king as he goeth out and as he cometh in. 9. And the captains over the hundreds did according to all things that Jehoiada the priest commanded: and they took every man his men that were to come in on the sabbath, with them that should go out on the sabbath, and came to Jehoiada the priest. 10, And to the captains over hundreds did the priest give king David's spears and shields, that were in the temple of the Lord. 11. And the guard stood, every man with his weapons in his hand, round about the king, from the right corner of the temple to the left corner of the temple, along by the altar and the temple. 12. And he brought forth the king's son, and put the crown upon him, and gave him the testimony; and they made him king, and anointed him; and they clapped their hands, and said, God save the king. 13. And when Athaliah heard the noise of the guard and of the people, she came to the people into the temple of the Lord. 14. And when she looked, behold, the king stood by a pillar, as the manner was, and the princes and the trumpeters by the king, and all the people of the land rejoiced, and blew with trumpets: and Athaliah rent her clothes, and cried, Treason, Treason. 15. But Jehoiada the priest commanded the captains of the hundreds, the officers of the host, and said unto them, Have her forth without the ranges: and him that followeth her kill with the sword. For the priest had said, Let her not be slain in the house of the Lord. 16. And they laid hands on her; and she went by the way by the which the horses came into the king's house: and there was she slain.'—2 KINGS xi. 1-16.

The king of Judah has been killed, his alliance with the king of Israel having involved him in the latter's fate. Jehu had also murdered 'the brethren of Ahaziah,' forty-two in number. Next, Athaliah, the mother of Ahaziah and a daughter of Ahab, killed all the males of the royal family, and planted herself on the throne. She had Jezebel's force of character, unscrupulousness and disregard of human life. She was a tigress of a woman, and, no doubt, her six years' usurpation was stained with blood and with the nameless abominations of Baal worship. Never had the kingdom of Judah been at a lower ebb. One infant was all that was left of David's descendants. The whole promises of God seemed to depend for fulfilment on one little, feeble life. The tree had been cut down, and there was but this one sucker pushing forth a tiny shoot from 'the root of Jesse.'

We have in the passage, first, the six years of hiding in the temple. It is a pathetic picture, that of the infant rescued by his brave aunt from the blood-bath, and stowed away in the storeroom where the mats and cushions which served for beds were kept when not in use, watched over by two loving and courageous women, and taught infantile lessons by the husband of his aunt, Jehoiada the high priest. Many must have been aware of his existence, and there must have been loyal guarding of the secret, or Athaliah's sword would have been reddened with the baby's blood. Like the child Samuel, he had the Temple for his home, and his first impressions would be of daily sacrifices and white-robed priests. It was a better school for him than if he had been in the palace close by. The opening flower would have been soon besmirched there, but in the holy calm of the Temple courts it unfolded unstained. A

Christian home should breathe the same atmosphere as surrounded Joash, and it, too, should be a temple, where holy peace rules, and where the first impressions printed on plastic little minds are of God and His service.

We have next the disclosure and coronation of the boy king. The narrative here has to be supplemented from that in 2 Chron. xxiii., which does not contradict that in this passage, as is often said, but completes it. It informs us that before the final scene in the Temple, Jehoiada had in Jerusalem assembled a large force of Levites and of the 'heads of the fathers' houses' from all the kingdom. That statement implies that the revolution was mainly religious in its motive, and was national in its extent. Obviously Jehoiada would have been courting destruction for Joash and himself unless he had made sure of a strong backing before he hoisted the standard of the house of David. There must, therefore, have been long preparation and much stir; and all the while the foreign woman was sitting in the palace, close by the Temple, and not a whisper reached her. Evidently she had no party in Judah, and held her own only by her indomitable will and by the help of foreign troops. Anybody who remembers how the Austrians in Italy were shunned, will understand how Athaliah heard nothing of the plot that was rapidly developing a stone's throw from her isolated throne. Strange delusion, to covet such a seat, yet no stranger than many another mistaking of serpents for fish, into which we fall!

Jehoiada's caution was as great as his daring. He does not appear to have given the Levites and elders any inkling of his purpose till he had them safe in the Temple, and then he opened his mind, swore them to stand by him, and 'showed them the king's son.' What a scene that would be—the seven-year-old child there among all these strange men, the joyful surprise flashing in their eyes, the exultation of the faithful women that had watched him so lovingly, the stern facing of the dangers ahead. Most of the assembly must have thought that none of David's house remained, and that thought would have had much to do with their submitting to Athaliah's usurpation. Now that they saw the true heir, they could not hesitate to risk their lives to set him on his throne. Show a man his true king, and many a tyranny submitted to before becomes at once intolerable. The boy Joash makes Athaliah look very ugly.

Jehoiada's plans are somewhat difficult to understand, owing to our ignorance of the details as to the usual arrangements of the guards of the palace, but the general drift of them is plain enough. The main thing was to secure the person of the king, and, for that purpose, the two companies of priests who were relieved on the Sabbath were for once kept on duty, and their numbers augmented by the company that would, in the ordinary course, have relieved them. This augmented force was so disposed as, first, to secure the Temple from attack; and, second, to 'compass the king'—in his chamber, that is. We learn from 2 Chronicles that it consisted of priests and Levites, and some would see in that statement a tampering with the account in this passage, in the interests of a later conception of the sanctity of the Temple and of the priestly order. Our narrative is said to make the foreign mercenaries of the palace guard the persons referred to; but surely that cannot be maintained in the face of the plain statement of verse 7, that they kept the watch of the Temple, for that was the office of the priests. Besides, how should foreign soldiers have needed to be armed from the Temple armoury? And is it probable on the face of it that the palace guard, who were Athaliah's men, and therefore antagonistic to Joash, and Baal worshippers, should have been gained over to his side, or should have been the guards of the house of Jehovah? If, however, we understand that these guards were Levites, all is plain, and the arming of them with 'the spears and shields that had been king David's' becomes intelligible, and would rouse them to enthusiasm and daring.

Not till all these dispositions for the boy king's safety, and for preventing an assault on the Temple, had been carried out, did the prudent Jehoiada venture to bring Joash out from his place of concealment. Note that in verse 12 he is not called 'the king,' as in the previous verses, but, as in verse 4, 'the king's son.' He was king by right, but not technically, till he had been presented to, and accepted by, the representatives of the people, had had 'the testimony' placed in his hands, and been anointed by the high-priest. So 'they *made* him king.' The three parts of the ceremony were all significant. The delivering of 'the testimony' (the Book of the Law—Deut. xvii 18, 19) taught him that he was no despot to rule by his own pleasure and for his own glory, but the viceroy of the true King of Judah, and himself subject to law. The people's making him king taught him and them that a true royalty rules over willing subjects, and both guarded the rights of the nation and set limits to the power of the ruler. The priest's anointing witnessed to the divine appointment of the monarch and the divine endowment with fitness for his office. Would that these truths were more recognised and felt by all rulers! What a different thing the page of history would be!

The vigilance of the tigress had been eluded, and Athaliah had a rude awakening. But she had her mother's courage, and as soon as she heard in the palace the shouts, she dashed to the Temple, alone as she was, and fronted the crowd. The sight might have made the boldest quail. Who was that child standing in the royal place? Where had he come from? How had he been hidden all these years? What was all this frenzy of rejoicing, this blare of trumpets, these ranks of grim men with weapons in their hands? The stunning truth fell on her; but, though she felt that all was lost, not a whit did she blench, but fronted them all as proudly as ever. One cannot but admire the dauntless woman, 'magnificent in sin.' But her cry of 'Treason! treason!'

brought none to her side. As she stood solitary there, she must have felt that her day was over, and that nothing remained but to die like a queen. Proudly as ever, she passed down the ranks and not a face looked pity on her, nor a voice blessed her. She was reaping what she had sown, and she who had killed without compunction the innocents who stood between her and her ambitions, was pitilessly slain, and all the land rejoiced at her death.

So ended the all but bloodless revolution which crushed Baal worship in Judah. It had been begun by Elijah and Elisha, but it was completed by a high priest. It was religious even more than political. It was a national movement, though Jehoiada's courage and wisdom engineered it to its triumph. It teaches us how God watches over His purposes and their instruments when they seem nearest to failure, for one poor infant was all that was left of the seed of David; and how, therefore, we are never to despair, even in the darkest hour, of the fulfilment of His promises. It teaches us how much one brave, good man and woman can do to change the whole face of things, and how often there needs but one man to direct and voice the thoughts and acts of the silent multitude, and to light a fire that consumes evil.

METHODICAL LIBERALITY

'4. And Jehoash said to the priests, All the money of the dedicated things that is brought into the house of the Lord, even the money of every one that passeth the account, the money that every man is set at, and all the money that cometh into any man's heart to bring into the house of the Lord, 5. Let the priests take it to them, every man of his acquaintance; and let them repair the breaches of the house, wheresoever any breach shall be found. 6. But it was so, that in the three and twentieth year of king Jehoash the priests had not repaired the breaches of the house. 7. Then king Jehoash called for Jehoiada the priest, and the other priests, and said unto them, Why repair ye not the breaches of the house? Now therefore receive no more money of your acquaintance, but deliver it for the breaches of the house. 8. And the priests consented to receive no more money of the people, neither to repair the breaches of the house. 9. But Jehoiada the priest took a chest, and bored a hole in the lid of it, and set it beside the altar, on the right side as one cometh into the house of the Lord: and the priests that kept the door put therein all the money that was brought into the house of the Lord. 10. And it was so, when they saw that there was much money in the chest, that the king's scribe and the high priest came up, and they put up in bags, and told the money that was found in the house of the Lord. 11. And they gave the money, being told, into the hands of them that did the work, that had the oversight of the house of the Lord: and they laid it out to the carpenters and builders that wrought upon the house of the Lord, 12. And to masons, and hewers of stone, and to buy timber and hewed stone to repair the breaches of the house of the Lord, and for all that wast laid out for the house to repair it. 13. Howbeit there were not made for the house of the Lord bowls of silver, snuffers, basons, trumpets, any vessels of gold, or vessels of silver, of the money that was brought into the house of the Lord: 14. But they gave that to the workmen, and repaired therewith the house of the Lord. 15. Moreover they reckoned not with the men, into whose hand they delivered the money to be bestowed on workmen: for they dealt faithfully.'—2 KINGS xii. 4-15.

'The sons of Athaliah, that wicked woman, had broken up the house of God,' says Chronicles. The dilapidation had not been complete, but had been extensive, as may be gathered from the large expenditure recorded in this passage for repairs, and the enumeration of the artisans employed. No doubt Joash was guided by Jehoiada in setting about the restoration, but the fact that he gives the orders, while the high priest is not mentioned, throws light on the relative position of the two authorities, and on the king's office as guardian of the Temple and official 'head of the church.' The story comes in refreshingly and strangely among the bloody pages in which it is embedded, and it suggests some lessons as to the virtue of plain common sense and business principles applied to religious affairs. If 'the outward business of the house of God' were always guided with as much practical reasonableness as Joash brought to bear on it, there would be fewer failures or sarcastic critics.

We note, first, the true source of money for religious purposes. There was a fixed amount for which 'each man is rated,' and that made the minimum, but there was also that which 'cometh into any man's heart to bring,' and that was infinitely more precious than the exacted tax. The former was appropriate to the Old Testament, of which the animating principle was law and the voice: 'Thou shalt' or 'Thou shalt not.' The latter alone fits the New Testament, of which the animating principle is love and the voice: 'Though I have all boldness in Christ to enjoin thee ... yet for love's sake I rather beseech.' What disasters and what stifling of the spirit of Christian liberality have marred the Church for many centuries, and in many lands, because the great anachronism has prevailed of binding its growing limbs in Jewish swaddling bands, and degrading Christian giving into an assessment! And how shrunken the stream that is squeezed out by such a process, compared with the abundant gush of the fountain of love opened in a grateful, trusting heart!

Next, we have the negligent, if not dishonest, officials. We do not know how long Joash tried the experiment of letting the priests receive the money and superintend the repairs; but probably the restoration project was begun early in his reign, and if so, he gave the experiment of trusting all to the officials, a fair, patient trial, till the twenty-third year of his reign. Years gone and nothing done, or at least nothing completed! We do not need to accuse them of intentional embezzlement, but certainly they were guilty of carelessly letting the money slip through their fingers, and a good deal of it stick to their hands. It is always the temptation of the clergy to think of their own support as a first charge on the church, nor is it quite unheard of that the ministry should be less enthusiastic in religious objects than the 'laity,' and should work the enthusiasm of the latter for their own advantage. Human nature is the same in Jerusalem in Joash's time, and to-day in Manchester, or New York, or Philadelphia, and all men who live by the gifts of Christian people have need to watch themselves, lest they, like Ezekiel's false shepherds, feed themselves and not the flock, and seek the wool and the fat and not the good of the sheep.

Next we have the application of businesslike methods to religious work. It was clearly time to take the whole matter out of the priests' hands, and Joash is not afraid to assume a high tone with the culprits, and even with Jehoiada as their official head. He was in some sense responsible for his subordinates, and probably, though his own hands were clean, he may have been too lax in looking after the disposal of the funds. Note that while Joash rebuked the priests, and determined the new arrangements, it was Jehoiada who carried them out and provided the chest for receiving the contributions. The king wills, the high priest executes, the rank and file of the priests, however against the grain, consent. The arrangement for collecting the contributions 'saved the faces' of the priests to some extent, for the gifts were handed to them, and by them put into the chest. But, of course, that was done at once, in the donor's presence. If changes involving loss of position are to work smoothly, it is wise to let the deposed officials down as easily as may be.

Similar common sense is shown in the second step, the arrangement for ascertaining the amounts given. The king's secretary and the high-priest (or a representative) jointly opened the chest, counted and bagged up the money. They checked each other, and prevented suspicion on either side. No man who regards his own reputation will consent to handle public money without some one to stand over him and see what he does with it. One would be wise always to suspect people who appeal for help 'for the Lord's work' and are too 'spiritual' to have such worldly things as committees or auditors of their books. Accurate accounts are as essential to Christian work as spirituality or enthusiasm. The next stage was to hand over the money to the 'contractors,' as we should call them; and there similar precautions were taken against possible peculation on the part of the two officials who had received the money, for it was apparently 'weighed out into the hands' of the overseers, who would thus be able to check what they received by what the secretary and the high-priest had taken from the chest, and would be responsible for the expenditure of the amount which the two officials knew that they had received.

But all this system of checks seems to break down at the very point where it should have worked most searchingly, for 'they reckoned not with the men, into whose hand they delivered the money' to pay the workmen, 'for they dealt faithfully.' That last clause looks like a hit at the priests who had not dealt so, and contrasts the methods of plain business men of no pretensions, with those of men whose very calling should have guaranteed their trustworthiness. The contrast has been repeated in times and places nearer home. But another suggestion may also be made about this singular lapse into what looks like unwise confidence. These overseers had proved their faithfulness and earned the right to be trusted entirely, and the way to get the best out of a man, if he has any reliableness in him, is to trust him utterly, and to show him that you do. 'It is a shame to tell Arnold a lie; he always believes us,' said the Rugby boys about their great head-master. There is a time for using all precautions, and a time for using none. Businesslike methods do not consist in spying at the heels of one's agents, but in picking the right men, and, having proved them, giving them a free hand. And is not that what the great Lord and Employer does with His servants, and is it not part of the reason why Jesus gets more out of us than any one else can do, that He trusts us more?

One more point may be noticed; namely, the order of precedence in which the necessary works were done. Not a coin went to provide the utensils for sacrifice till the Temple was completely repaired. After they had 'set up the house of God in its state,' as Chronicles tells us, they took the balance of the funds to the king and Jehoiada, and spent that on 'vessels for the house.' A clear insight to discern what most needs to be done, and a firm resolve to 'do the duty that lies nearest thee,' and to let everything else, however necessary, wait till it is done, is a great part of Christian prudence, and goes far to make works or lives truly prosperous. 'First things first'!—it is a maxim that carries us far and as right as far.

THE SPIRIT OF POWER

'And Elisha said to the king of Israel, Put thine hand upon the bow. And he put his hand upon it: and Elisha put his hands upon the king's hands.'— 2 KINGS xiii. 16.

This is part of one of the strangest narratives in the Old Testament. Elisha is on his deathbed, 'sick of the sickness' wherewith he 'should die.' A very different scene, that close sick-chamber, from the open plain beyond Jordan from which Elijah had gone up; a very different way of passing from life by wasting sickness than by fiery chariot! But God is as near His servant in the one place as in the other, and the slow wasting away is as much His messenger as the sudden apocalypse of the horsemen of fire. The king of Israel comes to the old prophet, and very significantly repeats over him his own exclamation over Elijah, 'My father! My father! the chariot of Israel and the horsemen thereof.' Elisha takes no notice of the grief and reverence expressed by the exclamation, but goes straight to his work, and what follows is remarkable indeed.

Here is a prophet dying; and his last words are not edifying moral and religious reflections, nor does he seem to be much concerned to leave with the king his final protest against Israel's sin, but his thoughts are all of warfare, and his last effort is to stir up the sluggish young monarch to some of his own enthusiasm in the conflict with the enemy. It does not sound like an edifying deathbed. People might have said, 'Ah! secular and political affairs should be all out of a man's mind when he comes to his last moments.' But Elisha thought that to stick to his life's work till the last breath was out of him, and to devote the last breath to stimulating successors who might catch up the torch that dropped from his failing hands, was no unworthy end of a prophet's life.

So there followed what perhaps is not very familiar to some of us, that strange scene in which the dying man is far fuller of energy and vigour than the young king, and takes the upper hand of him, giving him a series of curt, authoritative commands, each of which he punctiliously obeys. 'Take bow and arrow,' and he took them. Then the prophet lays his wasted hand for a moment on the strong, young hand, and having thus either in symbol or reality—never mind which—communicated power, he says to him, 'Fling open the casement towards the quarter where the enemy's territory lies,' and he flings it open. 'Now, shoot,' and he shoots. Then the old man gathers himself up on his bed, and with a triumphant shout exclaims, 'The Lord's arrow of victory!... Thou shalt smite the Syrians till they be consumed.'

That is not all. There is a second stage. The promise is given; the possibility is opened before the king, and now all depends on the question whether he will rise to the height of the occasion. So the prophet says to him, 'Take the sheaf of arrows in your hand'; and he takes them. And then he says, 'Now smite upon the ground.' It is a test. If he had been roused and stirred by what had gone before; if he had any earnestness of belief in the power that was communicated, and any eagerness of desire to realise the promises that had been given of complete victory, what would he have done? What would Elisha have done if he had had the quiver in his hand? This king smites three perfunctory taps on the floor, and having done what will satisfy the old man's whim, and what in decency he had to do, he stops, as if weary of the whole performance. So the prophet bursts out in indignation on his dying bed— 'Thou shouldst have smitten five or six times; then hadst thou conquered utterly. Now thou shalt conquer but thrice.' A strange story; very far away from our atmosphere and latitude! Yet are there not obviously in it great principles which may be disentangled from their singular setting, and fully applied to us? I think so. Let us try and draw them from it.

I. Here we have the power communicated.

Now the story seems to indicate that it was only for a moment that the prophet's hands were laid on the king's hands, because, after they had been so laid, he is bidden to go to the window and fling it open, and the bedridden man could not go there with him; then he is bidden to draw the bow, and another hand upon his would have been a hindrance rather than a help. So it was but a momentary touch, a communication of power in reality or in symbol that the muscular young hand needed, and the wasted old one could give. And is that not a parable for us? We, too, if we are Christian men and women, have a gospel of which the very kernel is that there is to us a communication of power, and the very name of that divine Spirit whom it is Christ's greatest work to send flashing and flaming through the world, is the 'Spirit of Power.' And so the old promise that ye shall be clothed with strength from on high is the standing prerogative of the Christian Church. There is not merely some partial communication, as when hand touched hand, but every organ is vitalised and quickened; as in the case of the other miracle of this prophet, when he stretched himself on the dead child eye to eye, and mouth to mouth, and hand to hand; and each part received the vitalising influence. We have, if we are Christian people, a Spirit given to us, and are 'strengthened with might by the Spirit in the inner man.'

That gift, that strength comes to us by contact, not with Elisha, but with Elisha's Lord and Master. Christ's touch, when He was on earth, brought sight to the blind, healing to the sick, vigour to the limbs of the lame, life to the dead. And you and I can have that touch, far more truly, and far more mightily operative upon us than they had, who only felt the contact of His finger, and only derived corporeal blessing. For we can draw near to Him, and in union with Him by faith and love and obedience, can have His Spirit in close contact with our spirits, and strengthening us for all service, and for every task. Brethren! that touch which gives strength is a real thing. It is no mere piece of mystical exaggeration when we speak of our spirits being in actual contact with Christ's Spirit. Many of us have no clear conception, and still less a firm realisation, of that closer than corporeal contact, more real than bodily presence, and more intimate than any possible physical union, which is the great gift of God in Jesus Christ, and brings to us, if we will, life and strength according to our need. I would that the popular Christianity of this day had a far larger infusion of the sound, mystical element that lies in the New Testament Christianity, and did not talk so exclusively about a Christ that is for us as to have all but lost sight of the second stage of our relation to Christ, and lost a faith in a Christ that is in us Brethren! He can lay His hand upon your spirit's hand. He can flash light into your spirit's eye from

His eye. He can put breath and eloquence into your spirit's lips from His lips, and His heart beating against yours can transfuse—if I may so say—into you His own life-blood, which cleanses from all sin, and fits for all conflict.

Then, further, let me remind you that this power, which is bestowed on condition of contact, is given before duties are commanded. This king, in our acted parable, first had the touch of Elisha's fingers, and then received the command from Elisha's lips, 'Shoot!' So Jesus Christ gives before He commands, and commands nothing which He has not fitted us to perform. He is not 'an austere man, reaping where He did not sow, and gathering where He did not straw'; but He comes first to us saying, 'I give thee Myself,' and then He looks us in the eyes and says, 'Wilt thou not give Me thyself?' He bestows the strength first, and He commands the consequent duty afterwards.

Further, this strength communicated is realised in the effort to obey Christ's great commands. Joash felt nothing when the prophet's hand was laid upon his but, perhaps, some tingling. But when he got the bow in his hand and drew the arrow to its head, the infused power stiffened his muscles and strengthened him to pull; and though he could not distinguish between his own natural corporeal ability and that which had been thus imparted to him, the two co-operated in the one act, and it was when he drew his bow that he felt his strength. 'Stretch forth thine hand,' said Christ to the lame man. But the very infirmity to be dealt with was his inability to stretch it forth. At the command he tried, and, to his wonder, the stiffened sinews relaxed, and the joint that had been immovable had free play, and he stretched out his hand, and it was restored whole as the other. So He gives what He commands, and in obeying the command we realise and are conscious of the power. Elisha and Joash but act an illustration of the great word of Paul: 'Work out your own salvation ... for it is God that worketh in you.'

II. And now, secondly, look at the perfected victory that is possible.

When the arrows, by God's strength operating through Joash's arm, had been shot, the prophet says, 'The arrow of the Lord's victory! ... thou shalt smite ... till thou have consumed.' Yes, of course; if the arrow is the Lord's arrow, and the strength is His strength, then the only issue corresponding to the power is perfect victory. I would that Christian people realised more than they do practically in their lives that while men's ideals and aims may be all unaccomplished, or but partially approximated to, since God is God, His nature is perfection, and nothing that He does can fall beneath His ideal and purpose in doing it. All that comes from Him must correspond to Him from whom it comes. He never leaves off till He has completed, nor can any one say about any of His work, 'He began to build, and was not able to finish.' So, Christian people! I would that we should rise to the height of our prerogatives, and realise the fact that perfect victory is possible, regard being had to the power which 'teaches our hands to war and our fingers to fight.' A great deal of not altogether profitable jangling goes on at present in reference to the question of whether absolute sinlessness is possible for a Christian man on earth. Whatever view we take upon that question, it ought not to hide from us the fact which should loom very much more largely in our daily operative belief than it does with most of us, that in so far as the power which is given to us is concerned, perfect victory is within our grasp, and is the only worthy and correspondent result to the perfect power which worketh in us. So there is no reason, as from any defect of the divine gift to the weakest of us, why our Christian lives should have ups and downs, why there should be interruptions in our devotion, fallings short in our consecration, contradictions in our conduct, slidings backward in our progress. There is no reason why, in our Christian year, there should be summer and winter; but according to the symbolical saying of one of the old prophets, 'The ploughman may overtake the reaper, and he that treadeth out the grapes him that soweth the seed.' In so far as our Christian life is concerned, the perfection of the power that is granted to us involves the possibility of perfection in the recipient.

And the same thing is true in reference to a Christian man's work in the world. God's Church has ample resources to overcome the evil of the world. The fire is tremendous, but the Christian Church has possession of the floods that can extinguish the fire. If we utilised all that we have, we might 'smite till we had consumed,' and turned the world into the Church of God. That is the ideal, the possibility, when we look at the Christian man as possessor of the communicated power of God. And then we turn to the reality, to our own consciences, to the state of our religious communities everywhere, and we see what seems to be blank contradiction of the possibility. Where is the explanation?

III. That brings me to my last point, the partial victory that is actually won.

'Thou shouldst have smitten five or six times; then hadst thou smitten the Syrians till they were consumed. But now thou shalt conquer but thrice.' All God's promises and prophecies are conditional. There is no such thing as an unconditional promise of victory or of defeat; there is always an 'if.' There is always man's freedom as a factor. It is strange. I suppose no thinking, metaphysical or theological, ever has solved or ever will, that great paradox of the power of a finite will to lift itself up in the face of, and antagonism to, an Infinite Will backed by infinite power, and to thwart its purposes. 'How often *would I* have gathered ... and ye *would not.*' Here is all the power for a perfect victory, and yet the man that has it has to be contented with a very partial one.

It is a solemn thought that the Church's unbelief can limit and hinder Christ's work in the world, and we have here another illustration of that truth. You will find now and then in the newspapers, stories—they may be true or false—about caterpillars stopping a train. There is an old legend of that fabulous creature the remora, a tiny thing that fastened itself to the keel of a ship, and arrested it in mid-ocean. That is what we do with God and His purposes, and with His power granted to us.

A low expectation limits the power. This king did not believe, did not expect, that he would conquer utterly, and so he did not. You believe that you can do a thing, and in nine cases out of ten that goes nine-tenths of the way towards doing it. If we cast ourselves into our fight expecting victory, the expectation will realise itself in nine cases out of ten. And the man who in faith refuses to say 'that beast of a word—impossible!' will find that 'all things are possible to him that believeth.' 'Expect great things of God,' and you will feel His power tingling to your very fingertips, and will be able to draw the arrow to its head, and send it whizzing home to its mark.

Small desires block the power. Where there is an iron-bound coast running in one straight line, the whole ocean may dash itself on the cliffs at the base, but it enters not into the land; but where the shore opens itself out into some deep gulf far inland, and broad across at the entrance, then the glad water rushes in and fills it all. Make room for God in your lives by your desires and you will get Him in the fullness of His power.

The use of our power increases our power. Joash had an unused quiver full of arrows, and he only smote thrice. 'To him that hath shall be given, and from him that hath not shall be taken.' The reason why many of us professing Christians have so little of the strength of God in our lives is because we have made so little use of the strength that we have. Stow away your seed-corn in a granary and do not let the air into it, and weevils and rats will consume it. Sow it broadcast on the fields with liberal hand, and it will spring up, 'some thirty, some sixty, some an hundredfold.' Use increases strength in all regions, and unused organs atrophy and wither.

So, dear friends! if we will keep ourselves in contact with Christ, and tremulously sensitive to His touch, if we will expect power according to our tasks and our needs, if we will desire more of His grace, and if we will honestly and manfully use the strength that we have, then He will 'teach our hands to war and our fingers to fight,' and will give us strength, 'so that a bow of brass is bent by' our arms, and we shall be 'more than conquerors through Him that loved us.'

A KINGDOM'S EPITAPH

'In the ninth year of Hoshea the king of Assyria took Samaria, and carried Israel away into Assyria, and placed them in Halah and in Habor by the river of Gozan, and in the cities of the Medes. 7. For so it was, that the children of Israel had sinned against the Lord their God, which had brought them up out of the land of Egypt, from under the hand of Pharaoh king of Egypt, and had feared other gods, 8. And walked in the statutes of the heathen, whom the Lord cast out from before the children of Israel, and of the kings of Israel, which they had made. 9. And the children of Israel did secretly those things that were not right against the Lord their God, and they built them high places in all their cities, from the tower of the watchmen to the fenced city. 10. And they set them up images and groves in every high hill, and under every green tree: 11. And there they burnt incense in all the high places, as did the heathen whom the Lord carried away before them; and wrought wicked things to provoke the Lord to anger: 12. For they served idols, whereof the Lord had said unto them, Ye shall not do this thing. 13. Yet the Lord testified against Israel, and against Judah, by all the prophets and by all the seers, saying, Turn ye from your evil ways, and keep My commandments and My statutes, according to all the law which I commanded your fathers, and which I sent to you by My servants the prophets. 14. Notwithstanding they would not hear, but hardened their necks, like to the neck of their fathers, that did not believe in the Lord their God. 15. And they rejected His statutes, and His covenant that He made with their fathers, and His testimonies which He testified against them; and they followed vanity, and became vain, and went after the heathen that were round about them, concerning whom the Lord had charged them, that they should not do like them. 16. And they left all the commandments of the Lord their God, and made them molten images, even two calves, and made a grove, and worshipped all the host of heaven, and served Baal. 17. And they caused their sons and their daughters to pass through the fire, and used divination and enchantments, and sold themselves to do evil in the sight of the Lord, to provoke Him to anger. 18. Therefore the Lord was very angry with Israel, and removed them out of His sight: there was none left but the tribe of Judah only.'—2 KINGS xvii. 6-18.

The brevity of the account of the fall of Samaria in verse 6 contrasts with the long enumeration of the sins which caused it, in the rest of this passage. Modern critics assume that verses 7-23 are 'an interpolation by the Deuteronomic writer,' apparently for no reason but because they trace Israel's fall to its cause in idolatry. But surely the bare notice in verse 6, immediately followed by verse 24, cannot have been all that the original historian had to say about so tragic an end of so large a part of the people of God. The whole purpose of the Old Testament history is not to chronicle events, but to declare God's dealings, and the fall of a kingdom was of little moment, except as revealing the righteousness of God.

The main part of this passage, then, is the exposition of the causes of the national ruin. It is a *post mortem* inquiry into the diseases that killed a kingdom. At first sight, these verses seem a mere heaping together, not without some repetition, of one or two charges; but, more closely looked at, they disclose a very striking progress of thought. In the centre stands verse 13, telling of the mission of the prophets. Before it, verses 7-12, narrate Israel's sin, which culminates in provoking the Lord to anger (ver. 11). After it, the sins are reiterated with noticeable increase of emphasis, and again culminate in provoking the Lord to anger (ver. 17). So we have two degrees of guilt—one before and one after the prophets' messages; and two kindlings of God's anger—one which led to the sending of the prophets, and one which led to the destruction of Israel. The lessons that flow from this obvious progress of thought are plain.

I. The less culpable apostasy before the prophets' warnings. The first words of verse 7, rendered as in the Revised Version, give the purpose of all that follows; namely, to declare the causes of the calamity just told. Note that the first characteristic of Israel's sin was ungrateful departure from God. There is a world of pathos and meaning in that 'their God,' which is enhanced by the allusion to the Egyptian deliverance. All sins are attempts to break the chain which binds us to God—a chain woven of a thousand linked benefits. All practically deny His possession of us, and ours of Him, and display the short memory which ingratitude has. All have that other feature hinted at here—the contrast, so absurd if it were not so sad, between the worth and power of the God who is left and the other gods who are preferred. The essential meanness and folly of Israel are repeated by every heart departing from the living God.

The double origin of the idolatry is next set forth. It was in part imported and in part home-made. We have little conception of the strength of faith and courage which were needed to keep the Jews from becoming idolaters, surrounded as they were by such. But the same are needed to-day to keep us from learning the ways of the world and getting a snare to our souls. Now, as ever, walking with God means walking in the opposite direction from the crowd, and that requires some firm nerve. The home-made idolatry is gibbeted as being according to 'the statutes of the kings.' What right had they to prescribe their subjects' religion? The influence of influential people, especially if exerted against the service of God, is hard to resist; but it is no excuse for sin that it is fashionable.

The blindness of Israel to the consequences of their sin is hinted in the reference to the fate of the nations whom they imitated. They had been cast out; would not their copyists learn the lesson? We, too, have examples enough of what godless lives come to, if we had the sense to profit by them. The God who cast out the vile Canaanites and all the rest of the wicked crew before the sons of the desert has not changed, and will treat Israel as He did them, if Israel come down to their level. Outward privileges make idolatry or any sin more sinful, and its punishment more severe.

Another characteristic of Israel's sin is its being done 'secretly.' Of the various meanings proposed for that word (ver. 9) the best seems to be that it refers to the attempt to combine the worship of God and of idols, of which the calf worship is an instance. Elijah had long ago taunted the people with trying 'to hobble on both knees,' or on 'two opinions' at once; and here the charge is of covering idolatry with a cloak of Jehovah worship. A varnish of religion is convenient and cheap, and often effectual in deceiving ourselves as well as others; but 'as a man thinketh in his heart, so is he,' whatever his cloak may be; and the thing which we count most precious and long most for is our god, whatever our professions of orthodox religion.

The idolatry is then described, in rapid touches, as universal. Wherever there was a solitary watchman's tower among the pastures there was a high place, and they were reared in every city. Images and Asherim deformed every hill-top and stood under every spreading tree. Everywhere incense loaded the heavy air with its foul fragrance. The old scenes of unnamable abomination, which had been so terribly avenged, seemed to have come back, and to cry aloud for another purging by fire and sword.

The terrible upshot of all was 'to provoke the Lord to anger.' The New Testament is as emphatic as the Old in asserting that there is the capacity of anger in the God whose name is love, and that sin calls it forth. The special characteristic of sin, by which it thus attracts that lightning, is that it is disobedience. As in the first sin, so in all others, God has said, 'Ye shall not do this thing'; and we say, 'Do it we will.' What can the end of that be but the anger of the Lord? 'Because of these things cometh the wrath of God upon the children of disobedience.'

II. Verse 13 gives the pleading of Jehovah. The mission of the prophets was God's reply to Israel's rebellion, and was equally the sign of His anger and of His love. The more sin abounds, the more does God multiply means to draw back to Himself. The deafer the ears, the louder the beseeching voice of His grieved and yet pitying love. His anger clothes itself in more stringent appeals and clearer revelations of Himself before it takes its slaughtering weapons in hand. The darker the background of sin, the brighter the beams of His light show against it. Man's sin is made the occasion for a more glorious display of God's character and heart. It is on the storm-cloud that the sun paints the rainbow. Each successive stage in man's departure from

God evoked a corresponding increase in the divine effort to attract him back, till 'last of all He sent unto them His Son.' In nature, attraction diminishes as distance increases; in the realms of grace, it grows with distance. The one desire of God's heart is that sinners would return from their evil ways, and He presses on them the solemn thought of the abundant intimations of His will which have been given from of old, and are pealed again into all ears by living voices. His law for us is not merely an old story spoken centuries ago, but is vocal in our consciences to-day, and fresh as when Sinai flamed and thundered above the camp, and the trumpet thrilled each heart.

III. The heavier sin that followed the divine pleading. That divine voice leaves no man as it finds him. If it does not sway him to obedience, it deepens his guilt, and makes him more obstinate. Like some perverse ox in the yoke, he stiffens his neck, and stands the very picture of brute obduracy. There is an awful alternative involved in our hearing of God's message, which never returns to Him void, but ever does something to the hearer, either softening or hardening, either scaling the eyes or adding another film on them, either being the 'savour of life unto life or of death unto death.' The mission of the prophets changed forgetfulness of God's 'statutes' into 'rejection' of them, and made idolatry self-conscious rebellion. Alas, that men should make what is meant to be a bond to unite them to God into a wedge to part them farther from Him! But how constantly that is the effect of the gospel, and for the same reason as in Israel—that they 'did not believe in the Lord their God'!

The miserable result on the sinners' own natures is described with pregnant brevity in verse 15. 'They followed vanity, and became vain.' The worshipper became like the thing worshipped, as is always the case. The idol is vanity, utter emptiness and nonentity; and whoever worships nothingness will become in his own inmost life as empty and vain as it is. That is the retribution attendant on all trust in, and longing after, the trifles of earth, that we come down to the level of what we set our hearts upon. We see the effects of that principle in the moral degradation of idolaters. Gods lustful, cruel, capricious, make men like themselves. We see it working upwards in Christianity, in which God becomes man that men may become like God, and of which the whole law is put into one precept, which is sure to be kept, in the measure of the reality of a man's religion. 'Be ye therefore imitators of God, as beloved children.'

In verses 16 and 17 the details of the idolatry follow the general statement, as in verses 9 to 12, but with additions and with increased severity of tone. We hear now of calves and star worship, and Baal, and burning children to Moloch, and divination and enchantment. The catalogue is enlarged, and there is added to it the terrible declaration that Israel had 'sold themselves to do evil in the sight of the Lord.' The same thing was said by Elijah to Ahab— a noble instance of courage. The sinner who steels himself against the divine remonstrance, does not merely go on in his old sins, but adds new ones. Begin with the calves, and fancy that you are worshipping Jehovah, and you will end with Baal and Moloch. Refuse to hear God's pleadings, and you will sell your freedom, and become the lowest and only real kind of slave—the bondsman of evil. When that point of entire abandonment to sin, which Paul calls being 'sold under sin,' is reached, as it may be reached, at all events by a nation, and corruption has struck too deep to be cast out, once again the anger of the Lord is provoked; but this time it comes in a different guise. The armies of the Assyrians, not the prophets, are its messengers now. Israel had made itself like the nations whom God had used it to destroy, and now it shall be destroyed as they were.

To be swept out of His sight is the fate of obstinate rejection of His commandments and pleadings. Israel made itself the slave of evil, and was made the captive of Assyria. Self-willed freedom, which does as it likes, and heeds not God, ends in bondage, and is itself bondage. God's anger against sin speaks pleadingly to us all, saying, 'Do not this abominable thing that I hate.' Well for us if we hearken to His voice when 'His anger is kindled but a little.' If we do not yield to Him, and cast away our idols, we shall become vain as they. Our evil will be more fatal, and our obstinacy more criminal, because He called, and we refused. 'Who may abide the day of His coming? and who shall stand when He appeareth?' These captives, dragging their weary limbs, with despair in their hearts, across the desert to a land of bondage, were but shadows, in the visible region of things, of the far more doleful and dreary fate that sooner or later must fall on those who would none of God's counsel, and despised all His reproof, but cling to their idol till they and it are destroyed together.

DIVIDED WORSHIP

'These nations feared the Lord, and served their own gods.'—2 KINGS xvii. 33.

The kingdom of Israel had come to its fated end. Its king and people had been carried away captives in accordance with the cruel policy of the great Eastern despotisms, which had so much to do with weakening them by their very conquests. The land had lain desolate and uncultivated for many years, savage beasts had increased in the untilled solitudes, even as weeds and nettles grew in the gardens and vineyards of Samaria. At last the king of Assyria resolved to people the country; and for this purpose he sent a mixed multitude from the different nationalities of his empire to the land of Israel. They were men of five nationalities, most of them recently conquered. Israel had been deported to different parts of the Assyrian empire; men from different parts of the empire were deported to the land of Israel. Such cruel uprootings seemed to be wisdom, but were really a policy that kept alive disaffection. It was the same mistake (and bore the same fruits) as Austria pursued in sending Hungarian regiments to keep down Venice, and Venetian-born soldiers to overawe Hungary.

These new settlers brought with them their national peculiarities, and among the rest, their gods. They knew nothing about the Jehovah whom they supposed to be the local deity of Israel; and when they were troubled by the wild beasts which had, of course, rapidly increased in the land, they attributed it to their neglect of His worship, and sent an embassy to the king of Assyria telling that as they 'know not the manners of the God of the land,' He has sent lions among them.

This is an instructive example of the heathen way of thinking. They have their local deities. Each land, each valley, each mountain top, has its own. They are ready to worship them all, for they have no real worship for any. Their reason for worship is to escape from harm, to pay the tribute to which the god has a right on his own territory, lest he should make it the worse for them if they neglect it. 'The mild tolerance of heathendom' simply means the utter absence of religion and an altogether inadequate notion of deity.

So the settlers have sent to them one of these schismatic priests who had belonged to the extinct sanctuary at Beth-el, and he, apparently, not having any truer notions of God or of worship than they had, nothing loth, teaches them the rites of the Israelite worship, which was not like that of Judah, as is distinctly stated in the context. This worship of Jehovah was, however, blended by them with their own national idolatry. How contemptuously the historian enumerates the hard names of their gods and the rabble rout of them which each nation made! 'The men of Babylon *made* Succoth-benoth' (probably a deity, though the name may mean booths for purposes of prostitution) and the others '*made* Nergal and Ashima and Nibhaz and Tartak.' What names, and what a pantheon! 'They feared the Lord and served their own gods.'

This was the beginning of the Samaritan people, whom we find through the rest of Scripture even down to the Acts of the Apostles, retaining some trace of their heathen origin. Simon Magus bewitched them in his sorceries. They began as heathen, though in lapse of years they came to be pure monotheists, even more rigid than the Jews themselves, and today, if you went to Nablus, you would find the small remnant of their descendants adhering to Moses and the law, guarding their sacred copy of the Pentateuch with unintelligent awe, and eating the Paschal Lamb with wild rites. They have changed the object of their worship, but one fears that it is little more real and deep than in old days, 2500 years ago, when their forefathers 'feared the Lord and served their own gods.'

Now I venture to take this verse as indicative of a tendency which belongs to a great many more people than the confused mass of settlers that were shot down on the hills of Israel by the king of Assyria. It is really a description of a great deal of what goes by the name of religion amongst us.

I. The Religion of Fear.

These people would never have thought about God if it had not been for the lions. When they did think of Him it was only to tremble before Him. The reason for their trembling was that they did not know the etiquette of His worship; that they thought of Him as having rights over them because they had come into His territory, which He would exact, or punish them for omitting. In a word, their notion of God was that of a jealous, capricious tyrant, whose ways were inscrutable to them, in whose territory they found themselves without their will, and who needed to be propitiated if they would live in peace.

And this is the thought which is most operative in many minds, though it is veiled in more seemly phrases, and which darkens and injures all those on whom it lays hold. Need I spend time in showing you how, point by point, this picture is a picture of many among us? How many of you think of God when you are ill, and forget Him when you are well? How many of you pour out a prayer when you are in trouble, and forget all about Him and it when you are prosperous? How many of you see God in your calamities and not in your joys? Why do people call sudden deaths and the like the 'visitation of God'? How many of us are like Italian sailors who burn candles and shriek out to the Madonna when the storm catches them, and get drunk in the first wine-shop which they come to when they land! Is not many a man's thought of God, 'I knew Thee that Thou wert an austere Man, and I was afraid'?

The popular religion is largely a religion of fear.

There is a fear which is right and noble. That is reverend, humble adoration at the sight or thought of God's great perfections. Angels veil their faces with their wings. Such awe has no thought of personal consequences— is inseparable from all true knowledge of God; for all greatness of character is perfected by love. Of such fear we are not now speaking.

Terror of God is deep in men's hearts.

Fear is the apprehension of personal evil from some person or thing. Now I believe that terror has its place in the human economy, and in religion, as the sense of pain has. There is something in man's relations to God to cause it.

The Bible sets forth 'the terror of the Lord,' that men may tremble before Him. Moses said, 'I exceedingly fear and quake.' But that terror is only right when it proceeds from a sense of God's holiness and a consciousness of my own sinfulness. It is not right when it is a mere dread of a hard tyrant. That terror is only right when it leads to a joyful acceptance of God's revelation of His love in Christ.

Fear was never meant to be permanent, it is only the alarum-bell which rings to wake up the soul that sleeps on when in mortal peril. And it should pass into penitence, faith, joy in Jesus. 'We have access with confidence by the faith of Him.' The brightness is great and awful, but go nearer, as you can in Jesus, and lo! there is love in the brightness. You see it all tender and sweet. A heart and a hand are there, and from the midst of it the Father's voice speaks, and says, 'My son, give Me thine heart.'

The religion of fear is worthless. It produces no holiness, it does nothing for a man, it does not bind him to God. He is none the stronger for it. It paralyses so far as it does anything.

It is spasmodic and intermittent. It is impossible to keep it up, so it comes in fits and starts. When the morning comes men laugh at their terrors. It leads to wild endeavours to forget God—atheism—to insensibility. He who begins by fearing when there was no need, ends by not fearing when he ought.

II. The Religion of Form.

The Samaritans' whole worship was outward worship. They did the things which the Beth-el priest taught them to do, and that was all.

And this again is a type, very common in our day. Religion must have forms. The forms often help to bring us the spirit. But we are always in danger of trusting to them too much.

How many of us have our Christianity only in outward seeming? The only thing that unites men to God is love.

So your external connection with God's worship is of no use at all unless you have that.

Church and chapel-goers are alike exposed to the danger of erecting the forms of worship to a place in which they cannot be put without marring the spirit of worship. Whether our worship be more or less symbolic, whether we have a more or less elaborate ritual, whether we think more or less of sacraments, whether we put hearing a sermon as more or less prominent, or even if we follow the formless forms of the Friends, we are all tempted to substitute our forms for the spirit which alone is worship.

III. The Religion of Compromise or Worldliness.

They had God and they had gods. They liked the latter best. They gave God formal worship, but they gave the others more active service.

Such a kind of religion is a type of much that we see around us; the attempt to be Christians and worldlings, the indecision under which many men labour all their lives, being drawn one way by their consciences, another by their inclinations.

You cannot unite the two. God requires all. He fills the heart, and claims supreme control over all the nature. There cannot be two supreme in the soul. It cannot be God and self. It must be God or self. You may look now one way and now another, but the way the heart goes is the thing. Mr. Facing-both-ways does not really face both ways. He only turns quickly round from one to the other.

Such divided religion is impossible in the nature of God—of the soul—of religion.

To attempt it, then, is really to decide against God.

It is weak and unmanly to be thus vague and decided by circumstances. You would have been a Mohammedan if you had been born in Turkey.

You ought to decide for God.

He claims, He deserves, He will reward and bless, your whole soul.

'Choose you this day whom ye will serve. If the Lord be God, follow Him' If Baal or Succoth-benoth, then follow him. 'You cannot serve God and Mammon.' 'He that is not for us is against us.' Be one thing or the other.

HEZEKIAH, A PATTERN OF DEVOUT LIFE

'Hezekiah trusted in the Lord God of Israel.... 6. He clave to the Lord, and departed not from following Him, but kept His commandments.'—2 KINGS xviii. 5,6.

Devout people in all ages and stations are very much like each other. The elements of godliness are always the same. This king of Israel, something like two thousand six hundred years ago, and the humblest Christian to-day have the family likeness on their faces. These words, which are an outline sketch of the king's character, are really a sketch of the religious life at all times and in all places. He realised it; why may not we? He achieved it amid much ignorance; why should not we amid our blaze of knowledge? He accomplished it amid the temptations of a monarchy; why should not we in our humbler spheres?

There are four things set forth here as constituting a religious life. We begin at the bottom with the foundation of everything. 'He trusted in the Lord God of Israel.' The Old Testament is just as emphatic in declaring that there is no religion without trust, and that trust is the very nerve and life-blood of religion, as is the New. Only that in the one half of the book our translators have chosen to use the word 'trust,' and in the other half of the book they have chosen to use, for the very same act, the word 'faith.' They have thus somewhat obscured the absolute identity which exists in the teaching of the Old and of the New Testament as regards the bond which unites men to God. That union always was, and always will be, begun in the simple attitude and exercise of trust, and everything else will come out of that, and without that nothing else will come.

So this king had a certain measure of knowledge about the character of God, and that measure of knowledge led him to lean all his weight upon the Lord. You and I know a great deal more about God and His ways and purposes than Hezekiah did, but we can make no better use of it than he did—translate our knowledge into faith, and rely with simple, absolute confidence on Him whose name we know in Christ more fully and blessedly than was possible to Hezekiah.

And need I remind you of how, in this life of which the outline is here given and the inmost secret is here disclosed, there were significant and magnificent instances of the power of humble trust to bring to an else helpless man all the blessings that he needs, and to put a crystal wall round about him that will preserve him from every evil, howsoever threatening it may seem?

'It has come addressed to me, but it is meant for Thee. Vindicate Thine own cause by delivering Thine own servant.' And so, 'when the morning dawned, they were all dead men,' and faith rejoiced in a perfect deliverance. And you and I may get the same answer, in the midst of all our trials, difficulties, toils, and conflicts, if only we will go the same way to get it, and let our faith work, as Hezekiah's worked, and take everything that troubles us to our Father in the heavens, and be quite sure that He is the God 'who daily bears our burdens.' Let us begin with the simple act of confidence in Him. That is the foundation, and on that we may build everything besides.

Let us see what this man further built upon it. The second story, if I may so say, of the temple-fortress of his life, upon the foundation of faith, was, 'He clave to the Lord.'

That is to say, the act of confidence must be followed and perfected by tenacious adherence with all the tendrils of a man's nature to the God in whom he says that he trusts. The metaphor is a very forcible one, so familiar in Scripture as that we are apt to overlook its emphasis. Let me recall one or two of the instances in which it is employed about other matters which throw light on its force here.

First of all, remember that sweet picture of the widow woman from Moab and the two daughters-in-law, one sent back, not reluctantly, to her home; and the other persisting in keeping by Naomi's side, in spite of difficulties and remonstrances. With kisses of real love Orpah went back, but she did go back, to her people and her gods, but 'Ruth clave unto her.' So should we cling to God, as Ruth flung her arms round Naomi, and twined her else lonely and desolate heart about her dear and only friend, for whose sweet sake she became a willing exile from kindred and country. Is that how we cleave to the Lord?

More sacred still are the lessons that are suggested by the fact that this is the word employed to describe the blessed and holy union of man and woman in pure wedded life, and I suppose some allusion to that use of the expression underlies its constant application to the relation of the believing soul to Jehovah. For by trust the soul is wedded to Him, and so 'joined to the Lord' as to be 'one spirit.'

Or if we do not care to go so deep as that, let us take the metaphor that lies in the word itself, without reference to its Scriptural applications. As the limpet holds on to its rock, as the ivy clings to the wall, as a shipwrecked sailor grasps the spar which keeps his head above water, so a Christian man ought to hold on to God, with all his energy, and with all parts of his nature. The metaphor implies tenacity; closeness of adhesion, in heart and will, in thought, in desire, and in all the parts of our receptive humanity, all of which can touch God and be touched by Him, and all of which are blessed only in the measure in which, yielding to Him, they are filled and steadied and glorified.

And there is implied, too, not only tenacity of adherence, but tenacity in the face of obstacles. There must be resistance to all the forces which would detach, if there is to be union with God in the midst of life in the world. Or, to recur for a moment to the figure that I employed a moment ago, as the sailor clings to a spar, though the waves dash round him, and his fingers get stiffened with cold and cramped with keeping the one position, and can scarcely hold on, but he knows that it is life to cling and death to loosen, and so tightens his grasp; thus have we to lay hold of God, and in spite of all obstacles, to keep hold of Him. Our grasp tends to slacken, and is feeble at the best, even if there were nothing outside of us to make it difficult for us to get a good grip. But there are howling winds and battering waves blowing and beating on us, and making it hard to keep our hold.

Do not let us yield to these, but in spite of them all let our hearts tighten round Him, for it is only in His sweet, eternal, perfect love that they can be at rest. And let our thoughts keep close to Him in spite of all distractions, for it is only in the measure in which His light fills our minds and His truth occupies our thoughts that our thinking spirits will be at rest. And let our desires, as the tentacles of some shell-fish fasten upon the rock, and feel out towards the ocean that is coming to it, let our desires go all out towards Him until they touch that after which they feel, and curl round it in repose and in blessedness.

The whole secret of a joyful, strong, noble Christian life lies here—that on the foundation of faith we should rear tenacious adherence to Him in spite of all obstacles. So it was a most encyclopaedic, though laconic, exhortation that that 'good man' sent down from Jerusalem to encourage the first heathen converts gave, when instead of all other instruction or advice, or inculcation of less important, and yet real, Christian duties, Barnabas exhorted them all 'that with purpose of heart'—the full devotion of their inmost natures—'they should cleave to the Lord.'

Then the third stage, or the third story, in this building is that, cleaving to the Lord, 'he departed not from following Him.' The metaphor of cleaving implies proximity and union; the metaphor of following implies distance which is being diminished. These two are incongruous, and the very incongruity helps to give point to the representation. The same two ideas of union and yet of pursuit are brought still more closely together in other parts of Scripture. For instance, there is a remarkable saying in one of the Psalms, translated in our Bible—'My soul followeth hard after Thee. Thy right hand upholdeth me,' where the expression 'followeth hard after' is a lame attempt at translating the perhaps impossible-to-be-translated fullness of the original, which reads 'My soul cleaveth after Thee.' It is an incongruous combination of ideas, by its very incongruity and paradoxical form suggesting a profound truth—viz. that in all the conscious union and tenacious adherence to God which makes the Christian life, there is ever, also, a sense of distance which kindles aspiration and leads to the effort after continual progress. However close we may be to God, it is always possible to press closer. However full may be the union, it may always be made fuller; and the cleaving spirit will always be longing for a closer contact and a more blessed sense of being in touch with God.

So, as we climb, new heights reveal themselves, and the further we advance in the Christian life the more are we conscious of the infinite depths that yet remain to be traversed. Hence arises one great element of the blessedness of being a Christian—namely, that we need not fear ever coming to the end of the growth in holiness and the increase of joy and power that are possible to us. So that weariness, and the sense of having reached the limits that are possible on a given path, which sooner or later fall upon men that live for anything but God, can never be ours if we live for Him. But the oldest and most experienced will have the same forward-looking glances of hope and forward-directed steps of strenuous effort as the youngest beginner on the path; and a Paul will be able to say when he is 'Paul the aged,' and 'the time of his departure is at hand,' that he 'forgets the things that are behind, and reaches forth unto the things that are before, while he presses towards the mark.' Let us be thankful for the endless progress which is possible to the Christian, and let us see to it that we are never paralysed into supposing that 'to-morrow must be *as* this day,' but trust the infinite resources of our God, and be sure that we growingly make our own the growing gifts which He bestows.

And so, lastly, the fourth element in this analysis of a devout life is 'He kept the commandments of the Lord.' That is the outcome of them all. Faith, adhesion, aspiration, and progress, all vindicate their value and reality in the simple, homely way of practical obedience.

Let us learn two things. One as to the worthlessness of all these others, if they do not issue in this. Not that these inward emotions are ever to be despised, but that, if they are genuine in our hearts, they cannot but manifest themselves in our lives. And so, dear Christian friends! do you not build upon your faith, on your adherence to God, on your aspirations after Him, unless you can bring into court, as witnesses for these, daily and hourly, your efforts after the conformity of your will to His, in the great things and in the small. Then, and only then, may we be sure that our confidence is not a delusion, and that it is to Him that we cleave when our feet tread in the paths of goodness.

And on the other hand, let us learn that all attempts to be obedient to a divine will which do not begin with trust and cleaving to Him are vain. There is no other way to get that conformity of will except by that union of spirit. All other attempts are beginning at the wrong end. You do not begin building your houses with the chimney-pots, but many a man who seeks to obey without trusting does precisely commit that fault. Let us be sure that the foundations are in, and then let us be sure that we do not stop half-way up, lest all that pass by should mock and say, 'This man began to build and was not able to finish.'

How many professing Christians' lives are half-finished and unroofed houses, because they have not 'added to their faith'—that is, to their 'cleaving to the Lord'—endless aspiration and continual progress, and to their aspiration and their progress the peaceable fruit of practical righteousness! If these things be in us and abound, they mark us as devout men after God's pattern. And if we want to be devout men after God's pattern, we must follow God's sequence, which begins with trust and ends with obedience.

'HE UTTERED HIS VOICE, THE EARTH MELTED'

'Then Isaiah the son of Amos sent to Hezekiah, saying, Thus saith the Lord God of Israel, That which thou hast prayed to Me against Sennacherib king of Assyria I have heard. 21. This is the word that the Lord hath spoken concerning him; The virgin, the daughter of Zion, hath despised thee, and laughed thee to scorn; the daughter of Jerusalem hath shaken her head at thee. 22. Whom hast thou reproached and blasphemed? and against whom hast thou exalted thy voice, and lifted up thine eyes on high? even against the Holy One of Israel.... 28. Because thy rage against Me and thy tumult is come up into Mine ears, therefore I will put My hook in thy nose, and My bridle in thy lips, and I will turn thee back by the way by which thou camest. 29. And this shall be a sign unto thee, Ye shall eat this year such things as grow of themselves, and in the second year that which springeth of the same; and in the third year sow ye, and reap, and plant vineyards, and eat the fruits thereof. 30. And the remnant that is escaped of the house of Judah shall yet again take root downward, and bear fruit upward. 31. For out of Jerusalem shall go forth a remnant, and they that escape out of mount Zion: the zeal of the Lord of hosts shall do this. 32. Therefore thus saith the Lord concerning the king of Assyria, He shall not come into this city, nor shoot an arrow there, nor come before it with shield, nor cast a bank against it. 33. By the way that he came, by the same shall he return, and shall not come into this city, saith the Lord. 34. For I will defend this city, to save it, for Mine own sake, and for My servant David's sake. 35. And it came to pass that night, that the angel of the Lord went out, and smote in the camp of the Assyrians an hundred fourscore and five thousand: and when they arose early in the morning, behold, they were all dead corpses. 36. So Sennacherib king of Assyria departed, and went and returned, and dwelt at Nineveh. 37. And it came to pass, as he was worshipping in the house of Nisroch his god, that Adrammelech and Sharezer his sons smote him with the sword; and they escaped into the land of Armenia: and Esarhaddon his son reigned in his stead.'—2 KINGS xix. 20-22; 28-37.

At an earlier stage of the Assyrian invasion Hezekiah had sent to Isaiah, asking him to pray to his God for deliverance, and had received an explicit assurance that the invasion would be foiled. When the second stage was reached, and Hezekiah was personally summoned to surrender, by a letter which scoffed at Isaiah's promise, he himself prayed before the Lord. Isaiah does not seem to have been present, and may not have known of the prayer. At all events, the answer was given to him to give to the king; and it is noteworthy that, as in the former case, he does not himself come, but sends to Hezekiah. He did come when he had to bring a message of death, and again when he had to rebuke (chap. xx.), but now he only sends. As the chosen speaker of Jehovah's will, he was mightier than kings, and must not imperil the dignity of the message by the behaviour of the messenger. In a sentence, Hezekiah's prayer is answered, and then the prophet, in Jehovah's name, bursts into a wonderful song of triumph over the defeated invader. 'I have heard.' That is enough. Hezekiah's prayer has, as it were, fired the fuse or pulled the trigger, and the explosion follows, and the shot is sped. 'Whereas thou hast prayed, ... I have heard,' is ever true, and God's hearing is God's acting in answer. The methods of His response vary, the fact that He responds to the cry of despair driven to faith by extremity of need does not vary.

But it is noteworthy that, with that brief, sufficient assurance, Hezekiah, as it were, is put aside, and instead of three fighters in the field, the king, with God to back him, and on the other side Sennacherib, two only, appear. It is a duel between Jehovah and the arrogant heathen who had despised Him. Jerusalem appears for a moment, in a magnificent piece of poetical scorn, as despising and making gestures of contempt at the baffled would-be conqueror, as Miriam and her maidens did by the Red Sea. The city is 'virgin,' as many a fortress in other lands has been named, because uncaptured. But she, too, passes out of sight, and Jehovah and Sennacherib stand opposed on the field. God speaks now not 'concerning,' but to, him, and indicts him for insane pride, which was really a denial of dependence on God, and passionate antagonism to Him, as manifested not only in his war against Jehovah's people, but also in the tone of his insolent defiances of Hezekiah, in which he scoffed at the vain trust which the latter was placing in his God, and paralleled Jehovah with the gods of the nations whom he had already conquered (Isaiah xix. 12).

The designation of God, characteristic of Isaiah, as 'the Holy One of Israel,' expresses at once His elevation above, and separation from, all mundane, creatural limitations, and His special relation to His people, and both thoughts intensify Sennacherib's sin. The Highest, before whose transcendent height all human elevations sink to a uniform level, has so joined Israel to Himself that to touch it is to strike at Him, and to vaunt one's self against it is to be arrogant towards God. That mighty name has received wider extension now, but the wider sweep does not bring diminished depth, and lowly souls who take that name for their strong tower can still run into it and be safe from 'the oppressor's wrong, the proud man's contumely,' and the strongest foes.

There is tremendous scorn in the threat with which the divine address to Sennacherib ends. The dreaded world-conqueror is no more in God's eyes than a wild beast, which He can ring and lead as He will, and not even as formidable as that, but like a horse or a mule, that can easily be bridled and directed. What majestic assertion lies in these figures and in 'My hook' and 'My bridle!' How many conquerors and mighty men since then have been so mastered, and their schemes balked! Sennacherib had to return by 'the way that he came,' and to tramp back, foiled and disappointed, over all the weary miles which he had trodden before with such insolent confidence of victory. A modern parallel is Napoleon's retreat from Moscow. But the same experience really befalls all who order life regardless of God. Their schemes may seem to succeed, but in deepest truth they fail, and the schemers never reach their goal.

In verse 29 the prophet turns away abruptly and almost contemptuously from Sennacherib to speak comfortably to Jerusalem, addressing Hezekiah first, but turning immediately to the people. The substance of his words to them is, first, the assurance that the Assyrian invasion had limits of time set to it by God; and, second, that beyond it lay prosperous times, when the prophetic visions of a flourishing Israel should be realised in fact. For two seed-times only field work was to be impossible on account of the Assyrian occupation, but it was to foam itself away, like a winter torrent, before a third season for sowing came round.

But how could this sequence of events, which required time for its unfolding, be 'a sign'? We must somewhat modify our notions of a sign to understand the prophet. The Scripture usage does not only designate by that name a present event or thing which guarantees the truth of a prophecy, but it sometimes means an event, or sequence of events, in the future, which, when they have come to pass in accordance with the divine prediction of them, will shed back light on other divine words or acts, and demonstrate that they were of God. Thus Moses was given as a sign of his mission the worshipping in Mount Sinai, which was to take place only after the Exodus. So with Isaiah's sign here. When the harvest of the third year was gathered in, then Israel would know that the prophet had spoken from God when he had sung Sennacherib's defeat. For the present, Hezekiah and Judah had to live by faith; but when the deliverance was complete, and they were enjoying the fruits of their labours and of God's salvation, then they could look back on the weary years, and recognise more clearly than while these were slowly passing how God had been in all the trouble, and had been carrying on His purposes of mercy through it all. And there will be a 'sign' for us in like manner when we look back from eternity on the transitory conflicts of earthly life, and are satisfied with the harvest which He has caused to spring from our poor sowings to the Spirit.

The definite promise of deliverance in verses 32-34 is addressed to Judah, and emphasises the completeness of the frustration of the invader's efforts. There is a climax in the enumeration of the things that he will not be allowed to do—he will not make his entry into the city, nor even shoot an arrow there, nor even make preparation for a siege. His whole design will be overturned, and as had already been said (ver. 28), he will retrace his steps a baffled man.

Note the strong antithesis: 'He shall not come into this city, ... for I will defend this city.' Zion is impregnable because Jehovah defends it. Sennacherib can do nothing, for he is fighting against God. And if we 'are come unto the city of the living God,' we can take the same promise for the strength of our lives. God saves Zion 'for His own sake,' for His name is concerned in its security, both because He has taken it for His own and because He has pledged His word to guard it. It would be a blot on His faithfulness, a slur on His power, if it should be conquered while it remains true to Him, its King. His honour is involved in protecting us if we enter into the strong city of which the builder and maker is God. And 'for David's sake,' too, He defends Zion, because He had sworn to David to dwell there. But Zion's security becomes an illusion if Zion breaks away from God. If it becomes as Sodom, it shares Sodom's fate.

It is remarkable that neither in the song of triumph nor in the prophecy of deliverance is there allusion to the destruction of the Assyrian army. How the exultant taunts of the one and the definite promises of the other were to be fulfilled was not declared till the event declared it. But faithful expectation had not long to wait, for 'that night' the blow fell, and no second was needed. We are not told where the Assyrian army was, but clearly it was not before Jerusalem. Nor do we learn what was the instrument of destruction wielded by the 'angel of the Lord,' if there was any. The catastrophe may have been brought about by a pestilence, but however effected, it was 'the act of God,' the fulfilment of His promise, the making bare of His arm. 'By terrible things in righteousness' did He answer the prayer of Hezekiah, and give to all humble souls who are oppressed and cry to Him a pledge that 'as they have heard, so' will they 'see, in the city of' their 'God.' How much more impressive is the stern, naked brevity of the Scriptural account than a more emotional expansion of it, like, for instance, Byron's well-known, and in their way powerful lines, would have been! To the writer of this book it seemed the most natural thing in the world that the foes of Zion should be annihilated by one blow of the divine hand. His business is to tell the facts; he leaves commentary and wonder and triumph or terror to others.

There is but one touch of patriotic exultation apparent in the half-sarcastic and half-rejoicing accumulation of synonyms descriptive of Sennacherib's retreat. He 'departed, and went and returned.' It is like the picture in Psalm xlviii., which probably refers to the same events: 'They saw it, and so they marvelled; they were troubled, and hasted away.'

About twenty years elapsed between Sennacherib's retreat and his assassination. During all that time he 'dwelt at Nineveh,' so far as Judah was concerned. He had had enough of attacking it and its God. But the notice of his death is introduced here, not only to complete the narrative, but to point a lesson, which is suggested by the fact that he was murdered 'as he was worshipping in the house of Nisroch his god.' Hezekiah had gone into the house of *his* God with Sennacherib's letter, and the dead corpses of an army showed what Jehovah could do for His servant; Sennacherib was praying in the temple of *his* god, and his corpse lay stretched before his idol, an object lesson of the impotence of Nisroch and all his like to hear or help their worshippers.

THE REDISCOVERED LAW AND ITS EFFECTS

'And Hilkiah the high priest said unto Shaphan the scribe, I have found the book of the law in the house of the Lord: and Hilkiah gave the book to Shaphan, and he read it. 9. And Shaphan the scribe came to the king, and brought the king word again, and said, Thy servants have gathered the money that was found in the house, and have delivered it into the hand of them that do the work, that have the oversight of the house of the Lord. 10. And Shaphan the scribe shewed the king, saying, Hilkiah the priest hath delivered me a book: and Shaphan read it before the king. 11. And it came to pass, when the king had heard the words of the book of the law, that he rent his clothes. 12. And the king commanded Hilkiah the priest, and Ahikam the son of Shaphan, and Achbor the son of Michaiah, and Shaphan the scribe, and Asahiah a servant of the king's, saying, 13. Go ye, enquire of the Lord for me, and for the people, and for all Judah, concerning the words of this book that is found: for great is the wrath of the Lord that is kindled against us, because our fathers have not hearkened unto the words of this book, to do according unto all that which is written concerning us. 14. So Hilkiah the priest, and Ahikam, and Achbor, and Shaphan, and Asahiah, went unto Huldah the prophetess, the wife of Shallum the son of Tikvah, the son of Harhas, keeper of the wardrobe; (now she dwelt in Jerusalem in the college;) and they communed with her. 15. And she said unto them, Thus saith the Lord God of Israel, Tell the man that sent you to me, 16. Thus saith the Lord, Behold, I will bring evil upon this place, and upon the inhabitants thereof, even all the words of the book which the king of Judah hath read: 17. Because they have forsaken Me, and have burnt incense unto other gods, that they might provoke Me to anger with all the works of their hands; therefore My wrath shall be kindled against this place, and shall not be quenched. 18. But to the king of Judah, which sent you to enquire of the Lord, thus shall ye say to him, Thus saith the Lord God of Israel, As touching the words which thou hast heard; 19. Because thine heart was tender, and thou hast humbled thyself before the Lord, when thou heardest what I speak against this place, and against the inhabitants thereof, that they should become a desolation and a curse, and hast rent thy clothes, and wept before Me; I also have heard thee, saith the Lord. 20. Behold, therefore, I will gather thee unto thy fathers, and thou shalt be gathered into thy grave in peace; and thine eyes shall not see all the evil which I will bring upon this place. And they brought the king word again.'—2 KINGS xxii. 8-20.

We get but a glimpse into a wild time of revolution and counter-revolution in the brief notice that the 'servants of Amon,' Josiah's father, conspired and murdered him in his palace, but were themselves killed by a popular rising, in which the 'people of the land made Josiah his son king in his stead,' and so no doubt balked the conspirators' plans. Poor boy! he was only eight years old when he made his first acquaintance with rebellion and bloodshed. There must have been some wise heads and strong arms and loyal hearts round him, but their names have perished. The name of David was still a spell in Judah, and guarded his childish descendant's royal rights. In the eighteenth year of his reign, the twenty-sixth of his age, he felt himself firm enough in the saddle to begin a work of religious reformation, and the first reward of his zeal was the finding of the book of the law. Josiah, like the rest of us, gained fuller knowledge of God's will in the act of trying to do it so far as he knew it. 'Light is sown for the upright.'

I. We have, first, the discovery of the law. The important and complicated critical questions raised by the narrative cannot be discussed here, nor do they affect the broad lines of teaching in the incident. Nothing is more truthful-like than the statement that, in course of the repairs of the Temple, the book should be found,—probably in the holiest place, to which the high priest would have exclusive access. How it came to have been lost is a more puzzling question; but if we recall that seventy-five years had passed since Hezekiah, and that these were almost entirely years of apostasy and of tumult, we shall not wonder that it was so. Unvalued things easily slip out of sight, and if the preservation of Scripture depended on the estimation which some of us have of it, it would have been lost long ago. But the fact of the loss suggests the wonder of the preservation. It would appear that this copy was the only one existing,—at all events, the only one known. It alone transmitted the law to later days, like some slender thread of water that finds its way through the sand and brings the river down to broad plains beyond. Think of the millions of copies now, and the one dusty, forgotten roll tossing unregarded in the dilapidated Temple, and be thankful for the Providence that has watched over the transmission. Let us take care, too, that the whole Scripture is not as much lost to us, though we have half a dozen Bibles each, as the roll was to Josiah and his men.

Hilkiah's announcement to Shaphan has a ring of wonder and of awe in it. It sounds as if he had not known that such a book was anywhere in the Temple. And it is noteworthy that not he, but Shaphan, is said to have read it. Perhaps he could not,—though, if he did not, how did he know what the book was? At all events, he and Shaphan seem to have felt the importance of the find, and to have consulted what was to be done. Observe how the latter goes cautiously to work, and at first only says that he has received 'a book.' He gives it no name, but leaves it to tell its own story,—which it was then, and is still, well able to do. Scripture is its own best credentials and witnesses whence it comes. Again Shaphan is the reader, as it was natural that a 'scribe' should be, and again the possibility is that Josiah could not read.

II. One can easily picture the scene while the reader's voice went steadily through the commandments, threatenings, and promises,—the deepening eagerness of the king, the gradual shaping out before his conscience of God's ideal for him and his people, and the gradual waking of the sense of sin in him, like a dormant serpent beginning to stir in the first spring sunshine.

The effect of God's law on the sinful heart is vividly pictured in Josiah's emotion. 'By the law is the knowledge of sin.' To many of us that law, in spite of our outward knowledge of it, is as completely absent from our consciousness as it had been from the most ignorant of Josiah's subjects; and if for once its searchlight were thrown into the hidden corners of our hearts and lives, it would show up in dreadful clearness the skulking foes that are stealing to assail us, and the foul things that have made good their lodgment in our hearts and lives. It always makes an epoch in a life when it is really brought to the standard of God's law; and it is well for us if, like Josiah, we rend our clothes, or rather 'our heart, and not our garments,' and take home the conviction, 'I have sinned against the Lord.'

The dread of punishment sprang up in the young king's heart, and though that emotion is not the highest motive for seeking the Lord, it is not an unworthy one, and is meant to lead on to nobler ones than itself. There is too much unwillingness, in many modern conceptions of Christ's gospel, to recognise the place which the apprehension of personal evil consequences from sin has in the initial stages of the process by which we are 'translated from the kingdom of darkness into that of God's dear Son.'

III. The message to Huldah is remarkable. The persons sent with it show its importance. The high priest, the royal secretary, and one of the king's personal attendants, who was, no doubt, in his confidence, and two other influential men, one of whom, Ahikam, is known as Jeremiah's staunch friend, would make some stir in 'the second quarter,' on their way to the modest house of the keeper of the wardrobe. The weight and number of the deputation did honour to the prophetess, as well as showed the king's anxiety as to the matter in hand. Jeremiah and Zephaniah were both living at this time, and we do not know why Huldah was preferred. Perhaps she was more accessible. But conjecture is idle. Enough that she was recognised as having, and declared herself to have, direct authoritative communications from God.

For what did Josiah need to inquire of the Lord 'concerning the words of this book'? They were plain enough. Did he hope to have their sternness somewhat mollified by the words of a prophetess who might be more amenable to entreaties or personal considerations than the unalterable page was? Evidently he recognised Huldah as speaking with divine authority, and he might have known that two depositories of God's voice could not contradict each other. But possibly his embassy simply reflected his extreme perturbation and alarm, and like many another man when God's law startles him into consciousness of sin, he betook himself to one who was supposed to be in God's counsels, half hoping for a mitigated sentence, and half uncertain of what he really wished. He confusedly groped for some support or guide. But, confused as he was, his message to the prophetess implied repentance, eager desire to know what to do, and humble docility. If dread of evil consequences leads us to such a temper, we shall hear, as Josiah did, answers of peace as authoritative and divine as were the threatenings that brought us to our senses and our knees.

IV. The answer which Josiah received falls into two parts, the former of which confirms the threatenings of evil to Jerusalem, while the latter casts a gleam athwart the thundercloud, and promises Josiah escape from the national calamities. Observe the difference in the designation given him in the two parts. When the threatenings are confirmed, his individuality is, as it were, sunk; for that part of the message applies to any and every member of the nation, and therefore he is simply called 'the man that sent you.' Any other man would have received the same answer. But when his own fate is to be disclosed, then he is 'the king of Judah, who sent you,' and is described by the official position which set him apart from his subjects.

Huldah has but to confirm the dread predictions of evil which the roll had contained. What else can a faithful messenger of God do than reiterate its threatenings? Vainly do men seek to induce the living prophet to soften down God's own warnings. Foolishly do they think that the messenger or the messenger's Sender has any 'pleasure in the death of the wicked'; and as foolishly do they take the message to be unkind, for surely to warn that destruction waits the evildoer is gracious. The signal-man who waves the red flag to stop the train rushing to ruin is a friend. Huldah was serving Judah best by plain reiteration of the 'words of the book.'

But the second half of her message told that in wrath God remembered mercy. And that is for ever true. His thunderbolts do not strike indiscriminately, even when they smite a nation. Judah's corruption had gone too far for recovery, and the carcase called for the gathering together of the vultures, but Josiah's penitence was not in vain. 'I have heard thee' is always said to the true penitent, and even if he is involved in widespread retribution, its strokes become different to him. Josiah was assured that the evil should not come in his days. But Huldah's promise seems contradicted by the circumstances of his death. It was a strange kind of being gathered to his grave in peace when he fell on the fatal field of Megiddo, and 'his servants carried him in a chariot dead, ... and buried him in his own sepulchre' (2 Kings xxiii. 30). But the promise is fulfilled in its real meaning by the fact that the threatenings which he was inquiring about did not fall on Judah in his time, and so far as these were concerned, he *did* come to his grave in peace.

THE END

'1. And it came to pass in the ninth year of his reign, in the tenth month, in the tenth day of the month, that Nebuchadnezzar king of Babylon came, he, and all his host, against Jerusalem, and pitched against it; and they built forts against it round about. 2. And the city was besieged unto the eleventh year of king Zedekiah. 3. And on the ninth day of the fourth month the famine prevailed in the city, and there was no bread for the people of the land. 4. And the city was broken up, and all the men of war fled by night by the way of the gate, between two walls, which is by the king's garden; (now the Chaldees were against the city round about;) and the king went the way toward the plain. 5. And the army of the Chaldees pursued after the king, and overtook him in the plains of Jericho: and all his army were scattered from him. 6. So they took the king, and brought him up to the king of Babylon to Riblah; and they gave judgment upon him. 7. And they slew the sons of Zedekiah before his eyes, and put out the eyes of Zedekiah, and bound him with fetters of brass, and carried him to Babylon. 8. And in the fifth month, on the seventh day of the month, which is the nineteenth year of king Nebuchadnezzar king of Babylon, came Nebuzar-adan, captain of the guard, a servant of the king of Babylon, unto Jerusalem: 9. And he burnt the house of the Lord, and the king's house, and all the houses of Jerusalem, and every great man's house burnt he with fire. 10. And all the army of the Chaldees, that were with the captain of the guard, brake down the walls of Jerusalem round about. 11. Now the rest of the people that were left in the city, and the fugitives that fell away to the king of Babylon, with the remnant of the multitude, did Nebuzar-adan, the captain of the guard, carry away. 12. But the captain of the guard left of the poor of the land to be vine-dressers and husbandmen.'—2 KINGS xxv. 1-12.

Eighteen months of long-drawn-out misery and daily increasing famine preceded the fall of the doomed city. The siege was a blockade. No assaults by the enemy, nor sorties by the inhabitants, are narrated, but the former grimly and watchfully drew their net closer, and the latter sat still in their despair. The passionless tone of the narrative here is very remarkable. Not a word escapes the writer to show his feelings, though he is telling his country's fall. We must turn to Lamentations for sighs and groans. There we have the emotions of devout hearts; here we have the calm record of God's judgment. It is all one long sentence, for in the Hebrew each verse begins with 'and,' clause heaped on clause, as if each were a footstep of the destroying angel in his slow, irresistible march.

The narrative falls into two principal parts—the fate of the king and that of the city. It is unnecessary to dwell on the details. The confusion of counsels, the party strife, the fierce hatred of God's prophet, the agony of famine, are all suppressed here, but painted with terrible vividness in the Book of Jeremiah. At last the fatal day came. On the north side a breach was made in the wall, and through it the fierce besiegers poured—the 'princes of the king of Babylon,' with their idolatrous and barbarous names, 'came in, and sat in the middle gate.' It was night. The sudden appearance of the conquerors in the heart of the city shot panic into the feeble king and his 'men of war' who had never struck one blow for deliverance; and they hurried under cover of darkness, and hidden between two walls, down the ravine to the king's garden, once the scene of pleasure, but waste now, and thence, as best they could, round or over Olivet to the road to Jericho. The king's flight by night had been foretold by Ezekiel far away in captivity (Ezek. xii. 12); and the same prophet received on that very day a divine message announcing the fall of the city, and bidding him 'write thee the name of the day, even of this selfsame day,' as that on which the king of Babylon 'drew close unto Jerusalem' (Ezek. xxiv. 1 *et seq.*).

Down the rocky road went the flying host, with 'their shaftless, broken bows' closely followed by the avenging foe with 'red pursuing spear.' Where Israel had first set foot on its inheritance, the last king of David's line was captured and his monarchy shattered. The scene of the first victory, when Jericho fell before unarmed men trusting in God, was the scene of the last defeat. The spot where the covenant was renewed, and the reproach of Israel rolled away, was the spot where the broken covenant was finally avenged and abrogated. The end came back to the beginning, and the cradle was the coffin.

Away up to Riblah, in the far north, under the shadow of Lebanon, the captive was dragged to meet the conqueror. The name of each is a profession of belief. The one means 'Jehovah is righteousness'; the other, 'Nebo, protect the crown.' The idol seemed to have overcome, but the defeat of the unbelieving confessor of the true God at the hands of the idolater is really the victory of the righteousness which the name celebrated and the bearer of the name insulted. His murdered sons were the last sight which he saw before he was blinded, according to the ferocious practice of the East. It was ingenuity of cruelty to let him see for so long, and then to give him that as the last thing seen, and therefore often remembered. Note how the enigma of Ezekiel's prophecy (Ezek. xii. 13) and its apparent contradiction of Jeremiah's (Jer. xxxii. 4; xxxiv. 3) are reconciled, and learn how easily the fact, when it comes, clears the riddles of prophecy, and how easily, probably, the whole facts, if we knew them, would clear the difficulties of Scripture history. The blinded king was harmless, but according to Jewish tradition, was set to work in a mill (though that is probably only an application of Samson's story), and according to Jeremiah (Jer. lii. 11), was kept in prison till his death. So ended the monarchy of Judah.

The fate of the city was not settled for a month, during which, no doubt, there was much consultation at Riblah whether to garrison or destroy it. The king of Babylon did not go in person, but despatched a force commanded by a high officer, to burn palace, Temple, the more important houses (the poorer people would probably be lodged in huts not worth burning), and to raze the fortifications. In accordance with the practice of the great Eastern despotisms, deportation followed victory—a clever though cruel device for securing conquests. But some were left behind; for the land, if deserted, would have fallen out of cultivation, and been profitless to Babylon. The bulk of the people of Jerusalem, the fugitives who had joined the invaders during the siege, and the mass of the general population, were carried off, in such a long string of misery as we may still see on the monuments, and a handful left behind, too poor to plot, and stirred to diligence by necessity. So ended the possession by Israel of its promised inheritance.

Now this fall of Jerusalem is like an object-lesson to teach everlasting truth as to the retributive providence of God. What does it say?

It declares plainly what brings down God's judgments. The terms on which Israel prospered and held its land were obedience to God's law. We cannot directly apply the principles of God's government of it to modern nations. The present analogue of Israel is the Church, not the nation. But when all deductions have been made, it is still true that a nation's religious attitude is a most potent factor in its prosperous development. It is not accidental that, on the whole, stagnant Europe and America are Roman Catholic, and the progressive parts Protestant. Nor was it causes independent of religion that scattered a decaying Christianity in the lands of the Eastern Church before the onslaught of wild Arabs, who, at all events, did believe in Allah. So there are abundant lessons for politics and sociology in the story of Jerusalem's fall.

But these lessons have direct application to the individual and to the Christian Church. All departure from God is ruin. We slay ourselves by forsaking Him, and every sinner is a suicide. We live under a moral government, and in a system of things so knit together as that even here every transgression receives its just recompense—if not visibly and palpably in outward circumstances, yet really and punctually in effects on mind and heart, which are more solemn and awful. 'Behold the righteous shall be recompensed in the earth: much more the wicked and the sinner.' Sin and sorrow are root and fruit.

Especially does that crash of Jerusalem's fall thunder the lesson to all churches that their life and prosperity are inseparably connected with faithful obedience and turning away from all worldliness, which is idolatry. They stand in the place that was made empty by Israel's later fall. Our very privileges call us to beware. 'Because of unbelief they were broken off, and thou standest by faith.' That great seven-branched candlestick was removed out of its place, and all that is left of it is its sculptured image among the spoils on the triumphal arch to its captor. Other lesser candlesticks have been removed from their places, and Turkish oppression brings night where Sardis and Laodicea once gave a feeble light. The warning is needed to-day; for worldliness is rampant in the Church. 'If God spared not the natural branches, take heed lest He also spare not thee.' The fall of Jerusalem is not merely a tragic story from the past. It is a revelation, for the present, of the everlasting truth, that the professing people of God deserve and receive the sorest chastisement, if they turn again to folly.

Further, we learn the method of present retribution. Nebuchadnezzar knew nothing of the purposes which he fulfilled. 'He meaneth not so, neither doth his heart think so.' He was but the 'axe' with which God hewed. Therefore, though he was God's tool, he was also responsible, and would be punished even for performing God's 'whole work upon Jerusalem,' because of 'the glory of his high looks.' The retribution of disobedience, so far as that retribution is outward, needs no 'miracle.' The ordinary operations of Providence amply suffice to bring it. If God wills to sting, He will 'hiss for the fly,' and it will come. The ferocity and ambition of a grim and bloody despot, impelled by vainglory and lust of cruel conquest, do God's work, and yet the doing is sin. The world is full of God's instruments, and He sends punishments by the ordinary play of motives and circumstances, which we best understand when we see behind all His mighty hand and sovereign will. The short-sighted view of history says 'Nebuchadnezzar captured Jerusalem B.C. so and so,' and then discourses about the tendencies of which Babylonia was exponent and creature. The deeper view says, God smote the disobedient city, as He had said, and Nebuchadnezzar was 'the rod of His anger.'

Again, we learn the Divine reluctance to smite. More than four hundred years had passed since Solomon began idolatry, and steadily, through all that time, a stream of prophecy of varying force and width had flowed, while smaller disasters had confirmed the prophets' voices. 'Rising up early and sending' his servants, God had been in earnest in seeking to save Israel from itself. Men said then, 'Where is the promise of His coming?' and mocked His warnings and would none of His reproof; but at last the hour struck and the crash came. 'As a dream when one awaketh; so, O Lord! when Thou awakest, Thou shalt despise their image.' His judgment seems to slumber, but its eyes are open, and it remains inactive, that His long-suffering may have free scope. As long as His gaze can discern the possibility of repentance, He will not strike; and when that is hopeless, He will not delay. The explanation of the marvellous tolerance of evil which sometimes tries faith and always evokes wonder, lies in the great words, which might well be written over the chair of every teacher of history: 'The Lord is not slack concerning His promise, as some men count slackness; but is long-suffering to us-ward.' Alas, that that divine patience should ever be twisted into the ground of indurated disobedience! 'Because sentence against an evil work is not executed speedily, therefore the heart of the sons of men is fully set in them to do evil.'

God's reluctance to punish is no reason for doubting that He will. Judgment is His 'strange work,' less congenial, if we may so paraphrase that strong word of the prophet's, than pure mercy, but it will be done nevertheless. The tears over Jerusalem that witnessed Christ's sorrow did not blind the eyes like a flame of fire, nor stay the outstretched hand of the Judge, when the time of her final fall came. The longer the delay, the worse the ruin. The more protracted the respite and the fuller it has been of entreaties to return, the more terrible the punishment. 'Behold, therefore, the goodness and severity of God: towards them which fell, severity; but toward thee, goodness, if thou continue in His goodness: otherwise thou also shalt be cut off.'

THE FIRST BOOK OF CHRONICLES

THE KING'S POTTERS

'There they dwelt with the king for his work.'—1 CHRON. iv. 23.

In these dry lists of names which abound in Chronicles, we now and then come across points of interest, oases in the desert, which need but to be pondered sympathetically to yield interesting suggestions. Here for example, buried in a dreary genealogical table, is a little touch which repays meditating on. Among the members of the tribe of Judah were a hereditary caste of potters who lived in 'Netaim and Gederah,' if we adhere to the Revised Version's text, or 'among plantations and hedges' if we prefer the margin. But they are also described as dwelling 'with the king.' That can only mean on the royal estates, for the king himself resided in Jerusalem. He, however, held large domains in the territory of Judah, on some of which these ceramic artists were settled down and followed their calling. They were kept on the royal estates and kept in comfort, not needing to till, but fed and cared for, that they might be free to mould, out of common clay, forms of beauty and 'vessels meet for the master's use.' Surely we may read into the brief statement of the text a meaning of which the writer of it never dreamt, and see in the description of these forgotten artisans, a symbol of our Christian relations to our Lord and of our life's work.

I. We, too, dwell with the King.

The Davidic king was in Jerusalem, and the potters were 'among plantations and hedges,' yet in a real sense they 'dwelt with the king,' though some of them might never have seen his face or trod the streets of the sacred city. Perhaps now and then he came to visit them on his outlying domains, but they were always parts of his household. And have we, Christ's servants, not His gracious parting word: 'I am with you always'? True, we are not beside Him in the great city, but He is beside us in His outlying domains, and we may be with Him in His glory, if while we still outwardly live among the 'plantations and hedges' of this life, we dwell in spirit, by faith and aspiration, with our risen and ascended Lord. If we so 'dwell with the King,' He will dwell with us, and fill our humble abode with the radiance of His presence, 'making that place of His feet glorious.' That He should be with us is supreme condescension, that we should be with Him is the perfection of exaltation. How low He stoops, how high we can rise! The vigour of our Christian life largely depends on our keeping vivid the consciousness of our communion with Jesus and the sense of His real presence with us. How life's burdens would be lightened if we faced them all in the strength of the felt nearness of our Lord! How impossible it would be that we should ever feel the dreary sense of solitude, if we felt that unseen, but most real, Presence wrapping us round! It is only when our faith in it has fallen asleep that any earthly good allures, or any earthly evil frightens us. To be sure, in our thrilling consciousness, that we dwell with Jesus is an impenetrable cuirass that blunts the points of all arrows and keeps the breast that wears it unwounded in the fray. The world has no voices which can make themselves heard above that low sovereign whisper: 'I am with you always, even to the end of the world'— and after the end has come, then we shall be with Him.

But we find in this notice a hint that leads us in yet another direction. They 'dwelt with the king' in the sense that they were housed and cared for on his lands. And in like manner, the true conception of the Christian life is that each of us is 'a sojourner with Thee,' set down on Christ's domains, and looked after by Him in regard to provision for outward wants. We have nothing in property, but all is His and held by His gift and to be used for Him. The slave owns nothing. The patch of ground which he cultivates for his food and what grows on it, are his master's. These workmen were not slaves, but they were not owners either. And we hold nothing as our own, if we are true to the terms on which it is given us to hold.

So if we rightly appreciate our position as dwelling on the King's lands, our delusion of possession will vanish, and we shall feel more keenly the pressure of responsibility while we feel less keenly the grip of anxiety. We are for the time being entrusted with a tiny piece of the royal estates. Let us not strut about as if we were owners, nor be for ever afraid that we shall not have enough for our needs. One sometimes comes on a model village close to the gates of some ducal palace, and notes how the lordly owner's honour prompts its being kept up to a high standard of comfort and beauty. We may be sure that the potters were well lodged and looked after, and that care for their personal wants was shifted from their shoulders to the king's. So should ours be. He will not leave His servants to starve. They should not dishonour Him and disturb themselves by worries and cares that would be reasonable only if they had no Provider. He has said, 'All things are given to Me of My Father,' and He gives us all that God has given Him.

II. We dwell with the King for His work.

The king's potters had not to till the land nor do any work but to mould clay into vessels for use and beauty. For that purpose they had their huts and bits of ground assigned them. So with us, Christ has a purpose in His provision for us. We are set down on His domains, and we enjoy His presence and providing in order that, set free from carking cares and low ends, we may, with free and joyous hearts, yield ourselves to His joyful service. The law of our life should be that we please not ourselves, nor consult our own will in choosing our tasks, nor seek our own profit or gratification in doing them, but ever ask of Him: 'Lord, what wilt Thou have me to do?' and when the answer comes, as come it will to all who ask with real desire to learn and with real inclination to do His will, that we 'make haste and delay not, but make haste to keep His commandments.' The spirit which should animate our active lives is plainly enough taught us in that little word, they 'dwelt with the king for his work.'

Nor are we to forget that, in a very profound sense, dwelling with the King must go before doing His work. Unless we are living continually under the operation of the stimulus of communion with Jesus, we shall have neither quickness of ear to know what He wishes us to do, nor any resolute concentration of ourselves on our Christ-appointed tasks. The spring of all noble living is communion with noble ideals, and fellowship with Jesus sets men agoing, as nothing else will, in practical lives of obedience to Jesus. Time given to silent, retired meditation on that sweet, sacred bond that knits the believing soul to the redeeming Lord is not lost with reference to active work for Jesus. The meditative and the practical life are not antagonistic, but complementary, Mary and Martha are sisters, though sometimes they differ, and foolish people try to set them against each other.

But we must beware of a common misconception of what the King's work is. The royal potters did not make only things of beauty, but very common vessels designed for common and ignoble uses. There were vessels of dishonour dried in their kilns as well as vessels 'meet for the master's use.' There is a usual and lamentable narrowing of the term 'Christian work,' to certain conventional forms of service, which has done and is doing an immense amount of harm. The King's work is far wider in scope than teaching in Sunday-schools, or visiting the sick, or any similar acts that are usually labelled with the name. It covers all the common duties of life. A shallow religion tickets some selected items with the name; a robuster, truer conception extends the designation to everything. It is not only when we are definitely trying to bring others into touch with Jesus that we are doing Him service, but we may be equally serving Him in everything. The difference between the king's work and the poor potters' own lay not so much in the nature as in the motive of it, and whatever we do for Christ's sake and with a view to His will is work that He owns, while a regard to self in our motive or in our end decisively strikes any service tainted by it out of the category.

We are to hallow all our deeds by drawing the motive for them from the King and by laying the fruits of them at His feet. Thus, and only thus, will the most 'secular' actions be sanctified and the narrowest life be widened to contain a present Christ.

There are subsidiary motives which may legitimately blend with the supreme one. The potters would be stimulated to work hard and with their utmost skill when they thought of how well they were paid in house and store for their work. We have ample reasons for dedicating our whole selves to Jesus when we think of His gift of Himself to us, of His wages beforehand, of His joyful presence with His eye ever on us, marking our purity of motive and our diligence.

There is a final thought that may well stimulate us to put all our skill and effort into our work. The potters' work went to Jerusalem. It was for the king. What can be too good for him? He will see it, therefore let us put our best into it. And we shall see it too, when we too enter 'the city of the great King.' Jars that perhaps were wrought by these very workmen of whom we have been speaking turn up to-day in the excavations in Palestine. So much has perished and they remain, speaking symbols of the solemn truth that nothing human ever dies. Our 'works do follow us.' Let us so live that these may be 'found unto praise and honour and glory' at the appearing of 'the King.'

DAVID'S CHORISTERS

'They stood in their office, according to their order.'—1 CHRON. vi. 32 (R.V. margin).

This brief note is buried in the catalogue of the singers appointed by David for 'the service of song in the house of the Lord.' The waves of their choral praise have long ages since ceased to eddy round the 'tabernacle of the tent of meeting,' and all that is left of their melodious companies is a dry list of names, in spite of which the dead owners of them are nameless. But the chronicler's description of them may carry some lessons for us, for is not the Church of Christ a choir, chosen to 'shew forth the praises of Him who has called us out of darkness into His marvellous light'? We take a permissible liberty with this fragment, when we use it to point lessons that may help that great band of choristers who are charged with the office of making the name of Jesus ring through the world. Now, in making such a use of the text, we may linger on each important word in it and find each fruitful in suggestions which we shall be the better for expanding in our own meditations.

We pause on the first word, which is rendered in the Authorised and Revised Versions 'waited,' and in the margin of the latter 'stood.' The former rendering brings into prominence the mental attitude with which the singers held themselves ready to take their turns in the service, the latter points rather to their bodily attitude as they fulfilled their office. We get a picture of the ranked files gathered round their three leaders, Heman, Asaph, and Ethan. These three names are familiar to us from the Psalter, but how all the ranks behind them have fallen dim to us, and how their song has floated into inaudible distance! They 'stood,' a melodious multitude, girt and attent on their song, or waiting their turn to fill the else silent air with the high praises of Jehovah, and glad when it came to their turn to open their lips in full-throated melody.

Now may we not catch the spirit of that long vanished chorus, and find in the two possible renderings of this word a twofold example, the faithful following of which would put new vigour into our service? We are called to a loftier office, and have heavenly harmonies entrusted to us to be made vocal by our lips, compared with which theirs were poor. 'They waited on' their office, and shall not we, in a higher fashion, wait on our ministry, and suffer no inferior claims to block our way or hamper our preparedness to discharge it? To let ourselves be entangled with 'the affairs of this life,' or to 'drowse in idle cell,' sleepily letting summonses that should wake us to work sound unheeded and almost unheard, is flagrant despite done to our high vocation as Christians. 'They also serve who only stand and wait,' but not if in their waiting their eyes are straying everywhere but to their Master's pointing hand or directing eye. The world is full of voices calling Christ's folk to help; but what a host of so-called Christians fail to hear these piteous and despairing cries, because the noise of their own whims, fancies, and self-centred desires keeps buzzing in their ears. A constant accompaniment of deafness is constant noises in the head; and the Christians who are hardest of hearing when Christ calls are generally afflicted with noises which are probably the cause, and not merely an accompaniment, of their deafness. For indeed it demands no little detachment of spirit from self and sense, from the world and its clamant suitors, if a Christian soul is to be ready to mark the first signal of the great Conductor's baton, and to answer the lightest whisper, intrusting it with a task for Him, with its self-consecrating 'Here am I. Send me.'

It used to be said that they who watched for providences never wanted providences to watch for; it is equally true that they who are on the watch for opportunities for service never fail to find them, and that ears pricked to 'hear what God the Lord shall speak,' summoning to work for Him, will not listen in vain. Paul saw in a vision 'a *man* of Macedonia' begging for his help, and 'straightway' he concluded that '*God* had called' him to preach in Europe. Happy are these Christian workers who hear God's voice speaking through men's needs, and recognise a divine imperative in human cries!

May we not see in the attitude of David's choristers as they sang, hints for our own discharge of the tasks of our Christian service? There was a curse of old on him who did the work of the Lord 'negligently,' and its weight falls still on workers and work. For who can measure the harm done to the Christian life of the negligent worker, and who can expect any blessing to come either to him or to others from such half-hearted seeming service? The devil's kingdom is not to be cast down nor Christ's to be builded up by workers who put less than their whole selves, the entire weight of their bodies, into their toil. A pavior on the street brings down his rammer at every stroke with an accompanying exclamation expressing effort, and there is no place in Christ's service for dainty people who will not sweat at their task, and are in mortal fear of over-work. Strenuousness, the gathering together of all our powers, are implied in the attitude of Heman and his band as they 'stood' in their office. Idle revellers might loll on their rose-strewn couches as they 'sing idle songs to the sound of the viol and devise for themselves instruments of music, like David,' but the austerer choir of the Temple despised ease, and stood ready for service and in the best bodily posture for song.

The second important word of the text brings other thoughts no less valuable and rich in practical counsel. The singers in the Temple stood in their 'office,' which was song. Their special work was praise. And that is the highest task of the Church. As a matter of fact, every period of quickened earnestness in the Church's life has been a period marked by a great outburst of Christian song. All intense emotion seeks expression in poetry, and music is the natural speech of a vivid faith. Luther chanted the Marseillaise of the Reformation, 'A safe stronghold our God is still,' and many another sweet strain blended strangely with the fiery and sometimes savage words from his lips. The Scottish Reformation, grim in some of its features as it was, had yet its 'Gude and Godly Ballads.' At the birth of Methodism, as round the cradle at Bethlehem, hovered as it were angel voices singing, 'Glory to God in the highest.' A flock of singing birds let loose attends every revival of Christian life.

The Church's praise is the noblest expression of the Church's life. Its hymns go deeper than its creeds, touch hearts more to the quick, minister to the faith which they enshrine, and often draw others to see the preciousness of the Christ whom they celebrate. How little we should have known of Old Testament religion, notwithstanding law and prophets, if the Psalter had perished!

And it is true, in a very deep sense, that we shall do more for Christ and men by voicing our own deep thankfulness for His great gifts and speaking simply our valuation of, and our thankfulness for, what we draw from Him than by any other form of so-called Christian work. We can offend none by saying: 'We have found the Messias,' and are adoringly glad that we have. The most effectual way of moving other souls to participate in our joy is to let our joy speak. 'If you wish me to weep,' your own tears must not be held back, and if you wish others to know the preciousness of Christ, you must ring out His name with fervour of emotion and the triumphant confidence. We are the 'secretaries of God's praise,' as George Herbert has it, for we have possession of His greatest gift, and have learned to know Him in loftier fashion than Heman's choristers dreamed of, having seen 'the glory of God in the face of Jesus Christ,' and tasted the sweetness of redeeming love. The Apocalyptic seer sets forth a great truth when he tells us that he first heard a new song from the lips of the representatives of the Church, who could sing, 'Thou wast slain and didst redeem us to God with Thy blood,' and then heard their adoration echoed from 'many angels round about the throne,' and finally heard the song reverberated from every created thing in heaven and earth, in the sea and all deep places. A praising Church has experiences of its own which angels cannot share, and it sets in motion the great sea of praise whose surges break in music and roll from every side of the universe in melodious thunder to the great white throne. Without our song even angel voices would lack somewhat.

'God said, "A praise is in Mine ear;
There is no doubt in it, no fear:
Clearer loves sound other ways:
I miss My little human praise."'

The song of the redeemed has in it a minor strain that gives a sweetness far more poignant than belongs to those who cannot say: 'Out of the depths I cried unto Thee.' 'The sweetest songs are those which tell of saddest thought,' and recount experiences of conquered sin and life springing from death.

But it is also true that no kind of Christian service will be effectual, if it lacks the element of grateful praise as its motive and mainspring. Perhaps there would be fewer complaints of toiling all night and wearily hauling in empty nets, if the nets were oftener let down not only 'at Thy word' but with glad remembrance of the fishermen's debt to Jesus, and in the spirit of praise. When all our work is a sacrifice of praise, it is pleasing to God and profitable to ourselves and to others. If we would oftener bethink ourselves, and herald every deed with a silent dedication of it and of ourselves to Him who died for us, we should less often have to complain that we have sowed much and brought back little. A pinch of incense cast into the common domestic fire makes its flame sacrificial and fragrant.

The last important word of the text is also fertile in hints for us. The singers stood in their office 'according to their order.' That last expression may either refer to rotation of service or to distribution of parts in the chorus. They did not sing in unison, grand as the effect of such a song from a multitude sometimes is, but they had their several parts. The harmonious complexity of a great chorus is the ideal for the Church. Paul puts the same thought in a sterner metaphor when he tells the Colossian Christians that he joys 'beholding your order and the steadfastness of your faith in Christ,' where he is evidently thinking of the Roman legion with its rigid discipline and its solid, irresistible, ranked weight. Division of function and consequent concordant action of different parts is the lesson taught by both metaphors, and by the many modern examples of the immense results gained in machinery that almost simulates vital action, and by organisations for great purposes in which men combine. The Church should be the highest example of such combination, for it is the shrine of the noblest life, even the life of its indwelling Lord. Every member of it should have and know his place. Every Christian should know his part in the great chorus, for he has a part, even if it is only that of tinkling the triangle in the orchestra or beating a drum. That division of function and concordance of action apply to all forms of the Church's action, and are enforced most chiefly by the great Apostolic metaphor of the body and its members. Paul did not delight in 'uniformity.' Inferiors calling themselves his successors have often aimed at enforcing it, but nature has been too strong for them, and the hedge will grow its own way in spite of pedants' shears. 'If the whole body were an eye, where the hearing?' The monotony of a church in which uniformity was the ideal would be intolerable. The chorus has its parts, and the soprano cannot say to the bass, 'I have no need of you,' nor the bass to the tenor, 'I have no need of thee.'

So let us see that we find our own place, and see that we fill it, singing our own part lustily, and not being either confused or made dumb because another has other notes to sing than are written on our score. Let us recognise unity made more melodious by diversity, the importance of the humblest, and 'having gifts differing according to the grace given unto us let us wait on our ministry,' and stand in our office according to our order.

DRILL AND ENTHUSIASM

'[Men that] could keep rank, they were not of double heart.'—1 CHRON. xii. 33.

These words come from the muster-roll of the hastily raised army that brought David up to Hebron and made him King. The catalogue abounds in brief characterisations of the qualities of each tribe's contingent. For example, Issachar had 'understanding of the times.' Our text is spoken of the warriors of Zebulon, who had left their hills and their flocks in the far north, and poured down from their seats by the blue waters of Tiberias to gather round their king. They were not only like their brethren expert in war and fully equipped, but they had some measure of discipline too, a rare thing in the days when there were no standing armies. They 'could keep rank,' could march together, had been drilled to some unanimity of step and action, could work and fight together, were an army, not a crowd, and not only so, but also 'they were not of double heart.' Each man, and the whole body, had a brave single resolve; they had one spirit animating the whole, and that was to make David king, an enthusiastic loyalty which made them brave, and a discipline which kept the courage from running to waste.

I take, then, this text as bringing before us two very important characteristics which ought to be found in every Christian church, and without which no real prosperity and growth is possible. These two may be put very briefly: organisation and enthusiastic devotion. These are both important, but in very different degrees. Organisation without valour is in a worse plight than valour without organisation. The one is fundamental, the other secondary. The one is the true cause, so far as men are concerned, of victory, the other is but the instrument by which the cause works. There have been many victories won by undisciplined valour, but disciplined cowardice and apathy come to no good.

These two have been separated and made antagonistic, and churches are to be found which glory in the one, and others in the other. Some have gone in for order, and are like butterflies in a cabinet all ticketed and displayed in place, but a pin is run through their bodies and they are dead; and others have prided themselves on unfettered freedom, and been not an army, but a mob. The true relation, of course, is that life should shape and inform organisation, and organisation should preserve, manifest and obey life. There must be body to hold spirit, there must be spirit to keep body from rotting.

I. Organisation.

This is not the strong point of Nonconformist churches. We pride ourselves on our individualism, and that is all very well. We believe in direct access of each soul to Christ, that men must come to Him one by one, that religion is purely a personal matter, and the firmness with which we hold this tends to make us weak in combined action. It cannot be truthfully denied that both in the relations of our churches to one another, and in the internal organisation of these, we are and have been too loosely compacted, and have forgotten that two is more than one *plus* one, so that we are only helping to redress the balance a little when we insist upon the importance of organisation in our churches.

And first of all—remember the principles in subordination to which our organisation must be framed.

What are we united by? Common love and faith to Christ, or rather Christ Himself. 'One is your Master, even Christ, and all ye are brethren.' So there must be nothing in our organisation which is inconsistent with Christ's supreme place among us, and with our individual obedience to Him. There are to be no 'lords over God's heritage' in the Church of Christ. There are churches in which the temptation to be such affects the official chiefly, and there are others, with a different polity, in which it is chiefly a Diotrephes, who loves to have pre-eminence. Character, zeal, social station, even wealth will always confer a certain influence, and their possessors will be tempted to set up their own will or opinions as dominant in the Church. Such men are sinning against the very bond of Christian union. Organisation which is bought by investing one man with authority, is too dearly purchased at the cost of individual development on the individual's own lines. A row of clipped yew-trees is not an inspiring sight.

And yet again what are we organised for? Not merely for our own growth or spiritual advantage, but also, and more especially, for spreading faith in Christ and advancing His glory. All our organisation, then, is but an arrangement for doing our work, and if it hinders that, it is cumbrous and must be cut away or modified, at all hazards. Ecclesiastical martinets are still to be found, to whom drill is all-important, and who see no use in irregular valour, but they are a diminishing number, and they may be recommended to ponder the old wise saying: 'Where no oxen are, the crib is clean, but much increase is by the strength of the ox.' If the one aim is a 'clean crib' the best way to secure that is to keep it empty; but if a harvest is the aim, there must be cultivation, and one must accept the consequences of having a strong team to plough. The end of drill is fighting. The parade-ground and its exercising is in order that a corps may be hurled against the enemy, or may stand unmoved, like a solid breakwater against a charge which it flings off in idle spray, and the end of the Church's organisation is that it may move *en masse*, without waste, against the enemy.

But a further guiding principle to shape Christian organisation is that of the Church as the body of Christ. That requires that there shall be work for every member. Christ has endowed His members with varying gifts, powers, opportunities, and has set them in diverse circumstances, that each may give his own contribution to the general stock of work. Our theory is that each man has his own proper gift from God, 'one after this manner, and another after that.' But what is our practice? Take any congregation of Christian people in any of our churches, and especially in the Free Churches of which I know most, and is there anything like this wide diversity of forms of service, to which each contributes? A handful of people do all the work, and the remainder are idlers. The same small section are in evidence always, and the rest are nowhere. There are but a few bits of coloured glass in a kaleidoscope, they take different patterns when the tube is turned, but they are always the same bits of glass.

There needs to be a far greater variety of forms of work for our people and more workers in the field. There are too few wheels for the quantity of water in the river, and, partly for that reason, the amount of water that runs waste over the sluice is deplorable. There is a danger in having too many spindles for the power available, but the danger in modern church organisation is exactly the other way.

Every one should have his own work. In all living creatures, differentiation of organs increases as the creature rises in the scale of being, from the simple sac which does everything up to the human body with a distinct function for every finger. It should not be possible for a lazy Christian to plead truly as his vindication that 'no man had hired' him. It should be the Church's business to find work for the unemployed.

The example in our text should enforce the necessity of united work. David's levies could keep rank. They did not let each man go at his own rate and by his own road, but kept together, shoulder to shoulder, with equal stride. They were content to co-operate and be each a part of a greater whole. That keeping rank is a difficult problem in all societies, where individual judgments, weaknesses, wills, and crotchets are at work, but it is apt to be especially difficult in Christian communities, where one may expect to find individual characteristics intensified, a luxuriant growth of personal peculiarities, an intense grip of partial aspects of the great truths and a corresponding dislike of other aspects of these, and of those whose favourite truths they are. One would do nothing to clip that growth, but still Christians who have not learned to subordinate themselves in and for united work are of little use to God or man. What does such united work require? Mainly the bridling of self, the curbing of one's own will, not insisting on forcing one's opinions on one's brother, not being careful of having one's place secured and one's honour asserted. Without such virtues no association of man could survive for a year. If the world managed its societies as the Church manages its unity, they would collapse quickly. Indeed it is a strong presumption in favour of Christianity that the Churches have not killed it long ago. Vanity, pride, self-importance, masterfulness, pettishness get full play among us. Diotrephes has many descendants to-day. A cotton mill, even if it were a co-operative one, could not work long without going into bankruptcy, if there were no more power of working together than some Christian congregations have. A watch would be a poor timekeeper, where every wheel tried to set the pace and be a mainspring, or sulked because the hands moved on the face in sight of all men, while it had to move round and fit into its brother wheel in the dark.

Subordination is required as well as co-operation. For if there be harmonious co-operation in varying offices, there must be degrees and ranks. The differences of power and gift make degrees, and in every society there will be leaders. Of course there is no commanding authority in the Churches. Its leaders are brethren, whose most imperative highest word is, 'We beseech you.'

Of course, too, these varieties and degrees do not mean real superiority or inferiority in the eye of God. From the highest point of view nothing is great or small, there is no higher or lower. The only measure is quality, the only gauge is motive. 'Small service is true service while it lasts.' He that receiveth a prophet in the name of a prophet, shall receive a prophet's reward. But yet there are, so far as our work here is concerned, degrees and orders, and we need a hearty and ungrudging recognition of superiority wherever we find it. If the 'brother of high degree' needs to be exhorted to beware of arrogance and imposing his own will on his fellows, the 'brother of low degree' needs not less to be exhorted to beware of letting envy and self-will hiss and snarl in his heart at those who are in higher positions than himself. If the chief of all needs to be reminded that in Christ's household preeminence means service, the lower no less needs to be reminded that in Christ's household service means pre-eminence.

So much, then, for organisation. It is perfectly reconcilable with democracy that is not mob-ocracy. In fact, democracy needs it most. If I may venture to speak to the members of the Free Churches, with which I am best acquainted, I would take upon myself to say that there is nothing which they need more than that they should show their polity to be capable of reconciling the freest development of the individual with the most efficient organisation of the community. The object is work for Christ, the bond of their fellowship is brotherly union with Christ. Many eyes are on them to-day, and the task is in their hands of showing that they can keep rank. The most perfect discipline in war in old times was found, not amongst the subjects of Eastern despots who were not free enough to learn to submit, but amongst the republics of Greece, where men were all on a level in the city, and fell into their places in the camp, because they loved liberty enough to know the worth of discipline, and so the slaves of Xerxes were scattered before the resistless onset of the phalanx of the free. The terrible legion which moved 'altogether when it moved at all,' and could be launched at the foe like one javelin of steel, had for its units free men and equals. There needs freedom for organisation. There needs organisation for freedom. Let us learn the lesson. 'God is not the author of confusion, but of order, in all churches of saints.'

II. Enthusiastic devotion.

These men came to bring David up to Hebron with one single purpose in their hearts. They had no sidelong glances to their own self-interest, they had no wavering loyalty, they had no trembling fears, so we may take their spirit as expressing generally the deepest requirements for prosperity in a church.

The foundation of all prosperity is a passion of personal attachment to Christ our King.

Christ is Christianity objective. Love to Christ is Christianity subjective. The whole stress of Christian character is laid on this. It is the mother of all grace and goodness, and in regard to the work of the Church, it is the ardour of a soul full of love to Jesus that conquers. The one thing in which all who have done much for Him have been alike in that single-hearted devotion.

But such love is the child of faith. It rests upon belief of truth, and is the response of man to God. Dwelling in the truth is the means of it. How our modern Christianity fails in this strong personal bond of familiar love!

Consider its effect on the individual.

It will give tenacity of purpose, will brace to strenuous effort, will subdue self, self-regard, self-importance, will subdue fear. It is the true anaesthetic. The soldier is unconscious of his wounds, while the glow of devotion is in his heart and the shout of the battle in his ears. It will give fertility of resource and patience.

Consider its effect on the community.

It will remove all difficulties in the way of discipline arising from vanity and self which can be subdued by no other means. That flame fuses all into one glowing mass like a stream that pours from the blast furnace. What a power a church would be which had this! It is itself victory. The men that go into battle with that one firm resolve, and care for nothing else, are sure to win. Think what one man can do who has resolved to sell his life dear!

Consider the worthlessness of discipline without this.

It is a poor mechanical accuracy. How easy to have too much machinery! How the French Revolution men swept the Austrian martinets before them! David was half-smothered in Saul's armour. On the other hand, this fervid flame needs control to make it last and work. Spirit and law are not incompatible. Valour may be disciplined, and the combination is irresistible.

And so here, till we exchange the close array of the battlefield for the open ranks of the festal procession on the Coronation day, and lay aside the helmet for the crown, the sword for the palm, the breastplate for the robe of peace, and stand for ever before the throne, in the peaceful ranks of 'the solemn troops and sweet societies' of the unwavering armies of the heavens who serve Him with a perfect heart, and burn unconsumed with the ardours of an immortal and ever brightening love, let us see to it that we too are 'men that can keep rank and are not of double heart.'

DAVID'S PROHIBITED DESIRE AND PERMITTED SERVICE

'Then he called for Solomon his son, and charged him to build an house for the Lord God of Israel. 7. And David said to Solomon, My son, as for me, it was in my mind to build an house unto the name of the Lord my God: 8. But the word of the Lord came to me, saying, Thou hast shed blood abundantly, and hast made great wars: thou shalt not build an house unto My name, because thou hast shed much blood upon the earth in My sight. 9. Behold, a son shall be born to thee, who shall be a man of rest; and I will give him rest from all his enemies round about: for his name shall be Solomon, and I will give peace and quietness unto Israel in his days. 10. He shall build an house for My name; and he shall be My son, and I will be his Father; and I will establish the throne of his kingdom over Israel for ever. 11. Now, my son, the Lord be with thee; and prosper thou, and build the house of the Lord thy God as He hath said of thee. 12. Only the Lord give thee wisdom and understanding, and give thee charge concerning Israel, that thou mayest keep the law of the Lord thy God, 13. Then shalt thou prosper, if thou takest heed to fulfil the statutes and judgments which the Lord charged Moses with concerning Israel: be strong, and of good courage; dread not, nor be dismayed. 14. Now, behold, in my trouble I have prepared for the house of the Lord an hundred thousand talents of gold, and a thousand thousand talents of silver; and of brass and iron without weight; for it is in abundance: timber also and stone have I prepared and thou mayest add thereto. 15. Moreover, there are workmen with thee in abundance, hewers and workers of stone and timber, and all manner of cunning men for every manner of work. 16. Of the gold, the silver, and the brass, and the iron, there is no number. Arise, therefore, and be doing, and the Lord be with thee.'—1 CHRON. xxii. 6-16.

This passage falls into three parts. In verses 6-10 the old king tells of the divine prohibition which checked his longing to build the Temple; in verses 11-13 he encourages his more fortunate successor, and points him to the only source of strength for his happy task; in verses 14-16 he enumerates the preparations which he had made, the possession of which laid stringent obligations on Solomon.

I. There is a tone of wistfulness in David's voice as he tells how his heart's desire had been prohibited. The account is substantially the same as we have in 2 Samuel vii. 4-16, but it adds as the reason for the prohibition David's warlike career. We may note the earnestness and the motive of the king's desire to build the Temple. 'It was in my heart'; that implies earnest longing and fixed purpose. He had brooded over the wish till it filled his mind, and was consolidated into a settled resolve. Many a musing, solitary moment had fed the fire before it burned its way out in the words addressed to Nathan. So should our whole souls be occupied with our parts in God's service, and so should our desires be strongly set towards carrying out what in solitary meditation we have felt borne in on us as our duty.

The moving spring of David's design is beautifully suggested in the simple words 'unto the name of the Lord my God.' David's religion was eminently a personal bond between him and God. We may almost say that he was the first to give utterance to that cry of the devout heart, 'My God,' and to translate the generalities of the name 'the God of Israel' into the individual appropriation expressed by the former designation. It occurs in many of the psalms attributed to him, and may fairly be regarded as a characteristic of his ardent and individualising devotion. The sense of a close, personal relation to God naturally prompted the impulse to build His house. We must claim our own portion in the universal blessings shrined in His name before we are moved to deeds of loving sacrifice. We must feel that Christ 'loved me, and gave Himself for me,' before we are melted into answering surrender.

The reason for the frustrating of David's desire, as here given, is his career as a warrior king. Not only was it incongruous that hands which had been reddened with blood should rear the Temple, but the fact that his reign had been largely occupied with fighting for the existence of the kingdom showed that the time for engaging in such a work, which would task the national resources, had not yet come. We may draw two valuable lessons from the prohibition. One is that it indicates the true character of the kingdom of God as a kingdom of peace, which is to be furthered, not by force, but in peace and gentleness. The other is that various epochs and men have different kinds of duties in relation to Christ's cause, some being called on to fight, and others to build, and that the one set of tasks may be as sacred and as necessary for the rearing of the Temple as the other. Militant epochs are not usually times for building. The men who have to do destructive work are not usually blessed with the opportunity or the power to carry out constructive work. Controversy has its sphere, but it is mostly preliminary to true 'edification.' In the broadest view all the activity of the Church on earth is militant, and we have to wait for the coming of the true 'Prince of peace' to build up the true Temple in the land of peace, whence all foes have been cast out for ever. To serve God in God's way, and to give up our cherished plans, is not easy; but David sets us an example of simple-hearted, cheerful acquiescence in a Providence that thwarted darling designs. There is often much self-will in what looks like enthusiastic perseverance in some form of service.

II. The charge to Solomon breathes no envy of his privilege, but earnest desire that he may be worthy of the honour which falls to him. Petitions and exhortations are closely blended in it, and, though the work which Solomon is called to do is of an external sort, the qualifications laid down for it are spiritual and moral. However 'secular' our work in connection with God's service may be, it will not be rightly done unless the highest motives are brought to bear on it, and it is performed as worship. The basis of all successful work is God's presence with us, so David prays for that to be granted to Solomon as the beginning of all his fitness for his task.

Next, David recalls to his son God's promise concerning him, that it may hearten him to undertake and to carry on the great work. A conviction that our service is appointed for us by God is essential for vigorous and successful Christian work. We must have, in some way or other, heard Him 'speak concerning us,' if we are to fling ourselves with energy into it.

The petitions in verse 12 seem to stretch beyond the necessities of the case, in so far as building the Temple is concerned. Wisdom and understanding, and a clear consciousness of the duty enjoined on him by God in reference to Israel, were surely more than that work required. But the qualifications for God's service, however the manner of service may be concerned with 'the outward business of the house of God,' are always these which David asked for Solomon. The highest result of true 'wisdom and understanding' given by God is keeping God's law; and keeping it is the one condition on which we shall obtain and retain that presence of God with us which David prayed for Solomon, and without which they labour in vain that build. A life conformed to God's will is the absolutely indispensable condition of all prosperity in direct Christian effort. The noblest exercise of our wisdom and understanding is to obey every word that we hear proceeding out of the mouth of God.

III. There is something very pathetic in the old king's enumeration of the treasures which, by the economies of a lifetime, he had amassed. The amount stated is enormous, and probably there is some clerical error in the numbers specified. Be that as it may, the sum was very large. It represented many an act of self-denial, many a resolute shearing off of superfluities and what might seem necessaries. It was the visible token of long years of fixed attention to one object. And that devotion was all the more noble because the result of it was never to be seen by the man who exercised it.

Therein David is but a very conspicuous example of a law which runs through all our work for God. None of us are privileged to perform completed tasks. 'One soweth and another reapeth.' We have to be content to do partial work, and to leave its completion to our successors. There is but one Builder of whom it can be said that His hands 'have laid the foundation of this house; His hands shall also finish it.' He who is the 'Alpha and Omega,' and He alone, begins and completes the work in which He has neither sharers nor predecessors nor successors. The rest of us do our little bit of the great work which lasts on through the ages, and, having inherited unfinished tasks, transmit them to those who come after us. It is privilege enough for any Christian to lay foundations on which coming days may build. We are like the workers on some great cathedral, which was begun long before the present generation of masons were born, and will not be finished until long after they have dropped trowel and mallet from their dead hands. Enough for us if we can lay one course of stones in that great structure. The greater our aims, the less share has each man in their attainment. But the division of labour is the multiplication of joy, and all who have shared in the toil will be united in the final triumph. It would be poor work that was capable of being begun and perfected in a lifetime. The labourer that dug and levelled the track and the engineer that drives the locomotive over it are partners. Solomon could not have built the Temple unless, through long, apparently idle, years, David had been patiently gathering together the wealth which he bequeathed. So, if our work is but preparatory for that of those who come after, let us not think it of slight importance, and let us be sure that all who have had any portion in the toil shall share in the victory, that 'he that soweth and he that reapeth may rejoice together.'

DAVID'S CHARGE TO SOLOMON

'And David assembled all the princes of Israel, the princes of the tribes, and the captains of the companies that ministered to the king by course, and the captains over the thousands, and captains over the hundreds, and the stewards over all the substance and possession of the king, and of his sons, with the officers, and with the mighty men, and with all the valiant men, unto Jerusalem. 2. Then David the king stood up upon his feet, and said, Hear me, my brethren, and my people: As for me, I had in mine heart to build an house of rest for the ark of the covenant of the Lord, and for the footstool of our God, and had made ready for the building: 3. But God said unto me, Thou shalt not build an house for My name, because thou hast been a man of war, and hast shed blood. 4. Howbeit the Lord God of Israel chose me before all the house of my father to be king over Israel for ever: for He hath chosen Judah to be the ruler; and of the house of Judah, the house of my father; and among the sons of my father He liked me to make me king over all Israel: 5. And of all my sons, (for the Lord hath given me many sons), he hath chosen Solomon my son to sit upon the throne of the kingdom of the Lord over Israel. 6. And He said unto me, Solomon thy son, he shall build My house and My courts: for I have chosen him to be My son, and I will be his father. 7. Moreover I will establish his kingdom for ever, if he be constant to do My commandments and My judgments, as at this day. 8. Now therefore in the sight of all Israel the congregation of the Lord, and in the audience of our God, keep and seek for all the commandments of the Lord your God: that ye may possess this good land, and leave it for an inheritance for your children after you for ever. 9. And thou, Solomon my son, know thou the God of thy father, and serve Him with a perfect heart and with a willing mind: for the Lord searcheth all hearts, and understandeth all the imaginations of the thoughts: if thou seek Him, He will be found of thee; but if thou forsake Him, He will cast thee off for ever. 10. Take heed now; for the Lord hath chosen thee to build an house for the sanctuary: be strong, and do it.'—1 CHRON. xxviii. 1-10.

David had established an elaborate organisation of royal officials, details of which occupy the preceding chapters and interrupt the course of the narrative. The passage picks up again the thread dropped at chapter xxiii. 1. The list of the members of the assembly called in verse 1 is interesting as showing how he tried to amalgamate the old with the new. The princes of Israel, the princes of the tribes, represented the primitive tribal organisation, and they receive precedence in virtue of the antiquity of their office. Then come successively David's immediate attendants, the military officials, the stewards of the royal estates, the 'officers' or eunuchs attached to the palace, and the faithful 'mighty men' who had fought by the king's side in the old days. It was an assembly of officials and soldiers whose adherence to Solomon it was all-important to secure, especially in regard to the project for building the Temple, which could not be carried through without their active support. The passage comprises only the beginning of the proceedings of this assembly of notables. The end is told in the next chapter; namely, that the Temple-building scheme was unanimously and enthusiastically adopted, and large donations given for it, and that Solomon's succession was accepted, and loyal submission offered by the assembly to him.

David's address to this gathering is directed to secure these two points. He begins by recalling his own intention to build the Temple and God's prohibition of it. The reason for that prohibition differs from that alleged by Nathan, but there is no contradiction between the two narratives, and the chronicler has already reported Nathan's words (chap. xvii. 3, etc.), so that the motive which is ascribed to many of the variations in this book, a priestly desire to exalt Temple and ritual, cannot have been at work here. Why should there not have been a divine communication to David as well as Nathan's message? That hands reddened with blood, even though it had been shed in justifiable war, were not fitted to build the Temple, was a thought so far in advance of David's time, and flowing from so spiritual a conception of God, that it may well have been breathed into David's spirit by a divine voice. Sword in one hand and trowel in the other are incongruous, notwithstanding Nehemiah's example. The Temple of the God of peace cannot be built except by men of peace. That is true in the widest and highest application. Jesus builds the true Temple. Controversy and strife do not. And, on a lower level, the prohibition is for ever valid. Men do not atone for a doubtful past by building churches, founding colleges, endowing religious or charitable institutions.

The speech next declares emphatically that the throne belongs to David and his descendants by real 'divine right,' and that God's choice is Solomon, who is to inherit both the promises and obligations of the office, and, among the latter, that of building the Temple. The unspoken inference is that loyalty to Solomon would be obedience to Jehovah. The connection between the true heavenly King and His earthly representative is strongly expressed in the remarkable phrase: 'He hath chosen Solomon ... to sit upon the throne of the kingdom of Jehovah,' which both consecrates and limits the rule of Solomon, making him but the viceroy of the true king of Israel. When Israel's kings remembered that, they flourished; when they forgot it, they destroyed their kingdom and themselves. The principle is as true to-day, and it applies to all forms of influence, authority, and gifts. They are God's, and we are but stewards.

The address to the assembly ends with the exhortation to these leaders to 'observe,' and not merely to observe, but also to 'seek out' God's commandments, and so to secure to the nation, whom they could guide, peaceful and prosperous days. It is not enough to do God's will as far as we know it; we must ever be endeavouring after clearer, deeper insight into it. Would that these words were written over the doors of all Senate and Parliament houses! What a different England we should see!

But Solomon was present as well as the notables, and it was well that, in their hearing, he should be reminded of his duties. David had previously in private taught him these, but this public 'charge' before the chief men of the kingdom bound them more solemnly upon him, and summoned a cloud of witnesses against him if he fell below the high ideal. It is pitched on a lofty key of spiritual religion, for it lays 'Know thou the God of thy fathers' as the foundation of everything. That knowledge is no mere intellectual apprehension, but, as always in Scripture, personal acquaintanceship with a Person, which involves communion with Him and love towards Him. For us, too, it is the seed of all strenuous discharge of our life's tasks, whether we are rulers or nobodies, and it means a much deeper experience than understanding or giving assent to a set of truths about God. We know one another when we summer and winter with each other, and not unless we love one another, and we know God on no other terms.

After such knowledge comes an outward life of service. Active obedience is the expression of inward communion, love, and trust. The spring that moves the hands on the dial is love, and, if the hands do not move, there is something wrong with the spring. Morality is the garment of religion; religion is the animating principle of morality. Faith without works is dead, and works without faith are dead too.

But even when we 'know God' we have to make efforts to have our service correspond with our knowledge, for we have wayward hearts and obstinate wills, which need to be stimulated, sometimes to be coerced and forcibly diverted from unworthy objects. Therefore the exhortation to serve God 'with a perfect heart and with a willing mind' is always needful and often hard. Entire surrender and glad obedience are the Christian ideal, and continual effort to approximate to it will be ours in the degree in which we 'know God.' There is no worse slavery than that of the half-hearted Christian whose yoke is not padded with love. Reluctant obedience is disobedience in God's sight.

David solemnly reminds Solomon of those 'pure eyes and perfect judgment,' not to frighten, but to enforce the thought of the need for whole-hearted and glad service, and of the worthlessness of external acts of apparent worship which have not such behind them. What a deal of seeming wheat would turn out to be chaff if that winnowing fan which is in Christ's hand were applied to it! How small our biggest heaps would become!

The solemn conditions of the continuance of God's favour and of the fulfilment of His promises are next plainly stated. God responds to our state of heart and mind. We determine His bearing to us. The seeker finds. If we move away from Him, He moves away from us. That is not, thank God! all the truth, or what would become of any of us? But it is true, and in a very solemn sense God is to us what we make Him. 'With the pure Thou wilt show Thyself pure; and with the perverse Thou wilt show Thyself froward.'

The charge ends with recalling the high honour and office to which Jehovah had designated Solomon, and with exhortations to 'take heed' and to 'be strong, and do it.' It is well for a young man to begin life with a high ideal of what he is called to be and do. But many of us have that, and miserably fail to realise it, for want of these two characteristics, which the sight of such an ideal ought to stamp on us. If we are to fulfil God's purposes with us, and to be such tools as He can use for building His true Temple, we must exercise self-control and 'take heed to our ways,' and we must brace ourselves against opposition and crush down our own timidity. It seems to be commanding an impossibility to say to a weak creature like any one of us, 'Be strong,' but the impossible becomes a possibility when the exhortation takes the full Christian form: 'Be strong in the Lord, and in the power of His might.'

THE WAVES OF TIME

'The times that went over him.'—1 CHRON. xxix. 30.

This is a fragment from the chronicler's close of his life of King David. He is referring in it to other written authorities in which there are fuller particulars concerning his hero; and he says, 'the acts of David the King, first and last, behold they are written in the book of Samuel the seer ... with all his reign and his might, and the times that went over him, and over all Israel, and over all the kingdoms of the countries.'

Now I have ventured to isolate these words, because they seem to me to suggest some very solemn and stimulating thoughts about the true nature of life. They refer, originally, to the strange vicissitudes and extremes of fortune and condition which characterised, so dramatically and remarkably, the life of King David. Shepherd-boy, soldier, court favourite, outlaw, freebooter and all but brigand; rebel, king, fugitive, saint, sinner, psalmist, penitent—he lived a life full of strongly marked alternations, and 'the times that went over him' were singularly separate and different from each other. There are very few of us who have such chequered lives as his. But the principle which dictated the selection by the chronicler of this somewhat strange phrase is true about the life of every man.

I. Note, first, 'the times' which make up each life.

Now, by the phrase here the writer does not merely mean the succession of moments, but he wishes to emphasise the view that these are epochs, sections of 'time,' each with its definite characteristics and its special opportunities, unlike the rest that lie on either side of it. The great broad field of time is portioned out, like the strips of peasant allotments, which show a little bit here, with one kind of crop upon it, bordered by another little morsel of ground bearing another kind of crop. So the whole is patchy, and yet all harmonises in effect if we look at it from high enough up. Thus each life is made up of a series, not merely of successive moments, but of well-marked epochs, each of which has its own character, its own responsibilities, its own opportunities, in each of which there is some special work to be done, some grace to be cultivated, some lesson to be learned, some sacrifice to be made; and if it is let slip it never comes back any more. 'It might have been once, and we missed it, and lost it for ever.' The times pass over us, and every single portion has its own errand to us. Unless we are wide awake we let it slip, and are the poorer to all eternity for not having had in our heads the eyes of the wise man which 'discern both time and judgment.' It is the same thought which is suggested by the well-known words of the cynical book of Ecclesiastes—'To every thing there is a season and a time'—an opportunity, and a definite period—'for every purpose that is under the sun.' It is the same thought which is suggested by Paul's words, 'As we have therefore opportunity, let us do good to all men. In due season we shall reap if we faint not.' There is 'a time for weeping and a time for laughing, a time for building up and a time for casting down.' It is the same thought of life, and its successive epochs of opportunity never returning, which finds expression in the threadbare lines about 'a tide in the affairs of men, which, taken at the flood, leads on to fortune,' and neglected, condemns the rest of a career to be hemmed in among creeks and shallows.

Through all the variety of human occupations, each moment comes to us with its own special mission, and yet, alas! to far too many of us the alternations do not suggest the question, what is it that I am hereby called upon to be or to do? what is the lesson that present circumstances are meant to teach, and the grace that my present condition is meant to force me to cultivate or exhibit? There is one point, as it were, upon the road where we may catch a view far away into the distance, and, if we are not on the lookout when we come there, we shall never get that glimpse at any other point along the path. The old alchemists used to believe that there was what they called the 'moment of projection,' when, into the heaving molten mass in their crucible, if they dropped the magic powder, the whole would turn into gold; an instant later and there would be explosion and death; an instant earlier and there would be no effect. And so God's moments come to us; every one of them—if we had eyes to see and hands to grasp—a crisis, affording opportunity for something for which all eternity will not afford a second opportunity, if the moment be let pass. 'The times went over him,' and your life and mine is parcelled out into seasons which have their special vocation for and message to us.

How solemn that makes our life! How it destroys the monotony that we sometimes complain of! How it heightens the low things and magnifies the apparently small ones! And how it calls upon us for a sharpened attention, that we miss not any of the blessings and gifts which God is meaning to bestow upon us through the ministry of each moment! How it calls upon us for not only sharpened attention, but for a desire to know the meaning of each of the hours and of every one of His providences! And how it bids us, as the only condition of understanding the times, so as to know what we ought to do, to keep our hearts in close union with Him, and ourselves ever standing, as becomes servants, girded and ready for work; and with the question on our lips and in our hearts, 'Lord, what wouldst Thou have me to do? and what wouldst Thou have me to do *now*?' The lesson of the day has to be learned in a day, and at the moment when it is put in practice.

II. Another thought suggested by this text is, the Power that moves the times.

As far as my text represents—and it is not intended to go to the bottom of everything—these times flow on over a man, as a river might. But is there any power that moves the stream? Unthinking and sense-bound men—and we are all such, in the measure in which we are unspiritual—are contented simply to accept the mechanical flow of the stream of time. We are all tempted not to look behind the moving screen to see the force that turns the wheel on which the painted scene Is stretched. But, Oh! how dreary a thing it is if all that we have to say about life is, 'The times pass over us,' like the blind rush of a stream, or the movement of the sea around our coasts, eating away here and depositing its spoils there, sometimes taking and sometimes giving, but all the work of mere eyeless and purposeless chance or of natural causes.

Oh, brethren! there is nothing more dismal or paralysing than the contemplation of the flow of the times over our heads, unless we see in their flow something far more than that.

It is very beautiful to notice that this same phrase, or at least the essential part of it, is employed in one of the Psalms ascribed to David, with a very significant addition. He says, 'My times are *in Thy hand.*' So, then, the passage of our epochs over us is not merely the aimless flow of a stream, but the movement of a current which God directs. Therefore, if at any time it goes over our heads and seems to overwhelm us, we can look up through the transparent water and say, '*Thy* waves and *Thy* billows have gone over me,' and so I die not of suffocation beneath them. God orders the times, and therefore, though, as the bitter ingenuity of Ecclesiastes, on the lookout for proofs of the vanity of life, complained, in a one-sided view, as an aggravation of man's lot, that there is a time for everything, yet that aspect of change is not its deepest or truest. True it is that sometimes birth and sometimes death, sometimes joy and sometimes sorrow, sometimes building up and sometimes casting down, follow each other with monotonous uniformity of variety, and seem to reduce life to a perpetual heaping up of what is as painfully to be cast down the next moment, like the pitiless sport of the wind amongst the sandhills of the desert. But the futility is only apparent, and the changes are not meant to occasion 'man's misery' to be 'great upon him,' as Ecclesiastes says they do. The diversity of the 'times' comes from a unity of purpose; and all the various methods of the divine Providence exercised upon us have one unchanging intention. The meaning of all the 'times' is that they should bring us nearer to God, and fill us more full of His power and grace. The web is one, however various may be the pattern wrought upon the tapestry. The resulting motion of the great machine is one, though there may be a wheel turning from left to right here, and another one that fits into it, turning from right to left there. The end of all the opposite motions is straight progress. So the varying times do all tend to the one great issue. Therefore let us seek to pursue, in all varying circumstances, the one purpose which God has in them all, which the Apostle states to be 'even your sanctification,' and let us understand how summer and winter, springtime and harvest, tempest and fair weather, do all together make up the year, and ensure the springing of the seed and the fruitfulness of the stalk.

III. Lastly, let me remind you, too, how eloquently the words of my text suggest the transiency of all the 'times.'

They 'passed over him' as the wind through an archway, that whistles and comes not again. The old, old thought, so threadbare and yet always so solemnising and pathetic, which we know so well that we forget it, and are so sure of that it has little effect on life, the old, old thought, 'this too will pass away,' underlies the phrase of my text,

How blessed it is, brethren! to cherish that wholesome sense of the transiency of things here below, only those who live under its habitual power can fairly estimate. It is thought to be melancholy. We are told that it spoils joys and kills interest, and I know not what beside. It spoils no joys that ought to be joys. It kills no interests that are not on other grounds unworthy to be cherished. Contrariwise, the more fully we are penetrated with the persistent conviction of the transiency of the things seen and temporal, the greater they become, by a strange paradox. For then only are they seen in their true magnitude and nobility, in their true solemnity and importance as having a bearing on the things that are eternal. Time is the 'ceaseless lackey of eternity,' and the things that pass over us may become, like the waves of the sea, the means of bearing us to the unmoving shore. Oh! if only in the midst of joys and sorrows, of heavy tasks and corroding cares, of weary work and wounded spirits, we could feel, 'but for a moment,' all would be different, and joy would come, and strength would come, and patience would come, and every grace would come, in the train of the wholesome conviction that 'here we have no continuing city.'

Cherish the thought. It will spoil nothing the spoiling of which will be a loss. It will heighten everything the possession of which is a gain. It will teach us to trust in the darkness, and to believe in the light. And when the times are dreariest, and frost binds the ground, we shall say, 'If winter comes, can spring be far behind?' The times roll over us, like the seas that break upon some isolated rock, and when the tide has fallen and the vain flood has subsided, the rock is there. If the world helps us to God, we need not mind though it passes, and the fashion thereof.

But do not let us forget that this text in its connection may teach us another thought. The transitory 'times that went over' Israel's king are all recorded imperishably on the pages here, and so, though condensed into narrow space, the record of the fleeting moments lives for ever, and 'the books shall be opened, and men shall be judged according to their works.' We are writing an imperishable record by our fleeting deeds. Half a dozen pages carry all the story of that stormy life of Israel's king. It takes a thousand rose-trees to make a vial full of essence of roses. The record and issues of life will be condensed into small compass, but the essence of it is eternal. We shall find it again, and have to drink as we have brewed when we get yonder. 'Be not deceived, God is not mocked, for whatsoever a man soweth that shall he also reap.' 'There is a time to sow,' and that is the present life; 'and there is a time to gather the fruits' of our sowing, and that is the time when times have ended and eternity is here.

THE SECOND BOOK OF CHRONICLES

THE DUTY OF EVERY DAY

'Then Solomon offered burnt offerings unto the Lord ... Even after a certain rate every day.'—(A.V.)

'Then Solomon offered burnt offerings unto the Lord, even as the duty of every day required it.'—2 Chron. viii. 12-13 (R. V.).

This is a description of the elaborate provision, in accordance with the commandment of Moses, which Solomon made for the worship in his new Temple. The writer is enlarging on the precise accordance of the ritual with the regulations laid down in the law. He expresses, by the phrase which we have taken as our text, not only the accordance of the worship with the commandment, but its unbroken continuity, and also the variety in it, according to the regulations for different days. For the verse runs on, 'on the Sabbaths, and on the new moons, and on the solemn feasts, three times in the year, even in the Feast of unleavened bread, and in the Feast of weeks, and in the Feast of Tabernacles.' There were, then, these characteristics in the ritual of Solomon's Temple, precise compliance with the Divine commandment, unbroken continuity, and beautiful flexibility and variety of method.

But passing altogether from the original application of the words, I venture to do now what I very seldom do, and that is, to take this verse as a kind of motto. 'Even according as the duty of every day required'; the phrase may suggest three thoughts: that each day has its own work, its own worship, and its own supplies, 'even as the duty of every day required.'

Each day has its own work.

Of course there is a great uniformity in our lives, and many of us who are set down to one continuous occupation can tell twelve months before what, in all probability, we shall be doing at each hour of each day in the week. But for all that, there is a certain individual physiognomy about each new day as it comes to us; and the oldest, most habitual, and therefore in some degree easiest and least stimulating, work has its own special characteristics as it comes again to us day by day for the hundredth time.

So there are three pieces of practical wisdom that I would suggest, and one is—be content to take your work in little bits as it comes. There is a great deal of practical wisdom in taking short views of things, for although we have often to look ahead, yet it is better on the whole that a man should, as far as he can, confine his anticipations to the day that is passing, and leave the day that is coming to look after itself. Take short views and be content to let each

- 73 -

day prescribe its tasks, and you have gone a long way to make all your days quiet and peaceful. For it is far more the anticipation of difficulties than the realisation of them that wears and wearies us. If a man says to himself, 'This sorrow that I am carrying, or this work that I have to do, is going to last for many days to come,' his heart will fail. If he said to himself, 'It will be no worse to-morrow than it is at this moment, and I can live through it, for am I not living through it at this moment, and getting power to endure or do at this moment? and to-morrow will probably be like today,' things would not be so difficult.

You remember the homely old parable of the clock on the stair that gave up ticking altogether because it began to calculate how many thousands of seconds there are in the year, and that twice that number of times it would have to wag backwards and forwards. The lesson that it learned was—tick one tick and never mind the next. You will be able to do it when the time to do it comes. Let us act 'as the duty of every day requireth.' 'Sufficient for the day is the work thereof.'

Then there is another piece of advice from this thought of each day having its own work, and that is—keep your ears open, and your eyes too, to learn the lesson of what the day's work is. There is generally abundance of direction for us if only we are content with the one-step-at-a-time direction, which we get, and if another condition is fulfilled, if we try to suppress our own wishes and the noisy babble of our own yelping inclinations, and take the whip to them until they cease their barking, that we may hear what God says. It is not because He does not speak, but because we are too anxious to have our own way to listen quietly to His voice, that we make most of our blunders as to what the duty of every day requires. If we will be still and listen, and stand in the attitude of the boy-prophet before the glimmering lamp in the sacred place, saying, 'Speak, Lord! for Thy servant heareth,' we shall get sufficient instruction for our next step.

Another piece of practical wisdom that I would suggest is that if every day has its own work, we should buckle ourselves to do the day's work before night falls and not leave any over for to-morrow, which will be quite full enough. 'Do the duty that lies nearest thee,' was the preaching of one of our sages, and it is wholesome advice. For when we do that duty, the doing of it has a wonderful power of opening up further steps, and showing us more clearly what is the next duty. Only let us be sure of this, that no moment comes from God which has not in it boundless possibilities; and that no moment comes from God which has not in it stringent obligations. We neither avail ourselves of the one, nor discharge the other, unless we come, morning by morning, to the new day that is dawning upon us, with some fresh consciousness of the large issues that may be wrapped in its unseen hours, and the great things for Him that we may do ere its evening falls.

Each day has its tasks, and if we do not do the tasks of each day in its day, we shall fling away life. If a man had L. 100,000 for a fortune, and turned it all into halfpence, and tossed them out of the window, he could soon get rid of his whole fortune. And if you fling away your moments or live without the consciousness of their solemn possibilities and mystic awfulness, you will find at the last that you have made 'ducks and drakes' of your years, and have flung them away in moments without knowing what you were doing, and without possibility of recovery. 'Take care of the pence, the pounds will take care of themselves.' Take care of the days, and the years will show a fair record.

Secondly, we have here the suggestion that every day has its own worship.

As I remarked at the beginning of my observations, the chronicler dwells, with a certain kind of satisfaction, in accordance with the tone of his whole writings, upon the external ritual of the Temple; and points out its entire conformity with the divine precept, and the unbroken continuity of worship day after day, year in year out, and the variation of the characteristics of that worship according as the day was more or less ritually important. From his words we may deduce a very needful though obvious and commonplace lesson. What we want is every-day religion, and that every-day religion is the only thing that will enable us to do what the duty of every day requires. But that every-day religion which will be our best ally, and power for the discharge of the obligations that each moment brings with it, must have its points of support, as it were, in special moments and methods of worship.

So, then, take that first thought: What we want is a religion that will go all through our lives. A great many of you keep your religion where you keep your best clothes: putting it on on Sunday and locking it away on the Sunday night in a wardrobe because it is not the dress that you go to work in. And some of you keep your religion in your pew, and lock it up in the little box where you put your hymn-books and your Bibles, which you read only once a week, devoting yourselves to ledgers or novels and newspapers for the rest of your time. We want a religion that will go all through our life; and if there is anything in our life that will not stand its presence, the sooner we get rid of that element the better. A mountain road has generally a living brooklet leaping and flashing by the side of it. So our lives will be dusty and dead and cold and poor and prosaic unless that river runs along by the roadside and makes music for us as it flows. Take your religion wherever you go. If you cannot take it in to any scenes or company, stop you outside.

There is nothing that will help a man to do his day's work so much as the realisation of Christ's Presence. And that realisation, along with its certain results, devotion of heart to Him and submission of will to His commandment, and desire to shape our lives to be like His, will make us

- 75 -

masters of all circumstances and strong enough for the hardest work that God can lay upon us.

There is nothing so sure to make life beautiful, and noble, and pure, and peaceful, and strong as this—the application to its monotonous trifles of religious principles. If you do not do little things as Christian men and women, and under the influence of Christian principle, pray *what* are you going to do under the influence of Christian principle? If you are keeping your religion to influence the crises of your lives, and are content to let the trifles be ruled by the devil or the world and yourselves, you will find out, when you come to the end, that there were perhaps three or four crises in your experience, and that all the rest of life was made of trifles, and that when the crises came you could not lay your hand on the religious principle that would have enabled you to deal with them. The sword had got so rusty in its scabbard because it had never been drawn for long years, that it could not be readily drawn in the moment of sudden peril; and if you could have drawn it, you would have found its edge blunted. Use your religion on the trifles, or you will not be able to make much of it in the crises. 'He that is faithful in that which is least is faithful also in much.' The worship of every day is the preparation for the work of that day.

Further, that worship, that religion, wearing its common, modest suit of workaday clothes, must also, if there is to be any power in it, have a certain variety in its methods. 'Solomon offered burnt offerings … on the Sabbaths, on the new moons,' which had a little more ceremonial than the Sabbaths, 'and on the solemn feasts three times in a year,' which had still more ceremonial than the new moons, 'even in the Feast of unleavened bread, and in the Feast of weeks, and in the Feast of tabernacles.' These were spring-tides when the sea of worship rose beyond its usual level, and they kept it from stagnating. We, too, if we wish to have this every-day religion running with any strength of scour and current through our lives, will need to have moments when it touches high-water mark, else it will not flush the foulness out of our hearts and our lives.

Lastly, take the other suggestion, that every day has its own supplies.

That does not lie in the text properly, but for the sake of completeness I add it. Every day has its own supplies. The manna fell every day, and was gathered and consumed on the day on which it fell. God gives us strength measured accurately by the needs of the day. You will get as much as you require, and if ever you do not get as much as you require, which is very often the case with Christian people, that is not because God did not send enough manna, but because their *omer* was not ready to catch it as it fell. The day's supply is measured by the day's need. Suppose an Israelite had sat in his tent and said, 'I am not going out to gather,' would he have had any in his empty vessel? Certainly not. The manna lay all around the tent, but each man had to go out and gather it. God makes no mistakes in His weights and measures. He gives us each sufficient strength to do His will and to walk in His ways; and if we do not do His will or walk in His ways, or if we find our burden too heavy, our sorrows too sharp, our loneliness too dreary, our difficulties too great, it is not because 'the Lord's hand is shortened that it cannot' supply, but because our hands are so slack that they will not take the sufficiency which He gives. In the midst of abundance we are starving. We let the water run idly through the open sluice instead of driving the wheels of life.

My friend! God's measure of supply is correct. If we were more faithful and humble, and if we understood better and felt more how deep is our need and how little is our strength, we should more continually be able to rejoice that He has given, and we have received, 'even as the duty of every day required.'

CONTRASTED SERVICES

'They shall be his servants: that they may know My service, and the service of the kingdoms of the countries.'—2 Chron. xii. 8.

Rehoboam was a self-willed, godless king who, like some other kings, learned nothing by experience. His kingdom was nearly wrecked at the very beginning of his reign, and was saved much more by the folly of his rival than by his own wisdom. Jeroboam's religious revolution drove all the worshippers of God among the northern kingdom into flight. They might have endured the separate monarchy, but they could not endure the separate Temple. So all priests and Levites in Israel, and all the adherents of the ancestral worship in the Temple at Jerusalem, withdrew to the southern kingdom and added much to its strength.

Rehoboam's narrow escape taught him neither moderation nor devotion, his new strength turned his head. He forsook the law of the Lord. The dreary series, so often illustrated in the history of Israel, came into operation. Prosperity produced irreligion; irreligion brought chastisement; chastisement brought repentance; repentance brought the removal of the invader—and then, like a spring released, back went king and nation to their old sin.

So here—Rehoboam's sins take visible form in Sheshak's army. He has sown the dragon's teeth and they spring up armed men. Shemaiah the prophet, the first of the long series of noble men who curbed the violence of Jewish monarchs, points the lesson of invasion in plain, blunt words: 'Ye have forsaken Me.' Then follow penitence and confession—and the promise that Jerusalem shall not be destroyed, but at the same time they are to be left as vassals and tributaries of Egypt—an anomalous position for them—and the reason is given in these words of our text.

I. The contrasted Masters.

Judah was too small to be independent of the powerful warlike states to its north and south, unless miraculously guarded and preserved. So it must either keep near God, and therefore free and safe from invasion, or else, departing from God and following its own ways, fall under alien dominion. Its experience was a type of that of universal humanity. Man is not independent. His mass is not enough for him to do without a central orb round which he may revolve. He has a choice of the form of service and the master that he will choose, but one or other must dominate his life and sway his motions. 'Ye cannot serve God and Mammon'; ye must serve God *or* Mammon. The solemn choice is presented to every man, but the misery of many lives is that they drift along, making their election unawares, and infallibly choosing the worse by the very act of lazily or weakly allowing accident to determine their lives. Not consciously and strongly to will the right, not resolutely and with coercion of the vagrant self to will to take God for our aim, is to choose the low, the wrong. Perhaps none, or very few of us, would deliberately say 'I choose Mammon, having carefully compared the claims of the opposite systems of life that solicit me, and with open-eyed scrutiny measured their courses, their goods and their ends.' But how many of us there are who have in effect made that choice, and never have given one moment's clear, patient examination of the grounds of our choice! The policy of drift is unworthy of a man and is sure to end in ruin.

It is not for me to attempt here to draw out the contrast between man's chief end and all other rival claimants of our lives. Each man must do that for himself, and I venture to assert that the more thoroughly the process of comparison is carried out, and the more complete the analysis not only of the rival claims and gifts, but of our capacities and needs, the more sun-clear will be the truth of the old, well-worn answer: 'Man's chief end is to glorify God and to enjoy Him for ever.' The old woman by her solitary fireside who has learned that and practises it, has chosen the better part which will last when many shining careers have sunk into darkness, and many will-o'-the-wisps, which have been pursued with immense acclamations, have danced away into the bog, and many a man who has been envied and admired has had to sum up his successful career in the sad words, 'I have played the fool and erred exceedingly.' I cannot pretend to conduct the investigation for you, but I can press on every one who does not wish to let accidents mould him, at least to recognise that there is a choice to be made, and to make it deliberately and with eyes open to the facts of the case. It is a shabby way of ruining yourself to do it for want of thought. The rabble of competitors of God catch more souls by accident than of set purpose. Most men are godless because they have never fairly faced the question: what does my soul require in order to reach its highest blessedness and its noblest energy?

II. The contrasted experience of the servants.

Judah learned that the yoke of obedience to God's law was a world lighter than the grinding oppression of the Egyptian invader.

God's service is freedom; the world's is slavery.

Liberty is unrestrained power to do what we ought. Man must be subject to law. The solemn imperative of duty is omnipresent and sovereign. To do as we like is not freedom, but bondage to self, and that usually our worst self, which means crushing or coercing the better self. The choice is to chain the beast in us or to clip the wings of the angel in us, and he is a fool who conceits himself free because he lets his inferior self have its full swing, and hustles his better self into bondage to clear the course for the other. There is but one deliverance from the sway of self, and it is realised in the liberty wherewith Christ has made us free. To make self our master inevitably leads to setting beggars on horseback and princes walking. Passion, the 'flesh' is terribly apt to usurp the throne within when once God is dethroned. Then indulgence feeds passion, and deeper draughts become necessary in order to produce the same effects, and cravings, once allowed free play, grow in ravenousness, while their pabulum steadily loses its power to satisfy. The experience of the undevout sensualist is but too faithful a type of that of all undevout livers, in the failure of delights to delight and of acquisitions to enrich, and in the bondage, often to nothing more worthy to be obeyed than mere habit, and in the hopeless incapacity to shake off the adamantine chains which they have themselves rivetted on their limbs. There are endless varieties in the forms which the service of self assumes, ranging from gross animalism, naked and unashamed, up to refined and cultured godlessness, but they are one in their inmost character, one in their disabling the spirit from a free choice of its course, one in the limitations which they impose on its aspirations and possibilities, one in the heavy yoke which they lay on their vassals. The true liberty is realised only when for love's dear sake we joyously serve God, and from the highest motive enrol ourselves in the household of the highest Person, and by the act become 'no more servants but sons.' Well may we all pray—

> 'Lord! bind me up, and let me lie
> A prisoner to my liberty,
> If such a state at all can be
> As an imprisonment, serving Thee.'

God's service brings solid good, the world's is vain and empty.

God's service brings an approving conscience, a calm heart, strength and gladness. It is in full accord with our best selves. Tranquil joys attend on it. 'In keeping Thy commandments there is great reward,' and that not merely bestowed after keeping, but realised and inherent in the very act. On the other side, think of the stings of conscience, the illusions on which those feed who will not eat of the heavenly food, the husks of the swine-trough, the ashes for bread, that self and the world, in all their forms set before men. A pathetic character in modern fiction says, 'If you make believe very much it is nice.' It takes a tremendous amount of make-believe to keep up an appetite for the world's dainties or to find its meats palatable, after a little while. No sin ever yields the fruit it was expected to produce, or if it does it brings something which was not expected, and the bitter tang of the addition spoils the whole. It may be wisely adapted to secure a given end, but that end is only a means to secure the real end, our substantial blessedness, and that is never attained but by one course of life, the life of service of God. We may indeed win a goodly garment, but the plague is in the stuff and, worn, it will burn into the bones like fire. I read somewhere lately of thieves who had stolen a cask of wine, and had their debauch, but they sickened and died. The cask was examined and a huge snake was found dead in it. Its poison had passed into the wine and killed the drinkers. That is how the world serves those who swill its cup. 'What fruit had ye then in those things whereof ye are *now* ashamed?' The threatening pronounced against Israel's disobedience enshrines an eternal truth: 'Because thou servedst not the Lord thy God with joyfulness, and with gladness of heart, by reason of the abundance of all things; therefore shalt thou serve thine enemies … in hunger and in thirst, and in nakedness and in want of all things.'

God's service has final issues and the world's service has final issues.

Only fools try to blink the fact that all our doings have consequences. And it augurs no less levity and insensibility to blink the other fact that these consequences show no indications of being broken short off at the end of our earthly life. Men die into another life, as they have ever, dimly and with many foolish accompaniments, believed; and dead, they are the men that they have made themselves while living. Character is eternal, memory is eternal, death puts the stamp of perpetuity on what life has evolved. Nothing human ever dies. The thought is too solemn to be vulgarised by pulpit rhetoric. Enough to say here that these two tremendous alternatives, Life and Death, express some little part of the eternal issues of our fleeting days. Looking fixedly into these two great symbols of the ultimate issues of these contrasted services, we can dimly see, as in the one, a wonder of resplendent glories moving in a sphere 'as calm as it is bright,' so, in the other, whirling clouds and jets of vapour as in the crater of a volcano. One shuddering glance over the rim of it should suffice to warn from lingering near, lest the unsteady soil should crumble beneath our feet.

But the true Lord of our lives loves us too well to let us experience all the bitter issues of our foolish rebellion against His authority, and yet He loves us too well not to let us taste something of them that we may 'know and see that it is an evil thing *and a bitter*, that thou hast forsaken the Lord thy God.' The experiences of the consequences of godless living are in some measure allowed to fall on us by God's love, lest we should persist in the evil and so bring down on ourselves still more fatal issues. It is mercy that here chastises the evildoer with whips, in hope of not having to chastise him with scorpions. God desires to teach us, by the pains and heartaches of an undevout life, by disappointments, foiled plans, wrecked hopes, inner poverty, the difference between His service and that of 'the kingdoms of the countries,' if haply He may not be forced to let the full flood of fatal results overwhelm us. It is best to be drawn to serve Him by the cords of love, but it is possible to have the beginnings of the desire so to serve roused by the far lower motives of weariness and disgust at the world's wages, and by dread of what these may prove when they are paid in full. Self-interest may sicken a man of serving Mammon, and may be transformed into the self-surrender which makes God's service possible and blessed. The flight into the city of refuge may be quickened by the fear of the pursuer, whose horse's hoofs are heard thundering on the road behind the fugitive, and whose spear is all but felt a yard from his back, but once within the shelter of the city wall, gratitude for deliverance will fill his heart and 'perfect love will cast out fear.'

The king concerning whom our text was spoken had to suffer humiliation by the Egyptian invasion. His sufferings were meant to be educational, and when they in some measure effected their purpose, God curbed the invader and granted some measure of deliverance. So is it with us, if, moved by whatever impulse, we betake ourselves to Jesus to save us from the bitter fruits of our evil lives. The extreme severity of the results of our sins does not fall on penitent, believing spirits, but some do fall. As the Psalmist says: 'Thou wast a God that forgavest them though Thou tookest vengeance of their inventions.' A profligate course of life may be forgiven, but health or fortune is ruined all the same. In brief, the so-called 'natural' consequences are not removed, though the sin which caused them is pardoned. Polluted memories, indulged habits, defiled imaginations, are not got rid of, though the sins that inflicted them are forgiven.

Is it not, then, the part of wise men to lay to heart the lessons of experience, and to let what we have learned of the bitter fruit of godless living turn us away from such service, and draw us by merciful chastisement to yield ourselves to God, whom to serve accords with our deepest needs and brings first fruits and pre-libations of blessedness and peace here, and fullness of joy with pleasures for evermore hereafter?

THE SECRET OF VICTORY

'The children of Judah prevailed, because they relied upon the Lord God of their fathers.'—2 CHRON. xiii. 18.

These words are the summing-up of the story of a strange old-world battle between Jeroboam, the adventurer who rent the kingdom, and Abijah, the son of the foolish Rehoboam, whose unseasonable blustering had played into the usurper's hands. The son was a wiser and better man than his father. It is characteristic of the ancient world, that before battle was joined Abijah made a long speech to the enemy, recounting the ritual deficiencies of the Northern kingdom, and proudly contrasting the punctilious correctness of the Temple service with the irregular cult set up by Jeroboam. He confidently pointed to the priests 'with their trumpets' in his army as the visible sign that 'God is with us at our head,' and while charging Israel with having 'forsaken the Lord our God,' to whom he and his people had kept true, besought them not to carry their rebellion to the extreme of fighting against their fathers' God, and assured them that no success could attend their weapons in such a strife. The passionate appeal had no effect, but while Abijah was orating, Jeroboam was carrying out a ruse, and planting part of his troops behind Judah, so as to put them between two fires and draw a net round the outnumbered and outmanoeuvred enemy.

Abijah and his men suddenly detected their desperate position, and did the only wise thing. When, with a shock of surprise, they saw that 'behold! the battle was before and behind them,' they 'cried unto the Lord, and the priests sounded with the trumpets.' The sharp, short cry from thousands of agitated men ringed round by foes, and the blare of the trumpets were both prayers, and heartened the suppliants for their whirlwind charge, before which the men of Israel, double in number as they were, broke and fled. The defeat was thorough, and, for a while, Rehoboam and his kingdom were 'brought under,' and a comparatively long peace followed. Our text gathers up the lesson taught, not to Judah or Israel alone, by victory and defeat, when it declares that to rely upon the Lord is to prevail. It opens for us the secret of victory, in that old far-off struggle and in to-day's conflicts.

I. We note the faith of the fighters.

'They relied,' says the chronicler, 'upon the Lord.' Now the word rendered 'relied' is one of several picturesque words by which the Old Testament, which we are sometimes told, with a great flourish of learning, has no mention of 'faith,' expresses 'trust,' by metaphors drawn from bodily actions which symbolise the spiritual act. The word here literally signifies to lean on, as a feeble hand might on a staff, or a tremulous arm on a strong one. And does not that picture carry with it much insight into what the essence of Old Testament 'trust' or New Testament 'faith' is? If we think of faith as leaning, we shall not fall into that starved misconception of it which takes it to be nothing more than intellectual assent. We shall see there is a far fuller pulse of feeling than that beating in it. A man who leans on some support, does so because he knows that his own strength is insufficient for his need. The consciousness of weakness is the beginning of faith. He who has never despaired of himself has scarcely trusted in God. Abijah's enemies were two to one of his own men. No wonder that they cried unto the Lord, and felt a stound of despair shake their courage. And who of us can face life with its heavy duties, its thick-clustering dangers and temptations, its certain struggles, its possible failures, and not feel the cold touch of dread gripping our hearts, though strong and brave? Surely he has had little experience, or has learned little wisdom from the experience he has had, who has yet to discover his own weakness. But the consciousness of weakness is by itself debilitating, and but increases the weakness of which it is painfully aware. There is no surer way to sap what strength we have than to tell ourselves what poor creatures we are. The purpose and end of self-contemplation which becomes aware of our own feebleness is to lead us to the contemplation of God, our immortal strength. Abijah's assurance that 'God is with us at our head' rang out triumphantly. Faith has an upper and an under side: the under side is self-distrust; the upper, trust in God. He will never lean all his weight on a prop, who fancies that he can stand alone, or has other stays to hold him up.

But Abijah's example teaches us another lesson—that for a vigorous faith, there must be obedience to all God's known will. True, thank God! faith often springs in its power in a soul that is conscious but of sin, but a continuance in disobedience will inevitably kill faith. It was because Abijah and his people had kept 'the charge of the Lord our God,' that they were sure that God was with them. We can only be sure of God to lean on when we are doing His will, and we shall do His will only as we are sure that we lean on Him. Our trust in Him will be strong and operative in the measure in which our lives are conformed to His commandments. Much elaborate dissertation has been devoted to expounding what faith is, and the strong, vivid Scriptural conception of it has been woefully darkened and overlaid with cobwebs of theology, but surely this eloquent metaphor of our text tells us more than do many learned volumes. It bids us lean on God, rest the whole weight of our needs, our weaknesses, and our sins on Him. Like any human friend or helper, He is better pleased when we lean hard on Him than when we gingerly put a finger on His arm, and lay no pressure on it, as we do when in ceremonial fashion we seem to accept another's support, and hold ourselves back from putting a weight on the offered arm. We cannot rely too utterly on Him. We honour Him most when we repose our whole selves on His strong arm.

II. The increase of faith by sudden fear.

'When Judah looked back, behold, the battle was before and behind them.' The shock of seeing the flashing spears in the rear would make the bravest hold their breath for one overwhelming moment, but the next moment their faith in God surged back with tenfold force, increased by the sudden new peril. The sharp collision of flint and steel struck out a spark of faith. 'What time I am afraid, I will trust in Thee,' said an expert in the genesis and growth of trust. Peril kills a feeble trust, but vivifies it, if strong. The recognition of danger is meant to drive us to God. If each fresh difficulty or danger makes us tighten our clasp of Him, and lean the harder on Him, it has done its highest service to us, and we have conquered it, and are the stronger because of it. The storm that makes the traveller, fighting with the wind and the rain in his face, clasp his cloak tighter round him, does him no harm. The purpose of our trials is to drive us to God, and a fair-weather faith which had all but fallen asleep is often roused to energy that works wonders, by the sudden dash of danger flung into and disturbing a life. It is wise seamanship to make a run to get snugly behind the breakwater when a sudden gale springs up.

III. The expression of faith in appeal to God.

When the ambush was unmasked, the surrounded men of Judah 'cried unto the Lord, and the priests sounded with the trumpets,' before they flung themselves on the enemy. We may be sure that their cry was short and sharp, and poignant with appeal to God. There would be no waste words, nor perfunctory petitions without wings of desire, in that cry. Should we not look for the essential elements of prayer rather to such cries, pressed from burdened hearts by a keen sense of absolute helplessness, and very careless of proprieties so long as they were shrill enough to pierce God's ear and touch His heart, than to the formal petitions of well-ordered worship? A single ejaculation flung heavenward in a moment of despair or agony is more precious in God's sight than a whole litany of half-hearted devotions.

The text puts in a striking form another lesson well worth learning, that, in the greatest crises, no time is better spent than time used for prayer. A rush on the enemy would not have served Abijah's purpose nearly so well as that moment's pause for crying to the Lord, before his charge. Hands lifted to heaven are nerved to clutch the sword and strike manfully. It is not only that Christ's soldiers are to fight and pray, but that they fight by praying. That is true in the small conflicts and antagonisms of the lives of each of us, and it is true in regard to the agelong battle against ignorance and sin. Christian's sword was named 'All-prayer.'

The priests, too, blew a prayer through their trumpets, for the ordinance had appointed that 'when ye go to war ... then shall ye sound an alarm with the trumpets; and ye shall be remembered before the Lord your God, and ye shall be saved from your enemies.' The clear, strident blare was not intended to hearten warriors, or to sing defiance, but to remind God of His promises, and to bring Him on to the battlefield, as He had said that He would be. The truest prayer is that which but picks up the arrows of promise shot from heaven to earth, and casts them back from earth to heaven. He prays best who fills his mouth with God's words, turning every 'I will' of His into 'Do Thou!'

IV. The strength that comes through faith.

'As the men of Judah shouted, it came to pass that God smote Jeroboam and all Israel before Abijah and Judah.' There is no such quickener of all a man's natural force as even the lowest forms of faith. He who throws himself into any enterprise sure of success will often succeed just because he was sure he would. The world's history is full of instances where men, with every odds against them, have plucked the flower safety out of the nettle danger, just because they trusted in their star, or their luck, or their destiny. We all know how a very crude faith turned a horde of wild Arabs into a conquering army, that in a century dominated the world from Damascus to Seville. The truth that is in 'Christian Science' is that many forms of disease yield to the patient's firm persuasion of recovery. And from these and many other facts the natural power of faith is beginning to dawn on the most matter-of-fact and unspiritual people. They are beginning to think that perhaps Christ was right after all in saying 'All things are possible to him that believeth,' and that it is not such a blunder after all to make faith the first step to all holiness and purity, and the secret of victory in life's tussle. Leaving out of view for the moment the supernatural effects of faith, which Christianity alleges are its constant consequences, it is clear that its natural effects are all in the direction of increasing the force of the trusting man. It calms, it heartens for all work, effort, and struggle. It imparts patience, it brightens hope, it forbids discouragement, it rebukes and cures despondency. And besides all this, there is the supernatural communication of a strength not our own, which is the constant result of Christian faith. Christian faith knits the soul and the Saviour in so close a union, that all that is Christ's becomes the Christian's, and every believer may hear His Lover's voice whispering to him what one of His servants once heard in an hour of despondency, 'My grace is sufficient for thee, for My power is made perfect in weakness.' Faith joins us to the Lord, and 'he that is joined to the Lord is one spirit'; and that Lord has said to all His disciples, 'I give thee Myself, and in Myself all that is Mine.' We do not go to warfare at our own charges, but there will pass into and abide in our hearts the warlike might of the true King and Captain of the Lord's host, and we shall hear the ring of His encouraging voice saying, 'Be of good cheer! I have overcome the world.'

ASA'S REFORMATION, AND CONSEQUENT PEACE AND VICTORY

'And Asa did that which was good and right in the eyes of the Lord his God; 3. For he took away the altars of the strange gods, and the high places, and brake down the images, and cut down the groves: 4. And commanded Judah to seek the Lord God of their fathers, and to do the law and the commandment. 5. Also he took away out of all the cities of Judah the high places and the images: and the kingdom was quiet before him. 6. And he built fenced cities in Judah: for the land had rest, and he had no war in those years; because the Lord had given him rest. 7. Therefore he said unto Judah, Let us build these cities, and make about them walls, and towers, gates, and bars, while the land is yet before us; because we have sought the Lord our God, we have sought Him, and He hath given us rest on every side. So they built and prospered. 8. And Asa had an army of men that bare targets and spears, out of Judah three hundred thousand; and out of Benjamin, that bare shields and drew bows, two hundred and fourscore thousand: all these were mighty men of valour.'—2 CHRON. xiv. 2-8.

Asa was Rehoboam's grandson, and came to the throne when a young man. The two preceding reigns had favoured idolatry, but the young king had a will of his own, and inaugurated a religious revolution, with which and its happy results this passage deals.

I. It first recounts the thorough clearance of idolatrous emblems and images which Asa made. 'Strange altars,'—that is, those dedicated to other gods; 'high places,'—that is, where illegal sacrifice to Jehovah was offered; 'pillars,'—that is, stone columns; and 'Asherim,'—that is, trees or wooden poles, survivals of ancient stone- or tree-worship; 'sun-images,'—that is, probably, pillars consecrated to Baal as sun-god, were all swept away. The enumeration vividly suggests the incongruous rabble of gods which had taken the place of the one Lord. How vainly we try to make up for His absence from our hearts by a multitude of finite delights and helpers! Their multiplicity proves the insufficiency of each and of all.

1 Kings xv. 13 adds a detail which brings out still more clearly Asa's reforming zeal; for it tells us that he had to fight against the influence of his mother, who had been prominent in supporting disgusting and immoral forms of worship, and who retained some authority, of which her son was strong enough to take the extreme step of depriving her. Remembering the Eastern reverence for a mother, we can estimate the effort which that

required, and the resolution which it implied. But 1 Kings differs from our narrative in stating that the 'high places' were not taken away—the explanation of the variation probably being that the one account tells what Asa attempted and commanded, and the other records the imperfect way in which his orders were carried out. They would be obeyed in Jerusalem and its neighbourhood, but in many a secluded corner the old rites would be observed.

It is vain to force religious revolutions. Laws which are not supported by the national conscience will only be obeyed where disobedience will involve penalties. If men's hearts cleave to Baal, they will not be turned into Jehovah-worshippers by a king's commands. Asa could command Judah to 'seek the Lord God of their fathers, and to do the law,' but he could not make them do it.

II. The chronicler brings out strongly the truth which runs through his whole book,—namely, the connection between honouring Jehovah and national prosperity. He did not import that thought into his narrative, but he insisted on it as moulding the history of Judah. Modern critics charge him with writing with a bias, but he learned the 'bias' from God's own declarations, and had it confirmed by observation, reflection, and experience. The whole history of Israel and Judah was one long illustration of the truth which he is constantly repeating. No doubt, the divine dealings with Israel brought obedience and well-being into closer connection than exists now; but in deepest truth the sure defence of our national prosperity is the same as theirs, and it is still the case that 'righteousness exalteth a nation.' 'The kingdom was quiet,' says the chronicler, 'and he had no war in those years; because the Lord had given him rest.' 1 Kings makes more of the standing enmity with the northern kingdom, and records scarcely anything of Asa's reign except the war which, as it says, was between him and Baasha of Israel 'all their days.' But, according to 2 Chronicles xvi. 1, Baasha did not proceed to war till Asa's thirty-sixth year, and the halcyon time of peace evidently followed immediately on the religious reformation at its very beginning.

Asa's experience embodies a truth which is substantially fulfilled in nations and in individuals; for obedience brings rest, often outward tranquillity, always inward calm. Note the heightened earnestness expressed in the repetition of the expression 'We have sought the Lord' in verse 7, and the grand assurance of His favour as the source of well-being in the clause which follows, 'and He hath given us rest on every side.' That is always so, and will be so with us. If we seek Him with our whole hearts, keeping Him ever before us amid the distractions of life, taking Him as our aim and desire, and ever stretching out the tendrils of our hearts to feel after Him and clasp Him, all around and within will be tranquil, and even in warfare we shall preserve unbroken peace.

Asa teaches us, too, the right use of tranquillity. He clearly and gratefully recognised God's hand in it, and traced it not to his own warlike skill or his people's prowess, but to Him. And he used the time of repose to strengthen his defences, and exercise his soldiers against possible assaults. We do not yet dwell in the land of peace, where it is safe to be without bolts and bars, but have ever to be on the watch for sudden attacks. Rest from war should give leisure for building not only fortresses, but temples, as was the case with Solomon. The time comes when, as in many an ancient fortified city of Europe, the ramparts may be levelled, and flowers bloom where sentries walked; but to-day we have to be on perpetual guard, and look to our fortifications, if we would not be overcome.

ASA'S PRAYER

'And Asa cried unto the Lord his God, and said, Lord, it is nothing with Thee to help, whether with many, or with them that have no power: help us, O Lord our God; for we rest on Thee, and in Thy Name we go against this multitude. O Lord, Thou art our God; let not man prevail against Thee.'—2 CHRON. xiv. 11.

This King Asa, Rehoboam's grandson, had had a long reign of peace, which the writer of the Book of Chronicles traces to the fact that he had rooted out idolatry from Judah, 'The land had rest, and he no war ... because the Lord had given him rest.'

But there came a time when the war-cloud began to roll threateningly over the land, and a great army—the numbers of which, from their immense magnitude, seem to be erroneously given—came up against him. Like a wise man he made his military dispositions first, and prayed next. He set his troops in order, and then he fell down on his knees, and spoke to God.

Now, it seems to me that this prayer contains the very essence of what ought to be the Christian attitude in reference to all the conditions and threatening dangers and conflicts of life; and so I wish to run over it, and bring out the salient points of it, as typical of what ought to be our disposition.

I. The wholesome consciousness of our own impotence.

It did not take much to convince Asa that he had 'no power.' His army, according to the numbers given of the two hosts, was outnumbered two to one; and so it did not require much reflection to say, 'We have no might.' But although perhaps not so sufficiently obvious to us, as truly as in the case in our text, if we look fairly in the face our duties, our tasks, our dangers, the possibilities of life and its certainties, the more humbly we think of our own capacity, the more wisely we shall think about God, and the more truly we shall estimate ourselves. The world says, 'Self-reliance is the conquering virtue'; Jesus says to us, 'Self-distrust is the condition of all victory.' And that does not mean any mere shuffling off of responsibility from our own shoulders, but it means looking the facts of our lives, and of our own characters, in the face. And if we will do that, however apparently easy may be our course, and however richly endowed in mind, body, or estate we may be, if we all do that honestly, we shall find that we each are like 'the man with ten thousand' that has to meet 'the King that comes against him with twenty thousand'; and we shall not 'desire conditions of peace' with our enemy, for that is not what in this case we have to do, but we shall look about us, and not keep our eyes on the horizon, and on the levels of earth, but look up to see if there is not there an Ally that we can bring into the field to redress the balance, and to make our ten as strong as the opposing twenty. Zerah the Ethiopian, who was coming down on Asa, is said to have had a million fighting-men at his back, but that is probably an erroneous figure, because Old Testament numbers are necessarily often unreliable. Asa had only half the number; so he said, 'What can I do?' And what *could* he do? He did the only thing possible, he 'grasped at God's skirts, and prayed,' and that made all the difference.

Now all that is true about the disproportion between the foes we have to face and fight and our own strength. It is eminently true about us Christian people, if we are doing any work for our Master. You hear people say, 'Look at the small number of professing Christians in this country, as compared with the numbers on the other side. What is the use of their trying to convert the world?' Well, think of the assembled Christian people, for instance, of Manchester, on the most charitable supposition, and the shallowest interpretation of that word 'Christian.' What are they among so many? A mere handful. If the Christian Church had to undertake the task of Christianising the world by its own strength, we might well despair of success and stop altogether. 'We have no might.' The disproportion both numerically and in all things that the world estimates as strength (which are many of them good things), is so great that we are in a worse case than Asa was. It is not two to one; it is twenty to one, or an even greater disproportion. But we are not only numerically weak. A multitude of non-effectives, mere camp followers, loosely attached, nominal Christians, have to be deducted from the muster-roll, and the few who are left are so feeble as well as few that they have more than enough to do in holding their own, to say nothing of dreaming of charging the wide-stretching lines of the enemy. So a profound self-distrust is our wisdom. But that should not paralyse us, but lead to something better, as it led Asa.

II. Summoning God into the field should follow wholesome self-distrust.

Asa uses a remarkable expression, which is, perhaps, scarcely reproduced adequately in our Authorised Version: 'It is nothing with Thee to help, whether with many or with them that have no power.' It is a strange phrase, but it seems most probable that the suggested rendering in the Revised Version is nearer the writer's meaning, which says, 'Lord! there is none beside Thee to help between the mighty and them that have no power,' which to our ears is a somewhat cumbrous way of saying that God, and God only, can adjust the difference between the mighty and the weak; can redress the balance, and by the laying of His hand upon the feeble hand can make it strong as the mailed fist to which it is opposed. If we know ourselves to be hopelessly outnumbered, and send to God for reinforcements, He will clash His sword into the scale, and make it go down. Asa turns to God and says, 'Thou only canst trim the scales and make the lighter of the two the heavier one by casting Thy might into it. So help us, O Lord our God!'

One man with God at his back is always in the majority; and, however many there may be on the other side, 'there are more that be with us than they that be with them.' *There* is encouragement for people who have to fight unpopular causes in the world, who have been accustomed to be in minorities all their days, in the midst of a wicked and perverse generation. Never mind about the numbers; bring God into the field, and the little band, which is compared in another place in these historical Books to 'two flocks of kids' fronting the enemy, that had flowed all over the land, is in the majority. 'God with us'; then we are strong.

The consciousness of weakness may unnerve a man; and that is why people in the world are always patting each other on the back and saying 'Be of good cheer, and rely upon yourself.' But the self-distrust that turns to God becomes the parent of a far more reliable self-reliance than that which trusts to men. My consciousness of need is my opening the door for God to come in. Just as you always find the lakes in the hollows, so you will always find the grace of God coming into men's hearts to strengthen them and make them victorious, when there has been the preparation of the lowered estimate of one's self. Hollow out your heart by self-distrust, and God will fill it with the flashing waters of His strength bestowed. The more I feel myself weak, the more I am meant not to fold my hands and say, 'I never can do that thing; it is of no use my trying to attempt it, I may as well give it up'; but to say, 'Lord I there is none beside Thee that can set the balance right between the mighty and him that hath no strength.' 'Help me, O Lord my God!' Just as those little hermit-crabs that you see upon the seashore, with soft bodies unprotected, make for the first empty shell they can find, and house in that and make it their fortress, our exposed natures, our unarmoured characters, our sense of weakness, ought to drive us to Him. As the unarmed population of a land invaded by the enemy pack their goods and hurry to the nearest fortified place, so when I say to myself I have no strength, let me say, 'Thou art my Rock, my Strength, my Fortress, and my Deliverer. My God, in whom I trust, my Buckler, and the Horn of my Salvation, and my high Tower.'

Now, there is one more word about this matter, and that is, the way by which we summon God into the field. Asa prays, 'Help us, O Lord our God! for we rest on Thee'; and the word that he employs for 'rest' is not a very frequent one. It carries with it a very striking picture. Let me illustrate it by a reference to another case where it is employed. It is used in that tragical story of the death of Saul, when the man that saw the last of him came to David and drew in a sentence the pathetic picture of the wearied, wounded, broken-hearted, discrowned, desperate monarch, *leaning on* his spear. You can understand how hard he leaned, with what a grip he held it, and how heavily his whole languid, powerless weight pressed upon it. And that is the word that is used here. 'We lean on Thee' as the wounded Saul leaned upon his spear. Is that a picture of your faith, my friend? Do you lean upon God like that, laying your hand upon Him till every vein on your hand stands out with the force and tension of the grasp? Or do you lean lightly, as a man that does not feel much the need of a support? Lean hard if you wish God to come quickly. 'We rest on Thee; help us, O Lord!'

III. Courageous advance should follow self-distrust and summoning God by faith.

It is well when self-distrust leads to confidence, when, as Charles Wesley has it in his great hymn:

'… I am weak,
But confident in self-despair.'

But that is not enough. It is better when self-distrust and confidence in God lead to courage, and as Asa goes on, 'Help us, for we rely on Thee, and in Thy name we go against this multitude.' Never mind though it is two to one. What does that matter? Prudence and calculation are well enough, but there is a great deal of very rank cowardice and want of faith in Christian people, both in regard to their own lives and in regard to Christian work in the world, which goes masquerading under much too respectable a name, and calls itself 'judicious caution' and 'prudence.' There is little ever done by that, especially in the Christian course; and the old motto of one of the French republicans holds good; 'Dare! dare! always dare!' You have more on your side than you have against you, and creeping prudence of calculation is not the temper in which the battle is won. 'Dash' is not always precipitate and presumptuous. If we have God with us, let us be bold in fronting the dangers and difficulties that beset us, and be sure that He will help us.

IV. And now the last point that I would notice is this—the all-powerful plea which God will answer.

'Thou art my God, let not man prevail against Thee.' That prayer covers two things. You may be quite sure that if God is your God you will not be beaten; and you may be quite sure that if you have made God's cause yours He will make your cause His, and again you will not be beaten.

'Thou art our God.' 'It takes two to make a bargain,' and God and we have both to act before He is truly ours. He gives Himself to us, but there is an act of ours required too, and you must take the God that is given to you, and make Him yours because you make yourselves His. And when I have taken Him for mine, and not unless I have, He is mine, to all intents of strength-giving and blessedness. When I can say, 'Thou art my God, and it is impossible that Thou wilt deny Thyself,' then nothing can snap that bond; and 'neither life nor death, nor angels, nor principalities, nor powers, nor things present, nor things to come, nor height, nor depth, nor any *other* creature' can do it. But there is a creature that can, and that is I. For I can separate *myself* from the love and the guardianship of God, and He can say to a man, 'I am thy God,' and the man *not* answer, 'Thou art my God.'

And then there is another plea here. 'Let not man prevail against Thee.' What business had Asa to identify his little kingdom and his victory with God's cause and God's conquest? Only this, that he had flung himself into God's arms, and because he had, and was trying to do what God would have him do, he was quite sure that it was not Asa but Jehovah that the million of Ethiopians were fighting against. People warn us against the fanaticism of taking for granted that our cause is God's cause. Well, we need the warning sometimes, but we may be quite sure of this, that if we have made God's cause ours, He will make our cause His, down to the minutest point in our daily lives.

And then, if thus we say in the depths of our hearts, and live accordingly, 'There is none other that fighteth for us, but only Thou, O God!' it will be with us as it was with Asa in the story before us, 'the enemy fled, and could not recover themselves, for they were destroyed before the Lord and before His hosts.'

THE SEARCH THAT ALWAYS FINDS

'They ... sought Him with their whole desire; and He was found of them: and the Lord gave them rest round about.'—2 CHRON. xv. 15.

These words occur in one of the least familiar passages of the Old Testament. They describe an incident in the reign of Asa, who was the grandson of Solomon's foolish son Rehoboam, and was consequently the third king of Judah after the secession of the North. He had just won a great victory, and was returning with his triumphant army to Jerusalem, when there met him a prophet, unknown otherwise, who poured out fiery words, exhorting Asa and his people to cleave to God and to cast away their idols. Asa, encouraged by the prophetic words of this bold speaker for God, screwed himself up, and was able to induce also his people, to effect a great religious reformation. He made a clean sweep of the idols, and gathered the sadly-dwindled nation together in Jerusalem, where they renewed the covenant with the Lord God of their fathers. The text sums up their work and its result. 'They sought Him with their whole heart, and He was found of them; and the Lord gave them rest round about.' The words express in simplest form what should be the chief desire of our hearts and occupation of our lives, and what will then be our peaceful experience. We shall best bring out these points if we take the words just as they lie, and consider the seeking, the finding which certainly crowns that seeking, and the rest which ensues on finding God.

I. The seeking.

Now, of course, there is no doubt that what the chronicler meant to describe by the phrase, 'seeking the Lord,' was largely the mere external acts of ritual worship, the superficial turning from idols to a purely external recognition of God as the God of Israel. But while there may have been nothing deeper than a change in the nominal object of nominal worship, so far as many were concerned, no doubt a very real turning of heart to God underlay the external change in many other cases, of which the destruction of idols and the renewed observance of the form of Jehovah's worship were the consequence and sign. That turning of mind, will, and affection towards God must be ours if we are to be among those wise and happy seekers who are sure to find that which—or rather Him whom—they seek and to rest in Him whom they find. That search is not after a lost treasure, nor does it imply ignorance of where its object is to be found. We seek that which we know, and which we may be assured of finding. Therefore there need be no tremors of uncertainty in our quest, and the blessedness of the search is as real as, though different from, the blessedness of the possession which ends it. The famous saying which prefers the search after, to the possession of truth, is more proud than wise; but the comparison which it institutes is so far true that there is a joy in the aspiration after and the efforts towards truth only less joyous than that which attends its attainment. But truth divorced from God is finite and may pall, become familiar and lose its radiance, like a gathered flower; and hence the preference for the search is intelligible though one-sided. But God does not pall, and the more we find Him the more we delight in Him; the highest bliss is to find Him, the next highest is to seek

Him; and, since seeking and finding Him are never wholly separate, these kindred joys blend their lights in the experience of all His children.

But our text lays emphasis on the whole-heartedness of the people's seeking of God. The search must be earnest and engaged in with the whole energy of our whole being, if any blessing is to come from it. Why! one reason why the great mass of professing Christians make so little of their religion is because they are only half-hearted in it. If you divide a river into two streams the force of each is less than half the power of the original current; and the chances are that you will make a stagnant marsh where there used to be a flowing stream. 'All in all, or not at all,' is the rule for life, in all departments. It is the rule in daily business. A man that puts only half himself in his profession or trade, while the other half of his wits is gone woolgathering and dreaming, is predestined from all eternity to fail. The same is true about our religion. If you and I attend to it as a kind of by-occupation; if we give the balance of our time and the superfluity of our energy, after we have done a hard day's work—say, an hour upon a Sunday—to seeking God, and devote all the rest of the week to seeking worldly prosperity, it is no wonder if our religion languishes, and is mainly a matter of forms, as it is with such hosts of people that call themselves Christians.

Oh! dear brethren, I do believe there is more unconscious unreality in the average Christian man's endeavour to be a better Christian than there is in almost anything else in the world:—

'One foot on sea, and one on shore,
To one thing constant never.'

That is why so many of us know nothing of a progressive strengthening of our faith, and an increasing conquest of ourselves, and a firmer grasp of God, and a fuller realisation of the blessedness of walking in His ways.

'They sought Him with all their heart.' That does not mean, remember, that there are to be no other desires, for it is a great mistake to pit religion against other things which are meant to be its instruments and its helps. We are not required to seek nothing else in order to seek God wholly. He demands no impossible and fantastic detachment of ourselves from the ordinary and legitimate occupations, affections, and duties of human life, but He does ask that the dominant desire after Him should be powerful enough to express itself through all our actions, and that we should seek for God in them, and for them in God.

Whilst thus we are to give the right interpretation to that whole-heartedness in our seeking God, on which the text lays stress, do not let us forget that the one token of it which the text specifies is, casting out our idols. There must be detachment if there is to be attachment. If some climbing plant, for instance, has twisted itself round the unprofitable thorns in the hedge, the gardener, before he can get it to go up the support that it is meant to encircle, has carefully to detach it from the stays to which it has wantonly clung, taking care that in the process he does not break its tendrils and destroy its power of growth. So, to train our souls to cleave to God, and to grow up round the great Stay that is provided for us, there is needed, as an essential part of the process, the voluntary, conscious, conscientious, and constant guarding of ourselves from the vagrancies of our desires, which send out their shoots away from Him; and when the objects of these become idols, then there is nothing for it but that, like Asa and his people, we should hew them to pieces and make a bonfire of them; and then renew our covenant before God. I desire to press that upon you and upon myself. The heart must be emptied of baser liquors, if the new wine of the Kingdom is to be poured into it.

True it is, of course—and thank God for it!—that the most powerful agent in effecting that detachment of ourselves from lower things is our fruition of higher. It is when God comes into the temple that Dagon falls on the threshold. It is when a new affection begins to spring in the heart that old loves are thrust out of it. But whilst that is true, it is also true that the two processes run on simultaneously; and that whilst, on the one hand, if we are ever to overcome our love of the world it must be through the love of God, on the other hand, if we are ever to be confirmed in a whole-hearted love of God, it must be through our conquest of our love of the world. 'Unite my heart to fear Thy name' was the profound prayer of the old Psalmist; and the 'heart,' according to Old Testament usage, is the central fountain from which flow all the streams of conscious life. To seek Him with the whole heart is to engage the whole self in the quest, and that is the only kind of seeking which has the certainty of success.

II. The finding which crowns such seeking.

'He was found of them.' Yes; anything is possible rather than that a whole-hearted search after God should be a vain search. For there are, in that case, two seekers—God is seeking for us more truly than we are seeking for Him. And if the mother is seeking her child, and the child its mother, it will be a very wide desert where they will not meet. 'The Father seeketh such to worship Him,' that is—the divine activity is going about the world, searching for the heart that turns to Him, and it cannot but be that they that seek Him shall find Him, or 'shall be found of Him.' Open the windows, and you cannot keep out the sunshine; open your lungs and you cannot keep out the air. 'In Him we live and move and have our being,' and if our desires turn, however blindly, to Him, and are accompanied with the appropriate action, heaven and earth are more likely to rush to ruin than such a searching to be frustrated of its aim.

Brethren! is there anything else in the world of which you can say, 'Seek, and ye shall find'? You, with white hairs on your heads, have you found anything else in which the chase was sure to result in the capture; in which capture was sure to yield all that the hunter had wished? There is only one direction for a man's desires and aims, in which disappointment is an impossibility. In all other regions the most that can be promised is 'Seek, and *perhaps* you will find'; and, when you have found, perhaps you will feel that the prize was not worth the finding. Or it is, 'Seek, and *possibly* you will find; and after you have found and kept for a little while, you will lose.' Though it may be

'Better to have loved and lost,
Than never to have loved at all,'

a treasure that slips out of our fingers is not the best treasure that we can search for. But here the assurance is, 'Seek, and ye *shall* find; and shall never lose. Find, and you shall always possess.'

What would you think of a company of gold-seekers, hunting about in some exhausted claim, for hypothetical grains, ragged, starving—and all the while in the next gully were lying lumps of gold for the picking up? And that figure fairly represents what people do and suffer who seek for good and do not seek for God.

III. The rest which ensues on finding God.

'The Lord gave them rest round about.' We believe that the Jewish nation was under special supernatural guidance, so that national adherence to the Law was always followed by external prosperity. That is not, of course, the case with us. But which is the better thing, 'rest round about' or rest within? We have no immunity from toil or conflict. Seeking God does not cover our heads from the storm of external calamities, nor arm our hearts against the darts and daggers of many a pain, anxiety, and care, but disturbance around is a very small matter if there be a better thing, rest within.

Do you remember who it was that said, 'In the world ye shall have tribulation … but in Me ye shall have peace'? Then we have, as it were, two abodes—one, as far as regards the life of sense, in the world of sense—another, as far as regards the inmost self, which may, if we will, be in Christ. A vessel with an outer casing and a layer of air between it and the inner will keep its contents hot. So we may have round us the very opposite of repose, and, if God so wills, let us not kick against His will; we may have conflict and stir and strife, and yet a better rest than that of my text may be ours. 'Rest round about' is sometimes good and sometimes bad. It is often bad, for it is the people that 'have no changes' who most usually 'do not fear God.' But rest within, that is sure to come when a man has sought with all his desire for God, whom he has found in all His fullness, is only good and best of all.

We all know, thank God! in worldly matters and in inferior degree, how blessed and restful it is when some strong affection is gratified, some cherished desire fulfilled. Though these satisfactions are not perpetual, nor perfect, they may teach us what a depth of blessed and calm repose, incapable of being broken by any storms or by any tasks, will come to and abide with the man whose deepest love is satisfied in God, and whose most ardent desires have found more than they sought for in Him. Be sure of this, dear friends! that if we do thus seek, and thus find, it is not in the power of anything 'that is at enmity with joy' utterly to 'abolish or destroy' the quietness of our hearts. 'Rest in the Lord, and wait patiently for Him.' They who thus repose will have peace in their hearts, even whilst tasks and temptations, changes and sorrows, disturb their outward lives. 'In the world ye shall have tribulation.' Be it so; it may be borne with submission and thankfulness if in Christ we have peace.

Thus we may have the peace of God, rest in and from Him, entering into us, and in due time, by His gracious guidance and help, we shall enter into eternal rest. Whilst to seek is to find Him, in a very deep and blessed sense, even in this life; in another aspect all our earthly life may be regarded as seeking after Him, and the future as the true finding of Him. That future will bring to those whose hearts have turned from the shows and vanities of time to God a possession of Him so much fuller than was experienced here that the lesser discoveries and enjoyments of Him which are experienced here, scarcely deserve in comparison to be called by the same name. So my text may be taken, as in its first part, a description of the blessed life here—'They sought Him with all their heart'—and in its second, as a shadowy vision of the yet more blessed life hereafter, 'He was found of them, and the Lord gave them rest round about,' as well as within, in the land of peace, where sorrow and sighing, and toil and care, shall pass from memory; and they that warred against us shall be far away.

JEHOSHAPHAT'S REFORM

'And Jehoshaphat his son reigned in his stead, and strengthened himself against Israel. 2. And he placed forces in all the fenced cities of Judah, and set garrisons in the land of Judah, and in the cities of Ephraim, which Asa his father had taken. 3. And the Lord was with Jehoshaphat, because he walked in the first ways of his father David, and sought not unto Baalim; 4. But sought to the Lord God of his father, and walked in His commandments, and not after the doings of Israel. 5. Therefore the Lord established the kingdom in his hand; and all Judah brought to Jehoshaphat presents; and he had riches and honour in abundance. 6. And his heart was lifted up in the ways of the Lord: moreover he took away the high places and groves out of Judah. 7. Also in the third year of his reign he sent to his princes, even to Ben-hail, and to Obadiah, and to Zechariah, and to Nethaneel, and to Michaiah, to teach in the cities of Judah. 8. And with them he sent Levites, even Shemaiah, and Nethaniah, and Zebadiah, and Asabel, and Shemiramoth, and Jehonathan, and Adonijah, and Tobijah, and Tobadonijah, Levites: and with them Elishama and Jehoram, priests. 9. And they taught in Judah, and had the book of the law of the Lord with them, and went about throughout all the cities of Judah, and taught the people. 10. And the fear of the Lord fell upon all the kingdoms of the lands that were round about Judah, so that they made no war against Jehoshaphat.'—2 CHRON. xvii. 1-10.

The first point to be noted in this passage is that Jehoshaphat followed in the steps of Asa his father. Stress is laid on his adherence to the ancestral faith, 'the first ways of his father David,'—before his great fall,—and the paternal example, 'he sought to the God of his father.' Such carrying on of a predecessor's work is rare in the line of kings of Judah, where father and son were seldom of the same mind in religion. The principle of hereditary monarchy secures peaceful succession, but not continuity of policy. Many a king of Judah had to say in his heart what Ecclesiastes puts into Solomon's mouth, 'I hated all my labour, ... seeing that I must leave it unto the man that shall be after me. And who knoweth whether he shall be a wise man or a fool?'

But it is not only in kings' houses that that experience is realised. Many a home is saddened to-day because the children do not seek the God of their fathers. 'Instead of the fathers' should 'come up thy children'; but, alas! grandmother Lois and mother Eunice do not always see the boy who has known the Scriptures from a child grow up into a Timothy, in whom their unfeigned faith lives again. The neglect of religious instruction in professedly Christian families, the inconsistent lives of parents or their too rigid restraints, or, sometimes, their too lax discipline, are to be blamed for many such cases. But there are many instances in which not the parents, but the children, are to be blamed. An earnest Sunday-school teacher may do much to lead the children of godly parents to their father's God. Blessed is the home where the golden chain of common faith binds hearts together, and family love is elevated and hallowed by common love of God!

Jehoshaphat's religion was, further, resolutely held in the face of prevailing opposition. 'The Baalim' were popular; it was fashionable to worship them. They were numerous, and all varieties of taste could find a Baal to please them. But this young king turned from the tempting ways that opened flower-strewn before him, and chose the narrow road that led upwards. 'So did not I, because of the fear of God,' might have been his motto. A similar determined setting of our faces God-ward, in spite of the crowd of tempting false deities around us, must mark us, if we are to have any religion worth calling by the name. This king recoiled from the example of the neighbouring monarchy, and walked 'not after the doings of Israel.' His seeking to God was very practical, for it was not shown simply by professed beliefs or by sentiment, but by ordering his life in obedience to God's will. The test of real religion is, after all, a life unlike the lives of the men who do not share our faith, and moulded in accordance with God's known will. It is vain to allege that we are seeking the Lord unless we are walking in His commandments.

Prosperity followed godliness, in accordance with the divinely appointed connection between them which characterised the Old Dispensation. 'Prosperity is the blessing of the Old Testament; adversity is the blessing of the New,' says Bacon. But the epigram is too neat to be entirely true, for the Book of Job and many a psalm show that the eternal problem of suffering innocence was raised by facts even in the old days, and in our days there are forms of well-being which are the natural fruits of well-doing. Still, the connection was closer in Judah than with us, and, in the case before us, the establishment of Jehoshaphat in the kingdom, his subjects' love, which showed itself in voluntary gifts over and above the taxes imposed, and his wealth and honour, were the direct results of his true religion.

A really devout man must be a propagandist. True faith cannot be hid nor be dumb. As certainly as light must radiate must faith strive to communicate itself. So the account of Jehoshaphat's efforts to spread the worship of Jehovah follows the account of his personal godliness. 'His heart was lifted up in the ways of the Lord.' There are two kinds of lifted-up hearts; one when pride, self-sufficiency, and forgetfulness of God, raise a man to a giddy height, from which God's judgments are sure to cast him down and break him in the fall; one when a lowly heart is raised to high courage and devotion, and 'set on high,' because it fears God's name. Such elevation is consistent with humility. It fears no fall; it is an elevation above earthly desires and terrors, neither of which can reach it, so as to hinder the man from walking in 'the ways of the Lord.' This king was lifted to it by his happy experience of the blessed effects of obedience. These encouraged him to vigorous efforts to spread the religion which had thus gladdened and brightened his own life. Is that the use we make of the ease which God gives us?

Jehoshaphat had to destroy first, in order to build up. The 'high places and Asherim' had to be taken out of Judah before the true worship could be established there. So it is still. The Christian has to carry a sword in the one hand, and a trowel in the other. Many a rotten old building, the stones of which have been cemented in blood, has to be swept away before the fair temple can be reared. The Devil is in possession of much of the world, and the lawful owner has to dispossess the 'squatter.' No one can suppose that society is organised on Christian principles even in so-called 'Christian countries'; and there is much overturning work to be done before He whose right it is to reign is really king over the whole earth. We, too, have our 'high places and Asherim' to root out.

But that destructive work is not to be done by force. Institutions can only be swept away when public opinion has grown to see their evils. Forcible reformations of manners, and, still more, of religion, never last, but are sure to be followed by violent rebounds to the old order. So, side by side with the removal of idolatry, this king took care to diffuse the knowledge of the true worship, by sending out a body of influential commissioners to teach in Judah. That was a new departure of great importance. It presents several interesting features. The composition of the staff of instructors is remarkable. The principal men in it are five court officers, next to whom, and subordinate, as is shown not only by the order of enumeration, but by the phrase 'with them,' were nine Levites, and, last and lowest of all, two priests. We might have expected that priests should be the most numerous and important members of such a body, and we are led to suspect that the priesthood was so corrupted as to be careless about religious reformation. A clerical order is not always the most ardent in religious revival. The commissioners were probably chosen, without regard to their being priests, Levites, or 'laymen,' because of their zeal in the worship of Jehovah; and the five 'princes' head the list in order to show the royal authority of the commission.

Another point is the emphasis with which their function of teaching is thrice mentioned in three verses. Apparently the bulk of the nation knew little or nothing of 'the law of the Lord,' either on its spiritual and moral or its ceremonial side; and Jehoshaphat's object was to effect an enlightened, not a forcible and superficial, change. God's way of influencing actions is to reveal Himself to the understanding and the heart, that these may move the will, and that may shape the deeds. Wise men will imitate God's way. Jehoshaphat did not issue royal commands, but sent out teachers. In chapter xix. we find him despatching 'judges' in similar fashion throughout Judah. They had the power to punish, but these teachers had only authority to explain and to exhort.

The present writer accepts the chronicler's statement that the teachers had 'the Book of the Law' with them, though he recognises it as possible that that 'Book' was not identical with the complete collection of documents which now bears the name. But, be that as it may, the incident of our text is remarkable as being the only recorded systematic and complete attempt to diffuse the remedy against idolatry throughout the kingdom, as putting religious reformation on its only sure ground, and as hinting at deep and widespread ignorance among the masses.

'When a man's ways please the Lord, He maketh even his enemies to be at peace with him.' So Judah found. 'A terror of the Lord fell upon all the kingdoms' around. No doubt, the news filtered to them of how Jehovah was exerting His might on the nation, and a certain indefinable awe of this so potent god, who was defeating the Baalim, made them think that peace was the best policy. Each nation was supposed to have its own god, and the national god was supposed to fight for his worshippers; so that war was a struggle of deities as well as of men, and the stronger god won. Here was a god who had reconquered his territory, and had cast out usurpers. Prudence dictated keeping on good terms with him. But it never occurred to any of these peoples that their own gods were any less real than Judah's, or that Judah's God could ever become theirs.

AMASIAH

'Amasiah, the son of Zichri, who willingly offered himself unto the Lord.'—1 CHRON. xvii, 16.

This is a scrap from the catalogue of Jehoshaphat's 'mighty men of valour'; and is Amasiah's sole record. We see him for a moment and hear his eulogium and then oblivion swallows him up. We do not know what it was that he did to earn it. But what a fate, to live to all generations by that one sentence!

I. Cheerful self-surrender the secret of all religion.

The words of our text contain a metaphor naturally drawn from the sacrificial system. It comes so easily to us that we scarcely recognise the metaphorical element, but the clear recognition of it gives great additional energy to the words. Amasiah was both sacrificer and sacrifice. His offering was self-immolation. As in all love, so in that noblest kind of it which clasps God, its perfect expression is, 'I give Thee my living, loving self.' Nor is it only sacrifice and sacrificer that are seen in deepest truth in the experience of the Christian life, but the reality of the Temple is also there, for 'Ye also … are built up a spiritual house, to be a holy priesthood, to offer up spiritual sacrifices.' Only when God dwells in us, shall we have the nerve and the firmness of hand to take the knife and 'slay before the Lord,' the awful Guest in the sanctuary within, the most precious of the children of our spirits.

The essence of the sacrifice of self is the sacrifice of will. In the Christian experience 'willingly offered' is almost tautology, for unwilling offerings are a contradiction and in fact there are no such things. The quality of unwillingness destroys the character of the offering and robs it of all sacredness. Reluctant Christianity is not Christianity. That noun and that adjective can never be buckled together.

The submission of will and the consequent surrender of myself and my powers, opportunities, and possessions, so that I do all, enjoy all, use all, and when need is, endure all with glad thankful reference to God is only possible to me in the measure in which my will is made flexible by love, and such will-subduing love comes only when we 'know and believe the love that God hath to us.' There is the point at which not a few moral and religious teachers go wrong and bewilder themselves and their disciples. There, too, is the point at which Christ and the Gospel of salvation through faith in Him stand forth as emancipating humanity from the dreary round of efforts and vain attempts to work up the condition needful for achieving the height of self-surrender, which is seen to be indispensable to all true nobleness of living, but is felt to be beyond the reach of the ordinary man. There, too, is the point at which many good people mar their lives as Christians. They waste their strength in trying to bring the jibbing horse up to the leap. They try to blow up a fire of devotion and to make themselves priests to offer themselves, but all the while the mutinous self recoils from the leap, and the fire burns smokily, and their sacrifice is laid on the altar with little joy, because they have not been careful and wise enough to begin at the beginning and to follow God's way of melting their wills, by love, the reflection of the Infinite love of God to them. God's priests offer themselves because they offer their wills; they offer their wills because they love God; they love God because they know that God loves them. That is the divine order. It is vain to try to accomplish the end by any other.

II. This willing offering hallows all life.

No syllable is left to tell us what Amasiah did to win this praise. Probably the words enshrine some now forgotten memory of his cheerful courage, some heroic feat on an unrecorded battlefield. Particulars are not given nor needed. Specific actions are unimportant; the spirit of a life can be told with very incomplete details, and it, not the details, is the important thing. Sometimes, as in many modern biographies, one 'cannot see the wood for the trees,' and misses the main drift and aim of a life in the chaos of a bewildering mass of nothings. How much more happy the lot of this man of whom we have only the generalised expression of the text, unweighted and undisturbed by petty incidents! It takes tons of rose leaves to make a tiny phial of otto of roses, but the fragrance is far more pungent in a drop of the distillation than in armfuls of leaves. Every life shrinks into very small compass, and the centuries do not tolerate long biographies. Shall we not seek to order our life so that Amasiah's epitaph may serve for us? It will be blessed if this—and nothing else—is known about us, that we 'willingly offered ourselves to the Lord.' My friend: will that be a true epitome of your life?

III. This willing offering is accepted by God.

We may hear a mightier voice behind the chronicler's, and the judgment of the Judge of all pronounced by His lips. It matters little what men say of one another, but it matters everything what God says of us. We are but too apt to forget that He is now saying something as to each of us, and that we have not to wait for death to put a final period to our activities, before our lives become fit subjects for God's judgment, Moment by moment we are writing our own sentences. But while it is good for us to remember the continuous judgment of God on each deed, it is not good to let dark thoughts of the principles of that judgment paralyse our activity or chill our confidence in His forgiving and accepting mercy. There is often a dark suspicion, like that of the one-talented servant, which blackens God's fair fame as being 'an austere Man,' making demands rather than imparting power, and the effect of such an ugly conception of Him is to cut the nerve of service and bury the talent, carefully folded up, it may be, but none the less earning nothing. 'If we call on Him as Father, who without respect of persons judgeth according to every man's work,' let us be sure that it will be a Fatherly judgment that He will pass upon us and our offerings. There is a wonderful collection on His altar of what many people would think rubbish, just as many a mother has laid away among her treasures some worthless article which her child had once given her—a weed plucked by the roadside in a long past summer day, some trifle of rare preciousness in the child's eyes, and of none in any others than her own. She opens her drawer and brings out the poor little thing, and her eyes fill and her heart fills as she looks. And does not God keep His children's gifts as lovingly, and set them in places of honour in the day when He 'makes up His jewels'? There are cups of cold water and widows' mites and much else that a supercilious world would call 'trash' stored there. Thank God! He accepts imperfect service, faltering faith, partial consecration, a little love. Even our poor offering may be an 'odour of a sweet smell,' ministering fragrance that is a delight to Him, if it is offered with the much incense of the great Sacrifice and through the mediation of the great High Priest.

The world forgot Amasiah, or never knew him, an obscure soldier in an obscure kingdom, but God did not forget, and here is his epitaph, and this is his memorial to all generations. Men's chronicles have no room for all the names that their wearers are eager to have inscribed on their crumbling and crowded pages, 'but the Lamb's Book of Life' has ample space on its radiant pages for all who desire to set their names there, and if ours are there, we need not envy the proudest whose titles and deeds fill the most conspicuous pages in the world's records. 'Then shall every man have praise of Christ,' and he who wins that guerdon needs nothing more, and can have nothing more to swell his blessedness.

'A MIRROR FOR MAGISTRATES'

'And Jehoshaphat the king of Judah returned to his house in peace to Jerusalem. 2. And Jehu the son of Hanani the seer went out to meet him, and said to king Jehoshaphat, Shouldest thou help the ungodly, and love them that hate the Lord? therefore is wrath upon thee from before the Lord. 3. Nevertheless there are good things found in thee, in that thou hast taken away the groves out of the land, and hast prepared thine heart to seek God. 4. And Jehoshaphat dwelt at Jerusalem: and he went out again through the people from Beer-sheba to mount Ephraim, and brought them back unto the Lord God of their fathers. 5. And he set judges in the land throughout all the fenced cities of Judah, city by city. 6. And said to the judges, Take heed what ye do: for ye judge not for man, but for the Lord, who is with you in the judgment. 7. Wherefore now let the fear of the Lord be upon you; take heed and do it: for there is no iniquity with the Lord our God, nor respect of persons, nor taking of gifts. 8. Moreover in Jerusalem did Jehoshaphat set of the Levites, and of the priests, and of the chief of the fathers of Israel, for the judgment of the Lord, and for controversies, when they returned to Jerusalem. 9. And he charged them, saying, Thus shall ye do in the fear of the Lord, faithfully, and with a perfect heart. 10. And what cause soever shall come to you of your brethren that dwell in their cities, between blood and blood, between law and commandment, statutes and judgments, ye shall even warn them that they trespass not against the Lord, and so wrath come upon you, and upon your brethren: this do, and ye shall not trespass. 11. And, behold, Amariah the chief priest is over you in all matters of the Lord; and Zebadiah the son of Ishmael, the ruler of the house of Judah, for all the king's matters: also the Levites shall be officers before you. Deal courageously, and the Lord shall be with the good.'—2 CHRON. XIX. 1-11.

Jehoshaphat is distinguished by two measures for his people's good: one, his sending out travelling preachers through the land (2 Chron. xvii. 7-9); another, this provision of local judges and a central court in Jerusalem. The former was begun as early as the third year of his reign, but was probably interrupted, like other good things, by his ill-omened alliance with Ahab. The prophet Jehu's plain speaking seems to have brought the king back to his better self, and its fruit was his going 'among the people,' from south to north, as a missionary, 'to bring them back to Jehovah.' The religious reformation was accompanied by his setting judges throughout the land. Our modern way of distinguishing between religious and civil concerns is foreign to Eastern thought, and was especially out of the question in a theocracy. Jehovah was the King of Judah; therefore the things that are Caesar's and the things that are God's coalesced, and these two objects of Jehoshaphat's journeyings were pursued simultaneously. We have travelled far from his simple institutions, and our course has not been all progress. His supreme concern was to deal out even-handed justice between man and man; is not ours rather to give ample doses of law? To him the judicial function was a copy of God's, and its exercise a true act of worship, done in His fear, and modelled after His pattern. The first impression made in one of our courts is scarcely that judge and counsel are engaged in worship.

There had been local judges before Jehoshaphat—elders in the villages, the 'heads of the fathers' houses' in the tribes. We do not know whether the great secession had flung the simple old machinery somewhat out of gear, or whether Jehoshaphat's action was simply to systematise and make universal the existing arrangements. But what concerns us most is to note that all the charge which he gives to these peasant magistrates bears on the religious aspect of their duties. They are to think themselves as acting for Jehovah and with Jehovah. If they recognise the former, they may be confident of the latter. They are to 'let the fear of Jehovah be upon you,' for that awe resting on a spirit will, like a burden or water-jar on a woman's shoulder, make the carriage upright and the steps firm. They are not only to act for and with Jehovah, but to do like Him, avoiding injustice, favouritism, and corruption, the plague-spots of Eastern law-courts. In such a state of society, the cases to be adjudicated were mostly such as mother-wit, honesty and the fear of God could solve; other times call for other qualifications. But still, let us learn from this charge that even in our necessarily complicated legal systems and political life, there is room and sore need for the application of the same principles. What a different world it would be if our judges and representatives carried some tincture of Jehoshaphat's simple and devout wisdom into their duties! Civic and political life ought to be as holy as that of cloister and cell. To judge righteously, to vote honestly, is as much worship as to pray. A politician may be 'a priest of the Most High God.'

And for us all the spirit of Jehoshaphat's charge is binding, and every trivial and secular task is to be discharged for God, with God, in the fear of God. 'On the bells of the horses shall be Holiness unto Jehovah.' If our religion does not drive the wheels of daily life, so much the worse for our life and our religion. But, above all, this charge reminds us that the secret of right living is to imitate God. These peasants were to find direction, as well as inspiration, in gazing on Jehovah's character, and trying to copy it. And we are to be 'imitators of God, as beloved children,' though our best efforts may only produce poor results. A masterpiece may be copied in some wretched little newspaper blotch, but the great artist will own it for a copy, and correct it into complete likeness.

The second step was to establish a 'supreme court' in Jerusalem, which had two divisions, ecclesiastical and civil, as we should say, the former presided over by the chief priest, and the latter by 'the ruler of the house of Judah.' Murder cases and the graver questions involving interpretation of the law were sent up thither, while the village judges had probably to decide only points that shrewdness and integrity could settle. But these superior judges, too, received charges as to moral, rather than intellectual or learned qualifications. Religiously, uprightly, 'with a perfect heart,' courageously, they were to act, 'and Jehovah be with the good!' That may be a prayer, like the old invocation with which heralds sent knights to tilt at each other, and with which, in some legal proceedings, the pleas are begun, 'God defend the right!' But more probably it is an assurance that God will guide the judges to favour the good cause, if they on their parts will bring the aforesaid qualities to their decisions. And are not these qualities just such as will, for the most part, give similar results to us, if in our various activities we exercise them? And may we not see a sequence worth our practically putting to the proof in these characteristics enjoined on Jehoshaphat's supreme court? Begin with 'the fear of the Lord'; that will help us to 'faithfulness and a perfect heart'; and these again by taking away occasions of ignoble fear, and knitting together the else tremulous and distracted nature, will make the fearful brave and the weak strong.

But another thought is suggested by Jehoshaphat's language. Note how this court does not seem to have inflicted punishments, but to have had only counsels and warnings to wield. It was a board of conciliation rather than a penal tribunal. Two things it had to do—to press upon the parties the weighty consideration that crimes against men were sins against God, and that the criminal drew down wrath on the community. This remarkable provision brings out strongly thoughts that modern society will be the better for incorporating. The best way to deal with men is to get at their hearts and consciences. The deeper aspect of civil crimes or wrongs to men should be pressed on the doer; namely, that they are sins against God. Again, all such acts are sins against the mystical sacred bond of brotherhood. Again, the solidarity of a nation makes it inevitable that 'one sinner destroyeth much good,' and pulls down with him, when God smites him, a multitude of innocents. So finely woven is the web of the national life that, if a thread run in any part of it, a great rent gapes. If one member sins, all the members suffer with it. And lastly, the cruellest thing that we can do is to be dumb when we see sin being committed. It is not public men, judges and the like, alone, who are called on thus to warn evil-doers, but all of us in our degree. If we do not, we are guilty along with a guilty nation; and it is only when, to the utmost of our power, we have warned our brethren as to national sins, that we can wash our hands in innocency, 'This do, and ye shall not be guilty.'

A STRANGE BATTLE

'We have no might against this great company that cometh against us; neither know we what to do: but our eyes are upon Thee.'—2 CHRON xx. 12.

A formidable combination of neighbouring nations, of which Moab and Ammon, the ancestral enemies of Judah, were the chief, was threatening Judah. Jehoshaphat, the king, was panic-stricken when he heard of the heavy war-cloud that was rolling on, ready to burst in thunder on his little kingdom. His first act was to muster the nation, not as a military levy but as suppliants, 'to seek help of the Lord.' The enemy was camping down by the banks of the Dead Sea, almost within striking distance of Jerusalem. It seemed a time for fighting, not for praying, but even at that critical moment, the king and the men, whom it might have appeared that plain duty called to arms, were gathered in the Temple, and, hampered by their wives and children, were praying. Would they not have done better if they had been sturdily marching through the wilderness of Judah to front their foes? Our text is the close and the climax of Jehoshaphat's prayer, and, as the event proved, it was the most powerful weapon that could have been employed, for the rest of the chapter tells the strangest story of a campaign that was ever written. No sword was drawn. The army was marshalled, but Levites with their instruments of music, not fighters with their spears, led the van, and as 'they began to sing and to praise,' sudden panic laid hold on the invading force, who turned their arms against each other. So when Judah came to some rising ground, on which stood a watch-tower commanding a view over the savage grimness of 'the wilderness,' it saw a field of corpses, stark and stiff and silent. Three days were spent in securing the booty, and on the fourth, Jehoshaphat and his men 'assembled themselves in the Valley of Blessing,' and thence returned a joyous multitude praising God for the victory which had been won for them without their having struck a blow. The whole story may yield large lessons, seasonable at all times. We deal with it, rather than with the fragment of the narrative which we have taken as our text.

I. We see here the confidence of despair.

Jehoshaphat's prayer had stayed itself on God's self-revelation in history, and on His gift of the land to their fathers. It had pleaded that the enemy's hostility was a poor 'reward' for Israel's ancient forbearance, and now, with a burst of agony, it casts down before God, as it were, Judah's desperate plight as outnumbered by the swarm of invaders and brought to their last shifts— 'we have no might against this great company … neither know we what to do.' But the very depth of despair sets them to climb to the height of trust. That is a mighty 'But,' which buckles into one sentence two such antitheses as confront us here. 'We know not what to do, but our eyes are upon Thee'—

blessed is the desperation which catches at God's hand; firm is the trust which leaps from despair!

The helplessness is always a fact, though most of us manage to get along for the most part without discovering it. We are all outnumbered and overborne by the claims, duties, hindrances, sorrows, and entanglements of life. He is not the wisest of men who, facing all that life may bring and take away, all that it must bring and take away, knows no quiver of nameless fear, but jauntily professes himself ready for all that life can inflict. But there come moments in every life when the false security in which shallow souls wrap themselves ignobly is broken up, and then often a paroxysm of terror or misery grips a man, for which he has no anodyne, and his despair is as unreasonable as his security. The meaning of all circumstances that force our helplessness on us is to open to us Jehoshaphat's refuge in his—'our eyes are upon Thee.' We need to be driven by the crowds of foes and dangers around to look upwards. Our props are struck away that we may cling to God. The tree has its lateral branches hewed off that it may shoot up heavenward. When the valley is filled with mist and swathed in evening gloom, it is the time to lift our gaze to the peaks that glow in perpetual sunshine. Wise and happy shall we be if the sense of helplessness begets in us the energy of a desperate faith. For these two, distrust of self and glad confidence in God, are not opposites, as naked distrust and trust are, but are complementary. He does not turn his eyes to God who has not turned them on himself, and seen there nothing to which to cling, nothing on which to lean. Astronomers tell us that there are double stars revolving round one axis and forming a unity, of which the one is black and the other brilliant. Self-distrust and trust in God are thus knit together and are really one.

II. We see here the peaceful assurance of victory that attends on faith.

A flash of inspiration came to one of the Levitical singers who had, no doubt, been deeply moved and had unconsciously fitted himself for receiving it. Divinely breathed confidence illuminated his waiting spirit, and a great message of encouragement poured from his lips. His words heartened the host more than a hundred trumpets braying in their ears. How much one man who has drunk in God's assurance of victory can do to send a thrill of his own courage through more timorous hearts! Courage is no less contagious than panic. This Levite becomes the commander of the army, and Jehoshaphat and his captains 'bow their heads' and accept his plan for to-morrow, hearing in his ringing accents a message from Jehovah. The instructions given and at once accepted are as unlike those of ordinary warfare as is the whole incident; for there is to be no sword drawn nor blow struck, but they are to 'stand still and see the salvation of the Lord.' They are told where to find the enemy and are bid to go forth in order of battle against them, and they are assured 'that the battle is not theirs, but God's.' No wonder that the message was hailed as from heaven, and put new heart into the host, or that, when the messenger's voice ceased, his brother Levites broke into shrill praise as for a victory already won. With what calm, triumphant hearts the camp would sleep that night!

May we not take that inspired Levite's message as one to ourselves in the midst of our many conflicts both in the outward life and in the inward? If we have truly grasped God's hands, and are fighting for what is accordant with His will, we have a right to feel that 'the battle is not ours but God's,' and to be sure that therefore we shall conquer. Of course we are not to say to ourselves, 'God will fight for us, and we need not strike a blow,' Jehoshaphat's example does not fit our case in that respect, and we may thank God that it does not. We have a better lot than to 'stand still and see the salvation of God,' for we are honoured by being allowed to share the stress of conflict and the glow of battle as well as in the shout of victory. But even in the struggles of outward life, and much more in those of our spiritual nature, every man who watches his own career will many a time have to recognise God's hand, unaided by any act of his own, striking for him and giving him victory; and in the spiritual life every Christian man knows that his best moments have come from the initiation of the Spirit who 'bloweth where He listeth.' How often we have been surprised by God's help; how often we have been quickened by God's inbreathed Spirit, and have been taught that the passivity of faith draws to us greater blessings than the activity of effort! 'They also serve who only stand and wait,' and they also conquer who in quietness and confidence keep themselves still and let God work for them and in them. The first great blessing of trust in God is that we may be at peace on the eve of battle, and the second is that in every battle it is, in truth, not we that fight, but God who fights for and in us.

III. We learn here the best preparation for the conflict.

When the morning dawned, the array was set in order and the march begun, and a strange array it was. In the van marched the Temple singers singing words that are music to us still: 'Give thanks unto the Lord, for His mercy endureth for ever,' and behind them came the ranks of Judah, no doubt swelling the volume of melody, that startled the wild creatures of the wilderness, and perhaps travelled through the still morning as far as the camp of the enemy. The singers had no armour nor weapons. They were clad in 'the beauty of holiness,' the priestly dress, and for sword and spear they carried harps and timbrels. Our best weapons are like their equipment.

We are most likely to conquer if we lift up the voice of thanks for victory in advance, and go into the battle expecting to triumph, because we trust in God. The world's expectation of success is too often a dream, a will-o'-the-wisp that tempts to bogs where the beguiled victim is choked, though even in the world it is often true; 'screw your courage to the sticking point, and we'll not fail.' But faith, that is the expectation of success based on God's help and inspiring to struggles for things dear to His heart, is wont to fulfil itself, and by bringing God into the fray, to secure the victory. A thankful heart not seldom brings into existence that for which it is thankful.

IV. We see here the victory and the praise for it.

The panic that laid hold on the enemy, and turned their swords against each other, was more natural in an undisciplined horde such as these irregular levies of ancient times, than it would be in a modern army. Once started, the infection would spread, so we need not wonder that by the time that Judah arrived on the field all was over. How often a like experience attends us! We quiver with apprehension of troubles that never attack us. We dread some impending battlefield, and when we reach it, Jehoshaphat's surprise is repeated, 'and, behold they were dead bodies, fallen to the earth.' Delivered from foes and fears, Judah's first impulse was to secure the booty, for they were keen after wealth, and their 'faith' was not very pure or elevating. But their last act was worthier, and fitly ended the strange campaign. They gathered in some wady among the grim cliffs of the wilderness of Judah, which broke the dreariness of that savage stretch of country with perhaps verdure and a brook, and there they 'blessed the Lord.' The chronicler gives a piece of popular etymology, in deriving the name, 'the valley of blessing,' from that morning's worship. Perhaps the name was older than that, and was given from a feeling of the contrast between the waste wilderness, which in its gaunt sterility seemed an accursed land, and the glen which with its trees and stream was indeed a 'valley of blessing.' If so, the name would be doubly appropriate after that day's experience. Be that as it may, here we have in vivid form the truth that all our struggles and fightings may end in a valley of blessing, which will ring with the praise of the God who fights for us. If we begin our warfare with an appeal to God, and with prayerful acknowledgment of our own impotence, we shall end it with thankful acknowledgment that we are 'more than conquerors through Him that loved us' and fought for us, and our choral song of praise will echo through the true Valley of Blessing, where no sound of enemies shall ever break the settled stillness, and the host of the redeemed, like that army of Judah, shall bear 'psalteries and harps and trumpets,' and shall need spear and sword no more at all for ever.

HOLDING FAST AND HELD FAST

'As they went forth Jehoshaphat stood and said, Believe in the Lord your God, so shall ye be established.'—2 CHRON. xx. 20.

Certainly no stronger army ever went forth to victory than these Jews, who poured out of Jerusalem that morning with no weapon in all their ranks, and having for their van, not their picked men, but singers who 'praised the beauty of holiness,' and chanted the old hymn, 'Give thanks unto the Lord, for His mercy endureth for ever.' That was all that men had to do in the battle, for as the shrill song rose in the morning air 'the Lord set liers in wait for the foe,' and they turned their swords against one another, so that when Jehoshaphat and his troops came in sight of the enemy the battle was over and the field strewn with corpses—so great and swift is the power of devout recognition of God's goodness and trust in His enduring mercy, even in the hour of extremest peril.

The exhortation in our text which is Jehoshaphat's final word to his army, has, in the original, a beauty and emphasis that are incapable of being preserved in translation. There is a play of words which cannot be reproduced in another language, though the sentiment of it may be explained. The two expressions for 'believing' and 'being established' are two varying forms of the same root-word; and although we can only imitate the original clumsily in our language, we might translate in some such way as this: 'Hold fast by the Lord your God, and you will be held fast,' or 'stay yourselves on Him and you will be stable.' These attempts at reproducing the similarity of sound between the two verbs in the two clauses of our text, rude as they are, preserve what is lost, so far as regards form, in the English translation, though that is correct as to the meaning of the command and promise. If we note this connection of the two clauses we just come to the general principle which lies here, that the true source of steadfastness in character and conduct, of victory over temptation, and of standing fast in slippery places, is simple reliance, or, to use the New Testament word, 'faith,' 'Believe and ye shall be established.' Put out your hand and clasp Him, and He puts out His hand and steadies you. But all the steadfastness and strength come from the mighty Hand that is outstretched, not from the tremulous one that grasps it.

So, then, keeping to the words of my text, let me suggest to you the large lessons that this saying teaches us, in regard to three things, which I may put as being the object, the nature, and the issues of faith; or, in other words, to whom we are to cling, how we are to cling, and what the consequence of the clinging is.

I. To whom we must cling.

'Stay yourselves on the Lord your God,' Well, then, faith is not believing a number of theological articles, nor is it even accepting the truth of the Gospel as it lies in Jesus Christ, but it is accepting the Christ whom the truth of the Gospel reveals to us. And, although we have to come to Him through the word that declares what He is, and what He has done for us, the act of believing on Him is something that lies beyond the mere understanding of, or giving credence to, the message that tells us who He is and what He has done. A man may have not the ghost of a doubt or hesitation about one tittle of revealed truth, and if you were to cross-question him, could answer satisfactorily all the questions of an orthodox inquisitor, and yet there may not be one faintest flicker of faith in that man's whole being, for all the correctness of his creed, and the comprehensiveness of it, too. Trust is more than assent. If it is a Person on whom our faith leans, then from that there follows clearly enough that the bond which binds us to Him must be something far warmer, far deeper, and far more under the control of our own will than the mere consent or assent of our brains to a set of revealed truths. 'The Lord your God,' and not even the Bible that tells you about Him; 'the Lord your God,' and not even the revealed truths that manifest Him, but Him as revealed by the truths—it is He that is the Object to which our faith clings.

Jehoshaphat, in the same breath in which he exhorted his people to 'believe in the Lord, that they might be established,' also said, 'Believe His prophets, so shall ye prosper.' The immediate reference, of course, was to the man who the day before had assured them of victory. But the wider truth suggested is, that the only way to get to God is through the word that speaks of Him, and which has come from the lips either of prophets or of the Son who has spoken more, and more sweetly and clearly, than all the prophets put together. If we are to believe God, we must believe the prophets that tell us of Him.

And then there is another suggestion that may be made. The Object of faith proposed to Judah is not only 'the Lord,' but 'the Lord *your* God.' I do not say that there can be no faith without the 'appropriating' action which takes the whole Godhead for mine, but I doubt very much whether there is any. And it seems to me that to a very large extent the difference between mere nominal, formal Christians and men who really are living by the power of faith in God as revealed in Jesus Christ, lies in that one little word, 'the Lord your God.' That a man shall put out a grasping hand, and say, 'I take for my own—for my very own—the universal blessing, I claim as my possession that God of the spirits of all flesh, I believe that He does stand in a real individualising relation to me, and I to Him,' is surely of the very essence of faith. There is no presumption, but the truest wisdom and lowliness in enclosing, if I may so say, a part of this great common for ours, and putting a hedge about it, as it were, and saying, 'That is mine.' We shall not have understood the sweetness and the power of the Gospel of Jesus Christ until we have pointed and condensed the general declaration, 'He so loved the world,' into the individualising and appropriating one, 'He loved me, and gave Himself for me.' Oh! if we could only apply that process thoroughly to all the broad glorious words and promises of Scripture, and feel that the whole incidence of them was meant to fall upon us, one by one, and that just as the sun, up in the heavens there, sends all his beams into the tiniest daisy on the grass, as if there was nothing else in the whole world, but only its little petals to be smoothed out and opened, I think our Christianity would be more real, and we should have more blessings in our hands. God in Christ and I, the only two beings in the universe, and all His fullness mine, and all my weakness supported and supplemented by Him—that is the view that we should sometimes take. We should set ourselves apart from all mankind, and claim Him as our very own, and so be filled with the fullness of God.

This, then, is the Object of faith, a Person who is all mine and all yours too. The beam of light that falls on my eye falls on yours, and no man makes a sunbeam the smaller because he sees by it; and in like manner we may each possess the whole of God for our very own property.

II. How we cling.

The metaphor, I suppose, is more eloquent than all explanations of it. 'Believe in the Lord'; hold fast by Him with a tight grip, continually renewed when it tends to slacken, as it surely will, and then you will be established.

We might run out into any number of figurative illustrations. Look at that little child beginning to learn to walk, how it fastens its little dimpled hands into its mother's apron, and so the tiny tottering feet get a kind of steadfastness into them. Look at that man lying at the door of the Temple, who never had walked since his mother's womb, and had lain there for forty years, with his poor weak ankles all atrophied by reason of their disuse. 'He held Peter and John.' Would not his grasp be tight? Would he not clasp their hands as his only stay? He had not become accustomed to the astounding miracle of walking, nor learned to balance himself and accomplish the still more astounding feat of standing steady. So he clutched at the two Apostles and was 'established.' Look at that man walking by a slippery path which he does not know, holding by the hand the guide who is able to direct and keep him up. See this other in some wild storm, with an arm round a steadfast tree-stem, to keep him from being blown over the precipice, how he clings like a limpet to a rock. And that is how we are to hold on to God, with what would be despair if it were not the perfection of confidence, with the clear sense that the only thing between us and ruin is the strong Hand that we clasp.

And what do we mean by clasping God? I mean making daily efforts to rivet our love on Him, and not to let the world, with all its delusive and cloying sweets, draw us away from Him. I mean continual and strenuous efforts to fix our *thoughts* upon Him, and not to allow the trivialities of life, or the claims of culture, or the necessities of our daily position so to absorb our minds as that thoughts of God are comparative strangers there, except, perhaps, sometimes on a Sunday, and now and then at the sleepy end, or the half-awake beginning, of a day. I mean continually repeated and strenuous efforts to cleave to Him by the submission of our *will*, letting Him 'do what seemeth Him good,' and not lifting ourselves up against Him, or perking our own inclinations, desires, and fancies in His face, as if we would induce Him to take them for His guides! And I mean that we should try to commit our *way* unto the Lord, 'to rest in the Lord, and wait patiently for Him.' The submissive will which cleaves to God's commandments, the waiting heart that clings to His love, the regulated thoughts that embrace His truth, and the childlike confidence that commits its path to Him—these are the elements of that steadfast adherence to the Lord which shall not be in vain.

III. The blessed effects of this clinging to God.

'So shall ye be established.' That follows, as a matter of course. The only way to make light things stable is to fasten them to something that is stable. And the only way to put any kind of calmness and fixedness, and yet progress—stability in the midst of progress, and progress in the midst of stability—into our lives, is by keeping firm hold of God. If we grasp His hand, then a calm serenity will be ours. In the midst of changes, sorrows, losses, disappointments, we shall not be blown about here and there by furious winds of fortune, nor will the heavy currents of the river of life sweep us away. We shall have a holdfast and a mooring. And although, like some light-ship anchored in the Channel, we may heave up and down with the waves, we shall keep in the same place, and be steadfast in the midst of mobility, and wholesomely mobile although anchored in the one spot where there is safety. As the issue of faith, of this throwing the responsibility for ourselves upon God, there will be quietness of heart, and continuance and persistence in righteousness, and steadfastness of purpose and continuity of advancement in the divine life. 'The law of the Lord is in his heart,' says one of the Psalms, 'none of his steps shall slide.' The man who walks holding God's hand can put down a firm foot, even when he is walking in slippery places. There will be decision, and strength, and persistence of continuous advance, in a life that derives its impulse and its motive power from communion with God in Jesus Christ.

There will be victory, not indeed after the fashion of that in this story before us. In it, of course, men had to do nothing but 'stand still and see the salvation of God.' That is the law for us, in regard to the initial blessings of acceptance, and forgiveness, and the communication of the divine life from above. We have to be simple recipients, and we have no co-operating share in that part of the work of our own salvation. But for the rest we have to help God. 'Work out your own salvation with fear and trembling, for it is God that worketh in you.' But none the less, 'This is the victory that over-cometh the world, even our faith,' and if we give heed to Jehoshaphat's commandment, and go out to battle as his people did, with the love and trust of God in our hearts, then we shall come back as they did, laden with spoil, and shall name the place which was the field of conflict 'the valley of blessing,' and return to Jerusalem 'with psalteries, and harps, and trumpets,' and 'God will give us rest from all our enemies round about us.'

JOASH

'And Joash did that which was right in the sight of the Lord all the days of Jehoiada the priest.... 17. Now after the death of Jehoiada came the princes of Judah, and made obeisance to the king. Then the king hearkened unto them.'—2 CHRON. xxiv. 2, 17.

Here we have the tragedy of a soul. Joash begins life well and for the greater part of it remains faithful to his conscience and to his duty, and then, when outward circumstances change, he casts all behind him, forgets the past and commits moral suicide. It is the sad old story, a bright commencement, an early promise all scattered to the winds. It is a strange story, too. This seven-year-old king had been saved when his father had been killed, and that true daughter of Jezebel, as well by nature as by blood, Athaliah, had murdered all his brothers and sisters, and made herself queen. He had been saved by the courage of a woman who might worthily stand by the side of Deborah and other Jewish heroines. By this woman, who was his aunt, he was hidden and brought up in the Temple until, whilst yet a mere boy, he came to the throne, the High Priest Jehoiada, the husband of his aunt, being his guardian during his nonage. He reigns well till the lad of seven becomes a mature man of thirty or thereabouts, and then Jehoiada dies, full of years and honours, and they fitly lay him among the kings of Judah, a worthy resting-place for one who had 'done good in Israel.' And now the weakling on the throne is left alone without the strong arm to guide him and keep him right, and we read that 'the princes of Judah came and made obeisance to him.' They take him on his weak side, and I dare say Jehoiada had been too true and too noble to do that, and though we are not told what means they took to flatter and coax him, we see very plainly what they were conspiring to do, for we read that 'they left the house of the Lord their God, the God of their fathers, and served groves and idols,' the groves here mentioned being symbols of Ashtaroth the goddess of the Sidonians. And so all the past is wiped out and Joash takes his place amongst the apostates. The story has solemn lessons.

I. Note the change from loyal adhesion to apostasy.

The strong man on whom Joash used to lean was away, and the poor, weak king went just where the wicked princes led him. It was probably out of sheer imbecility that he passed from the worship of God to the acknowledgment and service of idols.

The first point that I would insist upon is a well-worn and familiar one, as I am well aware, but I urge it upon you, and especially upon the younger portion of my audience. It is this, that there is no telling the amount of mischief that pure weakness of character may lead into. The worst men we come across in the Bible are not those who begin with a deliberate intention of doing evil. They are weak creatures, 'reeds shaken by the wind,' who have no power of resisting the force of circumstances. It is a truth which every one's experience confirms, that the mother of all possible badness is weakness, and that, not only as Milton's Satan puts it, 'To be weak is to be miserable,' but that weakness is wickedness sooner or later. The man who does not bar the doors and windows of his senses and his soul against temptation, is sure to make shipwreck of his life and in the end to become 'a fool.' There is so much wickedness lying round us in this world that any man who lets himself be shaped and coloured by that with which he comes in contact, is sure to go to the bad in the long run. Where a man lays himself open to the accidents of time and circumstances, the majority of these influences will be contrary to what is right and good. Therefore, he must gather himself together and learn to say 'No!' There is no foretelling the profound abysses into which a 'good, easy' nature, with plenty of high and pure impulses, perhaps, but which are written in water, may fall. 'Thou, therefore, young man! be strong in the grace that is in Christ Jesus.' Learn to say No! or else you will be sure to say Yes! in the wrong place, and then down you will go, like this Joash whose goodness depended on Jehoiada, and when he died, all the virtue that had characterised this life hitherto was laid with him in the dust.

Let us learn from this story in the next place, how little power of continuance there is in a merely traditional religion. Many of you call yourselves Christian people mainly because other people do the same. It is customary to respect and regard Christianity. You have been brought up in the midst of it. Our country is always considered a Christian land, and so, naturally, you tacitly accept the truth of a religion which is so influential. The lowest phase of this attitude is that which seeks some advantage from a church connection, like the foolish man in the Old Testament who thought he would do well because he had a Levite for his priest. Religion is the most personal thing about a man. To become a Christian is the most personal act one can perform. It is a thing that a man has to do for himself, and however friends and guides may help us in other matters, in trials and perplexities and difficulties, by their sympathy and experience, they are useless here. A man has here to act as if there were no other beings in the universe but a solitary God and himself, and unless we have ourselves done that act in the depths of our own personality, we have not done it at all. If you young people are good, just because you have pious parents who make you go to church or chapel on a Sunday, and keep you out of mischief during the week, your goodness is a sham. One great result of personal Christianity is to make a minister, a teacher, a guide, superfluous, and when such an one becomes so, his work has been successful and not till then. Unless you put forth for yourself the hand of faith and for yourself yield up the devotion and love of your own heart, your religion is nought.

However much active effort about the outside of religion there may be, it is of itself useless. It is without bottom and without reality. Here we have Joash busy with the externals of worship and actually deceiving himself thereby. It was a great deal easier to make that chest for contributions to a Temple Repairing Fund, and to get it well filled, and to patch up the house of the Lord, than for him to get down on his knees and pray, and he may have thought that to be busy about the house of God was to be devout. So it may be with many Sunday-school teachers and Church workers. Their religion may be as merely superficial and as little personal as this man's was. It is not for me to say so about A, B, or C. It is for you to ask of yourselves if it is so as to you. But I do say that there is nothing that masks his own soul from a man more than setting him to do something for Christianity and God's Church, while in his inmost self he has not yet yielded himself to God.

I look around and I see the devil slaying his thousands by setting them to work in Christian associations and leaving them no time to think about their own Christianity. My brother! if the cap fits, go home and put it on.

We see in Joash's life for how long a time a man may go on in this self-delusion of external and barren service and never know it. Joash came to the throne at the age of seven. Up till that age he had lived in the Temple in concealment. Until he was one and thirty he went on in a steady, upright course, never knowing that there was anything hollow in his life. Apparently, Jehoiada's long life of one hundred and thirty years extended over the greater part of Joash's reign, during most of which he had Jehoiada to direct him and keep him right, and all this tragedy comes at the tag end of it.

So he went on apparently all right, like a tree that has become quite hollow, till during some storm it is blown down and falls with a crash, and it is seen that for years it has been only the skin of a tree, bark outside, and inside—emptiness.

II. We come now to the second stage in the later life of Joash: His resistance to the divine pleading.

'And they left the house of the Lord God of their fathers, and served groves and idols, and wrath came upon Judah and Jerusalem for their trespass, yet He sent prophets to them to bring them again unto the Lord.' He sent with endless pity, with long-suffering patience. He would not be put away, and as they increased the distance between Him and them, He increased His energies to bring them back. But they lifted themselves up, Joash and his princes, and with that strange, awful power of resisting the attraction of the divine pleading, and hardening their hearts against the divine patience—'they would not.' And then comes the affecting episode of the death of the high priest Zechariah, who had succeeded to his father's place and likewise to his heroism, and who, with the Spirit of God upon him, stands up and pointing out his wickedness, rebukes the fallen monarch for his apostasy. Joash, doubtless stung to the quick by Zechariah's just reproaches, allowed the truculent princes to slay him in the court of the Temple, even between the very shrine and the altar.

What a picture we have here of the divine love which follows every wanderer with its pleadings and beseechings! It came to this man through the lips of a prophet. It comes to us all in daily blessings, sometimes in messages, like these poor words of mine. God will not let us ruin ourselves without pleading with us and wooing us to love Him and cling to Him. 'He rises up early' and daily sends us His messages, sometimes rebukes and voices in our conscience, sometimes sunset glows and starry heavens lifting our thoughts above this low earth, sometimes sorrows that are meant to 'drive us to His breast,' and above all, the 'Gospel of our salvation' in Christ, ever, in such a land as ours, sounding in our ears.

Still further, we see in Joash what a strange, awful strength of obstinate resistance, a character weak as regards its resistance to man, can put forth against God. He never attempted to say 'No!' to the princes of Judah, but he could say it again and again to his Father in heaven. He could not but yield to the temptations which were level with his eyes, and this poor creature, easily swayed by human allurements and influences, could gather himself together, standing, as it were, on his little pin point, and say to God, 'Thou dost call and I refuse.' What a paradox, and yet repetitions of it are sitting in these pews, only half aware that it is about them that I am speaking!

The ever-deepening evil which began with forsaking the house of the Lord and serving Ashtaroth, ends with Joash steeping his hands in blood. The murder of Zechariah was beyond the common count of crimes, for it was a foul desecration of the Temple, an act of the blackest ingratitude to the man who had saved his infant life, and put him on the throne, an outrage on the claims of family connections, for Joash and Zechariah were probably blood relations. My brother! once get your foot upon that steep incline of evil, once forsake the path of what is good and right and true, and you are very much like a climber who misses his footing up among the mountain peaks, and down he slides till he reaches the edge of the precipice and then in an instant is dashed to pieces at the bottom. Once put your foot on that slippery slope and you know not where you may fall to.

III. Last comes the final scene: The retribution.

We have that picture of Zechariah, solemnly lifting up his eyes to heaven and committing his cause to God. 'The Lord look upon it and require it,' says the martyr priest in the spirit of the old Law. The dying appeal was soon answered in the invasion of the Syrian army, a comparatively small company, into whose hands the Lord delivered a very great host of the Israelites. The defeat was complete, and possibly Joash's 'great diseases,' of which the narrative speaks, refer to wounds received in the fight. The end soon comes, for two of his servants, neither of them Hebrews, one being the son of an Ammonitess and the other the son of a Moabitess, who were truer to his religion than he had been, and resolved to revenge Zechariah's death, entered the room, of the wounded king in the fortress whither he had retired to hide himself after the fight, and 'slew him on his bed.' Imagine the grim scene— the two men stealing in, the sick man there on the bed helpless, the short ghastly struggle and the swift end. What an end for a life with such a beginning!

Now I am not going to dwell on this retribution, inflicted on Joash, or on that which comes to us if we are like him, through a loud-voiced conscience, and a memory which, though it may be dulled and hushed to sleep at present, is sure to wake some day here or yonder. But I beseech you to ask yourselves what your outlook is. 'Be not deceived, God is not mocked; for whatsoever a man soweth that shall he also reap.' Is that all? Zechariah said, 'The Lord look upon it and require it.' The great doctrine of retribution is true for ever. Yes; but our Zechariah lifts up his eyes to heaven and he says, 'Father! forgive them, for they know not what they do.' And so, dear brother! you and I, trusting to that dear Lord, may have all our apostasy forgiven, and be brought near by the blood of Christ. Let us say with the Apostle Peter, 'Lord, to whom shall we go but to Thee? Thou hast the words of eternal life.'

GLAD GIVERS AND FAITHFUL WORKERS

'And it came to pass after this, that Joash was minded to repair the house of the Lord. 5. And he gathered together the priests and the Levites, and said to them, go out unto the cities of Judah, and gather of all Israel money to repair the house of your God from year to year, and see that ye hasten the matter. Howbeit the Levites hastened it not. 6. And the king called for Jehoiada the chief, and said unto him, Why hast thou not required of the Levites to bring in out of Judah and out of Jerusalem the collection, according to the commandment of Moses the servant of the Lord, and of the congregation of Israel, for the tabernacle of witness' 7. For the sons of Athaliah, that wicked woman, had broken up the house of God: and also all the dedicated things of the house of the Lord did they bestow upon Baalim. 8. And at the king's commandment they made a chest, and set it without at the gate of the house of the Lord. 9. And they made a proclamation through Judah and Jerusalem, to bring in to the Lord the collection that Moses the servant of God laid upon Israel in the wilderness. 10. And all the princes and all the people rejoiced, and brought in, and cast into the chest, until they had made an end. 11. Now it came to pass, that at what time the chest was brought unto the king's office by the hand of the Levites, and when they saw that there was much money, the king's scribe and the high priest's officer came and emptied the chest, and took it, and carried it to his place again. Thus they did day by day, and gathered money in abundance. 12. And the king and Jehoiada gave it to such as did the work of the service of the house of the Lord, and hired masons and carpenters to repair the house of the Lord, and also such as wrought iron and brass to mend the house of the Lord. 13. So the workmen wrought, and the work was perfected by them, and they set the house of God in his state, and strengthened it. 11. And when they had finished it, they brought the rest of the money before the king and Jehoiada, whereof were made vessels for the house of the Lord, even vessels to minister, and to offer withal, and spoons, and vessels of gold and silver. And they offered burnt offerings in the house of the Lord continually all the days of Jehoiada.'—2 CHRON. xxiv. 4-14.

Joash owed his life and his throne to the high-priest Jehoiada, who was his uncle by marriage with the sister of Ahaziah, his father. Rescued by his aunt when an infant, he 'was with them, hid in the house of God six years,' and, when seven years old, was made king by Jehoiada's daring revolt against 'that wicked woman,' Athaliah. Jehoiada's influence was naturally paramount, and was as wholesome as strong. It is remarkable, however, that this impulse to repair the Temple seems to have originated with the king, not with the high-priest, though no doubt the spirit which conceived the impulse was largely moulded by the latter. The king, whose childhood had found a safe asylum in the Temple, might well desire its restoration, even apart from considerations of religion.

I. The story first brings into strong contrast the eager king, full of his purpose, and the sluggards to whom he had to entrust its execution. We can only guess the point in his reign at which Joash summoned the priests to his help. It was after his marriage (ver. 3), and considerably before the twenty-third year of his reign, at which time his patience was exhausted (2 Kings xii. 6). Some years were apparently wasted by the dawdling sluggishness of the priests, who, for some reason or other, did not go into the proposed restoration heartily. Joash seems to have suspected that they would push the work languidly; for there is a distinct tinge of suspicion and 'whipping up' in his injunction to 'hasten the matter.'

The first intention was to raise the funds by sending out the priests and Levites to collect locally the statutory half-shekel, as well as other contributions mentioned in 2 Kings xii. There we learn that each collector was to go to 'his acquaintance.' The subscription was to be spread over some years, and for a while Joash waited quietly; but in the twenty-third year of his reign (see 2 Kings), he could stand delay no longer. Whether the priests had been diligent in collecting or not, they had done nothing towards repairing. Perhaps they found it difficult to determine the proportion of the money which was needed for the ordinary expenses of worship, and for the restoration fund; and, as the former included their own dues and support, they would not be likely to set it down too low. Perhaps they did not much care to carry out a scheme which had not begun with themselves; for priests are not usually eager to promote ecclesiastical renovations suggested by laymen. Perhaps they did not care as much about the renovation as the king did, and smiled at his earnestness as a pious imagining. Possibly there was even deliberate embezzlement. But, at any rate, there was half-heartedness, and that always means languid work, and that always means failure. The earnest people are fretted continually by the indifferent. Every good scheme is held back, like a ship with a foul bottom, by the barnacles that stick to its keel and bring down its speed. Professional ecclesiastics in all ages have succumbed to the temptation of thinking that 'church property' was first of all to be used for their advantage, and, secondarily, for behoof of God's house. Eager zeal has in all ages to be yoked to torpid indifference, and to drag its unwilling companion along, like two dogs in a leash. Direct opposition is easier to bear than apparent assistance which tries to slow down to half speed.

Joash's command is imperative on all workers for God. 'See that ye hasten the matter,' for time is short, the fruit great, the evening shadows lengthening, the interests at stake all-important, and the Lord of the harvest will soon come to count our sheaves. Whatever work may be done without haste,

God's cannot be, and a heavy curse falls on him who 'does the work of the Lord negligently.' The runner who keeps well on this side of fatigue, panting, and sweat, has little chance of the crown.

II. The next step is the withdrawal of the work from the sluggards. They are relieved both of the collection and expenditure of the money. Apparently (2 Kings xii. 9) the contributors handed their donations to the doorkeepers, who put them into the chest with 'a hole in the lid of it,' in the sight of the donors. The arrangement was not flattering to the hierarchy, but as appearances were saved by Jehoiada's making the chest (see 2 Kings) they had to submit with the best grace they could. In our own times, we have seen the same thing often enough. When clergy have maladministered church property, Parliament has appointed ecclesiastical commissioners. Common sense prescribes taking slovenly work out of lazy hands. The more rigidly that principle is carried out in the church and the nation, at whatever cost of individual humiliation, the better for both. 'The tools to the hands that can use them' is the ideal for both. God's dealings follow the same law, both in withdrawing opportunities of service and in giving more of such. The reward for work is more work, and the punishment for sloth is compulsory idleness.

III. We are next shown the glad givers. Probably suspicion had been excited in others than the king, and had checked liberality. People will not give freely if the expenses of the collectors' support swallow up the funds. It is hard to get help for a vague scheme, which unites two objects, and only gives the balance, after the first is provided for, to the second and more important. So the whole nation, both high and low, was glad when the new arrangement brought a clear issue, and secured the right appropriation of the money.

No doubt, too, Joash's earnestness kindled others. Chronicles speaks only of the 'tax,'—that is, the half-shekel,—but Kings mentions two other sources, one of which is purely spontaneous gifts, and these are implied by the tone of verse 10, which lays stress on the gladness of the offerers. That is the incense which adds fragrance to our gifts. Grudging service is no service, and money given for ever so religious a purpose, without gladness because of the opportunity of giving, is not, in the deepest sense, given at all. Love is a longing to give to the beloved, and whoever truly loves God will know no keener delight than surrender for His dear sake. Pecuniary contributions for religious purposes afford a rough but real test of the depth of a man's religion; but it is one available only for himself, since the motive, and not the amount, is the determining element. We all need to bring our hearts more under the Influence of God's love to us, that our love to Him may be increased, and then to administer possessions, under the impulse to glad giving which enkindled love will always excite. Super-heated steam has most expansive power and driving force. These glad givers may remind us not only of the one condition of acceptable giving, but also of the need for clear and worthy objects, and of obvious disinterestedness in those who seek for money to help good causes. The smallest opening for suspicion that some of it sticks to the collector's fingers is fatal, as it should be.

IV. Joash was evidently a business-like king. We next hear of the precautions he took to secure the public confidence. There was a rough but sufficient audit. When the chest grew heavy, and sounded full, two officials received it at the 'king's office.' The Levites carried it there, but were not allowed to handle the contents. The two tellers represented the king and the chief priest, and thus both the civil and religious authorities were satisfied, and each officer was a check on the other. Public money should never be handled by a man alone; and an honest one will always wish, like Paul, to have a brother associated with him, that no man may blame him in his administration of it. If we take 'day by day' literally, we have a measure of the liberality which filled the chest daily; but, more probably, the expression simply means 'from time to time,' when occasion required.

V. The application of the money is next narrated. In this Jehoiada is associated with Joash, the king probably desiring to smooth over any slight that might seem to have been put on the priests, as well as being still under the influence of the high-priest's strong character and early kindness. Together they passed over the results of the contribution to the contractors, who in turn paid it in wages to the workmen who repaired the fabric, such as masons and carpenters, and to other artisans who restored other details, such as brass and iron work. The Second Book of Kings tells us that Joash's cautious provision against misappropriation seems to have deserted him at this stage; for no account was required of the workmen, 'for they dealt faithfully.' That is an indication of their goodwill. The humble craftsmen were more reliable than the priests. They had, no doubt, given their half-shekel like others, and now they gladly gave their work, and were not hirelings, though they were hired. We, too, have to give our money and our labour; and if our hearts are right, we shall give both with the same conscientious cheerfulness, and, if we are paid in coin for our work, will still do it for higher reasons and looking for other wages. These Temple workmen may stand as patterns of what religion should do for those of us whose lot is to work with our hands,—and not less for others who have to toil with their brains, and the sweat of whose brow is inside their heads. A Christian workman should be a 'faithful' workman, and will be so if he is full of faith.

Joash knew when to trust and when to keep a sharp eye on men. His experience with the priests had not soured him into suspecting everybody. Cynical disbelief in honesty is more foolish and hurtful to ourselves than even excessive trust. These workmen wrought all the more faithfully because they knew that they were trusted, and in nine cases out of ten men will try to live up to our valuation of them. The Rugby boys used to say, 'It's a shame to tell Arnold a lie, he always believes us.' Better to be cheated once than to treat the nine as rogues,—better for them and better for ourselves.

'Faithful' work is prosperous work. As verse 13 picturesquely says, 'Healing went up upon the work'; and the Temple was restored to its old fair proportions, and stood strong as before. Where there is conscientious effort, God's blessing is not withheld. Labour 'in the Lord' can never be empty labour, though even a prophet may often be tempted, in a moment of weary despondency, to complain, 'I have laboured in vain.' We may not see the results, nor have the workmen's joy of beholding the building rise, course by course, under our hands, but we shall see it one day, though now we have to work in the dark.

There seems a discrepancy between the statements in Chronicles and Kings as to the source from which the cost of the sacrificial vessels was defrayed, since, according to the former, it was from the restoration fund, which is expressly denied by the latter. The explanation seems reasonable, that, as Chronicles says, it was from the balance remaining after all restoration charges were liquidated, that this other expenditure was met. First, the whole amount was sacredly devoted to the purpose for which it had been asked, and then, when the honest overseers repaid the uncounted surplus, which they might have kept, it was found sufficient to meet the extra cost of furnishing. God blesses the faithful steward of his gifts with more than enough for the immediate service, and the best use of the surplus is to do more with it for Him. 'God is able to make all grace abound unto you; that ye, having always all sufficiency in every thing, may abound unto every good work, … being enriched in every thing unto all liberality.'

PRUDENCE AND FAITH

'And Amaziah said to the man of God, But what shall we do for the hundred talents which I have given to the army of Israel? And the man of God answered, The Lord is able to give thee much more than this.'—2 CHRON. xxv. 9.

The character of this Amaziah, one of the Kings of Judah, is summed up by the chronicler in a damning epigram: 'He did that which was right in the sight of the Lord, but not with a perfect heart.' He was one of your half-and-half people, or, as Hosea says, 'a cake not turned,' burnt black on one side, and raw dough on the other. So when he came to the throne, in the buoyancy and insolence of youth, he immediately began to aim at conquests in the neighbouring little states; and in order to strengthen himself he hired 'a hundred thousand mighty men of valour' out of Israel for a hundred talents of silver. To seek help from Israel was, in a prophet's eyes, equivalent to flinging off help from God. So a man of God comes to him, and warns him that the Lord is not with Israel, and that the alliance is not permissible for him. But, instead of yielding to the prophet's advice, he parries it with this misplaced question, 'But what shall we do for the hundred talents that I have given to the army of Israel?' He does not care to ask whether the counsel that he is receiving is right or wrong, or whether what he is intending to do is in conformity with, or in opposition to, the will of God, but, passing by all such questions, at once he fastens on the lower consideration of expediency—'What is to become of me if I do as this prophet would have me do? What a heavy loss one hundred talents will be! It is too much to sacrifice to a scruple of that sort. It cannot be done.'

A great many of us may take a lesson from this man. There are two things in my text—a misplaced question and a triumphant answer: 'What shall we do for the hundred talents?' 'The Lord is able to give thee much more than this.' Now, remarkably enough, both question and answer may be either very right or very wrong, according as they are taken, and I purpose to look at those two aspects of each.

I. A misplaced question.

I call it misplaced because Amaziah's fault, and the fault of a great many of us, was, not that he took consequences into account, but that he took them into account at the wrong time. The question should have come second, not first. Amaziah's first business should have been to see clearly what was duty; and then, and not till then, the next business should have been to consider consequences.

Consider the right place and way of putting this question. Many of us make shipwreck of our lives because, with our eyes shut, we determine upon some grand design, and fall under the condemnation of the man that 'began to build, and was not able to finish.' He drew a great plan of a stately mansion; and then found that he had neither money in the bank, nor stones in his quarry, to finish it, and so it stood—a ruin. All through our Lord's life He was engaged rather in repressing volunteers than in soliciting recruits, and He from time to time poured a douche of cold water upon swiftly effervescing desires to go after Him. When the multitudes followed Him, He turned and said to them, 'If you are counting on being My disciples, understand what it means: take up the cross and follow Me.' When an enthusiastic man, who had not looked consequences in the face, came rushing to Him and said: 'Lord, I will follow Thee whithersoever Thou goest,' His answer to him was another pull at the string of the shower bath: 'The Son of Man hath not where to lay His head.' When the two disciples came to him and said: 'Grant that we may sit, the one on Thy right hand and the other on Thy left, when Thou comest into Thy kingdom,' He said: 'Are ye able to drink of the cup that I drink of, and to be baptized with the baptism that I am baptized withal?' Look the facts in the face before you make your election. Jesus Christ will enlist no man under false pretences. Recruiting-sergeants tell country bumpkins or city louts wonderful stories of what they will get if they take the shilling and put on the king's uniform; but Jesus Christ does not recruit His soldiers in that fashion. If a man does not open his eyes to a clear vision of the consequences of his actions, his life will go to water in all directions. And there is no region in which such clear insight into what is going to follow upon my determinations and the part that I take is more necessary than in the Christian life. It is just because in certain types of character, 'the word is received with joy,' and springs up immediately, that when 'the sun is risen with a burning heat'—that is, as Christ explains, when the pinch of difficulty comes—'immediately they fall away,' and all their grand resolutions go to nothing. 'Lightly come, lightly go.' Let us face the facts of what is involved, in the way of sacrifice, surrender, loss, if we determine to be on Christ's side; and then, when the anticipated difficulties come, we shall neither be perplexed nor swept away, but be able quietly to say, 'I discounted it all beforehand; I knew it was coming.' The storm catches the ship that is carrying full sail and expecting nothing but light and favourable breezes; while the captain that looked into the weather quarter and saw the black cloud beginning to rise above the horizon, and took in his sails and made his vessel snug and tight, rides out the gale. It is wisdom that becomes a man, to ask this question, if first of all he has asked, 'What ought I to do?'

But we have here an instance of a right thing in a wrong place. It was right to ask the question, but wrong to ask it at that point. Amaziah thought nothing about duty. There sprang up in his mind at once the cowardly and ignoble thought: 'I cannot afford to do what is right, because it will cost me a hundred talents,' and that was his sin. Consequences may be, must be, faced in anticipation, or a man is a fool. He that allows the clearest perception of disagreeable consequences, such as pain, loss of ease, loss of reputation, loss of money, or any other harmful results that may follow, to frighten him out of the road that he knows he ought to take, is a worse fool still, for he is a coward and recreant to his own conscience.

We have to look into our own hearts for the most solemn and pressing illustrations of this sin, and I daresay we all of us can remember clear duties that we have neglected, because we did not like to face what would come from them. A man in business will say, 'I cannot afford to have such a high standard of morality; I shall be hopelessly run over in the race with my competitors if I do not do as they do,' or he will say, 'I durst not take a stand as an out-and-out Christian; I shall lose connections, I shall lose position. People will laugh at me. What am I to do for the hundred talents?'

But we can find the same thing in Churches. I do not mean to enter upon controversial questions, but as an instance, I may remind you that one great argument that our friends who believe in an Established Church are always bringing forward, is just a modern form of Amaziah's question, 'What shall we do for the hundred talents? How could the Church be maintained, how could its ministrations be continued, if its State-provided revenues were withdrawn or given up?' But it is not only Anglicans who put the consideration of the consequences of obedience in the wrong place. All the Churches are but too apt to let their eyes wander from reading the plain precepts of the New Testament to looking for the damaging results to be expected from keeping them. Do we not sometimes hear, as answer to would-be reformers, 'We cannot afford to give up this, that, or the other practice? We should not be able to hold our ground, unless we did so-and-so and so-and-so.'

But not only individuals or Churches are guilty in this matter. The nation takes a leaf out of Amaziah's book, and puts aside many plain duties, for no better reason than that it would cost too much to do them. 'What is the use of talking about suppressing the liquor traffic or housing the poor? Think of the cost.' The 'hundred talents' block the way and bribe the national conscience. For instance, the opium traffic; how is it defended? Some attempt is made to prove either that we did not force it upon China, or that the talk about the evils of opium is missionary fanaticism, but the sheet-anchor is: 'How are we ever to raise the Indian revenue if we give up the traffic?' That is exactly Amaziah over again, come from the dead, and resurrected in a very ugly shape.

So national policy and Church action, and—what is of far more importance to you and me than either the one or the other,—our own personal relation to Jesus Christ and discipleship to Him, have been hampered, and are being hampered, just by that persistent and unworthy attitude of looking at the consequences of doing plain duties, and permitting ourselves to be frightened from the duties because the consequences are unwelcome to us.

Prudence is all right, but when prudence takes command and presumes to guide conscience, then it is all wrong. In some courts of law and in certain cases, the judge has an assessor sitting beside him, an expert about some of the questions that are involved. Conscience is the judge, prudence the assessor. But if the assessor ventures up on the judgment-seat, and begins to give the decisions which it is not his business to give—for *his* only business is to give advice—then the only thing to do with the assessor is to tell him to hold his tongue and let the judge speak. It is no answer to the prophet's prohibition to say, 'But what shall I do for the hundred talents?' A yet better answer than the prophet gave Amaziah would have been, 'Never mind about the hundred talents; do what is right, and leave the rest to God.' However, that was not the answer.

II. The triumphant answer.

'The Lord is able to give thee much more than this.' Now, this answer, like the question, may be right or wrong, according as it is taken. In what aspect is it wrong? In what sense is it not true? I suppose this prophet did not mean more than the undeniable truth that God was able to give Amaziah more than a hundred talents. He was not thinking of the loftier meanings which we necessarily, as Christian people, at a later stage of Revelation, and with a clearer vision of many things, attach to the words. He simply meant, 'You will very likely get more than the hundred talents that you have lost, if you do what pleases God.' He was speaking from the point of view of the Old Testament; though even in the Old Testament we have instances enough that prosperity did not always attend righteousness. In the Old Testament we find the Book of Job, and the Book of Ecclesiastes, and many a psalm, all of which were written in order to grapple with the question, 'How is it that God does not give the good man more than the hundred talents that he has lost for the sake of being good?' It is not true, and it is a dangerous mistake to suggest that it is true, that a man in this world never loses by being a good, honest, consistent Christian. He often does lose a great deal, as far as this world is concerned; and he has to make up his mind to lose it, and it would be a very poor thing to say to him, 'Now, live like a Christian man, and if you are flinging away money or anything else because of your Christianity, you will get it back.' No; you will not, in a good many cases. Sometimes you will, and sometimes you will not. It does not matter whether you do or do not.

But the sense in which the triumphant answer of the prophet is true is a far higher one. 'The Lord is able to give thee much more than this,'—what is 'more'? a thousand talents? No; the 'much more' that Christianity has educated us to understand is meant in the depths of such a promise as this is, first of all, character. Every man that sacrifices anything to convictions of duty gains more than he loses thereby, because he gains an inward nobleness and strength, to say nothing of the genial warmth of an approving conscience. And whilst that is true in all regions of life, it is most especially true in regard to sacrifices made from Christian principle. No matter how disastrous may be the results externally, the inward results of faithfulness are so much greater and sweeter and nobler than all the external evil consequences that may follow, that it is 'good policy' for a man to beggar himself for Christ's sake, for the sake of the durable riches—which our Lord Himself explains to be synonymous with righteousness—which will come thereby. He that wins strength and Christ-likeness of character by sacrificing for Christ has won far more than he can ever lose.

He wins not only character, but a fuller capacity for a fuller possession of Jesus Christ Himself, and that is infinitely more than anything that any man has ever sacrificed for the sake of that dear Lord. Do you remember when it was that there was granted to the Apostle John the vision of the throned Christ, and that he felt laid upon him the touch of the vivifying Hand from Heaven? It was 'when I was in Patmos for the Word of God, and for the testimony of Jesus.' He lost Ephesus; he gained an open heaven and a visible Christ. Do you remember who it was that said, 'I have suffered the loss of all things, and do count them but dung, that I may win Christ'? It was a good bargain, Paul! The balance-sheet showed a heavy balance to your credit. Debit, 'all things'; credit, 'Christ.' 'The Lord is able to give thee much more than this.'

Remember the old prophecy: 'For brass I will bring gold; and for iron, silver.' The brass and the iron may be worth something, but if we barter them away and get instead gold and silver, we are gainers by the transaction. Fling out the ballast if you wish the balloon to rise. Let the hundred talents go if you wish to get 'the more than this.' And listen to the New Testament variation of this man of God's promise, 'If thou wilt have treasure in heaven, go and sell all that thou hast, and follow Me.'

JOTHAM

'So Jotham became mighty, because he prepared his ways before the Lord his God.'—2 CHRON. xxvii 6.

This King Jotham is one of the obscurer of the Jewish monarchs, and we know next to nothing about him. The most memorable event in his reign is that 'in the year when King Uzziah,' his father, 'died,' and consequently in Jotham's first year, Isaiah saw the Lord sitting in the Temple on the empty throne, and had the lips which were to utter so many immortal words touched with fire from the altar. Whether it were the effect of the prophet's words, or from other causes, the little that is told of him is good, and he is eulogised as having imitated his father's God-pleasing acts, and not having stained himself by repeating his father's sin. The rest that we hear of him in Chronicles is a mere sketch of campaigns, buildings, and victories, and then he and his reign are summed up in the words of our text, which is the analysis of the man and the disclosure of the secret of his prosperity: 'He became mighty, because he prepared his ways'—and, more than that, 'he prepared them before the Lord his God.'

So then, if we begin, as it were, at the bottom, as we ought to do, in studying a character, taking the deepest thing first, and laying hold upon the seminal and germinal principle of the whole, this text reminds us that—The secret of true strength lies in the continual recognition that life is lived 'Before the Lord our God.'

Now to say, 'Walk thou *before* Me,' the command given to Abraham, suggests a somewhat different modification of the idea from the apparently parallel phrase, 'to walk *with* God' which is declared to have been the life's habit of Enoch. The one expression suggests simple companionship and communion; the other suggests rather the vivid and continual realisation of the thought that we are 'ever in the great Taskmaster's eye.' To walk before God is to feel thrillingly and continually, and yet without being abased or crushed or discomposed, but rather being encouraged and quickened and calmed and ennobled and gladdened thereby: 'Thou God seest me.' It seems to me that one of the plainest pieces of Christian duty, and, alas! one of the most neglected of them, is the cultivation, definitely and consciously, by effort and by self-discipline, of that consciousness as a present factor in all our lives, and an influencing motive in everything that we do. If once we could bring before the eye of our minds that great, blazing, white throne, and Him that sits upon it, we should want nothing else to burn up the commonplaces of life, and to flash its insignificance into splendour and awfulness. We should want nothing else to lift us to a 'solemn scorn of ills,' and to deliver us from the false sweetnesses and fading delights that grow on the low levels of a sense-bound life! Brethren! our whole life would be transformed and glorified, and we should be different men and women if we ordered our ways as '*before the Lord our God.*' What meanness could live when we knew that it was seen by those pure Eyes? How we should be ashamed of ourselves, of our complaints, of our murmurings, of our reluctance to do our duty, of our puerile regrets for vanished blessings, and of all the low cares and desires that beset and spoil our lives, if once this thought, 'before God,' were habitual with us, and we walked in it as in an atmosphere!

Why is it not? and might it not be? and if it might not, ought it not to be? And what are we to say to Him whom we profess to love as our Supreme Good, if all the day long the thought of Him seldom comes into our minds, and if any triviality, held near the eye, is large enough and bright enough to shut Him out from our sight? With deep ethical significance and accuracy was the command given to Abraham as the sole, all-sufficient direction for both inward and outward life: 'Walk before Me and (so) be thou perfect.' For indeed the full realisation—adequate and constant and solid enough to be a motive—of 'Thou God seest me,' would be found to contain practical directions in regard to all moral difficulties, and would unfailingly detect the evil, howsoever wrapped up, and would carry in itself not only motive but impulse, not only law but power to fulfil it. The Master's eye makes diligent servants. How schoolboys bend themselves over their slates and quicken their effort when the teacher is walking behind the benches! And how a gang of idle labourers will buckle to the spade and tax their muscles in an altogether different fashion when the overseer appears upon the field! If we realised, as we should do, the presence in all our little daily life of that great, sovereign Lord, there would be less skulking, less superficially performed tasks, less jerry work put into our building; more of our strength cast into all our work, and less of ourselves in any of it.

Remember, too, how connected with this is another piece of effort needful in the religious life, and suggested by the last words of this text, 'Before the Lord *his* God.' Cultivate the habit of narrowing down the general truths of religion to their relation to yourselves. Do not be content with 'the Lord *our* God,' or 'the Lord the God of the whole earth,' but put a 'my' in, and realise not only the presence of a divine Inspector, but the closeness of the personal bond that unites to Him; and the individual responsibility, in all its width and depth and unshiftableness—if I may use such a word—which results therefrom. You cannot shake off or step out of the tasks that 'the Lord *your* God' lays upon you. You and He are as if alone in the world. Make Him your God by choice, by your own personal acceptance of His authority and dependence upon His power, and try to translate into daily life the great truth, 'Thou God seest *me*,' and bring it to bear upon the veriest trifles and smallest details.

Now the text follows the order of observation, so to speak, and mentions the outward facts of Jotham's success before it goes deeper and accounts for them. We have reversed the process and dealt first with the cause. The spring of all lay in his conscious recognition of his relation to God and God's to him. From that, of course, followed that he 'prepared,' according to the Authorised Version, or 'ordered,' according to the Revised Version, 'his ways.' There is an alternative rendering of the word rendered 'prepared' or 'ordered' given in the margin of the Authorised Version, which reads, 'established his ways.' Both the ideas of ordering and establishing are contained in the word.

Now that fact, that the same word means both these, conveys a piece of practical wisdom, which it will do us all good to note clearly and take to heart. For it teaches us that whatever is 'ordered' is firm, and whatever is disorderly, haphazard, done without the exercise of one's mind on the act, being chaotic, is necessarily short-lived.

The ordered life is the established life. The life of impulse, chance, passion, the life that is lived without choice and plan, without reflection and consideration of consequences, the following of nature, which some people tell us is the highest law, and which is woefully likely to degenerate into following the *lower* nature, which ought not to be followed, but covered and kept under hatches—such a life is sure to be a topsy-turvy life, which, being based upon the narrowest point, must, by the laws of equilibrium, topple over sooner or later. If you would have your lives established, they must be ordered. You must bring your brains to bear upon them, and you must bring more than brain, you must bring to bear on every part of them the spiritual instincts that are quickened by contact with the thought of the All-seeing God, and let these have the ordering of them. Such lives, and only such, will endure 'when all that seems shall suffer shock.' 'He that doeth the will of God abideth for ever.'

But the lesson that is pressed upon us by this word, understood in the other meanings of 'prepared' or 'ordered,' is that all our 'ways,' that is, our practical life, our acts, direction of mind, habits, should be regulated by continual consciousness of, and reference to, the All-discerning Eye that looks down upon us, and 'the God in whose hands our breath is, and whose are'—whether we make them so or not—'all our ways.' To translate that into less picturesque, and less forcible, but more modern words, it is just this: You Christian people ought to make it a point of duty to cultivate the habit of referring everything that you do to the will and judgment of God. Take Him into account in everything great or small, and in nothing say, 'Thus I will, thus I command. My will shall stand instead of all other reasons'; but say, 'Lord! by Thee and for Thee I try to do this'; and having done it, say, 'Lord! the seed is sown in Thy name; bless Thou the springing thereof.' Works thus begun, continued and ended, will never be put to confusion, and 'ways' thus ordered will be established. A path of righteousness like that can no more fail to be a way of peace than can God's throne ever totter or fall. An ordered life in which He is consulted, and which is all shaped at His bidding, and by His strength, and for His dear name, will 'stand four-square to all the winds that blow,' and, being founded upon a rock, will never fall.

But we may also note that in the strength of that thought, that we are before the Lord our God, we shall best establish our ways in the sense that we shall keep on steadily and doggedly on the path. Well begun may be half ended, but there is often a long dreary grind before it is wholly ended, and the last half of the march is the wearisome half. The Bible has a great deal to say about the need of obstinate persistence on the right road. 'Ye did run well, what did hinder you?' 'Cast not away your confidence, which hath great recompense of reward.' 'We are made partakers of Christ if we hold fast the beginning of our confidence firm unto the end.' 'He that overcometh and keepeth My words unto the end, to him will I give authority.' Lives which derive their impulse from communion with God will not come to a dead stop half-way on their road, like a motor the fuel of which fails; and it will be impossible for any man to 'endure unto the end' and so to be heir of the promise—'the same shall be saved,' unless he draws his persistency from Him who 'fainteth not, neither is weary' and who 'reneweth strength to them that have no might' so that in all the monotonous levels they shall 'walk and not faint,' and in all the crises, demanding brief spurts of energy, 'they shall run and not be weary,' and at last 'shall mount up with wings as eagles.' A path ordered and a path persisted in ought to be the path of every Christian man.

The text finally tells of the prosperity and growing power which attends such a course. 'Jotham became mighty.' That was simple outward blessing. His kingdom prospered, and, according to the theocratic constitution of Judah, faithfulness to God and material well-being went together. You cannot apply these words, of course, to the outward lives of Christians. It is no doubt true that 'Godliness *is* profitable for all things,' but there are a great many other things besides the godliness of the man that does them which determine whether a man's undertakings shall prosper in the world's sense or not. It would be a pitiable thing if the full revelation of God in Christ did not teach us Christians more about the meaning and the worth of outward success and inward prosperity than the Old Testament could teach. I hope we have learned that lesson; at least, it is not the fault of our lesson book if we have not. Although it is true that religion does make the best of both worlds, it does not do so by taking the world's estimate of what its best for to-day is, and giving a religious man *that*. Sometimes it does, and sometimes it does not, and whether it does or no depends on other considerations than the reality of the man's devotion. Good men are often made better by being made sad and unsuccessful. And if they are not bettered by adversity, it is not the fault of the discipline but of the people who undergo it.

But though the husk of my text falls away—and we should thank God that it has fallen away—the kernel of it is ever true. Whosoever will thus root his life in the living thought of a loving, divine Eye being perpetually upon him, and make that thought a motive for holiness and loving obedience and effort after service, will find that the true success, the only success and the only strength that are worth a man's ambition to desire or his effort to secure, will assuredly be his. He may be voted a failure as regards the world's prizes. But a man that 'orders his ways,' and perseveres in ways thus ordered, 'before the Lord' will for reward get more power to order his ways, and a purer and more thrilling, less interrupted and more childlike vision of the Face that looks upon him. God's 'eyes behold the upright,' and the upright behold His eyes, and in the interchange of glances there is power; and in that power is the highest reward for ordered lives. We shall get power to do, power to bear, power to think aright, power to love, power to will, power to behold, power to deny ourselves, 'power to become sons of God.' This is the success of life, when out of all its changes, and by reason of all its efforts, we realise more fully our filial possession of our Father, and our Father's changeless love to us. We shall become mighty with the might that is born of obedience and faith if we order our ways before the Lord our God. 'The path of the just is as the shining light, that shineth more and more until the noontide of the day.'

COSTLY AND FATAL HELP

'He sacrificed unto the gods of Damascus, which smote him: and he said, Because the gods of the kings of Syria help them, therefore will I sacrifice to them, that they may help me. But they were the ruin of him, and of all Israel.'—2 CHRON. xxviii. 23.

Ahaz came to the throne when a youth of twenty. From the beginning he reversed the policy of his father, and threw himself into the arms of the heathen party. In a comparatively short reign of sixteen years he stamped out the worship of God, and nearly ruined the kingdom.

He did not plunge into idolatry for want of good advice. The greatest of the prophets stood beside him. Isaiah addressed to him remonstrances which might have made the most reckless pause, and promises which might have kindled hope and courage in the bosom of despair. Hosea in the northern kingdom, Micah in Judah, and other less brilliant names were amongst the stars which shone even in that dark night. But their light was all in vain. The foolish lad had got the bit between his teeth, and, like many another young man, thought to show his 'breadth' and his 'spirit' by neglecting his father's counsellors, and abandoning his father's faith. He was ready to worship anything that called itself a god, always excepting Jehovah. He welcomed Baal, Moloch, Rimmon, and many more with an indiscriminate eagerness that would have been ludicrous if it had not been tragical. The more he multiplied his gods the more he multiplied his sorrows, and the more he multiplied his sorrows the more he multiplied his gods.

From all sides the invaders came. From north, northeast, east, south-east, south, they swarmed in upon him. They tore away the fringes of his kingdom; and hostile armies flaunted their banners beneath the very walls of Jerusalem.

And then, in his despair, like a scorpion in a circle of fire, he inflicted a deadly wound on himself by calling in the fatal help of Assyria. Nothing loth, that warlike power responded, scattered his less formidable foes, and then swallowed the prey which it had dragged from between the teeth of the Israelites and Syrians. The result of Ahaz's frantic appeals to false gods and faithless men may still be read on the cuneiform inscriptions, where, amidst a long list of unknown tributary kings, stands, with a Philistine on one side of him and an Ammonite on the other, the shameful record, 'Ahaz of Judah.'

That was what came of forsaking the God of his fathers. It is a type of what always has come, and always must come, of a godless life. That is the point of view from which I wish to look at the story, and at these words of my text which gather the whole spirit of it into one sentence.

I. First, then, let me ask you to notice how this narrative illustrates for us the crowd of vain helpers to which a man has to take when he turns his back upon God.

If we compare the narrative in our chapter with the parallel in the Second Book of Kings, we get a very vivid picture of the strange medley of idolatries which they introduced. Amongst Ahaz's new gods are, for instance, the golden calves of Israel and the ferocious Moloch of Ammon, to whom he sacrificed, passing through the fire at least one of his own children. The ancient sacred places of the Canaanites, on every high hill and beneath every conspicuous tree, again smoked with incense to half-forgotten local deities. In every open space in Jerusalem he planted a brand-new altar with a brand-new worship attendant upon it. In the Temple, he brushed aside the altar that Solomon had made and put up a new one, copied from one which he had seen at Damascus. The importation of the Damascene altar, I suppose, meant, as our text tells us, the importation of the Damascene gods along with it.

Side by side with that multiplication of false deities went the almost entire neglect of the worship of Jehovah, until at last, as his reign advanced and he floundered deeper into his troubles, the Temple was spoiled, everything in it that could be laid hands upon was sent to the melting-pot, to pay the Assyrian tribute; and then the doors were shut, the lamps extinguished, the fire quenched on the cold altars, and the silent Temple left to the bats and—*the Shekinah*; for God still abode in the deserted house.

Further, side by side with this appealing all round the horizon to whatsoever obscene and foul shape seemed to promise some help, there went the foolish appeal to the northern invaders to come and aid him, which they did, to his destruction. His whole career is that of a godless and desperate man who will grasp at anything that offers deliverance, and will worship any god or devil who will extricate him from his troubles.

Is the breed extinct, think you? Is there any one among us who, if he cannot get what he wants by fair ways, will try to get it by foul? Do none of you ever bow down to Satan for a slice of the kingdoms of this world? Ahaz has still plenty of brothers and sisters in all our churches and chapels.

This story illustrates for us what, alas! is only too true, both on the broad scale, as to the generation in which we live, and on the narrower field of our own individual lives. Look at the so-called cultured classes of Europe to-day; turning away, as so many of them are, from the Lord God of their fathers; what sort of gods are they worshipping instead? Scraps from Buddhism, the

Vedas, any sacred books but the Bible; quackeries, and charlatanism, arid dreams, and fragmentary philosophies all pieced together, to try and make up a whole, instead of the old-fashioned whole that they have left behind them. There are men and women in many congregations who, in modern fashion, are doing precisely the thing that Ahaz did—having abandoned Christianity, they are trying to make up for it by hastily stitching together shreds and patches that they have found in other systems. 'The garment is narrower than that a man can wrap himself in it,' and a creed patched together so will never make a seamless whole which can be trusted not to rend.

But look, further, how the same thing is true as to the individual lives of godless men.

Many of us are trying to make up for not having the One by seeking to stay our hearts on the many. But no accumulation of insufficiencies will ever make a sufficiency. You may fill the heaven all over with stars, bright and thickly set as those in the whitest spot in the galaxy, and it will be night still. Day needs the sun, and the sun is one, and when it comes the twinkling lights are forgotten. You cannot make up for God by any extended series of creatures, any more than a row of figures that stretched from here to *Sirius* and back again would approximate to infinitude.

The very fact of the multitude of helpers is a sign that none of them is sufficient. There is no end of 'cures' for toothache, that is to say there is none. There is no end of helps for men that have abandoned God, that is to say, every one in turn when it is tried, and the stress of the soul rests upon it, gives, and is found to be a broken staff that pierces the hand that leans upon it.

Consult your own experience. What is the meaning of the unrest and distraction that mark the lives of most of the men in this generation? Why is it that you hurry from business to pleasure, from pleasure to business, until it is scarcely possible to get a quiet breathing time for thought at all? Why is it but because one after another of your gods have proved insufficient, and so fresh altars must be built for fresh idolatries, and new experiments made, of which we can safely prophesy the result will be the old one. We have not got beyond St. Augustine's saying:—'Oh, God! my heart was made for Thee, and in Thee only doth it find repose.' The many idols, though you multiply them beyond count, all put together will never make the One God. You are seeking what you will never find. The many pearls that you seek will never be enough for you. The true wealth is One, 'One pearl of great price.'

II. So notice again how this story teaches the heavy cost of these helpers' help.

Ahaz had, as he thought, two strings to his bow. He had the gods of Damascus and of other lands on one hand, he had the king of Assyria on another. They both of them exacted onerous terms before they would stir a foot to his aid. As for the northern conqueror, all the wealth of the king and of the princes and of the Temple was sent to Assyria as the price of his hurtful help. As for the gods, his helpers, one of his sons at least went into the furnace to secure their favour; and what other sacrifices he may have made besides the sacrifice of his conscience and his soul, history does not tell us. These were considerable subsidies to have to be paid down before any aid was granted.

Do *you* buy this world's help any cheaper, my brother? You get nothing for nothing in that market. It is a big price that you have to pay before these mercenaries will come to fight on your side. Here is a man that 'succeeds in life,' as we call it. What does it cost him? Well! it has cost him the suppression, the atrophy by disuse, of many capacities in his soul which were far higher and nobler than those that have been exercised in his success. It has cost him all his days; it has possibly cost him the dying out of generous sympathies and the stimulating of unwholesome selfishness. Ah! he has bought his prosperity very dear. Political economists have much to say about the 'appreciation of gold.' I think if people would estimate what they pay for it, in an immense majority of cases, in treasure that cannot be weighed and stamped, they would find it to be about the dearest thing in God's universe; and that there are few men who make worse bargains than the men who give *themselves* for worldly success, even when they receive what they give themselves for.

There are some of you who know how much what you call enjoyment has cost you. Some of us have bought pleasure at the price of innocence, of moral dignity, of stained memories, of polluted imaginations, of an incapacity to rise above the flesh: and some of us have bought it at the price of health. The world has a way of getting more out of you than it gives to you.

At the best, if you are not Christian men and women, whether you are men of business, votaries of pleasure, seekers after culture and refinement or anything else, you have given Heaven to get earth. Is that a good bargain? Is it much wiser than that of a horde of naked savages that sell a great tract of fair country, with gold-bearing reefs in it, for a bottle of rum, and a yard or two of calico? What is the difference? You have been fooled out of the inheritance which God meant for you; and you have got for it transient satisfaction, and partial as it is transient. If you are not Christian people, you have to buy this world's wealth and goods at the price of God and of your own souls. And I ask you if that is an investment which recommends itself to your common sense. Oh! my brother; 'what shall it profit a man if he gain the whole world, and lose himself?' Answer the question.

III. Lastly, we may gather from this story an illustration of the fatal falsehood of the world's help.

Ahaz pauperised himself to buy the hireling swords of Assyria, and he got them; but, as it says in the narrative, 'the king came unto him, and distressed him, but strengthened him not.' He helped Ahaz at first. He scattered the armies of which the king of Judah was afraid like chaff, with his fierce and disciplined onset. And then, having driven them off the bleeding prey, he put his own paw upon it, and growled 'Mine!' And where he struck his claws there was little more hope of life for the prostrate creature below him.

Ay! and that is what this world always does. In the case before us there was providential guidance of the politics of the Eastern nations in order to bring about these results; and we do not look for anything of that sort. No! But there are natural laws at work today which are God's laws, and which ensure the worthlessness of the help bought so dear.

A godless life has at the best only partial satisfaction, and that partial satisfaction soon diminishes. 'Even in laughter the heart is sorrowful, and the end of that mirth is heaviness.'

That is the experience of all men, and I need not dwell upon the threadbare commonplaces which have survived from generation to generation, because each generation in turn has found them so piteously true, about the incompleteness and the fleetingness of all the joys and treasures of this life. The awful power of habit, if there were no other reason, takes the edge off all gratification except in so far as God is in it. Nothing fully retains its power to satisfy. Nothing has that power absolutely at any moment; but even what measure of it any of our possessions or pursuits may have for a time, soon, or at all events by degrees, passes away. The greater part of life is but like drinking out of empty cups, and the cups drop from our hands. What one of our purest and peacefullest poets said in his haste about all his kind is true in spirit of all godless lives:—

'We poets, in our youth, begin in gladness,
But thereof cometh, in the end, despondency and madness.'

'Vanity of vanities! saith'—not the Preacher only, but the inmost heart of every godless man and woman—'vanity of vanities! all is vanity!'

And do not forget that, partial and transient as these satisfactions of which I have been speaking are, they derive what power of helping and satisfying is in them only from the silence of our consciences, and our success in being able to shut out realities. One word, they say, spoken too loud, brings down the avalanche, and beneath its white, cold death, the active form is motionless and the beating heart lies still. One word from conscience, one touch of an awakened reflectiveness, one glance at the end—the coffin and the shroud and what comes after these—slay your worldly satisfactions as surely as that falling snow would crush some light-winged, gauzy butterfly that had been dancing at the cliff's foot. Your jewellery is all imitation. It is well enough for candle-light. Would you like to try the testing acid upon it? Here is a drop of it. 'Know thou that for all these things God will bring thee into judgment.' Does it smoke? or does it stand the test? Here is another drop. 'This night thy soul shall be required of thee.' Does it stand that test? My brother! do not be afraid to take in all the facts of your earthly life, and do not pretend to satisfy yourselves with satisfactions which dare not face realities, and shrivel up at their presence.

These fatal helpers come as friends and allies, and they remain as masters. Ahaz and a hundred other weak princes have tried the policy of sending for a strong foreign power to scatter their enemies, and it has always turned out one way. The foreigner has come and he has stopped. The auxiliary has become the lord, and he that called him to his aid becomes his tributary. Ay! and so it is with all the things of this world. Here is some pleasant indulgence that I call to my help lightly and thoughtlessly. It is very agreeable and does what I wanted with it, and I try it again. Still it answers to my call. And then after a while I say, 'I am going to give that up,' and I cannot, I have brought in a master when I thought I was only bringing in an ally that I could dismiss when I liked. The sides of the pit are very slippery; it is gay travelling down them, but when the animal is trapped at the bottom there is no possibility of getting up again. So some of you, dear friends! have got masters in your delights, masters in your pursuits, masters in your habits. These are your gods, these are your tyrants, and you will find out that they are so, if ever, in your own strength, you try to break away from them.

So let me plead with you. With some of you, perhaps, my voice, as a familiar voice, that in some measure, however undeservedly, you trust, may have influence. Let me plead with you—do not run after these will-o'-the-wisps that will only lure you into destruction, but follow the light of life which is Jesus Christ Himself. Do not take these tyrants for your helpers, who will master you under pretence of aiding you; and work their will of you instead of lightening your burden. The same unwise and hopeless mode of life, which we have been describing this evening by one symbolic illustration, as calling vain helpers to our aid, was presented by Ahaz's great contemporary Isaiah, in words which Ahaz himself may have heard, as 'striking a covenant with death, and making lies our refuge.' Some of us, alas! have been doing that all our lives. Let such hearken to the solemn words which may have rung in the ears of this unworthy king. 'Judgment also will I lay to the line, and righteousness to the plummet, and the hail shall sweep away the refuge of lies.' I come to you, dear friends! to press on your acceptance the true Guide and Helper—even Jesus Christ your Brother, in whose single Self you will find all that you have vainly sought dispersed 'at sundry times and in divers manners'—among creatures. Take Him for your Saviour by trusting your whole selves to Him. He is the Sacrifice by whose blood all our sins are washed away, and the Indweller, by whose Spirit all our spirits are ennobled and gladdened. I ask you to take Him for your Helper, who will never deceive you; to call whom to our aid is to be secure and victorious for ever. 'Behold! I lay in Zion for a foundation a stone, a tried stone, a precious cornerstone, a sure foundation: he that believeth shall not make haste.'

A GODLY REFORMATION

'Hezekiah began to reign when he was five and twenty years old, and he reigned nine and twenty years in Jerusalem. And his mother's name was Abijah, the daughter of Zechariah. 2. And he did that which was right in the sight of the Lord, according to all that David his father had done. 3. He in the first year of his reign, in the first mouth, opened the doors of the house of the Lord, and repaired them. 4. And he brought in the priests and the Levites, and gathered them together into the east street, 5. And said unto them, Hear me, ye Levites; Sanctify now yourselves, and sanctify the house of the Lord God of your fathers, and carry forth the filthiness out of the holy place. 6. For our fathers have trespassed, and done that which was evil in the eyes of the Lord our God, and have forsaken Him, and have turned away their faces from the habitation of the Lord, and turned their backs. 7. Also they have shut up the doors of the porch, and put out the lamps, and have not burnt incense, nor offered burnt-offerings in the holy place unto the God of Israel. 8. Wherefore the wrath of the Lord was upon Judah and Jerusalem, and He hath delivered them to trouble, to astonishment, and to hissing, as ye see with your eyes. 9. For, lo, our fathers have fallen by the sword; and our sons and our daughters and our wives are in captivity for this. 10. Now it is in mine heart to make a covenant with the Lord God of Israel, that His fierce wrath may turn away from us. 11. My sons, be not now negligent: for the Lord hath chosen you to stand before Him, to serve Him, and that ye should minister unto Him, and burn incense.'—2 CHRON. xxix. 1-11.

Hezekiah, the best of the later kings, had the worst for his father, and another almost as bad for his son. His own piety was probably deepened by the mad extravagance of his father's boundless idolatry, which brought the kingdom to the verge of ruin. Action and reaction are equal and contrary. Saints grown amidst fashionable and deep corruption are generally strong, and reformers usually arise from the midst of the systems which they overthrow. Hezekiah came to a tottering throne and an all but beggared nation, ringed around by triumphant enemies. His brave young heart did not quail. He sought 'first the kingdom of God, and His righteousness,' and of the two pressing needs for Judah, political peace and religious purity, he began with the last. The Book of Kings tells at most length the civil history; the Book of Chronicles, as usual, lays most stress on the ecclesiastical. The two complete each other. The present passage gives a beautiful picture of the vigorous, devout young king setting about the work of reformation.

We may note, first, his prompt action. Joash had to whip up the reluctant priests with his 'See that ye hasten the matter!' Hezekiah lets no grass grow under his feet, but begins his reforms with his reign. 'The first month' (ver. 3) possibly, indeed, means the first month of the calendar, not of Hezekiah, who may have come to the throne in the later part of the Jewish year; but, in any case, no time was lost. The statement in verse 3 may be taken as a general *resume* of what follows in detail, but this vigorous speech to the priests was clearly among the new king's first acts. No doubt his purpose had slowly grown while his father was affronting Heaven with his mania for idols. Such decisive, swift action does not come without protracted, previous brooding. The hidden fires gather slowly in the silent crater, however rapidly they burst out at last.

We can never begin good things too early, and when we come into new positions, it is always prudence as well as bravery to show our colours unmistakably from the first. Many a young man, launched among fresh associations, has been ruined because of beginning with temporising timidity. It is easier to take the right standing at first than to shift to it afterwards. Hezekiah might have been excused if he had thought that the wretched state of political affairs left by Ahaz needed his first attention. Edomites on the east, Philistines on the west and south, Syrians and Assyrians on the north, 'compassed him about like bees,' and worldly prudence would have said, 'Look after these enemies today, and the Temple tomorrow.' He was wiser than that, knowing that these were effects of the religious corruption, and so he went at that first. It is useless trying to mend a nation's fortunes unless you mend its morals and religion.

And there are some things which are best done quickly, both in individual and national life. Leaving off bad habits by degrees is not hopeful. The only thing to be done is to break with them utterly and at once. One strong, swift blow, right through the heart, kills the wild beast. Slighter cuts may make him bleed to death, but he may kill you first. The existing state was undeniably sinful. There was no need for deliberation as to that. Therefore there was no reason for delay. Let us learn the lesson that, where conscience has no doubts, we should have no dawdling. 'I made haste, and delayed not to keep thy commandment.'

Note, too, in Hezekiah's speech, the true order of religious reformation. The priests and Levites were not foremost in it, as indeed is only too often the case with ecclesiastics in all ages. Probably many of them had been content to serve Ahaz as priests of his multiform idolatry. At all events, they needed 'sanctifying,' though no doubt the word is here used in reference to merely ceremonial uncleanness. Still the requirement that they should cleanse themselves before they cleansed the Temple has more than ceremonial significance. Impure hands are not fit for the work of religious reformation, though they have often been employed in it. What was the weakness of the Reformation but that the passions of princes and nobles were so soon and generally enlisted for it, and marred it? He that enters into the holy place, especially if his errand be to cleanse it, must have 'clean hands, and a pure heart.' The hands that wielded the whip of small cords, and drove out the money-changers, were stainless, and therefore strong. Some of us are very fond of trying to set churches to rights. Let us begin with ourselves, lest, like careless servants, we leave dirty finger-marks where we have been 'cleaning.'

The next point in the speech is the profound and painful sense of existing corruption. Note the long-drawn-out enumeration of evils in verses 6 and 7, starting with the general recognition of the fathers' trespass, advancing to the more specific sin of forsaking Him and His house, and dwelling, finally, as with fascinated horror, on all the details of closed shrine and quenched lamps and cold altars. The historical truth of the picture is confirmed by the close of the previous chapter, and its vividness shows how deeply Hezekiah had felt the shame and sin of Ahaz. It is not easy to keep clear of the influence of prevailing corruptions of religion. Familiarity weakens abhorrence, and the stained embodiments of the ideal hide its purity from most eyes. But no man will be God's instrument to make society, the church, or the home, better, unless he feels keenly the existing evils. We do not need to cherish a censorious spirit, but we do need to guard against an unthinking acquiescence in the present state of things, and a self-complacent reluctance to admit their departure from the divine purpose for the church. There is need to-day for a like profound consciousness of evil, and like efforts after new purity. If we individually lived nearer God, we should be less acclimatised to the Church's imperfections. No doubt Hezekiah's clear sight of the sinfulness of the idolatry so universal round him was largely owing to Isaiah's influence. Eyes which have caught sight of the true King of Israel, and of the pure light of His kingdom, will be purged to discern the sore need for purifying the Lord's house.

The clear insight into the national sin gives as clear understanding of the national suffering. Hezekiah speaks, in verses 8 and 9, as the Law and the Prophets had been speaking for centuries, and as God's providence had been uttering in act all through the national history. But so slow are men to learn familiar truths that Ahaz had grasped at idol after idol to rescue him; 'but they were the ruin of him, and of all Israel.' How difficult it is to hammer plain truths, even with the mallet of troubles, into men's heads! How blind we all are to the causal connection between sin and sorrow! Hezekiah saw the iron link uniting them, and his whole policy was based upon that 'wherefore.' Of course, if we accept the Biblical statements as to the divine dealing with Israel and Judah, obedience and disobedience were there followed by reward and suffering more certainly and directly than is now the case in either national or individual life. But it still remains true that it is a 'bitter' as well as an 'evil' thing to depart from the living God. If we would find the cause of our own or of a nation's sorrows, we had better begin our search among our or its sins.

That phrase 'an astonishment, and an hissing' (ver. 8) is new. It appears for the first time in Micah (Micah vi. 16), and he, we know, exercised influence on Hezekiah (Jer. xxvi. 18, 19). Perhaps the king is here quoting the prophet.

The exposition of the sin and its fruit is followed by the king's resolve for himself, and, so far as may be, for his people. The phrase 'it is in my heart' expresses fixed determination, not mere wish. It is used by David and of him, in reference to his resolve to build the Temple. 'To make a covenant' probably means to renew the covenant, made long ago at Sinai, but broken by sin. The king has made up his mind, and announces his determination. He does not consult priests or people, but expects their acquiescence. So, in the early days of Christianity, the 'conversion' of a king meant that of his people. Of course, the power of the kings of Israel and Judah to change the national religion at their pleasure shows how slightly any religion had penetrated, and how much, at the best, it was a matter of mere ceremonial worship with the masses. People who worshipped Ahaz's rabble of gods and godlings to-day because he bade them, and Hezekiah's God to-morrow, had little worship for either, and were much the same through all changes.

Hezekiah was in earnest, and his resolve was none the less right because it was moved by a desire to turn away the fierce anger of the Lord. Dread of sin's consequences and a desire to escape these is no unworthy motive, however some superfine moralists nowadays may call it so. It is becoming unfashionable to preach 'the terror of the Lord.' The more is the pity, and the less is the likelihood of persuading men. But, however kindled, the firm determination (which does not wait for others to concur) that 'As for me, I will serve the Lord,' is the grand thing for us all to imitate. That strong young heart showed itself kingly in its resolve, as it had shown itself sensitive to evil and tender in contemplating the widespread sorrow. If we would brace our feeble wills, and screw them to the sticking-point of immovable determination to make a covenant with God, let us meditate on our departures from Him, the Lover and Benefactor of our souls, and on the dreadfulness of His anger and the misery of those who forsake Him.

Once more the king turns to the priests. He began and he finishes with them, as if he were not sure of their reliableness. His tone is kindly, 'My sons,' but yet monitory. They would not have been warned against 'negligence' unless they had obviously needed it, nor would they have been stimulated to their duties by reminding them of their prerogatives, unless they had been apt to slight these. Officials, whose business is concerned with the things of God, are often apt to drop into an easy-going pace. Negligent work may suit unimportant offices, but is hideously inconsistent with the tasks and aims of God's servants. If there is any work which has to be done 'with both hands, earnestly,' it is theirs. Unless we put all our strength into it, we shall get no good for ourselves or others out of it. The utmost tension of all powers, the utmost husbanding of every moment, is absolutely demanded by the greatness of the task; and the voice of the great Master says to all His servants, 'My sons, be not now negligent.' Ungirt loins and unlit lamps are fatal.

We should meditate, too, on the prerogatives and lofty offices to which Christ calls those who love Him; not to minister to self-complacency, as if we were so much better than other men, but to deepen our sense of responsibility, and stir us to strenuous efforts to be what we are called to be. If Christian people thought more earnestly on what Jesus Christ means them to be to the world, they would not so often counterwork His purpose and shirk their own duties. Crowns are heavy to wear. Gifts are calls to service. If we are chosen to be His ministers, we have solemn responsibilities. If we are to burn incense before Him, our censers need to be bright and free from strange fire. If we are the lights of the world, our business is to shine.

SACRIFICE RENEWED

'Then they went in to Hezekiah the king, and said, We have cleansed all the house of the Lord, and the altar of burnt-offering, with all the vessels thereof, and the shew-bread table, with all the vessels thereof. 19. Moreover, all the vessels, which king Ahaz in his reign did cast away in his transgression, have we prepared and sanctified, and, behold, they are before the altar of the Lord. 20. Then Hezekiah the king rose early, and gathered the rulers of the city, and went up to the house of the Lord. 21. And they brought seven bullocks, and seven rams, and seven lambs, and seven he goats, for a sin-offering for the kingdom, and for the sanctuary, and for Judah. And he commanded the priests, the sons of Aaron, to offer them on the altar of the Lord. 22. So they killed the bullocks, and the priests received the blood, and sprinkled it on the altar: likewise, when they had killed the rams, they sprinkled the blood upon the altar: they killed also the lambs, and they sprinkled the blood upon the altar. 23. And they brought forth the he goats for the sin-offering before the king and the congregation; and they laid their hands upon them. 24. And the priests killed them, and they made reconciliation with their blood upon the altar, to make an atonement for all Israel: for the king commanded that the burnt-offering and the sin-offering should be made for all Israel. 25. And he set the Levites in the house of the Lord with cymbals, with psalteries, and with harps, according to the commandment of David, and of Gad the king's seer, and Nathan the prophet: for so was the commandment of the Lord by His prophets. 26. And the Levites stood with the instruments of David, and the priests with the trumpets. 27. And Hezekiah commanded to offer the burnt-offering upon the altar. And when the burnt-offering began, the song of the Lord began also with the trumpets, and with the instruments ordained by David king of Israel. 28. And all the congregation worshipped, and the singers sang, and the trumpeters sounded: and all this continued until the burnt-offering was finished. 29. And when they had made an end of offering, the king and all that were present with him bowed themselves, and worshipped. 30. Moreover, Hezekiah the king and the princes commanded the Levites to sing praises unto the Lord with the words of David, and of Asaph the seer. And they sang praises with gladness, and they bowed their heads and worshipped. 31. Then Hezekiah answered and said, Now ye have consecrated yourselves unto the Lord, come near, and bring sacrifices and thank-offerings into the house of the Lord. And the congregation brought in sacrifices and thank-offerings; and as many as were of a free heart burnt offerings.—2 CHRON. xxix. 18-31.

Ahaz, Hezekiah's father, had wallowed in idolatry, worshipping any and every god but Jehovah. He had shut up the Temple, defiled the sacred vessels, and 'made him altars in every corner of Jerusalem.' And the result was that he brought the kingdom very near ruin, was not allowed to be buried in the tombs of the kings, and left his son a heavy task to patch up the mischief he had wrought. Hezekiah began at the right end of his task. 'In the first year of his reign, in the first month,' he set about restoring the worship of Jehovah. The relations with Syria and Damascus would come right if the relations with Judah's God were right. 'First things first' was his motto, and perhaps he discerned the true sequence more accurately than some great political pundits do nowadays. So neglected had the Temple been that a strong force of priests and Levites took a fortnight to 'carry forth the filthiness out of the holy place to the brook Kidron,' and to cleanse and ceremonially sanctify the sacred vessels. Then followed at once the re-establishment of the Temple worship, which is narrated in the passage.

The first thing to be noted is that the whole movement back to Jehovah was a one-man movement. It was Hezekiah's doing and his only. No priest is named as prominent in it, and the slowness of the whole order is especially branded in verse 34. No prophet is named; was there any one prompting the king? Perhaps Isaiah did, though his chapter i. with its scathing repudiation of 'the burnt offerings of rams and the fat of fed beasts,' suggests that he did not think the restoration of sacrifice so important as that the nation should 'cease to do evil and learn to do well.' The people acquiesced in the king's worship of Jehovah, as they had acquiesced in other kings' worship of Baal or Moloch or Hadad. When kings take to being religious reformers, they make swift converts, but their work is as slight as it is speedy, and as short-lived as it is rapid. Manasseh was Hezekiah's successor, and swept away all his work after twenty-nine years, and apparently the mass of his people followed him just as they had followed Hezekiah. Religion must be a matter of personal conviction and individual choice. Imposed from without, or adopted because other people adopt it, it is worthless.

Another point to notice is that Hezekiah's reformation was mainly directed to ritual, and does not seem to have included either theology or ethics. Was be quite right in his estimate of what was the first thing? Isaiah, in the passage already referred to, does not seem to think so. To him, as to all the prophets, foul hands could not bring acceptable sacrifices, and worship was an abomination unless preceded by obedience to the command: 'Put away the evil of your doings from before Mine eyes.' The filth in the hearts of the men of Judah was more 'rank, and smelt to heaven' more offensively, than that in the Temple, which took sixteen days to shovel into Kidron. No doubt ceremonial bulked more largely in the days of the Old Covenant than it does in those of the New, and both the then stage of revelation and the then spiritual stature of the recipients of revelation required that it should do so. But the true religious reformers, the prophets, were never weary of insisting that, even in those days, moral and spiritual reformation should come first, and that unless it did, ritual worship, though it were nominally offered to Jehovah, was as abhorrent to Him as if it had been avowedly offered to Baal. Not a little so-called Christian worship today, judged by the same test, is as truly heathen superstition as if it had been paid to Mumbo-Jumbo.

But when all deductions have been made, the scene depicted in the passage is not only an affecting, but an instructive one. Strangely unlike our notions of worship, and to us almost repulsive, must have been the slaying of three hundred and seventy animals and the offering of them as burnt offerings. Try to picture the rivers of blood, the contortions of the dumb brutes, the priests bedaubed with gore, the smell of the burnt flesh, the blare of the trumpets, the shouts of the worshippers, the clashing cymbals, and realise what a world parts it from 'They went up into the upper chamber where they were abiding ... these all with one accord continued steadfastly in prayer, with the women, and Mary, the mother of Jesus, and with His brethren'! Sacrifice has been the essential feature in all religions before Christ. It has dropped out of worship wherever Christ has been accepted. Why? Because it spoke of a deep, permanent, universal need, and because Christ was recognised as having met the need. People who deny the need, and people who deny that Jesus on the Cross has satisfied it, may be invited to explain these two facts, written large on the history of humanity.

That brings us to the most important aspect of Hezekiah's great sacrifice. It sets forth the stages by which men can approach to God. It is symbolic of spiritual facts, and prophetic of Christ's work and of our way of coming to God through Him. The first requisite for Judah's return to Jehovah, whom they had forsaken, was the presentation of a 'sin offering.' The king and the congregation laid their hands on the heads of the goats, thereby, as it were, transferring their own sinful personality to them. Thus laden with the nation's sins, they were slain, and in their death the nation, as it were, bore the penalty of its sin. Representation and substitution were dramatised in the sacrifice. The blood sprinkled on the altar (which had previously been 'sanctified' by sprinkling of blood, and so made capable of presenting what touched it to Jehovah), made 'atonement for all Israel.' We note in passing the emphasis of 'Israel' here, extending the benefit of the sacrifice to the separated tribes of the Northern Kingdom, in a gush of yearning love and desire that they, too, might be reconciled to Jehovah. And is not this the first step towards any man's reconciliation with God? Is not

'My faith would lay her hand
On that dear head of Thine,'

the true expression of the first requisite for us all? Jesus is the sin-offering for the world. In His death He bears the world's sin. His blood is presented to God, and if we have associated ourselves with Him by faith, that blood sprinkled on the altar covers all our sins.

Then followed in this parabolic ceremonial the burnt offering. And that is the second stage of our return to God, for it expresses the consecration of our forgiven selves, as being consumed by the holy and blessed fire of a self-devotion, kindled by the 'unspeakable gift,' which fire, burning away all foulness, will make us tenfold ourselves. That fire will burn up only our bonds, and we shall walk at liberty in it. And that burnt-offering will always be accompanied with 'the song of Jehovah,' and the joyful sound of the trumpets and 'the instruments of David.' The treasures of Christian poetry have always been inspired by the Cross, and the consequent rapture of self-surrender. Calvary is the true fountain of song.

The last stage in Hezekiah's great sacrifice was 'thank-offerings,' brought by 'as many as were of a willing heart.' And will not the self-devotion, kindled by the fire of love, speak in daily life by practical service, and the whole activities of the redeemed man be a long thank-offering for the Lamb who 'bears away the sins of the world'? And if we do not thus offer our whole lives to God, how shall we profess to have taken the priceless benefit of Christ's death? Hezekiah followed the order laid down in the Law, and it is the only order that leads to the goal. First, the atoning sacrifice of the slain Lamb; next, our identification with Him and it by faith; then the burnt-offering of a surrendered self, with the song of praise sounding ever through it; and last, the life of service, offering all our works to God, and so reaching the perfection of life on earth and antedating the felicities of heaven.

A LOVING CALL TO REUNION

'And Hezekiah sent to all Israel and Judah, and wrote letters also to Ephraim and Manasseh, that they should come to the house of the Lord at Jerusalem, to keep the passover unto the Lord God of Israel. 2. For the king had taken counsel, and his princes, and all the congregation in Jerusalem, to keep the passover in the second month. 3. For they could not keep it at that time, because the priests had not sanctified themselves sufficiently, neither had the people gathered themselves together to Jerusalem. 4. And the thing pleased the king and all the congregation. 5. So they established a decree to make proclamation throughout all Israel, from Beersheba even to Dan, that they should come to keep the passover unto the Lord God of Israel at Jerusalem: for they had not done it of a long time in such sort as it was written. 6. So the posts went with the letters from the king and his princes throughout all Israel and Judah, and according to the commandment of the king, saying, Ye children of Israel, turn again unto the Lord God of Abraham, Isaac, and Israel, and he will return to the remnant of you, that are escaped out of the hand of the kings of Assyria. 7. And be not ye like your fathers, and like your brethren, which trespassed against the Lord God of their fathers, who therefore gave them up to desolation, as ye see. 8. Now, be ye not stiffnecked, as your fathers were, but yield yourselves unto the Lord, and enter into His sanctuary, which He hath sanctified for ever: and serve the Lord your God, that the fierceness of His wrath may turn away from you. 9. For if ye turn again unto the Lord, your brethren and your children shall find compassion before them that lead them captive, so that they shall come again into this land: for the Lord your God is gracious and merciful, and will not turn away His face from you, if ye return unto Him. 10. So the posts passed from city to city through the country of Ephraim and Manasseh, even unto Zebulun: but they laughed them to scorn, and mocked them. 11. Nevertheless divers of Asher and Manasseh and of Zebulun humbled themselves, and came to Jerusalem. 12. Also in Judah the hand of God was to give them one heart to do the commandment of the king and of the princes, by the word of the Lord. 13. And there assembled at Jerusalem much people to keep the feast of unleavened bread in the second month, a very great congregation.'—2 CHRON. xxx. 1-13.

The date of Hezekiah's passover is uncertain, for, while the immediate connection of this narrative with the preceding account of his cleansing the Temple and restoring the sacrificial worship suggests that the passover followed directly on those events, which took place at the beginning of the reign, the language employed in the message to the northern tribes (vers. 6,7, 9) seems to imply the previous fall of the kingdom of Israel, If so, this passover did not occur till after 721 B.C., the date of the capture of Samaria, six years after Hezekiah's accession.

The sending of messengers from Jerusalem on such an errand would scarcely have been possible if the northern kingdom had still been independent. Perhaps its fall was thought by Hezekiah to open the door to drawing 'the remnant that were escaped' back to the ancient unity of worship, at all events, if not of polity. No doubt a large number had been left in the northern territory, and Hezekiah may have hoped that calamity had softened their enmity to his kingdom, and perhaps touched them with longings for the old worship. At all events, like a good man, he will stretch out a hand to the alienated brethren, now that evil days have fallen on them. The hour of an enemy's calamity should be our opportunity for seeking to help and proffering reconciliation. We may find that trouble inclines wanderers to come back to God.

The alteration of the time of keeping the passover from the thirteenth day of the first month to the same day of the second was in accordance with the liberty granted in Numbers ix. 10, 11, to persons unclean by contact with a dead body or 'in a journey afar off.' The decision to have the passover was not taken in time to allow of the necessary removal of uncleanness from the priests nor of the assembling of the people, and therefore the permission to defer it for a month was taken advantage of, in order to allow full time for the despatch of the messengers and the journeys of the farthest northern tribes. It is to be observed that Hezekiah took his subjects into counsel, since the step intended was much too great for him to venture on of his own mere motion. So the overtures went out clothed with the authority of the whole kingdom of Judah. It was the voice of a nation that sought to woo back the secessionists.

The messengers were instructed to supplement the official letters of invitation with earnest entreaties as from the king, of which the gist is given in verses 6-9. With the skill born of intense desire to draw the long-parted kingdoms together, the message touches on ancestral memories, recent bitter experiences, yearnings for the captive kinsfolk, the instinct of self-preservation, and rises at last into the clear light of full faith in, and insight into, God's infinite heart of pardoning pity.

Note the very first words, 'Ye children of Israel,' and consider the effect of this frank recognition of the northern kingdom as part of the undivided Israel. Such recognition might have been misunderstood or spurned when Samaria was gay and prosperous; but when its palaces were desolate, the effect of the old name, recalling happier days, must have been as if the elder brother had come out from the father's house and entreated the prodigal to come back to his place at the fireside. The battle would be more than half won if the appeal that was couched in the very name of Israel was heeded.

Note further how firmly and yet lovingly the sin of the northern kingdom is touched on. The name of Jehovah as the God of Abraham, Isaac, and Israel, recalls the ancient days when the undivided people worshipped Him, and the still more ancient, and, to hearers and speakers alike, more sacred, days when the patriarchs received wondrous tokens that He was their God, and they were His people; while the recurrence of 'Israel' as the name of Jacob adds force to its previous use as the name of all His descendants. The possible rejection of the invitation, on the ground which the men of the north, like the Samaritan woman, might have taken, that they were true to their fathers' worship, is cut away by the reminder that that worship was an innovation, since the fathers of the present generation had been apostate from the God of *their* fathers. The appeal to antiquity often lands men in a bog because it is not carried far enough back. 'The fathers' may lead astray, but if the antiquity to which we appeal is that of which the New Testament is the record, the more conservative we are, the nearer the truth shall we be.

Again, the message touched on a chord that might easily have given a jarring note; namely, the misfortunes of the kingdom. But it was done with so delicate a hand, and so entirely without a trace of rejoicing in a neighbour's calamities, that no susceptibilities could be ruffled, while yet the solemn lesson is unfalteringly pointed. 'He gave them up to desolation, as ye see.' Behind Assyria was Jehovah, and Israel's fall was not wholly explained by the disparity between its strength and the conquerors'. Under and through the play of criminal ambition, cruelty, and earthly politics, the unseen Hand wrought; and the teaching of all the Old Testament history is condensed into that one sad sentence, which points to facts as plain as tragical. In deepest truth it applies to each of us; for, if we trespass against God, we draw down evil on our heads with both hands, and shall find that sin brings the worst desolation—that which sheds gloom over a godless soul.

We note further the deep true insight into God's character and ways expressed in this message. There is a very striking variation in the three designations of Jehovah as 'the God of Abraham, Isaac, and Israel' (ver. 6), 'the god of their [that is, the preceding generation] fathers' (ver. 7), and 'your God' (ver. 8). The relation which had subsisted from of old had not been broken by man's apostasy, Jehovah still was, in a true sense, their God, even if His relation to them only bound Him not to leave them unpunished. So their very sufferings proved them His, for 'What son is he whom the father chasteneth not?' But strong, sunny confidence in God shines from the whole message, and reaches its climax in the closing assurance that He is merciful and gracious. The evil results of rebellion are not omitted, but they are not dwelt on. The true magnet to draw wanderers back to God is the loving proclamation of His love. Unless we are sure that He has a heart tender with all pity, and 'open as day to melting charity,' we shall not turn to Him with our hearts.

The message puts the response which it sought in a variety of ways; namely, turning to Jehovah, not being stiff-necked, yielding selves to Jehovah, entering into His sanctuary. More than outward participation in the passover ceremonial is involved. Submission of will, abandonment of former courses of action, docility of spirit ready to be directed anywhere, the habit of abiding with God by communion—all these, the standing characteristics of the religious life, are at least suggested by the invitations here. We are all summoned thus to yield ourselves to God, and especially to do so by surrendering our wills to Him, and to 'enter into His sanctuary,' by keeping up such communion with Him as that, however and wherever occupied, we shall still 'dwell in the house of the Lord all the days of our lives.'

And the summons to return unto God is addressed to us all even more urgently than to Israel. God Himself invites us by the voice of His providences, by His voice within, and by the voice of Jesus Himself, who is ever saying to each of us, by His death and passion, by His resurrection and ascension, 'Turn ye! turn ye! why will ye die?' and who has more than endorsed Hezekiah's messengers' assurance that 'Jehovah will not turn away His face from' us by His own gracious promise, 'Him that cometh to Me I will in no wise cast out.'

The king's message met a mingled reception. Some mocked, some were moved and accepted. So, alas! is it with the better message, which is either 'a savour of life unto life or of death unto death.' The same fire melts wax and hardens clay. May it be with all of us as it was in Judah—that we 'have one heart, to do the commandment' and to accept the merciful summons to the great passover!

A STRANGE REWARD FOR FAITHFULNESS

'After these things, and the establishment thereof, Sennacherib, king of Assyria, came.'—2 CHRON. XXXII. 1.

The Revised Version gives a much more accurate and significant rendering of a part of these words. It reads: 'After these things and *this faithfulness*,

Sennacherib, king of Assyria, came.' What are 'these things' and 'this faithfulness'? The former are the whole of the events connected with the religious reformation in Judah, which King Hezekiah inaugurated and carried through so brilliantly and successfully. This 'faithfulness' directly refers to a word in a couple of verses before the text: 'Thus did Hezekiah throughout all Judah; and he wrought that which was good and right and *faithfulness* before the Lord his God.' And, after these things, the re-establishment of religion and this 'faithfulness,' though Hezekiah was perfect before God in all ritual observances and in practical righteousness, and though he was seeking the Lord his God with all his heart, here is what came of it:—'After this faithfulness came' not blessings or prosperity, but 'Sennacherib, king of Assyria'! The chronicler not only tells this as singular, but one can feel that he is staggered by it. There is a tone of perplexity and wonder in his voice as he records that *this* was what followed the faithful righteousness and heart-devotion of the best king that ever sat on the throne of Judah. I think that this royal martyr's experience is really a mirror of the experience of devout men in all ages and a revelation of the great law and constant processes of the Divine Providence. And from that point of view I wish to speak now, not only on the words I have read, but on what follows them.

I. We have here the statement of the mystery.

It is the standing puzzle of the Old Testament, how good men come to be troubled, and how bad men come to be prosperous. And although we Christian men and women are a great deal too apt to suppose that we have outlived that rudimentary puzzle of the religious mind, yet I do not think by any means that we have. For we hear men, when the rod falls upon themselves, saying, 'What have I done that I should be smitten thus?' or when their friends suffer, saying, 'What a marvellous thing it is that such a good man as A, B, or C should have so much trouble!' or, when widespread calamities strike a community, standing aghast at the broad and dark shadows that fall upon a nation or a continent, and wondering what the meaning of all this heaped misery is, and why the world is thus allowed to run along its course surrounded by an atmosphere made up of the breath of sighs, and swathed in clouds which are moist with tears.

My text gives us an illustration in the sharpest form of the mystery. 'After these things and this faithfulness, Sennacherib came'—and he always comes in one shape or another. For, to begin with, a good man's goodness does not lift him out of the ordinary associations and contingencies and laws of life. If he has inherited a diseased constitution, his devotion will not make him a healthy man. If he has little common sense, his godliness will not make him prosper in worldly affairs. If he is tied to unfortunate connections, he will have to suffer. If he happens to be in a decaying branch of business, his prayers will not make him prosperous. If he falls in the way of poisonous gas from a sewer, his godliness will not exempt him from an attack of fever. So all round the horizon we see this: that the godly man is involved like any other man in the ordinary contingencies and possible evils of life. Then, have we to say that God has nothing to do with these?

Again, Hezekiah's story teaches us how second causes are God's instruments, and He is at the back of everything. There are two sources of our knowledge of the history of Judah in the time with which we are concerned. One is the Bible, the other is the Assyrian monuments; and it is a most curious contrast to read the two narratives of the same events, agreeing about the facts, but disagreeing utterly in the spirit. Why? Because the one tells the story from the world's point of view, and the other tells it from God's point of view. So when you take the one narrative, it is simply this: 'There was a conspiracy down in the south against the political supremacy of Assyria, and a lot of little confederate kinglets gathered themselves; and Hezekiah, of Judah, was one, along with So-and-So of such-and-such a petty land, and they leaned upon Egypt; and I, Sennacherib, came down among them, and they tumbled to pieces, and that is all.' Then the Bible comes in, and it says that God ordered all those political complications, and that they were all the working out of His purposes, and that 'the axe in His hand' as Isaiah has it so picturesquely, was this proud king of Assyria, with his boastful mouth and vainglorious words.

Now, that is the principle by which we have to estimate all the events that befall us. There are two ways of looking at them. You may look at them from the under side or from the top side. You may see them as they appear to men who cannot look beyond their noses and only have concern with the visible cranks and shafting, or you may look at them from the engine-room and take account of the invisible power that drives them all. In the one case you will regard it as a mystery that good men should have to suffer so; in the other case, you will say, 'It is the Lord, let Him do'—even when He does it through Sennacherib and his like, 'let Him do what seemeth Him good.'

Then there is another thing to be taken into account—that is, that the better a man is, the more faithful he is and the more closely he cleaves to God, and seeks, like this king, to do, with all his heart, all his work in the service of the House of God and to seek his God, the more sure is he to bring down upon himself certain forms of trouble and trial. The rebellion which, from the Assyrian side of the river, seemed to be a mere political revolt, from the Jordan side of the river seemed to be closely connected with the religious reformation. And it was just because Hezekiah and his people came back to God that they rebelled against the King of Assyria and served him not. If you provoke Sennacherib, Sennacherib will be down upon you very quickly. That is to say, being translated, if you will live like Christian men and women and fling down the gage of battle to the world and to the evil that lies in every one of us, and say, 'No, I have nothing to do with you. My law is not your law, and, God helping me, my practice shall not be your practice,' then you will find out that the power that you have defied has a very long arm and a very tight grasp, and you will have to make up your minds that, in some shape or other, the old law will be fulfilled about you. Through much tribulation we must enter the Kingdom.

II. Now, secondly, my text and its context solve the mystery which it raises.

The chronicler, as I said, wishes us to notice the sequence, strange as it is, and to wonder at it for a moment, in order that we may be prepared the better to take in the grand explanation that follows. And the explanation lies in the facts that ensue.

Did Sennacherib come to destroy? By no means! Here were the results: first, a stirring to wholesome energy and activity. If annoyances and troubles and sorrows, great or small, do nothing else for us, they would be clear and simple gain if they woke us up, for the half of men pass half of their lives half-asleep. And anybody that has ever come through a great sorrow and can remember what deep fountains were opened in his heart that he knew nothing about before, and how powers that were all unsuspected by himself suddenly came to him, and how life, instead of being a trivial succession of nothings, all at once became significant and solemn—any man who can remember that, will feel that if there were nothing else that his troubles did for him than to shake him out of torpor and rouse him to a tension of wholesome activity, so that he cried out:

'Call forth thy powers, my soul! and dare
The conflict of unequal war,'

he would have occasion to bless God for the roughest handling. The tropics are very pleasant for lazy people, but they sap the constitution and make work impossible; and after a man has lived for a while in their perpetual summer, he begins to long for damp and mist and frost and east winds which bring bracing to the system and make him fit to work. God takes us often into very ungenial climates, and the vindication of it is that we may be set to active service. That was the first good thing that Sennacherib's coming did.

The next was that his invasion increased dependence upon God. You will remember the story of the insolent taunts and vulgar vaunting by him and his servants, and the one answer that was given: 'Hezekiah, the king, and Isaiah the son of Amoz the prophet, prayed and cried to God.' Ah! dear brethren, any thing that drives us to His breast is blessing. We may call it evil when we speak from the point of view of the foolish senses and the quivering heart, but if it blows us into His arms, any wind, the roughest and the fiercest, is to be welcomed more than lazy calms or gentle zephyrs. If, realising our own weakness and impotence, we are made to hang more completely upon Him, then let us be thankful for whatever has been the means of such a blessed issue. That was the second good thing that Sennacherib did.

The third good thing that he—not exactly did—but that was done through him, was that experience of God's delivering power was enriched. You remember the miracle of the destruction of the army. I need not dilate upon it. A man who can look back and say, 'Thou hast been with me in six troubles,' need never be afraid of the seventh; and he who has hung upon that strong rope when he has been swinging away down in the darkness and asphyxiating atmosphere of the pit, and has been drawn up into the sunshine again, will trust it for all coming time. If there were no other explanation, the enlarged and deepened experience of the realities of God's Gospel and of God's grace, which are bought only by sorrow, would be a sufficient explanation of any sorrow that any of us have ever had to carry.

'Well roars the storm to him who hears
A deeper voice across the storm.'

There are large tracts of Scripture which have no meaning, no blessedness to us until they have been interpreted to us by losses and sorrows. We never know the worth of the lighthouse until the November darkness and the howling winds come down upon us, and then we appreciate its preciousness.

So, dear friends! the upshot of the whole is just that old teaching, that if we realised what life is for, we should wonder less at the sorrows that are in it. For life is meant to make us partakers of His holiness, not to make us happy. Our happiness is a secondary purpose, not out of view of the Divine love, but it is not the primary one. And the direct intention and mission of sorrow, like the direct intention and mission of joy, are to further that great purpose, that we 'should be partakers of His holiness.' 'Every branch in Me that beareth fruit, He purgeth it, that it may bring forth more fruit.'

III. Lastly, my text suggests a warning against letting prosperity undo adversity's work.

Hezekiah came bravely through his trials. They did exactly what God wanted them to do; they drove him to God, they forced him down upon his knees. When Sennacherib's letter came, he took it to the Temple and spread it before God, and said, 'O Lord! it is Thy business. It is addressed to me, but it is meant for Thee; do Thou answer it.' And so he received the help that he wanted. But he broke down after that. He was 'exalted'; and the allies, his neighbours, that had not lifted a finger to help him when he needed their help, sent him presents which would have been a great deal more seasonable when he was struggling for his life with Sennacherib. What 'came after

(God's) faithfulness'? This—'his heart was lifted up, and he rendered not according to the benefit rendered to him.' Therefore the blow had to come down again. A great many people take refuge in archways when it rains, and run out as soon as it holds up, and a great many people take religion as an umbrella, to put down when the sunshine comes. We cross the bridge and forget it, and when the leprosy is out of us we do not care to go back and give thanks. Sometimes too, we begin to think, 'After all, it was we that killed Sennacherib's army, and not the angel.' And so, like dull scholars, we need the lesson repeated once, twice, thrice, 'here a little and there a little, precept upon precept, line upon line.' There is none of us that has so laid to heart our past difficulties and trials that it is safe for God to burn the rod as long as we are in this life.

Dear friends! do not let it be said of us, 'In vain have I smitten thy children. They have received no correction'; but rather let us keep close to Him, and seek to learn the sweet and loving meaning of His sharpest strokes. Then the little book, 'written within and without with lamentation and woe,' which we all in our turn have to absorb and make our own, may be 'bitter in the mouth,' but will be 'sweet as honey' thereafter.

MANASSEH'S SIN AND REPENTANCE

'So Manasseh made Judah and the inhabitants of Jerusalem to err, and to do worse than the heathen, whom the Lord had destroyed before the children of Israel. 10. And the Lord spake to Manasseh, and to his people: but they would not hearken. 11. Wherefore the Lord brought upon them the captains of the host of the king of Assyria, which took Manasseh among the thorns, and bound him with fetters, and carried him to Babylon. 12. And when he was in affliction, he besought the Lord his God, and humbled himself greatly before the God of his fathers, 13. And prayed unto him: and he was intreated of him, and heard his supplication, and brought him again to Jerusalem into his kingdom. Then Manasseh knew that the Lord He was God. 14. Now after this he built a wall without the city of David, on the west side of Gihon, in the valley, even to the entering in at the fish gate, and compassed about Ophel, and raised it up a very great height, and put captains of war in all the fenced cities of Judah. 15. And he took away the strange gods, and the idol out of the house of the Lord, and all the altars that he had built in the mount of the house of the Lord, and in Jerusalem, and cast them out of the city. 16. And he repaired the altar of the Lord, and sacrificed thereon peace offerings and thank offerings, and commanded Judah to serve the Lord God of Israel.'—2 CHRON. xxxiii. 9-16.

The story of Manasseh's sin and repentance may stand as a typical example. Its historical authenticity is denied on the ground that it appears only in this Book of Chronicles. I must leave others to discuss that matter; my purpose is to bring out the teaching contained in the story.

The first point in it is the stern indictment against Manasseh and his people. The experience which has saddened many a humbler home was repeated in the royal house, where a Hezekiah was followed by a Manasseh, who scorned all that his father had worshipped, and worshipped all that his father had loathed. Happily the father's eyes were closed long before the idolatrous bias of his son could have disclosed itself. Succeeding to the throne at twelve years of age, he could not have begun his evil ways at once, and probably would have been preserved from them if his father had lived long enough to mould his character. A child of twelve, flung on to a throne, was likely to catch the infection of any sin that was in the atmosphere. The narrative specifies two points in which, as he matured in years, and was confirmed in his course of conduct, he went wrong: first, in his idolatry; and second, in his contempt of remonstrances and warnings. As to the former, the preceding context gives a terrible picture. He was smitten with a very delirium of idolatry, and wallowed in any and every sort of false worship. No matter what strange god was presented, there were hospitality, an altar, and an offering for him. Baal, Moloch, 'the host of heaven,' wizards, enchanters, anybody who pretended to have any sort of black art, all were welcome, and the more the better. No doubt, this eager acceptance of a miscellaneous multitude of deities was partly reaction from the monotheism of the former reign, but also it was the natural result of being surrounded by the worshippers of these various gods; and it was an unconscious confession of the insufficiency of each and all of them to fill the void in the heart, and satisfy the needs of the spirit. There are 'gods many, and lords many,' because they are insufficient; 'the Lord our God is one Lord,' because He, in His single Self, is more than all these, and is enough for any and every man.

We may note, too, that at the beginning of the chapter Manasseh is said to have done '*like* unto the abominations of the heathen,' while in verse 9 he is said to have done 'evil *more* than did the nations.' When a worshipper of Jehovah does *like* the heathen, he does *worse* than they. An apostate Christian is more guilty than one who has never 'tasted the good word of God,' and is likely to push his sins to a more flagrant wickedness. 'The corruption of the best is the worst.' We cannot do what the world does without being more deeply guilty than they.

The narrative lays stress on the fact that the king's inclination to idolatry was agreeable to the people. The kings, who fought against it, had to resist the popular current, but at the least encouragement from those in high places the nation was ready to slide back. Rulers who wish to lower the standard of morality or religion have an easy task; but the people who follow their lead are not free from guilt, though they can plead that they only followed. The second count in the indictment is the refusal of king and people to listen to God's remonstrances. 2 Kings, chap. xxi., gives the prophets' warnings at greater length. 'They would not hearken'—can anything madder and sadder be said of any of us than that? Is it not the very sin of sins, and the climax of suicidal folly, that God should call and men stop their ears? And yet how many of us pay no more regard to His voice, in His providences, in our own consciences, in history, in Scripture, and, most penetrating and beseeching of all, in Christ, than to idle wind whistling through an archway! Our own evil deeds stop our ears, and the stopped ears make further evil deeds more easy.

The second step in this typical story is merciful chastisement, meant to secure a hearing for God's voice. 2 Kings tells the threat, but not the fulfilment; Chronicles tells the fulfilment, but not the threat. We note how emphatically God's hand is recognised behind the political complications which brought the Assyrians to Jerusalem, and how particularly it is stated that the invasion was not headed by Esarhaddon, but by his generals. The place of Manasseh's captivity also is specified, not as Nineveh, as might have been expected, but as Babylon. These details, especially the last, look like genuine history. It is history which carries a lesson. Here is one conspicuous instance of the divine method, which is working to-day as it did then. God's hand is behind the secondary causes of events. Our sorrows and 'misfortunes' are sent to us by Him, not hurled at us by human hands only, or occurring by the working of impersonal laws. They are meant to make us bethink ourselves, and drop evil things from our hands and hearts. It is best to be guided by His eye, and not need 'bit and bridle'; but if we make ourselves stubborn as 'the mule, which has no understanding,' it is second best that we should taste the whip, that it may bring us to run in harness on the road which He wills. If we habitually looked at calamities as His loving chastisement, intended to draw us to Himself, we should not have to stand perplexed so often at what we call the mysteries of His providence.

The next step in the story is the yielding of the sinful heart when smitten. The worst affliction is an affliction wasted, which does us no good. And God has often to lament, 'In vain have I smitten your children; they received no correction.' Sorrow has in itself no power to effect the purpose for which it is sent; but all depends on how we take it. It sometimes makes us hard, bitter, obstinate in clinging to evil. A heart that has been disciplined by it, and still is undisciplined, is like iron hammered on an anvil, and made the more close-grained thereby. But this king took his chastisement wisely. An accepted sorrow is an angel in disguise, and nothing which drives us to God is a calamity. Manasseh praying was freer in his chains than ever he had been in his prosperity. Manasseh humbling himself greatly before God was higher than when, in the pride of his heart, he shut God out from it.

Affliction should clear our sight, that we may see ourselves as we are; and, if we do, there will be an end of high looks, and we shall 'take the lowest room.' Thus humbled, we shall pray as the self-confident and outwardly prosperous cannot do. Sorrow has done its best on us when, like some strong hand on our shoulders, it has brought us to our knees. No affliction has yielded its full blessing to us unless it has thus set us by Manasseh's side.

The next step in the story is the loving answer to the humbled heart, and the restoration to the kingdom. 'He was entreated of him.' No doubt, political circumstances brought about Manasseh's reinstatement, as they had brought about his captivity, but it was God that 'brought him again to his kingdom.' We may not receive again lost good things, but we may be quite sure that God never fails to hear the cry of the humble, and that, if there is one voice that more surely reaches His ear and moves His heart than another, it is the voice of His chastened children, who cry to Him out of the depths, and there have learned their own sin and sore need. He will be entreated of them, and, whether He gives back lost good or not, He will give Himself, in whom all good is comprehended. Manasseh's experience may be repeated in us.

And the best part of it was, not that he received back his kingdom, but that 'then Manasseh knew that the Lord He was God.' The name had been but a name to him, but now it had become a reality. Our traditional, second-hand belief in God is superficial and largely unreal till it is deepened and vivified by experience. If we have cried to Him, and been lightened, then we have a ground of conviction that cannot be shaken. Formerly we could at most say, 'I believe in God,' or, 'I think there is a God,' but now we can say, 'I know,' and no criticism nor contradiction can shake that. Such knowledge is not the knowledge won by the understanding alone, but it is acquaintance with a living Person, like the knowledge which loving souls have of each other; and he who has that knowledge as the issue of his own experience may smile at doubts and questionings, and say with the Apostle of Love, 'We know that we are of God, ... and we know that the Son of God is come, and hath given us an understanding, that we may know Him that is true.' Then, if we have that knowledge, we shall listen to the same Apostle's commandment, 'Keep yourselves from idols,' even as the issue of Manasseh's knowledge of God was that 'he took away the strange gods, and the idol out of the house of the Lord.'

JOSIAH

'Josiah was eight years old when he began to reign, and he reigned in Jerusalem one and thirty years. 2. And he did that which was right in the sight of the Lord, and walked in the ways of David his father, and declined neither to the right hand, nor to the left. 3. For in the eighth year of his reign, while he was yet young, he began to seek after the God of David his father: and in the twelfth year he began to purge Judah and Jerusalem from the high places, and the groves, and the carved images, and the molten images. 4. And they brake down the altars of Baalim in his presence; and the images, that were on high above them, he cut down; and the groves, and the carved images, and the molten images, he brake in pieces, and made dust of them, and strowed it upon the graves of them that had sacrificed unto them. 5. And he burnt the bones of the priests upon their altars, and cleansed Judah and Jerusalem. 6. And so did he in the cities of Manasseh, and Ephraim, and Simeon, even unto Naphtali, with their mattocks round about. 7. And when he had broken down the altars and the groves, and had beaten the graven images into powder, and cut down all the idols throughout all the land of Israel, he returned to Jerusalem. 8. Now in the eighteenth year of his reign, when he had purged the land, and the house, he sent Shaphan the son of Azaliah, and Maaseiah the governor of the city, and Joah the son of Joahaz the recorder, to repair the house of the Lord his God. 9. And when they came to Hilkiah the high priest, they delivered the money that was brought into the house of God, which the Levites that kept the doors had gathered of the hand of Manasseh and Ephraim, and of all the remnant of Israel, and of all Judah and Benjamin; and they returned to Jerusalem. 10. And they put it in the hand of the workmen that had the oversight of the house of the Lord, and they gave it to the workmen that wrought in the house of the Lord, to repair and amend the house: 11. Even to the artificers and builders gave they it, to buy hewn stone, and timber for couplings, and to floor the houses which the kings of Judah had destroyed. 12. And the men did the work faithfully: and the overseers of them were Jahath and Obadiah, the Levites, of the sons of Merari; and Zechariah and Meshullam, of the sons of the Kohathites, to set it forward; and other of the Levites, all that could skill of instruments of musick. 13. Also they were over the bearers of burdens, and were overseers of all that wrought the work in any manner of service: and of the Levites there were scribes, and officers, and porters.'—2 CHRON. xxxiv. 1-13.

Another boy king, even younger than his grandfather Manasseh had been at his accession, and another reversal of the father's religion! These vibrations from idolatry to Jehovah-worship, at the pleasure of the king, sadly tell how little the people cared whom they worshipped, and how purely a matter of ceremonies and names both their idolatry and their Jehovah-worship were. The religion of the court was the religion of the nation, only idolatry was more congenial than the service of God. How far the child monarch Josiah had a deeper sense of what that service meant we cannot decide, but the little outline sketch of him in verses 2 and 3 is at least suggestive of his having it, and may well stand as a fair portrait of early godliness.

A child eight years old, who had been lifted on to the throne of a murdered father, must have had a strong will and a love of goodness to have resisted the corrupting influences of royalty in a land full of idols. Here again we see that, great as may be the power of circumstances, they do not determine character; for it is always open to us either to determine whether we yield to them or resist them. The prevailing idolatry influenced the boy, but it influenced him to hate it with all his heart. So out of the nettle danger we may pluck the flower safety. The men who have smitten down some evil institution have generally been brought up so as to feel its full force.

'He did that which was right in the eyes of Jehovah'—that may mean simply that he worshipped Jehovah by outward ceremonies, but it probably means more; namely, that his life was pure and God-pleasing, or, as we should say, clean and moral, free from the foul vices which solicit a young prince. 'He walked in the ways of David his father'—not being one of the 'emancipated' youths who think it manly to throw off the restraints of their fathers' faith and morals. He 'turned not aside to the right hand or to the left'—but marched right onwards on the road that conscience traced out for him, though tempting voices called to him from many a side-alley that seemed to lead to pleasant places. 'While he was yet young, he began to seek after the God of David his father'—at the critical age of sixteen, when Easterns are older than we, in the flush of early manhood, he awoke to deeper experiences and felt the need for a closer touch of God. A career thus begun will generally prelude a life pure, strenuous, and blessed with a clearer and clearer vision of the God who is always found of them that seek Him. Such a childhood, blossoming into such a boyhood, and flowering in such a manhood, is possible to every child among us. It will 'still bring forth fruit in old age.'

The two incidents which the passage narrates, the purging of the land and the repair of the Temple, are told in inverted order in 2 Kings, but the order here is probably the more accurate, as dates are given, whereas in 2 Kings, though the purging is related after the Temple restoration, it is not said to have occurred after. But the order is of small consequence. What is important is the fiery energy of Josiah in the work of destruction of the idols. Here, there, everywhere, he flames and consumes. He darts a flash even into the desolate ruins of the Israelitish kingdom, where the idols had survived their devotees and still bewitched the scanty fragments of Israel that remained. The altars of stone were thrown down, the wooden sun-pillars were cut to pieces, the metal images were broken and ground to powder. A clean sweep was made.

A dash of ferocity mingled with contempt appears in Josiah's scattering the 'dust' of the images on the graves of their worshippers, as if he said: 'There you lie together, pounded idols and dead worshippers, neither able to help the other!' The same feelings prompted digging up the skeletons of priests and burning the bones on the very altars that they had served, thus defiling the altars and executing judgment on the priests. No doubt there were much violence and a strong strain of the 'wrath of man' in all this. Iconoclasts are wont to be 'violent'; and men without convictions, or who are partisans of what the iconoclasts are rooting out, are horrified at their want of 'moderation.' But though violence is always unchristian, indifference to rampant evils is not conspicuously more Christian, and, on the whole, you cannot throttle snakes in a graceful attitude or without using some force to compress the sinuous neck.

The restoration of the Temple comes after the cleansing of the land, in Chronicles, and naturally in the order of events, for the casting out of idols must always precede the building or repairing of the Temple of God. Destructive work is very poor unless it is for the purpose of clearing a space to build the Temple on. Happy the man or the age which is able to do both! Josiah and Joash worked at restoring the Temple in much the same fashion, but Josiah had a priesthood more interested than Joash had.

But we may note one or two points in his restoration. He had put his personal effort into the preparatory extirpation of idols, but he did not need to do so now. He could work this time by deputy. And it is noteworthy that he chose 'laymen' to carry out the restoration. Perhaps he knew how Joash had been balked by the knavery of the priests who were diligent in collecting money, but slow in spending it on the Temple. At all events, he delegated the work to three highly-placed officials, the secretary of state, the governor of Jerusalem, and the official historian.

It appears that for some time a collection had been going on for Temple repairs; probably it had been begun six years before, when the 'purging' of the land began. It had been carried on by the Levites, and had been contributed to even by 'the remnant of Israel' in the northern kingdom, who, in their forlorn weakness, had begun to feel the drawings of ancient brotherhood and the tie of a common worship. This fund was in the keeping of the high priest, and the three commissioners were instructed to require it from him. Here 2 Kings is clearer than our passage, and shows that what the three officials had mainly to do was to get the money from Hilkiah, and to hand it over to the superintendents of the works.

There are two remarkable points in the narrative; one is the observation that 'the men did the work faithfully,' which comes in rather enigmatically here, but in 2 Kings is given as the reason why no accounts were kept. Not an example to be imitated, and the sure way to lead subordinates sooner or later to deal unfaithfully; but a pleasant indication of the spirit animating all concerned.

Surely these men worked 'as ever in the great Taskmaster's eye.' That is what makes us work faithfully, whether we have any earthly overseer or audit or no. Another noteworthy matter is that not only were the superintendents of the work—the 'contractors,' as we might say—Levites, but so were also the inferior superintendents, or, as we might say, 'foremen.'

And not only so, but they were those that 'were skilful with instruments of music.' What were musicians doing there? Did the building rise

'with the sound Of dulcet symphonies and voices sweet?'

May we not gather from this singular notice the great thought that for all rearing of the true Temple, harps of praise are no less necessary than swords or trowels, and that we shall do no right work for God or man unless we do it as with melody in our hearts? Our lives must be full of music if we are to lay even one stone in the Temple.

JOSIAH AND THE NEWLY FOUND LAW

'And when they brought out the money that was brought into the house of the Lord, Hilkiah the priest found a book of the law of the Lord given by Moses. 15. And Hilkiah answered and said to Shaphan the scribe, I have found the book of the law in the house of the Lord. And Hilkiah delivered the book to Shaphan. 16 And Shaphan carried the book to the king, and brought the king word back again, saying, All that was committed to thy servants, they do it. 17. And they have gathered together the money that was found in the house of the Lord, and have delivered it into the hand of the overseers, and to the hand of the workmen. 18. Then Shaphan the scribe told the king, saying, Hilkiah the priest hath given me a book. And Shaphan read it before the king. 19. And it came to pass, when the king had heard the words of the law, that he rent his clothes. 20. And the king commanded Hilkiah, and Ahikam the son of Shaphan, and Abdon the son of Micah, and Shaphan the scribe, and Asaiah a servant of the king's, saying, 21. Go, enquire of the Lord for me, and for them that are left in Israel and in Judah, concerning the words of the book that is found: for great is the wrath of the Lord that is poured out upon us, because our fathers have not kept the word of the Lord, to do after all that is written in this book. 22. And Hilkiah, and they that the king had appointed, went to Huldah the prophetess, the wife of Shallum the son of Tikvath, the son of Hasrah, keeper of the wardrobe; (now she dwelt in Jerusalem in the college;) and they spake to her to that effect. 23. And she answered them, Thus saith the Lord God of Israel, Tell ye the man that sent you to me. 24. Thus saith the Lord, Behold, I will bring evil upon this place, and upon the inhabitants thereof, even all the curses that are written in the book which they have read before the king of Judah: 25. Because they have forsaken Me, and have burned incense unto other gods, that they might provoke Me to anger with all the works of their hands; therefore My wrath shall be poured out upon this place, and shall not be quenched. 26. And as for the king of Judah, who sent you to enquire of the Lord, so shall ye say unto him, Thus saith the Lord God of Israel concerning the words which thou hast heard; 27. Because thine heart was tender, and thou didst humble thyself before God, when thou heardest His words against this place, and against the inhabitants thereof, and humbledst thyself before Me, and did rendst thy clothes, and weep before Me; I have even heard thee also, saith the Lord. 28. Behold, I will gather thee to thy fathers, and thou shalt be gathered to thy grave in peace, neither shall thine eyes see all the evil that I will bring upon this place, and upon the inhabitants of the same. So they brought the king word again.'—2 CHRON. xxxiv. 14-28.

About one hundred years separated Hezekiah's restoration from Josiah's. Neither was more than a momentary arrest of the strong tide running in the opposite direction; and Josiah's was too near the edge of the cataract to last, or to avert the plunge. There is nothing more tragical than the working of the law which often sets the children's teeth on edge by reason of the fathers' eating of sour grapes.

I. The first point in this passage is the discovery of the book of the Law.

The book had been lost before it was found. For how long we do not know, but the fact that it had been so carelessly kept is eloquent of the indifference of priests and kings, its appointed guardians. Lawbreakers have a direct interest in getting rid of lawbooks, just as shopkeepers who use short yardsticks and light weights are not anxious the standards should be easily accessible. If we do not make God's law our guide, we shall wish to put it out of sight, that it may not be our accuser. What more sad or certain sign of evil can there be than that we had rather not 'hear what God the Lord will speak'?

The straightforward story of our passage gives a most natural explanation of the find. Hilkiah was likely to have had dark corners cleared out in preparation for repairs and in storing the subscriptions, and many a mislaid thing would turn up. If it be possible that the book of the Law should have been neglected (and the religious corruption of the last hundred years makes that only too certain), its discovery in some dusty recess is very intelligible, and would not have been doubted but for the exigencies of a theory. 'Reading between the lines' is fascinating, but risky; for the reader is very likely unconsciously to do what Hilkiah is said to have done—namely, to invent what he thinks he finds.

Accepting the narrative as it stands, we may see in it a striking instance of the indestructibleness of God's Word. His law is imperishable, and its written embodiment seems as if it, too, had a charmed life. When we consider the perils attending the transmission of ancient manuscripts, the necessary scarcity of copies before the invention of printing, the scattering of the Jewish people, it does appear as if a divine hand had guarded the venerable book. How came this strange people, who never kept their Law, to swim through all their troubles, like Caesar with his commentaries between his teeth, bearing aloft and dry, the Word which they obeyed so badly? 'Write it ... in a book, that it may be for the time to come for ever and ever.' The permanence of the written Word, the providence that has watched over it, the romantic history of its preservation through ages of neglect, and the imperishable gift to the world of an objective standard of duty, remaining the same from age to age, are all suggested by this reappearance of the forgotten Law.

It may suggest, too, that honest efforts after reformation are usually rewarded by clearer knowledge of God's will. If Hilkiah had not been busy in setting wrong things right, he would not have found the book in its dark hiding-place. We are told that the coincidence of the discovery at the nick of time is suspicious. So it is, if you do not believe in Providence. If you do, the coincidence is but one instance of His sending gifts of the right sort at the right moment. It is not the first time nor the last that the attempt to keep God's law has led to larger knowledge of the law. It is not the first time nor the last that God has sent to His faithful servants an opportune gift. What the world calls accidental coincidence deeper wisdom discerns to be the touch of God's hand.

Again, the discovery reminds us that the true basis of all religious reform is the Word of God. Josiah had begun to restore the Temple, but he did not know till he heard the Law read how great the task was which he had taken in hand. That recovered book gave impulse and direction to his efforts. The nearest parallel is the rediscovery of the Bible in the sixteenth century, or, if we may take one incident as a symbol of the whole, Luther's finding the dusty Latin Bible among the neglected convent books. The only reformation for an effete or secularised church is in its return to the Bible. Faded flowers will lift up their heads when plunged in water. The old Bible, discovered and applied anew, must underlie all real renovation of dead or moribund Christianity.

II. The next point here is the effect of the rediscovered Law. Shaphan was closely connected with Josiah, as his office made him a confidant. It is ordinarily taken for granted that he and the other persons named in this lesson formed a little knot of earnest Jehovah worshippers, fully sympathising with the Reformation, and that among them lay the authorship of the book. But we know nothing about them except what is told here and in the parallel in Kings. One of them, Ahikam, was a friend and protector of Jeremiah, and Shaphan the scribe was the father of another of Jeremiah's friends. They may all have been in accord with the king, or they may not.

At all events, Shaphan took the book to Josiah. We can picture the scene—the deepening awe of both men as the whole extent of the nation's departure from God became clearer and clearer, the tremulous tones of the reader, and the silent, fixed attention of the listener as the solemn threatenings came from Shaphan's reluctant, pallid lips. There was enough in them to touch a harder heart than Josiah's. We cannot suppose that, knowing the history of the past, and being sufficiently enlightened to 'seek after the God of David his father,' he did not know in a general way that sin meant sorrow, and national disobedience national death. But we all have the faculty of blunting the cutting edge of truth, especially if it has been familiar, so that some novelty in the manner of its presentation, or even its repetition without novelty sometimes, may turn commonplace and impotent truth into a mighty instrument to shake and melt.

So it seems to have been with Josiah. Whether new or old, the Word found him as it had never done before. The venerable copy from which Shaphan read, the coincidence of its discovery just then, the dishonour done to it for so long, may all have helped the impression. However it arose, it was made. If a man will give God's Word a fair hearing, and be honest with himself, it will bring him to his knees. No man rightly uses God's law who is not convinced by it of his sin, and impelled to that self-abased sorrow of which the rent royal robes were the passionate expression. Josiah was wise when he did not turn his thoughts to other people's sins, but began with his own, even whilst he included others. The first function of the law is to arouse the knowledge of sin, as Paul profoundly teaches. Without that penitent knowledge religion is superficial, and reformation merely external. Unless we 'abhor ourselves, and repent in dust and ashes,' Scripture has not done its work on us, and all our reading of it is in vain. Nor is there any good reason why familiarity with it should weaken its power. But, alas! it too often does. How many of us would stand in awe of God's judgments if we heard them for the first time, but listen to them unmoved, as to thunder without lightning, merely because wo know them so well! That is a reason for attending to them, not for neglecting.

Josiah's sense of sin led him to long for a further word from God; and so he called these attendants named in verse 20, and sent them to 'enquire of the Lord … concerning the words of the book.' What more did he wish to know? The words were plain enough, and their application to Israel and him indubitable. Clearly, he could only wish to know whether there was any possibility of averting the judgments, and, if so, what was the means. The awakened conscience instinctively feels that threatenings cannot be God's last words to it, but must have been given that they might not need to be fulfilled. We do not rightly sorrow for sin unless it quickens in us a desire for a word from God to tell us how to escape. The Law prepares for the Gospel, and is incomplete without it. 'The soul that sinneth, it shall die,' cannot be all which a God of pity and love has to say. A faint promise of life lies in the very fact of threatening death, faint indeed, but sufficient to awaken earnest desire for yet another word from the Lord. We rightly use the solemn revelations of God's law when we are driven by them to cry, 'What must I do to be saved?'

III. So we come to the last point, the double-edged message of the prophetess. Josiah does not seem to have told his messengers where to go; but they knew, and went straight to a very unlikely person, the wife of an obscure man, only known as his father's son. Where was Jeremiah of Anathoth? Perhaps not in the city at the time. There had been prophetesses in Israel before. Miriam, Deborah, the wife of Isaiah, are instances of 'your daughters' prophesying; and this embassy to Huldah is in full accord with the high position which women held in that state, of which the framework was shaped by God Himself. In Christ Jesus 'there is neither male nor female,' and Judaism approximated much more closely to that ideal than other lands did.

Huldah's message has two parts: one the confirmation of the threatenings of the Law; one the assurance to Josiah of acceptance of his repentance and gracious promise of escape from the coming storm. These two are precisely equivalent to the double aspect of the Gospel, which completes the Law, endorsing its sentence and pointing the way of escape.

Note that the former part addresses Josiah as 'the man that sent you,' but the latter names him. The embassy had probably not disclosed his name, and Huldah at first keeps up the veil, since the personality of the sender had nothing to do with her answer; but when she comes to speak of pardon and God's favour, there must be no vagueness in the destination of the message, and the penitent heart must be tenderly bound up by a word from God straight to itself. The threatenings are general, but each single soul that is sorry for sin may take as its very own the promise of forgiveness. God's great 'Whosoever' is for me as certainly as if my name stood on the page.

The terrible message of the inevitableness of the destruction hanging over Jerusalem is precisely parallel with the burden of all Jeremiah's teaching. It was too late to avert the fall. The external judgments must come now, for the emphasis of the prophecy is in its last words, it 'shall not be quenched.' But that did not mean that repentance was too late to alter the whole character of the punishment, which would be fatherly chastisement if meekly accepted. So, too, Jeremiah taught, when he exhorted submission to the 'Chaldees.' It is never too late to seek mercy, though it may be too late to hope for averting the outward consequences of sin.

As for Josiah, his penitence was accepted, and he was assured that he would be gathered to his fathers. That expression, as is clear from the places where it occurs, is not a synonym for either death or burial, from both of which it is distinguished, but is a dim promise of being united, beyond the grave, with the fathers, who, in some one condition, which we may call a place, are gathered into a restful company, and wander no more as pilgrims and sojourners in this lonely and changeful life.

Josiah died in battle. Was that going to his grave in peace? Surely yes! if, dying, he felt God's presence, and in the darkness saw a great light. He who thus dies, though it be in the thick of battle, and with his heart's blood pouring from an arrow-wound down on the floor of the chariot, dies in peace, and into peace.

THE FALL OF JUDAH

'Zedekiah was one and twenty years old when he began to reign, and reigned eleven years in Jerusalem. 12. And he did that which was evil in the sight of the Lord his God, and humbled not himself before Jeremiah the prophet speaking from the mouth of the Lord. 13. And he also rebelled against king Nebuchadnezzar, who had made him swear by God: but he stiffened his neck, and hardened his heart from turning unto the Lord God of Israel. 14. Moreover all the chief of the priests, and the people, transgressed very much after all the abominations of the heathen; and polluted the house of the Lord which he had hallowed in Jerusalem. 15. And the Lord God of their fathers sent to them by His messengers, rising up betimes, and sending; because He had compassion on His people, and on His dwelling-place: 16. But they mocked the messengers of God, and despised His words, and misused His prophets, until the wrath of the Lord arose against His people, till there was no remedy. 17. Therefore he brought upon them the king of the Chaldees, who slew their young men with the sword in the house of their sanctuary, and had no compassion upon young man or maiden, old man, or him that stooped for age: he gave them all into his hand. 18. And all the vessels of the house of God, great and small, and the treasures of the house of the Lord, and the treasures of the king, and of his princes; all these he brought to Babylon. 19. And they burnt the house of God, and brake down the wall of Jerusalem, and burnt all the palaces thereof with fire, and destroyed all the goodly vessels thereof. 20. And them that had escaped from the sword carried he away to Babylon; where they were servants to him and his sons until the reign of the kingdom of Persia: 21. To fulfil the word of the Lord by the mouth of Jeremiah, until the land had enjoyed her sabbaths; for as long as she lay desolate she kept sabbath, to fulfil threescore and ten years.'—2 CHRON. xxxvi 11-21.

Bigness is not greatness, nor littleness smallness. Nebuchadnezzar's conquest of Judah was, in his eyes, one of the least important of his many victories, but it is the only one of them which survives in the world's memory and keeps his name as a household word. The Jews were a mere handful, and their country a narrow strip of land between the desert and the sea; but little Judaea, like little Greece, has taught the world. The tragedy of its fall has importance quite disproportioned to its apparent magnitude. Our passage brings together Judah's sin and Judah's punishment, and we shall best gather the lessons of its fall by following the order of the text.

Consider the sin. There is nothing more remarkable than the tone in which the chronicler, like all the Old Testament writers, deals with the national sin. Patriotic historians make it a point of pride and duty to gloss over their country's faults, but these singular narrators paint them as strongly as they can. Their love of their country impels them to 'make known to Israel its transgression and to Judah its sin.' There are tears in their eyes, as who can doubt? But there is no faltering in their voices as they speak. A higher feeling than misguided 'patriotism' moves them. Loyalty to Israel's God forces them to deal honestly with Israel's sin. That is the highest kind of love of country, and might well be commended to loudmouthed 'patriots' in modern lands.

Look at the piled-up clauses of the long indictment of Judah in verses 12 to 16. Slow, passionless, unsparing, the catalogue enumerates the whole black list. It is like the long-drawn blast of the angel of judgment's trumpet. Any trace of heated emotion would have weakened the impression. The nation's sin was so crimson as to need no heightening of colour. With like judicial calmness, with like completeness, omitting nothing, does 'the book,' which will one day be opened, set down every man's deeds, and he will be 'judged according to the things that are written in this book.' Some of us will find our page sad reading.

But the points brought out in this indictment are instructive. Judah's idolatry and 'trespass after all the abominations of the heathen' is, of course, prominent, but the spirit which led to their idolatry, rather than the idolatry itself, is dwelt on. Zedekiah's doing 'evil in the sight of the Lord' is regarded as aggravated by his not humbling himself before Jeremiah, and the head and front of his offending is that 'he stiffened his neck and hardened his heart from turning unto the Lord.' Similarly, the people's sin reaches its climax in their 'mocking' and 'scoffing' at the prophets and 'despising' God's words by them. So then, an evil life has its roots in an alienated heart, and the source of all sin is an obstinate self-will. That is the sulphur-spring from which nothing but unwholesome streams can flow, and the greatest of all sins is refusing to hear God's voice when He speaks to us.

Further, this indictment brings out the patient love of God seeking, in spite of all their deafness, to find a way to the sinners' ears and hearts. In a bold transference to Him of men's ways, He is said to have 'risen early' to send the prophets. Surely that means earnest effort. The depths of God's heart are disclosed when we are bidden to think of His compassion as the motive for the prophet's messages and threatenings. What a wonderful and heart-melting revelation of God's placableness, wistful hoping against hope, and reluctance to abandon the most indurated sinner, is given in that centuries-long conflict of the patient God with treacherous Israel! That divine charity suffered long and was kind, endured all things and hoped all things.

Consider the punishment. The tragic details of the punishment are enumerated with the same completeness and suppression of emotion as those of the sin. The fact that all these were divine judgments brings the chronicler to the Psalmist's attitude. 'I was dumb, I opened not my mouth because Thou didst it.' Sorrow and pity have their place, but the awed recognition of God's hand outstretched in righteous retribution must come first. Modern sentimentalists, who are so tenderhearted as to be shocked at the Christian teachings of judgment, might learn a lesson here.

The first point to note is that a time arrives when even God can hope for no amendment and is driven to change His methods. His patience is not exhausted, but man's obstinacy makes another treatment inevitable. God lavished benefits and pleadings for long years in vain, till He saw that there was 'no remedy.' Only then did He, as if reluctantly forced, do 'His work, His strange work.' Behold, therefore, the 'goodness and severity' of God, goodness in His long delay, severity in the final blow, and learn that His purpose is the same though His methods are opposite.

To the chronicler God is the true Actor in human affairs. Nebuchadnezzar thought of his conquest as won by his own arm. Secular historians treat the fall of Zedekiah as simply the result of the political conditions of the time, and sometimes seem to think that it could not be a divine judgment because it was brought about by natural causes. But this old chronicler sees deeper, and to him, as to us, if we are wise, 'the history of the world is the judgment of the world.' The Nebuchadnezzars are God's axes with which He hews down fruitless trees. They are responsible for their acts, but they are His instruments, and it is His hand that wields them.

The iron band that binds sin and suffering is disclosed in Judah's fall. We cannot allege that the same close connection between godlessness and national disaster is exemplified now as it was in Israel. Nor can we contend that for individuals suffering is always the fruit of sin. But it is still true that 'righteousness exalteth a nation,' and that 'by the soul only are the nations great,' in the true sense of the word. To depart from God is always 'a bitter and an evil thing' for communities and individuals, however sweet draughts of outward prosperity may for a time mask the bitterness. Not armies nor fleets, not ships, colonies and commerce, not millionaires and trusts, not politicians and diplomatists, but the fear of the Lord and the keeping of His commandments, are the true life of a nation. If Christian men lived up to the ideal set them by Jesus, 'Ye are the salt of the land,' and sought more earnestly and wisely to leaven their nation, they would be doing more than any others to guarantee its perpetual prosperity.

The closing words of this chapter, not included in the passage, are significant. They are the first words of the Book of Ezra. Whoever put them here perhaps wished to show a far-off dawn following the stormy sunset. He opens a 'door of hope' in 'the valley of trouble.' It is an Old Testament version of 'God hath not cast away His people whom He foreknew.' It throws a beam of light on the black last page of the chronicle, and reveals that God's chastisement was in love, that it was meant for discipline, not for destruction, that it was educational, and that the rod was burned when the lesson had been learned. It was learned, for the Captivity cured the nation of hankering after idolatry, and whatever defects it brought back from Babylon, it brought back a passionate abhorrence of all the gods of the nations.

EZRA

THE EVE OF THE RESTORATION

'Now in the first year of Cyrus king of Persia, that the word of the Lord by the mouth of Jeremiah might be fulfilled, the Lord stirred up the spirit of Cyrus king of Persia, that he made a proclamation throughout all his kingdom, and put it also in writing, saying, 2. Thus saith Cyrus king of Persia, The Lord God of heaven hath given me all the kingdoms of the earth; and He hath charged me to build Him a house at Jerusalem, which is in Judah. 3. Who is there among you of all His people? his God be with him, and let him go up to Jerusalem, which is in Judah, and build the house of the Lord God of Israel (He is the God), which is in Jerusalem. 4. And whosoever remaineth in any place where he sojourneth, let the men of his place help him with silver, and with gold, and with goods, and with beasts, besides the freewill offering for the house of God that is in Jerusalem. 5. Then rose up the chief of the fathers of Judah and Benjamin, and the priests, and the Levites, with all them whose spirit God had raised, to go up to build the house of the Lord which is in Jerusalem. 6. And all they that were about them strengthened their hands with vessels of silver, with gold, with goods, and with beasts, and with precious things, besides all that was willingly offered. 7. Also Cyrus the king brought forth the vessels of the house of the Lord, which Nebuchadnezzar had brought forth out of Jerusalem, and had put them in the house of his gods; 8. Even those did Cyrus king of Persia bring forth by the hand of Mithredath the treasurer, and numbered them unto Sheshbazzar, the prince of Judah. 9. And this is the number of them: thirty chargers of gold, a thousand chargers of silver, nine and twenty knives, 10. Thirty basons of gold, silver basons of a second sort four hundred and ten, and other vessels a thousand. 11. All the vessels of gold and of silver were five thousand and four hundred. All these did Sheshbazzar bring up with them of the captivity that were brought up from Babylon unto Jerusalem.'—EZRA i. 1-11.

Cyrus captured Babylon 538 B.C., and the 'first year' here is the first after that event. The predicted seventy years' captivity had nearly run out, having in part done their work on the exiles. Colours burned in on china are permanent; and the furnace of bondage had, at least, effected this, that it fixed monotheism for ever in the inmost substance of the Jewish people. But the bulk of them seem to have had little of either religious or patriotic enthusiasm, and preferred Babylonia to Judea. We are here told of the beginning of the return of a portion of the exiles—forty-two thousand, in round numbers.

'The Lord stirred up the spirit of Cyrus.' That unveils the deepest cause of what fell into place, to the superficial observers, as one among many political events of similar complexion. We find among the inscriptions a cylinder written by order of Cyrus, which shows that he reversed the Babylonian policy of deporting conquered nations. 'All their peoples,' says he, in reference to a number of nations of whom he found members in exile in Babylonia, 'I assembled and restored to their lands and the gods ... whom Nabonidos ... had brought into Babylon, I settled in peace in their sanctuaries' (Sayce, *Fresh Light from the Ancient Monuments*, p. 148). It was, then, part of a wider movement, which sent back Zerubbabel and his people to Jerusalem, and began the rebuilding of the Temple. No doubt, Cyrus had seen that the old plan simply brought an element of possible rebellion into the midst of the country, and acted on grounds of political prudence.

But our passage digs deeper to find the true cause. Cyrus was God's instrument, and the statesman's insight was the result of God's illumination. The divine causality moves men, when they move themselves. It was not only in the history of the chosen people that God's purpose is wrought out by more or less conscious and willing instruments. The principle laid down by the writer of this book is of universal application, and the true 'philosophy of history' must recognise as underlying all other so-called causes and forces the one uncaused Cause, of whose purposes kings and politicians are the executants, even while they freely act according to their own judgments, and, it may be, in utter unconsciousness of Him. It concerns our tranquillity and hopefulness, in the contemplation of the bewildering maze and often heart-breaking tragedy of mundane affairs, to hold fast by the conviction that God's unseen Hand moves the pieces on the board, and presides over all the complications. The difference between 'sacred' and 'profane' history is not that one is under His direct control, and the other is not. What was true of Cyrus and his policy is as true of England. Would that politicians and all men recognised the fact as clearly as this historian did!

I. Cyrus's proclamation sounds as if he were a Jehovah-worshipper, but it is to be feared that his religion was of a very accommodating kind. It used to be said that, as a Persian, he was a monotheist, and would consequently be in sympathy with the Jews; but the same cylinder already quoted shatters that idea, and shows him to have been a polytheist, ready to worship the gods of Babylon. He there ascribes his conquest to 'Merodach, the great lord,' and distinctly calls himself that god's 'worshipper.' Like other polytheists, he had room in his pantheon for the gods of other nations, and admitted into it the deities of the conquered peoples.

The use of the name 'Jehovah' would, no doubt, be most simply accounted for by the supposition that Cyrus recognised the sole divinity of the God of Israel; but that solution conflicts with all that is known of him, and with his characterisation in Isaiah xlv. as 'not knowing' Jehovah. More probably, his confession of Jehovah as the God of heaven was consistent in his mind with a similar confession as to Bel-Merodach or the supreme god of any other of the conquered nations. There is, however no improbability in the supposition that the prophecies concerning him in Isaiah xlv, may have been brought to his knowledge, and be referred to in the proclamation as the 'charge' given to him to build Jehovah's Temple. But we must not exaggerate the depth or exclusiveness of his belief in the God of the Jews.

Cyrus's profession of faith, then, is an example of official and skin-deep religion, of which public and individual life afford plentiful instances in all ages and faiths. If we are to take their own word for it, most great conquerors have been very religious men, and have asked a blessing over many a bloody feast. All religions are equally true to cynical politicians, who are ready to join in worshipping 'Jehovah, Jove, or Lord,' as may suit their policy. Nor is it only in high places that such loosely worn professions are found. Perhaps there is no region of life in which insincerity, which is often quite unconscious, is so rife as in regard to religious belief. But unless my religion is everything, it is nothing. 'All in all, or not at all,' is the requirement of the great Lover of souls. What a winnowing of chaff from wheat there would be, if that test could visibly separate the mass which is gathered on His threshing-floor, the Church!

Cyrus's belief in Jehovah illustrates the attitude which was natural to a polytheist, and is so difficult for us to enter into. A vague belief in One Supreme, above all other gods, and variously named by different nations, is buried beneath mountains of myths about lesser gods, but sometimes comes to light in many pagan minds. This blind creed, if creed it can be called, is joined with the recognition of deities belonging to each nation, whose worship is to be co-extensive with the race of which they are patrons, and who may be absorbed into the pantheon of a conqueror, just as a vanquished king may be allowed an honourable captivity at the victor's capital. Thus Cyrus could in a sense worship Jehovah, the God of Israel, without thereby being rebellious to Merodach.

There are people, even among so-called Christians, who try the same immoral and impossible division of what must in its very nature be wholly given to One Supreme. To 'serve God and mammon' is demonstrably an absurd attempt. The love and trust and obedience which are worthy of Him must be wholehearted, whole-souled, whole-willed. It is as impossible to love God with part of one's self as it is for a husband to love his wife with half his heart, and another woman with the rest. To divide love is to slay it. Cyrus had some kind of belief in Jehovah; but his own words, so wonderfully recovered in the inscription already referred to, proved that he had not listened to the command, 'Him only shalt thou serve.' That command grips us as closely as it did the Jews, and is as truly broken by thousands calling themselves Christians as by any idolaters.

The substance of the proclamation is a permission to return to any one who wished to do so, a sanction of the rebuilding of the Temple, and an order to the native inhabitants to render help in money, goods, and beasts. A further contribution towards the building was suggested as 'a free-will offering.' The return, then, was not to be at the expense of the king, nor was any tax laid on for it; but neighbourly goodwill, born of seventy years of association, was invoked, and, as we find, not in vain. God had given the people favour in the eyes of those who had carried them captive.

II. The long years of residence in Babylonia had weakened the homesickness which the first generation of captives had, no doubt, painfully experienced, and but a small part of them cared to avail themselves of the opportunity of return. One reason is frankly given by Josephus: 'Many remained in Babylon, not wishing to leave their possessions behind them.' 'The heads of the fathers' houses [who may have exercised some sort of government among the captives], the priests and Levites,' made the bulk of the emigrants; but in each class it was only those 'whose spirit God had stirred up' (as he had done Cyrus') that were devout or patriotic enough to face the wrench of removal and the difficulties of repeopling a wasted land. There was nothing to tempt any others, and the brave little band had need of all their fortitude. But no heart in which the flame of devotion burned, or in which were felt the drawings of that passionate love of the city and soil where God dwelt (which in the best days of the nation was inseparable from devotion), could remain behind. The departing contingent, then, were the best part of the whole; and the lingerers were held back by love of ease, faint-heartedness, love of wealth, and the like ignoble motives.

How many of us have had great opportunities offered for service, which we have let slip in like manner! To have doors opened which we are too lazy, too cowardly, too much afraid of self-denial, to enter, is the tragedy and the crime of many a life. It is easier to live among the low levels of the plain of Babylon, than to take to the dangers and privations of the weary tramp across the desert. The ruins of Jerusalem are a much less comfortable abode than the well-furnished houses which have to be left. Prudence says, 'Be content where you are, and let other people take the trouble of such mad schemes as rebuilding the Temple.' A thousand excuses sing in our ears, and we let the moment in which alone some noble resolve is possible slide past us, and the rest of life is empty of another such. Neglected opportunities, unobeyed calls to high deeds, we all have in our lives. The saddest of all words is, 'It might have been.' How much wiser, happier, nobler, were the daring souls that rose to the occasion, and flung ease and wealth and companionship behind them, because they heard the divine command couched in the royal permission, and humbly answered, 'Here am I; send me'!

III. The third point in the passage is singular—the inventory of the Temple vessels returned by Cyrus. As to its particulars, we need only note that Sheshbazzar is the same as Zerubbabel; that the exact translation of some of the names of the vessels is doubtful; and that the numbers given under each head do not correspond with the sum total, the discrepancy indicating error somewhere in the numbers.

But is not this dry enumeration a strange item to come in the forefront of the narrative of such an event? We might have expected some kind of production of the enthusiasm of the returning exiles, some account of how they were sent on their journey, something which we should have felt worthier of the occasion than a list of bowls and nine-and-twenty knives. But it is of a piece with the whole of the first part of this Book of Ezra, which is mostly taken up with a similar catalogue of the members of the expedition. The list here indicates the pride and joy with which the long hidden and often desecrated vessels were received. We can see the priests and Levites gazing at them as they were brought forth, their hearts, and perhaps their eyes, filling with sacred memories. The Lord had 'turned again the captivity of Zion,' and these sacred vessels lay there, glittering before them, to assure them that they were not as 'them that dream.' Small things become great when they are the witnesses of a great thing.

We must remember, too, how strong a hold the externals of worship had on the devout Jew. His faith was much more tied to form than ours ought to be, and the restoration of the sacrificial implements as a pledge of the re-establishment of the Temple worship would seem the beginning of a new epoch of closer relation to Jehovah. It is almost within the lifetime of living men that all Scotland was thrilled with emotion by the discovery, in a neglected chamber, of a chest in which lay, forgotten, the crown and sceptre of the Stuarts. A like wave of feeling passed over the exiles as they had given back to their custody these Temple vessels. Sacreder ones are given into our hands, to carry across a more dangerous desert. Let us hear the charge, 'Be ye clean, that bear the vessels of the Lord,' and see that we carry them, untarnished and unlost, to 'the house of the Lord which is in Jerusalem.'

ALTAR AND TEMPLE

'And when the seventh month was come, and the children of Israel were in the cities, the people gathered themselves together as one man to Jerusalem. 2. Then stood up Jeshua the son of Jozadak, and his brethren the priests, and Zerubbabel the son of Shealtiel, and his brethren, and builded the altar of the God of Israel, to offer burnt offerings thereon, as it is written in the law of Moses the man of God. 3. And they set the altar upon his bases; for fear was upon them because of the people of those countries; and they offered burnt offerings thereon unto the Lord, even burnt offerings morning and evening. 4. They kept also the feast of tabernacles, as it is written, and offered the daily burnt offerings by number, according to the custom, as the duty of every day required; 5. And afterward offered the continual burnt offering, both of the new moons, and of all the set feasts of the Lord that were consecrated, and of every one that willingly offered a freewill offering unto the Lord. 6. From the first day of the seventh month began they to offer burnt offerings unto the Lord. But the foundation of the Temple of the Lord was not yet laid. 7. They gave money also unto the masons, and to the carpenters; and meat, and drink, and oil, unto them of Zidon, and to them of Tyre, to bring cedar trees from Lebanon to the sea of Joppa, according to the grant that they had of Cyrus king of Persia. 8. Now in the second year of their coming unto the house of God at Jerusalem, in the second month, began Zerubbabel the son of Shealtiel, and Jeshua the son of Jozadak, and the remnant of their brethren the priests and the Levites, and all they that were come out of the captivity unto Jerusalem; and appointed the Levites, from twenty years old and upward, to set forward the work of the house of the Lord. 9. Then stood Jeshua with his sons and his brethren, Kadmiel and his sons, the sons of Judah, together, to set forward the workmen in the house of God: the sons of Henadad, with their sons and their brethren the Levites. 10. And when the builders laid the foundation of the Temple of the Lord, they set the priests in their apparel with trumpets, and the Levites, the sons of Asaph, with cymbals, to praise the Lord, after the ordinance of David king of Israel. 11. And they sang together by course in praising and giving thanks unto the Lord; because He is good, for His mercy endureth for ever toward Israel. And all the people shouted with a great shout, when they praised the Lord, because the foundation of the house of the Lord was laid. 12. But many of the priests and Levites and chief of the fathers, who were ancient men, that had seen the first house, when the foundation of this house was laid before their eyes, wept with a loud voice; and many shouted aloud for joy: 13. So that the people could not discern the noise of the shout of joy from the noise of the weeping of the people: for the people shouted with a loud shout, and the noise was heard afar off.'—EZRA iii. 1-13.

What an opportunity of 'picturesque' writing the author of this book has missed by his silence about the incidents of the march across the dreary levels from Babylon to the verge of Syria! But the very silence is eloquent. It reveals the purpose of the book, which is to tell of the re-establishment of the Temple and its worship. No doubt the tone of the whole is somewhat prosaic, and indicative of an age in which the externals of worship bulked largely; but still the central point of the narrative was really the centre-point of the events. The austere simplicity of biblical history shows the real points of importance better than more artistic elaboration would do.

This passage has two main incidents—the renewal of the sacrifices, and the beginning of rebuilding the Temple.

The date given in verse 1 is significant. The first day of the seventh month was the commencement of the great festival of tabernacles, the most joyous feast of the year, crowded with reminiscences from the remote antiquity of the Exodus, and from the dedication of Solomon's Temple. How long had passed since Cyrus' decree had been issued we do not know, nor whether his 'first year' was reckoned by the same chronology as the Jewish year, of which we here arrive at the seventh month. But the journey across the desert must have taken some months, and the previous preparations could not have been suddenly got through, so that there can have been but a short time between the arrival in Judea and the gathering together 'as one man to Jerusalem.'

There was barely interval enough for the returning exiles to take possession of their ancestral fields before they were called to leave them unguarded and hasten to the desolate city. Surely their glad and unanimous obedience to the summons, or, as it may even have been, their spontaneous assemblage unsummoned, is no small token of their ardour of devotion, even if they were somewhat slavishly tied to externals. It would take a good deal to draw a band of new settlers in our days to leave their lots and set to putting up a church before they had built themselves houses.

The leaders of the band of returned exiles demand a brief notice. They are Jeshua, or Joshua, and Zerubbabel. In verse 2 the ecclesiastical dignitary comes first, but in verse 8 the civil. Similarly in Ezra ii. 2, Zerubbabel precedes Jeshua. In Haggai, the priest is pre-eminent; in Zechariah the prince. The truth seems to be that each was supreme in his own department, and that they understood each other cordially, or, Zechariah says, 'the counsel of peace' was 'between them both.' It is sometimes bad for the people when priests and rulers lay their heads together; but it is even worse when they pull different ways, and subjects are torn in two by conflicting obligations.

Jeshua was the grandson of Seraiah, the unfortunate high-priest whose eyes Nebuchadnezzar put out after the fall of Jerusalem. His son Jozadak succeeded to the dignity, though there could be no sacrifices in Babylon, and after him his son Jeshua. He cannot have been a young man at the date of the return; but age had not dimmed his enthusiasm, and the high-priest was where he ought to have been, in the forefront of the returning exiles. His name recalls the other Joshua, likewise a leader from captivity and the desert; and, if we appreciate the significance attached to names in Scripture, we shall scarcely suppose it accidental that these two, who had similar work to do, bore the same name as the solitary third, of whom they were pale shadows, the greater Joshua, who brings His people from bondage into His own land of peace, and builds the Temple.

Zerubbabel ('Sown in Babylon') belonged to a collateral branch of the royal family. The direct Davidic line through Solomon died with the wretched Zedekiah and Jeconiah, but the descendants of another son of David's, Nathan, still survived. Their representative was one Salathiel, who, on the failure of the direct line, was regarded as the 'son of Jeconiah' (1 Chron. iii. 17). He seems to have had no son, and Zerubbabel, who was really his nephew (1 Chron. iii. 19), was legally adopted as his son. In this makeshift fashion, some shadow of the ancient royalty still presided over the restored people. We see Zerubbabel better in Haggai and Zechariah than in Ezra, and can discern the outline of a strong, bold, prompt nature. He had a hard task, and he did it like a man. Patient, yet vigorous, glowing with enthusiasm, yet clear-eyed, self-forgetful, and brave, he has had scant justice done him, and ought to be a very much more familiar and honoured figure than he is. 'Who art thou, O great mountain? Before Zerubbabel thou shalt become a plain.' Great mountains only become plains before men of strong wills and fixed faith.

There is something very pathetic in the picture of the assembled people groping amid the ruins on the Temple hill, to find 'the bases,' the half-obliterated outlines, of the foundations of the old altar of burnt offerings. What memories of Araunah's threshing-floor, and of the hovering angel of destruction, and of the glories of Solomon's dedication, and of the long centuries during which the column of smoke had gone up continually from that spot, and of the tragical day when the fire was quenched, and of the fifty years of extinction, must have filled their hearts! What a conflict of gladness and sorrow must have troubled their spirits as the flame again shot upwards from the hearth of God, cold for so long!

But the reason for their so quickly rearing the altar is noteworthy. It was because 'fear was upon them because of the people of the countries.' The state of the Holy Land at the return must be clearly comprehended. Samaria and the central district were in the hands of bitter enemies. Across Jordan in the east, down on the Philistine plain in the west, and in the south where Edom bore sway, eager enemies sulkily watched the small beginnings of a movement which they were interested in thwarting. There was only the territory of Judah and Benjamin left free for the exiles, and they had reason for their fears; for their neighbours knew that if restitution was to be the order of the day, they would have to disgorge a good deal. What was the defence against such foes which these frightened men thought most impregnable? That altar!

No doubt, much superstition mingled with their religion. Haggai leaves us under no illusions as to their moral and spiritual condition. They were no patterns of devoutness or of morality. But still, what they did carries an eternal truth; and they were reverting to the original terms of Israel's tenure of their land when they acted on the conviction that their worship of Jehovah according to His commandment was their surest way of finding shelter from all their enemies. There are differences plain enough between their condition and ours; but it is as true for us as ever it was for them, that our safety is in God, and that, if we want to find shelter from impending dangers, we shall be wiser to betake ourselves to the altar and sit suppliant there than to make defences for ourselves. The ruined Jerusalem was better guarded by that altar than if its fallen walls had been rebuilt.

The whole ritual was restored, as the narrative tells with obvious satisfaction in the enumeration. To us this punctilious attention to the minutiae of sacrificial worship sounds trivial. But we equally err if we try to bring such externalities into the worship of the Christian Church, and if we are blind to their worth at an earlier stage.

There cannot be a temple without an altar, but there may be an altar without a temple. God meets men at the place of sacrifice, even though there be no house for His name. The order of events here teaches us what is essential for communion with God. It is the altar. Sacrifice laid there is accepted, whether it stand on a bare hill-top, or have round it the courts of the Lord's house.

The second part of the passage narrates the laying of the foundations of the Temple. There had been contracts entered into with masons and carpenters, and arrangements made with the Phoenicians for timber, as soon as the exiles had returned; but of course some time elapsed before the stone and timber were sufficient to make a beginning with. Note in verse 7 the reference to Cyrus' grant as enabling the people to get these stores together. Whether the whole preparations, or only the transport of cedar wood, is intended to be traced to the influence of that decree, there seems to be a tacit contrast, in the writer's mind, with the glorious days when no heathen king had to be consulted, and Hiram and Solomon worked together like brothers. Now, so fallen are we, that Tyre and Sidon will not look at us unless we bring Cyrus' rescript in our hands!

If the 'years' in verses 1 and 8 are calculated from the same beginning, some seven months were spent in preparation, and then the foundation was laid. Two things are noted—the humble attempt at making some kind of a display on the occasion, and the conflict of feeling in the onlookers. They had managed to get some copies of the prescribed vestments; and the narrator emphasises the fact that the priests were 'in their apparel,' and that the Levites had cymbals, so that some approach to the pomp of Solomon's dedication was possible. They did their best to adhere to the ancient prescriptions, and it was no mere narrow love of ritual that influenced them. However we may breathe a freer air of worship, we cannot but sympathise with that earnest attempt to do everything 'according to the order of David king of Israel.' Not only punctiliousness as to ritual, but the magnetism of glorious memories, prescribed the reproduction of that past. Rites long proscribed become very sacred, and the downtrodden successors of mighty men will cling with firm grasp to what the greater fathers did.

The ancient strain which still rings from Christian lips, and bids fair to be as eternal as the mercies which it hymns, rose with strange pathos from the lips of the crowd on the desolate Temple mountain, ringed about by the waste solitudes of the city: 'For He is good, for His mercy endureth for ever toward Israel.' It needed some faith to sing that song then, even with the glow of return upon them. What of all the weary years? What of the empty homesteads, and the surrounding enemies, and the brethren still in Babylon? No doubt some at least of the rejoicing multitude had learned what the captivity was meant to teach, and had come to bless God, both for the long years of exile, which had burned away much dross, and for the incomplete work of restoration, surrounded though they were with foes, and little as was their strength to fight. The trustful heart finds occasion for unmingled praise in the most mingled cup of joy and sorrow.

There can have been very few in that crowd who had seen the former Temple, and their memories of its splendour must have been very dim. But partly remembrance and partly hearsay made the contrast of the past glories and the present poverty painful. Hence that pathetic and profoundly significant incident of the blended shouts of the young and tears of the old. One can fancy that each sound jarred on the ears of those who uttered the other. But each was wholly natural to the years of the two classes. Sad memories gather, like evening mists, round aged lives, and the temptation of the old is unduly to exalt the past, and unduly to depreciate the present. Welcoming shouts for the new befit young lips, and they care little about the ruins that have to be carted off the ground for the foundations of the temple which they are to have a hand in building. However imperfect, it is better to them than the old house where the fathers worshipped.

But each class should try to understand the other's feelings. The friends of the old should not give a churlish welcome to the new, nor those of the new forget the old. It is hard to blend the two, either in individual life or in a wider sphere of thought or act. The seniors think the juniors revolutionary and irreverent; the juniors think the seniors fossils. It is possible to unite the shout of joy and the weeping. Unless a spirit of reverent regard for the past presides over the progressive movements of this or any day, they will not lay a solid foundation for the temple of the future. We want the old and the young to work side by side, if the work is to last and the sanctuary is to be ample enough to embrace all shades of character and tendencies of thought. If either the grey beards of Solomon's court or the hot heads of Rehoboam's get the reins in their hands, they will upset the chariot. That mingled sound of weeping and joy from the Temple hill tells a more excellent way.

BUILDING IN TROUBLOUS TIMES

'Now when the adversaries of Judah and Benjamin heard that the children of the captivity builded the temple unto the Lord God of Israel; 2. Then they came to Zerubbabel, and to the chief of the fathers, and said unto them, Let us build with you: for we seek your God, as ye do; and we do sacrifice unto Him since the days of Esar-haddon king of Assur, which brought us up hither. 3. But Zerubbabel, and Joshua, and the rest of the chief of the fathers of Israel, said unto them, Ye have nothing to do with us to build an house unto our God; but we ourselves together will build unto the Lord God of Israel, as king Cyrus the king of Persia hath commanded us. 4. Then the people of the land weakened the hands of the people of Judah, and troubled them in building, 5. And hired counsellors against them, to frustrate their purpose, all the days of Cyrus king of Persia, even until the reign of Darius king of Persia.'—EZRA iv. 1-5.

Opposition began as soon as the foundations were laid, as is usually the case with all great attempts to build God's house. It came from the Samaritans, the mingled people who were partly descendants of the ancient remnant of the northern kingdom, left behind after the removal by deportation of the bulk of its population, and partly the descendants of successive layers of immigrants, planted in the empty territory by successive Assyrian and Babylonian kings. Esar-haddon was the first who had sent colonists, about one hundred and thirty years before the return. The writer calls the Samaritans 'the adversaries,' though they began by offers of friendship and alliance. The name implies that these offers were perfidious, and a move in the struggle.

One can easily understand that the Samaritans looked with suspicion on the new arrivals, the ancient possessors of the land, coming under the auspices of the new dynasty, and likely to interfere with their position if not reduced to inferiority or neutralised somehow. The proposal to unite in building the Temple was a political move; for, in old-world ideas, co-operation in Temple-building was incorporation in national unity. The calculation, no doubt, was that if the returning exiles could be united with the much more numerous Samaritans, they would soon be absorbed in them. The only chance for the smaller body was to keep itself apart, and to run the risk of its isolation.

The insincere request was based on an untruth, for the Samaritans did not worship Jehovah as the Jews, but along with their own gods (2 Kings xvii. 25-41). To divide His dominion with others was to dethrone Him altogether.

It therefore became an act of faithfulness to Jehovah to reject the entangling alliance. To have accepted it would have been tantamount to frustrating the very purpose of the return, and consenting to be muzzled about the sin of idolatry. But the chief lesson which exile had burned in on the Jewish mind was a loathing of idolatry, which is in remarkable contrast to the inclination to it that had marked their previous history. So one answer only was possible, and it was given with unwelcome plainness of speech, which might have been more courteous, and not less firm. It flatly denied any common ground; it claimed exclusive relation to 'our God,' which meant, 'not yours'; it underscored the claim by reiterating that Jehovah was the 'God of Israel'; it put forward the decree of Cyrus, as leaving no option but to confine the builders to the people whom it had empowered to build.

Now, it is easy to represent this as a piece of impolitic narrowness, and to say that its surly bigotry was rightly punished by the evils that it brought down on the returning exiles. The temper of much flaccid Christianity at present delights to expand in a lazy and foolish 'liberality,' which will welcome anybody to come and take a hand at the building, and accepts any profession of unity in worship. But there is no surer way of taking the earnestness out of Christian work and workers than drafting into it a mass of non-Christians, whatever their motives may be. Cold water poured into a boiling pot will soon stop its bubbling, and bring down its temperature. The churches are clogged and impeded, and their whole tone lowered and chilled, by a mass of worldly men and women. Nothing is gained, and much is in danger of being lost, by obliterating the lines between the church and the world. The Jew who thought little of the difference between the Samaritan worship with its polytheism, and his own monotheism, was in peril of dropping to the Samaritan level. The Samaritan who was accepted as a true worshipper of Jehovah, though he had a bevy of other gods in addition, would have been confirmed in his belief that the differences were unimportant. So both would have been harmed by what called itself 'liberality,' and was in reality indifference.

No doubt, Zerubbabel had counted the cost of faithfulness, and he soon had to pay it. The would-be friends threw off the mask, and, as they could not hinder by pretending to help, took a plainer way to stop progress. All the weapons that Eastern subtlety and intrigue could use were persistently employed to 'weaken the hands' of the builders, and the most potent of all methods, bribery to Persian officials, was freely used. The opponents triumphed, and the little community began to taste the bitterness of high hopes disappointed and noble enterprises frustrated. How differently things had turned out from the expectations with which the company had set forth from Babylon! The rough awakening to realities disillusions us all when we come to turn dreams into facts. The beginning of laying the Temple foundations is put in 536 B.C.; the first year of Darius was 522. How soon after the commencement of the work the Samaritan tricks succeeded we do not know, but it must have been some time before the death of Cyrus in 529. For weary years then the sanguine band had to wait idly, and no doubt enthusiasm died out: they had enough to do in keeping themselves alive, and in holding their own amidst enemies. They needed, as we all do, patience, and a willingness to wait for God's own time to fulfil His own promise.

THE NEW TEMPLE AND ITS WORSHIP

'And the elders of the Jews builded, and they prospered through the prophesying of Haggai the prophet and Zechariah the son of Iddo: and they builded, and finished it, according to the commandment of the God of Israel, and according to the commandment of Cyrus, and Darius, and Artaxerxes king of Persia. 15. And this house was finished on the third day of the month Adar, which was in the sixth year of the reign of Darius the king. 16. And the children of Israel, the priests, and the Levites, and the rest of the children of the captivity, kept the dedication of this house of God with joy, 17. And offered at the dedication of this house of God an hundred bullocks, two hundred rams, four hundred lambs; and for a sin offering for all Israel, twelve he-goats, according to the number of the tribes of Israel. 18. And they set the priests in their divisions, and the Levites in their courses, for the service of God, which is at Jerusalem; as it is written in the book of Moses. 19. And the children of the captivity kept the passover upon the fourteenth day of the first month. 20. For the priests and the Levites were purified together, all of them were pure, and killed the passover for all the children of the captivity, and for their brethren the priests, and for themselves. 21. And the children of Israel, which were come again out of captivity, and all such as had separated themselves unto them from the filthiness of the heathen of the land, to seek the Lord God of Israel, did eat, 22. And kept the feast of unleavened bread seven days with joy: for the Lord had made them joyful, and turned the heart of the king of Assyria unto them, to strengthen their hands in the work of the house of God, the God of Israel.'—EZRA. vi. 14-22.

There are three events recorded in this passage,—the completion of the Temple, its dedication, and the keeping of the passover some weeks thereafter. Four years intervene between the resumption of building and its successful finish, much of which time had been occupied by the interference of the Persian governor, which compelled a reference to Darius, and resulted in his confirmation of Cyrus' charter. The king's stringent orders silenced opposition, and seem to have been loyally, however unwillingly, obeyed. About twenty-three years passed between the return of the exiles and the completion of the Temple.

I. The prosperous close of the long task (vers. 14, 15). The narrative enumerates three points in reference to the completion of the Temple which are very significant, and, taken together, set forth the stimulus and law and helps of work for God.

It is expressive of deep truth that first in order is named, as the cause of success, 'the prophesying of Haggai and Zechariah.' 'Practical men,' no doubt, then as always, set little store by the two prophets' fiery words, and thought that a couple of masons would have done more for the building than they did. The contempt for 'ideas' is the mark of shallow and vulgar minds. Nothing is more practical than principles and motives which underlie and inform work, and these two prophets did more for building the Temple by their words than an army of labourers with their hands. 'There are diversities of operations,' and it is not given to every man to handle a trowel; but no good work will be prosperously accomplished unless there be engaged in it prophets who rouse and rebuke and hearten, and toilers who by their words are encouraged and saved from forgetting the sacred motives and great ends of their work in the monotony and multiplicity of details.

Still more important is the next point mentioned. The work was done 'according to the commandment of the God of Israel.' There is peculiar beauty and pathos in that name, which is common in Ezra. It speaks of the sense of unity in the nation, though but a fragment of it had come back. There was still an Israel, after all the dreary years, and in spite of present separation. God was still its God, though He had hidden His face for so long. An inextinguishable faith, wistful but assured, in His unalterable promise, throbs in that name, so little warranted by a superficial view of circumstances, but so amply vindicated by a deeper insight. His 'commandment' is at once the warrant and the standard for the work of building. In His service we are to be sure that He bids, and then to carry out His will whoever opposes.

We are to make certain that our building is 'according to the pattern showed in the mount,' and, if so, to stick to it in every point. There is no room for more than one architect in rearing the temple. The working drawings must come from Him. We are only His workmen. And though we may know no more of the general plan of the structure than the day-labourer who carries a hod does, we must be sure that we have His orders for our little bit of work, and then we may be at rest even while we toil. They who build according to His commandment build for eternity, and their work shall stand the trial by fire. That motive turns what without it were but 'wood, hay, stubble,' into 'gold and silver and precious stones.'

The last point is that the work was done according to the commandment of the heathen kings. We need not discuss the chronological difficulty arising from the mention of Artaxerxes here. The only king of that name who can be meant reigned fifty years after the events here narrated. The mention of him here has been explained by 'the consideration that he contributed to the maintenance, though not to the building, of the Temple.' Whatever is the solution, the intention of the mention of the names of the friendly monarchs is plain. 'The king's heart is in the hand of the Lord as the watercourses; He turneth it whithersoever He will.' The wonderful providence, surpassing all hopes, which gave the people 'favour in the eyes of them that carried them captive,' animates the writer's thankfulness, while he recounts that miracle that the commandment of God was re-echoed by such lips. The repetition of the word in both clauses underscores, as it were, the remarkable concurrence.

II. The dedication of the Temple (vers. 16-18). How long the dedication was after the completion is not specified. The month Adar was the last of the Jewish year, and corresponded nearly with our March. Probably the ceremonial of dedication followed immediately on the completion of the building. Probably few, if any, of the aged men, who had wept at the founding, survived to see the completion of the Temple. A new generation had no such sad contrasts of present lowliness and former glory to shade their gladness. So many dangers surmounted, so many long years of toil interrupted and hope deferred, gave keener edge to joy in the fair result of them all.

We may cherish the expectation that our long tasks, and often disappointments, will have like ending if they have been met and done in like spirit, having been stimulated by prophets and commanded by God. It is not wholesome nor grateful to depreciate present blessings by contrasting them with vanished good. Let us take what God gives to-day, and not embitter it by remembering yesterday with vain regret. There is a remembrance of the former more splendid Temple in the name of the new one, which is thrice repeated in the passage,—'this house.' But that phrase expresses gratitude quite as much as, or more than, regret. The former house is gone, but there is still 'this house,' and it is as truly God's as the other was. Let us grasp the blessings we have, and be sure that in them is continued the substance of those we have lost.

The offerings were poor, if compared with Solomon's 'two and twenty thousand oxen, and an hundred and twenty thousand sheep' (1 Kings viii. 63), and no doubt the despisers of the 'day of small things,' whom Zechariah had rebuked, would be at their depreciating work again. But 'if there be first a willing mind, it is accepted according to that a man hath, and not according to that he hath not.' The thankfulness of the offerers, not the number of their bullocks and rams, made the sacrifice well pleasing. But it would not have been so if the exiles' resources had been equal to the great King's. How many cattle had they in their stalls at home, not how many they brought to the

Temple, was the important question. The man who says, 'Oh! God accepts small offerings,' and gives a mite while he keeps talents, might as well keep his mite too; for certainly God will not have it.

A significant part of the offerings was the 'twelve he-goats, according to the number of the tribes of Israel.' These spoke of the same confidence as we have already noticed as being expressed by the designation of 'the God of Israel.' Possibly scattered members of all the tribes had come back, and so there was a kind of skeleton framework of the nation present at the dedication; but, whether that be so or not, that handful of people was not Israel. Thousands of their brethren still lingered in exile, and the hope of their return must have been faint. Yet God's promise remained, and Israel was immortal. The tribes were still twelve, and the sacrifices were still theirs. A thrill of emotion must have touched many hearts as the twelve goats were led up to the altar. So an Englishman feels as he looks at the crosses on the Union Jack.

But there was more than patriotism in that sacrifice. It witnessed to unshaken faith. And there was still more expressed in it than the offerers dreamed; for it prophesied of that transformation of the national into the spiritual Israel, in virtue of which the promises remain true, and are inherited by the Church of Christ in all lands.

The re-establishment of the Temple worship with the appointment of priests and Levites, according to the ancient ordinance, naturally followed on the dedication.

III. The celebration of the Passover (vers. 19-22). It took place on the fourteenth day of the first month, and probably, therefore, very soon after the dedication. They 'kept the feast, … for the priests and Levites were purified together.' The zeal of the sacerdotal class in attending to the prescriptions for ceremonial purity made it possible that the feast should be observed. How much of real devotion, and how much of mere eagerness to secure their official position, mingled with this zeal, cannot be determined. Probably there was a touch of both. Scrupulous observance of ritual is easy religion, especially if one's position is improved by it. But the connection pointed out by the writer is capable of wide applications. The true purity and earnestness of preachers and teachers of all degrees has much to do with their hearers' and scholars' participation in the blessings of the Gospel. If priests are not pure, they cannot kill the passover. Earnest teachers make earnest scholars. Foul hands cannot dispense the bread of life.

There is a slight deviation from the law in the ritual as here stated, since it was prescribed that each householder should kill the passover lamb for his house. But from the time of Hezekiah the Levites seem to have done it for the congregation (2 Chron. xxx. 17), and afterwards for the priests also (2 Chron. xxxv. 11, 14).

Verse 21 tells that not only the returned exiles, but also 'all such as had separated themselves unto them from the filthiness of the heathen of the land, to seek the Lord God of Israel,' ate the passover. It may be questioned whether these latter were Israelites, the descendants of the residue who had not been deported, but who had fallen into idolatry during the exile, or heathens of the mixed populations who had been settled in the vacant country. The emphasis put on their turning to Israel and Israel's God seems to favour the latter supposition. But in any case, the fact presents us with an illustration of the proper effect of the presence anywhere of a company of God's true worshippers. If we purify ourselves, and keep the feast of the true passover with joy as well as purity, we shall not want for outsiders who will separate themselves from the more subtle and not less dangerous idolatries of modern life, to seek the Lord God of Israel. If His Israel is what it ought to be, it will attract. A bit of scrap-iron in contact with a magnet is a magnet. They who live in touch with Him who said, 'I will draw all men unto Me' will share His attractive power in the measure of their union with Him.

The week after the passover feast was, according to the ritual, observed as the feast of unleavened bread. The narrative touches lightly on the ceremonial, and dwells in conclusion on the joy of the worshippers and its cause. They do well to be glad whom God makes glad. All other joy bears in it the seeds of death. It is, in one aspect, the end of God's dealings, that we should be glad in Him. Wise men will not regard that as a less noble end than making us pure; in fact, the two are united. The 'blessed God' is glad in our gladness when it is His gladness.

Notice the exulting wonder with which God's miracle of mercy is reported in its source and its glorious result. The heart of the king was turned to them, and no power but God's could have done that. The issue of that divine intervention was the completed Temple, in which once more the God of that Israel which He had so marvellously restored dwelt in the midst of His people.

GOD THE JOY-BRINGER

'They kept the feast ... seven days with joy; for the Lord had made them joyful.'—EZRA vi. 22.

Twenty years of hard work and many disappointments and dangers had at last, for the Israelites returning from the captivity, been crowned by the completion of the Temple. It was a poor affair as compared with the magnificent house that had stood upon Zion; and so some of them 'despised the day of small things.' They were ringed about by enemies; they were feeble in themselves; there was a great deal to darken their prospects and to sadden their hearts; and yet, when memories of the ancient days came back, and once more they saw the sacrificial smoke rising from the long cold and ruined altar, they rejoiced in God, and they kept the passover amid the ruins, as my text tells us, for the 'seven days' of the statutory period 'with joy,' because, in spite of all, 'the Lord had made them joyful.'

I think if we take this simple saying we get two or three thoughts, not altogether irrelevant to universal experience, about the true and the counterfeit gladnesses possible to us all.

I. Look at that great and wonderful thought—God the joy-maker.

We do not often realise how glad God is when we are glad, and how worthy an object of much that He does is simply the prosperity and the blessedness of human hearts. The poorest creature that lives has a right to ask from God the satisfaction of its instincts, and every man has a claim on God—because he is God's creature—to make him glad. God honours all cheques legitimately drawn on Him, and answers all claims, and regards Himself as occupied in a manner entirely congruous with His magnificence and His infinitude, when He stoops to put some kind of vibrating gladness into the wings of a gnat that dances for an hour in the sunshine, and into the heart of a man that lives his time for only a very little longer.

God is the Joy-maker. There are far more magnificent and sublime thoughts about Him than that; but I do not know that there is any that ought to come nearer to our hearts, and to silence more of our grumblings and of our distrust, than the belief that the gladness of His children is an end contemplated by Him in all that He does. Whether we think it of small importance or no, He does not think it so, that all mankind should rejoice in Himself. And this is a marvellous revelation to break out of the very heart of that comparatively hard system of ancient Judaism. 'The Lord hath made them joyful.'

Turning away from the immediate connection of these words, let me remind you of the great outlines of the divine provision for gladdening men's hearts. I was going to say that God had only one way of making us glad; and perhaps that is in the deepest sense true. That way is by putting Himself into us. He gives us Himself to make us glad; for nothing else will do it—or, at least, though there may be many subordinate sources of joy, if there be in the innermost shrine of our spirits an empty place, where the Shekinah ought to shine, no other joys will suffice to settle and to rejoice the soul. The secret of all true human well-being is close communion with God; and when He looks at the poorest of us, desiring to make us blessed, He can but say, 'I will give Myself to that poor man; to that ignorant creature; to that wayward and prodigal child; to that harlot in her corruption; to that worldling in his narrow godlessness; I will give Myself, if they will have Me.' And thus, and only thus, does He make us truly, perfectly, and for ever glad.

Besides that, or rather as a sequel and consequence of that, there come such other God-given blessings as these to which my text refers. What were the outward reasons for the restored exiles' gladness? 'The Lord had made them joyful, and turned the heart of the king ... unto them to strengthen their hands in the work of the house of God, the God of Israel.'

So, then, He pours into men's lives by His providences the secondary and lower gifts which men, according to changing circumstances, need; and He also satisfies the permanent physical necessities of all orders of beings to whom He has given life. He gives Himself for the spirit; He gives whatever is contributory to any kind of gladness; and if we are wise we shall trace all to Him. He is the Joy-giver; and that man has not yet understood either the sanctity of life or the full sweetness of its sweetest things unless he sees, written over every one of them, the name of God, their giver. Your common mercies are His love tokens, and they all come to us, just as the gifts of parents to their children do, with this on the fly-leaf, 'With a father's love.' Whatever comes to God's child with that inscription, surely it ought to kindle a thrill of gladness. That 'the king of Assyria's heart is turned'; shall we thank the king of Assyria? Yes and No! For it was God who 'turned' it. Oh! to carry the quiet confidence of that thought into all our daily life, and see His name written upon everything that contributes to make us blessed. God is the true Source and Maker of every joy.

And by the side of that we must put this other thought—there are sources of joy with which He has nothing to do. There are people who are joyful—and there are some of them listening now—not because God made them joyful, but because 'the world, the devil, and the flesh' have given them ghastly caricatures of the true gladness. And these rival sources of blessedness, the existence of which my text suggests, are the enemies of all that is good and noble in us and in our joys. God made these men joyful, and so their gladness was wholesome.

II. Note the consequent obligation and wisdom of taking our God-given joys.

'They kept the feast with joy, for the Lord had made them joyful.' Then it is our obligation to accept and use what it is His blessedness to give. Be sure you take Him. When He is waiting to pour all His love into your heart, and all His sweetness into your sensitive spirit, to calm your anxieties, to deepen your blessedness, to strengthen everything that is good in you, to be to you a stay in the midst of crumbling prosperity, and a Light in the midst of gathering darkness, be sure that you take the joy that waits your acceptance.

Do not let it be said that, when the Lord Christ has come down from heaven, and lived upon earth, and gone back to heaven, and sent His Spirit to dwell in you, you lock the door against the entrance of the joy-bringing Messenger, and are sad and restless and discontented because you have shut out the God who desires to abide in your hearts.

'They kept the feast with joy, because the Lord had made them joyful.' Oh! how many Christian men and women there are, who in the midst of the abundant and wonderful provision for continual cheerfulness and buoyancy of spirit given to them in the promises of the Gospel, in the gifts of Christ, in the indwelling of the Divine Spirit, do yet go through life creeping and sad, burdened and anxious, perplexed and at their wits' end, just because they will not have the God who yearns to come to them, or at least will not have Him in anything like the fullness and the completeness in which He desires to bestow Himself. If God gives, surely we are bound to receive. It is an obligation upon Christian men and women, which they do not sufficiently realise, to be glad, and it is a commandment needing to be reiterated. 'Rejoice in the Lord always; and again I say, rejoice.' Would that Christian experience in this generation was more alive to the obligation and the blessedness of perpetual joy arising from perpetual communion with Him.

Further, another obligation is to recognise Him in all common mercies, because He is at the back of them all. Let them always proclaim Him to us. Oh! if we did not go through the world blinded to the real Power that underlies all its motions, we should feel that everything was vocal to us of the loving-kindness of our Father in heaven. Link Him, dear friend! with everything that makes your heart glad; with everything pleasant that comes to you. There is nothing good or sweet but it flows from Him. There is no common delight of flesh or sense, of sight or taste or smell, no little enjoyment that makes the moment pass more brightly, no drop of oil that eases the friction of the wheels of life, but it may be elevated into greatness and nobleness, and will then first be understood in its true significance, if it is connected with Him. God does not desire to be put away high up on a pedestal above our lives, as if He regulated the great things and the trifles regulated themselves; but He seeks to come, as air into the lungs, into every particle of the mass of life, and to fill it all with His own purifying presence.

Recognise Him in common joys. If, when we sit down to partake of them, we would say to ourselves, 'The Lord has made us joyful,' all our home delights, all our social pleasures, all our intellectual and all our sensuous ones—rest and food and drink and all other goods for the body—they would all be felt to be great, as they indeed are. Enjoyed in Him, the smallest is great; without Him, the greatest is small. 'The Lord made them joyful'; and what is large enough for Him to give ought not to be too small for us to receive with recognition of His hand.

Another piece of wholesome counsel in this matter is—Be sure that you use the joys which God does give. Many good people seem to think that it is somehow devout and becoming to pitch most of their songs in a minor key, and to be habitually talking about trials and disappointments, and 'a desert land,' and 'Brief life is here our portion,' and so on, and so on. There are two ways in which you can look at the world and at everything that befalls you. There is enough in everybody's life to make him sad if he sulkily selects these things to dwell upon. There is enough in everybody's life to make him continually glad if he wisely picks out these to think about. It depends altogether on the angle at which you look at your life what you see in it. For instance, you know how children do when they get a bit of a willow wand into their possession. They cut off rings of bark, and get the switch alternately white and black, white and black, and so on right away to the tip. Whether will you look at the white rings or the black ones? They are both there. But if you rightly look at the black you will find out that there is white below it, and it only needs a very little stripping off of a film to make it into white too. Or, to put it into simpler words, no Christian man has the right to regard anything that God's Providence brings to him as such unmingled evil that it ought to make him sad. We are bound to 'rejoice in the Lord always.'

I know how hard it is, but sure am I that it is possible for a man, if he keeps near Jesus Christ, to reproduce Paul's paradox of being 'sorrowful yet always rejoicing,' and even in the midst of darkness and losses and sorrows and blighted hopes and disappointed aims to rejoice in the Lord, and to 'keep the feast with gladness, because the Lord has made him joyful.' Nor do we discharge our duty, unless side by side with the sorrow which is legitimate, which is blessed, strengthening, purifying, calming, moderating, there is also 'joy unspeakable and full of glory.'

Again, be sure that you limit your delights to God-made joys. Too many of us have what parts of our nature recognise as satisfaction, and are glad to have, apart from Him. There is nothing sadder than the joys that come into a life, and do not come from God. Oh! let us see to it that we do not fill our cisterns with poisonous sewage when God is waiting to fill them with the pure 'river of the water of life.' Do not let us draw our blessedness from the world and its evils. Does my joy help me to come near to God? Does it interfere with my communion with Him? Does it aid me in the consecration of myself? Does my conscience go with it when my conscience is most awake? Do I recognise Him as the Giver of the thing that is so blessed? If we can say Yes! to these questions, we can venture to believe that our blessedness comes from God, and leads to God, however homely, however sensuous and material may be its immediate occasion. But if not, then the less we have to do with such sham gladness the better. 'Even in laughter the heart is sorrowful, and the end of that mirth is heaviness.' The alternative presented for the choice of each of us is whether we will have surface joy and a centre of dark discontent, or surface sorrow and a centre of calm blessedness. The film of stagnant water on a pond full of rottenness simulates the glories of the rainbow, in which pure sunshine falls upon the pure drops, but it is only painted corruption after all, a sign of rotting; and if a man puts his lips to it it will kill him. Such is the joy which is apart from God. It is the 'crackling of thorns under a pot'—the more fiercely they burn the sooner they are ashes. And, on the other hand, 'these things have I spoken unto you that My joy might remain in you, and that your joy might be full.'

It is not 'for seven days' that we 'keep the feast' if God has 'made us joyful,' but for all the rest of the days of time, and for the endless years of the calm gladnesses of the heavens.

HEROIC FAITH

'I was ashamed to require of the king a band of soldiers and horsemen to help us against the enemy in the way: because we had spoken unto the king, saying, The hand of our God is upon them all for good that seek Him.... 23. So we fasted and besought our God for this.... 31. The hand of our God was upon us, and He delivered us from the hand of the enemy, and of such as lay in wait by the way. 32. And we came to Jerusalem.'—EZRA viii. 22, 23, 31, 32.

The memory of Ezra the scribe has scarcely had fairplay among Bible-reading people. True, neither his character nor the incidents of his life reach the height of interest or of grandeur belonging to the earlier men and their times. He is no hero, or prophet; only a scribe; and there is a certain narrowness as well as a prosaic turn about his mind, and altogether one feels that he is a smaller man than the Elijahs and Davids of the older days. But the homely garb of the scribe covered a very brave devout heart, and the story of his life deserves to be more familiar to us than it is.

This scrap from the account of his preparations for the march from Babylon to Jerusalem gives us a glimpse of a high-toned faith, and a noble strain of feeling. He and his company had a long weary journey of four months before them. They had had little experience of arms and warfare, or of hardships and desert marches, in their Babylonian homes. Their caravan was made unwieldy and feeble by the presence of a large proportion of women and children. They had much valuable property with them. The stony desert, which stretches unbroken from the Euphrates to the uplands on the east of Jordan, was infested then as now by wild bands of marauders, who might easily swoop down on the encumbered march of Ezra and his men, and make a clean sweep of all which they had. And he knew that he had but to ask and have an escort from the king that would ensure their safety till they saw Jerusalem. Artaxerxes' surname, 'the long-handed,' may have described a physical peculiarity, but it also expressed the reach of his power; his arm could reach these wandering plunderers, and if Ezra and his troop were visibly under his protection, they could march secure. So it was not a small exercise of trust in a higher Hand that is told us here so simply. It took some strength of principle to abstain from asking what it would have been so natural to ask, so easy to get, so comfortable to have. But, as he says, he remembered how confidently he has spoken of God's defence, and he feels that he must be true to his professed creed, even if it deprives him of the king's guards. He halts his followers for three days at the last station before the desert, and there, with fasting and prayer, they put themselves in God's hand; and then the band, with their wives and little ones, and their substance,—a heavily-loaded and feeble caravan,—fling themselves into the dangers of the long, dreary, robber-haunted march. Did not the scribe's robe cover as brave a heart as ever beat beneath a breastplate?

That symbolic phrase, 'the hand of our God,' as expressive of the divine protection, occurs with remarkable frequency in the books of Ezra and Nehemiah, and though not peculiar to them, is yet strikingly characteristic of them. It has a certain beauty and force of its own. The hand is of course the seat of active power. It is on or over a man like some great shield held aloft above him, below which there is safe hiding. So that great Hand bends itself over us, and we are secure beneath its hollow. As a child sometimes carries a tender-winged butterfly in the globe of its two hands that the bloom on the wings may not be ruffled by fluttering, so He carries our feeble, unarmoured souls enclosed in the covert of His Almighty hand. 'Who hath measured the waters in the hollow of His hand?' 'Who hath gathered the wind in His fists?' In that curved palm where all the seas lie as a very little thing, we are held; the grasp that keeps back the tempests from their wild rush, keeps us, too, from being smitten by their blast. As a father may lay his own large muscular hand on his child's tiny fingers to help him, or as 'Elisha put his hands on the king's hands,' that the contact might strengthen him to shoot the 'arrow of the Lord's deliverance,' so the hand of our God is upon us to impart power as well as protection; and our 'bow abides in strength,' when 'the arms of our hands are made strong by the hands of the mighty God of Jacob.' That was Ezra's faith, and that should be ours.

Note Ezra's sensitive shrinking from anything like inconsistency between his creed and his practice. It was easy to talk about God's protection when he was safe behind the walls of Babylon; but now the pinch had come. There was a real danger before him and his unwarlike followers. No doubt, too, there were plenty of people who would have been delighted to catch him tripping; and he felt that his cheeks would have tingled with shame if they had been able to say, 'Ah! that is what all his fine professions come to, is it?

He wants a convoy, does he? We thought as much. It is always so with these people who talk in that style. They are just like the rest of us when the pinch comes.' So, with a high and keen sense of what was required by his avowed principles, he will have no guards for the road. *There* was a man whose religion was at any rate not a fair-weather religion. It did not go off in fine speeches about trusting to the protection of God, spoken from behind the skirts of the king, or from the middle of a phalanx of his soldiers. He clearly meant what he said, and believed every word of it as a prose fact, which was solid enough to build conduct on.

I am afraid a great many of us would rather have tried to reconcile our asking for a band of horsemen with our professed trust in God's hand; and there would have been plenty of excuses very ready about using means as well as exercising faith, and not being called upon to abandon advantages, and not pushing a good principle to Quixotic lengths, and so on, and so on. But whatever truth there is in such considerations, at any rate we may well learn the lesson of this story—to be true to our professed principles; to beware of making our religion a matter of words; to live, when the time for putting them into practice comes, by the maxims which we have been forward to proclaim when there was no risk in applying them; and to try sometimes to look at our lives with the eyes of people who do not share our faith, that we may bring our actions up to the mark of what they expect of us. If 'the Church' would oftener think of what 'the world' looks for from it, it would seldomer have cause to be ashamed of the terrible gap between its words and its deeds.

Especially in regard to this matter of trust in an unseen Hand, and reliance on visible helps, we all need to be very rigid in our self-inspection. Faith in the good hand of God upon us for good should often lead to the abandonment, and always to the subordination, of material aids. It is a question of detail, which each man must settle for himself as each occasion arises, whether in any given case abandonment or subordination is our duty. This is not the place to enter on so large and difficult a question. But, at all events, let us remember, and try to work into our own lives, that principle which the easy-going Christianity of this day has honeycombed with so many exceptions, that it scarcely has any whole surface left at all; that the absolute surrender and forsaking of external helps and goods is sometimes essential to the preservation and due expression of reliance on God.

There is very little fear of any of us pushing that principle to Quixotic lengths. The danger is all the other way. So it is worth while to notice that we have here an instance of a man's being carried by a certain lofty enthusiasm further than the mere law of duty would take him. There would have been no harm in Ezra's asking an escort, seeing that his whole enterprise was made possible by the king's support. He would not have been 'leaning on an arm of flesh' by availing himself of the royal troops, any more than when he used the royal firman. But a true man often feels that he cannot do the things which he might without sin do. 'All things are lawful for me, but all things are not expedient,' said Paul. The same Apostle eagerly contended that he had a perfect right to money support from the Gentile Churches; and then, in the next breath, flamed up into, 'I have used none of these things, for it were better for me to die, than that any man should make my glorying void.' A sensitive spirit, or one profoundly stirred by religious emotion, will, like the apostle whose feet were moved by love, far outrun the slower soul, whose steps are only impelled by the thought of duty. Better that the cup should run over than that it should not be full. Where we delight to do His will, there will often be more than a scrupulously regulated enough; and where there is not sometimes that 'more,' there will never be enough.

'Give all thou canst; high Heaven rejects the lore
Of nicely calculated less or more.'

What shall we say of people who profess that God is their portion, and are as eager in the scramble for money as anybody? What kind of a commentary will sharp-sighted, sharp-tongued observers have a right to make on us, whose creed is so unlike theirs, while our lives are identical? Do you believe, friends! that 'the hand of our God is upon all them for good that seek Him'? Then, do you not think that racing after the prizes of this world, with flushed cheeks and labouring breath, or longing, with a gnawing hunger of heart, for any earthly good, or lamenting over the removal of creatural defences and joys, as if heaven were empty because some one's place here is, or as if God were dead because dear ones die, may well be a shame to us, and a taunt on the lips of our enemies? Let us learn again the lesson from this old story,—that if our faith in God is not the veriest sham, it demands and will produce, the abandonment sometimes and the subordination always, of external helps and material good.

Notice, too, Ezra's preparation for receiving the divine help. There, by the river Ahava, he halts his company like a prudent leader, to repair omissions, and put the last touches to their organisation before facing the wilderness. But he has another purpose also. 'I proclaimed a fast there, to seek of God a right way for us.' There was no foolhardiness in his courage; he was well aware of all the possible dangers on the road; and whilst he is confident of the divine protection, he knows that, in his own quiet, matter-of-fact words, it is given 'to all them that *seek* Him.' So his faith not only impels him to the renunciation of the Babylonian guard, but to earnest supplication for the defence in which he is so confident. He is sure it will be given—so sure, that he will have no other shield; and yet he fasts and prays that he and his company may receive it. He prays because he is sure that he will receive it, and does receive it because he prays and is sure.

So for us, the condition and preparation on and by which we are sheltered by that great Hand, is the faith that asks, and the asking of faith. We must forsake the earthly props, but we must also believingly desire to be upheld by the heavenly arms. We make God responsible for our safety when we abandon other defence, and commit ourselves to Him. With eyes open to our dangers, and full consciousness of our own unarmed and unwarlike weakness, let us solemnly commend ourselves to Him, rolling all our burden on His strong arms, knowing that He is able to keep that which we have committed to Him. He will accept the trust, and set His guards about us. As the song of the returning exiles, which may have been sung by the river Ahava, has it: 'My help cometh from the Lord. The Lord is thy keeper. The Lord is thy shade upon thy right hand.'

So our story ends with the triumphant vindication of this Quixotic faith. A flash of joyful feeling breaks through the simple narrative, as it tells how the words spoken before the king came true in the experience of the weaponless pilgrims: 'The hand of our God *was* upon us, and He delivered us from the hand of the enemy, and of such as lay in wait by the way; and we came to Jerusalem.' It was no rash venture that we made. He was all that we hoped and asked. Through all the weary march He led us. From the wild, desert-born robbers, that watched us from afar, ready to come down on us, from ambushes and hidden perils, He kept us, because we had none other help, and all our hope was in Him. The ventures of faith are ever rewarded. We cannot set our expectations from God too high. What we dare scarcely hope now we shall one day remember. When we come to tell the completed story of our lives, we shall have to record the fulfilment of all God's promises, and the accomplishment of all our prayers that were built on these. Here let us cry, 'Be Thy hand upon us.' Here let us trust, Thy hand will be upon us. Then we shall have to say, 'The hand of our God was upon us,' and as we look from the watch-towers of the city, on the desert that stretches to its very walls, and remember all the way by which He led us, we shall rejoice over His vindication of our poor faith, and praise Him that 'not one thing hath failed of all the things which the Lord our God spake concerning us.'

THE CHARGE OF THE PILGRIM PRIESTS

'Watch ye, and keep them, until ye weigh them … at Jerusalem, in the chambers of the house of the Lord.'—EZRA viii. 29.

The little band of Jews, seventeen hundred in number, returning from Babylon, had just started on that long pilgrimage, and made a brief halt in order to get everything in order for their transit across the desert; when their leader Ezra, taking count of his men, discovers that amongst them there are none of the priests or Levites. He then takes measures to reinforce his little army with a contingent of these, and entrusts to their special care a very valuable treasure in gold, and silver, and sacred vessels, which had been given to them for use in the house of the Lord. The words which I have taken as text are a portion of the charge which he gave to those twelve priestly guardians of the precious things, that were to be used in worship when they got back to the Temple. 'Watch and keep them, until ye weigh them in the chambers of the house of the Lord.'

So I think I may venture, without being unduly fanciful, to take these words as a type of the injunctions which are given to us Christian people; and to see in them a striking and picturesque representation of the duties that devolve upon us in the course of our journey across the desert to the Temple-Home above.

And to begin with, let me remind you, for a moment or two, what the precious treasure is which is thus entrusted to our keeping and care. We can scarcely, in such a connection and with such a metaphor, forget the words of our Lord about a certain king that went to receive his kingdom, and to return; who called together his servants, and gave to each of them according to their several ability, with the injunction to trade upon that until he came. The same metaphor which our Master employed lies in this story before us—in the one case, sacrificial vessels and sacred treasures; in the other case, the talents out of the rich possessions of the departing king.

Nor can we forget either the other phase of the same figure which the Apostle employs when he says to his 'own son' and substitute, Timothy: 'That good thing which was committed unto thee, keep by the Holy Ghost which dwelleth in us,' nor that other word to the same Timothy, which says: 'O Timothy! keep that which was committed to thy trust, and avoid profane and vain babblings, and oppositions of science, falsely so called.' In these quotations, the treasure, and the rich deposit, is the faith once delivered to the saints; the solemn message of love and peace in Jesus Christ, which was entrusted, first of all to those preachers, but as truly to every one of Christ's disciples.

So, then, the metaphor is capable of two applications. The first is to the rich treasure and solemn trust of our own nature, of our own souls; the faculties and capacities, precious beyond all count, rich beyond all else that a man has ever received. Nothing that you have is half so much as that which you are. The possession of a soul that knows and loves, and can obey; that trusts and desires; that can yearn and reach out to Jesus Christ, and to God in Christ; of a conscience that can yield to His command; and faculties of comprehending and understanding what comes to them from Jesus Christ— that is more than any other possession, treasure, or trust. That which you and I carry with us—the infinite possibilities of these awful spirits of ours—the tremendous faculties which are given to every human soul, and which, like a candle plunged into oxygen, are meant to burn far more brightly under the stimulus of Christian faith and the possession of God's truth, are the rich deposit committed to our charge. You priests of the living God, you men and women, you say that you are Christ's, and therefore are consecrated to a nobler priesthood than any other—to you is given this solemn charge: 'That good thing which is committed unto thee, keep by the Holy Ghost that dwelleth in you.' The precious treasure of your own natures, your own hearts, your own understandings, wills, consciences, desires—keep these, until they are weighed in the house of the Lord in Jerusalem.

And in like manner, taking the other aspect of the metaphor—we have given to us, in order that we may do something with it, that great deposit and treasure of truth, which is all embodied and incarnated in Jesus Christ our Lord. It is bestowed upon us that we may use it for ourselves, and in order that we may carry it triumphantly all through the world. Possession involves responsibility always. The word of salvation is given to us. If we go tampering with it, by erroneous apprehension, by unfair usage, by failing to apply it to our own daily life; then it will fade and disappear from our grasp. It is given to us in order that we may keep it safe, and carry it high up across the desert, as becomes the priests of the most high God.

The treasure is first—our own selves—with all that we are and may be, under the stimulating and quickening influence of His grace and Spirit. The treasure is next—His great word of salvation, once delivered unto the saints, and to be handed on, without diminution or alteration in its fair perspective and manifold harmonies, to the generations that are to come. So, think of yourselves as the priests of God, journeying through the wilderness, with the treasures of the Temple and the vessels of the sacrifice for your special deposit and charge.

Further, I touch on the command, the guardianship that is here set forth. 'Watch ye, and keep them.' That is to say, I suppose, according to the ordinary idiom of the Old Testament, 'Watch, in order that you may keep.' Or to translate it into other words: The treasure which is given into our hands requires, for its safe preservation, unceasing vigilance. Take the picture of my text: These Jews were four months, according to the narrative, in travelling from their first station upon their journey to Jerusalem across the desert. There were enemies lying in wait for them by the way. With noble self-restraint and grand chivalry, the leader of the little band says: 'I was ashamed to require of the king a band of soldiers and horsemen, to help us against the enemy in the way; because we had spoken unto the king, saying, The hand of our God is upon all them for good that seek Him; but His power and His wrath is against all that forsake Him.' And so they would not go to him, cap in hand, and ask him to give them a guard to take care of them; but 'We fasted and besought our God for this; and He was intreated of us.'

Thus the little company, without arms, without protection, with nothing but a prayer and a trust to make them strong, flung themselves into the pathless desert with all those precious things in their possession; and all the precaution which Ezra took was to lay hold of the priests in the little party, and to say: 'Here! all through the march do you stick by these precious things. Whoever sleeps, do you watch. Whoever is careless, be you vigilant. Take these for your charge, and remember I weigh them here before we start, and they will be all weighed again when we get there. So be alert.'

And is not that exactly what Christ says to us? 'Watch; keep them; be vigilant, that ye may keep; and keep them, because they will be weighed and registered when you arrive there.'

I cannot do more than touch upon two or three of the ways in which this charge may be worked out, in its application for ourselves, beginning with that first one which is implied in the words of the text—*unslumbering vigilance*; then *trust*, like the trust which is glorified in the context, depending only on 'the good hand of our God upon us'; then *purity*, because, as Ezra said, 'Ye are holy unto the Lord. The vessels are holy also'; and therefore ye are the fit persons to guard them. And besides these, there is, in our keeping our trust, a method which does not apply to the incident before us; namely, *use*, in order to their preservation.

That is to say, first of all, no slumber; not a moment's relaxation; or some of those who lie in wait for us on the way will be down upon us, and some of the precious things will go. While all the rest of the wearied camp slept, the guardians of the treasure had to outwatch the stars. While others might straggle on the march, lingering here or there, or resting on some patch of green, they had to close up round their precious charge; others might let their eyes wander from the path, they had ever to look to their charge. For them the journey had a double burden, and unslumbering vigilance was their constant duty.

We likewise have unslumberingly and ceaselessly to watch over that which is committed to our charge. For, depend upon it, if for an instant we turn away our heads, the thievish birds that flutter over us will be down upon the precious seed that is in our basket, or that we have sown in the furrows, and it will be gone. Watch, that ye may keep.

And then, still further, see how in this story before us there are brought out very picturesquely, and very simply, deeper lessons still. It is not enough that a man shall be for ever keeping his eye upon his own character and his own faculties, and seeking sedulously to cultivate and improve them, as he that must give an account. There must be another look than that. Ezra said, in effect, 'Not all the cohorts of Babylon can help us; and we do not want them. We have one strong hand that will keep us safe'; and so he, and his men, with all this mass of wealth, so tempting to the wild robbers that haunted the road, flung themselves into the desert, knowing that all along it there were, as he says, 'such as lay in wait for them.' His confidence was: 'God will bring us all safe out to the end there; and we shall carry every glittering piece of the precious things that we brought out of Babylon right into the Temple of Jerusalem.' Yet he says, 'Watch ye and keep them.'

What does that come to in reference to our religious experience? Why this: 'Work out your own salvation with fear and trembling; for it is God that worketh in you, both to will and to do of His own good pleasure.' You do not need these external helps. Fling yourself wholly upon His keeping hand, and also watch and keep yourselves. 'I know in whom I have believed, and that He is able to keep that which I have committed unto Him against that day,' is the complement of the other words, 'That good thing which was committed unto thee, keep by the Holy Ghost.'

So guardianship is, first, unceasing vigilance; and then it is lowly trust. And besides that, it is *punctilious purity.* 'I said unto them, Ye are holy unto the Lord; the vessels are holy unto the Lord. Watch ye, and keep them.'

It was fitting that priests should carry the things that belonged to the Temple. No other hands but consecrated hands had a right to touch them. To none other guardianship but the guardianship of the possessors of a symbolic and ceremonial purity, could the vessels of a symbolic and ceremonial worship be entrusted; and to none others but the possessors of real and spiritual holiness can the treasures of the true Temple, of an inward and spiritual worship, be entrusted. 'Be ye clean that bear the vessels of the Lord,' said Isaiah using a kindred metaphor. The only way to keep our treasure undiminished and untarnished, is to keep ourselves pure and clean.

And, lastly, we have to exercise a guardianship which not only means unslumbering vigilance, lowly trust, punctilious purity, but also requires the constant use of the treasure.

'Watch ye, and keep them.' Although the vessels which those priests bore through the desert were used for no service during all the weary march, they weighed just the same when they got to the end as at the beginning; though, no doubt, even their fine gold had become dim and tarnished through disuse. But if we do not use the vessels that are entrusted to our care, *they* will *not* weigh the same. The man that wrapped up his talent in the napkin, and said, 'Lo, there thou hast that is thine,' was too sanguine. There was never an unused talent rolled up in a handkerchief yet, but when it was taken out and put into the scales it was lighter than when it was committed to the keeping of the earth. Gifts that are used fructify. Capacities that are strained to the uttermost increase. Service strengthens the power for service; and just as the reward for work is more work, the way for making ourselves fit for bigger things is to do the things that are lying by us. The blacksmith's arm, the sailor's eye, the organs of any piece of handicraft, as we all know, are strengthened by exercise; and so it is in this higher region.

And so, dear brethren, take these four words—vigilance, trust, purity, exercise. 'Watch ye, and keep them, until they are weighed in the chambers of the House of the Lord.'

And, lastly, think of that weighing in the House of the Lord. Cannot you see the picture of the little band when they finally reach the goal of their pilgrimage; and three days after they arrived, as the narrative tells us, went up into the Temple, and there, by number and by weight, rendered up their charge, and were clear of their responsibility? 'And the first came and said, Lord, thy pound hath gained ten pounds. And he said, Well, thou good servant, because thou hast been faithful in a very little, have thou authority over ten cities.'

Oh! how that thought of the day when they would empty out the rich treasure upon the marble pavement, and clash the golden vessels into the scales, must have filled their hearts with vigilance during all the weary watches, when desert stars looked down upon the slumbering encampment, and they paced wakeful all the night. And how the thought, too, must have filled their hearts with joy, when they tried to picture to themselves the sigh of satisfaction, and the sense of relief with which, after all the perils, their 'feet would stand within thy gates, O Jerusalem,' and they would be able to say, 'That which thou hast given us, we have kept, and nothing of it is lost.'

A lifetime would be a small expenditure to secure that; and though it cannot be that you and I will meet the trial and the weighing of that great day without many failures and much loss, yet we may say: 'I know in whom I have believed, and that He is able to keep my deposit—whether it be in the sense of that which I have committed unto Him, or in the sense of that which He has committed unto me—against that day.' We may hope that, by His gracious help and His pitying acceptance, even such careless stewards and negligent watchers as we are, may lay ourselves down in peace at the last, saying, 'I have kept the faith,' and may be awakened by the word, 'Well done! good and faithful servant.'

THE BOOK OF NEHEMIAH

A REFORMER'S SCHOOLING

'The words of Nehemiah the son of Hachaliah. And it came to pass in the month Chislev, in the twentieth year, as I was in Shushan the palace, 2. That Hanani, one of my brethren, came, he and certain men of Judah; and I asked them concerning the Jews that had escaped, which were left of the captivity, and concerning Jerusalem. 3. And they said unto me, The remnant that are left of the captivity there in the province are in great affliction and reproach: the wall of Jerusalem also is broken down, and the gates thereof are burned with fire. 4. And it came to pass, when I heard these words, that I sat down and wept, and mourned certain days, and fasted, and prayed before the God of heaven, 5. And said, I beseech Thee, O Lord God of heaven, the great and terrible God, that keepeth covenant and mercy for them that love Him and observe His commandments: 6. Let Thine ear now be attentive, and Thine eyes open, that Thou mayest hear the prayer of Thy servant, which I pray before Thee now, day and night, for the children of Israel Thy servants, and confess the sins of the children of Israel, which we have sinned against Thee: both I and my father's house have sinned. 7. We have dealt very corruptly against Thee, and have not kept the commandments, nor the statutes, nor the judgments, which Thou commandedst Thy servant Moses. 8. Remember, I beseech Thee, the word that Thou commandedst Thy servant Moses, saying, If ye transgress, I will scatter you abroad among the nations: 9. But if ye turn unto Me, and keep My commandments, and do them; though there were of you cast out unto the uttermost part of the heaven, yet will I gather them from thence, and will bring them unto the place that I have chosen to set My name there. 10. Now these are Thy servants and Thy people, whom Thou hast redeemed by Thy great power, and by Thy strong hand. 11. O Lord, I beseech Thee, let now Thine ear be attentive to the prayer of Thy servant, and to the prayer of Thy servants, who desire to fear Thy name: and prosper, I pray Thee, Thy servant this day, and grant him mercy in the sight of this man. For I was the king's cupbearer.'—NEH. i. 1-11.

The date of the completion of the Temple is 516 B.C.; that of Nehemiah's arrival 445 B.C. The colony of returned exiles seems to have made little progress during that long period. Its members settled down, and much of their enthusiasm cooled, as we see from the reforms which Ezra had to inaugurate fourteen years before Nehemiah. The majority of men, even if touched by spiritual fervour, find it hard to keep on the high levels for long. Breathing is easier lower down. As is often the case, a brighter flame of zeal burned in the bosoms of sympathisers at a distance than in those of the actual workers, whose contact with hard realities and petty details disenchanted them. Thus the impulse to nobler action came, not from one of the colony, but from a Jew in the court of the Persian king.

This passage tells us how God prepared a man for a great work, and how the man prepared himself.

I. Sad tidings and their effect on a devout servant of God (vs. 1-4). The time and place are precisely given. 'The month Chislev' corresponds to the end of November and beginning of December. 'The twentieth year' is that of Artaxerxes (Neh. ii. 1). 'Shushan,' or Susa, was the royal winter residence, and 'the palace' was 'a distinct quarter of the city, occupying an artificial eminence.' Note the absence of the name of the king. Nehemiah is so familiar with his greatness that he takes for granted that every reader can fill the gaps. But, though the omission shows how large a space the court occupied in his thoughts, a true Jewish heart beat below the courtier's robe. That flexibility which enabled them to stand as trusted servants of the kings of many lands, and yet that inflexible adherence to, and undying love of, Israel, has always been a national characteristic. We can think of this youthful cup-bearer as yearning for one glimpse of the 'mountains round about Jerusalem' while he filled his post in Shushan.

His longings were kindled into resolve by intercourse with a little party of Jews from Judaea, among whom was his own brother. They had been to see how things went there, and the fact that one of them was a member of Nehemiah's family seems to imply that the same sentiments belonged to the whole household. Eager questions brought out sorrowful answers. The condition of the 'remnant' was one of 'great affliction and reproach,' and the ground of the reproach was probably (Neh. ii. 17; iv. 2-4) the still ruined fortifications.

It has been supposed that the breaking down of the walls and burning of the gates, mentioned in verse 3, were recent, and subsequent to the events recorded in Ezra; but it is more probable that the project for rebuilding the defences, which had been stopped by superior orders (Ezra iv. 12-16), had not been resumed, and that the melancholy ruins were those which had met the eyes of Zerubbabel nearly a hundred years before. Communication between Shushan and Jerusalem cannot have been so infrequent that the facts now borne in on Nehemiah might not have been known before. But the impression made by facts depends largely on their narrator, and not a little on the mood of the hearer. It was one thing to hear general statements, and another to sit with one's brother, and see through his eyes the dismal failure of the 'remnant' to carry out the purpose of their return. So the story, whether fresh or repeated with fresh force, made a deep dint in the young cupbearer's heart, and changed his life's outlook. God prepares His servants for their work by laying on their souls a sorrowful realisation of the miseries which other men regard, and they themselves have often regarded, very lightly. The men who have been raised up to do great work for God and men, have always to begin by greatly and sadly feeling the weight of the sins and sorrows which they are destined to remove. No man will do worthy work at rebuilding the walls who has not wept over the ruins.

So Nehemiah prepared himself for his work by brooding over the tidings with tears, by fasting and by prayer. There is no other way of preparation. Without the sad sense of men's sorrows, there will be no earnestness in alleviating them, nor self-sacrificing devotion; and without much prayer there will be little consciousness of weakness or dependence on divine help.

Note the grand and apparently immediate resolution to throw up brilliant prospects and face a life of danger and suffering and toil. Nehemiah was evidently a favourite with the king, and had the ball at his foot. But the ruins on Zion were more attractive to him than the splendours of Shushan, and he willingly flung away his chances of a great career to take his share of 'affliction and reproach.' He has never had justice done him in popular estimation. He is not one of the well-known biblical examples of heroic self-abandonment; but he did just what Moses did, and the eulogium of the Epistle to the Hebrews fits him as well as the lawgiver; for he too chose 'rather to suffer with the people of God than to enjoy pleasures for a season.' So must we all, in our several ways, do, if we would have a share in building the walls of the city of God.

II. The prayer (vs. 5-11). The course of thought in this prayer is very instructive. It begins with solemnly laying before God His own great name, as the mightiest plea with Him, and the strongest encouragement to the suppliant. That commencement is no mere proper invocation, conventionally regarded as the right way of beginning, but it expresses the petitioner's effort to lay hold on God's character as the ground of his hope of answer. The terms employed remarkably blend what Nehemiah had learned from Persian religion and what from a better source. He calls upon Jehovah, the great name which was the special possession of Israel. He also uses the characteristic Persian designation of 'the God of heaven,' and identifies the bearer of that name, not with the god to whom it was originally applied, but with Israel's Jehovah. He takes the crown from the head of the false deity, and lays it at the feet of the God of his fathers. Whatsoever names for the Supreme Excellence any tongues have coined, they all belong to our God, in so far as they are true and noble. The modern 'science of comparative religion' yields many treasures which should be laid up in Jehovah's Temple.

But the rest of the designations are taken from the Old Testament, as was fitting. The prayer throughout is full of allusions and quotations, and shows how this cupbearer of Artaxerxes had fed his young soul on God's word, and drawn thence the true nourishment of high and holy thoughts and strenuous resolutions and self-sacrificing deeds. Prayers which are cast in the mould of God's own revelation of Himself will not fail of answer. True prayer catches up the promises that flutter down to us, and flings them up again like arrows.

The prayer here is all built, then, on that name of Jehovah, and on what the name involves, chiefly on the thought of God as keeping covenant and mercy. He has bound Himself in solemn, irrefragable compact, to a certain line of action. Men 'know where to have Him,' if we may venture on the familiar expression. He has given us a chart of His course, and He will adhere to it. Therefore we can go to Him with our prayers, so long as we keep these within the ample space of His covenant, and ourselves within its terms, by loving obedience.

The petition that God's ears might be sharpened and His eyes open to the prayer is cast in a familiar mould. It boldly transfers to Him not only the semblance of man's form, but also the likeness of His processes of action. Hearing the cry for help precedes active intervention in the case of men's help, and the strong imagery of the prayer conceives of similar sequence in God. But the figure is transparent, and the 'anthropomorphism' so plain that no mistakes can arise in its interpretation.

Note, too, the light touch with which the suppliant's relation to God ('Thy servant') and his long-continued cry ('day and night') are but just brought in for a moment as pleas for a gracious hearing. The prayer is 'for Thy servants the children of Israel,' in which designation, as the next clauses show, the relation established by God, and not the conduct of men, is pleaded as a reason for an answer.

The mention of that relation brings at once to Nehemiah's mind the terrible unfaithfulness to it which had marked, and still continued to mark, the whole nation. So lowly confession follows (vs. 6, 7). Unprofitable servants they had indeed been. The more loftily we think of our privileges, the more clearly should we discern our sins. Nothing leads a true heart to such self-ashamed penitence as reflection on God's mercy. If a man thinks that God has taken him for a servant, the thought should bow him with conscious unworthiness, not lift him in self-satisfaction. Nehemiah's confession not only sprung from the thought of Israel's vocation, so poorly fulfilled, but it also laid the groundwork for further petitions. It is useless to ask God to help us to repair the wastes if we do not cast out the sins which have made them. The beginning of all true healing of sorrow is confession of sins. Many promising schemes for the alleviation of national and other distresses have come to nothing because, unlike Nehemiah's, they did not begin with prayer, or prayed for help without acknowledging sin.

And the man who is to do work for God and to get God to bless his work must not be content with acknowledging other people's sins, but must always say, 'We have sinned,' and not seldom say, 'I have sinned.' That penitent consciousness of evil is indispensible to all who would make their fellows happier. God works with bruised reeds. The sense of individual transgression gives wonderful tenderness, patience amid gainsaying, submission in failure, dependence on God in difficulty, and lowliness in success. Without it we shall do little for ourselves or for anybody else.

The prayer next reminds God of His own words (vs. 8,9), freely quoted and combined from several passages (Lev. xxvi. 33-45; Deut. iv. 25-31, etc.). The application of these passages to the then condition of things is at first sight somewhat loose, since part of the people were already restored; and the purport of the prayer is not the restoration of the remainder, but the deliverance of those already in the land from their distresses. Still, the promise gives encouragement to the prayer and is powerful with God, inasmuch as it could not be said to have been fulfilled by so incomplete a restoration as that as that at present realised. What God does must be perfectly done; and His great word is not exhausted so long as any fuller accomplishment of it can be imagined.

The reminder of the promise is clinched (v. 10) by the same appeal as formerly to the relation to Himself into which God had been pleased to bring the nation, with an added reference to former deeds, such as the Exodus, in which His strong hand had delivered them. We are always sure of an answer if we ask God not to contradict Himself. Since He has begun He will make an end. It will never be said of Him that He 'began to build and was not able to finish.' His past is a mirror in which we can read His future. The return from Babylon is implied in the Exodus.

A reiteration of earlier words follows, with the addition that Nehemiah now binds, as it were, his single prayer in a bundle with those of the like-minded in Israel. He gathers single ears into a sheaf, which he brings as a 'wave-offering.' And then, in one humble little sentence at the end, he puts his only personal request. The modesty of the man is lovely. His prayer has been all for the people. Remarkably enough, there is no definite petition in it. He never once says right out what he so earnestly desires, and the absence of specific requests might be laid hold of by sceptical critics as an argument against the genuineness of the prayer. But it is rather a subtle trait, on which no forger would have been likely to hit. Sometimes silence is the very result of entire occupation of mind with a thought. He says nothing about the particular nature of his request, just because he is so full of it. But he does ask for favour in the eyes of 'this man,' and that he may be prospered 'this day.'

So this was his morning prayer on that eventful day, which was to settle his life's work. The certain days of solitary meditation on his nation's griefs had led to a resolution. He says nothing about his long brooding, his slow decision, his conflicts with lower projects of personal ambition. He 'burns his own smoke,' as we all should learn to do. But he asks that the capricious and potent will of the king may be inclined to grant his request. If our morning supplication is 'Prosper Thy servant this day,' and our purposes are for God's glory, we need not fear facing anybody. However powerful Artaxerxes was, he was but 'this man,' not God. The phrase does not indicate contempt or undervaluing of the solid reality of his absolute power over Nehemiah, but simply expresses the conviction that the king, too, was a subject of God's, and that his heart was in the hand of Jehovah, to mould as He would. The consciousness of dependence on God and the habit of communion with Him give a man a clear sight of the limitations of earthly dignities, and a modest boldness which is equally remote from rudeness and servility.

Thus prepared for whatever might be the issue of that eventful day, the young cupbearer rose from his knees, drew a long breath, and went to his work. Well for us if we go to ours, whether it be a day of crisis or of commonplace, in like fashion! Then we shall have like defence and like calmness of heart.

THE CHURCH AND SOCIAL EVILS

'It came to pass, when I heard these words, that I sat down and wept, and mourned certain days, and fasted, and prayed before the God of heaven.'—NEH. i. 4.

Ninety years had passed since the returning exiles had arrived at Jerusalem. They had encountered many difficulties which had marred their progress and cooled their enthusiasm. The Temple, indeed, was rebuilt, but Jerusalem lay in ruins, and its walls remained as they had been left, by Nebuchadnezzar's siege, some century and a half before. A little party of pious pilgrims had gone from Persia to the city, and had come back to Shushan with a sad story of weakness and despondency, affliction and hostility. One of the travellers had a brother, a youth named Nehemiah, who was a cup-bearer in the court of the Persian king. Living in a palace, and surrounded with luxury, his heart was with his brethren; and the ruins of Jerusalem were dearer to him than the pomp of Shushan.

My text tells how the young cupbearer was affected by the tidings, and how he wept and prayed before God. The accurate dates given in this book show that this period of brooding contemplation of the miseries of his brethren lasted for four months. Then he took a great resolution, flung up brilliant prospects, identified himself with the afflicted colony, and asked for leave to go and share, and, if it might be, to redress, the sorrows which had made so deep a dint upon his heart.

Now, I think that this vivid description, drawn by himself, of the emotions excited in Nehemiah by his countrymen's sorrows, which influenced his whole future, contains some very plain lessons for Christian people, the observance of which is every day becoming more imperative by reason of the drift of public opinion, and the new prominence which is being given to so-called 'social questions.' I wish to gather up one or two of these lessons for you now.

I. First, then, note the plain Christian duty of sympathetic contemplation of surrounding sorrows. Nehemiah might have made a great many very good excuses for treating lightly the tidings that his brother had brought him. He might have said: 'Jerusalem is a long way off. I have my own work to do; it is no part of my business to rebuild the walls of Jerusalem. I am the King's cupbearer. They went with their eyes open, and experience has shown that the people who knew when they were well off, and stayed where they were, were a great deal wiser.' These were not his excuses. He let the tidings fill his heart, and burn there.

Now, the first condition of sympathy is knowledge; and the second is attending to what we do know. Nehemiah had probably known, in a kind of vague way, for many a day how things were going in Palestine. Communications between it and Persia were not so difficult but that there would come plenty of Government despatches; and a man at headquarters who had the ear of the monarch, was not likely to be ignorant of what was going on in that part of his dominions. But there is all the difference between hearing vague general reports, and sitting and hearing your own brother tell you what he had seen with his own eyes. So the impression which had existed before was all inoperative until it was kindled by attention to the facts which all the time had been, in some degree, known.

Now, how many of us are there that know—and don't know—what is going on round about us in the slums and back courts of this city? How many of us are there who are habitually ignorant of what we actually know, because we never, as we say, 'give heed' to it. 'I did not think of that,' is a very poor excuse about matters concerning which there is knowledge, whether there is thought or not. And so I want to press upon all you Christian people the plain duty of knowing what you do know, and of giving an ample place in your thoughts to the stark staring facts around us.

Why! loads of people at present seem to think that the miseries, and hideous vices, and sodden immorality, and utter heathenism, which are found down amongst the foundations of every civic community are as indispensable to progress as the noise of the wheels of a train is to its advancement, or as the bilge-water in a wooden ship is to keep its seams tight. So we prate about 'civilisation,' which means turning men into cities. If agglomerating people into these great communities, which makes so awful a feature of modern life, be necessarily attended by such abominations as we live amongst and never think about, then, better that there had never been civilisation in such a sense at all. Every consideration of communion with and conformity to Jesus Christ, of loyalty to His words, of a true sense of brotherhood and of lower things—such as self-interest—every consideration demands that Christian people shall take to their hearts, in a fashion that the churches have never done yet, 'the condition of England question,' and shall ask, 'Lord! what wouldst Thou have me to do?'

I do not care to enter upon controversy raised by recent utterances, the motive of which may be worthy of admiration, though the expression cannot be acquitted of the charge of exaggeration, to the effect that the Christian churches as a whole have been careless of the condition of the people. It is not true in its absolute sense. I suppose that, taking the country over, the majority of the members of, at all events the Nonconformist churches and congregations, are in receipt of weekly wages or belong to the upper ranks of the working-classes, and that the lever which has lifted them to these upper ranks has been God's Gospel. I suppose it will be admitted that the past indifference with which we are charged belonged to the whole community, and that the new sense of responsibility which has marked, and blessedly marked, recent years, is largely owing to political and other causes which have lately come into operation. I suppose it will not be denied that, to a very large extent, any efforts which have been made in the past for the social, intellectual, and moral, and religious elevation of the people have had their impulse, and to a large extent their support, both pecuniary and active, from Christian churches and individuals. All that is perfectly true and, I believe, undeniable. But it is also true that there remains an enormous, shameful, dead mass of inertness in our churches, and that, unless we can break up that, the omens are bad, bad for society, worse for the church. If cholera is raging in the slums, the suburbs will not escape. If the hovels are infected, the mansions will have to pay their tribute to the disease. If we do not recognise the brotherhood of the suffering and the sinful, in any other fashion—'Then,' as a great teacher told us a generation ago now, and nobody paid any attention to him, 'then they will begin and show you that they are your brethren by killing some of you.' And so self-preservation conjoins with loftier motives to make this sympathetic observation of the surrounding sorrows the plainest of Christian duties.

II. Secondly, such a realisation of the dark facts is indispensable to all true work for alleviating them.

There is no way of helping men out by bearing what they bear. No man will ever lighten a sorrow of which he has not himself felt the pressure. Jesus Christ's Cross, to which we are ever appealing as the ground of our redemption and the anchor of our hope, is these, thank God! But it is more than these. It is the pattern for our lives, and it lays down, with stringent accuracy and completeness, the enduring conditions of helping the sinful and the sorrowful. The 'saviours of society' have still, in lower fashion, to be crucified. Jesus Christ would never have been 'the Lamb of God that bore away the sins of the world' unless He Himself had 'taken our infirmities and borne our sicknesses.' No work of any real use will be done except by those whose hearts have bled with the feeling of the miseries which they set themselves to cure.

Oh! we all want a far fuller realisation of that sympathetic spirit of the pitying Christ, if we are ever to be of any use in the world, or to help the miseries of any of our brethren. Such a sorrowful and participating contemplation of men's sorrows springing from men's sins will give tenderness to our words, will give patience, will soften our whole bearing. Help that is flung to people, as you might fling a bone to a dog, hurts those whom it tries to help, and patronising help is help that does little good, and lecturing help does little more. You must take blind beggars by the hand if you are going to make them see; and you must not be afraid to lay your white, clean fingers upon the feculent masses of corruption in the leper's glistening whiteness if you are going to make him whole. Go down in order to lift, and remember that without sympathy there is no sufficient help, and without communion with Christ there is no sufficient sympathy.

III. Thirdly, such realisation of surrounding sorrows should drive to communion with God.

Nehemiah wept and mourned, and that was well. But between his weeping and mourning and his practical work there had to be still another link of connection. 'He wept and mourned,' and because he was sad he turned to God, 'and I fasted and prayed certain days.' There he got at once comfort for his sorrows, his sympathies, and deepening of his sympathies, and thence he drew inspiration that made him a hero and a martyr. So all true service for the world must begin with close communion with God.

There was a book published several years since which made a great noise in its little day, and called itself *The Service of Man*, which service it proposed to substitute for the effete conception of worship as the service of God. The service of man is, then, best done when it is the service of God. I suppose nowadays it is 'old-fashioned' and 'narrow,' which is the sin of sins at present, but I for my part have very little faith in the persistence and wide operation of any philanthropic motives except the highest—namely, compassion caught from Jesus Christ. I do not believe that you will get men, year in and year out, to devote themselves in any considerable numbers to the service of man unless you appeal to this highest of motives. You may enlist a little corps—and God forbid that I should deny such a plain fact—of selecter spirits to do purely secular alleviative work, with an entire ignoring of Christian motives, but you will never get the army of workers that is needed to grapple with the facts of our present condition, unless you touch the very deepest springs of conduct, and these are to be found in communion with God. All the rest is surface drainage. Get down to the love of God, and the love of men therefrom, and you have got an Artesian well which will bubble up unfailingly.

And I have not much faith in remedies which ignore religion, and are brought, without communion with God, as sufficient for the disease. I do not want to say one word that might seem to depreciate what are good and valid and noble efforts in their several spheres. There is no need for antagonism—rather, Christian men are bound by every consideration to help to the utmost of their power, even in the incomplete attempts that are made to grapple with social problems. There is room enough for us all. But sure I am that until grapes and waterbeds cure smallpox, and a spoonful of cold water puts out Vesuvius, you will not cure the evils of the body politic by any lesser means than the application of the Gospel of Jesus Christ.

We hear a great deal to-day about a 'social gospel,' and I am glad of the conception, and of the favour which it receives. Only let us remember that the Gospel is social *second*, and individual *first*. And that if you get the love of God and obedience to Jesus Christ into a man's heart it will be like putting gas into a balloon, it will go up, and the man will get out of the slums fast enough; and he will not be a slave to the vices of the world much longer, and you will have done more for him and for the wide circle that he may influence than by any other means. I do not want to depreciate any helpers, but I say it is the work of the Christian church to carry to the world the only thing that will make men deeply and abidingly happy, because it will make them good.

IV. And so, lastly, such sympathy should be the parent of a noble, self-sacrificing life. Look at the man in our text. He had the ball at his feet. He had the *entree* of a court, and the ear of a king. Brilliant prospects were opening before him, but his brethren's sufferings drew him, and with a noble resolution of self-sacrifice, he shut himself out from the former and went into the wilderness. He is one of the Scripture characters that never have had due honour—a hero, a saint, a martyr, a reformer. He did, though in a smaller sphere, the very same thing that the writer of the Epistle to the Hebrews magnified with his splendid eloquence, in reference to the great Lawgiver, 'And chose rather to suffer affliction with the people of God,' and to turn his back upon the dazzlements of a court, than to 'enjoy the pleasures of sin for a season,' whilst his brethren were suffering.

Now, dear friends! the letter of the example may be put aside; the spirit of it must be observed. If Christians are to do the work that they can do, and that Christ has put them into this world that they may do, there must be self-sacrifice with it. There is no shirking that obligation, and there is no discharging our duty without it. You and I, in our several ways, are as much under the sway of that absolute law, that 'if a corn of wheat fall into the ground and die, it brings forth fruit,' as ever was Jesus Christ or His Apostles. I have nothing to say about the manner of the sacrifice. It is no part of my business to prescribe to you details of duty. It is my business to insist on the principles which must regulate these, and of these principles in application to Christian service there is none more stringent than—'I will not offer unto my God burnt-offering of that which doth cost me nothing.'

I am sure that, under God, the great remedy for social evils lies mainly here, that the bulk of professing Christians shall recognise and discharge their responsibilities. It is not ministers, city missionaries, Bible-women, or any other paid people that can do the work. It is by Christian men and by Christian women, and, if I might use a very vulgar distinction which has a meaning in the present connection, very specially by Christian ladies, taking their part in the work amongst the degraded and the outcasts, that our sorest difficulties and problems will be solved. If a church does not face these, well, all I can say is, its light will go out; and the sooner the better. 'If thou forbear to deliver them that are appointed to death, and say, Behold! I knew it not, shall not He that weigheth the hearts consider it, and shall He not render to every man according to his work?' And, on the other hand, there are no blessings more rich, select, sweet, and abiding, than are to be found in sharing the sorrow of the Man of Sorrows, and carrying the message of His pity and His redemption to an outcast world. 'If thou draw out thy soul to the hungry, and satisfy the afflicted soul, the Lord shall satisfy thy soul; and thou shalt be as a watered garden, and as a spring of water whose waters fail not.'

'OVER AGAINST HIS HOUSE'

'The priests repaired every one over against his house.'—NEH. iii. 28.

The condition of our great cities has lately been forced upon public attention, and all kinds of men have been offering their panaceas. I am not about to enter upon that discussion, but I am glad to seize the opportunity of saying one or two things which I think very much need to be said to individual Christian people about their duty in the matter. 'Every man over against his house' is the principle I desire to commend to you as going a long way to solve the problem of how to sweeten the foul life of our modern cities.

The story from which my text is taken does not need to detain us long. Nehemiah and his little band of exiles have come back to a ruined Jerusalem. Their first care is to provide for their safety, and the first step is to know the exact extent of their defencelessness. So we have the account of Nehemiah's midnight ride amongst the ruins of the broken walls. And then we read of the co-operation of all classes in the work of reconstruction. 'Many hands made light work.' Men and women, priests and nobles, goldsmiths, apothecaries, merchants, all seized trowel or spade, and wheeled and piled. One man puts up a long length of wall, another can only manage a little bit; another undertakes the locks, bolts, and bars for the gates. Roughly and hastily the work is done. The result, of course, is very unlike the stately structures of Solomon's or of Herod's time, but it is enough for shelter. We can imagine the sigh of relief with which the workers looked upon the completed circle of their rude fortifications.

The principle of division of labour in our text is repeated several times in this list of the builders. It was a natural one; a man would work all the better when he saw his own roof mutely appealing to be defended, and thought of the dear ones that were there. But I take these words mainly as suggesting some thoughts applicable to the duties of Christian people in view of the spiritual wants of our great cities.

I. I need not do more than say a word or two about the ruins which need repair. If I dwell rather upon the dark side than on the bright side of city life I shall not be understood, as forgetting that the very causes which intensify the evil of a great city quicken the good—the friction of multitudes and the impetus thereby given to all kinds of mental activity. Here amongst us there is much that is admirable and noble—much public spirit, much wise and benevolent expenditure of thought and toil for the general good, much conjoint action by men of different parties, earnest antagonism and earnest co-operation, and a free, bracing intellectual atmosphere, which stimulates activity. All that is true, though, on the other hand, it is not good to live always within hearing of the clatter of machinery and the strife of tongues; and the wisdom that is born of solitary meditation and quiet thought is less frequently met with in cities than is the cleverness that is born of intercourse with men, and newspaper reading.

But there is a tragic other side to all that, which mostly we make up our minds to say little about and to forget. The indifference which has made that ignorance possible, and has in its turn been fed by the ignorance, is in some respects a more shocking phenomenon than the vicious life which it has allowed to rot and to reek unheeded.

Most of us have got so familiarised with the evils that stare us in the face every time we go out upon the pavements, that we have come to think of them as being inseparable from our modern life, like the noise of a carriage wheel from its rotation. And is it so then? Is it indeed inevitable that within a stone's throw of our churches and chapels there should be thousands of men and women that have never been inside a place of worship since they were christened; and have no more religion than a horse? Must it be that the shining structure of our modern society, like an old Mexican temple, must be built upon a layer of living men, flung in for a foundation? Can it not be helped that there should be streets in our cities into which it is unfit for a decent woman to go by day alone, and unsafe for a brave man to venture after nightfall? Must men and women huddle together in dens where decency is as impossible as it is for swine in a sty? Is it an indispensable part of our material progress and wonderful civilisation that vice and crime and utter irreligion and hopeless squalor should go with it? Can all that bilge water really not be pumped out of the ship? If it be so, then I venture to say that, to a very large extent, progress is a delusion, and that the simple life of agricultural communities is better than this unwholesome aggregation of men.

The beginning of Nehemiah's work of repair was that sad midnight ride round the ruined walls. So there is a solemn obligation laid on Christian people to acquaint themselves with the awful facts, and then to meditate on them, till sacred, Christ-like compassion, pressing against the flood-gates of the heart, flings them open, and lets out a stream of helpful pity and saving deeds.

II. So much for my first point. My second is—the ruin is to be repaired mainly by the old Gospel of Jesus Christ. Far be it from me to pit remedies against each other. The causes are complicated, and the cure must be as manifold as the causes. For my own part I believe that, in regard to the condition of the lowest of our outcast population, drink and lust have done it almost all, and that for all but an infinitesimal portion of it, intemperance is directly or indirectly the cause. That has to be fought by the distinct preaching of abstinence, and by the invoking of legislative restrictions upon the traffic. Wretched homes have to be dealt with by sanitary reform, which may require municipal and parliamentary action. Domestic discomfort has to be dealt with by teaching wives the principles of domestic economy. The gracious influence of art and music, pictures and window-gardening, and the like, will lend their aid to soften and refine. Coffee taverns, baths and wash-houses, workmen's clubs, and many other agencies are doing real and good work. I for one say, 'God speed to them all,' and willingly help them so far as I can.

But, as a Christian man, I believe that I know a thing that if lodged in a man's heart will do pretty nearly all which they aspire to do; and whilst I rejoice in the multiplied agencies for social elevation, I believe that I shall best serve my generation, and I believe that ninety-nine out of a hundred of you will do so too, by trying to get men to love and fear Jesus Christ the Saviour. If you can get His love into a man's heart, that will produce new tastes and new inclinations, which will reform, and sweeten, and purify faster than anything else does.

They tell us that Nonconformist ministers are never seen in the slums; well, that is a libel! But I should like to ask why it is that the Roman Catholic priest is seen there more than the Nonconformist minister? Because the one man's congregation is there, and the other man's is not—which, being translated into other words, is this: the religion of Jesus Christ mostly keeps people out of the slums, and certainly it will take a man out of them if once it gets into his heart, more certainly and quickly than anything else will.

So, dear friends! if we have in our hearts and in our hands this great message of God's love, we have in our possession the germ out of which all things that are lovely and of good report will grow. It will purify, elevate, and sweeten society, because it will make individuals pure and strong, and homes holy and happy. We do not need to draw comparisons between this and other means of reparation, and still less to feel any antagonism to them or the benevolent men who work them; but we should fix it in our minds that the principles of Christ's Gospel adhered to by individuals, and therefore by communities, would have rendered such a condition of things impossible, and that the true repair of the ruin wrought by evil and ignorance, in the single soul, in the family, the city, the nation, the world, is to be found in building anew on the One Foundation which God has laid, even Jesus Christ, the Living Stone, whose pure life passes into all that are grounded and founded on Him.

III. Lastly, this remedy is to be applied by the individual action of Christian men and women on the people nearest them.

'The priests repaired every one over against his house.' We are always tempted, in the face of large disasters, to look for heroic and large remedies, and to invoke corporate action of some sort, which is a great deal easier for most of us than the personal effort that is required. When a great scandal and danger like this of the condition of the lower layers of our civic population is presented before men, for one man that says, 'What can *I* do?' there are twenty who say, 'Somebody should do something. Government should do something. The Corporation should do something. This, that, or the other aggregate of men should do something.' And the individual calmly and comfortably slips his neck out of the collar and leaves it on the shoulders of these abstractions.

As I have said, there are plenty of things that need to be done by these somebodies. But what they do (they will be a long time in doing it), when they do get to work will only touch the fringe of the question, and the substance and the centre of it you can set to work upon this very day if you like, and not wait for anybody either to set you the example or to show you the way.

If you want to do people good you can; but you must pay the price for it. That price is personal sacrifice and effort. The example of Jesus Christ is the all-instructive one in the case. People talk about Him being their Pattern, but they often forget that whatever more there was in Christ's Cross and Passion there was this in it:—the exemplification for all time of the one law by which any reformation can be wrought on men—that a sympathising man shall give himself to do it, and that by personal influence alone men will be drawn and won from out of the darkness and filth. A loving heart and a sympathetic word, the exhibition of a Christian life and conduct, the fact of going down into the midst of evil and trying to lift men out of it, are the old-fashioned and only magnets by which men are drawn to purer and higher life. That is God's way of saving the world—by the action of single souls on single souls. Masses of men can neither save nor be saved. Not in groups, but one by one, particle by particle, soul by soul, Christ draws men to Himself, and He does His work in the world through single souls on fire with His love, and tender with pity learned of Him.

So, dear friends! do not think that any organisation, any corporate activity, any substitution of vicarious service, will solve the problem. It will not. There is only one way of doing it, the old way that we must tread if we are going to do anything for God and our fellows: 'The priests repaired every one over against his house.'

Let me briefly point out some very plain and obvious things which bear upon this matter of individual action. Let me remind you that if you are a Christian man you have in your possession the thing which will cure the world's woe, and possession involves responsibility. What would you think of a man that had a specific for some pestilence that was raging in a city, and was contented to keep it for his own use, or at most for his family's use, when his brethren were dying by the thousand, and their corpses polluting the air? And what shall we say of men and women who call themselves Christians, who have some faith in that great Lord and His mighty sacrifice; who know that the men they meet with every day of their lives are dying for want of it, and who yet themselves do absolutely nothing to spread His name, and to heal men's hurts? What shall we say? God forbid that we should say they are not Christians! but God forbid that anybody should flatter them with the notion that they are anything but most inconsistent Christians!

Still further, need I remind you that if we have found anything in Jesus Christ which has been peace and rest for ourselves, Christ has thereby called us to this work? He has found and saved us, not only for our own personal good. That, of course, is the prime purpose of our salvation, but not its exclusive purpose. He has saved us, too, in order that the Word may be spread through us to those beyond. 'The Kingdom of Heaven is like leaven, which a woman took and hid in three measures of meal until the whole was leavened,' and every little bit of the dough, as it received into itself the leaven, and was transformed, became a medium for transmitting the transformation to the next particle beyond it and so the whole was at last permeated by the power. We get the grace for ourselves that we may pass it on; and as the Apostle says: 'God hath shined into our hearts that we might give the light of the knowledge of the glory of God in the face of Jesus Christ.'

And you can do it, you Christian men and women, every one of you, and preach Him to somebody. The possession of His love gives the commission; ay! and it gives the power. There is nothing so mighty as the confession of personal experience. Do not you think that when that first of Christian converts, and first of Christian preachers went to his brother, all full of what he had discovered, his simple saying, 'We have found the Messias,' was a better sermon than a far more elaborate proclamation would have been? My brother! if you have found Him, you can say so; and if you can say so, and your character and your life confirm the words of your lips, you will have done more to spread His name than much eloquence and many an orator. All can preach who can say, 'We have found the Christ.'

The last word I have to say is this: there is no other body that can do it but you. They say:—'What an awful thing it is that there are no churches or chapels in these outcast districts!' If there were they would be what the churches and chapels are now—half empty. Bricks and mortar built up into ecclesiastical forms are not the way to evangelise this or any other country. It is a very easy thing to build churches and chapels. It is not such an easy thing—I believe it is an impossible thing (and that the sooner the Christian church gives up the attempt the better)—to get the godless classes into any church or chapel. Conducted on the principles upon which churches and chapels must needs at present be conducted, they are for another class altogether; and we had better recognise it, because then we shall feel that no multiplication of buildings like this in which we now are, for instance, is any direct contribution to the evangelisation of the waste spots of the country, except in so far as from a centre like this there ought to go out much influence which will originate direct missionary action in places and fashions adapted to the outlying community.

Professional work is not what we want. Any man, be he minister, clergyman, Bible-reader, city missionary, who goes among our godless population with the suspicion of pay about him is the weaker for that. What is needed besides is that ladies and gentlemen that are a little higher up in the social scale than these poor creatures, should go to them themselves; and excavate and work. Preach, if you like, in the technical sense; have meetings, I suppose, necessarily; but the personal contact is the thing, the familiar talk, the simple exhibition of a loving Christian heart, and the unconventional proclamation in free conversation of the broad message of the love of God in Jesus Christ. Why, if all the people in this chapel who can do that would do it, and keep on doing it, who can tell what an influence would come from some hundreds of new workers for Christ? And why should the existence of a church in which the workers are as numerous as the Christians be an Utopian dream? It is simply the dream that perhaps a church might be conceived to exist, all the members of which had found out their plainest, most imperative duty, and were really trying to do it.

No carelessness, no indolence, no plea of timidity or business shift the obligation from your shoulders if you are a Christian. It is your business, and no paid agents can represent you. You cannot buy yourselves substitutes in Christ's army, as they used to do in the militia, by a guinea subscription. We are thankful for the money, because there are kinds of work to be done that unpaid effort will not do. But men ask for your money; Jesus Christ asks for yourself, for your work, and will not let you off as having done your duty because you have paid your subscription. No doubt there are some of you who, from various circumstances, cannot yourselves do work amongst the masses of the outcast population. Well, but you have got people by your side whom you can help. The question which I wish to ask of my Christian brethren and sisters now is this: Is there a man, woman, or child living to whom you ever spoke a word about Jesus Christ? Is there? If not, do not you think it is time that you began?

There are people in your houses, people that sit by you in your counting-house, on your college benches, who work by your side in mill or factory or warehouse, who cross your path in a hundred ways, and God has given them to you that you may bring them to Him. Do you set yourself, dear brother, to work and try to bring them. Oh! if you lived nearer Jesus Christ you would catch the sacred fire from Him; and like a bit of cold iron lying beside a magnet, touching Him, you would yourselves become magnetic and draw men out of their evil and up to God.

Let me commend to you the old pattern: 'The priests repaired every one over against his house'; and beseech you to take the trowel and spade, or anything that comes handiest, and build, in the bit nearest you, some living stones on the true Foundation.

DISCOURAGEMENTS AND COURAGE

'Nevertheless we made our prayer unto our God, and set a watch against them day and night, because of them. 10. And Judah said, The strength of the bearers of burdens is decayed, and there is much rubbish; so that we are not able to build the wall. 11. And our adversaries said, They shall not know, neither see, till we come in the midst among them, and slay them, and cause the work to cease. 12. And it came to pass, that when the Jews which dwelt by them came, they said unto us ten times, From all places whence ye shall return unto us they will be upon you. 13. Therefore set I in the lower places behind the wall, and on the higher places, I even set the people after their families with their swords, their spears, and their bows. 14. And I looked and rose up, and said unto the nobles, and to the rulers, and to the rest of the people, Be not ye afraid of them: remember the Lord, which is great and terrible, and fight for your brethren, your sons, and your daughters, your wives, and your houses. 15. And it came to pass, when our enemies heard that it was known unto us, and God had brought their counsel to nought, that we returned all of us to the wall, every one unto his work. 16. And it came to pass from that time forth, that the half of my servants wrought in the work, and the other half of them held both the spears, the shields, and the bows, and the habergeons; and the rulers were behind all the house of Judah. 17. They which builded on the wall, and they that bare burdens, with those that laded, every one with one of his hands wrought in the work, and with the other hand held a weapon. 18. For the builders, every one had his sword girded by his side, and so builded. And he that sounded the trumpet was by me. 19. And I said unto the nobles, and to the rulers, and to the rest of the people, The work is great and large, and we are separated upon the wall, one far from another. 20. In what place therefore ye hear the sound of the trumpet, resort ye thither unto us: our God shall fight for us. 21. So we laboured in the work: and half of them held the spears from the rising of the morning till the stars appeared.'—Neh. iv. 9-21.

Common hatred has a wonderful power of uniting former foes. Samaritans, wild Arabs of the desert, Ammonites, and inhabitants of Ashdod in the Philistine plain would have been brought together for no noble work, but mischief and malice fused them for a time into one. God's work is attacked from all sides. Herod and Pilate can shake hands over their joint antagonism.

This passage paints vividly the discouragements which are apt to dog all good work, and the courage which refuses to be discouraged, and conquers by bold persistence. The first verse (v. 9) may stand as a summary of the whole, though it refers to the preceding, not to the following, verses. The true way to meet opposition is twofold—prayer and prudent watchfulness.

'Pray to God, and keep your powder dry,' is not a bad compendium of the duty of a Christian soldier. The union of appeal to God with the full use of common sense, watchfulness, and prudence, would dissipate many hindrances to successful service.

I. In verses 10-12 Nehemiah tells, in his simple way, of the difficulties from three several quarters which threatened to stop his work. He had trouble from the workmen, from the enemies, and from the mass of Jews not resident in Jerusalem. The enthusiasm of the builders had cooled, and the magnitude of their task began to frighten them. Verse 6 tells us that the wall was completed 'unto the half of it'; that is, to one-half the height, and half-way through is just the critical time in all protracted work. The fervour of beginning has passed; the animation from seeing the end at hand has not sprung up. There is a dreary stretch in the centre, where it takes much faith and self-command to plod on unfainting. Half-way to Australia from England is the region of sickening calms. It is easier to work in the fresh morning or in the cool evening than at midday. So in every great movement there are short-winded people who sit down and pant very soon, and their prudence croaks out undeniable facts. No doubt strength does become exhausted; no doubt there is 'much rubbish' (literally 'dust'). What then? The conclusion drawn is not so unquestionable as the premises. 'We cannot build the wall' Why not? Have you not built half of it? And was not the first half more embarrassed by rubbish than the second will be?

It is a great piece of Christian duty to recognise difficulties, and not be cowed by them. The true inference from the facts would have been, 'so that we must put all our strength into the work, and trust in our God to help us.' We may not be responsible for discouragements suggesting themselves, but we are responsible for letting them become dissuasives. Our one question should be, Has God appointed the work? If so, it has to be done, however little our strength, and however mountainous the accumulations of rubbish.

The second part in the trio was taken by the enemies—Sanballat and Tobiah and the rest. They laid their plans for a sudden swoop down on Jerusalem, and calculated that, if they could surprise the builders at their work, they would have no weapons to show fight with, and so would be easily despatched. Killing the builders was but a means; the desired end is significantly put last (v. 11), as being the stopping of the abhorred work. But killing the workmen does not cause the work to cease when it is God's work, as the history of the Church in all ages shows. Conspirators should hold their tongues. It was not a hopeful way of beginning an attack, of which the essence was secrecy and suddenness, to talk about it. 'A bird of the air carries the matter.'

The third voice is that of the Jews in other parts of the land, and especially those living on the borders of Samaria, next door to Sanballat. Verse 12 is probably best taken as in the Revised Version, which makes 'Ye must return to us' the imperative and often-repeated summons from these to the contingents from their respective places of abode, who had gone up to Jerusalem to help in building. Alarms of invasion made the scattered villagers wish to have all their men capable of bearing arms back again to defend their own homes. It was a most natural demand, but in this case, as so often, audacity is truest prudence; and in all high causes there come times when men have to trust their homes and dear ones to God's protection. The necessity is heartrending, and we may well pray that we may not be exposed to it; but if it clearly arises, a devout man can have no doubt of his duty. How many American citizens had to face it in the great Civil War! And how character is ennobled by even so severe a sacrifice!

II. The calm heroism of Nehemiah and his wise action in the emergency are told in verses 13-15. He made a demonstration in force, which at once showed that the scheme of a surprise was blown to pieces. It is difficult to make out the exact localities in which he planted his men. 'The lower places behind the wall' probably means the points at which the new fortifications were lowest, which would be the most exposed to assault; and the 'higher places' (Auth. Ver.), or 'open places' (Rev. Ver.), describes the same places from another point of view. They afforded room for posting troops because they were without buildings. At any rate, the walls were manned, and the enemy would have to deal, not with unarmed labourers, but with prepared soldiers. The work was stopped, and trowel and spade exchanged for sword and spear. 'And I looked,' says Nehemiah. His careful eye travelled over the lines, and, seeing all in order, he cheered the little army with ringing words. He had prayed (Neh. i. 5) to 'the great and terrible God,' and now he bids his men remember Him, and thence draw strength and courage. The only real antagonist of fear is faith. If we can grasp God, we shall not dread Sanballat and his crew. Unless we do, the world is full of dangers which it is not folly to fear.

Note, too, that the people are animated for the fight by reminding them of the dear ones whose lives and honour hung on the issue. Nothing is said about fighting for God and His Temple and city, but the motives adduced are not less sacred. Family love is God's best of earthly gifts, and, though it is sometimes duty to 'forget thine own people, and thy father's house,' as we have just seen, nothing short of these highest obligations can supersede the sweet one of straining every nerve for the well-being of dear ones in the hallowed circle of home.

So the plan of a sudden rush came to nothing. It does not appear that the enemy was in sight; but the news of the demonstration soon reached them, and was effectual. Prompt preparation against possible dangers is often the means of turning them aside. Watchfulness is indispensable to vigour of Christian character and efficiency of work. Suspicion is hateful and weakening; but a man who tries to serve God in such a world as this had need to be like the living creatures in the Revelation, having 'eyes all over.' 'Blessed is the man that [in that sense] feareth always.'

The upshot of the alarm is very beautifully told: 'We returned all of us to the wall, every one unto his work.' No time was wasted in jubilation. The work was the main thing, and the moment the interruption was ended, back to it they all went. It is a fine illustration of persistent discharge of duty, and of that most valuable quality, the ability and inclination to keep up the main purpose of a life continuous through interruptions, like a stream of sweet water running through a bog.

III. The remainder of the passage tells us of the standing arrangements made in consequence of the alarm (vs. 16-21). First we hear what Nehemiah did with his own special 'servants,' whether these were slaves who had accompanied him from Shushan (as Stanley supposes), or his body-guard as a Persian official. He divided them into two parts—one to work, one to watch. But he did not carry out this plan with the mass of the people, probably because it would have too largely diminished the number of builders. So he armed them all. The labourers who carried stones, mortar, and the like, could do their work after a fashion with one hand, and so they had a weapon in the other. If they worked in pairs, that would be all the easier. The actual builders needed both hands, and so they had swords stuck in their girdles. No doubt such arrangements hindered progress, but they were necessary. The lesson often drawn from them is no doubt true, that God's workers must be prepared for warfare as well as building. There have been epochs in which that necessity was realised in a very sad manner; and the Church on earth will always have to be the Church militant. But it is well to remember that building is the end, and fighting is but the means. The trowel, not the sword, is the natural instrument. Controversy is second best—a necessity, no doubt, but an unwelcome one, and only permissible as a subsidiary help to doing the true work, rearing the walls of the city of God.

'He that soundeth the trumpet was by me.' The gallant leader was everywhere, animating by his presence. He meant to be in the thick of the fight, if it should come. And so he kept the trumpeter by his side, and gave orders that when he sounded all should hurry to the place; for there the enemy would be, and Nehemiah would be where they were. 'The work is great and large, and we are separated ... one far from another.' How naturally the words lend themselves to the old lesson so often drawn from them! God's servants are widely parted, by distance, by time, and, alas! by less justifiable causes. Unless they draw together they will be overwhelmed, taken in detail, and crushed. They must rally to help each other against the common foe.

Thank God! the longing for manifest Christian unity is deeper to-day than ever it was. But much remains to be done before it is adequately fulfilled in the recognition of the common bond of brotherhood, which binds us all in one family, if we have one Father. English and American Christians are bound to seek the tightening of the bonds between them and to set themselves against politicians who may seek to keep apart those who both in the flesh and in the spirit are brothers. All Christians have one great Captain; and He will be in the forefront of every battle. His clear trumpet-call should gather all His servants to His side.

The closing verse tells again how Nehemiah's immediate dependants divided work and watching, and adds to the picture the continuousness of their toil from the first grey of morning till darkness showed the stars and ended another day of toil. Happy they who thus 'from morn till noon, from noon till dewy eve,' labour in the work of the Lord! For them, every new morning will dawn with new strength, and every evening be calm with the consciousness of 'something attempted, something done.'

AN ANCIENT NONCONFORMIST

'… So did not I, because of the fear of God.'—Neh. v. 15.

I do not suppose that the ordinary Bible-reader knows very much about Nehemiah. He is one of the neglected great men of Scripture. He was no prophet, he had no glowing words, he had no lofty visions, he had no special commission, he did not live in the heroic age. There was a certain harshness and dryness; a tendency towards what, when it was more fully developed, became Pharisaism, in the man, which somewhat covers the essential nobleness of his character. But he was brave, cautious, circumspect, disinterested; and he had Jerusalem in his heart.

The words that I have read are a little fragment of his autobiography which deal with a prosaic enough matter, but carry in them large principles. When he was appointed governor of the little colony of returned exiles in Palestine, he found that his predecessors, like Turkish pashas and Chinese mandarins to-day, had been in the habit of 'squeezing' the people of their Government, and that they had requisitioned sufficient supplies of provisions to keep the governor's table well spread. It was the custom. Nobody would have wondered if Nehemiah had conformed to it; but he felt that he must have his hands clean. Why did he not do what everybody else had done in like circumstances? His answer is beautifully simple: 'Because of the fear of God.' His religion went down into the little duties of common life, and imposed upon him a standard far above the maxims that were prevalent round about him. And so, if you will take these words, and disengage them from the small matter concerning which they were originally spoken, I think you will find in them thoughts as to the attitude which we should take to prevalent practices, the motive which should impel us to a sturdy non-compliance, and the power which will enable us to walk on a solitary road. 'So did not I, because of the fear of God.' Now, then, these are my three points:—

I. The attitude to prevalent practices.

Nehemiah would not conform. And unless you can say 'No!' and do it very often, your life will be shattered from the beginning. That non-compliance with customary maxims and practices is the beginning, or, at least, one of the foundation-stones, of all nobleness and strength, of all blessedness and power. Of course it is utterly impossible for a man to denude himself of the influences that are brought to bear upon him by the circumstances in which he lives, and the trend of opinion, and the maxims and practices of the world, in the corner, and at the time, in which his lot is cast. But, on the other hand, be sure of this, that unless you are in a very deep and not at all a technical sense of the word, 'Nonconformists,' you will come to no good. None! It is so easy to do as others do, partly because of laziness, partly because of cowardice, partly because of the instinctive imitation which is in us all. Men are gregarious. One great teacher has drawn an illustration from a flock of sheep, and says that if we hold up a stick, and the first of the flock jumps over it, and then if we take away the stick, all the rest of the flock will jump when they come to the point where the first did so. A great many of us adopt our creeds and opinions, and shape our lives for no better reason than because people round us are thinking in a certain direction, and living in a certain way. It saves a great deal of trouble, and it gratifies a certain strange instinct that is in us all, and it avoids dangers and conflicts that we should, when we are at Rome, do as the Romans do. 'So did not I, because of the fear of God.'

Now, brethren! I ask you to take this plain principle of the necessity of non-compliance (which I suppose I do not need to do much to establish, because, theoretically, we most of us admit it), and apply it all round the circumference of your lives. Apply it to your opinions. There is no tyranny like the tyranny of a majority in a democratic country like ours. It is quite as harsh as the tyranny of the old-fashioned despots. Unless you resolve steadfastly to see with your own eyes, to use your own brains, to stand on your own feet, to be a voice and not an echo, you will be helplessly enslaved by the fashion of the hour, and the opinions that prevail.

'What everybody says'—perhaps—'is true.' What most people say, at any given time, is very likely to be false. Truth has always lived with minorities, so do not let the current of widespread opinion sweep you away, but try to have a mind of your own, and not to be brow-beaten or overborne because the majority of the people round about you are giving utterance, and it may be unmeasured utterance, to any opinions.

Now, there is one direction in which I wish to urge that especially—and now I speak mainly to the young men in my congregation—and that is, in regard to the attitude that so many amongst us are taking to Christian truth. If you have honestly thought out the subject to the best of your ability, and have come to conclusions diverse from those which men like me hold dearer than their lives, that is another matter. But I know that very widely there is spread to-day the fashion of unbelief. So many influential men, leaders of opinion, teachers and preachers, are giving up the old-fashioned Evangelical faith, that it takes a strong man to say that he sticks by it. It is a poor reason to give for your attitude, that unbelief is in the air, and nobody believes those old doctrines now. That may be. There are currents of opinion that are transitory, and that is one of them, depend upon it. But at all events do not be fooled out of your faith, as some of you are tending to be, for no better reason than because other people have given it up. An iceberg lowers the temperature all round it, and the iceberg of unbelief is amongst us to-day, and it has chilled a great many people who could not tell why they have lost the fervour of their faith.

On the other hand, let me remind you that a mere traditional religion, which is only orthodox because other people are so, and has not verified its beliefs by personal experience, is quite as deleterious as an imitative unbelief. Doubtless, I speak to some who plume themselves on 'never having been affected by these currents of popular opinion,' but whose unblemished and unquestioned orthodoxy has no more vitality in it than the other people's heterodoxy. The one man has said, 'What is everywhere always, and by all believed, I believe'; and the other man has said, 'What the select spirits of this day disbelieve, I disbelieve,' and the belief of one and the unbelief of the other are equally worthless, and really identical.

But it is not only, nor mainly, in reference to opinion that I would urge upon you this nonconformity with prevalent practices as the measure of most that is noble in us. I dare not talk to you as if I knew much about the details of Manchester commercial life, but I can say this much, that it is no excuse for shady practices in your trade to say, 'It is the custom of the trade, and everybody does it.' Nehemiah might have said: 'There never was a governor yet but took his forty shekels a day's worth'—about L. 1,800 of our money—'of provisions from these poor people, and I am not going to give it up because of a scruple. It is the custom, and because it is the custom I can do it.' I am not going into details. It is commonly understood that preachers know nothing about business; that may be true, or it may not. But this, I am sure, is a word in season for some of my friends this evening—do not hide behind the trade. Come out into the open, and deal with the questions of morality involved in your commercial life, as you will have to deal with them hereafter, by yourself. Never mind about other people. 'Oh,' but you say, 'that involves loss.' Very likely! Nehemiah was a poorer man because he fed all these one hundred and fifty Jews at his table, but he did not mind that. It may involve loss, but you will keep God, and that is gain.

Turn this searchlight in another direction. I see a number of young people in my congregation at this moment, young men who are perhaps just beginning their career in this city, and who possibly have been startled when they heard the kind of talk that was going on at the next desk, or from the man that sits beside them on the benches at College. Do not be tempted to follow that multitude to do evil. Unless you are prepared to say 'No!' to a great deal that will be pushed into your face in this great city, as sure as you are living you will make shipwreck of your lives. Do you think that in the forty years and more that I have stood here I have not seen successive generations of young men come into Manchester? I could people many of these pews with the faces of such, who came here buoyant, full of hope, full of high resolves, and with a mother's benediction hanging over their heads, and who got into a bad set, and had not the strength to say 'No,' and they went down and down and down, and then presently somebody asked, 'Where is so-and-so?' 'Oh! his health broke down, and he has gone home to die.' 'His bones are full of the iniquity of his youth'—and he made shipwreck of prospects and of life, because he did not pull himself together when the temptation came, and say, 'So did not I, because of the fear of God.'

II. Now let me ask you to turn with me to the second thought that my text suggests to me; that is,

The motive that impels to this sturdy non-compliance.

Nehemiah puts it in Old Testament phraseology, 'the fear of God'; the New Testament equivalent is 'the love of Christ.' And if you want to take the power and the life out of both phrases, in order to find a modern conventional equivalent, you will say 'religion.' I prefer the old-fashioned language. 'The love of Christ' impels to this non-compliance. Now, my point is this, that Jesus Christ requires from each of us that we shall abstain, restrict ourselves, refuse to do a great many things that are being done round us.

I need not remind you of how continually He spoke about taking up the cross. I need not do more than just remind you of His parable of the two ways, but ask you, whilst you think of it, to note that all the characteristics of each of the ways which He sets forth are given by Him as reasons for refusing the one and walking in the other. For example, 'Enter ye in at the strait gate, for strait is the gate'—that is a reason for going in; 'and narrow is the way'—

that is a reason for going in; 'and few there be that find it'—that is a reason for going in. 'Wide is the gate'—that is a reason for stopping out; 'and broad is the way'—that is a reason for stopping out; 'and many there be that go in thereat'—that is a reason for stopping out. Is not that what I said, that the minority is generally right and the majority wrong? Just because there are so many people on the path, suspect it, and expect that the path with fewer travellers is probably the better and the higher.

But to pass from that, what did Jesus Christ mean by His continual contrast between His disciples and the world? What did He mean by 'the world'? This fair universe, with all its possibilities of help and blessing, and all its educational influences? By no means. He meant by 'the world' the aggregate of things and men considered as separate from God. And when He applied the term to men only, He meant by it very much what we mean when we talk about society. Society is not organised on Christian principles; we all know that, and until it is, if a man is going to be a Christian he must not conform to the world. 'Know ye not that whosoever is a friend of the world is an enemy of God.'

I would press upon you, dear friends! that our Christianity is nothing unless it leads us to a standard, and a course of conduct in conformity with that standard, which will be in diametrical opposition to a great deal of what is patted on the back, and petted and praised by society. Now, there is an easy-going kind of Christianity which does not recognise that, and which is in great favour with many people to-day, and is called 'liberality' and 'breadth,' and 'conciliating and commending Christianity to outsiders,' and I know not what besides. Well, Christ's words seem to me to come down like a hammer upon that sort of thing. Depend upon it, 'the world'—I mean by that the aggregate of godless men organised as they are in society—does not think much of these trimmers. It may dislike an out-and-out Christian, but it knows him when it sees him, and it has a kind of hostile respect for him which the other people will never get. You remember the story of the man that was seeking for a coachman, and whose question to each applicant was, 'How near can you drive to the edge of a precipice?' He took the man who said: 'I would keep away from it as far as I could.' And the so-called Christian people that seem to be bent on showing how much their lives can be made to assimilate to the lives of men that have no sympathy with their creeds, are like the rash Jehus that tried to go as near the edge as they could. But the consistent Christian will keep as far away from it as he can. There are some of us who seem as if we were most anxious to show that we, whose creed is absolutely inconsistent with the world's practices, can live lives which are all but identical with these practices. Jesus Christ says, through the lips of His Apostle, what He often said in other language by His own lips when He was here on earth: 'Be ye not conformed to the world.'

Surely such a command as that, just because it involves difficulty, self-restraint, self-denial, and sometimes self-crucifixion, ought to appeal, and does appeal, to all that is noble in humanity, in a fashion that that smooth, easy-going gospel of living on the level of the people round us never can do. For remember that Christ's commandment not to be conformed to the world is the consequence of His commandment to be conformed to Himself. 'Thus did not I' comes second; 'This one thing I do' comes first. You will misunderstand the whole genius of the Gospel if you suppose that, as a law of life, it is perpetually pulling men short up, and saying: Don't, don't, don't! There is a Christianity of that sort which is mainly prohibition and restriction, but it is not Christ's Christianity. He begins by enjoining: 'This do in remembrance of Me,' and the man that has accepted that commandment must necessarily say, as he looks out on the world, and its practices: 'So did not I, because of the fear of God.'

III. And now one last word—my text not only suggests the motive which impels to this non-compliance, but also the power which enables us to exercise it.

'The fear of God,' or, taking the New Testament equivalent, 'the love of Christ,' makes it possible for a man, with all his weakness and dependence on surroundings, with all his instinctive desire to be like the folk that are near him, to take that brave attitude, and to refuse to be one of the crowd that runs after evil and lies. I have no time to dwell upon this aspect of my subject, as I should be glad to have done. Let me sum up in a sentence or two what I would have said. Christ will enable you to take this necessary attitude because, in Himself He gives you the Example which it is always safe to follow. The instinct of imitation is planted in us for a good end, and because it is in us, examples of nobility appeal to us. And because it is in us Jesus Christ has lived the life that it is possible for, and therefore incumbent on, us to live. It is safe to imitate Him, and it is easy not to do as men do, if once our main idea is to do as Christ did.

He makes it possible for us, because He gives the strongest possible motive for the life that He prescribes. As the Apostle puts it, 'Ye are bought with a price, be not the servants of men.' There is nothing that will so deliver us from the tyranny of majorities, and of what we call general opinion and ordinary custom, as to feel that we belong to Him because He died for us. Men become very insignificant when Christ speaks, and the charter of our freedom from them lies in our redemption by the blood of Jesus Christ.

Jesus Christ being our Redeemer is our Judge, and moment by moment He is estimating our conduct, and judging our actions as they are done. 'With me it is a very small matter to be judged of you or of man's judgment. He that judgeth me is the Lord.' Never mind what the people round you say; you do not take your orders from them, and you do not answer to them. Like some official abroad, appointed by the Crown, you do not report to the local authorities; you report to headquarters, and what He thinks about you is the only important thing. So 'the fear of man which bringeth a snare' dwindles down into very minute dimensions when we think of the Pattern, the Redeemer and the Judge to whom we give account.

And so, dear friends! if we will only open our hearts, by quiet humble faith, for the coming of Jesus Christ into our lives, then we shall be able to resist, to refuse compliance, to stand firm, though alone. The servant of Christ is the master of all men. 'All things are yours, whether Paul, or Apollos, or Cephas—all are yours, and ye are Christ's.'

READING THE LAW WITH TEARS AND JOY

'And all the people gathered themselves together as one man into the street that was before the water gate; and they spake unto Ezra the scribe to bring the book of the law of Moses, which the Lord had commanded to Israel. 2. And Ezra the priest brought the law before the congregation both of men and women, and all that could hear with understanding, upon the first day of the seventh month. 3. And he read therein before the street that was before the water gate, from the morning until midday, before the men and the women, and those that could understand; and the ears of all the people were attentive unto the book of the law. 4. And Ezra the scribe stood upon a pulpit of wood, which they had made for the purpose; and beside him stood Mattithiah, and Shema, and Anaiah, and Urijah, and Hilkiah, and Maaseiah, on his right hand; and on his left hand Pedaiah, and Mishael, and Malchiah, and Hashum, and Hashbadana, Zechariah, and Meshullam. 5. And Ezra opened the book in the sight of all the people; (for he was above all the people); and when he opened it, all the people stood up: 6. And Ezra blessed the Lord, the great God. And all the people answered, Amen, Amen, with lifting up their hands: and they bowed their heads, and worshipped the Lord with their faces to the ground. 7. Also Jeshua, and Bani, and Sherebiah, Jemin, Akkub, Shabbethai, Hodijah, Maaseiah, Kelita, Azariah, Jozabad, Hanan, Pelaiah, and the Levites, caused the people to understand the law: and the people stood in their place. 8. So they read in the book in the law of God distinctly, and gave the sense, and caused them to understand the reading. 9. And Nehemiah, which is the Tirashatha, and Ezra the priest the scribe, and the Levites that taught the people, said unto all the people, This day is holy unto the Lord your God; mourn not, nor weep. For all the people wept, when they heard the words of the law. 10. Then he said unto them, Go your way, eat the fat, and drink the sweet, and send portions unto them for whom nothing is prepared: for this day is holy unto our Lord: neither be ye sorry; for the joy of the Lord is your strength. 11. So the Levites stilled all the people, saying, Hold your peace, for the day is holy; neither be ye grieved. 12. And all the people went their way to eat, and to drink, and to send portions, and to make great mirth, because they had understood the words that were declared unto them.'—Neh. viii. 1-12.

The wall was finished on the twenty-fifth day of the month Elul, which was the sixth month. The events recorded in this passage took place on the first day of the seventh month. The year is not given, but the natural inference is that it was the same as that of the finishing of the wall; namely, the twentieth of Artaxerxes. If so, the completion of the fortifications to which Nehemiah had set himself, was immediately followed by this reading of the law, in which Ezra takes the lead. The two men stand in a similar relative position to that of Zerubbabel and Joshua, the one representing the civil and the other the religious authority.

According to Ezra vii. 9, Ezra had gone to Jerusalem about thirteen years before Nehemiah, and had had a weary time of fighting against the corruptions which had crept in among the returned captives. The arrival of Nehemiah would be hailed as bringing fresh, young enthusiasm, none the less welcome and powerful because it had the king's authority entrusted to it. Evidently the two men thoroughly understood one another, and pulled together heartily. We heard nothing about Ezra while the wall was being built. But now he is the principal figure, and Nehemiah is barely mentioned. The reasons for Ezra's taking the prominent part in the reading of the law are given in the two titles by which he is designated in two successive verses (vers. 1,2). He was 'the scribe' and also 'the priest,' and in both capacities was the natural person for such a work.

The seventh month was the festival month of the year, its first day being that of the Feast of trumpets, and the great Feast of tabernacles as well as the solemn day of atonement occurring in it. Possibly, the prospect of the coming of the times for these celebrations may have led to the people's wish to hear the law, that they might duly observe the appointed ceremonial. At all events, the first thing to note is that it was in consequence of the people's wish that the law was read in their hearing. Neither Ezra nor Nehemiah originated the gathering together. They obeyed a popular impulse which they had not created. We must not, indeed, give the multitude credit for much more than the wish to have their ceremonial right. But there was at least that wish, and possibly something deeper and more spiritual. The walls were completed; but the true defence of Israel was in God, and the condition of His defending was Israel's obedience to His law. The people were, in some measure, beginning to realise that condition with new clearness, in consequence of the new fervour which Nehemiah had brought.

It is singular that, during his thirteen years of residence, Ezra is not recorded to have promulgated the law, though it lay at the basis of the drastic reforms which he was able to carry through. Probably he had not been silent, but the solemn public recitation of the law was felt to be appropriate on occasion of completing the wall. Whether the people had heard it before, or, as seems implied, it was strange to them, their desire to hear it may stand as a pattern for us of that earnest wish to know God's will which is never cherished in vain. He who does not intend to obey does not wish to know the law. If we have no longing to know what the will of the Lord is, we may be very sure that we prefer our own to His. If we desire to know it, we shall desire to understand the Book which contains so much of it. Any true religion in the heart will make us eager to perceive, and willing to be guided by, the will of God, revealed mainly in Scripture, in the Person, works, and words of Jesus, and also in waiting hearts by the Spirit, and in those things which the world calls 'circumstances' and faith names 'providences.'

II. Verses 2-8 appear to tell the same incidents twice over—first, more generally in verses 2 and 8, and then more minutely. Such expanded repetition is characteristic of the Old Testament historical style. It is somewhat difficult to make sure of the real circumstances. Clearly enough there was a solemn assembly of men, women, and children in a great open space outside one of the gates, and there, from dawn till noon, the law was read and explained. But whether Ezra read it all, while the Levites named in verse 7 explained or paraphrased or translated it, or whether they all read in turns, or whether there were a number of groups, each of which had a teacher who both read and expounded, is hard to determine. At all events, Ezra was the principal figure, and began the reading.

It was a picturesque scene. The sun, rising over the slopes of Olivet, would fall on the gathered crowd, if the water-gate was, as is probable, on the east or south-east side of the city. Beneath the fresh fortifications probably, which would act as a sounding-board for the reader, was set up a scaffold high above the crowd, large enough to hold Ezra and thirteen supporters— principal men, no doubt—seven on one side of him and six on the other. Probably a name has dropped out, and the numbers were equal. There, in the morning light, with the new walls for a background, stood Ezra on his rostrum, and amid reverent silence, lifted high the sacred roll. A common impulse swayed the crowd, and brought them all to their feet—token at once of respect and obedient attention. Probably many of them had never seen a sacred roll. To them all it was comparatively unfamiliar. No wonder that, as Ezra's voice rose in prayer, the whole assembly fell on their faces in adoration, and every lip responded 'Amen! amen!'

Much superstition may have mingled with the reverence. No doubt, there was then what we are often solemnly warned against now, bibliolatry. But in this time of critical investigation it is not the divine element in Scripture which is likely to be exaggerated; and few are likely to go wrong in the direction of paying too much reverence to the Book in which, as is still believed, God has revealed His will and Himself. While welcoming all investigations which throw light on its origin or its meaning, and perfectly recognising the human element in it, we should learn the lesson taught by that waiting crowd prone on their faces, and blessing God for His word. Such attitude must ever precede reading it, if we are to read aright.

Hour after hour the recitation went on. We must let the question of the precise form of the events remain undetermined. It is somewhat singular that thirteen names are enumerated as of the men who stood by Ezra, and thirteen as those of the readers or expounders. It may be the case that the former number is complete, though uneven, and that there was some reason unknown for dividing the audience into just so many sections. The second set of thirteen was not composed of the same men as the first. They seem to have been Levites, whose office of assisting at the menial parts of the sacrifices was now elevated into that of setting forth the law. Probably the portions read were such as bore especially on ritual, though the tears of the listeners are sufficient proof that they had heard some things that went deeper than that.

The word rendered 'distinctly' in the Revised Version (margin, *with* an *interpretation*) is ambiguous, and may either mean that the Levites explained or that they translated the words. The former is the more probable, as there is no reason to suppose that the audience, most of whom had been born in the land, were ignorant of Hebrew. But if the ritual had been irregularly observed, and the circle of ideas in the law become unfamiliar, many explanations would be necessary. It strikes one as touching and strange that such an assembly should be needed after so many centuries of national existence. It sums up in one vivid picture the sin and suffering of the nation. To observe that law had been the condition of their prosperity. To bind it on their hearts should have been their delight and would have been their life; and here, after all these generations, the best of the nation are assembled, so ignorant of it that they cannot even understand it when they hear it. Absorption with worldly things has an awful power of dulling spiritual apprehension. Neglect of God's law weakens the power of understanding it.

This scene was in the truest sense a 'revival.' We may learn the true way of bringing men back to God; namely, the faithful exposition and enforcement of God's will and word. We may learn, too, what should be the aim of public teachers of religion; namely, first and foremost, the clear setting forth of God's truth. Their first business is to 'give the sense, so that they understand the reading'; and that, not for merely intellectual purposes, but that, like the crowd outside the water-gate on that hot noonday, men may be moved to penitence, and then lifted to the joy of the Lord.

The first day of the seventh month was the Feast of trumpets; and when the reading was over, and its effects of tears and sorrow for disobedience were seen, the preachers changed their tone, to bring consolation and exhort to gladness. Nehemiah had taken no part in reading the law, as Ezra the priest and his Levites were more appropriately set to that. But he joins them in exhorting the people to dry their tears, and go joyfully to the feast. These exhortations contain many thoughts universally applicable. They teach that even those who are most conscious of sin and breaches of God's law should weep indeed, but should swiftly pass from tears to joy. They do not teach how that passage is to be effected; and in so far they are imperfect, and need to be supplemented by the New Testament teaching of forgiveness through the sacrifice of Jesus Christ. But in their clear discernment that sorrow is not meant to be a permanent characteristic of religion, and that gladness is a more acceptable offering than tears, they teach a valuable lesson, needed always by men who fancy that they must atone for their sins by their own sadness, and that religion is gloomy, harsh, and crabbed.

Further, these exhortations to festal gladness breathe the characteristic Old Testament tone of wholesome enjoyment of material good as a part of religion. The way of looking at eating and drinking and the like, as capable of being made acts of worship, has been too often forgotten by two kinds of men—saints who have sought sanctity in asceticism; and sensualists who have taken deep draughts of such pleasures without calling on the name of the Lord, and so have failed to find His gifts a cup of salvation. It is possible to 'eat and drink and see God' as the elders of Israel did on Sinai.

Further, the plain duty of remembering the needy while we enjoy God's gifts is beautifully enjoined here. The principle underlying the commandment to 'send portions to them for whom nothing is provided'—that is, for whom no feast has been dressed—is that all gifts are held in trust, that nothing is bestowed on us for our own good only, but that we are in all things stewards. The law extends to the smallest and to the greatest possessions. We have no right to feast on anything unless we share it, whether it be festal dainties or the bread that came down from heaven. To divide our portion with others is the way to make our portion greater as well as sweeter.

Further, 'the joy of the Lord is your strength.' By *strength* here seems to be meant a *stronghold*. If we fix our desires on God, and have trained our hearts to find sweeter delights in communion with Him than in any earthly good, our religion will have lifted us above mists and clouds into clear air above, where sorrows and changes will have little power to affect us. If we are to rejoice in the Lord, it will be possible for us to 'rejoice always,' and that joy will be as a refuge from all the ills that flesh is heir to. Dwelling in God, we shall dwell safely, and be far from the fear of evil.

THE JOY OF THE LORD

'The joy of the Lord is your strength.'—Neh. viii. 10.

Judaism, in its formal and ceremonial aspect, was a religion of gladness. The feast was the great act of worship. It is not to be wondered at, that Christianity, the perfecting of that ancient system, has been less markedly felt to be a religion of joy; for it brings with it far deeper and more solemn views about man in his nature, condition, responsibilities, destinies, than ever prevailed before, under any system of worship. And yet all deep religion ought to be joyful, and all strong religion assuredly will be so.

Here, in the incident before us, there has come a time in Nehemiah's great enterprise, when the law, long forgotten, long broken by the captives, is now to be established again as the rule of the newly-founded commonwealth. Naturally enough there comes a remembrance of many sins in the past history of the people; and tears not unnaturally mingle with the thankfulness that again they are a nation, having a divine worship and a divine law in their midst. The leader of them, knowing for one thing that if the spirits of his people once began to flag, they could not face nor conquer the difficulties of their position, said to them, 'This day is holy unto the Lord: this feast that we are keeping is a day of devout worship; therefore mourn not, nor weep: go your way; eat the fat, and drink the sweet, and send portions unto them for whom nothing is prepared; neither be ye sorry, for the joy of the Lord is your strength.' You will make nothing of it by indulgence in lamentation and in mourning. You will have no more power for obedience, you will not be fit for your work, if you fall into a desponding state. Be thankful and glad; and remember that the purest worship is the worship of God-fixed joy, 'the joy of the Lord is your strength.' And that is as true, brethren! with regard to us, as it ever was in these old times; and we, I think, need the lesson contained in this saying of Nehemiah's, because of some prevalent tendencies amongst us, no less than these Jews did. Take some simple thoughts suggested by this text which are both important in themselves and needful to be made emphatic because so often forgotten in the ordinary type of Christian character. They are these. Religious Joy is the natural result of faith. It is a Christian duty. It is an important element in Christian strength.

I. Joy in the Lord is the natural result of Christian Faith.

There is a natural adaptation or provision in the Gospel, both by what it brings to us and by what it takes away from us, to make a calm, and settled, and deep gladness, the prevalent temper of the Christian spirit. In what it gives us, I say, and in what it takes away from us. It gives us what we call well a sense of acceptance with God, it gives us God for the rest of our spirits, it gives us the communion with Him which in proportion as it is real, will be still, and in proportion as it is still, will be all bright and joyful. It takes away from us the fear that lies before us, the strifes that lie within us, the desperate conflict that is waged between a man's conscience and his inclinations, between his will and his passions, which tears the heart asunder, and always makes sorrow and tumult wherever it comes. It takes away the sense of sin. It gives us, instead of the torpid conscience, or the angrily-stinging conscience—a conscience all calm from its accusations, with all the sting drawn out of it:—for quiet peace lies in the heart of the man that is trusting in the Lord. The Gospel works joy, because the soul is at rest in God; joy, because every function of the spiritual nature has found now its haven and its object; joy, because health has come, and the healthy working of the body or of the spirit is itself a gladness; joy, because the dim future is painted (where it is painted at all) with shapes of light and beauty, and because the very vagueness of these is an element in the greatness of its revelation. The joy that is in Christ is deep and abiding. Faith in Him naturally works gladness.

I do not forget that, on the other side, it is equally true that the Christian faith has as marked and almost as strong an adaptation to produce a solemn *sorrow*—solemn, manly, noble, and strong. 'As sorrowful, yet always rejoicing,' is the rule of the Christian life. If we think of what our faith does; of the light that it casts upon our condition, upon our nature, upon our responsibilities, upon our sins, and upon our destinies, we can easily see how, if gladness be one part of its operation, no less really and truly is sadness another. Brethren! all great thoughts have a solemn quiet in them, which not unfrequently merges into a still sorrow. There is nothing more contemptible in itself, and there is no more sure mark of a trivial nature and a trivial round of occupations, than unshaded gladness, that rests on no deep foundations of quiet, patient grief; grief, because I know what I am and what I ought to be; grief, because I have learnt the 'exceeding sinfulness of sin'; grief, because, looking out upon the world, I see, as other men do not see, hell-fire burning at the back of the mirth and the laughter, and know what it is that men are hurrying to! Do you remember who it was that stood by the side of the one poor dumb man, whose tongue He was going to loose, and looking up to heaven, *sighed* before He could say, 'Be opened'? Do you remember that of Him it is said, 'God hath anointed Thee with the oil of gladness above Thy fellows'; and also, 'a Man of sorrows, and acquainted with grief'? And do you not think that both these characteristics are to be repeated in the operations of His Gospel upon every heart that receives it? And if, by the hopes it breathes into us, by the fears that it takes away from us, by the union with God that it accomplishes for us, by the fellowship that it implants in us, it indeed anoints us all 'with the oil of gladness'; yet, on the other hand, by the sense of mine own sin that it teaches me; by the conflict with weakness which it makes to be the law of my life; by the clear vision which it gives me of 'the law of my members warring against the law of my mind, and bringing me into subjection'; by the intensity which it breathes into all my nature, and by the thoughts that it presents of what sin leads to, and what the world at present is, the Gospel, wheresoever it comes, will infuse a wise, valiant sadness as the very foundation of character. Yes, joy, but sorrow too! the joy of the Lord, but sorrow as we look on our own sin and the world's woe! the head anointed with the oil of gladness, but also crowned with thorns!

These two are not contradictory. These two states of mind, both of them the natural operations of any deep faith, may co-exist and blend into one another, so as that the gladness is sobered, and chastened, and made manly and noble; and that the sorrow is like some thundercloud, all streaked with bars of sunshine, that pierce into its deepest depths. The joy lives in the midst of the sorrow; the sorrow springs from the same root as the gladness. The two do not clash against each other, or reduce the emotion to a neutral indifference, but they blend into one another; just as, in the Arctic regions, deep down beneath the cold snow, with its white desolation and its barren death, you will find the budding of the early spring flowers and the fresh green grass; just as some kinds of fire burn below the water; just as, in the midst of the barren and undrinkable sea, there may be welling up some little fountain of fresh water that comes from a deeper depth than the great ocean around it, and pours its sweet streams along the surface of the salt waste. Gladness, because I love, for love *is* gladness; gladness, because I trust, for trust *is* gladness; gladness, because I obey, for obedience is a meat that others know not of, and light comes when we do His will! But sorrow, because still I am wrestling with sin; sorrow, because still I have not perfect fellowship; sorrow, because mine eye, purified by my living with God, sees earth, and sin, and life, and death, and the generations of men, and the darkness beyond, in some measure as God sees them! And yet, the sorrow is surface, and the joy is central; the sorrow springs from circumstance, and the gladness from the essence of the thing;—and therefore the sorrow is transitory, and the gladness is perennial. For the Christian life is all like one of those sweet spring showers in early April, when the rain-drops weave for us a mist that hides the sunshine; and yet the hidden sun is in every sparkling drop, and they are all saturated and steeped in its light. 'The joy of the Lord' is the natural result and offspring of all Christian faith.

II. And now, secondly, the 'joy of the Lord' or rejoicing in God, is a matter of Christian duty.

It is a commandment here, and it is a command in the New Testament as well. 'Neither be ye sorry, for the joy of the Lord is your strength.' I need not quote to you the frequent repetitions of the same injunction which the Apostle Paul gives us, 'Rejoice in the Lord always, and again I say, Rejoice'; 'Rejoice evermore,' and the like. The fact that this joy is enjoined us suggests to us a thought or two, worth looking at.

You may say with truth, 'My emotions of joy and sorrow are not under my own control: I cannot help being glad and sad as circumstances dictate.' But yet here it lies, a commandment. It is a duty, a thing that the Apostle enjoins; in which, of course, is implied, that somehow or other it is to a large extent within one's own power, and that even the indulgence in this emotion, and the degree to which a Christian life shall be a cheerful life, is dependent in a large measure on our own volitions, and stands on the same footing as our obedience to God's other commandments.

We *can* to a very great extent control even our own emotions; but then, besides, we can do more than that. It may be quite true, that you cannot help feeling sorrowful in the presence of sorrowful thoughts, and glad in the presence of thoughts that naturally kindle gladness. But I will tell you what you can do or refrain from doing—you can either go and stand in the light, or you can go and stand in the shadow. You can either fix your attention upon, and make the predominant subject of your religious contemplations, a truth which shall make you glad and strong, or a half-truth, which shall make you sorrowful, and therefore weak. Your meditations may either centre mainly upon your own selves, your faults and failings, and the like; or they may centre mainly upon God and His love, Christ and His grace, the Holy Spirit and His communion. You may either fill your soul with joyful thoughts, or though a true Christian, a real, devout, God-accepted believer, you may be so misapprehending the nature of the Gospel, and your relation to it, its promises and precepts, its duties and predictions, as that the prevalent tinge and cast of your religion shall be solemn and almost gloomy, and not lighted up and irradiated with the felt sense of God's presence—with the strong, healthy consciousness that you are a forgiven and justified man, and that you are going to be a glorified one.

And thus far (and it is a long way) by the selection or the rejection of the appropriate and proper subjects which shall make the main portion of our religious contemplation, and shall be the food of our devout thoughts, we can determine the complexion of our religious life. Just as you inject colouring matter into the fibres of some anatomical preparation; so a Christian may, as it were, inject into all the veins of his religious character and life, either the bright tints of gladness or the dark ones of self-despondency; and the result will be according to the thing that he has put into them. If your thoughts are chiefly occupied with God, and what He has done and is for you, then you will have peaceful joy. If, on the other hand, they are bent ever on yourself and your own unbelief, then you will always be sad. You can make your choice.

Christian men, the joy of the Lord is a duty. It is so because, as we have seen, it is the natural effect of faith, because we can do much to regulate our emotions directly, and much more to determine them by determining what set of thoughts shall engage us. A wise and strong faith is our duty. To keep our emotional nature well under control of reason and will is our duty. To lose thoughts of ourselves in God's truth about Himself is our duty. If we do these things, we cannot fail to have Christ's joy remaining in us, and making ours full. If we have not that blessed possession abiding with us, which He lived and died to give us, there is something wrong in us somewhere.

It seems to me that this is a truth which we have great need, my friends, to lay to heart. It is of no great consequence that we should practically confute the impotent old sneer about religion as being a gloomy thing. One does not need to mind much what some people say on that matter. The world would call 'the joy of the Lord' gloom, just as much as it calls 'godly sorrow' gloom. But we are losing for ourselves a power and an energy of which we have no conception, unless we feel that joy is a duty, and unless we believe that not to be joyful in the Lord is, therefore, more than a misfortune, it is a fault.

I do not forget that the comparative absence of this happy, peaceful sense of acceptance, harmony, oneness with God, springs sometimes from temperament, and depends on our natural disposition. Of course the natural character determines to a large extent the perspective of our conceptions of Christian truth, and the colouring of our inner religious life. I do not mean to say, for a moment, that there is one uniform type to which all must be conformed, or they sin. There is indeed one type, the perfect manhood of Jesus, but it is all comprehensive, and each variety of our fragmentary manhood finds its own perfecting, and not its transmutation to another fashion of man, in being conformed to Him. Some of us are naturally fainthearted, timid, sceptical of any success, grave, melancholy, or hard to stir to any emotion. To such there will be an added difficulty in making quiet confident joy any very familiar guest in their home or in their place of prayer. But even such should remember that the 'powers of the world to come,' the energies of the Gospel, are given to us for the very express purpose of overcoming, as well as of hallowing, natural dispositions. If it be our duty to rejoice in the Lord, it is no sufficient excuse to urge for not responding to the reiterated call, 'I myself am disposed to sadness.'

Whilst making all allowances for the diversities of character, which will always operate to diversify the cast of the inner life in each individual, we think that, in the great majority of instances, there are two things, both faults, which have a great deal more to do with the absence of joy from much Christian experience, than any unfortunate natural tendency to the dark side of things. The one is, an actual deficiency in the depth and reality of our faith; and the other is, a misapprehension of the position which we have a right to take and are bound to take.

There is an actual deficiency in our faith. Oh, brethren! it is not to be wondered at that Christians do not find that the Lord with them is the Lord their strength and joy, as well as the Lord 'their righteousness'; when the amount of their fellowship with Him is so small, and the depth of it so shallow, as we usually find it. The first true vision that a sinful soul has of God, the imperfect beginnings of religion, usually are accompanied with intense self-abhorrence, and sorrowing tears of penitence. A further closer vision of the love of God in Jesus Christ brings with it 'joy and peace in believing.' But the prolongation of these throughout life requires the steadfast continuousness of gaze towards Him. It is only where there is much faith and consequent love that there is much joy. Let us search our own hearts. If there is but little heat around the bulb of the thermometer, no wonder that the mercury marks a low degree. If there is but small faith, there will not be much gladness. The road into Giant Despair's castle is through doubt, which doubt comes from an absence, a sinful absence, in our own experience, of the felt presence of God, and the felt force of the verities of His Gospel.

But then, besides that, there is another fault: not a fault in the sense of crime or sin, but a fault (and a great one) in the sense of error and misapprehension. We as Christians do not take the position which we have a right to take and that we are bound to take. Men venture themselves upon God's word as they do on doubtful ice, timidly putting a light foot out, to feel if it will bear them, and always having the tacit fear, 'Now, it is going to crack!' You must cast yourselves on God's Gospel with all your weight, without any hanging back, without any doubt, without even the shadow of a suspicion that it will *give*—that the firm, pure floor will give, and let you through into the water! A Christian shrink from saying what the Apostle said, 'I *know* in whom I have believed, and am persuaded that He is able to keep that which I have committed to Him until that day'! A Christian fancy that salvation is a future thing, and forget that it is a present thing! A Christian tremble to profess 'assurance of hope,' forgetting that there is no hope strong enough to bear the stress of a life's sorrows, which is not a conviction certain as one's own existence! Brethren! understand that the Gospel is a Gospel which brings a present salvation; and try to feel that it is not presumption, but simply acting out the very fundamental principle of it, when you are not afraid to say, 'I *know* that my Redeemer is yonder, and I *know* that He loves me!' Try to feel, I say, that by faith you have a right to take that position, 'Now, we *know* that we are the sons of God'; that you have a right to claim for yourselves, and that you are falling beneath the loftiness of the gift that is given to you unless you do claim for yourselves, the place of sons, accepted, loved, sure to be glorified at God's right hand. Am I teaching presumption? am I teaching carelessness, or a dispensing with self-examination? No, but I am saying this: If a man have once felt, and feel, in however small and feeble a degree, and depressed by whatsoever sense of daily transgressions, if he feel, faint like the first movement of an imprisoned bird in its egg, the feeble pulse of an almost imperceptible and fluttering faith beat—then that man has a right to say, 'God is mine!'

As one of our great teachers, little remembered now said, 'Let me take my personal salvation for granted'—and what? and 'be idle?' No; 'and *work* from it.' Ay, brethren! a Christian is not to be for ever asking himself, 'Am I a Christian?' He is not to be for ever looking into himself for marks and signs that he is. He *is* to look into himself to discover sins, that he may by God's help cast them out, to discover sins that shall teach him to say with greater thankfulness, 'What a redemption this is which I possess!' but he is to base his convictions that he is God's child upon something other than his own characteristics and the feebleness of his own strength. He is to have 'joy in the Lord' whatever may be his sorrow from outward things. And I believe that if Christian people would lay that thought to heart, they would understand better how the natural operation of the Gospel is to make them glad, and how rejoicing in the Lord is a Christian duty.

III. And now with regard to the other thought that still remains to be considered, namely, that rejoicing in the Lord is a source of strength,—I have already anticipated, fragmentarily, nearly all that I could have said here in a more systematic form. All gladness has something to do with our efficiency; for it is the prerogative of man that his force comes from his mind, and not from his body. That old song about a sad heart tiring in a mile, is as true in regard to the Gospel, and the works of Christian people, as in any other case. If we have hearts full of light, and souls at rest in Christ, and the wealth and blessedness of a tranquil gladness lying there, and filling our being; work will be easy, endurance will be easy, sorrow will be bearable, trials will not be so very hard, and above all temptations we shall be lifted, and set upon a rock. If the soul is full, and full of joy, what side of it will be exposed to the assault of any temptation? If the appeal be to fear, the gladness that is there is an answer. If the appeal be to passion, desire, wish for pleasure of any sort, there is no need for any more-the heart is *full*. And so the gladness which rests in Christ will be a gladness which will fit us for all service and for all endurance, which will be unbroken by any sorrow, and, like the magic shield of the old legends, invisible, impenetrable, in its crystalline purity will stand before the tempted heart, and will repel all the 'fiery darts of the wicked.'

'The joy of the Lord is your strength,' my brother! Nothing else is. No vehement resolutions, no sense of his own sinfulness, nor even contrite remembrance of past failures, ever yet made a man strong. It made him weak that he might become strong, and when it had done that it had done its work. For strength there must be hope, for strength there must be joy. If the arm is to smite with vigour, it must smite at the bidding of a calm and light heart. Christian work is of such a sort as that the most dangerous opponent to it is simple despondency and simple sorrow. 'The joy of the Lord is your strength.'

Well, then! there are two questions: How comes it that so much of the world's joy is weakness? and how comes it that so much of the world's notion of religion is gloom and sadness? Answer them for yourselves, and remember: you are weak unless you are glad; you are not glad and strong unless your faith and hope are fixed in Christ, and unless you are working from and not towards the sense of pardon, from and not towards the conviction of acceptance with God!

SABBATH OBSERVANCE

'In those days saw I in Judah some treading wine presses on the sabbath, and bringing in sheaves, and lading asses; as also wine, grapes, and figs, and all manner of burdens, which they brought into Jerusalem on the sabbath day: and I testified against them in the day wherein they sold victuals. 16. There dwelt men of Tyre also therein, which brought fish, and all manner of ware, and sold on the sabbath unto the children of Judah, and in Jerusalem. 17. Then I contended with the nobles of Judah, and said unto them, What evil thing is this that ye do, and profane the sabbath day? 18. Did not your fathers thus, and did not our God bring all this evil upon us, and upon this city? yet ye bring more wrath upon Israel by profaning the sabbath, 19. And it came to pass, that when the gates of Jerusalem began to be dark before the sabbath, I commanded that the gates should be shut, and charged that they should not be opened till after the sabbath: and some of my servants set I at the gates, that there should no burden be brought in on the sabbath day. 20. So the merchants and sellers of all kind of ware lodged without Jerusalem once or twice. 21. Then I testified against them, and said unto them, Why lodge ye about the wall? if ye do so again, I will lay hands on you. From that time forth came they no more on the sabbath. 22. And I commanded the Levites that they should cleanse themselves, and that they should come and keep the gates, to sanctify the sabbath day. Remember me, O my God, concerning this also, and spare me according to the greatness of Thy mercy.'—NEH. xiii. 15-22.

Many religious and moral reformations depend for their vitality on one man, and droop if his influence be withdrawn. It was so with Nehemiah's work. He toiled for twelve years in Jerusalem, and then returned for 'certain days' to the king at Babylon. The length of his absence is not given; but it was long enough to let much of his work be undone, and to give him much trouble to restore it to the condition in which he had left it. This last chapter of his book is but a sad close for a record which began with such high hope, and tells of such strenuous, self-sacrificing effort. The last page of many a reformer's history has been, like Nehemiah's, a sad account of efforts to stem the ebbing tide of enthusiasm and the flowing tide of worldliness. The heavy stone is rolled a little way up hill, and, as soon as one strong hand is withdrawn, down it tumbles again to its old place. The evanescence of great men's work makes much of the tragedy of history.

Our passage is particularly concerned with Nehemiah's efforts to enforce Sabbath observance. The rest of the chapter is occupied with similar efforts to set right other irregularities of a ceremonial character, such as the exclusion of Gentiles from the Temple, the exaction of the 'portions of the Levites,' and the like. The passage falls into three parts—the abuse (vs. 15, 16), the vigorous remedies (vs. 17-22), and the prayer (v. 22).

I. The abuse consisted in Sabbath work and trading. Nehemiah found, on his return, that the people 'in Judaea'—that is, in the country districts— carried on their farm labour and also brought their produce to market to Jerusalem on the Sabbath. So he 'testified against them in the day wherein they sold victuals'; that is, probably meaning that he warned them either in person or by messengers before taking further steps. Not only did Jews break the sacred day, but they let heathen do so too. The narrative tells, with a kind of horror, the many aggravations of this piece of wickedness. 'They'— Gentiles with whom contact defiled—'sold on the Sabbath'—the day of rest—'to the children of Judah'—God's people—'in Jerusalem'—the Holy City. It was a many-barrelled crime. Tyre was far from Jerusalem, and one does not see how fish could have been brought in good condition. Perhaps their perishableness was the excuse for allowing their sale on the Sabbath, as is sometimes the case in fishing-villages even in Sabbath-keeping Scotland. Such was the abuse with which Nehemiah struggled.

It is easy to pooh-pooh his crusade against Sabbath labour as mere scrupulousness about externals. But it is a blunder and an injustice to a noble character if we forget that the stage of revelation at which he stood necessarily made him more dependent on externals than Christians are or should be. But his vindication does not need such considerations. He had a truer insight into what active men needed for vigorous working days, and what devout men needed for healthy religion, than many moderns who smile at his eagerness about 'mere externalisms.'

It is easy to ridicule the Jewish Sabbath and 'the Puritan Sunday.' No doubt there have been and are well-meant but mistaken efforts to insist on too rigid observance. No doubt it has been often forgotten by good people that the Christian Lord's Day is not the Jewish Sabbath. Of course the religious observance of the day is not a fit subject for legislation. But the need for a seventh day of rest is impressed on our physical and intellectual nature; and devout hearts will joyfully find their best rest in Christian worship and service. The vigour of religious life demands special seasons set apart for worship. Unless there be such reservoirs along the road, there will be but a thin trickle of a brook by the way. It is all very well to talk about religion diffused through the life, but it will not be so diffused unless it is concentrated at certain times.

They are no benefactors to the community who seek to break down and relax the stringency of the prohibition of labour. If once the idea that Sunday is a day of amusement take root, the amusement of some will require the hard work of others, and the custom of work will tend to extend, till rest becomes the exception, and work the rule. There never was a time when men lived so furiously fast as now. The pace of modern life demands Sunday rest more than ever. If a railway car is run continually it will wear out sooner than if it were laid aside for a day or two occasionally; and if it is run at express speed it will need the rest more. We are all going at top speed; and there would be more breakdowns if it were not for that blessed institution which some people think they are promoting the public good by destroying—a seventh day of rest.

Our great trading centres in England have the same foreign element to complicate matters as Nehemiah had to deal with. The Tyrian fishmongers knew and cared nothing for Israel's Jehovah or Sabbath, and their presence would increase the tendency to disregard the day. So with us, foreigners of many nationalities, but alike in their disregard of our religious observances, leaven the society, and help to mould the opinions and practices, of our great cities. That is a very real source of danger in regard to Sabbath observance and many other things; and Christian people should be on their guard against it.

II. The vigorous remedies applied by Nehemiah were administered first to the rulers. He sent for the nobles, and laid the blame at their doors. 'Ye profane the day,' said he. Men in authority are responsible for crimes which they could check, but prefer to wink at. Nehemiah seems to trace all the national calamities to the breach of the Sabbath; but of course he is simply laying stress on the sin about which he is speaking, as any man who sets himself earnestly to work to fight any form of evil is apt to do. Then the men who are not in earnest cry out about 'exaggeration.' Many other sins besides Sabbath-breaking had a share in sending Israel into captivity; and if

Nehemiah had been fighting with idolatrous tendencies he would have isolated idolatry as the cause of its calamities, just as, when fighting against Sabbath-breaking, he emphasises that sin.

Nehemiah was governor for the Persian king, and so had a right to rate these nobles. In this day the people have the same right, and there are many social sins for which they should arraign civic and other authorities. Christian principles unflinchingly insisted on by Christian people, and brought to bear, by ballot-boxes and other persuasive ways, on what stands for conscience in some high places, would make a wonderful difference on many of the abominations of our cities. Go to the 'nobles' first, and lay the burden on the backs that ought to carry it.

Then Nehemiah took practical measures by shutting the city gates on the eve of the Sabbath, and putting some of his own servants as a watch. The thing seems to have been done without any notice; so when the country folk came in, as usual, on the Sabbath, they could not get into the city, and camped outside, making a visible temptation to the citizens, to slip out and do a little business, if they could manage to elude the guards. Once or twice this happened; and then Nehemiah himself seems to have taken them in hand, with a very plain and sufficiently emphatic warning: 'If ye do so again, I will lay hands on you.'

Of course, 'from that time they came no more on the Sabbath,' as was natural after such a volley. A man with a good strong will is apt to get his own way, even when he is not clothed with the authority of a governor. Then Nehemiah strengthened the guard, or perhaps withdrew his own servants and substituted for them Levites, whose official position would put them in full sympathy with his efforts. That priestly guard would be inflexible, and with its appointment the abuse appears to have been crushed.

The example of Nehemiah's enforcing Sabbath observance is not to be taken as a pattern for Christian communities, without many limitations. But it appears to the present writer that it is perfectly legitimate for the civil power to insist upon, and if necessary to enforce, the observance of Sunday as a day of rest; and that, since legitimate, it is for the well-being of the community that it should do so. Tyrians might believe anything they chose, and use the day of rest as they thought proper, so long as they did not sell fish on it. We do not interfere with religious convictions when we enjoin Sunday observance. Nehemiah's argument has sometimes to be used, even about such a matter: 'If ye do so again, I will lay hands on you.'

The methods adopted may yield suggestions for all who would aim at reforming abuses or public immoralities. One most necessary step is to cut off, as far as possible, opportunities for the sin. There will be no trade if you shut the gates the night before. There will be little drunkenness if there are no liquor shops. It is quite true that people cannot be made virtuous by legislation, but it is also true that they may be saved from temptations to become vicious by it.

Another hint comes from Nehemiah's vigorous word to the country folk outside the wall. There is need for very strong determination and much sanctified obstinacy in fighting popular abuses. They die hard. It is permissible to invoke the aid of the lawful authority. But a man with strong convictions and earnest purpose will be able to impress his convictions on a mass, even if he have no guards at his back. The one thing needful for Christian reformers is, not the power to appeal to force, but the force which they can carry within them. And it is better when the traders love the Sabbath too well to wish to drive bargains on it, than when they are hindered from doing as they wish by Nehemiah's strong will or formidable threats.

Once more, the guard of Levites may suggest that the execution of measures for the reformation of manners or morals is best entrusted to those who are in sympathy with them. Levites made faithful watchmen. Many a promising measure for reformation has come to nothing because committed to the hands of functionaries who did not care for its success. The instruments are almost as important as the measures which they carry out.

III. Nehemiah's prayer occurs thrice in this chapter, at the close of each section recounting his reforming acts. In the first instance (v. 14) it is most full, and puts very plainly the merit of good deeds as a plea with God. The same thing is implied in its form in verse 22. But while, no doubt, the tone of the prayer is startling to us, and is not such as should be offered now by Christians, it but echoes the principle of retribution which underlies the law. 'This do, and thou shalt live,' was the very foundation of Nehemiah's form of God's revelation. We do not plead our own merits, because we are not under the law, but under grace, and the principle underlying the gospel is life by impartation of unmerited mercy and divine life. But the law of retribution still remains valid for Christians in so far as that God will never forget any of their works, and will give them full recompense for their work of faith and labour of love. Eternal life here and hereafter is wholly the gift of God; but that fact does not exclude the notion of 'the recompense of reward' from the Christian conception of the future. It becomes not us to present our good deeds before the Judge, since they are stained and imperfect, and the goodness in them is His gift. But it becomes Him to crown them with His gracious approbation, and to proportion the cities ruled in that future world to the talents faithfully used here. We need not be afraid of obscuring the truth that we are saved 'not of works, lest any man should boast,' though we insist that a Christian man is rewarded according to his works.

Nehemiah had no false notion of his own goodness; for, while he asked for recompense for these good deeds of his, he could not but add, 'Spare me according to the greatness of Thy mercy.' He who asks to be 'spared' must know himself in peril of destruction; and he who invokes 'mercy' must think that, if he were dealt with according to justice, he would be in evil case. So the consciousness of weakness and sin is an integral part of this prayer, and that takes all the apparent self-righteousness out of the previous petition. However worthy of and sure of reward a Christian man's acts of love and efforts for the spread of God's honour may be, the doer of them must still be 'looking for the mercy of our Lord Jesus Christ unto eternal life.'

THE BOOK OF ESTHER

THE NET SPREAD

'After these things did king Ahasuerus promote Haman the son of Hammedatha the Agagite, and advanced him, and set his seat above all the princes that were with him. 2. And all the king's servants, that were in the king's gate, bowed, and reverenced Haman: for the king had so commanded concerning him. But Mordecai bowed not, nor did him reverence. 3. Then the king's servants which were in the king's gate, said unto Mordecai, Why transgressest thou the king's commandment? 4. Now it came to pass, when they spake daily unto him, and he hearkened not unto them, that they told Haman, to see whether Mordecai's matters would stand: for he had told them that he was a Jew. 5. And when Haman saw that Mordecai bowed not, nor did him reverence, then was Haman full of wrath. 6. And he thought scorn to lay hands on Mordecai alone; for they had showed him the people of Mordecai: wherefore Haman sought to destroy all the Jews that were throughout the whole kingdom of Ahasuerus, even the people of Mordecai. 7. In the first month, that is, the month Nisan, in the twelfth year of king Ahasuerus, they cast Pur, that is, the lot, before Haman from day to day, and from month to month, to the twelfth month, that is, the month Adar. 8. And Haman said unto king Ahasuerus, There is a certain people scattered abroad and dispersed among the people in all the provinces of thy kingdom; and their laws are diverse from all people; neither keep they the king's laws: therefore it is not for the king's profit to suffer them. 9. If it please the king, let it be written that they may be destroyed: and I will pay ten thousand talents of silver to the hands of those that have the charge of the business, to bring it into the king's treasuries. 10. And the king took his ring from his hand, and gave it unto Haman the son of Hammedatha the Agagite, the Jews' enemy. 11. And the king said unto Haman, The silver is given to thee, the people also, to do with them as it seemeth good to thee.'—ESTHER iii. 1-11.

The stage of this passage is filled by three strongly marked and strongly contrasted figures: Mordecai, Haman, and Ahasuerus; a sturdy nonconformist, an arrogant and vindictive minister of state, and a despotic and careless king. These three are the visible persons, but behind them is an unseen and unnamed Presence, the God of Israel, who still protects His exiled people.

We note, first, the sturdy nonconformist. 'The reverence' which the king had commanded his servants to show to Haman was not simply a sign of respect, but an act of worship. Eastern adulation regarded a monarch as in some sense a god, and we know that divine honours were in later times paid to Roman emperors, and many Christians martyred for refusing to render them. The command indicates that Ahasuerus desired Haman to be regarded as his representative, and possessing at least some reflection of godhead from him. European ambassadors to Eastern courts have often refused to prostrate themselves before the monarch on the ground of its being degradation to their dignity; but Mordecai stood erect while the crowd of servants lay flat on their faces, as the great man passed through the gate, because he would have no share in an act of worship to any but Jehovah. He might have compromised with conscience, and found some plausible excuses if he had wished. He could have put his own private interpretation on the prostration, and said to himself, 'I have nothing to do with the meaning that others attach to bowing before Haman. I mean by it only due honour to the second man in the kingdom.' But the monotheism of his race was too deeply ingrained in him, and so he kept 'a stiff backbone' and 'bowed not down.'

That his refusal was based on religious scruples is the natural inference from his having told his fellow-porters that he was a Jew. That fact would explain his attitude, but would also isolate him still more. His obstinacy piqued them, and they reported his contumacy to the great man, thus at once gratifying personal dislike, racial hatred, and religious antagonism, and recommending themselves to Haman as solicitous for his dignity. We too are sometimes placed in circumstances where we are tempted to take part in what may be called constructive idolatry. There arise, in our necessary co-operation with those who do not share in our faith, occasions when we are expected to unite in acts which we are thought very straitlaced for refusing to do, but which, conscience tells us, cannot be done without practical disloyalty to Jesus Christ. Whenever that inner voice says 'Don't,' we must disregard the persistent solicitations of others, and be ready to be singular, and run any risk rather than comply. 'So did not I, because of the fear of God,' has to be our motto, whatever fellow-servants may say. The gate of Ahasuerus's palace was not a favourable soil for the growth of a devout soul, but flowers can bloom on dunghills, and there have been 'saints' in 'Caesar's household.'

Haman is a sharp contrast to Mordecai. He is the type of the unworthy characters that climb or crawl to power in a despotic monarchy, vindictive, arrogant, cunning, totally oblivious of the good of the subjects, using his position for his own advantage, and ferociously cruel. He had naturally not noticed the one erect figure among the crowd of abject ones, but the insignificant Jew became important when pointed out. If he had bowed, he would have been one more nobody, but his not bowing made him somebody who had to be crushed. The childish burst of passion is very characteristic, and not less true to life is the extension of the anger and thirst for vengeance to 'all the Jews that were throughout the whole kingdom of Ahasuerus.' They were 'the people of Mordecai,' and that was enough. 'He thought scorn to lay hands on Mordecai alone.' What a perverted notion of personal dignity which thought the sacrifice of the one offender beneath it, and could only be satisfied by a blood-bath into which a nation should be plunged! Such an extreme of frantic lust for murder is only possible in such a state as Ahasuerus's Persia, but the prostitution of public position to personal ends, and the adoption of political measures at the bidding of wounded vanity, and to gratify blind hatred of a race, is possible still, and it becomes all Christian men to use their influence that the public acts of their nation shall be clear of that taint.

Haman was as superstitious as cruel, and so he sought for auguries from heaven for his hellish purpose, and cast the lot to find the favourable day for bringing it about. He is not the only one who has sought divine approval for wicked public acts. Religion has been used to varnish many a crime, and *Te Deums* sung for many a victory which was little better than Haman's plot.

The crafty denunciation of the Jews to the king is a good specimen of the way in which a despot is hoodwinked by his favourites, and made their tool. It was no doubt true that the Jews' laws were 'diverse from those of every people,' but it was not true that they did not 'keep the king's laws,' except in so far as these required worship of other gods. In all their long dispersion they have been remarkable for two things,—their tenacious adherence to the Law, so far as possible in exile, and their obedience to the law of the country of their sojourn. No doubt, the exiles in Persian territory presented the same characteristics. But Haman has had many followers in resenting the distinctiveness of the Jew, and charging on them crimes of which they were innocent. From Mordecai onwards it has been so, and Europe is to-day disgraced by a crusade against them less excusable than Haman's. Hatred still masks itself under the disguise of political expediency, and says, 'It is not for the king's profit to suffer them.'

But the true half of the charge was a eulogium, for it implied that the scattered exiles were faithful to God's laws, and were marked off by their lives. That ought to be true of professing Christians. They should obviously be living by other principles than the world adopts. The enemy's charge 'shall turn unto you for a testimony.' Happy shall we be if observers are prompted to say of us that 'our laws are diverse' from those of ungodly men around us!

The great bribe which Haman offered to the king is variously estimated as equal to from three to four millions sterling. He, no doubt, reckoned on making more than that out of the confiscation of Jewish property. That such an offer should have been made by the chief minister to the king, and that for such a purpose, reveals a depth of corruption which would be incredible if similar horrors were not recorded of other Eastern despots. But with Turkey still astonishing the world, no one can call Haman's offer too atrocious to be true.

Ahasuerus is the vain-glorious king known to us as Xerxes. His conduct in the affair corresponds well enough with his known character. The lives of thousands of law-abiding subjects are tossed to the favourite without inquiry or hesitation. He does not even ask the name of the 'certain people,' much less require proof of the charge against them. The insanity of weakening his empire by killing so many of its inhabitants does not strike him, nor does he ever seem to think that he has duties to those under his rule. Careless of the sanctity of human life, too indolent to take trouble to see things with his own eyes, apparently without the rudiments of the idea of justice, he wallowed in a sty of self-indulgence, and, while greedy of adulation and the semblance of power, let the reality slip from his hands into those of the favourite, who played on his vices as on an instrument, and pulled the strings that moved the puppet. We do not produce kings of that sort nowadays, but King Demos has his own vices, and is as easily blinded and swayed as Ahasuerus. In every form of government, monarchy or republic, there will be would-be leaders, who seek to gain influence and carry their objects by tickling vanity, operating on vices, calumniating innocent men, and the other arts of the demagogue. Where the power is in the hands of the people, the people is very apt to take its responsibilities as lightly as Ahasuerus did his, and to let itself be led blindfold by men with personal ends to serve, and hiding them under the veil of eager desire for the public good. Christians should 'play the citizen as it becomes the gospel of Christ,' and take care that they are not beguiled into national enmities and public injustice by the specious talk of modern Hamans.

ESTHER'S VENTURE

'Again Esther spake unto Hatach, and gave him commandment unto Mordecai: 11. All the king's servants, and the people of the king's provinces, do know, that whosoever, whether man or woman, shall come unto the king into the inner court, who is not called, there is one law of his to put him to death, except such to whom the king shall hold out the golden sceptre, that he may live: but I have not been called to come in unto the king these thirty days. 12. And they told to Mordecai Esther's words. 13. Then Mordecai commanded to answer Esther, Think not with thyself that thou shalt escape in the king's house, more than all the Jews. 14. For if thou altogether holdest thy peace at this time, then shall there enlargement and deliverance arise to the Jews from another place; but thou and thy father's house shall be destroyed: and who knoweth whether thou art come to the kingdom for such a time as this? 15. Then Esther bade them return Mordecai this answer, 16. Go, gather together all the Jews that are present in Shushan, and fast ye for me, and neither eat nor drink three days, night or day: I also and my maidens will fast likewise; and so will I go in unto the king, which is not according to the law: and if I perish, I perish. 17. So Mordecai went his way, and did according to all that Esther had commanded him. 'Now it came to pass on the third day, that Esther put on her royal apparel, and stood in the inner court of the king's house, over against the king's house: and the king sat upon his royal throne in the royal house, over against the gate of the house. 2. And it was so, when the king saw Esther the queen standing in the court, that she obtained favour in his sight: and the king held out to Esther the golden sceptre that was in his hand. So Esther drew near, and touched the top of the sceptre. 3. Then said the king unto her, What wilt thou, queen Esther? and what is thy request? it shall be even given thee to the half of the kingdom.'- ESTHER iv. 10-17; v. 1-3.

Patriotism is more evident than religion in the Book of Esther. To turn to it after the fervours of prophets and the continual recognition of God in history which marks the other historical books, is like coming down from heaven to earth, as Ewald says. But that difference in tone probably accurately represents the difference between the saints and heroes of an earlier age and the Jews in Persia, in whom national feeling was stronger than devotion. The picture of their characteristics deducible from this Book shows many of the traits which have marked them ever since,—accommodating flexibility, strangely united with unbending tenacity; a capacity for securing the favour of influential people, and willingness to stretch conscience in securing it; reticence and diplomacy; and, beneath all, unquenchable devotion to Israel, which burns alike in the politic Mordecai and the lovely Esther.

There is not much audible religion in either, but in this lesson Mordecai impressively enforces his assurance that Israel cannot perish, and his belief in Providence setting people in their places for great unselfish ends; and Esther is ready to die, if need be, in trying to save her people, and thinks that fasting and prayer will help her in her daring attempt. These two cousins, unlike in so much, were alike in their devotion to Israel; and though they said little about their religion, they acted it, which is better.

It is very like Jews that the relationship between Mordecai and Esther should have been kept dark. Nobody but one or two trusted servants knew that the porter was the queen's cousin, and probably her Jewish birth was also unknown. Secrecy is, no doubt, the armour of oppressed nations; but it is peculiarly agreeable to the descendants of Jacob, who was a master of the art. There must have been wonderful self-command on both sides to keep such a secret, and true affection, to preserve intercourse through apparent indifference.

Our passage begins in the middle of Esther's conversation with the confidential go-between, who told her of the insane decree for the destruction of the Jews, and of Mordecai's request that she should appeal to the king. She reminds him of what he knew well enough, the law that unsummoned intruders into the presence are liable to death; and adds what, of course, he did not know, that she had not been summoned for a month. We need not dwell on this ridiculously arrogant law, but may remark that the substantial accuracy of the statement is confirmed by classical and other authors, and may pause for a moment to note the glimpse given here of the delirium of self-importance in which these Persian kings lived, and to see in it no small cause of their vices and disasters. What chance of knowing facts or of living a wholesome life had a man shut off thus from all but lickspittles and slaves? No wonder that the victims of such dignity beat the sea with rods, when it was rude enough to wreck their ships! No wonder that they wallowed in sensuality, and lost pith and manhood! No wonder that Greece crushed their unwieldy armies and fleets!

And what a glimpse into their heart-emptiness and degradation of sacred ties is given in the fact that Esther the queen had not seen Ahasuerus for a month, though living in the same palace, and his favourite wife! No doubt, the experiences of exile had something to do in later ages with the decided preference of the Jew for monogamy.

But, passing from this, we need only observe how clearly Esther sees and how calmly she tells Mordecai the tremendous risk which following his counsel would bring. Note that she does not refuse. She simply puts the case plainly, as if she invited further communication. 'This is how things stand. Do you still wish me to run the risk?' That is poor courage which has to shut its eyes in order to keep itself up to the mark. Unfortunately, the temperament which clearly sees dangers and that which dares them are not often found together in due proportion, and so men are over-rash and over-cautious. This young queen with her clear eyes saw, and with her brave heart was ready to face, peril to her life. Unless we fully realise difficulties and dangers beforehand, our enthusiasm for great causes will ooze out at our fingers' ends at the first rude assault of these. So let us count the cost before we take up arms, and let us take up arms after we have counted the cost. Cautious courage, courageous caution, are good guides. Either alone is a bad one.

Mordecai's grand message is a condensed statement of the great reasons which always exist for self-sacrificing efforts for others' good. His words are none the less saturated with devout thought because they do not name God. This porter at the palace gate had not the tongue of a psalmist or of a prophet. He was a plain man, not uninfluenced by his pagan surroundings, and perhaps he was careful to adapt his message to the lips of the Gentile messenger, and therefore did not more definitely use the sacred name.

It is very striking that Mordecai makes no attempt to minimise Esther's peril in doing as he wished. He knew that she would take her life in her hand, and he expects her to be willing to do it, as he would have been willing. It is grand when love exhorts loved ones to a course which may bring death to them, and lifelong loneliness and quenched hopes to it. Think of Mordecai's years of care over and pride in his fair young cousin, and how many joys and soaring visions would perish with her, and then estimate the heroic self-sacrifice he exercised in urging her to her course.

His first appeal is on the lowest ground. Pure selfishness should send her to the king; for, if she did not go, she would not escape the common ruin. So, on the one hand, she had to face certain destruction; and, on the other, there were possible success and escape. It may seem unlikely that the general massacre should include the favourite queen, and especially as her nationality was apparently a secret. But when a mob has once tasted blood, its appetite is great and its scent keen, and there are always informers at hand to point to hidden victims. The argument holds in reference to many forms of conflict with national and social evils. If Christian people allow vice and godlessness to riot unchecked, they will not escape the contagion, in some form or other. How many good men's sons have been swept away by the immoralities of great cities! How few families there are in which there is not 'one dead,' the victim of drink and dissipation! How the godliness of the Church is cooled down by the low temperature around! At the very lowest, self-preservation should enlist all good men in a sacred war against the sins which are slaying their countrymen. If smallpox breaks out in the slums, it will come uptown into the grand houses, and the outcasts will prove that they are the rich man's brethren by infecting him, and perhaps killing him.

Mordecai goes back to the same argument in the later part of his answer, when he foretells the destruction of Esther and her father's house. There he puts it, however, in a rather different light. The destruction is not now, as before, her participation in the common tragedy, but her exceptional ruin while Israel is preserved. The unfaithful one, who could have intervened to save, and did not, will have a special infliction of punishment. That is true in many applications. Certainly, neglect to do what we can do for others does always bring some penalty on the slothful coward; and there is no more short-sighted policy than that which shirks plain duties of beneficence from regard to self.

But higher considerations than selfish ones are appealed to. Mordecai is sure that deliverance will come. He does not know whence, but come it will. How did he arrive at that serene confidence? Certainly because he trusted God's ancient promises, and believed in the indestructibility of the nation which a divine hand protected. How does such a confidence agree with fear of 'destruction'? The two parts of Mordecai's message sound contradictory;

but he might well dread the threatened catastrophe, and yet be sure that through any disaster Israel as a nation would pass, cast down, no doubt, but not destroyed.

How did it agree with his earnestness in trying to secure Esther's help? If he was certain of the issue, why should he have troubled her or himself? Just for the same reason that the discernment of God's purposes and absolute reliance on these stimulate, and do not paralyse, devout activity in helping to carry them out. If we are sure that a given course, however full of peril and inconvenience, is in the line of God's purposes, that is a reason for strenuous effort to carry it out. Since some men are to be honoured to be His instruments, shall not we be willing to offer ourselves? There is a holy and noble ambition which covets the dignity of being used by Him. They who believe that their work helps forward what is dear to God's heart may well do with their might what they find to do, and not be too careful to keep on the safe side in doing it. The honour is more than the danger. 'Here am I; take me,' should be the Christian feeling about all such work.

The last argument in this noble summary of motives for self-sacrifice for others' good is the thought of God's purpose in giving Esther her position. It carries large truth applicable to us all. The source of all endowments of position, possessions, or capacities, is God. His purpose in them all goes far beyond the happiness of the receiver. Dignities and gifts of every sort are ours for use in carrying out His great designs of good to our fellows. Esther was made queen, not that she might live in luxury and be the plaything of a king, but that she might serve Israel. Power is duty. Responsibility is measured by capacity. Obligation attends advantages. Gifts are burdens. All men are stewards, and God gives His servants their 'talents,' not for selfish squandering or hoarding, but to trade with, and to pay the profits to Him. This penetrating insight into the source and intention of all which we have, carries a solemn lesson for us all.

The fair young heroine's soul rose to the occasion, and responded with a swift determination to her older cousin's lofty words. Her pathetic request for the prayers of the people for whose sake she was facing death was surely more than superstition. Little as she says about her faith in God, it obviously underlay her courage. A soul that dares death in obedience to His will and in dependence on His aid, demonstrates its godliness more forcibly in silence than by many professions.

'If I perish, I perish!' Think of the fair, soft lips set to utter that grand surrender, and of all the flowery and silken cords which bound the young heart to life, so bright and desirable as was assured to her. Note the resolute calmness, the Spartan brevity, the clear sight of the possible fatal issue, the absolute submission. No higher strain has ever come from human lips. This womanly soul was of the same stock as a Miriam, a Deborah, Jephthah's daughter; and the same fire burned in her,—utter devotion to Israel because entire consecration to Israel's God. Religion and patriotism were to her inseparable. What was her individual life compared with her people's weal and her God's will? She was ready without a murmur to lay her young radiant life down. Such ecstasy of willing self-sacrifice raises its subject above all fears and dissolves all hindrances. It may be wrought out in uneventful details of our small lives, and may illuminate these as truly as it sheds imperishable lustre over the lovely figure standing in the palace court, and waiting for life or death at the will of a sensual tyrant.

The scene there need not detain us. We can fancy Esther's beating heart putting fire in her cheek, and her subdued excitement making her beauty more splendid as she stood. What a contrast between her and the arrogant king on his throne! He was a voluptuary, ruined morally by unchecked licence,—a monster, as he could hardly help being, of lust, self will, and caprice. She was at that moment an incarnation of self-sacrifice and pure enthusiasm. The blind world thought that he was the greater; but how ludicrous his condescension, how vulgar his pomp, how coarse his kindness, how gross his prodigal promises by the side of the heroine of faith, whose life he held in his capricious hand!

How amazed the king would have been if he had been told that one of his chief titles to be remembered would be that moment's interview! Ahasuerus is the type of swollen self-indulgence, which always degrades and coarsens; Esther is the type of self-sacrifice which as uniformly refines, elevates, and arrays with new beauty and power. If we would reach the highest nobleness possible to us, we must stand with Esther at the gate, and not envy or imitate Ahasuerus on his gaudy throne. 'He that loveth his life shall lose it; and he that loseth his life for My sake and the gospel's, the same shall find it.'

MORDECAI AND ESTHER

'For if thou altogether holdest thy peace at this time, then shall there enlargement and deliverance arise to the Jews from another place; but thou and thy father's house shall be destroyed: and who knoweth whether thou art come to the kingdom for such a time as this?'—ESTHER iv. 14.

All Christians are agreed in holding the principles which underlie our missionary operations. They all believe that the world is a fallen world, that without Christ the fallen world is a lost world, that the preaching of the Gospel is the way to bring Christ to those who need Him, that to the Church is committed the ministry of reconciliation.

These are the grand truths from which the grand missionary enterprise has sprung. It is not my intention to enlarge on them now. But in this and in all cases, there are secondary motives besides, and inferior to those which are derived from the real fundamental principles. We are stimulated to action not only because we hold certain great principles, but because they are reinforced by certain subordinate considerations.

It is the duty of all Christians to promote the missionary cause on the lofty grounds already referred to. Besides that, it may be in a special way our duty for some additional reasons drawn from peculiarities in our condition. Circumstances do not make duties, but they may bring a special weight of obligation on us to do them. Times again do not make duties, but they too make a thing a special duty now. The consideration of consequences may not decide us in matters of conscience, but it may allowably come in to deter us from what is on higher grounds a sin to be avoided, or a good deed to be done. Success or failure is an alternative that must not be thought of when we are asking ourselves, 'Ought I to do this?' but when we have answered that question, we may go to work with a lighter heart and a firmer hand if we are sure that we are not going to fail.

All these are inferior considerations which do not avail to determine duty and do not go deep enough to constitute the real foundation of our obligation. They are considerations which can scarcely be shut out, and should be taken in determining the weight of our obligation, in shaping the selection of our duties, in stimulating the zeal and sedulousness with which we do what we know to be right.

To a consideration of some of these secondary reasons for energy in the work of missions I ask your attention. The verse which I have selected for my text is spoken by Mordecai to Esther, when urging her to her perilous patriotism. It singularly blends the statesman and the believer. He sees that if she selfishly refuses to identify herself with her people, in their calamity, the wave that sweeps them away will not be stayed outside her royal dwelling; he knows too much of courts to think that she can stand against that burst of popular fury should it break out. But he looks on as a devout man believing God's promises, and seeing past all instruments; he warns her that 'deliverance and enlargement shall arise.' He is no fatalist; he believes in man's work, therefore he urges her to let herself be the instrument by which God's work shall be done. He is no atheist; he believes in God's sovereign power and unchangeable faithfulness, therefore he looks without dismay to the possibility of her failure. He knows that if she is idle, all the evil will come on her head, who has been unfaithful, and that in spite of that God's faithfulness shall not be made of none effect. He believes that she has been raised to her position for God's sake, for her brethren's sake, not her own.

'Who knoweth whether thou art come to the kingdom for such a time as this?' There speaks the devout statesman, the court-experienced believer. He has seen favourites tended and tossed aside, viziers powerful and beheaded, kings half deified and deserted in their utmost need. Sitting at the gate there, he has seen generations of Hamans go out and in; he has seen the craft, the cruelty, the lusts which have been the apparent causes of the puppets' rise and fall, and he has looked beyond it all and believed in a Hand that pulled the wires, in a King of Kings who raiseth up one and setteth down another. So he believes that his Esther has come to the kingdom by God's appointment, to do God's work at God's time. And these convictions keep him calm and stir her.

We may find here a series of considerations having a special bearing on this missionary work. To them I ask your attention.

I. God gives us our position that we may use it for His cause, for the spread of the Gospel.

In most general terms.

(a) No man has anything for his own sake—no man liveth to himself. We come to the kingdom for others. Here we touch the foundation of all authority; we learn the awful burden of all talents, the dreadful weight of every gift.

(b) No man receives the Gospel for his own sake. We are not non-conductors, but stand all linked hand in hand. We are members of the body that the blood may flow freely through us. For no loftier reason did God light the candle than that it might give light. We are beacons kindled to transmit, till every sister light flashes back the ray.

(c) We especially have received a position in the world for the conversion of the world. Our national character and position unite that of the Jew in his two stages—we are set to be the 'light of the world,' and we are 'tribes of the wandering foot.' Our history, all, has tended to this function, our local position, our laws, our commerce. We are citizens of a nation which 'as a nest has found the riches' of the peoples. In every land our people dwell.

Think of our colonies. Think that we are brought into contact with heathen, whether we will or not. We cannot help influencing them. 'Through you the name of God is blasphemed amongst the Gentiles.' Think of our sailors. Why this position? What is plainer than that all this is in order that the Gospel might be spread? God has ever let the Gospel follow in the tracks made for it by commercial law.

This object does not exclude others. Our language, our literature, our other rich spiritual treasures, we hold them all that we may impart. But remember that all these other good things that England has will spread themselves with little effort, people will be glad to get them. But the Gospel will not be spread so. It must be taken to those who do not want it. It must be held forth with outstretched hands to 'a disobedient and gainsaying people.' It is found of them that seek it not.

Like the Lord we must go to the wanderers, we must find them as they lie panting and thirsty in the wild wilderness. Therefore Christian men must make special earnest efforts or the work will not be done. They must be as the 'dew that tarrieth not for man, nor waiteth for the sons of men.'

And again, such action does not involve approval of the means by which such a position has become ours. Mordecai knew what vile passions had been at work to put Esther there, and did not forget poor Vashti, and we have no need to hide conviction that England's place has often been won by wrong, been kept by violence and fraud, that, as she has strode to empire, her foot has trodden on many a venerable throne unjustly thrown down, and her skirts have been dabbled with 'the blood of poor innocents,' splashed there with her armed hoof. Be it so!—Still! 'Thou makest the wrath of man to praise Thee.' Still—'we are debtors both to the Greek and barbarian,' and all the more debtors because of ills inflicted. God has laid on us a solemn responsibility. Over all the dust of base intrigues, and the smoke of bloody battles, and the hubbub of busy commerce, His hand has been working, and though we have been sinful, He has given us a place and a power, mighty and awful. We have received these not for our own glory, not that we should boast of our dominion, not that we should gather tribute of gain and glory from subject peoples, not even that we should carry to them the great though lesser blessings of language, united order, peaceful commerce, sway over brute nature, but that we should give them what will make them men— Christ.

We have a work to do, an awful work. To us all as Christians, to us especially as citizens of this land and members of this race, to us and to our brethren across the Atlantic the message comes, by our history, our manners, etc., as plainly as if it were written in every wave that beats around our coast. 'Ye are my witnesses, saith the Lord.'

II. God lays upon us special missionary work by the special characteristics of the times.

'Such a time as this!' Was there ever such a time?

Look at the condition of heathenism. It is everywhere tottering. 'The idols are on the beasts, Bel boweth down.' The grim gods sit half famished already. There is a crack in every temple wall. Mahommedanism, Buddhism, Brahminism—they are none of them progressive. They are none of them vital. Think how only the Gospel outleaps space and time. How all these systems are of time and devoured by it, as Saturn eats his own children. They are of the things that can be shaken, and their being shaken makes more certain the remaining of the things that cannot be shaken.

Look at the fields open. India, China, Japan, Africa, in a word, 'The field is the world' in a degree in which it never was before. 'Such a time'—a time of seething, and we can determine the cosmos; a plastic time, and we can mould it; it is a deluge, push the ark boldly out and ransom some.

III. If we neglect the voice of God's providence, harm comes on us.

The gifts unimproved are apt to be lost. One knows not all the conditions on which England holds her sway, nor do we fathom the strange way in which spiritual characteristics are inwrought with material interests. But we believe in a providential government of the world, and of this we may be very sure, that all advantages not used for God are held by a very precarious tenure.

The fact is that selfishness is the ruin of any people. When you have a 'Christian' nation not using their position for God's glory, they are using it for their own sakes; and that indicates a state of mind which will lead to numberless other evils in their relation to men, many of which have a direct tendency to rob them of their advantages. For instance, a selfish nation will never hold conquests with a firm grasp. If we do not bind subject peoples to us by benefits, we shall repel them by hatreds. Think of India and its lessons, or of South Africa and its. We have seen the tide of material prosperity ebb away from many a nation and land, and I for my part believe in the Hand of God in history, and believe that the tide follows the motions of the heavens.

The history of the Jewish people is not an exception to the laws of God's government of the world, but a specimen of it. They who were made a hearth in which the embers of divine truth were kept in a dark world, when they began to think that they had the truth in order that they might be different from other people, and forgot that they were different from others in order that they might first preserve and then impart the truth to all, lost the light and heat of it, stiffened into formal hypocrisy and malice and all uncharitableness, and then the Roman sword smote their national life in twain.

Whatever is not used for God becomes a snare first, then injures the possessors, and tends to destroy the possessors. The march of Providence goes on. Its purposes will be effected. Whatever stands in the way will be mowed remorselessly down, if need be. Helps that have become hindrances will go. The kingdoms of this world will have to fall; and if we are not helping and hasting the coming of the Lord we shall be destroyed by the brightness of His coming. The chariot rolls on. For men and for nations there is only the choice of yoking themselves to the car, and finding themselves borne along rather than bearing it, and partaking the triumph, or of being crushed beneath its awful wheels as they bound along their certain road, bearing Him who rides 'forth prosperously because of truth and meekness and righteousness.'

IV. Though we be unfaithful, God's purpose of mercy to the world shall be accomplished.

'Deliverance and enlargement shall arise from another place.' So it is certain that God from eternity has willed that all flesh should see His salvation. He loves the heathen better than we do. Christ has died not for our sins only, but for the sins of the whole world. God hath made of one blood all nations of men. The race is one in its need. The race is one in its goal. The Gospel is fit for all men. The Gospel is preached to all men. The Gospel shall yet be received by a world, and from every corner of a believing earth will rise one roll of praise to one Father, and the race shall be one in its hopes, one in its Lord, one in faith, one in baptism, one in one God and Father of us all. That grand unity shall certainly come. That true unity and fraternity shall be realised. The blissful wave of the knowledge of the Lord shall cover and hide and flow rejoicingly over all national distinctions. 'In that day Israel shall be the third with Egypt and with Assyria, a blessing in the midst of the earth.'

This is as certain as the efficacy of a Saviour's blood can make it, as certain as the universal adaptation and design of a preached Gospel can make it, as certain as the oneness of human nature can make it, as certain as the power of a Comforter who shall convince the world of sin, of righteousness, and judgment can make it, as certain as the misery of man can make it, as certain as the promises of God who cannot lie can make it, as certain as His faithfulness who hangs the rainbow in the heavens and enters into an everlasting covenant with all the earth can make it.

And this accumulation of certainties does not depend on the faithfulness of men. In the width of that mighty result the failure of some single agent may be eliminated. Nay, more, though all men failed, God hath instruments, and will use them Himself, if need were.

Only we may share the triumph and partake of the blessed result. Decide for yourself, what share you will have in that marvellous day. Let your work be such as that it shall abide. Stonehenge, cathedrals, temples stand when all else has passed away. Work for God abides and outlasts everything beside, and the smallest service for Him is only made to flash forth light by the glorifying and revealing fires of that awful day which will burn up the wood, the hay, and the stubble, and flow with beautifying brightness and be flashed back with double splendour from 'the gold, the silver, and the precious stones,' the abiding workmanship of devout hearts in that everlasting tabernacle which shall not be taken down, the ransomed souls builded together, ransomed by our preaching, and 'builded up together for a temple of God by the Spirit.'

THE NET BROKEN

'And Esther spake yet again before the king, and fell down at his feet, and besought him with tears to put away the mischief of Haman the Agagite, and his device that he had devised against the Jews. 4. Then the king held out the golden sceptre toward Esther. So Esther arose, and stood before the king, 5. And said, If it please the king, and if I have found favour in his sight, and the thing seem right before the king, and I be pleasing in his eyes, let it be written to reverse the letters devised by Haman the son of Hammedatha the Agagite, which he wrote to destroy the Jews which are in all the king's provinces: 6. For how can I endure to see the evil that shall come unto my people? or how can I endure to see the destruction of my kindred? 7. Then the king Ahasuerus said unto Esther the queen, and to Mordecai the Jew, Behold, I have given Esther the house of Haman, and him they have hanged upon the gallows, because he laid his hand upon the Jews. 8. Write ye also for the Jews, as it liketh you, in the king's name, and seal it with the king's ring: for the writing which is written in the king's name, and sealed with the king's ring, may no man reverse. 15. And Mordecai went out from the presence of the king in royal apparel of blue and white, and with a great crown of gold, and with a garment of fine linen and purple: and the city of Shushan rejoiced and was glad. 16. The Jews had light, and gladness, and joy, and honour. 17. And in every province, and in every city, whithersoever the king's commandment and his decree came, the Jews had joy and gladness, a feast and a good day. And many of the people of the land became Jews; for the fear of the Jews fell upon them.'—ESTHER viii. 3-8,15-17.

The spirit of this passage may perhaps be best caught by taking the three persons appearing in it, and the One who does not appear, but acts unseen through them all.

I. The heroine of the whole book and of this chapter is Esther, one of the sweetest and noblest of the women of Scripture. The orphan girl who had grown up into beauty under the care of her uncle Mordecai, and was lifted suddenly from sheltered obscurity into the 'fierce light that beats upon a throne,' like some flower culled in a shady nook and set in a king's bosom, was true to her childhood's protector and to her people, and kept her sweet, brave gentleness unspoiled by the rapid elevation which ruins so many characters. Her Jewish name of Hadassah ('myrtle') well befits her, for she is clothed with unostentatious beauty, pure and fragrant as the blossoms that brides twine in their hair. But, withal, she has a true woman's courage which is always ready to endure any evil and dare any danger at the bidding of her heart. She took her life in her hand when she sought an audience of Ahasuerus uninvited, and she knew that she did. Nothing in literature is nobler than her quiet words, which measure her danger without shrinking, and front it without heroics: 'If I perish, I perish!'

The danger was not past, though she was queen and beloved; for a despot's love is a shifting sand-bank, which may yield anchorage to-day, and to-morrow may be washed away. So she counted not her life dear unto herself when, for the second time, as in our passage, she ventured, uninvited, into the king's presence. The womanly courage that risks life for love's sake is nobler than the soldier's that feels the lust of battle maddening him.

Esther's words to the king are full of tact. She begins with what seems to have been the form of address prescribed by custom, for it is used by her in her former requests (chap. v. 8; vii. 3). But she adds a variation of the formula, tinged with more personal reference to the king's feeling towards her, as well as breathing entire submission to his estimate of what was fitting. 'If the thing seem right before the king,' appeals to the sense of justice that lay dormant beneath the monarch's arbitrary will; 'and I be pleasing in his eyes,' drew him by the charm of her beauty. She avoided making the king responsible for the plot, and laid it at the door of the dead and discredited Haman. It was his device, and since he had fallen, his policy could be reversed without hurting the king's dignity. And then with fine tact, as well as with a burst of genuine feeling, she flings all her personal influence into the scale, and seeks to move the king, not by appeals to his justice or royal duty, but to his love for her, which surely could not bear to see her suffer. One may say that it was a low motive to appeal to, to ask the despot to save a people in order to keep one woman from sorrow; and so it was. It was Ahasuerus's fault that such a reason had more weight with him than nobler ones. It was not Esther's that she used her power over him to carry her point. She used the weapons that she had, and that she knew would be efficacious. The purpose for which she used them is her justification.

Esther may well teach her sisters to-day to be brave and gentle, to use their influence over men for high purposes of public good, to be the inspirers of their husbands, lovers, brothers, for all noble thinking and doing; to make the cause of the oppressed their own, to be the apostles of mercy and the hinderers of wrong, to keep true to their early associations if prosperity comes to them, and to cherish sympathy with their nation so deep that they cannot 'endure to see the evil that shall come unto them' without using all their womanly influence to avert it.

II. Ahasuerus plays a sorry part beside Esther. He knows no law but his own will, and that is moved, not by conscience or reason, but by ignoble passions and sensual desires. He tosses his subjects' lives as trivial gifts to any who ask for them. Haman's wife knew that he had only to 'speak to the king,' and Mordecai would be hanged; Haman had no difficulty in securing the royal mandate for the murder of all the Jews. Sated with the indulgence of low desires, he let all power slip from his idle hands, and his manhood was rotted away by wallowing in the pigsty of voluptuousness. But he was tenacious of the semblance of authority, and demanded the appearance of abject submission from the 'servants' who were his masters. He yielded to Esther's prayer as lightly as to Haman's plot. Whether the Jews were wiped out or not mattered nothing to him, so long as he had no trouble in the affair.

To shift all responsibility off his own shoulders on to somebody else's was his one aim. He was as untrue to his duty when he gave his signet to Mordecai, and bade him and Esther do as they liked, as when he had given it to Haman. And with all this slothful indifference to his duty, he was sensitive to etiquette, and its cobwebs held him whom the cords of his royal obligations could not hold. It mattered not to him that the edict which he allowed Mordecai to promulgate practically lit the flames of civil war. He had washed his hands of the whole business.

It is a hideous picture of an Eastern despot, and has been said to be unhistorical and unbelievable. But the world has seen many examples of rulers whom the possession of unlimited and irresponsible power has corrupted in like fashion. And others than rulers may take the warning that to live to self is the mother of all sins and crimes; that no man can safely make his own will and his own passions his guides; that there is no slavery so abject as that of the man who is tyrannised by his lower nature; that there is a temptation besetting us all to take the advantages and neglect the duties of our position, and that to yield to it is sure to end in moral ruin. We are all kings, even if our kingdom be only our own selves, and we shall rule wisely only if we rule as God's viceroys, and think more of duty than of delight.

III. Mordecai is a kind of duplicate of Joseph, and embodies valuable lessons. Contented acceptance of obscurity and neglect of his services, faithfulness to his people and his God in the foul atmosphere of such a court, wise reticence, patient discharge of small duties, undoubting hope when things looked blackest fed by stedfast faith in God, unchangedness of character and purpose when lifted to supreme dignity, the use of influence and place, not for himself, but for his people,—all these are traits which may be imitated in any life. We should be the same men, whether we sit unnoticed among the lackeys at the gate, or are bearing the brunt of the hatred of powerful foes, or are clothed 'in royal apparel of blue and white, and with a great crown of gold.' These gauds were nothing to Mordecai, and earthly honours should never turn our heads. He valued power because it enabled him to save his brethren, and we should cultivate the same spirit. The political world, with its fierce struggles for personal ends, its often disregard of the public good, and its use of place and power for 'making a pile' or helping relations up, would be much the better for some infusion of the spirit of Mordecai.

IV. But we must not look only at the visible persons and forces. This book of Esther does not say much about God, but His presence broods over it all, and is the real spring that moves the movers that are seen. It is all a lesson of how God works out His purposes through men that seem to themselves to be working out theirs. The king's criminal abandonment to lust and luxury, Haman's meanly personal pique, Esther's beauty, the fall of the favourite, the long past services of Mordecai, even the king's sleepless night, are all threads in the web, and God is the weaver. The story raises the whole question of the standing miracle of the co-existence and co-operation of the divine and the human. Man is free and responsible, God is sovereign and all-pervading. He 'makes the wrath of man to praise Him, and with the remainder thereof He girdeth Himself.' To-day, as then, He is working out His deep designs through men whom He has raised up, though they have not known Him. Amid the clash of contending interests and worldly passions His solemn purpose steadily advances to its end, like the irresistible ocean current, which persists through all storms that agitate the surface, and draws them into the drift of its silent trend. Ahasuerus, Haman, Esther, Mordecai, are His instruments, and yet each of them is the doer of his or her deed, and has to answer to Him for it.

THE BOOK OF JOB

SORROW THAT WORSHIPS

'Naked came I out of my mother's womb, and naked shall I return thither: the Lord gave, and the Lord hath taken away; blessed be the name of the Lord.'—JOB i. 21.

This book of Job wrestles with the problem of the meaning of the mystery of sorrow. Whether history or a parable, its worth is the same, as tortured hearts have felt for countless centuries, and will feel to the end. Perhaps no picture that was ever painted is grander and more touching than that of the man of Uz, in the antique wealth and happiness of his brighter days, rich, joyful, with his children round him, living in men's honour, and walking upright before God. Then come the dramatic completeness and suddenness of his great trials. One day strips him of all, and stripped of all he rises to a loftier dignity, for there is a majesty as well as an isolation in his sorrow.

How many spirits tossed by afflictions have found peace in these words! How many quivering lips have tried to utter their grave, calm accents! To how many of us are they hallowed by memories of times when they stood between us and despair!

They seem to me to say everything that can be said about our trials and losses, to set forth the whole truth of the facts, and to present the whole series of feelings with which good men may and should be exercised.

I. The vindication of sorrow.

He 'rent his clothes'—the signs and tokens of inward desolation and loss.

It is worth our while to stay for one moment with the thought that we are meant to feel grief. God sends sorrows in order that they may pain. Sorrow has its manifold uses in our lives and on our hearts. It is natural. That is enough. God set the fountain of tears in our souls. We are bidden not to 'despise the chastening of the Lord.' It is they who are 'exercised' thereby to whom the chastisement is blessed.

It is sanctioned by Christ. He wept. He bade the women of Jerusalem weep for themselves and for their children.

Religion does not destroy the natural emotions—sorrow as little as any other. It guides, controls, curbs, comforts, and brings blessings out of it. So do not aim at an impossible stoicism, but permit nature to have its way, and look at the picture of this manly sorrow of Job's—calm, silent, unless when stung by the undeserved reproaches of these three 'orthodox liars for God,' and going to God and worshipping.

II. The recognition of loss and sorrow as the law of life.

'Naked came I out of my mother's womb.'

We need not dwell on the figure 'mother,' suggesting the grave as the kindly mother's bosom that gathers us all in, and the thought that perhaps gleams forth that death, too, is a kind of birth.

But the truth picturesquely set forth is just the old and simple one—that all possessions are transient.

The naked self gets clothed and lapped round with possessions, but they are all outside of it, apart from its individuality. It has been without them. It will be without them. Death at the end will rob us of them all.

The inevitable law of loss is fixed and certain. We are losing something every moment—not only possessions, but all our dearest ties are knit but for a time, and sure to be snapped. They go, and then after a while we go.

The independence of each soul of all its possessions and relations is as certain as the loss of them. They may go and we are made naked, but still we exist all the same. We have to learn the hard lesson which sounds so unfeeling, that we can live on in spite of all losses. Nothing, no one, is necessary to us.

All this is very cold and miserable; it is the standing point of law and necessity. An atheist could say it. It is the beginning of the Christian contemplation of life, but only the beginning.

III. The recognition of God in the law.

'The Lord gave, and the Lord hath taken away.' That is a step far beyond the former. To bring in the thought of *the Lord* makes a world of difference.

The tendency is to look only at the second cause. In Job's case there were two classes of agencies, men, Chaldeans and Sabeans, and natural causes, fire and wind, but he did not stop with these.

The grand corrective of that tendency lies in the full theistic idea, that God is the sole cause of all. The immanence of Deity in all things and events is our refuge from the soul-crushing tyranny of the reign of law.

That devout recognition of God in law is eminently to be made in regard to death, as Job does in the text: 'The number of his months is with Thee.' Death is not any more nor any less under His control than all other human incidents are. It has no special sanctity, nor abnormally close connection with His will, but it no more is exempt from such connection than all the other events of life. The connection is real. He opens the gate of the grave and no man shuts. He shuts, and no man opens.

Job did not forget the Lord's gifts even while he was writhing under the stroke of His withdrawings. Alas! that it should so often need sorrow to bear into our hearts that we owe all to Him, but even then, if not before, it is well to remember how much good we have received of the Lord, and the remembrance should not be 'a sorrow's crown of sorrow,' but a thankful one.

IV. The thankful resignation to God's loving administration of the law.

The preceding words might be said with mere submission to an irresistible power, but this last sentence climbs to the highest of the true Christian idea. It recognises in loss and sorrow a reason for praise.

Why?

Because we may be sure that all loss is for our good.

Because we may be sure that all loss is from a loving God. In loss of dear ones, *our* gain is in drawing nearer to God, in being taught more to long for heaven. In our relation to them, a loftier love, a hallowing of all the past. *Their* gain is in their entrance to heaven, and all the glory that they have reached.

This blessing of God for loss is not inconsistent with sorrow, but anticipates the future when we shall know all and bless Him for all.

THE PEACEABLE FRUITS OF SORROWS RIGHTLY BORNE

'Behold, happy is the man whom God correcteth: therefore despise not thou the chastening of the Almighty: 18. For He maketh sore, and bindeth up: He woundeth, and His hands make whole. 19. He shall deliver thee in six troubles: yea, in seven there shall no evil touch thee. 20. In famine He shall redeem thee from death: and in war from the power of the sword. 21. Thou shalt be hid from the scourge of the tongue: neither shalt thou be afraid of destruction when it cometh. 22. At destruction and famine thou shalt laugh: neither shalt thou be afraid of the beasts of the earth. 23. For thou shalt be in league with the stones of the field: and the beasts of the field shall be at peace with thee. 24. And thou shalt know that thy tabernacle shall be in peace; and thou shalt visit thy habitation, and shalt not sin. 25. Thou shalt know also that thy seed shall be great, and thine offspring as the grass of the earth. 26. Thou shalt come to thy grave in a full age, like as a shock of corn cometh in in his season. 27. Lo this, we have searched it, so it is; hear it, and know thou it for thy good.'—JOB v. 17-27.

The close of the Book of Job shows that his friends' speeches were defective, and in part erroneous. They all proceeded on the assumption that suffering was the fruit of sin—a principle which, though true in general, is not to be unconditionally applied to specific cases. They all forgot that good men might be exposed to it, not as punishment, nor even as correction, but as trial, to 'know what was in their hearts.'

Eliphaz is the best of the three friends, and his speeches embody much permanent truth, and rise, as in this passage, to a high level of literary and artistic beauty. There are few lovelier passages in Scripture than this glowing description of the prosperity of the man who accepts God's chastisements; and, on the whole, the picture is true. But the underlying belief in the uniform coincidence of inward goodness and outward good needs to be modified by the deeper teaching of the New Testament before it can be regarded as covering all the facts of life.

Eliphaz is gathering up, in our passage, the threads of his speech. He bases upon all that he has been saying the exhortation to Job to be thankful for his sorrows. With a grand paradox, he declares the man who is afflicted to be happy. And therein he strikes an eternally true note. It is good to be made to drink a cup of sorrow. Flesh calls pain evil, but spirit knows it to be good. The list of our blessings is not only written in bright inks, but many are inscribed in black. And the reason why the sad heart should be a happy heart is because, as Eliphaz believed, sadness is God's fatherly correction, intended to better the subject of it. 'Whom the Lord loveth He chasteneth,' says the Epistle to the Hebrews, in full accord with Eliphaz.

But his well-meant and true words flew wide of their mark, for two reasons. They were chillingly didactic, and it is vinegar upon nitre to stand over an agonised soul and preach platitudes in an unsympathetic voice. And they assumed unusual sin in Job as the explanation of his unparalleled pains, while the prologue tells us that his sufferings were not fruits of his sin, but trials of his righteousness. He was horrified at Job's words, which seemed to him full of rebellion and irreverence; and he made no allowance for the wild cries of an agonised heart when he solemnly warned the sufferer against 'despising' God's chastening. A more sympathetic ear would have detected the accent of faith in the groans.

The collocation, in verse 18, of making sore and binding up, does not merely express sequence, but also purpose. The wounding is in order to healing. The wounds are merciful surgery; and their intention is health, like the cuts that lay open an ulcer, or the scratches for vaccination. The view of suffering in these two verses is not complete, but it goes far toward completeness in tracing it to God, in asserting its disciplinary intention, in pointing to the divine healing which is meant to follow, and in exhorting to submission. We may recall the beautiful expansion of that exhortation in Hebrews, where 'faint not' is added to 'despise not,' so including the two opposite and yet closely connected forms of misuse of sorrow, according as we stiffen our wills against it, and try to make light of it, or yield so utterly to it as to collapse. Either extreme equally misses the corrective purpose of the grief.

On this general statement follows a charming picture of the blessedness which attends the man who has taken his chastisement rightly. After the thunderstorm come sunshine and blue, and the song of birds. But, lovely as it is, and capable of application in many points to the life of every man who trustfully yields to God's will, it must not be taken as a literally and absolutely true statement of God's dealings with His children. If so regarded, it would hopelessly be shattered against facts; for the world is full of instances of saintly men and women who have not experienced in their outward lives such sunny calm and prosperity stretching to old age as are here promised. Eliphaz is not meant to be the interpreter of the mysteries of Providence, and his solution is decisively rejected at the close. But still there is much in this picture which finds fulfilment in all devout lives in a higher sense than his intended meaning.

The first point is that the devout soul is exempt from calamities which assail those around it. These are such as are ordinarily in Scripture recognised as God's judgments upon a people. Famine and war devastate, but the devout soul abides in peace, and is satisfied. Now it is not true that faith and submission make a wall round a man, so that he escapes from such calamities. In the supernatural system of the Old Testament such exemptions were more usual than with us, though this very Book of Job and many a psalm show that devout hearts had even then to wrestle with the problem of the prosperity of the wicked and the indiscriminate fall of widespread calamities on the good and bad.

But in its deepest sense (which, however, is not Eliphaz's sense) the faithful man is saved from the evils which he, in common with his faithless neighbour, experiences. Two men are smitten down by the same disease, or lie dying on a battlefield, shattered by the same shell, and the one receives the fulfilment of the promise, 'there shall no evil touch thee,' and the other does not. For the evil in the evil is all sucked out of it, and the poison is wiped off the arrow which strikes him who is united to God by faith and submission. Two women are grinding at the same millstone, and the same blow kills them both; but the one is delivered, and the other is not. They who pass through an evil, and are not drawn away from God by it, but brought nearer to Him, are hid from its power. To die may be our deliverance from death.

Eliphaz's promises rise still higher in verses 22 and 23, in which is set forth a truth that in its deepest meaning is of universal application. The wild beasts of the earth and the stones of the field will be in league with the man who submits to God's will. Of course the beasts come into view as destructive, and the stones as injuring the fertility of the fields. There is, probably, allusion to the story of Paradise and the Fall. Man's relation to nature was disturbed by sin; it will be rectified by his return to God. Such a doctrine of the effects of sin in perverting man's relation to creatures runs all through Scripture, and is not to be put aside as mere symbolism.

But the large truth underlying the words here is that, if we are servants of God, we are masters of everything. 'All things work together for good to them that love God.' All things serve the soul that serves God; as, on the other hand, all are against him that does not, and 'the stars in their courses fight against' those who fight against Him. All things are ours, if we are Christ's. The many mediaeval legends of saints attended by animals, from St. Jerome and his lion downwards to St. Francis preaching to the birds, echo the thoughts here. A gentle, pure soul, living in amity with dumb creatures, has wonderful power to attract them. They who are at peace with God can scarcely be at war with any of God's creatures. Gentleness is stronger than iron bands. 'Cords of love' draw most surely.

Peace and prosperity in home and possessions are the next blessings promised (ver. 24). 'Thou shalt visit [look over] thy household, and shalt miss nothing.' No cattle have strayed or been devoured by evil beasts, or stolen, as all Job's had been. Alas! Eliphaz knew nothing about commercial crises, and the great system of credit by which one scoundrel's fall may bring down hundreds of good men and patient widows, who look over their possessions and find nothing but worthless shares. Yet even for those who find all at once that the herd is cut off from the stall, their tabernacle may still be in peace, and though the fold be empty they may miss nothing, if in the empty place they find God. That is what Christians may make out of the words; but it is not what was originally meant by them.

In like manner the next blessing, that of a numerous posterity, does not depend on moral or religious condition, as Eliphaz would make out, and in modern days is not always regarded as a blessing. But note the singular heartlessness betrayed in telling Job, all whose flocks and herds had been carried off, and his children laid dead in their festival chamber, that abundant possessions and offspring were the token of God's favour. The speaker seems serenely unconscious that he was saying anything that could drive a knife into the tortured man. He is so carried along on the waves of his own eloquence, and so absorbed in stringing together the elements of an artistic whole, that he forgets the very sorrows which he came to comfort. There are not a few pious exhorters of bleeding hearts who are chargeable with the same sin. The only hand that will bind up without hurting is a hand that is sympathetic to the finger-tips. No eloquence or poetic beauty or presentation of undeniable truths will do as substitutes for that.

The last blessing promised is that which the Old Testament places so high in the list of good things—long life. The lovely metaphor in which that promise is couched has become familiar to us all. The ripe corn gathered into a sheaf at harvest-time suggests festival rather than sadness. It speaks of growth accomplished, of fruit matured, of the ministries of sun and rain received and used, and of a joyful gathering into the great storehouse. There is no reference in the speech to the uses of the sheaf after it is harvested, but we can scarcely avoid following its history a little farther than the 'grave' which to Eliphaz seems the garner. Are all these matured powers to have no field for action? Were all these miracles of vegetation set in motion only in order to grow a crop which should be reaped, and there an end? What is to be done with the precious fruit which has taken so long time and so much cultivation to grow? Surely it is not the intention of the Lord of the harvest to let it rot when it has been gathered. Surely we are grown here and ripened and carried hence for something.

But that is not in our passage. This, however, may be drawn from it—that maturity does not depend on length of days; and, however Eliphaz meant to promise long life, the reality is that the devout soul may reckon on complete life, whether it be long or short. God will not call His children home till their schooling is done; and, however green and young the corn may seem to our eyes, He knows which heads in the great harvest-field are ready for removal, and gathers only these. The child whose little coffin may be carried under a boy's arm may be ripe for harvesting. Not length of days, but likeness to God, makes maturity; and if we die according to the will of God, it cannot but be that we shall come to our grave in a full age, whatever be the number of years carved on our tombstones.

The speech ends with a somewhat self-complacent exhortation to the poor, tortured man: 'We have searched it, so it is.' We wise men pledge our wisdom and our reputation that this is true. Great is authority. An ounce of sympathy would have done more to commend the doctrine than a ton of dogmatic self-confidence. 'Hear it, and know thou it for thyself.' Take it into thy mind. Take it into thy mind and heart, and take it for thy good. It was a frosty ending, exasperating in its air of patronage, of superior wisdom, and in its lack of any note of feeling. So, of course, it set Job's impatience alight, and his next speech is more desperate than his former. When will well-meaning comforters learn not to rub salt into wounds while they seem to be dressing them?

TWO KINDS OF HOPE

'Whose hope shall be cut off, and whose trust shall be a spider's web.'—
JOB viii. 14.

'And hope maketh not ashamed.'—ROMANS v. 5.

These two texts take opposite sides. Bildad was not the wisest of Job's
friends, and he gives utterance to solemn commonplaces with partial truth in
them. In the rough it is true that the hope of the ungodly perishes, and the
limits of the truth are concealed by the splendour of the imagery and the
perfection of artistic form in which the well-worn platitude is draped. The
spider's web stretched glittering in the dewy morning on the plants, shaking
its threaded tears in the wind, the flag in the dry bed of a nullah withering
while yet green, the wall on which leaning a man will fall, are vivid illustrations
of hopes that collapse and fail. But my other text has to do with hopes that
do not fail. Paul thinks that he knows of hope that maketh not ashamed, that
is, which never disappoints. Bildad was right if he was thinking, as he was, of
hopes fixed on earth; the Apostle was right, for he was thinking of hopes set
on God. It is a commonplace that 'hope springs immortal in the human
breast'; it is equally a commonplace that hopes are disappointed. What is the
conclusion from these two universal experiences? Is it the cynical one that it
is all illusion, or is it that somewhere there must be an object on which hope
may twine its tendrils without fear? God has given the faculty, and we may
be sure that it is not given to be for ever balked. We must hope. Our hope
may be our worst enemy; it may and should be our purest joy.

Let us then simply consider these two sorts of hope, the earthly and the
heavenly, in their working in the three great realms of life, death, and eternity.

I. In life.

The faculty is inseparable from man's consciousness of immortality and
of an indefinitely expansible nature which ever makes him discontented with
the present. It has great purposes to perform in strengthening him for work,
in helping him over sorrows, in making him buoyant and elastic, in painting
for him the walls of the dungeon, and hiding for him the weight of the fetters.

But for what did he receive this great gift? Mainly that he might pass
beyond the temporal and hold converse with the skies. Its true sphere is the
unseen future which is at God's right hand.

We may run a series of antitheses, *e.g.*—

Earthly hope is so uncertain that its larger part is often fear.

Heavenly hope is fixed and sure. It is as certain as history.

Earthly hope realised is always less blessed than we expected. How universal the experience that there is little to choose between a gratified and a frustrated hope! The wonders inside the caravan are never so wonderful as the canvas pictures outside.

Heavenly hopes ever surpass the most rapturous anticipation. 'The half hath not been told.'

Earthly hopes are necessarily short-winged. They are settled one way or another, and sink hull down below our horizon.

Heavenly hope sets its object far off, and because a lifetime only attains it in part, it blesses a lifetime and outlasts it.

II. Hope in death.

That last hour ends for us all alike our earthly joys and relations. The slow years slip away, and each bears with it hopes that have been outlived, whether fulfilled or disappointed. One by one the lights that we kindle in our hall flicker out, and death quenches the last of them. But there is one light that burns on clear through the article of death, like the lamp in the magician's tomb. 'The righteous hath hope in his death.' We can each settle for ourselves whether we shall carry that radiant angel with her white wings into the great darkness, or shall sadly part with her before we part with life. To the earthly soul that last earthly hour is a black wall beyond which it cannot look. To the God-trusting soul the darkness is peopled with bright-faced hopes.

III. Hope in eternity.

It is not for our tongues to speak of what must, in the natural working out of consequences, be the ultimate condition of a soul which has not set its hopes on the God who alone is the right Object of the blessed but yet awful capacity of hoping, when all the fleeting objects which it sought as solace and mask of its own true poverty are clean gone from its grasp. Dante's tremendous words are more than enough to move wholesome horror in any thinking soul: 'Leave hope behind, all ye who enter here.' They are said to be unfeeling, grim, and mediaeval, incredible in this enlightened age; but is there any way out of them, if we take into account what our nature is moulded to need and cling to, and what 'godless' men have done with it?

But let us turn to the brighter of these texts. 'Hope maketh not ashamed.' There will be an internal increase of blessedness, power, purity in that future, a fuller possession of God, a reaching out after completer likeness to Him. So if we can think of days in that calm state where time will be no more, 'to-morrow shall be as this day and much more abundant,' and the angel Hope, who kept us company through all the weary marches of earth, will attend on us still, only having laid aside the uncertainty that sometime veiled her smiles, but retaining all the buoyant eagerness for the ever unfolding wonders which gave us courage and cheer in the days of our flesh.

JOB'S QUESTION, JESUS' ANSWER

'If a man die, shall he live again?'—JOB xiv. 14.

'… I am the resurrection, and the life: he that believeth in Me, though he were dead, yet shall he live: 26. And whosoever liveth and believeth in Me shall never die.'—JOHN xi. 25, 26.

Job's question waited long for an answer. Weary centuries rolled away; but at last the doubting, almost despairing, cry put into the mouth of the man of sorrows of the Old Testament is answered by the Man of Sorrows of the New. The answer in words is this second text which may almost be supposed to allude to the ancient question. The answer, in fact, is the resurrection of Christ. Apart from this answer there is none.

So we may take these two texts to help us to grasp more clearly and feel more profoundly what the world owes to that great fact which we are naturally led to think of to-day.

I. The ancient and ever returning question.

The Book of Job is probably a late part of the Old Testament. It deals with problems which indicate some advance in religious thought. Solemn and magnificent, and for the most part sad; it is like a Titan struggling with large problems, and seldom attaining to positive conclusions in which the heart or the head can rest in peace. Here all Job's mind is clouded with a doubt. He has just given utterance to an intense longing for a life beyond the grave. His abode in Sheol is thought of as in some sense a breach in the continuity of his consciousness, but even that would be tolerable, if only he could be sure that, after many days, God would remember him. Then that longing gives way before the torturing question of the text, which dashes aside the tremulous hope with its insistent interrogation. It is not denial, but it is a doubt which palsies hope. But though he has no certainty, he cannot part with the possibility, and so goes on to imagine how blessed it would be if his longing were fulfilled. He thinks that such a renewed life would be like the 'release' of a sentry who had long stood on guard; he thinks of it as his swift, joyous 'answer' to God's summons, which would draw him out from the sad crowd of pale shadows and bring him back to warmth and reality. His hope takes a more daring flight still, and he thinks of God as yearning for His creature, as His creature yearns for Him, and having 'a desire to the work of His hands,' as if His heaven would be incomplete without His servant. But the rapture and the vision pass, and the rest of the chapter is all clouded over, and the devout hope loses its light. Once again it gathers brightness in the twenty-first chapter, where the possibility flashes out starlike, that 'after my skin hath been thus destroyed, yet from my flesh shall I see God.'

These fluctuations of hope and doubt reveal to us the attitude of devout souls in Israel at a late era of the national life. And if they show us their high-water mark, we need not suppose that similar souls outside the Old Testament circle had solid certainty where these had but a variable hope. We know how large a development the doctrine of a future life had in Assyria and in Egypt, and I suppose we are entitled to say that men have always had the idea of a future. They have always had the thought, sometimes as a fear, sometimes as a hope, but never as a certainty. It has lacked not only certainty but distinctness. It has lacked solidity also, the power to hold its own and sustain itself against the weighty pressure of intrusive things seen and temporal.

But we need not go to the ends of the earth or to past generations for examples of a doubting, superficial hold of the truth that man lives through death and after it. We have only to look around us, and, alas! we have only to look within us. This age is asking the question again, and answering it in many tones, sometimes of indifferent disregard, sometimes flaunting a stark negative without reasoned foundation, sometimes with affirmatives with as little reason as these negatives. The modern world is caught in the rush and whirl of life, has its own sorrows to front, its own battles to fight, and large sections of it have never come as near an answer to Job's question as Job did.

II. Christ's all-sufficing answer.

He gave it there, by the grave of Lazarus, to that weeping sister, but He spoke these great words of calm assurance to all the world. One cannot but note the difference between His attitude in the presence of the great Mystery and that of all other teachers. How calmly, certainly, and confidently He speaks!

Mark that Jesus, even at that hour of agony, turns Martha's thoughts to Himself. What He is is the all-important thing for her to know. If she understands Him, life and death will have no insoluble problems nor any hopelessness for her. 'I am the Resurrection and the Life.' She had risen in her grief to a lofty height in believing that 'even now'—at this moment when help is vain and hope is dead—'whatsoever thou wilt ask of God, God will give it thee,' but Jesus offers to her a loftier conception of Him when He lays a sovereign hand on resurrection and life, and discloses that both inhere in Him, and from Him flow to all who shall possess them. He claims to have in Himself the fountain of life, in all possible senses of the word, as well as in the special sense relevant at that sad hour. Further, He tells Martha that by faith in Him any and all may possess that life. And then He majestically goes on to declare that the life which He gives is immune from, and untouched by, death. The believer shall live though he dies, the living believer shall never die. It is clear that, in these two great statements, to die is used in two different meanings, referring in the former case to the physical fact, and in the latter carrying a heavier weight of significance, namely the pregnant sense which it usually has in this Gospel, of separation from God and consequently from the true life of the soul. Physical death is not the termination of human life. The grim fact touches only the surface life, and has nothing to do with the essential, personal being. He that believes on Jesus, and he only, truly lives, and his union with Jesus secures his possession of that eternal life, which victoriously persists through the apparent, superficial change which men call death. Nothing dies but the death which surrounds the faithful soul. For it to die is to live more fully, more triumphantly, more blessedly. So though the act of physical death remains, its whole character is changed. Hence the New Testament euphemisms for death are much more than euphemisms. Men christen it by names which drape its ugliness, because they fear it so much, but Faith can play with Leviathan, because it fears it not at all. Hence such names as 'sleep,' 'exodus,' are tokens of the victory won for all believers by Jesus. He will show Martha the hope for all His followers which begins to dawn even in the calling of her brother back from the grip of death. And He shows us the great truth that His being the 'Life' necessarily involved His being also the 'Resurrection,' for His life-communicating work could not be accomplished till His all-quickening vitality had flowed over into, and flooded with its own conquering tides, not only the spirit which believes but its humble companion, the soul, and its yet humbler, the body. A bodily life is essential to perfect manhood, and Jesus will not stay His hand till every believer is full-summed in all his powers, and is perfect in body, soul, and spirit, after the image of Him who redeemed Him.

III. The pledge for the truth of the answer.

The words of Jesus are only words. These precious words, spoken to that one weeping sister in a little Jewish village, and which have brought hope to millions ever since, are as baseless as all the other dreams and longings of the heart, unless Jesus confirms them by fact. If He did not rise from the dead, they are but another of the noble, exalted, but futile delusions of which the world has many others. If Christ be not risen, His words of consolation are swelling words of emptiness; His whole claims are ended, and the age-old question which Job asked is unanswered still, and will always remain unanswered. If Christ be not risen, the hopeless colloquy between Jehovah and the prophet sums up all that can be said of the future life: 'Son of man, can these bones live?' And I answered, 'O Lord God, Thou knowest!'

But Christ's resurrection is a fact which, taken in connection with His words while on earth, endorses these and establishes His claims to be the Declarer of the name of God, the Saviour of the world. It gives us demonstration of the continuity of life through and after death. Taken along with His ascension, which is but, so to speak, the prolongation of the point into a line, it declares that a glorified body and an abode in a heavenly home are waiting for all who by faith become here partakers in Jesus and are quickened by sharing in His life.

So in despite of sense and doubt and fear, notwithstanding teachers who, like the supercilious philosophers on Mars Hill, mock when they hear of a resurrection from the dead, we should rejoice in the great light which has shined into the region of the shadow of death, we should clasp His divine and most faithful answer to that old, despairing question, as the anchor of our souls, and lift up our hearts in thanksgiving in the triumphant challenge, 'O death! where is thy sting? O grave! where is thy victory?'

KNOWLEDGE AND PEACE

'Acquaint now thyself with Him, and be at peace: thereby good shall come unto thee.'—JOB xxii. 21.

In the sense in which the speaker meant them, these words are not true. They mean little more than 'It pays to be religious.' What kind of notion of acquaintance with God Eliphaz may have had, one scarcely knows, but at any rate, the whole meaning of the text on his lips is poor and selfish.

The peace promised is evidently only outward tranquillity and freedom from trouble, and the good that is to come to Job is plainly mere worldly prosperity. This strain of thought is expressed even more clearly in that extraordinary bit of bathos, which with solemn irony the great dramatist who wrote this book makes this Eliphaz utter immediately after the text, 'The Almighty shall be thy defence and—thou shalt have plenty of silver!' It has not been left for commercial Englishmen to recommend religion on the ground that it produces successful merchants and makes the best of both worlds.

These friends of Job's all err in believing that suffering is always and only the measure of sin, and that you can tell a man's great guilt by observing his great sorrows. And so they have two main subjects on which they preach at their poor friend, pouring vitriol into his wounds: first, how wicked he must be to be so haunted by sorrows; second, how surely he will be delivered if he will only be religious after their pattern, that is, speak platitudes of conventional devotion and say, I submit.

This is the meaning of our text as it stands. But we may surely find a higher sense in which it is true and take that to heart.

I. What is acquainting oneself with God?

The first thing to note is that this acquaintance depends on us. So then there must have been a previous objective manifestation on His part. Of course there must be a God to know, and there must be a way of knowing Him. For us Jesus Christ is the Revealer. What men know of God apart from Him is dim, shadowy, indistinct; it lacks certainty, and so is not knowledge. I venture to say that there is nothing between cultivated men and the loss of certain knowledge of God and conviction of His Being, but the historical revelation of Jesus Christ. The Christ reveals the inmost character of God, and that not in words but in deeds. Without Him no man knows God; 'No man knoweth the Father save the Son, and he to whom the Son will reveal Him.'

So then the objective revelation having been made, we must on our part embrace that revelation as ours. The act of so accepting begins with the familiar act of faith, which includes both an exercise of the understanding, as it embraces the facts of Christ's revelation of the Father, and of the will as it casts itself upon and submits to Him. But that exercise of faith is but the point which has to be drawn out into a golden line, woven into the whole length of a life. And it is in the continuity of that line that the average Christian so sadly fails, and because of that failure his acquaintance with God is so distant. How little time or thought we give to the character of God as revealed in Jesus Christ! We must be on intimate terms with Him. To know God, as to know a man, we must 'live with' Him, must summer and winter with Him, must bring Him into the pettinesses of daily life, must let our love set to Him, must be in sympathy with Him, our wills being tuned to make harmony with His, our whole nature being in accord with His. That is work more than enough for a lifetime, enough to task it, enough to bless it.

II. The peace of acquaintance with God.

Eliphaz meant nothing more than mere earthly tranquillity and exemption from trouble, but his words are true in a far loftier region.

Knowledge of God as He really is brings peace, because His heart is full of love. We do but need to know the actual state of the heart of God towards us to be lapped and folded in peace that nothing outside of God and ourselves can destroy. If we lived under the constant benediction of the deepest truth in the universe, 'God is love,' our peace would be full. That is enough, if we believe it to bring peace. The thought of God which alarms and terrifies cannot be a true thought. But, alas! in proportion as we know ourselves, it becomes difficult to believe that God is love. The stings of conscience hiss prophecies to us of that in God which cannot but be antagonistic to that in us which conscience condemns. Only when our thought of God is drawn from the revelation of Him in Jesus Christ, does it become possible for any man to grasp in one act of his consciousness the conviction, I am a sinner, and the conquering conviction, God is Love, and only Love to me. So the old exhortation, 'Acquaint thyself with God and be at peace,' comes to be in Christian language: 'Behold God in Jesus, and thou shalt possess the peace of God to keep thy heart and mind.'

Knowledge of God gives peace, because in it we find the satisfaction of our whole nature. Thereby we are freed from the unrest of tumultuous passions and storms of self-will. The internecine war between the better and the worse selves within ceases to rage, and when we have become God's friends, that in us which is meant to rule rules, and that in us which is meant to serve serves, and the inner kingdom is no longer torn asunder but is harmonised with itself.

Knowledge of God brings peace amid all changes, for he who has God for his continual Companion draws little of his supplies from without, and can be tranquil when the seas roar and are troubled and the mountains are cast into the midst of the sea. He bears all his treasures with him, and need fear no loss of any real good. And at last the angel of peace will lead us through the momentary darkness and guide us, after a passing shadow on our path, into 'the land of peace wherein we trusted,' while yet in the land of warfare. Jesus still whispers the ancient salutation with which He greeted the company in the upper room on the evening of the day of resurrection, as He comes to His servants here, and it will be His welcome to them when He receives them above.

III. The true good from acquaintance with God.

As we have already said, Eliphaz was only thinking, on Old Testament lines, that prosperity in material things was the theocratic reward of allegiance to Jehovah. He was rubbing vitriol into Job's sores, and avowedly regarding him as a fear-inspiring instance of the converse principle. But we have a better meaning breathed into his words, since Jesus has taught us what is the true good for a man all the days of his life. Acquaintance with God is, not merely procures, good. To know Him, to clasp Him to our hearts as our Friend, our Infinite Lover, our Source of all peace and joy, to mould our wills to His and let Him dominate our whole selves, to seek our wellbeing in Him alone—what else or more can a soul need to be filled with all good? Acquaintance with God brings Him in all His sufficiency to inhabit else empty hearts. It changes the worst, according to the judgment of sense, into the best, transforming sorrow into loving discipline, interpreting its meaning, fitting us to 'bear it, and securing to us its blessings. To him that is a friend of God,

'All is right that seems most wrong
If it be His sweet will.'

To be acquainted with God is the quintessence of good. 'This is life eternal, to know Thee, the only true God, and Jesus Christ whom Thou hast sent.'

WHAT LIFE MAY BE MADE

'For then shalt thou have thy delight in the Almighty, and shalt lift up thy face unto God. 27. Thou shalt make thy prayer unto Him, and He shall hear thee, and thou shalt pay thy vows. 28. Thou shalt also decree a thing, and it shall be established unto thee: and the light shall shine upon thy ways. 29. When men are cast down, then thou shalt say, … lifting up; and He shall save the humble person.'—JOB xxii. 26-29.

These words are a fragment of one of the speeches of Job's friends, in which the speaker has been harping on the old theme that affliction is the consequence and evidence of sin. He has much ado to square his theory with facts, and especially with the fact which brought him to Job's dunghill. But he gets over the difficulty by the simple method of assuming that, since his theory must be true, there must be unknown facts which vindicate it in Job's case; and since affliction is a sign of sin, Job's afflictions are proof that he has been a sinner. So he charges him with grossest crimes, without a shadow of other reason; and after having poured this oil of vitriol into his wounds by way of consolation, he advises him to be good, on the decidedly low and selfish ground that it will pay.

His often-quoted exhortation, 'Acquaint thyself with God, and be at peace: thereby good shall come unto thee,' is, in his meaning of it, an undisguised appeal to purely selfish considerations, and its promise is not in accordance with facts. Whether that saying is noble and true or ignoble and false, depends on the meanings attached to 'peace' and 'good.' A similar flaw mars the words of our text, as understood by the speaker. But they can be raised to a higher level than that on which he placed them, and regarded as describing the sweet and wonderful prerogatives of the devout life. So understood, they may rebuke and stimulate and encourage us to make our lives conformed to the ideal here.

I. I note, first, that life may be full of delight and confidence in God.

'Then shalt thou delight thyself in the Almighty, and shalt lift up thy face unto God.' Now when we 'delight' in a thing or a person, we recognise that that thing, or person, fits into a cleft in our hearts, and corresponds to some need in our natures. We not only recognise its good, sweetness, and adaptation to ourselves, but we actually possess in real fruition the sweetness that we recognise, and the good which we apprehend in it. And so these things, the recognition of the supreme sweetness and all-perfect adaptation and sufficiency of God to all that I need; the suppression of tastes and desires which may conflict with that sweetness, and the actual enjoyment and fruition of the sweetness and preciousness which I apprehend—these things are the very heart of a man's religion. Without delight in God, there is no real religion.

The bulk of men are so sunken and embruted in animal tastes and sensuous desires and fleeting delights, that they have no care for the pure and calm joys which come to those who live near God. But above these stand the men, of whom there are a good many amongst us, whose religion is a matter of fear or of duty or of effort. And above them there stand the men who serve because they trust God, but whose religion is seeking rather than finding, and either from deficient consecration or from false conceptions of Him and of their relation to Him, is overshadowed by an unnatural and unwholesome gloom. And all these kinds of religion, the religion of fear, of duty, of effort, of seeking, and of doubt fighting with faith, are at the best wofully imperfect, and are, some of them, radically erroneous types of the religious life. He is the truly devout man who not only knows God to be great and holy, but feels Him to be sweet and sufficient; who not only fears, but loves; who not only seeks and longs, but possesses; or, in one word, true religion is delighting in God.

So herein is supplied a very sharp test for us. Do our tastes and inclinations set towards Him, and is He better to us than anything beside? Is God to me my dearest faith, the very home of my heart, to which I instinctively turn? Is the brightness of my day the light of His face? Is He the gladness of my joy? Is my Christianity a mill-horse round of service that I am not glad to render? Do I worship because I think it is duty, and are my prayers compulsory and mechanical; or do I worship because my heart goes out to Him? And is my life calm and sweet because I 'delight in the Lord'?

The next words of my text will help us to answer. 'Thou shalt lift up thy face unto God.' That is a clear enough metaphor to express frank confidence of approach to Him. The head hangs down in the consciousness of demerit and sin. 'Mine iniquities have taken hold upon me,' wailed the Psalmist, 'so that I am not able to look up.' But it is possible for men to go into God's presence with a sense of peace, and to hold up their heads before their Judge and look Him in the eyes and not be afraid. And unless we have that confidence in Him, not because of our merits, but because of His certain love, there will be no 'delight in the Lord.' And there will be no such confidence in Him unless we have 'access with confidence by faith' in that Christ who has taken away our sins, and prepared the way for us into the Father's presence, and by whose death and sacrifice, and by it alone, we sinful men, with open face and uplifted foreheads, can stand to receive upon our visage the full beams of His light, and expatiate and be glad therein. There is no religion worth naming, of which the inmost characteristic is not delight in God. There is no 'delighting in God' possible for sinful men unless they can come to Him with frank confidence, and there is no such confidence possible for us unless we apprehend by faith, and thereby make our own, the great work of Jesus Christ our Lord.

II. So, secondly, note, such a life of delighting in God will be blessed by the frankest intercourse with Him.

'Thou shalt make thy prayer unto Him, and He shall hear thee, and thou shalt pay thy vows.' These are three stages of this blessed communion that is possible for men. And note, prayer is not regarded in this aspect as duty, nor is it even dwelt upon as privilege, but as being the natural outcome and issue of that delighting in God and confident access to Him which have preceded. That is to say, if a man really has set his heart on God, and knows that in Him is all that he needs, then, of course, he will tell Him everything. As surely as the sunshine draws out the odours from the opening petals of the flowers, will the warmth of the felt divine light and love draw from our hearts the sweet confidence, which it is impossible not to give to Him in whom we delight.

If you have to be driven to prayer by a sense of duty, and if there be no impulse in your heart whispering ever to you, 'Tell your Love about it!' you have much need to examine into the reality, and certainly into the depth of your religion. For as surely as instinctive impulse, which needs no spurring from conscience or will, leads us to breathe our confidences to those that we love best, and makes us restless whilst we have a secret hid from them, so surely will a true love to God make it the most natural thing in the world to put all our circumstances, wants, and feeling into the shape of prayers. They may be in briefest words. They may scarcely be vocalised at all, but there will be, if there be a true love to Him, an instinctive turning to Him in every circumstance; and the single-worded cry, if it be no more, for help is sufficient. The arrow may be shot towards Heaven, though it be but slender and short, and it will reach its goal.

For my text goes on to the second stage, 'He shall hear thee.' That was not true as Eliphaz meant it. But it is true if we remember the preceding conditions. The fundamental passage, which I suppose underlies part, at least, of our text, is that great word in the psalm, 'Delight thyself in the Lord, and He shall give thee the desires of thine heart.' Does that mean that if a man loves God he may get everything he wants? Yes! and No! If it is supposed to mean that our religion is a kind of key to God's storehouse, enabling us to go in there and rifle it at our pleasure, then it is not true; if it means that a man who delights himself in God will have his supreme desire set upon God, and so will be sure to get it, then it is true. Fulfil the conditions and you are sure of the promise. If our prayer in its deepest essence be 'Not my will, but Thine,' it will be answered. When the desires of our heart are for God, and for conformity to His will, as they will be when we 'delight ourselves in Him,' then we get our heart's desires. There is no promise of our being able to impose our wills upon God, which would be a calamity, and not a blessing, but a promise that they who make Him their joy and their desire will never be defrauded of their desire nor robbed of their joy.

And so the third stage of this frank intercourse comes. 'Thou shalt pay thy vows.' All life may become a thank-offering to God for the benefits that have flowed unceasing from His hands. First a prayer, then the answer, then the rendered thank-offering. Thus, in swift alternation and reciprocity, is carried on the commerce between Heaven and earth, between man and God. The desires rise to Heaven, but Heaven comes down to earth first; and prayer is not the initial stage, but the second, in the process. God first gives His promise, and the best prayer is the catching up of God's promise and tossing it back again whence it came. Then comes the second downward motion, which is the answer to prayer, in blessing, and on it follows, finally, the reflection upwards, in thankful surrender and service, of the love that has descended on us, in answer to our desires. So like sunbeams from a mirror, or heat from polished metal, backwards and forwards, in continual alternation and reciprocation of influence and of love, flash and travel bright gleams between the soul and God. 'Truth springs out of the earth, and righteousness looks down from Heaven. Our God shall give that which is good, and the earth shall yield her increase.' Is there any other life of which such alternation is the privilege and the joy?

III. Then thirdly, such a life will neither know failure nor darkness.

'Thou shalt also decree a thing, and it shall be established unto thee, and the light shall shine upon thy ways.' Then is my will to be omnipotent, and am I to be delivered from the experiences of disappointments and failures and frustrated plans that are common to all humanity, and an essential part of its discipline, because I am a Christian man? Eliphaz may have meant that, but we know something far nobler. Again, I say, remember the conditions precedent. First of all, there must be the delight in God, and the desire towards Him, the submission of the will to Him, and the waiting before Him for guidance. I decree a thing—if I am a true Christian, and in the measure in which I am—only when I am quite sure that God has decreed it. And it is only His decrees, registered in the chancery of my will, of which I may be certain that they shall be established. There will be no failures to the man whose life's purpose is to serve God, and to grow like Him; but if our purpose is anything less than that, or if we go arbitrarily and self-willedly resolving and saying, 'Thus I will; thus I command; let my will stand instead of all reason,' we shall have our contemptuous 'decrees' disestablished many a time. If we run our heads against stone walls in that fashion, the walls will stand, and our heads will be broken. To serve Him and to fall into the line of His purpose, and to determine nothing, nor obstinately want anything until we are sure that it is His will—that is the secret of never failing in what we undertake.

We must understand a little more deeply than we are apt to do what is meant by 'success,' before we predict unfailing success for any man. But if we have obeyed the commandment from the psalm already quoted, which may be again alluded to in the words of my text—'Commit thy way unto the Lord; trust also in Him'—we shall inherit the ancient promise, 'and He shall bring it to pass.' 'All things work together for good to them that love God,' and in the measure of our love to Him are our discernment and realisation of what is truly good. Religion gives no screen to keep the weather off us, but it gives us an insight into the truth that storms and rain are good for the only crop that is worth growing here. If we understand what we are here for, we shall be very slow to call sorrow evil, and to crown joy with the exclusive title of blessing and good; and we shall have a deeper canon of interpretation for the words of my text than he who is represented as speaking them ever dreamed of.

So with the promise of light to shine upon our paths. It is 'the light which never was on sea or land,' and not the material light which sense-bound eyes can see. That may all go. But if we have God in our hearts, there will be a light upon our way 'which knows no variableness, neither shadow of turning.' The Arctic winter, sunless though it be, has a bright heaven radiant with myriad stars, and flashing with strange lights born of no material or visible orb. And so you and I, if we delight ourselves 'in the Lord,' will have an unsetting sun to light our paths; 'and at eventide,' and in the mirkest midnight, 'there will be light' in the darkness.

IV. Lastly, such a life will be always hopeful, and finally crowned with deliverance.

'When they'—that is, the ways that he has been speaking about—'when they are cast down, thou shalt say, Lifting up.' That is an exclamation or a prayer, and we might simply render, 'thou shalt say, Up!' Even in so blessed a life as has been described, times will come when the path plunges downwards into some 'valley of the shadow of death.' But even then the traveller will bate no jot of hope. He will in his heart say 'Up!' even while sense says 'Down!' either as expressing indomitable confidence and good cheer in the face of depressing circumstances, or as pouring out a prayer to Him who 'has showed him great and sore troubles' that He would 'bring him up again from the depths of the earth.' The devout life is largely independent of circumstances, and is upheld and calmed by a quiet certainty that the general trend of its path is upward, which enables it to trudge hopefully down an occasional dip in the road.

Such an obstinate hopefulness and cheery confidence are the natural result of the experiences already described in the text. If we delight in God, hold communion with Him and have known Him as answering prayer, prospering our purposes and illuminating our paths, how shall we not hope? Nothing need depress nor perturb those whose joys and treasures are safe above the region of change and loss. If our riches are there where neither moth, rust, nor thieves can reach, our hearts will be there also, and an inward voice will keep singing, 'Lift up your heart.' It is the prerogative of experience to light up the future. It is the privilege of Christian experience to make hope certainty. If we live the life outlined in these verses we shall be able to bring June into December, and feel the future warmth whilst our bones are chilled with the present cold. 'When the paths are made low, thou shalt say, Up!'

And the end will vindicate such confidence. For the issue of all will be, 'He will save the humble person'; namely, the man who is of the character described, and who is 'lowly of eyes' in conscious unworthiness, even while he lifts up his face to God in confidence in his Father's love. The 'saving' meant here is, of course, temporary and temporal deliverance from passing outward peril. But we may permissibly give it wider and deeper meaning. Continuous partial deliverances lead on to and bring about final full salvation.

We read that into the words, of course. But nothing less than a complete and conclusive deliverance can be the legitimate end of the experience of the Christian life here. Absurdity can no further go than to suppose that a soul which has delighted itself in God, and looked in His face with frank confidence, and poured out his desires to Him, and been the recipient of numberless answers, and the seat of numberless thank-offerings, has travelled along life's common way in cheerful godliness, has had the light of heaven shining on the path, and has found an immortal hope springing as the natural result of present experience, shall at the last be frustrated of all, and lie down in unconscious sleep, which is nothingness. If that were the end of a Christian life, then 'the pillared firmament were rottenness, and earth's base built on stubble.' No, no! A heaven of endless blessedness and close communion with God is the only possible ending to the facts of the devout life on earth.

We have such a life offered to us all and made possible through faith in Jesus Christ, in whom we may delight ourselves in the Lord, by whom we have 'access with confidence,' who is Himself the light of our hope, the answer of our prayers, the joy of our hearts, and who will 'deliver us from every evil work' as we travel along the road; 'and save us' at last 'into His heavenly kingdom,' where we shall be joined to the Delight of our souls, and drink for evermore of the fountain of life.

'THE END OF THE LORD'

'Then Job answered the Lord, and said, 2. I know that Thou canst do every thing, and that no thought can he withholden from Thee. 3. Who is he that hideth counsel without knowledge? therefore have I uttered that I understood not; things too wonderful for me, which I knew not. 4. Hear, I beseech Thee, and I will speak: I will demand of Thee, and declare Thou unto me. 5. I have heard of Thee by the hearing of the ear: but now mine eye seeth Thee. 6. Wherefore I abhor myself, and repent in dust and ashes. 7. And it was so, that after the Lord had spoken these words unto Job, the Lord said to Eliphaz the Temanite, My wrath is kindled against thee, and against thy two friends: for ye have not spoken of Me the thing that is right, as My servant Job hath. 8. Therefore take unto you now seven bullocks and seven rams, and go to My servant Job, and offer up for yourselves a burnt offering; and My servant Job shall pray for you: for him will I accept: lest I deal with you after your folly, in that ye have not spoken of Me the thing which is right, like My servant Job. 9. So Eliphaz the Temanite and Bildad the Shuhite and Zophar the Naamathite went, and did according as the Lord commanded them: the Lord also accepted Job. 10. And the Lord turned the captivity of Job, when he prayed for his friends: also the Lord gave Job twice as much as he had before.'—JOB xlii. 1-10.

The close of the Book of Job must be taken in connection with its prologue, in order to get the full view of its solution of the mystery of pain and suffering. Indeed the prologue is more completely the solution than the ending is; for it shows the purpose of Job's trials as being, not his punishment, but his testing. The whole theory that individual sorrows were the result of individual sins, in the support of which Job's friends poured out so many eloquent and heartless commonplaces, is discredited from the beginning. The magnificent prologue shows the source and purpose of sorrow. The epilogue in this last chapter shows the effect of it in a good man's character, and afterwards in his life.

So we have the grim thing lighted up, as it were, at the two ends. Suffering comes with the mission of trying what stuff a man is made of, and it leads to closer knowledge of God, which is blessed; to lowlier self-estimation, which is also blessed; and to renewed outward blessings, which hide the old scars and gladden the tortured heart.

Job's final word to God is in beautiful contrast with much of his former unmeasured utterances. It breathes lowliness, submission, and contented acquiescence in a providence partially understood. It does not put into Job's mouth a solution of the problem, but shows how its pressure is lightened by getting closer to God. Each verse presents a distinct element of thought and feeling.

First comes, remarkably enough, not what might have been expected, namely, a recognition of God's righteousness, which had been the attribute impugned by Job's hasty words, but of His omnipotence. God 'can do everything,' and none of His 'thoughts' or purposes can be 'restrained' (Rev. Ver.). There had been frequent recognitions of that attribute in the earlier speeches, but these had lacked the element of submission, and been complaint rather than adoration. Now, the same conviction has different companions in Job's mind, and so has different effects, and is really different in itself. The Titan on his rock, with the vulture tearing at his liver, sullenly recognised Jove's power, but was a rebel still. Such had been Job's earlier attitude, but now that thought comes to him along with submission, and so is blessed. Its recurrence here, as in a very real sense a new conviction, teaches us how old beliefs may flash out into new significance when seen from a fresh point of view, and how the very same thought of God may be an argument for arraigning and for vindicating His providence.

The prominence given, both in the magnificent chapters in which God answers Job out of the whirlwind and in this final confession, to power instead of goodness, rests upon the unspoken principle that 'the divine nature is not a segment, but a circle. Any one divine attribute implies all others. Omnipotence cannot exist apart from righteousness' (Davidson's *Job*, Cambridge Bible for Schools). A mere naked omnipotence is not God. If we rightly understand His power, we can rest upon it as a Hand sustaining, not crushing, us. 'He doeth all things well' is a conviction as closely connected with 'I know that Thou canst do all things' as light is with heat.

The second step in Job's confession is the acknowledgment of the incompleteness of his and all men's materials and capacities for judging God's providence. Verse 3 begins with quoting God's rebuke (Job xxxviii 2). It had cut deep, and now Job makes it his own confession. We should thus appropriate as our own God's merciful indictments, and when He asks, 'Who is it?' should answer with lowliness, 'Lord, it is I.' Job had been a critic; he is a worshipper. He had tried to fathom the bottomless, and been angry because his short measuring-line had not reached the depths. But now he acknowledges that he had been talking about what passed his comprehension, and also that his words had been foolish in their rashness.

Is then the solution of the whole only that old commonplace of the unsearchableness of the divine judgments? Not altogether; for the prologue gives, if not a complete, yet a real, key to them. But still, after all partial solutions, there remains the inscrutable element in them. The mystery of pain and suffering is still a mystery; and while general principles, taught us even more clearly in the New Testament than in this book, do lighten the 'weight of all this unintelligible world,' we have still to take Job's language as the last word on the matter, and say, 'How unsearchable are His judgments, and His ways past finding out!'

For individuals, and on the wider field of the world, God's way is in the sea; but that does not bewilder those who also know that it is also in the sanctuary. Job's confession as to his rash speeches is the best estimate of many elaborate attempts to 'vindicate the ways of God to man.' It is better to trust than to criticise, better to wait than to seek prematurely to understand.

Verse 4, like verse 3, quotes the words of God (Job xxxviii. 3; xl. 7). They yield a good meaning, if regarded as a repetition of God's challenge, for the purpose of disclaiming any such presumptuous contest. But they are perhaps better understood as expressing Job's longing, in his new condition of humility, for fuller light, and his new recognition of the way to pierce to a deeper understanding of the mystery, by illumination from God granted in answer to his prayer. He had tried to solve his problem by much, and sometimes barely reverent, thinking. He had racked brain and heart in the effort, but he has learned a more excellent way, as the Psalmist had, who said, 'When I thought, in order to know this, it was too painful for me, until I went into the sanctuary of God; then understood I.' Prayer will do more for clearing mysteries than speculation, however acute, and it will change the aspect of the mysteries which it does not clear from being awful to being solemn—veils covering depths of love, not clouds obscuring the sun.

The centre of all Job's confession is in verse 5, which contrasts his former and present knowledge of God, as being mere hearsay before, and eyesight now. A clearer understanding, but still more, a sense of His nearness, and an acquaintance at first hand, are implied in the bold words, which must not be interpreted of any outward revelation to sense, but of the direct, full, thrilling consciousness of God which makes all men's words about Him seem poor. That change was the master transformation in Job's case, as it is for us all. Get closer to God, realise His presence, live beneath His eye and with your eyes fixed on Him, and ancient puzzles will puzzle no longer, and wounds will cease to smart, and instead of angry expostulation or bewildered attempts at construing His dealings, there will come submission, and with submission, peace.

The cure for questionings of His providence is experience of His nearness, and blessedness therein. Things that loomed large dwindle, and dangers melt away. The landscape is the same in shadow and sunshine; but when the sun comes out, even snow and ice sparkle, and tender beauty starts into visibility in grim things. So, if we see God, the black places of life are lighted; and we cease to feel the pressure of many difficulties of speculation and practice, both as regards His general providence and His revelation in law and gospel.

The end of the whole matter is Job's retractation of his words and his repentance. 'I abhor' has no object expressed, and is better taken as referring to the previous speeches than to 'myself.' He means thereby to withdraw them all. The next clause, 'I repent in dust and ashes,' carries the confession a step farther. He recognises guilt in his rash speeches, and bows before his God confessing his sin. Where are his assertions of innocence gone? One sight of God has scattered them, as it ever does. A man who has learned his own sinfulness will find few difficulties and no occasions for complaint in God's dealings with him. If we would see aright the meaning of our sorrows, we must look at them on our knees. Get near to God in heart-knowledge of Him, and that will teach our sinfulness, and the two knowledges will combine to explain much of the meaning of sorrow, and to make the unexplained residue not hard to endure.

The epilogue in prose which follows Job's confession, tells of the divine estimate of the three friends, of Job's sacrifice for them, and of his renewed outward prosperity. The men who had tried to vindicate God's righteousness are charged with not having spoken that which is right; the man who has passionately impugned it is declared to have thus spoken. No doubt, Eliphaz and his colleagues had said a great many most excellent, pious things, and Job as many wild and untrue ones. But their foundation principle was not a true representation of God's providence, since it was the uniform connection of sin with sorrow, and the accurate proportion which these bore to each other.

Job, on the other hand, had spoken truth in his denials of these principles, and in his longings to have the righteousness of God set in clear relation to his own afflictions. We must remember, too, that the friends were talking commonplaces learned by rote, while Job's words came scalding hot from his heart. Most excellent truth may be so spoken as to be wrong; and it is so, if spoken heartlessly, regardless of sympathy, and flung at sufferers like a stone, rather than laid on their hearts as a balm. God lets a true heart dare much in speech; for He knows that the sputter and foam prove that 'the heart's deeps boil in earnest.'

Job is put in the place of intercessor for the three—a profound humiliation for them and an honour for him. They obeyed at once, showing that they have learned their lesson, as well as Job his. An incidental lesson from that final picture of the sufferer become the priest requiting accusations with intercession, is the duty of cherishing kind feelings and doing kind acts to those who say hard things of us. It would be harder for some of us to offer sacrifices for our Eliphazes than to argue with them. And yet another is that sorrow has for one of its purposes to make the heart more tender, both for the sorrows and the faults of others.

Note, too, that it was 'when Job prayed for his friends' that the Lord turned his captivity. That is a proverbial expression, bearing witness, probably, to the deep traces left by the Exodus, for reversing calamity. The turning-point was not merely the confession, but the act, of beneficence. So, in ministering to others, one's own griefs may be soothed.

The restoration of outward good in double measure is not meant as the statement of a universal law of Providence, and still less as a solution of the problem of the book. But it is putting the truth that sorrows, rightly borne, yield peaceable fruit at the last, in the form appropriate to the stage of revelation which the whole book represents; that is, one in which the doctrine of immortality, though it sometimes rises before Job's mind as an aspiration of faith, is not set in full light.

To us, living in the blaze of light which Jesus Christ has let into the darkness of the future, the 'end of the Lord' is that heaven should crown the sorrows of His children on earth. We can speak of light, transitory affliction working out an eternal weight of glory. The book of Job is expressing substantially the same expectation, when it paints the calm after the storm and the restoration in double portion of vanished blessings. Many desolate yet trusting sufferers know how little such an issue is possible for their grief, but if they have more of God in clearer sight of Him, they will find empty places in their hearts and homes filled.

THE PROVERBS

A YOUNG MAN'S BEST COUNSELLOR

'The proverbs of Solomon the son of David, king of Israel; 2. To know wisdom and instruction; to perceive the words of understanding; 3. To receive the instruction of wisdom, justice, and judgment, and equity; 4. To give subtilty to the simple, to the young man knowledge and discretion, 5. A wise man will hear, and will increase learning; and a man of understanding shall attain unto wise counsels: 6. To understand a proverb, and the interpretation; the words of the wise, and their dark sayings. 7. The fear of the Lord is the beginning of knowledge: but fools despise wisdom and instruction. 8. My son, hear the instruction of thy father, and forsake not the law of thy mother: 9. For they shall be an ornament of grace unto thy head, and chains about thy neck. 10. My son, if sinners entice thee, consent thou not. 11. If they say, Come with us, let us lay wait for blood, let us lurk privily for the innocent without cause: 12. Let us swallow them up alive as the grave; and whole, as those that go down into the pit: 13. We shall find all precious substance, we shall fill our houses with spoil: 14. Cast in thy lot among us; let us all have one purse: 15. My son, walk not thou in the way with them; refrain thy foot from their path: 16. For their feet run to evil, and make haste to shed blood. 17. (Surely in vain the net is spread in the sight of any bird:) 18. And they lay wait for their own blood; they lurk privily for their own lives. 19. So arc the ways of every one that is greedy of gain; which taketh away the life of the owners thereof.'—PROV. i. 1-19.

This passage contains the general introduction to the book of Proverbs. It falls into three parts—a statement of the purpose of the book (vs. 1-6); a summary of its foundation principles, and of the teachings to which men ought to listen (vs. 7-9); and an antithetic statement of the voices to which they should be deaf (vs. 10-19).

I. The aim of the book is stated to be twofold—to enable men, especially the young, to 'know wisdom,' and to help them to 'discern the words of understanding'; that is, to familiarise, by the study of the book, with the characteristics of wise teachings, so that there may be no mistaking seducing words of folly for these. These two aims are expanded in the remaining verses, the latter of them being resumed in verse 6, while the former occupies the other verses.

We note how emphatically the field in which this wisdom is to be exercised is declared to be the moral conduct of life. 'Righteousness and judgment and equity' are 'wise dealing,' and the end of true wisdom is to practise these. The wider horizon of modern science and speculation includes much in the notion of wisdom which has no bearing on conduct. But the intellectual progress (and conceit) of to-day will be none the worse for the reminder that a man may take in knowledge till he is ignorant, and that, however enriched with science and philosophy, if he does not practise righteousness, he is a fool.

We note also the special destination of the book—for the young. Youth, by reason of hot blood and inexperience, needs such portable medicines as are packed in these proverbs, many of them the condensation into a vivid sentence of world-wide truths. There are few better guides for a young man than this book of homely sagacity, which is wisdom about the world without being tainted by the bad sort of worldly wisdom. But unfortunately those who need it most relish it least, and we have for the most part to rediscover its truths for ourselves by our own, often bitter, experience.

We note, further, the clear statement of the way by which incipient 'wisdom' will grow, and of the certainty of its growth if it is real. It is the 'wise man' who will 'increase in learning,' the 'man of understanding' who 'attains unto sound counsels.' The treasures are thrown away on him who has no heart for them. You may lavish wisdom on the 'fool,' and it will run off him like water off a rock, fertilising nothing, and stopping outside him.

The Bible would not have met all our needs, nor gone with us into all regions of our experience, if it had not had this book of shrewd, practical common-sense. Christianity is the perfection of common sense. 'Godliness hath promise of the life which now is.' The wisdom of the serpent, which Jesus enjoins, has none of the serpent's venom in it. It is no sign of spirituality of mind to be above such mundane considerations as this book urges. If we hold our heads too high to look to our road and our feet, we are sure to fall into a pit.

II. Verses 7-9 may be regarded as a summary statement of the principle on which the whole book is based, and of the duty which it enjoins. The principle is that true wisdom is based on religion, and the duty is to listen to parental instruction. 'My son,' is the address of a teacher to his disciples, rather than of a father to his child. The characteristic Old Testament designation of religion as 'the fear of Jehovah' corresponds to the Old Testament revelation of Him as the Holy One,—that is, as Him who is infinitely separated from creatural being and limitations. Therefore is He 'to be had in reverence of all' who would be 'about Him'; that fear of reverential awe in which no slavish dread mingles, and which is perfectly consistent with aspiration, trust, and love. The Old Testament reveals Him as separate from men; the New Testament reveals Him as united to men in the divine man, Christ Jesus. Therefore its keynote is the designation of religion as 'the love of God'; but that name is no contradiction of the earlier, but the completion of it.

That fear is the beginning or basis of wisdom, because wisdom is conceived of as God's gift, and the surest way to get it is to 'ask of God' (Jas. i. 5). Religion is, further, the foundation of wisdom, inasmuch as irreligion is the supreme folly of creatures so dependent on God, and so hungering after Him in the depths of their being, as we are. In whatever directions a godless man may be wise, in the most important matter of all, his relations to God, he is unwise, and the epitaph for all such is 'Thou fool!'

Further, religion is the fountain of wisdom, in the sense of the word in which this book uses it, since it opens out into principles of action, motives, and communicated powers, which lead to right apprehension and willing discharge of the duties of life. Godless men may be scientists, philosophers, encyclopaedias of knowledge, but for want of religion, they blunder in the direction of their lives, and lack wisdom enough to keep them from wrecking the ship on the rocks.

The Israelitish parent was enjoined to teach his or her children the law of the Lord. Here the children are enjoined to listen to the instruction. Reverence for traditional wisdom was characteristic of that state of society, and since a divine revelation stood at the beginning of the nation's history, it was not unreasonable to look back for light. Nowadays, a belief's being our fathers' is with many a reason for not making it ours. But perhaps that is no more rational than the blind adherence to the old with which this emancipated generation reproaches its predecessors. Possibly there are some 'old lamps' better than the new ones now hawked about the streets by so many loud-voiced vendors. The youth of this day have much need of the exhortation to listen to the 'instruction' (by which is meant, not only teaching by word, but discipline by act) of their fathers, and to the gentler voice of the mother telling of law in accents of love. These precepts obeyed will be fairer ornaments than jewelled necklaces and wreathed chaplets.

III. On one side of the young man are those who would point him to the fear of Jehovah; on the other are seducing whispers, tempting him to sin. That is the position in which we all stand. It is not enough to listen to the nobler voice. We have resolutely to stop our ears to the baser, which is often the louder. Facile yielding to the cunning inducements which strew every path, and especially that of the young, is fatal. If we cannot say 'No' to the base, we shall not say 'Yes' to the noble voice. To be weak is generally to be wicked; for in this world the tempters are more numerous, and to sense and flesh, more potent than those who invite to good.

The example selected of such enticers is not of the kind that most of us are in danger from. But the sort of inducements held out are in all cases substantially the same. 'Precious substance' of one sort or another is dangled before dazzled eyes; jovial companionship draws young hearts. The right or wrong of the thing is not mentioned, and even murder and robbery are presented as rather pleasant excitement, and worth doing for the sake of what is got thereby. Are the desirable consequences so sure? Is there no chance of being caught red-handed, and stoned then and there, as a murderer? The tempters are discreetly silent about that possibility, as all tempters are. Sin always deceives, and its baits artfully hide the hook; but the cruel barb is there, below the gay silk and coloured dressing, and it—not the false appearance of food which lured the fish—is what sticks in the bleeding mouth.

The teacher goes on, in verses 15 to 19, to supply the truth which the tempters tried to ignore. He does so in three weighty sentences, which strip the tinsel off the temptation, and show its real ugliness. The flowery way to which they coax is a way of 'evil'; that should be enough to settle the question. The first thing to ask about any course is not whether it is agreeable or disagreeable, but Is it right or wrong? Verse 17 is ambiguous, but probably the 'net' means the tempters' speech in verses 11 to 14, and the 'bird' is the young man supposed to be addressed. The sense will then be, 'Surely you are not foolish enough to fly right into the meshes, and to go with your eyes open into so transparent sin!'

Verse 18 points to the grim possibility already referred to, that the would-be murderers will be caught and executed. But its lesson is wider than that one case, and declares the great solemn truth that all sin is suicide. Who ever breaks God's law slays himself.

What is true about 'covetousness,' as verse 19 tells, is true about all kinds of sin—that it takes away the life of those who yield to it, even though it may also fill their purses, or in other ways may gratify their desires. Surely it is folly to pursue a course which, however it may succeed in its immediate aims, brings real death, by separation from God, along with it. He is not a very wise man who ties his gold round him when the ship founders. He is not parted from his treasure certainly, but it helps to sink him. We may get what we want by sinning, but we get also what we did not want or reckon on—that is, eternal death. 'This their way is their folly.' Yet, strange to tell, their posterity 'approve their sayings,' and follow their doings.

WISDOM'S CALL

'Wisdom crieth without; she uttereth her voice in the streets: 21. She crieth in the chief place of concourse, in the openings of the gates: in the city she uttereth her words, saying, 22. How long, ye simple ones, will ye love simplicity? and the scorners delight in their scorning, and fools hate knowledge? 23. Turn you at my reproof: behold, I will pour out my Spirit unto you, I will make known my words unto you. 24. Because I have called, and ye refused; I have stretched out my hand, and no man regarded; 25. But ye have set at nought all my counsel, and would none of my reproof: 26. I also will laugh at your calamity; I will mock when your fear cometh; 27. When your fear cometh as desolation, and your destruction cometh as a whirlwind; when distress and anguish cometh upon you. 28. Then shall they call upon me, but I will not answer; they shall seek me early, but they shall not find me: 29. For that they hated knowledge, and did not choose the fear of the Lord: 30. They would none of my counsel; they despised all my reproof. 31. Therefore shall they eat of the fruit of their own way, and be filled with their own devices. 32. For the turning away of the simple shall slay them, and the prosperity of fools shall destroy them. 33. But whoso hearkeneth unto me shall dwell safely, and shall be quiet from fear of evil.'—PROVERBS i. 20-33.

Our passage begins with a striking picture. A fair and queenly woman stands in the crowded resorts of men, and lifts up a voice of sweet entreaty—authoritative as well as sweet. Her name is Wisdom. The word is in the plural in the Hebrew, as if to teach that in this serene and lovely form all manifold wisdoms are gathered and made one. Who then is she? It is easy to say 'a poetical personification,' but that does not add much to our understanding. It is clear that this book means much more by Wisdom than a human quality merely; for august and divine attributes are given to her, and she is the co-eternal associate of God Himself. Dwelling in His bosom, she thence comes forth to inspire all human good deeds, to plead evermore with men, to enrich those who listen to her with choicest gifts. Intellectual clearness, moral goodness, religious devotion, are all combined in the idea of Wisdom as belonging to men.

The divine source of all, and the correspondence between the human and the divine nature, are taught in the residence of this personified Wisdom with God before she dwelt with men. The whole of the manifold revelations, by which God makes known any part of His will to men, are her voice. Especially the call contained in the Old Testament revelation is the summons of Wisdom. But whether the writer of this book had any inkling of deeper truth still, or not, we cannot but connect the incomplete personification of divine Wisdom here with its complete incarnation in a Person who is 'the power of God and the wisdom of God,' and who embodies the lineaments of the grand picture of a Wisdom crying in the streets, even while it is true of Him that 'He does not strive nor cry, nor cause His voice to be heard in the streets'; for the crying, which is denied to be His, is ostentatious and noisy, and the crying which is asserted to be hers is the plain, clear, universal appeal of divine love as well as wisdom. The light of Christ 'lighteth every man that cometh into the world.'

The call of Wisdom in this passage begins with remonstrance and plain speech, giving their right names to men who neglect her voice. The first step in delivering men from evil—that is, from foolish—courses is to put very clearly before them the true character of their acts, and still more of their inclinations. Gracious offers and rich promises come after; but the initial message of Wisdom to such men as we are must be the accusation of folly. 'When she is come, she will convict the world of sin.'

The three designations of men in verse 22 are probably arranged so as to make a climax. First come 'the simple,' or, as the word means, 'open.' There is a *sancta simplicitas*, a holy ignorance of evil, which is sister to the highest wisdom. It is well to be ignorant as well as 'innocent of much transgression'; and there is no more mistaken and usually insincere excuse for going into foul places than the plea that it is best to know the evil and so choose the good. That knowledge comes surely and soon enough without our seeking it. But there is a fatal simplicity, open-eared, like Eve, to the Tempter's whisper, which believes the false promises of sin, and as Bunyan has taught us, is companion of sloth and presumption.

Next come 'scorners,' who mock at good. A man must have gone a long way down hill before he begins to gibe at virtue and godliness. But the descent is steep, though the distance is long; and the 'simple' who begins to do what is wrong will come to sneer at what is right.

Then last comes the 'fool,' the name which, in Proverbs, is shorthand for mental stupidity, moral obstinacy, and dogged godlessness,—a foul compound, but one which is realised oftener than we think. A great many very superior intellects, cultivated ladies and gentlemen, university graduates, and the like, would be unceremoniously set down by divine wisdom as fools; and surely if account is taken of the whole compass and duration of our being, and of all our relations to things and persons seen and unseen, nothing can be more stupid than godlessness, however cultured. The word literally means coarse or thick, and may suggest the idea of stolid insensibility as the last stage in the downward progress.

But note that the charge is directed, not against deeds, but dispositions. Perverted love and perverted hatred underlie acts. The simple love simplicity, preferring to be unwarned against evil; the scorner finds delight in letting his rank tongue blossom into speech; and the false direction given to love gives a fatal twist to its corresponding hate, so that the fool detests 'knowledge' as a thief the policeman's lantern. You cannot love what you should loathe, without loathing what you should love. Inner longings and revulsions settle character and acts.

Verse 23 passes into entreaty; for it is vain to rouse conscience by plain speech, unless something is offered to make better life possible. The divine Wisdom comes with a rod, but also with gifts; but if the rod is kissed, the rewards are possessed. The relation of clauses in verse 23 is that the first is the condition of the fulfilment of the second and third. If we turn at her reproof, two great gifts will be bestowed. Her spirit within will make us quick to hear and receive her words sounding without. Whatever other good follows on yielding to the call of divine Wisdom (and the remaining early chapters of Proverbs magnificently detail the many rich gifts that do follow), chief of all are spirits swift to hear and docile to obey her voice, and then actual communications to purged ears. Outward revelation without prepared hearts is water spilt upon rock. Prepared hearts without a message to them would be but multiplication of vain longings; and God never stultifies Himself, or gives mouths without sending meat to fill them. To the submissive spirit, there will not lack either disposition to hear or clear utterance of His will.

But now comes a pause. Wisdom has made her offers in the crowded streets, and amid all the noise and bustle her voice has rung out. What is the result? Nothing. Not a head has been turned, nor an eye lifted. The bustle goes on as before. 'They bought, they sold,' as if no voice had spoken. So, after the disappointed waiting of Wisdom, her voice peals out again, but this time with severity in its tones. Note how, in verses 24 and 25, the sin of sins against the pleading Wisdom of God is represented as being simple indifference. 'Ye refused,' 'no man regarded,' 'set at nought,' 'would none of'—these are the things which bring down the heavy judgments. It does not need violent opposition or black crime to wreck a soul. Simply doing nothing when God speaks is enough to effect destruction. There is no need to lift up angry arms in hostility. If we keep them hanging listless by our sides, it is sufficient. The gift escapes us, if we simply keep our hands shut or held behind our backs. Alas, for ears which have not heard, for seeing eyes which have not seen because they loved evil simplicity and hated knowledge!

Then note the terrible retribution. That is an awful picture of the mocking laughter of Wisdom, accompanying the rush of the whirlwind and the groans of anguish and shrieks of terror. It is even more solemn and dreadful than the parallel representations in Psalm ii., for there the laughter indicates God's knowledge that the schemes of opponents are vain, but here it figures pleasure in calamities. Of course it is to be remembered that the Wisdom thus represented is not to be identified with God; but still the imagery is startling, and needs to be taken along with declarations that God has 'no pleasure in the death of the sinner,' and to be interpreted as indicating, with daring anthropomorphism, the inevitable character of the 'destruction,' and the uselessness of appeals to the Wisdom once despised. But we joyfully remember that the Incarnate Wisdom, fairer than the ancient personification, wept over the city which He knew must perish.

Verses 28-31 carry on the picture of too late repentance and inevitable retribution. They who let Wisdom cry, and paid no heed, shall cry to her in their turn, and be unnoticed. They whom she vainly sought shall vainly seek for her. Actions have their consequences, which are not annihilated because the doers do not like them. Thoughts have theirs; for the foolish not only eat of the fruit of their ways or doings, but are filled with their own devices or counsels. 'Whatsoever a man soweth, that shall he also reap.' That inexorable law works, deaf to all cries, in the field of earthly life, both as regards condition and character; and that field of its operation is all that the writer of this book has in view. He is not denying the possibility of forgiveness, nor the efficacy of repentance, nor is he asserting that a penitent soul ever seeks God in vain; but he is declaring that it is too late to cry out for deliverance from consequences of folly when the consequences have us in their grip, and that wishes for deliverance are vain, though sighs of repentance are not. We cannot reap where we have not sowed. We must reap what we have. If we are such sluggards that we will 'not plough in winter by reason of the cold,' we shall 'beg in harvest and have nothing.'

But though the writer had probably only this life in view, Jesus Christ has extended the teaching to the next, when He has told of those who will seek to enter in and not be able. The experience of the fruits of their godlessness will make godless men wish to escape eating the fruits—and that wish shall be vain. It is not for us to enlarge on such words, but it is for us all to lay them to heart, and to take heed that we listen now to the beseeching call of the heavenly Wisdom in its tenderest and noblest form, as it appeared in Christ, the Incarnate Word.

Verses 32 and 33 generalise the preceding promises and warnings in a great antithesis. 'The backsliding [or, turning away] of the simple slays them.' There is allusion to Wisdom's call in verse 23. The simple had turned, but in the wrong direction—away from and not towards her. To turn away from heavenly Wisdom is to set one's face toward destruction. It cannot be too earnestly reiterated that we must make our choice of one of two directions for ourselves—either towards God, to seek whom is life, to find whom is heaven; or away from Him, to turn our backs on whom is to embrace unrest, and to be separate from whom is death. 'The security of fools,' by which is meant, not their safety, but their fancy that they are safe, 'destroys them.' No man is in such danger as the careless man of the world who thinks that he is all right. A traveller along the edge of a precipice in the night, who goes on as if he walked a broad road and takes no heed to his footing, will soon repent his rashness at the bottom, mangled and bruised. A man who in this changing world fancies that he sits as a king, and sees no sorrow, will have a rude wakening. A moment's heed saves hours of pain.

The alternative to this suicidal folly is in listening to Wisdom's call. Whoever does that will 'dwell safely,' not in fancied but real security; and in his quiet heart there need be no unrest from feared evils, for he will have hold of a charm which turns evils into good, and with such a guide he cannot go astray, nor with such a defender be wounded to death, nor with such a companion ever be solitary. If Christ be our Light, we shall not walk in darkness. If He be our Wisdom, we shall not err. If He be our Life, we shall never see death. If He is our Good, we shall fear no evil.

THE SECRET OF WELL-BEING

'My son, forget not my law; but let thine heart keep my commandments. 2. For length of days, and long life, and peace, shall they add to thee. 3. Let not mercy and truth forsake thee: bind them about thy neck; write them upon the table of thine heart: 4. So shalt thou find favour and good understanding in the sight of God and man. 5. Trust in the Lord with all thine heart; and lean not unto thine own understanding. 6. In all thy ways acknowledge Him, and He shall direct thy paths. 7. Be not wise in thine own eyes: fear the Lord, and depart from evil. 8. It shall be health to thy navel, and marrow to thy bones. 9. Honour the Lord with thy substance, and with the firstfruits of all thine increase: 10. So shall thy barns be filled with plenty, and thy presses shall burst out with new wine.'—PROVERBS iii. 1-10.

The first ten verses of this passage form a series of five couplets, which enforce on the young various phases of goodness by their tendency to secure happiness or blessedness of various sorts. The underlying axiom is that, in a world ruled by a good Being, obedience must lead to well-being; but while that is in the general true, exceptions do occur, and good men do encounter evil times. Therefore the glowing promises of these verses are followed by two verses which deal with the explanation of good men's afflictions, as being results and tokens of God's fatherly love.

The first couplet is general in character. It inculcates obedience to the precepts of the teacher, and gives as reason the assurance that thereby long life and peace will be secured. True to the Old Testament conception of revelation as a law, the teacher sets obedience in the forefront. He is sure that his teaching contains the sufficient guide for conduct, and coincides with the divine will. He calls, in the first instance, for inward willing acceptance of His commandments; for it is the heart, not primarily the hands, which he desires should 'keep' them. The mother of all graces of conduct is the bowing of the will to divine authority. The will is the man, and where it ceases to lift itself up in self-sacrificing and self-determining rebellion, and dissolves into running waters of submission, these will flow through the life and make it pure. To obey self is sin, to obey God is righteousness. The issues of such obedience are 'length of days … and peace.'

Even if we allow for the difference between the Old and the New Testaments, it remains true that a life conformed to God's will tends to longevity, and that many forms of sin do shorten men's days. Passion and indulged appetites eat away the very flesh, and many a man's 'bones are full of the sin of his youth.' The profligate has usually 'a short life,' whether he succeeds in making it 'merry' or not.

'Peace' is a wide word, including all well-being. Ease-loving Orientals, especially when living in warlike times, naturally used the phrase as a shorthand expression for all good. Busy Westerns, torn by the distractions and rapid movement of modern life, echo the sigh for repose which breathes in the word. 'There is no joy but calm,' and the sure way to deepest peace is to give up self-will and live in obedience.

The second couplet deals with our relations to one another, and puts forward the two virtues of 'loving-kindness and truth'—that is truth, or faithfulness—as all-inclusive. They are the two which are often jointly ascribed to God, especially in the Psalms. Our attitude to one another should be moulded in God's to us all. The tiniest crystal has the same facets and angles as the largest. The giant hexagonal pillars of basalt, like our Scottish Staffa, are identical in form with the microscopic crystals of the same substance. God is our Pattern; goodness is likeness to Him.

These graces are to be bound about the neck, perhaps as an ornament, but more probably as a yoke by which the harnessed ox draws its burden. If we have them, they will fit us to bear one another's burdens, and will lead to all human duties to our fellows.

These graces are also to be written on the 'table of the heart'; that is, are to be objects of habitual meditation with aspiration. If so, they will come to sight in life. He who practises them will 'find favour with God and man,' for God looks with complacency on those who display the right attitude to men; and men for the most part treat us as we treat them. There are surly natures which are not won by kindness, like black tarns among the hills, that are gloomy even in sunshine, and requite evil for good; but the most of men reflect our feelings to them.

'Good understanding' is another result. It is 'found' when it is attributed to us, so that the expression substantially means that the possessors of these graces will win the reputation of being really wise, not only in the fallible judgment of men, but before the pure eyes of the all-seeing God. Really wise policy coincides with loving-kindness and truth.

The remaining couplets refer to our relations to God. The New Testament is significantly anticipated in the pre-eminence given to trust; that is, faith. Nor less significant and profound is the association of self-distrust with trust in the Lord. The two things are inseparable. They are but the under and upper sides of one thing, or like the two growths that come from a seed—one striking downwards becomes the root; one piercing upwards becomes the stalk. The double attitude of trust and distrust finds expression in acknowledging Him in all our ways; that is, ordering our conduct under a constant consciousness of His presence, in accordance with His will, and in dependence on His help.

Such a relation to God will certainly, and with no exceptions, issue in His 'directing our paths,' by which is meant that He will be not only our Guide, but also our Roadmaker, showing us the way and clearing obstacles from it. Calm certitude follows on willingness to accept God's will, and whoever seeks only to go where God sends him will neither be left doubtful whither he should go, nor find his road blocked.

The fourth couplet is, in its first part, in inverted parallelism with the third; for it begins with self-distrust, and proceeds thence to 'fear of the Lord,' which corresponds to, and is, in fact, but one phase of, trust in Him. It is the reverent awe which has no torment, and is then purest when faith is strongest. It necessarily leads to departing from evil. Morality has its roots in religion. There is no such magnet to draw men from sin as the happy fear of God, which is likewise faith. Whoever separates devoutness from purity of life, this teacher does not. He knows nothing of religion which permits association with iniquity. Such conduct will tend to physical well-being, and in a deeper sense will secure soundness of life. Godlessness is the true sickness. He only is healthy who has a healthy, because healed, soul.

The fifth couplet appears at first as being a drop to a lower region. A regulation of the Mosaic law may strike some as out of place here. But it is to be remembered that our modern distinction of ceremonial and moral law was non-existent for Israel, and that the command has a wider application than to Jewish tithes. To 'honour God with our substance' is not necessarily to give it away for religious purposes, but to use it devoutly and as He approves.

Christianity has more to say about the distribution, as well as the acquisition, of wealth, than professing Christians, especially in commercial communities, practically recognise. This precept grips us tight, and is much more than a ceremonial regulation. Many causes besides the devout use of property tend to wealth in our highly artificial state of society. The world tries to get it by shrewdness, unscrupulousness, and by many other vices which are elevated to the rank of virtues; but he who honours the Lord in getting and spending will generally have as much as his true needs and regulated desires require.

THE GIFTS OF HEAVENLY WISDOM

'My son, despise not the chastening of the Lord; neither be weary of His correction: 12. For whom the Lord loveth He correcteth; even as a father the son in whom he delighteth. 13. Happy is the man that findeth wisdom, and the man that getteth understanding. 14. For the merchandise of it is better than the merchandise of silver, and the gain thereof than fine gold. 15. She is more precious than rubies: and all the things thou canst desire are not to be compared unto her. 16. Length of days is in her right hand; and in her left hand riches and honour. 17. Her ways are ways of pleasantness, and all her paths are peace. 18. She is a tree of life to them that lay hold upon her: and happy is every one that retaineth her. 19. The Lord by wisdom hath founded the earth; by understanding hath He established the heavens. 20. By His knowledge the depths are broken up, and the clouds drop down the dew. 21. My son, let not them depart from thine eyes: keep sound wisdom and discretion: 22. So shall they be life unto thy soul, and grace to thy neck. 23. Then shalt thou walk in thy way safely, and thy foot shall not stumble. 24. When thou liest down, thou shalt not be afraid: yea, thou shalt lie down, and thy sleep shall be sweet.'—PROVERBS iii. 11-24.

The repetition of the words 'my son' at the beginning of this passage marks a new section, which extends to verse 20, inclusively, another section being similarly marked as commencing in verse 21. The fatherly counsels of these early chapters are largely reiterations of the same ideas, being line upon line. 'To write the same things to you, to me indeed is not grievous, but for you it is safe.' Many strokes drive the nail home. Exhortations to get Wisdom, based upon the blessings she brings, are the staple of the whole. If we look carefully at the section (vers. 11-20), we find in it a central core (vers. 13-18), setting forth the blessings which Wisdom gives, preceded by two verses, inculcating the right acceptance of God's chastisements which are one chief means of attaining Wisdom, and followed by two verses (vers. 19, 20), which exalt her as being divine as well as human. So the portraiture of her working in humanity is framed by a prologue and epilogue, setting forth two aspects of her relation to God; namely, that she is imparted by Him through the discipline of trouble, and that she dwells in His bosom and is the agent of His creative work.

The prologue, then, points to sorrow and trouble, rightly accepted, as one chief means by which we acquire heavenly Wisdom. Note the profound insight into the meaning of sorrows. They are 'instruction' and 'reproof.' The thought of the Book of Job is here fully incorporated and assimilated. Griefs and pains are not tokens of anger, nor punishments of sin, but love-gifts meant to help to the acquisition of wisdom. They do not come because the sufferers are wicked, but in order to make them good or better. Tempests are meant to blow us into port. The lights are lowered in the theatre that fairer scenes may become visible on the thin screen between us and eternity. Other supports are struck away that we may lean hard on God. The voice of all experience of earthly loss and bitterness is, 'Wisdom is the principal thing; therefore get Wisdom.' God himself becomes our Schoolmaster, and through the voice of the human teacher we hear His deeper tones saying, 'My son, despise not the chastening.'

Note, too, the assurance that all discipline is the fruit of Fatherly love. How many sad hearts in all ages these few words have calmed and braced! How sharp a test of our childlike spirit our acceptance of them, when our own hearts are sore, is! How deep the peace which they bring when really believed! How far they go to solve the mystery of pain, and turn darkness into a solemn light!

Note, further, that the words 'despise' and 'be weary' both imply rather rejection with loathing, and thus express unsubmissive impatience which gets no good from discipline. The beautiful rendering of the Septuagint, which has been made familiar by its adoption in Hebrews, makes the two words express two opposite faults. They 'despise' who steel their wills against the rod, and make as if they did not feel the pain; they 'faint' who collapse beneath the blows, which they feel so much that they lose sight of their purpose. Dogged insensibility and utter prostration are equally harmful. He who meets life's teachings, which are a Father's correction, with either, has little prospect of getting Wisdom.

Then follows the main part of this section (vers. 13-18),—the praise of Wisdom as in herself most precious, and as bestowing highest good. 'The man that findeth Wisdom' reminds us of the peasant in Christ's parable, who found treasure hidden in a field, and the 'merchandise' in verse 14, of the trader seeking goodly pearls. But the finding in verse 13 is not like the rustic's in the parable, who was seeking nothing when a chance stroke of his plough or kick of his heel laid bare the glittering gold. It is the finding which rewards seeking. The figure of acquiring by trading, like that of the pearl-merchant in the companion parable, implies pains, effort, willingness to part with something in order to attain.

The nature of the price is not here in question. We know who has said, 'I counsel thee to buy of Me gold tried in the fire.' We buy heavenly Wisdom when we surrender ourselves. The price is desire to possess, and willingness to accept as an undeserved, unearned gift. But that does not come into view in our lesson. Only this is strongly put in it—that this heavenly Wisdom outshines all jewels, outweighs all wealth, and is indeed the only true riches. 'Rubies' is probably rather to be taken as 'corals,' which seem to have been very highly prized by the Jews, and, no doubt, found their way to them from the Indian Ocean via the Red Sea. The word rendered 'things thou canst desire' is better taken as meaning 'jewels.'

This noble and conclusive depreciation of material wealth in comparison with Wisdom, which is not merely intellectual, but rests on the fear of the Lord, and is goodness as well as understanding, never needed preaching with more emphasis than in our day, when more and more the commercial spirit invades every region of life, and rich men are the aristocrats and envied types of success. When will England and America believe the religion which they profess, and adjust their estimates of the best things accordingly? How many so-called Christian parents would think their son mad if he said, 'I do not care about getting rich; my goal is to be wise with God's Wisdom'? How few of us order our lives on the footing of this old teacher's lesson, and act out the belief that Wisdom is more than wealth! The man who heaps millions together, and masses it, fails in life, however a vulgar world and a nominal church may admire and glorify him. The man who wins Wisdom succeeds, however bare may be his cupboard, and however people may pity him for having failed in life, because he has not drawn prizes in the Devil's lottery. His blank is a prize, and their prizes are blanks. This decisive subordination of material to spiritual good is too plainly duty and common sense to need being dwelt upon; but, alas! like a great many other most obvious, accepted truths, it is disregarded as universally as believed.

The inseparable accompaniments of Wisdom are next eloquently described. The picture is the poetical clothing of the idea that all material good will come to him who despises it all and clasps Wisdom to his heart. Some things flow from Wisdom possessed as usual consequences; some are inseparable from her. The gift in her right hand is length of days; that in her left, which, by its position, is suggested as inferior to the former, is wealth and honour—two goods which will attend the long life. No doubt such promises are to be taken with limitations; but there need be no doubt that, on the whole, loyal devotion to and real possession of heavenly Wisdom do tend in the direction of lengthening lives, which are by it delivered from vices and anxieties which cut many a career short, and of gathering round silver hairs reverence and troops of friends.

These are the usual consequences, and may be fairly brought into view as secondary encouragements to seek Wisdom. But if she is sought for the sake of getting these attendant blessings, she will not be found. She must be loved for herself, not for her dowry, or she will not be won. At the same time, the overstrained and fantastic morality, which stigmatises regard to the blessed results of a religious life as selfishness, finds no support in Scripture, as it has none in common sense. Would there were more of such selfishness!

Sometimes Wisdom's hands do not hold these outward gifts. But the connection between her and the next blessings spoken of is inseparable. Her ways are pleasantness and peace. 'In keeping'—not *for* keeping—'her commandments is great reward.' Inward delight and deep tranquillity of heart attend every step taken in obedience to Wisdom. The course of conduct so prescribed will often involve painful crucifying of the lower nature, but its pleasure far outweighs its pain. It will often be strewn with sharp flints, or may even have red-hot ploughshares laid on it, as in old ordeal trials; but still it will be pleasant to the true self. Sin is a blunder as well as a crime, and enlightened self-interest would point out the same course as the highest law of Wisdom. In reality, duty and delight are co-extensive. They are two names for one thing—one taken from consideration of its obligation; the other, from observation of its issues. 'Calm pleasures there abide.' The only complete peace, which fills and quiets the whole man, comes from obeying Wisdom, or what is the same thing, from following Christ. There is no other way of bringing all our nature into accord with itself, ending the war between conscience and inclination, between flesh and spirit. There is no other way of bringing us into amity with all circumstances, so that fortunate or adverse shall be recognised as good, and nothing be able to agitate us very much. Peace with ourselves, the world, and God, is always the consequence of listening to Wisdom.

The whole fair picture is summed up in verse 18: 'She is a tree of life to them that lay hold upon her.' This is a distinct allusion to the narrative of Genesis. The flaming sword of the cherub guard is sheathed, and access to the tree, which gives immortal life to those who eat, is open to us. Mark how that great word 'life' is here gathering to itself at least the beginnings of higher conceptions than those of simple existence. It is swelling like a bud, and preparing to open and disclose the perfect flower, the life which stands in the knowledge of God and the Christ whom He has sent. Jesus, the incarnate Wisdom, is Himself 'the Tree of Life in the midst of the paradise of God.' The condition of access to it is 'laying hold' by the outstretched hand of faith, and keeping hold with holy obstinacy of grip, in spite of all temptations to slack our grasp. That retaining is the condition of true blessedness.

Verses 19 and 20 invest the idea of Wisdom with still loftier sublimity, since they declare that it is an attribute of God Himself by which creation came into being. The meaning of the writer is inadequately grasped if we take it to be only that creation shows God's Wisdom. This personified Wisdom dwells with God, is the agent of creation, comes with invitations to men, may be possessed by them, and showers blessings on them. The planet Neptune was divined before it was discovered, by reason of perturbations in the movements of the exterior members of the system, unaccountable unless some great globe of light, hitherto unseen, were swaying them in their orbits. Do we not see here like influence streaming from the unrisen light of Christ? Personification prepares for Incarnation. There is One who has been with the Father from the beginning, by whom all things came into being, whose voice sounds to all, who is the Tree of Life, whom we may all possess, and with whose own peace we may be peaceful and blessed for evermore.

Verses 21-24 belong to the next section of the great discourse or hymn. They add little to the preceding. But we may observe the earnest exhortation to let wisdom and understanding be ever in sight. Eyes are apt to stray and clouds to hide the sun. Effort is needed to counteract the tendency to slide out of consciousness, which our weakness imposes on the most certain and important truths. A Wisdom which we do not think about is as good or as bad as non-existent for us. One prime condition of healthy spiritual life is the habit of meditation, thereby renewing our gaze upon the facts of God's revelation and the bearing of these on our conduct.

The blessings flowing from Wisdom are again dilated on, from a somewhat different point of view. She is the giver of life. And then she adorns the life she gives. One has seen homely faces so refined and glorified by the fair soul that shone through them as to be, 'as it were, the face of an angel.' Gracefulness should be the outward token of inward grace. Some good people forget that they are bound to 'adorn the doctrine.' But they who have drunk most deeply of the fountain of Wisdom will find that, like the fabled spring, its waters confer strange loveliness. Lives spent in communion with Jesus will be lovely, however homely their surroundings, and however vulgar eyes, taught only to admire staring colours, may find them dull. The world saw 'no beauty that they should desire Him,' in Him whom holy souls and heavenly angels and the divine Father deemed 'fairer than the sons of men'!

Safety and firm footing in active life will be ours if we walk in Wisdom's ways. He who follows Christ's footsteps will tread surely, and not fear foes. Quiet repose in hours of rest will be his. A day filled with happy service will be followed by a night full of calm slumber, 'Whether we sleep or wake, we live' with Him; and, if we do both, sleeping and waking will be blessed, and our lives will move on gently to the time when days and nights shall melt into one, and there will be no need for repose; for there will be no work that wearies and no hands that droop. The last lying down in the grave will be attended with no terrors. The last sleep there shall be sweet; for it will really be awaking to the full possession of the personal Wisdom, who is our Christ, our Life in death, our Heaven in heaven.

THE TWO PATHS

'Hear, O my son, and receive my sayings; and the years of thy life shall be many. 11. I have taught thee in the way of wisdom; I have led thee in right paths. 12. When thou goest, thy steps shall not be straitened; and when thou runnest, thou shalt not stumble. 13. Take fast hold of instruction; let her not go: keep her; for she is thy life. 14. Enter not into the path of the wicked, and go not in the way of evil men. 15. Avoid it, pass not by it, turn from it, and pass away. 16. For they sleep not, except they have done mischief; and their sleep is taken away, unless they cause some to fall. 17. For they eat the bread of wickedness, and drink the wine of violence. 18. But the path of the just is as the shining light, that shineth more and more unto the perfect day. 19. The way of the wicked is as darkness; they know not at what they stumble.'— PROVERBS iv. 10-19.

This passage includes much more than temperance or any other single virtue. It is a perfectly general exhortation to that practical wisdom which walks in the path of righteousness. The principles laid down here are true in regard to drunkenness and abstinence, but they are intended to receive a wider application, and to that wider application we must first look. The theme is the old, familiar one of the two paths, and the aim is to recommend the better way by setting forth the contrasted effects of walking in it and in the other.

The general call to listen in verse 10 is characteristically enforced by the Old Testament assurance that obedience prolongs life. That is a New Testament truth as well; for there is nothing more certain than that a life in conformity with God's will, which is the same thing as a life in conformity with physical laws, tends to longevity. The experience of any doctor will show that. Here in England we have statistics which prove that total abstainers are a long-lived people, and some insurance offices construct their tables accordingly.

After that general call to listen comes, in verse 11, the description of the path in which long life is to be found. It is 'the way of Wisdom'—that is, that which Wisdom prescribes, and in which therefore it is wise to walk. It is always foolish to do wrong. The rough title of an old play is *The Devil is an Ass*, and if that is not true about him, it is absolutely true about those who listen to his lies. Sin is the stupidest thing in the universe, for it ignores the plainest facts, and never gets what it flings away so much to secure.

Another aspect of the path is presented in the designation 'paths of uprightness,' which seems to be equivalent to those which belong to, or perhaps which consist of, uprightness. The idea of straightness or evenness is the primary meaning of the word, and is, of course, appropriate to the image of a path. In the moral view, it suggests how much more simple and easy a course of rectitude is than one of sin. The one goes straight and unswerving to its end; the other is crooked, devious, intricate, and wanders from the true goal. A crooked road is a long road, and an up-and-down road is a tiring road. Wisdom's way is straight, level, and steadily approaches its aim.

In verse 13 the image of the path is dropped for the moment, and the picture of the way of uprightness and its travellers is translated into the plain exhortation to keep fast hold of 'instruction,' which is substantially equivalent to the queenly Wisdom of these early chapters of Proverbs. The earnestness of the repeated exhortations implies the strength of the forces that tend to sweep us, especially those of us who are young, from our grasp of that Wisdom. Hands become slack, and many a good gift drops from nerveless fingers; thieves abound who will filch away 'instruction,' if we do not resolutely hold tight by it. Who would walk through the slums of a city holding jewels with a careless grasp, and never looking at them? How many would he have left if he did? We do not need to do anything to lose instruction. If we will only do nothing to keep it, the world and our own hearts will make sure that we lose it. And if we lose it, we lose ourselves; for 'she is thy life,' and the mere bodily life, that is lived without her, is not worth calling the life of a man.

Verses 14 to 17 give the picture of the other path, in terrible contrast with the preceding. It is noteworthy that, while in the former the designation was the 'path of uprightness' or of 'wisdom,' and the description therefore was mainly of the characteristics of the path, here the designation is 'the path of the *wicked*,' and the description is mainly of the travellers on it. Righteousness was dealt with, as it were, in the abstract; but wickedness is too awful and dark to be painted thus, and is only set forth in the concrete, as seen in its doers. Now, it is significant that the first exhortation here is of a negative character. In contrast with the reiterated exhortations to keep wisdom, here are reiterated counsels to steer clear of evil. It is all about us, and we have to make a strong effort to keep it at arm's-length. 'Whom resist' is imperative. True, negative virtue is incomplete, but there will be no positive virtue without it. We must be accustomed to say 'No,' or we shall come to little good. An outer belt of firs is sometimes planted round a centre of more tender and valuable wood to shelter the young trees; so we have to make a fence of abstinences round our plantation of positive virtues. The decalogue is mostly prohibitions. 'So did *not* I, because of the fear of God' must be our motto. In this light, entire abstinence from intoxicants is seen to be part of the 'way of Wisdom.' It is one, and, in the present state of England and America, perhaps the most important, of the ways by which we can 'turn from' the path of the wicked and 'pass on.'

The picture of the wicked in verses 16 and 17 is that of very grossly criminal sinners. They are only content when they have done harm, and delight in making others as bad as themselves. But, diabolical as such a disposition is, one sees it only too often in full operation. How many a drunkard or impure man finds a fiendish pleasure in getting hold of some innocent lad, and 'putting him up to a thing or two,' which means teaching him the vices from which the teacher has ceased to get much pleasure, and which he has to spice with the condiment of seeing an unaccustomed sinner's eagerness! Such people infest our streets, and there is only one way for a young man to be safe from them,—'avoid, pass not by, turn from, and pass on.' The reference to 'bread' and 'wine' in verse 17 seems simply to mean that the wicked men's living is won by their 'wickedness,' which procures bread, and by their 'violence,' which brings them wine. It is the way by which these are obtained that is culpable. We may contrast this foul source of a degraded living with verse 13, where 'instruction' is set forth as 'the life' of the upright.

Verses 18 and 19 bring more closely together the two paths, and set them in final, forcible contrast. The phrase 'the perfect day' might be rendered, vividly though clumsily, 'the steady of the day'—that is, noon, when the sun seems to stand still in the meridian. So the image compares the path of the just to the growing brightness of morning dawn, becoming more and more fervid and lustrous, till the climax of an Eastern midday. No more sublime figure of the continuous progress in goodness, brightness, and joy, which is the best reward of walking in the paths of uprightness, can be imagined; and it is as true as it is sublime. Blessed they who in the morning of their days begin to walk in the way of wisdom; for, in most cases, years will strengthen their uprightness, and to that progress there will be no termination, nor will the midday sun have to decline westward to diminishing splendour or dismal setting, but that noontide glory will be enhanced, and made eternal in a new heaven. The brighter the light, the darker the shadow. That blaze of growing glory, possible for us all, makes the tragic gloom to which evil men condemn themselves the thicker and more doleful, as some dungeon in an Eastern prison seems pitch dark to one coming in from the blaze outside. 'How great is that darkness!' It is the darkness of sin, of ignorance, of sorrow, and what adds deeper gloom to it is that every soul that sits in that shadow of death might have been shining, a sun, in the spacious heaven of God's love.

MONOTONY AND CRISES

'When thou goest, thy steps shall not be straitened; and when thou runnest, thou shalt not stumble.'—PROVERBS iv. 12.

The old metaphor likening life to a path has many felicities in it. It suggests constant change, it suggests continuous progress in one direction, and that all our days are linked together, and are not isolated fragments; and it suggests an aim and an end. So we find it perpetually in this Book of Proverbs. Here the 'way' has a specific designation, 'the way of Wisdom'—that is to say, the way which Wisdom teaches, and the way on which Wisdom accompanies us, and the way which leads to Wisdom. Now, these two clauses of my text are not merely an instance of the peculiar feature of Hebrew poetry called parallelism, in which two clauses, substantially the same, occur, but with a little pleasing difference. 'When thou goest'—that is, the monotonous tramp, tramp, tramp of slow walking along the path of an uneventful daily life, the humdrum 'one foot up and another foot down' which makes the most of our days. 'When thou runnest'—that points to the crises, the sudden spurts, the necessarily brief bursts of more than usual energy and effort and difficulty. And about both of them, the humdrum and the exciting, the monotonous and the startling, the promise comes that if we walk in the path of Wisdom we shall not get disgusted with the one and we shall not be overwhelmed by the other. 'When thou walkest, thy steps shall not be straitened; when thou runnest, thou shalt not stumble.'

But before I deal with these two clauses specifically, let me recall to you the condition, and the sole condition, upon which either of them can be fulfilled in our daily lives. The book from which my text is taken is probably one of the very latest in the Old Testament, and you catch in it a very significant and marvellous development of the Old Testament thought. For there rises up, out of these early chapters of the Book of Proverbs, that august and serene figure of the queenly Wisdom, which is more than a personification and is less than a person and a prophecy. It means more than the wise man that spoke it saw; it means for us Christ, 'the Power of God and the Wisdom of God.' And so instead of keeping ourselves merely to the word of the Book of Proverbs, we must grasp the thing that shines through the word, and realise that the writer's visions can only become realities when the serene and august Wisdom that he saw shimmering through the darkness took to itself a human Form, and 'the Word became flesh, and dwelt among us.'

With that heightening of the meaning of the phrase, 'the path of Wisdom' assumes a heightened meaning too, for it is the path of the personal Wisdom, the Incarnate Wisdom, Christ Himself. And what does it *then* come to be to obey this command to walk in the way of Wisdom? Put it into three sentences. Let the Christ who is not only wise, but Wisdom, choose your path, and be sure that by the submission of your will all your paths are His, and not only yours. Make His path yours by following in His steps, and do in your place what you think Christ would have done if He had been there. Keep company with Him on the road. If we will do these three things—if we will say to Him, 'Lord, when Thou sayest go, I go; when Thou biddest me come, I come; I am Thy slave, and I rejoice in the bondage more than in all licentious liberty, and what Thou biddest me do, I do'—if you will further say, 'As Thou art, so am I in the world'—and if you will further say, 'Leave me not alone, and let me cling to Thee on the road, as a little child holds on by her mother's skirt or her father's hand,' then, and only then, will you walk in the path of Wisdom.

Now, then, these three things—submission of will, conformity of conduct, closeness of companionship—these three things being understood, let us look for a moment at the blessings that this text promises, and first at the promise for long uneventful stretches of our daily life. That, of course, is mainly the largest proportion of all our lives. Perhaps nine-tenths at least of all our days and years fall under the terms of this first promise, 'When thou walkest.' For many miles there comes nothing particular, nothing at all exciting, nothing new, nothing to break the plod, plod, plod along the road. Everything is as it was yesterday, and the day before that, and as it will be to-morrow, and the day after that, in all probability. 'The trivial round, the common task' make up by far the largest percentage of our lives. It is as in wine, the immense proportion of it is nothing but water, and only a small proportion of alcohol is diffused through the great mass of the tamer liquid.

Now, then, if Jesus Christ is not to help us in the monotony of our daily lives, what, in the name of common sense, is His help good for? If it is not true that He will be with us, not only in the moments of crisis, but in the long commonplace hours, we may as well have no Christ at all, for all that I can see. Unless the trivial is His field, there is very little field for Him, in your life or mine. And so it should come to all of us who have to take up this daily burden of small, monotonous, constantly recurring, and therefore often wearisome, duties, as even a more blessed promise than the other one, that 'when thou walkest, thy steps shall not be straitened.'

I remember hearing of a man that got so disgusted with having to dress and undress himself every day that he committed suicide to escape from the necessity. That is a very extreme form of the feeling that comes over us all sometimes, when we wake in a morning and look before us along the stretch of dead level, which is a great deal more wearisome when it lasts long than are the cheerful vicissitudes of up hill and down dale. We all know the deadening influence of a habit. We all know the sense of disgust that comes over us at times, and of utter weariness, just because we have been doing the same things day after day for so long. I know only one infallible way of preventing the common from becoming commonplace, of preventing the small from becoming trivial, of preventing the familiar from becoming contemptible, and it is to link it all to Jesus Christ, and to say, 'For Thy sake, and unto Thee, I do this'; then, not only will the rough places become plain, and the crooked things straight, and not only will the mountains be brought low, but the valleys of the commonplace will be exalted. 'Thy steps shall not be straitened.' 'I will make his feet as hind's feet,' says one of the old prophets. What a picture of light, buoyant, graceful movement that is! And each of us may have that, instead of the grind, grind, grind! tramp, tramp, tramp! along the level and commonplace road of our daily lives, if we will. Walk in the path of Christ, with Christ, towards Christ, and 'thy steps shall not be straitened.'

Now, there is another aspect of this same promise—viz. if we thus are in the path of Incarnate Wisdom, we shall not feel the restrictions of the road to be restraints. 'Thy steps shall not be straitened'; although there is a wall on either side, and the road is the narrow way that leads to life, it is broad enough for the sober man, because he goes in a straight line, and does not need half the road to roll about in. The limits which love imposes, and the limits which love accepts, are not narrowing. 'I will walk at liberty, for—I do as I like.' No! that is slavery; but, 'I will walk at liberty, for I keep Thy precepts'; and I do not want to go vagrantising at large, but limit myself thankfully to the way which Thou dost mark out. 'Thy steps shall not be straitened.' So much for the first of these promises.

Now what about the other one? 'When thou runnest, thou shalt not stumble.'

As I have said, the former promise applies to the hours and the years of life. The latter applies to but a few moments of each man's life. Cast your thoughts back over your own days, and however changeful, eventful, perhaps adventurous, and as we people call it, romantic, some parts of our lives may have been, yet for all that you can put the turning-points, the crises that have called for great efforts, and the gathering of yourselves up, and the calling forth of all your powers to do and to dare, you can put them all inside of a week, in most cases. 'When thou runnest, thou shalt not stumble.' The greater the speed, the greater the risk of stumbling over some obstacle in the way. We all know how many men there are that do very well in the uneventful commonplaces of life, but bring them face to face with some great difficulty or some great trial, and there is a dismal failure. Jesus Christ is ready to make us fit for anything in the way of difficulty, in the way of trial, that can come storming upon us from out of the dark. And He will make us so fit if we follow the injunctions to which I have already been referring. Without His help it is almost certain that when we have to run, our ankles will give, or there will be a stone in the road that we never thought of, and the excitement will sweep us away from principle, and we shall lose our hold on Him; and then it is all up with us.

There is a wonderful saying in one of the prophets, which uses this same metaphor of my text with a difference, where it speaks of the divine guidance of Israel as being like that of a horse in the wilderness. Fancy the poor, nervous, tremulous creature trying to keep its footing upon the smooth granite slabs of Sinai. Travellers dare not take their horses on mountain journeys, because they are highly nervous and are not sure-footed enough. And, so says the old prophet, that gracious Hand will be laid on the bridle, and hold the nervous creature's head up as it goes sliding over the slippery rocks, and so He will bring it down to rest in the valley. 'Now unto Him that is able to keep us from stumbling,' as is the true rendering, 'and to present us faultless ... be glory.' Trust Him, keep near Him, let Him choose your way, and try to be like Him in it; and whatever great occasions may arise in your lives, either of sorrow or of duty, you will be equal to them.

But remember the virtue that comes out victorious in the crisis must have been nourished and cultivated in the humdrum moments. For it is no time to make one's first acquaintance with Jesus Christ when the eyeballs of some ravenous wild beast are staring into ours, and its mouth is open to swallow us. Unless He has kept our feet from being straitened in the quiet walk, He will not be able to keep us from stumbling in the vehement run.

One word more. This same distinction is drawn by one of the prophets, who adds another clause to it. Isaiah, or the author of the second portion of the book which goes by his name, puts in wonderful connection the two thoughts of my text with analogous thoughts in regard to God, when he says, 'Hast thou not known, hast thou not heard, that the everlasting God, the Lord, the Creator of the ends of the earth, fainteth not, neither is weary?' and immediately goes on to say, 'They that wait on the Lord shall renew their strength. They shall run and not be weary, they shall walk and not faint.' So it is from God, the unfainting and the unwearied, that the strength comes which makes our steps buoyant with energy amidst the commonplace, and steadfast and established at the crises of our lives. But before these two great promises is put another one: 'They shall mount up with wings as eagles,' and therefore both the other become possible. That is to say, fellowship with God in the heavens, which is made possible on earth by communion with Christ, is the condition both of the unwearied running and of unfainting walking. If we will keep in the path of Christ, He will take care of the commonplace dreary tracts and of the brief moments of strain and effort, and will bring us at last where He has gone, if, looking unto Him, we 'run with patience the race,' and walk with cheerfulness the road, 'that is set before us.'

FROM DAWN TO NOON

'The path of the just is as the shining light, that shineth more and more unto the perfect day.'—PROVERBS iv. 18.

'Then shall the righteous shine forth as the sun in the kingdom of their father.—MATT. xiii. 43.

The metaphor common to both these texts is not infrequent throughout Scripture. In one of the oldest parts of the Old Testament, Deborah's triumphal song, we find, 'Let all them that love Thee be as the sun when he goeth forth in his might.' In one of the latest parts of the Old Testament, Daniel's prophecy, we read, 'They that be wise shall shine as the brightness of the firmament; and they that turn many to righteousness as the stars for ever and ever.' Then in the New Testament we have Christ's comparison of His servants to light, and the great promise which I have read as my second text. The upshot of them all is this—the most radiant thing on earth is the character of a good man. The world calls men of genius and intellectual force its lights. The divine estimate, which is the true one, confers the name on righteousness.

But my first text follows out another analogy; not only brightness, but progressive brightness, is the characteristic of the righteous man.

We are to think of the strong Eastern sun, whose blinding light steadily increases till the noontide. 'The perfect day' is a somewhat unfortunate translation. What is meant is the point of time at which the day culminates, and for a moment, the sun seems to stand steady, up in those southern lands, in the very zenith, raying down 'the arrows that fly by noonday.' The text does not go any further, it does not talk about the sad diminution of the afternoon. The parallel does not hold; though, if we consult appearance and sense alone, it seems to hold only too well. For, sadder than the setting of the suns, which rise again to-morrow, is the sinking into darkness of death, from which there seems to be no emerging. But my second text comes in to tell us that death is but as the shadow of eclipse which passes, and with it pass obscuring clouds and envious mists, and 'then shall the righteous blaze forth like the sun in their Heavenly Father's kingdom.'

And so the two texts speak to us of the progressive brightness, and the ultimate, which is also the progressive, radiance of the righteous.

I. In looking at them together, then, I would notice, first, what a Christian life is meant to be.

I must not linger on the lovely thoughts that are suggested by that attractive metaphor of life. It must be enough, for our present purpose, to say that the light of the Christian life, like its type in the heavens, may be analysed into three beams—purity, knowledge, blessedness. And these three, blended together, make the pure whiteness of a Christian soul.

But what I wish rather to dwell upon is the other thought, the intention that every Christian life should be a life of increasing lustre, uninterrupted, and the natural result of increasing communion with, and conformity to, the very fountain itself of heavenly radiance.

Remember how emphatically, in all sorts of ways, progress is laid down in Scripture as the mark of a religious life. There is the emblem of my text. There is our Lord's beautiful one of vegetable growth: 'First the blade, then the ear, then the full corn in the ear.' There is the other metaphor of the stages of human life, 'babes in Christ,' young men in Him, old men and fathers. There is the metaphor of the growth of the body. There is the metaphor of the gradual building up of a structure. We are to 'edify ourselves together,' and to 'build ourselves up on our most holy faith.' There is the other emblem of a race—continual advance as the result of continual exertion, and the use of the powers bestowed upon us.

And so in all these ways, and in many others that I need not now touch upon, Scripture lays it down as a rule that life in the highest region, like life in the lowest, is marked by continual growth. It is so in regard to all other things. Continuity in any kind of practice gives increasing power in the art. The artisan, the blacksmith with his hammer, the skilled artificer at his trade, the student at his subject, the good man in his course of life, and the bad man in his, do equally show that use becomes second nature. And so, in passing, let me say what incalculable importance there is in our getting habit, with all its mystical power to mould life, on the side of righteousness, and of becoming accustomed to do good, and so being unfamiliar with evil.

Let me remind you, too, how this intention of continuous growth is marked by the gifts that are bestowed upon us in Jesus Christ. He gives us—and it is by no means the least of the gifts that He bestows—an absolutely unattainable aim as the object of our efforts. For He bids us not only be 'perfect, as our Father in Heaven is perfect,' but He bids us be entirely conformed to His own Self. The misery of men is that they pursue aims so narrow and so shabby that they can be attained, and are therefore left behind, to sink hull down on the backward horizon. But to have before us an aim which is absolutely unreachable, instead of being, as ignorant people say, an occasion of despair and of idleness, is, on the contrary, the very salt of life. It keeps us young, it makes hope immortal, it emancipates from lower pursuits, it diminishes the weight of sorrows, it administers an anaesthetic to every pain. If you want to keep life fresh, seek for that which you can never fully find.

Christ gives us infinite powers to reach that unattainable aim, for He gives us access to all His own fullness, and there is more in His storehouses than we can ever take, not to say more than we can ever hope to exhaust. And therefore, because of the aim that is set before us, and because of the powers that are bestowed upon us to reach it, there is stamped upon every Christian life unmistakably as God's purpose and ideal concerning it, that it should for ever and for ever be growing nearer and nearer, as some ascending spiral that ever circles closer and closer, and yet never absolutely unites with the great central Perfection which is Himself.

So, brethren, for every one of us, if we are Christian people at all, 'this is the will of God, even your perfection.'

II. Consider the sad contrast of too many Christian lives.

I would not speak in terms that might seem to be reproach and scolding. The matter is far too serious, the disease far too widespread, to need or to warrant any exaggeration. But, dear brethren, there are many so-called and, in a fashion, really Christian people to whom Christ and His work are mainly, if not exclusively, the means of escaping the consequences of sin—a kind of 'fire-escape.' And to very many it comes as a new thought, in so far as their practical lives are concerned, that these ought to be lives of steadily increasing deliverance from the love and the power of sin, and steadily increasing appropriation and manifestation of Christ's granted righteousness. There are, I think, many of us from whom the very notion of progress has faded away. I am sure there are some of us who were a great deal farther on on the path of the Christian life years ago, when we first felt that Christ was anything to us, than we are to-day. 'When for the time ye ought to be teachers, ye have need that one teach you which be the first principles of the oracles of God.'

There is an old saying of one of the prophets that a child would die a hundred years old, which in a very sad sense is true about very many folk within the pale of the Christian Church who are seventy-year-old babes still, and will die so. Suns 'growing brighter and brighter until the noonday!' Ah! there are many of us who are a great deal more like those strange variable stars that sometimes burst out in the heavens into a great blaze, that brings them up to the brightness of stars of the first magnitude, for a day or two; and then they dwindle until they become little specks of light that the telescope can hardly see.

And there are hosts of us who are instances, if not of arrested, at any rate of unsymmetrical, development. The head, perhaps, is cultivated; the intellectual apprehension of Christianity increases, while the emotional, and the moral, and the practical part of it are all neglected. Or the converse may be the case; and we may be full of gush and of good emotion, and of fervour when we come to worship or to pray, and our lives may not be a hair the better for it all. Or there may be a disproportion because of an exclusive attention to conduct and the practical side of Christianity, while the rational side of it, which should be the basis of all, and the emotional side of it, which should be the driving power of all, are comparatively neglected.

So, dear brethren! what with interruptions, what with growing by fits and starts, and long, dreary winters like the Arctic winters, coming in between the two or three days of rapid, and therefore brief and unwholesome, development, we must all, I think, take to heart the condemnation suggested by this text when we compare the reality of our lives with the divine intention concerning them. Let us ask ourselves, 'Have I more command over myself than I had twenty years ago? Do I live nearer Jesus Christ today than I did yesterday? Have I more of His Spirit in me? Am I growing? Would the people that know me best say that I am growing in the grace and knowledge of my Lord and Saviour?' Astronomers tell us that there are dark suns, that have burnt themselves out, and are wandering unseen through the skies. I wonder if there are any extinguished suns of that sort listening to me at this moment.

III. How the divine purpose concerning us may be realised by us.

Now the *Alpha* and the *Omega* of this, the one means which includes all other, is laid down by Jesus Christ Himself in another metaphor when He said, 'Abide in Me, and I in you; so shall ye bring forth much fruit.' Our path will brighten, not because of any radiance in ourselves, but in proportion as we draw nearer and nearer to the Fountain of heavenly radiance.

The planets that move round the sun, further away than we are on earth, get less of its light and heat; and those that circle around it within the limits of our orbit, get proportionately more. The nearer we are to Him, the more we shall shine. The sun shines by its own light, drawn indeed from the shrinkage of its mass, so that it gives away its very life in warming and illuminating its subject-worlds. But we shine only by reflected light, and therefore the nearer we keep to Him the more shall we be radiant.

That keeping in touch with Jesus Christ is mainly to be secured by the direction of thought, and love, and trust to Him. If we follow close upon Him we shall not walk in darkness. It is to be secured and maintained very largely by what I am afraid is much neglected by Christian people of all sorts nowadays, and that is the devotional use of their Bibles. That is the food by which we grow. It is to be secured and maintained still more largely by that which I, again, am afraid is but very imperfectly attained to by Christian people now, and that is, the habit of prayer. It is to be secured and maintained, again, by the honest conforming of our lives, day by day, to the present amount of our knowledge of Him and of His will. Whosoever will make all his life the manifestation of his belief, and turn all his creed into principles of action, will grow both in the comprehensiveness, and in the depths of his Christian character. 'Ye are the light in the Lord.' Keep in Him, and you will become brighter and brighter. So shall we 'go from strength to strength, till we appear before God in Zion.'

IV. Lastly, what brighter rising will follow the earthly setting?

My second text comes in here. Beauty, intellect, power, goodness; all go down into the dark. The sun sets, and there is left a sad and fading glow in the darkening pensive sky, which may recall the vanished light for a little while to a few faithful hearts, but steadily passes into the ashen grey of forgetfulness.

But 'then shall the righteous blaze forth like the sun, in their Heavenly Father's kingdom.' The momentary setting is but apparent. And ere it is well accomplished, a new sun swims into the 'ampler ether, the diviner air' of that future life, 'and with new spangled beams, flames in the forehead of the morning sky.'

The reason for that inherent brightness suggested in our second text is that the soul of the righteous man passes from earth into a region out of which we 'gather all things that offend, and them that do iniquity.' There are other reasons for it, but that is the one which our Lord dwells on. Or, to put it into modern scientific language, environment corresponds to character. So, when the clouds have rolled away, and no more mists from the undrained swamps of selfishness and sin and animal nature rise up to hide the radiance, there shall be a fuller flood of light poured from the re-created sun.

That brightness thus promised has for its highest and most blessed character that it is conformity to the Lord Himself. For, as you may remember, the last use of this emblem that we find in Scripture refers not to the servant but to the Master, whom His beloved disciple in Apocalyptic vision saw, with His 'countenance as the sun shining in his strength.' Thus 'we shall be like Him, for we shall see Him as He is.' And therefore that radiance of the sainted dead is progressive, too. For it has an infinite fulness to draw upon, and the soul that is joined to Jesus Christ, and derives its lustre from Him, cannot die until it has outgrown Jesus and emptied God. The sun will one day be a dark, cold ball. We shall outlast it.

But, brethren, remember that it is only those who here on earth have progressively appropriated the brightness that Christ bestows who have a right to reckon on that better rising. It is contrary to all probability to believe that the passage from life can change the ingrained direction and set of a man's nature. We know nothing that warrants us in affirming that death can revolutionise character. Do not trust your future to such a dim peradventure. Here is a plain truth. They who on earth are as 'the shining light that shineth more and more unto the perfect day,' shall, beyond the shadow of eclipse, shine on as the sun does, behind the opaque, intervening body, all unconscious of what looks to mortal eyes on earth an eclipse, and 'shall blaze out like the sun in their Heavenly Father's kingdom.' For all that we know and are taught by experience, religious and moral distinctions are eternal. 'He that is righteous, let him be righteous still; and he that is filthy, let him be filthy still.'

KEEPING AND KEPT

'Keep thy heart with all diligence; for out of it are the issues of life.'— PROVERBS iv. 23.

'Kept by the power of God through faith unto salvation.'—1 PETER 1. 5.

The former of these texts imposes a stringent duty, the latter promises divine help to perform it. The relation between them is that between the Law and the Gospel. The Law commands, the Gospel gives power to obey. The Law pays no attention to man's weakness, and points no finger to the source of strength. Its office is to set clearly forth what we ought to be, not to aid us in becoming so. 'Here is your duty, do it' is, doubtless, a needful message, but it is a chilly one, and it may well be doubted if it ever rouses a soul to right action. Moralists have hammered away at preaching self-restraint and a close watch over the fountain of actions within from the beginning, but their exhortations have little effect unless they can add to their icy injunctions the warmth of the promise of our second text, and point to a divine Keeper who will make duty possible. We must be kept by God, if we are ever to succeed in keeping our wayward hearts.

I. Without our guarding our hearts, no noble life is possible.

The Old Testament psychology differs from our popular allocation of certain faculties to bodily organs. We use head and heart, roughly speaking, as being respectively the seats of thought and of emotion. But the Old Testament locates in the heart the centre of personal being. It is not merely the home of the affections, but the seat of will, moral purpose. As this text says, 'the issues of life' flow from it in all the multitudinous variety of their forms. The stream parts into many heads, but it has one fountain. To the Hebrew thinkers the heart was the indivisible, central unity which manifested itself in the whole of the outward life. 'As a man thinketh in his heart, so is he.' The heart is the man. And that personal centre has a moral character which comes to light in, and gives unity and character to, all his deeds.

That solemn thought that every one of us has a definite moral character, and that our deeds are not an accidental set of outward actions but flow from an inner fountain, needs to be driven home to our consciences, for most of the actions of most men are done so mechanically, and reflected on so little by the doers, that the conviction of their having any moral character at all, or of our incurring any responsibility for them, is almost extinct in us, unless when something startles conscience into protest.

It is this shrouded inner self to which supreme care is to be directed. All noble ethical teaching concurs in this—that a man who seeks to be right must keep, in the sense both of watching and of guarding, his inner self. Conduct is more easily regulated than character—and less worth regulating. It avails little to plant watchers on the stream half way to the sea. Control must be exercised at the source, if it is to be effectual. The counsel of our first text is a commonplace of all wholesome moral teaching since the beginning of the world. The phrase 'with all diligence' is literally 'above all guarding,' and energetically expresses the supremacy of this keeping. It should be the foremost, all-pervading aim of every wise man who would not let his life run to waste. It may be turned into more modern language, meaning just what this ancient sage meant, if we put it as, 'Guard thy character with more carefulness than thou dost thy most precious possessions, for it needs continual watchfulness, and, untended, will go to rack and ruin.' The exhortation finds a response in every heart, and may seem too familiar and trite to bear dwelling on, but we may be allowed to touch lightly on one or two of the plain reasons which enforce it on every man who is not what Proverbs very unpolitely calls 'a fool.'

That guarding is plainly imposed as necessary, by the very constitution of our manhood. Our nature is evidently not a republic, but a monarchy. It is full of blind impulses, and hungry desires, which take no heed of any law but their own satisfaction. If the reins are thrown on the necks of these untamed horses, they will drag the man to destruction. They are only safe when they are curbed and bitted, and held well in. Then there are tastes and inclinations which need guidance and are plainly meant to be subordinate. The will is to govern all the lower self, and conscience is to govern the will. Unmistakably there are parts of every man's nature which are meant to serve, and parts which are appointed to rule, and to let the servants usurp the place of the rulers is to bring about as wild a confusion within as the Ecclesiast lamented that he had seen in the anarchic times when he wrote—princes walking and beggars on horseback. As George Herbert has it—

'Give not thy humours way;
God gave them to thee under lock and key.'

Then, further, that guarding is plainly imperative, because there is an outer world which appeals to our needs and desires, irrespective altogether of right and wrong and of the moral consequences of gratifying these. Put a loaf before a starving man and his impulse will be to clutch and devour it, without regard to whether it is his or no. Show any of our animal propensities its appropriate food, and it asks no questions as to right or wrong, but is stirred to grasp its natural food. And even the higher and nobler parts of our nature are but too apt to seek their gratification without having the license of conscience for doing so, and sometimes in defiance of its plain prohibitions. It is never safe to trust the guidance of life to tastes, inclinations, or to anything but clear reason, set in motion by calm will, and acting under the approbation of 'the Lord Chief Justice, Conscience.'

But again, seeing that the world has more evil than good in it, the keeping of the heart will always consist rather in repelling solicitations to yielding to evil. In short, the power and the habit of sternly saying 'No' to the whole crowd of tempters is always the main secret of a noble life. 'He that hath no rule over his own spirit is like a city broken down and without walls.'

II. There is no effectual guarding unless God guards.

The counsel in Proverbs is not mere toothless moral commonplace, but is associated, in the preceding chapter, with fatherly advice to 'let thine heart keep my commandments' and to 'trust in the Lord with all thine heart.' The heart that so trusts will be safely guarded, and only such a heart will be. The inherent weakness of all attempts at self-keeping is that keeper and kept being one and the same personality, the more we need to be kept the less able we are to effect it. If in the very garrison are traitors, how shall the fortress be defended? If, then, we are to exercise an effectual guard over our characters and control over our natures, we must have an outward standard of right and wrong which shall not be deflected by variations in our temperature. We need a fixed light to steer towards, which is stable on the stable shore, and is not tossing up and down on our decks. We shall cleanse our way only when we 'take heed thereto, according to Thy word.' For even God's viceroy within, the sovereign conscience, can be warped, perverted, silenced, and is not immune from the spreading infection of evil. When it turns to God, as a mirror to the sun, it is irradiated and flashes bright illumination into dark corners, but its power depends on its being thus lit by radiations from the very Light of Life. And if we are ever to have a coercive power over the rebellious powers within, we must have God's power breathed into us, giving grip and energy to all the good within, quickening every lofty desire, satisfying every aspiration that feels after Him, cowing all our evil and being the very self of ourselves.

We need an outward motive which will stimulate and stir to effort. Our wills are lamed for good, and the world has strong charms that appeal to us. And if we are not to yield to these, there must be somewhere a stronger motive than any that the sorceress world has in its stores, that shall constrainingly draw us to ways that, because they tend upward, and yield no pabulum for the lower self, are difficult for sluggish feet. To the writer of this Book of Proverbs the name of God bore in it such a motive. To us the name of Jesus, which is Love, bears a yet mightier appeal, and the motive which lies in His death for us is strong enough, and it alone is strong enough, to fire our whole selves with enthusiastic, grateful love, which will burn up our sloth, and sweep our evil out of our hearts, and make us swift and glad to do all that may please Him. If there must be fresh reinforcements thrown into the town of Mansoul, as there must be if it is not to be captured, there is one sure way of securing these. Our second text tells us whence the relieving force must come. If we are to keep our hearts with all diligence, we must be 'kept by the power of God,' and that power is not merely to make diversion outside the beleaguered fortress which may force the besiegers to retreat and give up their effort, but is to enter in and possess the soul which it wills to defend. It is when the enemy sees that new succours have, in some mysterious way, been introduced, that he gives up his siege. It is God in us that is our security.

III. There is no keeping by God without faith.

Peter was an expert in such matters, for he had had a bitter experience to teach him how soon and surely self-confidence became self-despair. 'Though all should forsake Thee, yet will not I,' was said but a few hours before he denied Jesus. His faith failed, and then the divine guard that was keeping his soul passed thence, and, left alone, he fell.

That divine Power is exerted for our keeping on condition of our trusting ourselves to Him and trusting Him for ourselves. And that condition is no arbitrary one, but is prescribed by the very nature of divine help and of human faith. If God could keep our souls without our trust in Him He would. He does so keep them as far as is possible, but for all the choicer blessings of His giving, and especially for that of keeping us free from the domination of our lower selves, there must be in us faith if there is to be in God help. The hand that lays hold on God in Christ must be stretched out and must grasp His warm, gentle, and strong hand, if the tingling touch of it is to infuse strength. If the relieving force is victoriously to enter our hearts, we must throw open the gates and welcome it. Faith is but the open door for God's entrance. It has no efficacy in itself any more than a door has, but all its blessedness depends on what it admits into the hidden chambers of the heart.

I reiterate what I have tried to show in these poor words. There is no noble life without our guarding our hearts; there is no effectual guarding unless God guards; there is no divine guarding unless through our faith. It is vain to preach self-governing and self-keeping. Unless we can tell the beleaguered heart, 'The Lord is thy Keeper; He will keep thee from all evil; He will keep thy soul,' we only add one more impossible command to a man's burden. And we do not apprehend nor experience the divine keeping in its most blessed and fullest reality, unless we find it in Jesus, who is 'able to keep us from falling, and to present us faultless before the presence of His glory with exceeding joy.'

THE CORDS OF SIN

'His own iniquities shall take the wicked himself, and he shall be holden with the cords of his sins.'—PROVERBS v. 22.

In Hosea's tender picture of the divine training of Israel which, alas! failed of its effect, we read, 'I drew them with cords of a man,' which is further explained as being 'with bands of love.' The metaphor in the prophet's mind is probably that of a child being 'taught to go' and upheld in its first tottering steps by leading-strings. God drew Israel, though Israel did not yield to the drawing. But if these gentle, attractive influences, which ever are raying out from Him, are resisted, another set of cords, not now sustaining and attracting, but hampering and fettering, twine themselves round the rebellious life, and the man is like a wild creature snared in the hunter's toils, enmeshed in a net, and with its once free limbs restrained. The choice is open to us all, whether we will let God draw us to Himself with the sweet manlike cords of His educative and forbearing love, or, flinging off these, which only foolish self-will construes into limitations, shall condemn ourselves to be prisoned within the narrow room of our own sins. We may choose which condition shall be ours, but one or other of them must be ours. We may either be drawn by the silken cord of God's love or we may be 'holden by the cords' of our sins.

In both clauses of our text evil deeds done are regarded as having a strange, solemn life apart from the doer of them, by which they become influential factors in his subsequent life. Their issues on others may be important, but their issues on him are the most important of all. The recoil of the gun on the shoulder of him who fired it is certain, whether the cartridge that flew from its muzzle wounded anything or not. 'His own iniquities shall take the wicked'—they ring him round, a grim company to whom he has given an independent being, and who have now 'taken' him prisoner and laid violent hands on him. A long since forgotten novel told of the fate of 'a modern Prometheus,' who made and put life into a dreadful creature in man's shape, that became the curse of its creator's life. That tragedy is repeated over and over again. We have not done with our evil deeds when we have done them, but they, in a very terrible sense, begin to be when they are done. We sow the seeds broadcast, and the seed springs up dragon's teeth.

The view of human experience set forth, especially in the second clause of this text, directs our gaze into dark places, into which it is not pleasant to look, and many of you will accuse me of preaching gloomily if I try to turn a reflective eye inwards upon them, but no one will be able to accuse me of not preaching truly. It is impossible to enumerate all the cords that make up the net in which our own evil doings hold us meshed, but let me point out some of these.

I. Our evil deeds become evil habits.

We all know that anything once done becomes easier to do again. That is true about both good and bad actions, but 'ill weeds grow apace,' and it is infinitely easier to form a bad habit than a good one. The young shoot is green and flexible at first, but it soon becomes woody and grows high and strikes deep. We can all verify the statement of our text by recalling the tremors of conscience, the self-disgust, the dread of discovery which accompanied the first commission of some evil deed, and the silence of undisturbed, almost unconscious facility, that accompanied later repetitions of it. Sins of sense and animal passion afford the most conspicuous instances of this, but it is by no means confined to these. We have but to look steadily at our own lives to be aware of the working of this solemn law in them, however clear we may be of the grosser forms of evil deeds. For us all it is true that custom presses on us 'with a weight, heavy as frost and deep almost as life,' and that it is as hard for the Ethiopian to change his skin or the leopard his spots as for those who 'are accustomed to do evil' to 'do good.'

But experience teaches not only that evil deeds quickly consolidate into evil habits, but that as the habit grips us faster, the poor pleasure for the sake of which the acts are done diminishes. The zest which partially concealed the bitter taste of the once eagerly swallowed morsel is all but gone, but the morsel is still sought and swallowed. Impulses wax as motives wane, the victim is like an ox tempted on the road to the slaughter-house at first by succulent fodder held before it, and at last driven into it by pricking goads and heavy blows. Many a man is so completely wrapped in the net which his own evil deeds have made for him, that he commits the sin once more, not because he finds any pleasure in it, but for no better reason than that he has already committed it often, and the habit is his master.

There are many forms of evil which compel us to repeat them for other reasons than the force of habit. For instance, a fraudulent book-keeper has to go on making false entries in his employer's books in order to hide his peculations. Whoever steps on to the steeply sloping road to which self-pleasing invites us, soon finds that he is on an inclined plane well greased, and that compulsion is on him to go on, though he may recoil from the descent, and be shudderingly aware of what the end must be. Let no man say, 'I will do this doubtful thing once only, and never again.' Sin is like an octopus, and if the loathly thing gets the tip of one slender filament round a man, it will envelop him altogether and drag him down to the cruel beak.

Let us then remember how swiftly deeds become habits, and how the fetters, which were silken at first, rapidly are exchanged for iron chains, and how the craving increases as fast as the pleasure from gratifying it diminishes. Let us remember that there are many kinds of evil which seem to force their own repetition, in order to escape their consequences and to hide the sin. Let us remember that no man can venture to say, 'This once only will I do this thing.' Let us remember that acts become habits with dreadful swiftness, and let us beware that we do not forge chains of darkness for ourselves out of our own godless deeds.

II. Our evil deeds imprison us for good.

The tragedy of human life is that we weave for ourselves manacles that fetter us from following and securing the one good for which we are made. Our evil past holds us in a firm grip. The cords which confine our limbs are of our own spinning. What but ourselves is the reason why so many of us do not yield to God's merciful drawings of us to Himself? We have riveted the chains and twined the net that holds us captive, by our own acts. It is we ourselves who have paralysed our wills, so that we see the light of God but as a faint gleam far away, and dare not move to follow the gleam. It is we who have smothered or silenced our conscience and perverted our tastes, and done violence to all in us that 'thirsteth for God, even the living God.' Alas! how many of us have let some strong evil habit gain such a grip of us that it has overborne our higher impulses, and silenced the voice within us that cries out for the living God! We are kept back from Him by our worse selves, and whoever lets that which is lowest in him keep him from following after God, who is his 'being's end and aim,' is caught and prisoned by the cords woven and knitted out of his sins. Are there none of us who know, when they are honest with themselves, that they would have been true Christians long since, had it not been for one darling evil that they cannot make up their minds to cast off? Wills disabled from strongly willing the good, consciences silenced as when the tongue is taken out of a bell-buoy on a shoal, tastes perverted and set seeking amid the transitory treasures of earth for what God only can give them, these are the 'cords' out of which are knotted the nets that hold so many of us captive, and hinder our feet from following after God, even the living God, in following and possessing whom is the only liberty of soul, the one real joy of life.

III. Our evil deeds work their own punishment.

I do not venture to speak of the issues beyond the grave. It is not for a man to press these on his brethren. But even from the standpoint of this Book of Proverbs, it is certain that 'the righteous shall be recompensed in the earth, much more the wicked and the sinner.' Probably it was the earthly consequences of wrongdoing that were in the mind of the proverb-maker.

And we are not to let our Christian enlightenment as to the future rob us of the certainty, written large on human life here and now, that with whatever apparent exceptions in regard to prosperous sin and tried righteousness, it is yet true that 'every transgression and disobedience receives its just recompense of reward.' Life is full of consequences of evil-doing. Even here and now we reap as we have sown. Every sin is a mistake, even if we confine our view to the consequences sought for in this life by it, and the consequences actually encountered. 'A rogue is a roundabout fool.' True, we believe that there is a future reaping so complete that it makes the partial harvests gathered here seem of small account. But the framer of this proverb, who had little knowledge of that future, had seen enough in the meditative survey of this present to make him sure that the consequences of evil-doing were certain, and in a very true sense, penal. And leaving out of sight all that lies in the dark beyond, surely if we sum up the lamed aspirations, the perverted tastes, the ossifying of noble emotions, the destruction of the balance of the nature, the blinding of the eye of the soul, the lowering and narrowing of the whole nature, and many another wound to the best in man that come as the sure issue of evil deeds, we do not need to doubt that every sinful man is miserably 'holden with the cords of his sin.' Life is the time for sowing, but it is a time for reaping too, and we do not need to wait for death to experience the truth of the solemn warning that 'he who soweth to the flesh shall of the flesh reap corruption.' Let us, then, do no deeds without asking ourselves, What will the harvest be? and if from any deeds that we have done we have to reap sorrow or inward darkness, let us be thankful that by experience our Father is teaching us how bitter as well as evil a thing it is to forsake Him, and cast off His fear from our wayward spirits.

IV. The cords can be loosened.

Bitter experience teaches that the imprisoning net clings too tightly to be stripped from our limbs by our own efforts. Nay rather, the net and the captive are one, and he who tries to cast off the oppression which hinders him from following that which is good is trying to cast off himself. The desperate problem that fronts every effort at self-emendation has two bristling impossibilities in it: one, how to annihilate the past; one, how to extirpate the evil that is part of my very self, and yet to keep the self entire. The very terms of the problem show it to be insoluble, and the climax of all honest efforts at making a clean thing of an unclean by means within reach of the unclean thing itself, is the despairing cry, 'O wretched man that I am! who shall deliver me out of the body of this death?'

But to men writhing in the grip of a sinful past, or paralysed beyond writhing, and indifferent, because hopeless, or because they have come to like their captivity, comes one whose name is 'the Breaker,' whose mission it is to proclaim liberty to the captives, and whose hand laid on the cords that bind a soul, causes them to drop harmless from the limbs and sets the bondsman free. Many tongues praise Jesus for many great gifts, but His proper work, and that peculiar to Himself alone, is His work on the sin and the sins of the world. He deals with that which no man can deal with for himself or by his own power. He can cancel our past, so that it shall not govern our future. He can give new power to fight the old habits. He can give a new life which owes nothing to the former self, and is free from taint from it. He can break the entail of sin, the 'law of the spirit of life in Christ Jesus' can make any of us, even him who is most tied and bound by the chain of his sins, 'free from the law of sin and death.' We cannot break the chains that fetter us, and our own struggles, like the plungings of a wild beast caught in the toils, but draw the bonds tighter. But the chains that cannot be broken can be melted, and it may befall each of us as it befell the three Hebrews in the furnace, when the king 'was astonished' and asked, 'Did not we cast three men bound into the midst of the fire?' and wonderingly declared, 'Lo, I see four men loose walking in the midst of the fire, and the aspect of the fourth is like a son of the gods.'

WISDOM'S GIFT

'That I may cause those that love me to inherit substance.'—PROVERBS viii. 21.

The word here rendered 'substance' is peculiar. Indeed, it is used in a unique construction in this passage. It means 'being' or 'existence,' and seems to have been laid hold of by the Hebrew thinkers, from whom the books commonly called 'the Wisdom Books' come, as one of their almost technical expressions. 'Substance' may be used in our translation in its philosophical meaning as the supposed reality underlying appearances, but if we observe that in the parallel following clause we find 'treasures,' it seems more likely that in the text, it is to be taken in its secondary, and much debased meaning of wealth, material possessions. But the prize held out here to the lovers of heavenly wisdom is much more than worldly good. In deepest truth, the being which is theirs is God Himself. They who love and seek the wisdom of this book possess Him, and in possessing Him become possessed of their own true being. They are owners and lords of themselves, and have in their hearts a fountain of life, because they have God dwelling with and in them.

I. The quest which always finds.

'Those who love wisdom' might be a Hebrew translation of 'philosopher,' and possibly the Jewish teachers of wisdom were influenced by Greece, but their conception of wisdom has a deeper source than the Greek had, and what they meant by loving it was a widely different attitude of mind and heart from that of the Greek philosopher. It could never be said of the disciples of a Plato that their quest was sure to end in finding what they sought. Many a man then, and many a man since, and many a man to-day, has 'followed knowledge, like a sinking star,' and has only caught a glimmer of a far-off and dubious light. There is only one search which is certain always to find what it seeks, and that is the search which knows where the object of it is, and seeks not as for something the locality of which is unknown, but as for that which the place of which is certain. The manifold voices of human aims cry, 'Who will show us any good?' The seeker who is sure to find is he who prays, 'Lord, lift Thou up the light of Thy countenance upon us.' The heart that truly and supremely affects God is never condemned to seek in vain. The Wisdom of this book herself is presented as proclaiming, 'They that seek me earnestly shall find me,' and humble souls in every age since then have set to their seal that the word is true to their experience. For there are two seekers in every such case, God and man. 'The Father seeketh such to worship Him,' and His love goes through the world, yearning and searching for hearts that will turn to Him. The shepherd seeks for the lost sheep, and lays it on his shoulders to bear it back to the fold. Jesus Christ is the incarnation of the seeking love of God. And the human seeker finds God, or rather is found by God, for no aspiration after Him is vain, no longing unresponded to, no effort to find Him unresponded to. We have as much of God as we wish, as much as our desires have fitted us to receive. The all-penetrating atmosphere enters every chink open to it, and no seeking soul has ever had to say, 'I sought Him but found Him not.'

Is there any other quest of which the same can be said? Are not all paths of human effort strewed with the skeletons of men who have fretted and toiled away their lives in vain attempts to grasp aims that have eluded their grip? Do we not all know the sickness of disappointed effort, or the sadder sickness of successful effort, which has secured the apparent good and found it not so good after all? The Christian life is, amid all the failures of human effort, the only life in which the seeking after good is but a little less blessed than the finding of it is, and in which it is always true that 'he that seeketh findeth.' Nor does such finding deaden the spirit of seeking, for in every finding there is a fresh discovery of new depths in God, and a consequent quickening of desire to press further into the abyss of His Being, so that aspiration and fruition ever beget each other, and the upward, Godward progress of the soul is eternal.

II. The finding that is always blessed.

We have seen that being is the gift promised to the lovers of wisdom, and that the promise may either be referred to the possession of God, who is the fountain of all being, or to the true possession of ourselves, which is a consequence of our possession of Him. In either aspect, that possession is blessedness. If we have God, we have real life. We truly own ourselves when we have God. We really live when God lives in us, the life of our lives. We are ourselves, when we have ceased to be ourselves, and have taken God to be the Self of ourselves.

Such a life, God-possessing, brings the one good which corresponds to our whole nature. All other good is fragmentary, and being fragmentary is inadequate, as men's restless search after various forms of good but too sadly proves. Why does the merchantman wander over sea and land seeking for many goodly pearls? Because he has not found one of great price, but tries to make up by their number for the insufficiency of each. But the soul is made, not to find its wealth in the manifold but in the one, and no aggregation of incompletenesses will make up completeness, nor any number of partial satisfactions of this and the other appetite or desire make a man feel that he has enough and more than enough. We must have all good in one Person, if we are ever to know the rest of full satisfaction. It will be fatal to our blessedness if we have to resort to a hundred different sources for different supplies. The true blessedness is simple and yet infinitely complex, for it comes from possessing the one Person in whom dwell for us all forms of good, whether good be understood as intellectual or moral or emotional. That which cannot be everything to the soul that seeks is scarcely worth the seeking, and certainly is not wisely proposed as the object of a life's search, for such a life will be a failure if it fails to find its object, and scarcely less tragically, though perhaps less conspicuously, a failure if it finds it. All other good is but apparent; God is the one real object that meets all man's desires and needs, and makes him blessed with real blessedness, and fills the cup of life with the draught that slakes thirst and satisfies the thirstiest.

III. The blessedness that always lasts.

He who finds God, as every one of us may find Him, in Christ, has found a Good that cannot change, pass, or grow stale. His blessedness will always last, as long as he keeps fast hold of that which he has, and lets no man take his crown.

For the Christian's good is the only one that does not intend to grow old and pall. We can never exhaust God. We need never grow weary of Him. Possession robs other wealth of its glamour, and other pleasures of their poignant sweetness. We grow weary of most good things, and those which we have long had, we generally find get somewhat faded and stale. Habit is a fatal enemy to enjoyment. But it only adds to the joy which springs from the possession of God in Christ. Swedenborg said that the oldest angels look the youngest, and they who have longest experience of the joy of fellowship with God are they who enjoy each instance of it most. We can never drink the chalice of His love to the dregs, and it will be fresh and sparkling as long as we have lips that can absorb it. He keeps the good wine till the last.

The Christian's good is the only good which cannot be taken away. Loss and change beggars the millionaire sometimes, and the possibility of loss shadows all earthly good with pale foreboding. Everything that is outside the substance of the soul can be withdrawn, but the possession of God in Christ is so intimate and inward, so interwoven with the very deepest roots of the Christian's personal being, that it cannot be taken out from these by any shocks of time or change. There is but one hand that can end that possession and that is his own. He can withdraw himself from God, by giving himself over to sin and the world. He can empty the shrine and compel the indwelling deity to say, as the legend told was heard in the Temple the night before Roman soldiers desecrated the Holy of Holies: Let us depart. But besides himself, 'neither things present, nor things to come, nor height nor depth, nor any other creature' has power to take away that faithful God to whom a poor soul clings, and in whom whoso thus clings finds its unchangeable good.

The Christian's good is the only one from which we cannot be taken. A grim psalm paints for us the life and end of men 'who trust in the multitude of their possessions,' and whose 'inward thought is that they have founded families that will last.' It tells how 'this their way is folly,' and yet is approved with acclamations by the crowd. It lets us see the founder of a family, the possessor of broad acres, going down to the grave, carrying nothing away, stripped of his glory and with Death for his shepherd, who has driven his flock from pleasant pastures here into the dreariness of Sheol. But that shepherd has a double office. Some he separates from all their possessions, hopes, and joys. Some he, stern though his aspect and harsh though his guidance, leads up to the green pastures of God, and as the last messenger of the love of God in Christ, unites the souls that found God amid the distractions of earth with the God whom they will know better and possess more fully and blessedly, amid the unending felicities and progressive blessednesses of Heaven.

WISDOM AND CHRIST

'Then I was by him, as one brought up with him: and I was daily his delight, rejoicing always before him; 31. Rejoicing in the habitable part of his earth; and my delights were with the sons of men.'—PROVERBS viii. 30, 31.

There is a singular difference between the two portions of this Book of Proverbs. The bulk of it, beginning with chapter x., contains a collection of isolated maxims which may be described as the product of sanctified common sense. They are shrewd and homely, but not remarkably spiritual or elevated. To these is prefixed this introductory portion, continuous, lofty in style, and in its personification of divine wisdom, rising to great sublimity both of thought and of expression. It seems as if the main body of the book had been fitted with an introduction by another hand than that of the compilers of the various sets of proverbial sayings. It is apparently due to an intellectual movement, perhaps not uninfluenced by Greek thought, and chronologically the latest of the elements composing the Old Testament scriptures. In place of the lyric fervour of prophets, and the devout intuition of psalmists, we have the praise of Wisdom. But that noble portrait is no copy of the Greek conception, but contains features peculiar to itself. She stands opposed to blatant, meretricious Folly, and seeks to draw men to herself by lofty motives and offering pure delights. She is not a person, but she is a personification of an aspect of the divine nature, and seeing that she is held forth as willing to bestow herself on men, that queenly figure shadows the great truth of God's self-communication as being the end and climax of all His revelation.

We are on the wrong tack when we look for more or less complete resemblances between the 'Wisdom' of Proverbs and the 'Sophia' of Greek thinkers. It is much rather an anticipation, imperfect but real, of Jesus than a pale reflection of Greek thought. The way for the perfect revelation of God in the incarnation was prepared by prophet and psalmist. Was it not also prepared by this vision of a Wisdom which was always with God, and yet had its delights with the sons of men, and whilst 'rejoicing always before Him,' yet rejoiced in the habitable parts of the earth?

Let us then look, however imperfect our gaze may be, at the self-revelation in Proverbs of the personified divine Wisdom, and compare it with the revelation of the incarnate divine Word.

I. The Self-revelation of Wisdom.

The words translated in Authorised Version, 'As one brought up with him,' are rendered in Revised Version, 'as a master workman,' and seem intended to represent Wisdom—that is, of course, the divine Wisdom—as having been God's agent in the creative act. In the preceding context, she triumphantly proclaims her existence before His 'works of old,' and that she was with God, 'or ever the earth was.' Before the everlasting mountains she was, before fountains flashed in the light and refreshed the earth, her waters flowed. But that presence is not all, Wisdom was the divine agent in creation. That thought goes beyond the ancient one: 'He spake and it was done.' Genesis regards the divine command as the cause of creatural being. God said, 'Let there be—and there was': the forthputting of His will was the impulse to which creatures sprang into existence at response. That is a great thought, but the meditative thinker in our text has pondered over the facts of creation, and notwithstanding all their apparent incompletenesses and errors, has risen to the conclusion that they can all be vindicated as 'very good.' To him, this wonderful universe is not only the product of a sovereign will, but of one guided in its operations by all-seeing Wisdom.

Then the relation of this divine Wisdom to God is represented as being a continual delight and a childlike rejoicing in Him, or as the word literally means, a 'sporting' in Him. Whatever energy of creative action is suggested by the preceding figure of a 'master workman,' that energy had no effort. To the divine Wisdom creation was an easy task. She was not so occupied with it as to interrupt her delight in contemplating God, and her task gave her infinite satisfaction, for she 'rejoiced always' before Him, and she rejoiced in His habitable earth. The writer does not shrink from ascribing to the agent of creation something like the glow of satisfaction that we feel over a piece of well-done work, the poet's or the painter's rapture as he sees his thoughts bodied forth in melody or glowing on canvas.

But there is a greater thought than these here, for the writer adds, 'and my delight was with the sons of men.' It is noteworthy that the same word is used in the preceding verse. The 'delight of the heavenly Wisdom in God' is not unlike that directed to man. 'The sons of men' are the last, noblest work of Creation, and on them, as the shining apex, her delight settles. The words describe not only what was true when man came into being, as the utmost possible climax of creatural excellence, but are the revelation of what still remains true.

One cannot but feel how in all this most striking disclosure of the depths of God, a deeper mystery is on the verge of revelation. There is here, as we have said, a personification, but there seems to be a Person shining through, or dimly discerned moving behind, the curtain. Wisdom is the agent of creation. She creates with ease, and in creating delights in God as well as in her work, which calls for no effort in doing, and done, is all very good. She delights most of all in the sons of men, and that delight is permanent. Does not this unknown Jewish thinker, too, belong, as well as prophet and psalmist, to those who went before crying, Hosanna to Him that cometh in the name of the Lord? Let us turn to the New Testament and find an answer to the question.

II. The higher revelation of the divine Word.

There can be no doubt that the New Testament is committed to the teaching that the Eternal Word of God, who was incarnate in Jesus, was the agent of creation. John, in his profound prologue to the Gospel, utters the deepest truths in brief sentences of monosyllables, and utters them without a trace of feeling that they needed proof. To him they are axiomatic and self evident. 'All things were made by Him.' The words are the words of a child; the thought takes a flight beyond the furthest reach of the mind of men. Paul, too, adds his Amen when he proclaims that 'All things have been created through Him and unto Him, and He is before all things, and in Him all things hold together.' The writer of Hebrews declares a Son 'through whom also He made the worlds, and who upholds all things by the word of His power' and does not scruple at transferring to Jesus the grand poetry of the Psalmist who hymned 'Thou, Lord, in the beginning, hast laid the foundation of the earth, and the heavens are the work of Thy hands.' We speak of things too deep for us when we speak of persons in the Godhead, but yet we know that the Eternal Word, which was from the beginning, was made flesh and dwelt among us. The personified Wisdom of Proverbs is the personal Word of John's prologue. John almost quotes the former when he says 'the same was in the beginning with God.' for his word recalls the grand declaration, 'The Lord possessed me in the beginning of His way ... I was set up in the beginning or ever the earth was.' Then there are two beginnings, one lost in the depths of timeless being, one, the commencement of creative activity, and that Word was with God in the remotest, as in the nearer, beginning.

But the ancient vision of the Jewish thinker anticipated the perfect revelation of the New Testament still further, in its thought of an unbroken communion between the personified Wisdom and God. That dim thought of perfect communion and interchange of delights flashes into wondrous clearness when we think of Him who spake of 'the glory which I had with Thee before the foundation of the world,' and calmly declared: 'Thou lovedst me before the foundation of the world.' Into that depth of mutual love we cannot look, and our eyes are too dim-sighted to bear the blaze of that flashing interchange of glory, but we shall rob the earthly life of Jesus of its pathos and saving power, if we do not recognise that in Him the personification of Proverbs has become a person, and that when He became flesh, He not only took on Him the garment of mortality, but laid aside 'the visible robes of His imperial majesty,' and that His being found in fashion as a man was humbling Himself beyond all humiliation that afterwards was His.

But still further, the Gospel reality fills out and completes the personification of Proverbs in that it shows us a divine person who so turned to 'the sons of men' that He took on Him their nature and Himself bore their sicknesses. The Jewish writer had great thoughts of the divine condescension, and was sure that God's love still rested on men, sinful as they were, but not even he could foresee the miracle of long-suffering love in the Incarnate Jesus, and he had no power of insight into the depths of the heart of God, that enabled him to foresee the sufferings and death of Jesus. Till that supreme self-sacrifice was a fact, it was inconceivable. Alas, now that it is a fact, to how many hearts that need it most is it still incredible. But passing all anticipation as it is, it is the root of all joy, the ground of all hope, and to millions of sinful souls it is their only refuge, and their sovereign example and pattern of life.

The Jewish thinker had a glimpse of a divine wisdom which delighted in man, but he did not dream of the divine stooping to share in man's sorrows, or of its so loving humanity as to take on itself its limitations, not only to pity these as God's images, but to take part of the same and to die. That man should minister to the divine delight is wonderful, but that God should participate in man's grief passes wonder. Thereby a new tenderness is given to the ancient personification, and the august form of the divine Wisdom softens and melts into the yet more august and tender likeness of the divine Love. Nor is there only an adumbration of the redeeming love of Jesus as He dwells among us here, but we have to remember that Jesus delights in the sons of men when they love Him back again. All the sweet mysteries of our loving communion with Him, and of His joy in our faith, love, and obedience, all the secret treasures of His self-impartation to, and abiding in, souls that open themselves to His entrance, are suggested in that thought. We can minister to the joy of Jesus, and when He is welcomed into any heart, and any man's love answers His, He sees of the travail of His soul and is satisfied.

III. The call of the personal Word to each of us.

The Wisdom of Proverbs is portrayed in her queenly dignity, as calling men to herself, and promising them the satisfaction of all their needs. She describes herself that the description may draw men to her. The self-revelation of God is His mightiest means of attracting men to Him. We but need to know Him as He really is, in order to love Him and cling to Him. A fairer form than hers has drawn near to us, and calls us with tenderer invitations and better promises. The divine Wisdom has become Man with 'sweet human hands and lips and eyes.' Such was His delight in the sons of men that He emptied Himself of His glory, and finished a greater work than that over which he presided when the mountains were settled and the hills brought forth. Now He calls us, and His summons is tenderer, and gives promise of loftier blessings than the call of Wisdom was and did. She called to the simple, 'Come eat ye of my bread, and drink of the wine which I have mingled.' He invites us: 'If any man thirst, let him come unto Me and drink,' and He furnishes a table for us, and calls us to eat of the bread which is His body broken for us, and to drink of the wine which is His blood shed for many for the remission of sins. She promises 'riches and honour, yea, durable riches and righteousness.' His voice vibrates with sympathy, and calls the weary and heavy laden, of whom she scarcely thinks, and offers to them a gift, which may seem humble enough beside her more dazzling offers of fruit, better than gold and revenues, better than choice silver, but which come closer to universal wants, the gift of rest, which is really what all men long for, and none but they who take His yoke upon them possess. 'See that ye refuse not Him that speaketh,' for if they escaped not when they refused her that spake through the Jewish thinker's lips of old, 'much more shall not we escape, if we turn away from Him that beseecheth us from heaven.' Jesus is the power of God and the wisdom of God, and it is in Him crucified that our weakness and our folly are made strong and wise, and Wisdom's ancient promise is fulfilled: 'Whoso findeth me findeth life, and shall obtain favour of the Lord.'

THE TWO-FOLD ASPECT OF THE DIVINE WORKING

'The way of the Lord is strength to the upright: but destruction shall be to the workers of iniquity.'—PROVERBS x. 29.

You observe that the words 'shall be,' in the last clause, are a supplement. They are quite unnecessary, and in fact they rather hinder the sense. They destroy the completeness of the antithesis between the two halves of the verse. If you leave them out, and suppose that the 'way of the Lord' is what is spoken of in both clauses, you get a far deeper and fuller meaning. 'The way of the Lord is strength to the upright; but destruction to the workers of iniquity.' It is the same way which is strength to one man and ruin to another, and the moral nature of the man determines which it shall be to him. That is a penetrating word, which goes deep down. The unknown thinkers, to whose keen insight into the facts of human life we are indebted for this Book of Proverbs, had pondered for many an hour over the perplexed and complicated fates of men, and they crystallised their reflections at last in this thought. They have in it struck upon a principle which explains a great many things, and teaches us a great many solemn lessons. Let us try to get a hold of what is meant, and then to look at some applications and illustrations of the principle.

I. First, then, let me just try to put clearly the meaning and bearing of these words. 'The way of the Lord' means, sometimes in the Old Testament and sometimes in the New, religion, considered as the way in which God desires a man to walk. So we read in the New Testament of 'the way' as the designation of the profession and practice of Christianity; and 'the way of the Lord' is often used in the Psalms for the path which He traces for man by His sovereign will.

But that, of course, is not the meaning here. Here it means, not the road in which God prescribes that we should walk, but that road in which He Himself walks; or, in other words, the sum of the divine action, the solemn footsteps of God through creation, providence, and history. 'His goings forth are from everlasting.' 'His way is in the sea.' 'His way is in the sanctuary.' Modern language has a whole set of phrases which mean the same thing as the Jew meant by 'the way of the Lord,' only that God is left out. They talk about the 'current of events,' 'the general tendency of things,' 'the laws of human affairs,' and so on. I, for my part, prefer the old-fashioned 'Hebraism.' To many modern thinkers the whole drift and tendency of human affairs affords no sign of a person directing these. They hear the clashing and grinding of opposing forces, the thunder as of falling avalanches, and the moaning as of a homeless wind, but they hear the sounds of no footfalls echoing down the ages. This ancient teacher had keener ears. Well for us if we share his faith, and see in all the else distracting mysteries of life and history, 'the way of the Lord!'

But not only does the expression point to the operation of a personal divine Will in human affairs, but it conceives of that operation as one, a uniform and consistent whole. However complicated, and sometimes apparently contradictory, the individual events were, there was a unity in them, and they all converged on one result. The writer does not speak of 'ways,' but of 'the way,' as a grand unity. It is all one continuous, connected, consistent mode of operation from beginning to end.

The author of this proverb believed something more about the way of the Lord. He believed that although it is higher than our way, still, a man can know something about it; and that whatever may be enigmatical, and sometimes almost heart-breaking, in it, one thing is sure—that as we have been taught of late years in another dialect, it 'makes for righteousness.' 'Clouds and darkness are round about Him,' but the Old Testament writers never falter in the conviction, which was the soul of all their heroism and the life blood of their religion, that in the hearts of the clouds and darkness, 'Justice and judgment are the foundations of His throne.' The way of the Lord, says this old thinker, *is* hard to understand, very complicated, full of all manner of perplexities and difficulties, and yet on the whole the clear drift and tendency of the whole thing is discernible, and it is this: it is all on the side of good. Everything that is good, and everything that does good, is an ally of God's, and may be sure of the divine favour and of the divine blessing resting upon it.

And just because that is so clear, the other side is as true; the same way, the same set of facts, the same continuous stream of tendency, which is all with and for every form of good, is all against every form of evil. Or, as one of the Psalmists puts the same idea, 'The eyes of the Lord are upon the righteous, and His ears are open unto their cry. The face of the Lord is against them that do evil.' The same eye that beams in lambent love on 'the righteous' burns terribly to the evil doer. 'The face of the Lord' means the side of the divine nature which is turned to us, and is manifested by His self-revealing activity, so that the expression comes near in meaning to 'the way of the

Lord,' and the thought in both cases is the same, that by the eternal law of His being, God's actions must all be for the good and against the evil.

They do not change, but a man's character determines which aspect of them he sees and has to experience. God's way has a bright side and a dark. You may take which you like. You can lay hold of the thing by whichever handle you choose. On the one side it is convex, on the other concave. You can approach it from either side, as you please. 'The way of the Lord' must touch *your* 'way.' Your cannot alter that necessity. Your path must either run parallel in the same direction with His, and then all His power will be an impulse to bear you onward; or it must run in the opposite direction, and then all His power will be for your ruin, and the collision with it will crush you as a ship is crushed like an egg-shell, when it strikes an iceberg. You can choose which of these shall befall you.

And there is a still more striking beauty about the saying, if we give the full literal meaning to the word 'strength.' It is used by our translators, I suppose, in a somewhat archaic and peculiar signification, namely, that of a stronghold. At all events the Hebrew means a fortress, a place where men may live safe and secure; and if we take that meaning, the passage gains greatly in force and beauty. This 'way of the Lord' is like a castle for the shelter of the shelterless good man, and behind those strong bulwarks he dwells impregnable and safe. Just as a fortress is a security to the garrison, and a frowning menace to the besiegers or enemies, so the 'name of the Lord is a strong tower,' and the 'way of the Lord' is a fortress. If you choose to take shelter within it, its massive walls are your security and your joy. If you do not, they frown down grimly upon you, a menace and a terror. How differently, eight hundred years ago, Normans and Saxons looked at the square towers that were built all over England to bridle the inhabitants! To the one they were the sign of the security of their dominion; to the other they were the sign of their slavery and submission. Torture and prison-houses they might become; frowning portents they necessarily were. 'The way of the Lord' is a castle fortress to the man that does good, and to the man that does evil it is a threatening prison, which may become a hell of torture. It is 'ruin to the workers of iniquity.' I pray you, settle for yourself which of these it is to be to you.

II. And now let me say a word or two by way of application, or illustration, of these principles that are here.

First, let me remind you how the order of the universe is such that righteousness is life and sin is death. This universe and the fortunes of men are complicated and strange. It is hard to trace any laws, except purely physical ones, at work. Still, on the whole, things do work so that goodness is blessedness, and badness is ruin. That is, of course, not always true in regard of outward things, but even about them it is more often and obviously true than we sometimes recognise. Hence all nations have their proverbs, embodying the generalised experience of centuries, and asserting that, on the whole, 'honesty is the best policy,' and that it is always a blunder to do wrong. What modern phraseology calls 'laws of nature,' the Bible calls 'the way of the Lord'; and the manner in which these help a man who conforms to them, and hurt or kill him if he does not, is an illustration on a lower level of the principle of our text. This tremendous congeries of powers in the midst of which we live does not care whether we go with it or against it, only if we do the one we shall prosper, and if we do the other we shall very likely be made an end of. Try to stop a train, and it will run over you and murder you; get into it, and it will carry you smoothly along. Our lives are surrounded with powers, which will carry our messages and be our slaves if we know how to command nature by obeying it, or will impassively strike us dead if we do not.

Again, in our physical life, as a rule, virtue makes strength, sin brings punishment. 'Riotous living' makes diseased bodies. Sins in the flesh are avenged in the flesh, and there is no need for a miracle to bring it about that he who sows to the flesh shall 'of the flesh reap corruption.' God entrusts the punishment of the breach of the laws of temperance and morality in the body to the 'natural' operation of such breach. The inevitable connection between sins against the body and disease in the body, is an instance of the way of the Lord—the same set of principles and facts—being strength to one man and destruction to another. Hundreds of young men in Manchester—some of whom are listening to me now, no doubt—are killing themselves, or at least are ruining their health, by flying in the face of the plain laws of purity and self-control. They think that they must 'have their fling,' and 'obey their instincts,' and so on. Well, if they must, then another 'must' will insist upon coming into play—and they must reap as they have sown, and drink as they have brewed, and the grim saying of this book about profligate young men will be fulfilled in many of them. 'His bones are full of the iniquity of his youth, which shall lie down with him in the grave.' Be not deceived, God is not mocked, and His way avenges bodily transgressions by bodily sufferings.

And then, in higher regions, on the whole, goodness makes blessedness, and evil brings ruin. All the powers of God's universe, and all the tenderness of God's heart are on the side of the man that does right. The stars in their courses fight against the man that fights against Him; and on the other side, in yielding thyself to the will of God and following the dictates of His commandments, 'Thou shalt make a league with the beasts of the field, and the stones of the field shall be at peace with thee.' All things serve the soul that serves God, and all war against him who wars against his Maker. The way of the Lord cannot but further and help all who love and serve Him. For them all things must work together for good. By the very laws of God's own being, which necessarily shape all His actions, the whole 'stream of tendency without us makes for righteousness.' In the one course of life we go with the stream of divine activity which pours from the throne of God. In the other we are like men trying to row a boat *up* Niagara. All the rush of the mighty torrent will batter us back. Our work will be doomed to destruction, and ourselves to shame. For ever and ever to be good is to be well. An eternal truth lies in the facts that the same word 'good' means pleasant and right, and that sin and sorrow are both called 'evil.' All sin is self-inflicted sorrow, and every 'rogue is a roundabout fool.' So ask yourselves the question: 'Is my life in harmony with, or opposed to, these omnipotent laws which rule the whole field of life?'

Still further, this same fact of the two-fold aspect and operation of the one way of the Lord will be made yet more evident in the future. It becomes us to speak very reverently and reticently about the matter, but I can conceive it possible that the one manifestation of God in a future life may be in substance the same, and yet that it may produce opposite effects upon oppositely disposed souls. According to the old mystical illustration, the same heat that melts wax hardens clay, and the same apocalypse of the divine nature in another world may to one man be life and joy, and to another man may be terror and despair. I do not dwell upon that; it is far too awful a thing for us to speak about to one another, but it is worth your taking to heart when you are indulging in easy anticipations that of course God is merciful and will bless and save everybody after he dies. Perhaps—I do not go any further than a perhaps—perhaps God cannot, and perhaps if a man has got himself into such a condition as it is possible for a man to get into, perhaps, like light upon a diseased eye, the purest beam may be the most exquisite pain, and the natural instinct may be to 'call upon the rocks and the hills to fall upon them' and cover them up in a more genial darkness from that Face, to see which should be life and blessedness.

People speak of future rewards and punishments as if they were given and inflicted by simple and divine volition, and did not stand in any necessary connection with holiness on the one hand or with sin on the other. I do not deny that some portion of both bliss and sorrow may be of such a character. But there is a very important and wide region in which our actions here must automatically bring consequences hereafter of joy or sorrow, without any special retributive action of God's.

We have only to keep in view one or two things about the future which we know to be true, and we shall see this. Suppose a man with his memory of all his past life perfect, and his conscience stimulated to greater sensitiveness and clearer judgment, and all opportunities ended of gratifying tastes and appetites, whose food is in this world, while yet the soul has become dependent on them for ease and comfort, What more is needed to make a hell? And the supposition is but the statement of a fact. We seem to forget much; but when the waters are drained off all the lost things will be found at the bottom. Conscience gets dulled and sophisticated here. But the icy cold of death will wake it up, and the new position will give new insight into the true character of our actions. You see how often a man at the end of life has his eyes cleared to see his faults. But how much more will that be the case hereafter! When the rush of passion is past, and you are far enough from your life to view it as a whole, holding it at arm's length, you will see better what it looks like. There is nothing improbable in supposing that inclinations and tastes which have been nourished for a lifetime may survive the possibility of indulging them in another life, as they often do in this; and what can be worse than such a thirst for one drop of water, which never can be tasted more? These things are certain, and no more is needed to make sin produce, by necessary consequence, misery, and ruin; while similarly, goodness brings joy, peace, and blessing.

But again, the self-revelation of God has this same double aspect.

'The way of the Lord' may mean His process by which He reveals His character. Every truth concerning Him may be either a joy or a terror to men. All His 'attributes' are builded into 'a strong tower, into which the righteous runneth, and is safe,' or else they are builded into a prison and torture-house. So the thought of God may either be a happy and strengthening one, or an unwelcome one. 'I remembered God, and was troubled' says one Psalmist. What an awful confession—that the thought of God disturbed him! The thought of God to some of us is a very unwelcome one, as unwelcome as the thought of a detective to a company of thieves. Is not that dreadful? Music is a torture to some ears: and there are people who have so alienated their hearts and wills from God that the Name which should be 'their dearest faith' is not only their 'ghastliest doubt,' but their greatest pain. O brethren, the thought of God and all that wonderful complex of mighty attributes and beauties which make His Name should be our delight, the key to all treasures, the end of all sorrows, our light in darkness, our life in death, our all in all. It is either that to us, or it is something that we would fain forget. Which is it to you?

Especially the Gospel has this double aspect. Our text speaks of the distinction between the righteous and evil doers; but how to pass from the one class to the other, it does not tell us. The Gospel is the answer to that question. It tells us that though we are all 'workers of iniquity,' and must, therefore, if such a text as this were the last word to be spoken on the matter, share in the ruin which smites the opponent of the divine will, we may pass from that class; and by simple faith in Him who died on the Cross for all workers of iniquity, may become of those righteous on whose side God works in all His way, who have all His attributes drawn up like an embattled army in their defence, and have His mighty name for their refuge.

As the very crown of the ways of God, the work of Christ and the record of it in the Gospel have most eminently this double aspect. God meant nothing but the salvation of the whole world when He sent us this Gospel. His 'way' therein was pure, unmingled, universal love. We can make that great message untroubled blessing by simply accepting it. Nothing more is needed but to take God at His word, and to close with His sincere and earnest invitation. Then Christ's work becomes the fortress in which we are guarded from sin and guilt, from the arrows of conscience, and the fiery darts of temptation. But if not accepted, then it is not passive, it is not nothing. If rejected, it does more harm to a man than anything else can, just because, if accepted, it would have done him more good. The brighter the light, the darker the shadow. The pillar which symbolised the presence of God sent down influences on either side; to the trembling crowd of the Israelites on the one hand, to the pursuing ranks of the Egyptians on the other; and though the pillar was one, opposite effects streamed from it, and it was 'a cloud and darkness to them, but it gave light by night to these.' Everything depends on which side of the pillar you choose to see. The ark of God, which brought dismay and death among false gods and their worshippers, brought blessing into the humble house of Obed Edom, the man of Gath, with whom it rested for three months before it was set in its place in the city of David. That which is meant to be the savour of life unto life must either be that or the savour of death unto death.

Jesus Christ is *something* to each of us. For you who have heard His name ever since you were children, your relation to Him settles your condition and your prospects, and moulds your character. Either He is for you the tried corner-stone, the sure foundation, on which whosoever builds will not be confounded, or He is the stone of stumbling, against which whosoever stumbles will be broken, and which will crush to powder whomsoever it falls upon, 'This Child is set for the rise' or for the fall of all who hear His name. He leaves no man at the level at which He found him, but either lifts him up nearer to God, and purity and joy, or sinks him into an ever-descending pit of darkening separation from all these. Which is He to you? Something He must be—your strength or your ruin. If you commit your souls to Him in humble faith, He will be your peace, your life, your Heaven. If you turn from His offered grace, He will be your pain, your death, your torture. 'What maketh Heaven, that maketh hell.' Which do you choose Him to be?

THE MANY-SIDED CONTRAST OF WISDOM AND FOLLY

'Whoso loveth instruction loveth knowledge: but he that hateth reproof is brutish. 2. A good man obtaineth favour of the Lord: but a man of wicked devices will he condemn. 3. A man shall not be established by wickedness; but the root of the righteous shall not be moved. 4. A virtuous woman is a crown to her husband: but she that maketh ashamed is as rottenness in his bones. 5. The thoughts of the righteous are right: but the counsels of the wicked are deceit. 6. The words of the wicked are to lie in wait for blood: but the mouth of the upright shall deliver them. 7. The wicked are overthrown, and are not: but the house of the righteous shall stand. 8. A man shall be commended according to his wisdom: but he that is of a perverse heart shall be despised. 9. He that is despised, and hath a servant, is better than he that honoureth himself, and lacketh bread. 10. A righteous man regardeth the life of his beast: but the tender mercies of the wicked are cruel. 11. He that tilleth his land shall be satisfied with bread: but he that followeth vain persons is void of understanding. 12. The wicked desireth the net of evil men: but the root of the righteous yieldeth fruit. 13. The wicked is snared by the transgression of his lips: but the just shall come out of trouble. 14. A man shall be satisfied with good by the fruit of his mouth; and the recompence of a man's hands shall be rendered unto him. 15. The way of a fool is right in his own eyes: but he that hearkeneth unto counsel is wise.'—PROVERBS xii. 1-15.

The verses of the present passage are a specimen of the main body of the Book of Proverbs. They are not a building, but a heap. The stones seldom have any mortar between them, and connection or progress is for the most part sought in vain. But one great antithesis runs through the whole—the contrast of wisdom or righteousness with folly or wickedness. The compiler or author is never weary of setting out that opposition in all possible lights. It is, in his view, the one difference worth noting between men, and it determines their whole character and fortunes. The book traverses with keen observation all the realm of life, and everywhere finds confirmation of its great principle that goodness is wisdom and sin folly.

There is something extremely impressive in this continual reiteration of that contrast. As we read, we feel as if, after all, there were nothing in the world but it and its results. That profound sense of the existence and far-reaching scope of the division of men into two classes is not the least of the benefits which a thoughtful study of Proverbs brings to us. In this lesson it is useless to attempt to classify the verses. Slight traces of grouping appear here and there; but, on the whole, we have a set of miscellaneous aphorisms turning on the great contrast, and setting in various lights the characters and fates of the righteous and the wicked.

The first mark of difference is the opposite feeling about discipline. If a man is wise, he will love 'knowledge'; and if he loves knowledge, he will love the means to it, and therefore will not kick against correction. That is another view of trials from the one which inculcates devout submission to a Father. It regards only the benefits to ourselves. If we want to be taught anything, we shall not flinch from the rod. There must be pains undergone in order to win knowledge of any sort, and the man who rebels against these shows that he had rather be comfortable and ignorant than wise. A pupil who will not stand having his exercises corrected will not learn his faults. On the other hand, hating reproof is 'brutish' in the most literal sense; for it is the characteristic of animals that they do not understand the purpose of pain, and never advance because they do not. Men can grow because they can submit to discipline; beasts cannot improve because, except partially and in a few cases, they cannot accept correction.

The first proverb deals with wisdom or goodness in its inner source; namely, a docile disposition. The two next deal with its consequences. It secures God's favour, while its opposite is condemned; and then, as a consequence of this, the good man is established and the wicked swept away. The manifestations of God's favour and its opposite are not to be thrown forward to a future life. Continuously the sunshine of divine love falls on the one man, and already the other is condemned. It needs some strength of faith to look through the shows of prosperity often attending plain wickedness, and believe that it is always a blunder to do wrong.

But a moderate experience of life will supply many instances of prosperous villainy in trade and politics which melted away like mist. The shore is strewn with wrecks, dashed to pieces because righteousness did not steer. Every exchange gives examples in plenty. How many seemingly solid structures built on wrong every man has seen in his lifetime crumble like the cloud masses which the wind piles in the sky and then dissipates! The root of the righteous is in God, and therefore he is firm. The contrast is like that of Psalm i.—between the tree with strong roots and waving greenery, and the chaff, rootless, and therefore whirled out of the threshing-floor.

The universal contrast is next applied to women; and in accordance with the subordinate position they held in old days, the bearing of her goodness is principally regarded as affecting her husband. That does not cover the whole ground, of course. But wherever there is a true marriage, the wife will not think that woman's rights are infringed because one chief issue of her beauty of virtue is the honour and joy it reflects upon him who has her heart. 'A virtuous woman' is not only one who possesses the one virtue to which the phrase has been so miserably confined, but who is 'a woman of strength'—no doll or plaything, but

'A perfect woman, nobly planned
To warn, to comfort, and command.'

The gnawing misery of being fastened like two dogs in a leash to one who 'causes shame' is vividly portrayed by that strong figure, that she is like 'rottenness in his bones,' eating away strength, and inflicting disfigurement and torture.

Then come a pair of verses describing the inward and outward work of the two kinds of men as these affect others. The former verses dealt with their effects on the actors; the present, with their bearing on others. Inwardly, the good man has thoughts which scrupulously keep the balance true and are just to his fellows, while the wicked plans to deceive for his own profit. When thoughts are translated into speech, deceit bears fruit in words which are like ambushes of murderers, laying traps to destroy, while the righteous man's words are like angels of deliverance to the unsuspecting who are ready to fall into the snare. Selfishness, which is the root of wickedness, will be cruelty and injustice when necessary for its ends. The man who is wise because God is his centre and aim will be merciful and helpful. The basis of philanthropy is religion. The solemn importance attached to speech is observable. Words can slay as truly as swords. Now that the press has multiplied the power of speech, and the world is buzzing with the clatter of tongues, we all need to lay to heart the responsibilities and magic power of spoken and printed words, and 'to set a watch on the door of our lips.'

Then follow a couple of verses dealing with the consequences to men themselves of their contrasted characters. The first of these (verse 7) recurs to the thought of verse 3, but with a difference. Not only the righteous himself, but his house, shall be established. The solidarity of the family and the entail of goodness are strongly insisted on in the Old Testament, though limitations are fully recognised. If a good man's son continues his father's character, he will prolong his father's blessings; and in normal conditions, a parent's wisdom passes on to his children. Something is wrong when, as is so often the case, it does not; and it is not always the children's fault.

The overthrow of the wicked is set in striking contrast with their plots to overthrow others. Their mischief comes back, like an Australian boomerang, to the hand that flings it; and contrariwise, delivering others is a sure way of establishing one's self. Exceptions there are, for the world-scheme is too complicated to be condensed into a formula; but all proverbs speak of the average usual results of virtue and vice, and those of this book do the same. Verse 8 asserts that, on the whole, honour attends goodness, and contempt wickedness. Of course, companions in dissipation extol each other's vices, and launch the old threadbare sneers at goodness. But if wisdom were not set uppermost in men's secret judgment, there would be no hypocrites, and their existence proves the truth of the proverb.

Verse 9 seems suggested by 'despised' in verse 8. There are two kinds of contempt—one which brands sin deservedly, one which vulgarly despises everybody who is not rich. A man need not mind, though his modest household is treated with contempt, if quiet righteousness reigns in it. It is better to be contented with little, and humble in a lowly place, than to be proud and hungry, as many were in the writer's time and since. A foolish world set on wealth may despise, but its contempt breaks no bones. Self-conceit is poor diet.

This seems to be the first of a little cluster of proverbs bearing on domestic life. It prefers modest mediocrity of station, such as Agur desired. Its successor shows how the contrasted qualities come out in the two men's relation to their domestic animals. Goodness sweeps a wide circle touching the throne of God and the stall of the cattle. It was not Coleridge who found out that 'He prayeth best who loveth best' but this old proverb-maker; and he could speak the thought without the poet's exaggeration, which robs his expression of it of half its value. The original says 'knoweth the soul' which may indeed mean, 'regardeth the life' but rather seems to suggest sympathetic interest in leading to an understanding of the dumb creature, which must precede all wise care for its well-being. It is a part of religion to try to enter into the mysterious feelings of our humble dependants in farmyard and stable. On the other hand, for want of such sympathetic interest, even when the 'wicked' means to be kind, he does harm; or the word rendered 'tender mercies' may here mean the feelings (literally, 'bowels') which, in their intense selfishness, are cruel even to animals.

Verse 11 has no connection with the preceding, unless the link is common reference to home life and business. It contrasts the sure results of honest industry with the folly of speculation. The Revised Version margin 'vain things' is better than the text 'vain persons,' which would give no antithesis to the patient tilling of the first clause. That verse would make an admirable motto to be stretched across the Stock Exchange, and like places on both sides of the Atlantic. How many ruined homes and heart-broken wives witness in America and England to its truth! The vulgar English proverb, 'What comes over the Devil's back goes under his belly,' says the same thing. The only way to get honest wealth is to work for it. Gambling in all its forms is rank folly.

So the next proverb (verse 12) continues the same thought, and puts it in a somewhat difficult phrase. It goes a little deeper than the former, showing that the covetousness which follows after vain things, is really wicked lusting for unrighteous gain. 'The net of evildoers' is better taken as in the margin (Rev. Ver.) 'prey' or 'spoil,' and the meaning seems to be as just stated. Such hankering for riches, no matter how obtained, or such envying of the booty which admittedly has been won by roguery, is a mark of the wicked. How many professing church members have known that feeling in thinking of the millions of some railway king! Would they like the proverb to be applied to them?

The contrast to this is 'the root of the righteous yields fruit,' or 'shoots forth,' We have heard (verse 3) that it shall never be moved, being fixed in God; now we are told that it will produce all that is needful. A life rooted in God will unfold into all necessary good, which will be better than the spoil of the wicked. There are two ways of getting on—to struggle and fight and trample down rivals; one, to keep near God and wait for him. 'Ye fight and war; ye have not, because ye ask not.'

The next two proverbs have in common a reference to the effect of speech upon the speaker. 'In the transgression of the lips is an evil snare'; that is, sinful words ensnare their utterer, and whoever else he harms, he himself is harmed most. The reflex influence on character of our utterances is not present to us, as it should be. They leave stains on lips and heart. Thoughts expressed are more definite and permanent thereby. A vicious thought clothed in speech has new power over the speaker. If we would escape from that danger, we must *be* righteous, and *speak* righteousness; and then the same cause will deepen our convictions of 'whatsoever things are lovely and of good report.'

Verse 14 insists on this opposite side of the truth. Good words will bring forth fruit, which will satisfy the speaker, because, whatever effects his words may have on others, they will leave strengthened goodness and love of it in himself. 'If the house be worthy, your peace shall rest upon it; if not, it shall return to you again.' That reaction of words on oneself is but one case of the universal law of consequences coming back on us. We are the architects of our own destinies. Every deed has an immortal life, and returns, either like a raven or a dove, to the man who sent it out on its flight. It comes back either croaking with blood on its beak, or cooing with an olive branch in its mouth. All life is at once sowing and reaping. A harvest comes in which retribution will be even more entire and accurate.

The last proverb of the passage gives a familiar antithesis, and partially returns to the thought of verse 1. The fool has no standard of conduct but his own notions, and is absurdly complacent as to all his doings. The wise seeks better guidance than his own, and is docile, because he is not so ridiculously sure of his infallibility. No type of weak wickedness is more abominable to the proverbialist than that of pert self-conceit, which knows so little that it thinks it knows everything, and is 'as untameable as a fly.' But in the wisest sense, it is true that a mark of folly is self-opinionativeness; that a man who has himself for teacher has a fool for scholar; that the test of wisdom is willingness to be taught; and, especially, that to bring a docile, humble spirit to the Source of all wisdom, and to ask counsel of God, is the beginning of true insight, and that the self-sufficiency which is the essence of sin, is never more fatal than when it is ignorant of guilt, and therefore spurns a Saviour.

THE POOR RICH AND THE RICH POOR

'There is that maketh himself rich, yet hath nothing; there is that maketh himself poor, yet hath great riches.'—PROVERBS xiii. 7.

Two singularly-contrasted characters are set in opposition here. One, that of a man who lives like a millionaire and is a pauper; another, that of a man who lives like a pauper and is rich. The latter character, that of a man who hides and hoards his wealth, was, perhaps, more common in the days when this collection of Proverbs was put together, because in all ill-governed countries, to show wealth is a short way to get rid of it. But they have their modern representatives. We who live in a commercial community have seen many a blown-out bubble soaring and glittering, and then collapsing into a drop of soapsuds, and on the other hand, we are always hearing of notes and bank-books being found stowed away in some wretched hovel where a miser has died.

Now, I do not suppose that the author of this proverb attached any kind of moral to it in his own mind. It is simply a jotting of an observation drawn from a wide experience; and if he meant to teach any lesson by it, I suppose it was nothing more than that in regard to money, as to other things, we should avoid extremes, and should try to show what we are, and to be what we seem. But whilst thus I do not take it that there is any kind of moral or religious lesson in the writer's mind, I may venture, perhaps, to take this saying as being a picturesque illustration, putting in vivid fashion certain great truths which apply in all regions of life, and which find their highest application in regard to Christianity, and our relation to Jesus Christ. There, too, 'there is that maketh himself rich, and yet hath nothing; and there is that maketh himself poor, and yet'—or one might, perhaps, say *therefore*—'hath great riches.' It is from that point of view that I wish to look at the words at this time. I must begin with recalling to your mind,

I. Our universal poverty.

Whatever a man may think about himself, however he may estimate himself and conceit himself, there stand out two salient facts, the fact of universal dependence, and the fact of universal sinfulness, which ought to bear into every heart the consciousness of this poverty. A word or two about each of these two facts.

First, the fact of universal dependence. Now, wise men and deep thinkers have found a very hard problem in the question of how it is possible that there should be an infinite God and a finite universe standing, as it were, over against Him. I am not going to trouble you with the all-but-just-succeeding answers to that great problem which the various systems of thinking have given. These lie apart from my present purpose. But what I would point out is that, whatever else may be dark and difficult about the co-existence of these two, the infinite God and the finite universe, this at least is sun-clear, that the creature depends absolutely for everything on that infinite Creator. People talk sometimes, and we are all too apt to think, as if God had made the world and left it. And we are all too apt to think that, however we may owe the origination of our own personal existence to a divine act, the act was done when we began to be, and the life was given as a gift that could be separated from the Bestower. But that is not the state of the case at all. The real fact is that life is only continued because of the continued operation on every living thing, just as being is only continued by reason of the continued operation on every existing thing, of the Divine Power. 'In Him we live,' and the life is the result of the perpetual impartation from Himself 'in whom all things consist,' according to the profound word of the Apostle. Their being depends on their union with Him. If it were possible to cut a sunbeam in two, so that the further half of it should be separated from its vital union with the great central fire from which it rushed long, long ago, that further half would pale into darkness. And if you cut the connection between God and the creature, the creature shrivels into nothing. By Him the spring buds around us unfold themselves; by Him all things are. So, at the very foundation of our being there lies absolute dependence.

In like manner, all that we call faculties, capacities, and the like, are, in a far deeper sense than the conventional use of the word 'gift' implies, bestowments from Him. The Old Testament goes to the root of the matter when, speaking of the artistic and aesthetic skill of the workers in the fine arts in the Tabernacle, it says, 'the Spirit of the Lord' taught Bezaleel; and when, even in regard to the brute strength of Samson—surely the strangest hero of faith that ever existed—it says that when 'the Spirit of the Lord came upon him,' into his giant hands there was infused the strength by which he tore the lion's jaws asunder. In like manner, all the faculties that men possess they have simply because He has given them. 'What hast thou that thou hast not received? If thou hast received, why dost thou boast thyself?' So there is a great psalm that gathers everything that makes up human life, and traces it all to God, when it says, 'They shall be abundantly satisfied with the fatness of Thy house,' for from God comes all that sustains us; 'Thou shalt make them drink of the river of Thy pleasures,' for from God comes all that gladdens us; 'with Thee is the fountain of life,' for from Him flow all the tiny streams that make the life of all that live; 'in Thy light shall we see light,' for every power of perceiving, and all grace and lustre of purity, owe their source to Him. As well, then, might the pitcher boast itself of the sparkling water that it only holds, as well might the earthen jar plume itself on the treasure that has been deposited in it, as we make ourselves rich because of the riches that we have received. 'Let not the wise man glory in his wisdom, neither let the mighty man glory in his strength. Let not the rich man glory in his riches; but he that glorieth, let him glory in the Lord.'

Then, turn for a moment to the second of the facts on which this universal poverty depends, and that is the fact of universal sinfulness. Ah! there is one thing that is our own—

'If any power we have, it is to will.'

We have that strange faculty, which nobody has ever thoroughly explained yet, but which we all know to exist, of wrenching ourselves so far away from God, 'in whom we live and move and have our being,' that we can make our thoughts and ways, not merely lower than, but contradictory of, and antagonistic to, His thoughts, and His ways. Conscience tells us, and we all know it, that we are the causes of our own actions, though from Him come the powers by which we do them. The electricity comes from the central powerstation, but it depends on us what sort of wheels we make it drive, and what kind of work we set it to do. Make all allowances you like for circumstances—what they call nowadays 'environment,' by which formidable word some people seem to think that they have explained away a great many difficulties—make all allowances you like for inheritance—what they now call 'heredity,' by which other magic word people seem to think that they may largely obliterate the sense of responsibility and sin—allow as much as you like, in reason, for these, and there remains the indestructible consciousness in every man, 'I did it, and it was my fault that I did it; and the moral guilt remains.'

So, then, there are these two things, universal dependence and universal sinfulness, and on them is built the declaration of universal poverty. Duty is debt. Everybody knows that the two words come from the same root. What we ought is what we owe. We all owe an obedience which none of us has rendered. Ten thousand talents is the debt and—'they had nothing to pay.' We are like bankrupts that begin business with a borrowed capital, by reason of our absolute dependence; and so manage their concerns as to find themselves inextricably entangled in a labyrinth of obligations which they cannot discharge. We are all paupers. And so I come to the second point, and that is—

II. The poor rich man.

'There is that maketh himself rich, and yet hath nothing.' That describes accurately the type of man of whom there are thousands; of whom there are dozens listening to me at this moment; who ignores dependence and is not conscious of sin, and so struts about in self-complacent satisfaction with himself, and knows nothing of his true condition. There is nothing more tragic—and so it would be seen to be if it were not so common—than that a man, laden, as we each of us are, with a burden of evil that we cannot get rid of, should yet conceit himself to possess merits, virtues, graces, that ought to secure for him the admiration of his fellows, or, at least, to exempt him from their censure, and which he thinks, when he thinks about it at all, may perhaps secure for him the approbation of God. 'The deceitfulness of sin' is one of its mightiest powers. There is nothing that so blinds a man to the real moral character of actions as that obstinate self-complacency which approves of a thing because it is mine. You condemn in other people the very things you do yourself. You see all their ugliness in them; you do not recognise it when it is your deed. Many of you have never ventured upon a careful examination and appraisement of your own moral and religious character. You durst not, for you are afraid that it would turn out badly. So, like some insolvent who has not the courage to face the facts, you take refuge in defective bookkeeping, and think that that is as good as being solvent. Then you have far too low a standard, and one of the main reasons why you have so low a standard is just because the sins that you do have dulled your consciences, and like the Styrian peasants that eat arsenic, the poison does not poison you, and you do not feel yourself any the worse for it. Dear brethren! these are very rude things for me to say to you. I am saying them to myself as much as to you, and I would to God that you would listen to them, not because I say them, but because they are true. The great bulk of us know our own moral characters just as little as we know the sound of our own voices. I suppose if you could hear yourself speak you would say, 'I never knew that my voice sounded like that.' And I am quite sure that many of you, if the curtain could be drawn aside which is largely woven out of the black yarn of your own evil thoughts, and you could see yourselves as in a mirror, you would say, 'I had no notion that I looked like that.' 'There is that maketh himself rich, and yet hath nothing.'

Ay! and more than that. The making of yourself rich is the sure way to prevent yourself from ever being so. We see that in all other regions of life. If a student says to himself, 'Oh! I know all that subject,' the chances are that he will not get it up any more; and the further chance is that he will be 'ploughed' when the examination-day comes. If the artist stands before the picture, and says to himself, 'Well done, that is the realisation of my ideal!' he will paint no more anything worth looking at. And in any department, when a man says 'Lo! I have attained,' then he ceases to advance.

Now, bring all that to bear upon religion, upon Christ and His salvation, upon our own spiritual and religious and moral condition. The sense of imperfection is the salt of approximation to perfection. And the man that says 'I am rich' is condemning himself to poverty and pauperism. If you do not know your need, you will not go to look for the supply of it. If you fancy yourselves to be quite well, though a mortal disease has gripped you, you will take no medicine, nor have recourse to any physician. If you think that you have enough good to show for man's judgment and for God's, and have not been convinced of your dependence and your sinfulness, then Jesus Christ will be very little to you, and His great work as the Redeemer and Saviour of His people from their sins will be nothing to you. And so you will condemn yourselves to have nothing unto the very end.

I believe that this generation needs few things more than it needs a deepened consciousness of the reality of sin and of the depth and damnable nature of it. It is because people feel so little of the burden of their transgression that they care so little for that gentle Hand that lifts away their burden. It is because from much of popular religion—and, alas! that I should have to say it, from much of popular preaching—there has vanished the deep wholesome sense of poverty, that, from so much of popular religion, and preaching too, there has faded away the central light of the Gospel, the proclamation of the Cross by which is taken away the sin of the whole world.

So, lastly, my text brings before us—

III. The rich poor man.

'There is that maketh himself poor and yet'—or, as varied, the expression is, 'therefore hath great riches.' Jesus Christ has lifted the thoughts in my text into the very region into which I am trying to bring them, when in the first of all the Beatitudes, as they are called, 'He opened His mouth and said, Blessed are the poor in spirit, for theirs is the Kingdom of Heaven.' Poor, and therefore an owner of a kingdom! Now I need not, at this stage of my sermon, insist upon the fact that that consciousness of poverty is the only fitting attitude for any of us to take up in view of the two facts with which I started, the fact of our dependence and the fact of our sinfulness. What absurdity it seems for a man about whom these two things are true, that, as I said, he began with a borrowed capital, and has only incurred greater debts in his transactions, there should be any foothold left in his own estimation on which he can stand and claim to be anything but the pauper that he is. Oh! brethren, of all the hallucinations that we put upon ourselves in trying to believe that things are as we wish, there is none more subtle, more obstinate, more deeply dangerous than this, that a man full of evil should be so ignorant of his evil as to say, like that Pharisee in our Lord's parable, 'I thank Thee that I am not as other men are. I give tithes ... I pray ... I am this, that, and the other thing; not like that wretched publican over there.' Yes, this is the fit attitude for us,—'He would not so much as lift up his eyes to heaven.'

Then let me remind you that this wholesome recognition of facts about ourselves as they are is the sure way to possess the wealth. Of course, it is possible for a man by some mighty influence or other brought to bear upon him, to see himself as God sees him, and then, if there is nothing more than that, he is tortured with 'the sorrow that worketh death.' Judas 'went out and hanged himself'; Peter 'went out and wept bitterly.' The one was sent 'to his own place,' wherever that was; the other was sent foremost of the Twelve. If you see your poverty, let self-distrust be the nadir, the lowest point, and let faith be the complementary high point, the zenith. The rebound from self-distrust to trust in Christ is that which makes the consciousness of poverty the condition of receiving wealth.

And what wealth it is!—the wealth of a peaceful conscience, of a quiet heart, of lofty aims, of a pure mind, of strength according to our need, of an immortal hope, of a treasure in the heavens that faileth not, 'where neither moth nor rust doth corrupt; where thieves do not break through nor steal.' Blessed be God! the more we have the riches of glory in Christ Jesus, the more shall we feel that we have nothing, and that all is His, and none of it ours. And so, as the rivers run in the valleys, and the high mountain-tops are dry and barren, the grace which makes us rich will run in the low ground of our conscious humiliation and nothingness.

Dear brother! do you estimate yourself as you are? Have you taken stock of yourself? Have you got away from the hallucination of possessing wealth? Has your sense of need led you to cease from trust in yourself, and to put all your trust in Jesus Christ? Have you taken the wealth which He freely gives to all who sue *in forma pauperis?* He does not ask you to bring anything but debts and sins, emptiness and weakness, and penitent faith. He will strengthen the weakness, fill the emptiness, forgive the sins, cancel the debts, and make you 'rich toward God.' I beseech you to listen to Him, speaking from heaven, and taking up the strain of this text: 'Because thou sayest I am rich, and increased with goods, and have need of nothing; and knowest not that thou art wretched, and miserable, and poor, and blind, and naked, I counsel thee to buy of Me gold tried in the fire, that thou mayest be rich.' And then you will be of those blessed poor ones who are 'rich through faith, and heirs of the Kingdom.'

THE TILLAGE OF THE POOR

'Much food is in the tillage of the poor.'—PROVERBS xiii. 23.

Palestine was a land of small peasant proprietors, and the institution of the Jubilee was intended to prevent the acquisition of large estates by any Israelite. The consequence, as intended, was a level of modest prosperity. It was 'the tillage of the poor,' the careful, diligent husbandry of the man who had only a little patch of land to look after, that filled the storehouses of the Holy Land. Hence the proverb of our text arose. It preserves the picture of the economical conditions in which it originated, and it is capable of, and is intended to have, an application to all forms and fields of work. In all it is true that the bulk of the harvested results are due, not to the large labours of the few, but to the minute, unnoticed toils of the many. Small service is true service, and the aggregate of such produces large crops. Spade husbandry gets most out of the ground. The labourer's allotment of half an acre is generally more prolific than the average of the squire's estate. Much may be made of slender gifts, small resources, and limited opportunities if carefully cultivated, as they should be, and as their very slenderness should stimulate their being.

One of the psalms accuses 'the children of Ephraim' because, 'being armed and carrying bows, they turned back in the day of battle.' That saying deduces obligation from equipment, and preaches a stringent code of duty to those who are in any direction largely gifted. Power to its last particle is duty, and not small is the crime of those who, with great capacities, have small desire to use them, and leave the brunt of the battle to half-trained soldiers, badly armed.

But the imagery of the fight is not sufficient to include all aspects of Christian effort. The peaceful toil of the 'husbandman that labours' stands, in one of Paul's letters, side by side with the heroism of the 'man that warreth.' Our text gives us the former image, and so supplements that other.

It completes the lesson of the psalm in another respect, as insisting on the importance, not of the well endowed, but of the slenderly furnished, who are immensely in the majority. This text is a message to ordinary, mediocre people, without much ability or influence.

I. It teaches, first, the responsibility of small gifts.

It is no mere accident that in our Lord's great parable He represents the man with the *one* talent as the hider of his gift. There is a certain pleasure in doing what we can do, or fancy we can do, well. There is a certain pleasure in the exercise of any kind of gift, be it of body or mind; but when we know that we are but very slightly gifted by Him, there is a temptation to say, 'Oh!

it does not matter much whether I contribute my share to this, that, or the other work or no. I am but a poor man. My half-crown will make but a small difference in the total. I am possessed of very little leisure. The few minutes that I can spare for individual cultivation, or for benevolent work, will not matter at all. I am only an insignificant unit; nobody pays any attention to my opinion. It does not in the least signify whether I make my influence felt in regard of social, religious, or political questions, and the like. I can leave all that to the more influential men. My littleness at least has the prerogative of immunity. My little finger would produce such a slight impact on the scale that it is indifferent whether I apply it or not. It is a good deal easier for me to wrap up my talent—which, after all, is only a threepenny bit, and not a talent—and put it away and do nothing.'

Yes, but then you forget, dear friend! that responsibility does not diminish with the size of the gifts, but that there is as great responsibility for the use of the smallest as for the use of the largest, and that although it does not matter very much to anybody but yourself what you do, it matters all the world to you.

But then, besides that, my text tells us that it does matter whether the poor man sets himself to make the most of his little patch of ground or not. 'There is much food in the tillage of the poor.' The slenderly endowed are the immense majority. There is a genius or two here and there, dotted along the line of the world's and the Church's history. The great men and wise men and mighty men and wealthy men may be counted by units, but the men that are not very much of anything are to be counted by millions. And unless we can find some stringent law of responsibility that applies to them, the bulk of the human race will be under no obligation to do anything either for God or for their fellows, or for themselves. If I am absolved from the task of bringing my weight to bear on the side of right because my weight is infinitesimal, and I am only one in a million, suppose all the million were to plead the same excuse; what then? Then there would not be any weight on the side of the right at all. The barns in Palestine were not filled by farming on a great scale like that pursued away out on the western prairies, where one man will own, and his servants will plough a furrow for miles long, but they were filled by the small industries of the owners of tiny patches.

The 'tillage of the poor,' meaning thereby not the mendicant, but the peasant owner of a little plot, yielded the bulk of the 'food.' The wholesome old proverb, 'many littles make a mickle,' is as true about the influence brought to bear in the world to arrest evil and to sweeten corruption as it is about anything besides. Christ has a great deal more need of the cultivation of the small patches that He gives to the most of us than He has even of the cultivation of the large estates that He bestows on a few. Responsibility is not to be measured by amount of gift, but is equally stringent, entire, and absolute whatsoever be the magnitude of the endowments from which it arises.

Let me remind you, too, how the same virtues and excellences can be practised in the administering of the smallest as in that of the greatest gifts. Men say—I dare say some of you have said—'Oh! if I were eloquent like So-and-so; rich like somebody else; a man of weight and importance like some other, how I would consecrate my powers to the Master! But I am slow of speech, or nobody minds me, or I have but very little that I can give.' Yes! 'He that is faithful in that which is least is faithful also in much.' If you do not utilise the capacity possessed, to increase the estate would only be to increase the crop of weeds from its uncultivated clods. We never palm off a greater deception on ourselves than when we try to hoodwink conscience by pleading bounded gifts as an excuse for boundless indolence, and to persuade ourselves that if we could do more we should be less inclined to do nothing. The most largely endowed has no more obligation and no fairer field than the most slenderly gifted lies under and possesses.

All service coming from the same motive and tending to the same end is the same with God. Not the magnitude of the act, but the motive thereof, determines the whole character of the life of which it is a part. The same graces of obedience, consecration, quick sympathy, self-denying effort may be cultivated and manifested in the spending of a halfpenny as in the administration of millions. The smallest rainbow in the tiniest drop that hangs from some sooty eave and catches the sunlight has precisely the same lines, in the same order, as the great arch that strides across half the sky. If you go to the Giant's Causeway, or to the other end of it amongst the Scotch Hebrides, you will find the hexagonal basaltic pillars all of identically the same pattern and shape, whether their height be measured by feet or by tenths of an inch. Big or little, they obey exactly the same law. There is 'much food in the tillage of the poor.'

II. But now, note, again, how there must be a diligent cultivation of the small gifts.

The inventor of this proverb had looked carefully and sympathetically at the way in which the little peasant proprietors worked; and he saw in that a pattern for all life. It is not always the case, of course, that a little holding means good husbandry, but it is generally so; and you will find few waste corners and few unweeded patches on the ground of a man whose whole ground is measured by rods instead of by miles. There will usually be little waste time, and few neglected opportunities of working in the case of the peasant whose subsistence, with that of his family, depends on the diligent and wise cropping of the little patch that does belong to him.

And so, dear brethren! if you and I have to take our place in the ranks of the one-talented men, the commonplace run of ordinary people, the more reason for us to enlarge our gifts by a sedulous diligence, by an unwearied perseverance, by a keen look-out for all opportunities of service, and above all by a prayerful dependence upon Him from whom alone comes the power to toil, and who alone gives the increase. The less we are conscious of large gifts the more we should be bowed in dependence on Him from whom cometh 'every good and perfect gift'; and who gives according to His wisdom; and the more earnestly should we use that slender possession which God may have given us. Industry applied to small natural capacity will do far more than larger power rusted away by sloth. You all know that it is so in regard of daily life, and common business, and the acquisition of mundane sciences and arts. It is just as true in regard to the Christian race, and to the Christian Church's work of witness.

Who are they who have done the most in this world for God and for men? The largely endowed men? 'Not many wise, not many mighty, not many noble are called.' The coral insect is microscopic, but it will build up from the profoundest depth of the ocean a reef against which the whole Pacific may dash in vain. It is the small gifts that, after all, are the important ones. So let us cultivate them the more earnestly the more humbly we think of our own capacity. 'Play well thy part; there all the honour lies.' God, who has builded up some of the towering Alps out of mica-flakes, builds up His Church out of infinitesimally small particles—slenderly endowed men touched by the consecration of His love.

III. Lastly, let me remind you of the harvest reaped from these slender gifts when sedulously tilled.

Two great results of such conscientious cultivation and use of small resources and opportunities may be suggested as included in that abundant 'food' of which the text speaks.

The faithfully used faculty increases. 'To him that hath shall be given.' 'Oh! if I had a wider sphere how I would flame in it, and fill it!' Then twinkle your best in your little sphere, and that will bring a wider one some time or other. For, as a rule, and in the general, though with exceptions, opportunities come to the man that can use them; and roughly, but yet substantially, men are set in this world where they can shine to the most advantage to God. Fill your place; and if you, like Paul, have borne witness for the Master in little Jerusalem, He will not keep you there, but carry you to bear witness for Him in imperial Rome itself.

The old fable of the man who told his children to dig all over the field and they would find treasure, has its true application in regard to Christian effort and faithful stewardship of the gifts bestowed upon us. The sons found no gold, but they improved the field, and secured its bearing golden harvests, and they strengthened their own muscles, which was better than gold. So if we want larger endowments let us honestly use what we possess, and use will make growth.

The other issue, about which I need not say more than a word, is that the final reward of all faithful service—'Enter thou into the joy of thy Lord' is said, not to the brilliant, but to the 'faithful' servant. In that great parable, which is the very text-book of this whole subject of gifts and responsibilities and recompense, the men who were entrusted with unequal sums used these unequal sums with equal diligence, as is manifest by the fact that they realised an equal rate of increase. He that got two talents made two more out of them, and he that had five did no more; for he, too, but doubled his capital. So, because the poorer servant with his two, and the richer with his ten, had equally cultivated their diversely-measured estates, they were identical in reward; and to each of them the same thing is said: 'Enter thou into the joy of thy Lord.' It matters little whether we copy some great picture upon a canvas as big as the side of a house, or upon a thumbnail; the main thing is that we copy it. If we truly employ whatsoever gifts God has given to us, then we shall be accepted according to that we have, and not according to that we have not.

SIN THE MOCKER

'Fools make a mock at sin; but among the righteous there is favour.'— Proverbs xiv, 9.

The wisdom of this Book of Proverbs is not simply intellectual, but it has its roots in reverence and obedience to God, and for its accompaniment, righteousness. The wise man is the good man, and the good man is the godly man. And as is wisdom, so its opposite, folly, is not only intellectual feebleness—the bad man is a fool, and the godless is a bad man. The greatest amount of brain-power cultivated to the highest degree does not make a man wise, and about many a student and thinker God pronounces the sentence 'Thou fool!'

That does not mean that all sin is ignorance, as we sometimes hear it said with a great show of tolerant profundity. There is some ignorance in all sin, but the essence of sin is the aversion of the will from a law and from a Person, not the defect of the understanding. So far from all sin being but ignorance, and therefore blameless, there is no sin without knowledge, and the measure of ignorance is the measure of blamelessness; unless the ignorance be itself, as it often is, criminal. Ignorance is one thing, folly is another.

One more remark by way of introduction must be made on the language of our text. The margin of the Revised Version correctly turns it completely round, and for 'the foolish make a mock at guilt,' would read, 'guilt mocketh at the foolish.' In the original the verb in our text is in the singular, and the only singular noun to go with it is 'guilt.' The thought then here is, that sin tempts men into its clutches, and then gibes and taunts them. It is a solemn and painful subject, but perhaps this text rightly pondered may help to save some of us from hearing the mocking laugh which echoes through the empty chambers of many an empty soul.

I. Sin mocks us by its broken promises.

The object immediately sought by any wrong act may be attained. In sins of sense, the appetite is gratified; in other sins, the desire that urged to them attains its end. But what then? The temptation lay in the imagination that, the wrong thing being done, an inward good would result, and it does not; for even if the immediate object be secured, other results, all unforeseen, force themselves on us which spoil the hoped for good. The sickle cuts down tares as well as wheat, and the reaper's hands are filled with poisonous growths as well as with corn. There is a revulsion of feeling from the thing that before the sin was done attracted. The hideous story of the sin of David's son, Amnon, puts in ugliest shape the universal experience of men who are tempted to sin and are victims of the revulsion that follows—He 'hated her exceedingly, so that the hatred wherewith he hated her was greater than the love wherewith he had loved her.' Conscience, which was overpowered and unheard amid the loud cries of desire, speaks. We find out the narrow limits of satisfaction. The satisfied appetite has no further driving power, but lies down to sleep off its debauch, and ceases to be a factor for the time. Inward discord, the schism between duty and inclination, sets up strife in the very sanctuary of the soul. We are dimly conscious of the evil done as robbing us of power to do right. We cannot pray, and would be glad to forget God. And a self thus racked, impoverished, and weakened, is what a man gains by the sin that promised him so much and hid so much from him.

Or if these consequences are in any measure silenced and stifled, a still more melancholy mockery betrays him, in the continuance of the illusion that he is happy and all is well, when all the while he is driving headlong to destruction. Many a man orders his life so that it is like a ship that sails with huzzas and bedizened with flags while a favouring breeze fills its sails, but comes back to port battered and all but waterlogged, with its canvas 'lean, rent, and beggared by the strumpet wind.' It is always a mistake to try to buy happiness by doing wrong. The price is rigorously demanded, but the *quid pro quo* is not given, or if it seems to be so, there is something else given too, which takes all the savour out of the composite whole. The 'Folly' of the earlier half of this book woos men by her sweet invitations, and promises the sweetness of stolen waters and the pleasantness of bread eaten in secret, but she hides the fact, which the listener to her seducing voice has to find out for himself after he has drunk of the stolen waters and tasted the maddening pleasantness of her bread eaten in secret, that 'her guests are in the depths of Sheol.' The temptations that seek to win us to do wrong and dazzle us by fair visions are but 'juggling fiends that keep the word of promise to the ear, and break it to the hope.'

II. Sin mocks fools by making them its slaves.

There is not only a revulsion of feeling from the evil thing done that was so tempting before, but there is a dreadful change in the voice of the temptress. Before her victim had done the sin, she whispered hints of how little a thing it was. 'Don't make such a mountain of a molehill. It is a very small matter. You can easily give it up when you like.' But when the deed is done, then her mocking laugh rings out, 'I have got you now and you cannot get away.' The prey is seduced into the trap by a carefully prepared bait, and as soon as its hesitating foot steps on to the slippery floor, down falls the door and escape is impossible, We are tempted to sin by the delusion that we are shaking off restraints that fetter our manhood, and that it is spirited to do as we like, and as soon as we have sinned we discover that we were pleasing not ourselves but a taskmaster, and that while the voice said, 'Show yourself a man, beyond these petty, old-fashioned maxims'; the meaning of it was, 'Become my slave.'

Sin grows in accordance with an awful necessity, so that it is never in a sinner's power to promise himself 'It is only this one time that I will do the wrong thing. Let me have one lapse and I will abjure the evil for ever after.' We have to reckon with the tremendous power of habit, and to bethink ourselves that a man may never commit a given sin, but that if he has committed it once, it is all but impossible that he will stop there. The incline is too slippery and the ice too smooth to risk a foot on it. Habit dominates, outward circumstances press, there springs up a need for repeating the draught, and for its being more highly spiced. Sin begets sin as fast as the green flies which infest rose-bushes. One has heard of slavers on the African coast speaking negroes fair, and tempting them on board by wonderful promises, but once the poor creatures are in the ship, then on with the hatches and, if need be, the chains.

III. Sin mocks fools by unforeseen consequences.

These are carefully concealed or madly disregarded, while we are in the stage of merely being tempted, but when we have done the evil, they are unmasked, like a battery against a detachment that has been trapped. The previous denial that anything will come of the sin, and the subsequent proclamation that this ugly issue has come of it, are both parts of sin's mockery, and one knows not which is the more fiendish, the laugh with which she promises impunity or that with which she tells of the certainty of retribution. We may be mocked, but 'God is not mocked. Whatever a man soweth, that'—and not some other growth—'shall he also reap.' We dwell in an all-related order of things, in which no act but has its appropriate consequences, and in which it is only fools who say to themselves, 'I did not think it would matter much.' Each act of ours is at once sowing and reaping; a sowing, inasmuch as it sets in motion a train the issues of which may not be realised by us till the act has long been forgotten; a reaping, inasmuch as what we are and do to-day is the product of what we were and did in a forgotten past. We are what we are, because we were long ago what we were. As in these composite photographs, which are produced by laying one individual likeness on another, our present selves have our past selves preserved in them. We do not need to bring in a divine Judge into human life in order to be sure that, by the play of the natural laws of cause and effect, 'every transgression and disobedience receives its just recompense of reward.' Given the world as it is, and the continuous identity of a man, and you have all that is needed for an Iliad of woes flowing from every life that makes terms with sin. If we gather into one dismal pile the weakening of power for good, the strengthening of impulses to evil, the inward poverty, the unrest, the gnawings of conscience or its silence, the slavery under evil often loathed even while it is being obeyed, the dreary sense of inability to mend oneself, and often the wreck of outward life which dog our sins like sleuth-hounds, surely we shall not need to imagine a future tribunal in order to be sure that sin is a murderess, or to hear her laugh as she mocks her helpless victims.

But as surely as there are in this present world experiences which must be regarded as consequences of sin, so surely do they all assume a more dreadful character and take on the office of prophets of a future. If man lives beyond the grave, there is nothing to suggest that he will there put off character as he puts off the bodily life. He will be there what he has made himself here. Only he will be so more intensely, more completely. The judgments of earth foretell and foreshadow a judgment beyond earth.

There is but one more word that I would say, and it is this. Jesus has come to set the captives of sin free from its mockery, its tyranny, its worst consequences. He breaks the power of past evil to domineer over us. He gives us a new life within, which has no heritage of evil to pervert it, no memories of evil to discourage it, no bias towards evil to lead it astray. As for the sins that we have done, He is ready to forgive, to seal to us God's forgiveness, and to take from our own self-condemnation all its bitterness and much of its hopelessness. For the past, His blood has taken away its guilt and power. For the future it sets us free from the mockery of our sin, and assures us of a future which will not be weakened or pained by remembrances of a sinful past. Sin mocks at fools, but they who have Christ for their Redeemer, their Righteousness, and their Life can smile at her impotent rage, and mock at her and her impotent attempts to terrify them and assert her lost power with vain threats.

HOLLOW LAUGHTER, SOLID JOY

'Even in laughter the heart is sorrowful; and the end of that mirth is heaviness.'—PROVERBS xiv. 13.

'These things have I spoken unto you, that My joy may be in you, and that your joy may be fulfilled.'—JOHN xv. 11 (R.V.).

A poet, who used to be more fashionable than he is now, pronounces 'happiness' to be our being's end and aim. That is not true, except under great limitations and with many explanations. It may be regarded as God's end, but it is ruinous to make it man's aim. It is by no means the highest conception of the Gospel to say that it makes men happy, however true it may be. The highest is that it makes them good. I put these two texts together, not only because they bring out the contrast between the laughter which is hollow and fleeting and the joy which is perfect and perpetual, but also because they suggest to us the difference in kind and object between earthly and heavenly joys; which difference underlies the other between the boisterous laughter in which is no mirth and no continuance and the joy which is deep and abiding.

In the comparison which I desire to make between these two texts we must begin with that which is deepest, and consider—

I. The respective objects of earthly and heavenly joy.

Our Lord's wonderful words suggest that they who accept His sayings, that they who have His word abiding in them, have in a very deep sense His joy implanted in their hearts, to brighten and elevate their joys as the sunshine flashes into silver the ripples of the lake. What then were the sources of the calm joys of 'the Man of Sorrows'? Surely His was the perfect instance of 'rejoicing in the Lord always'—an unbroken communion with the Father. The consciousness that the divine pleasure ever rested on Him, and that all His thoughts, emotions, purposes, and acts were in perfect harmony with the perfect will of the perfect God, filled His humanity up to the very brim with gladness which the world could not take away, and which remains for us for ever as a type to which all our gladness must be conformed if it is to be worthy of Him and of us. As one of the Psalmists says, God is to be 'the gladness of our joy.' It is in Him, gazed upon by the faith and love of an obedient spirit, sought after by aspiration and possessed inwardly in peaceful communion, confirmed by union with Him in the acts of daily obedience, that the true joy of every human life is to be realised. They who have drunk of this deep fountain of gladness will not express their joy in boisterous laughter, which is the hollower the louder it is, and the less lasting the more noisy, but will manifest itself 'in the depth and not the tumult of the soul.'

Nor must we forget that 'My joy' co-existed with a profound experience of sorrow to which no human sorrow was ever like. Let us not forget that, while His joy filled His soul to the brim, He was 'acquainted with grief'; and let us not wonder if the strange surface contradiction is repeated in ourselves. It is more Christlike to have inexpressibly deep joy with surface sorrow, than to have a shallow laughter masking a hurtful sorrow.

We have to set the sources of earthly gladness side by side with those of Christ's joy to be aware of a contrast. His sprang from within, the world's is drawn from without. His came from union with the Father, the world's largely depends on ignoring God. His needed no supplies from the gratifications ministered by sense, and so independent of the presence or absence of such; the world's need the constant contributions of outward good, and when these are cut off they droop and die. He who depends on outward circumstances for his joy is the slave of externals and the sport of time and chance.

II. The Christian's joy is full, the world's partial.

All human joys touch but part of our nature, the divine fills and satisfies all. In the former there is always some portion of us unsatisfied, like the deep pits on the moon's surface into which no light shines, and which show black on the silver face. No human joys wait to still conscience, which sits at the banquet like the skeleton that Egyptian feasters set at their tables. The old story told of a magician's palace blazing with lighted windows, but there was always one dark;—what shrouded figure sat behind it? Is there not always a surly 'elder brother' who will not come in however the musicians may pipe and the servants dance? Appetite may be satisfied, but what of conscience, and reason, and the higher aspirations of the soul? The laughter that echoes through the soul is the hollower the louder it is, and reverberates most through empty spaces.

But when Christ's joy remains in us our joy will be full. Its flowing tide will rush into and placidly occupy all the else oozy shallows of our hearts, even into the narrowest crannies its penetrating waters will pass, and everywhere will bring a flashing surface that will reflect in our hearts the calm blue above. We need nothing else if we have Christ and His joy within us. If we have everything else, we need His joy within us, else ours will never be full.

III. The heavenly joys are perpetual, the earthly joys transient.

Many of our earthly joys die in the very act of being enjoyed. Those which depend on the gratification of some appetite expire in fruition, and at each recurrence are less and less complete. The influence of habit works in two ways to rob all such joys of their power to minister to us—it increases the appetite and decreases the power of the object to satisfy. Some are followed by swift revulsion and remorse; all soon become stale; some are followed by quick remorse; some are necessarily left behind as we go on in life. To the old man the pleasures of youth are but like children's toys long since outgrown and left behind. All are at the mercy of externals. Those which we have not left we have to leave. The saddest lives are those of pleasure-seekers, and the saddest deaths are those of the men who sought for joy where it was not to be found, and sought for their gratification in a world which leaves them, and which they have to leave.

There is a realm where abide 'fullness of joy and pleasures for ever more.' Surely they order their lives most wisely who look for their joys to nothing that earth holds, and have taken for their own the ancient vow: 'Though the fig-tree shall not blossom, neither shall fruit be in the vine.... Yet I will rejoice in the Lord, I will joy in the God of my salvation.' If 'My joy' abides in us in its calm and changeless depth, our joy will be 'full' whatever our circumstances may be; and we shall hear at last the welcome: 'Enter thou into the joy of thy Lord.'

SATISFIED FROM SELF

'... A good man shall be satisfied from himself.'—PROVERBS xiv. 14.

At first sight this saying strikes one as somewhat unlike the ordinary Scripture tone, and savouring rather of a Stoical self-complacency; but we recall parallel sayings, such as Christ's words, 'The water that I shall give him shall be in him a well of water'; and the Apostle's, 'Then shall he have rejoicing in himself alone.' We further note that the text has an antithetic parallel in the preceding clause, where the picture is drawn of 'a backslider in heart,' as 'filled with his own ways'; so that both clauses set forth the familiar but solemn thought that a man's deeds react upon the doer, and apart from all thoughts of divine judgment, themselves bring certain retribution. To grasp the inwardness of this saying we must note that—

I. Goodness comes from godliness.

There is no more striking proof that most men are bad than the notion which they have of what is good. The word has been degraded to mean in common speech little more than amiability, and is applied with little discrimination to characters of which little more can be said than that they are facile and indulgent of evil. 'A good fellow' may be a very bad man. At the highest the epithet connotes merely more or less admirable motives and more or less admirable deeds as their results, whilst often its use is no more than a piece of unmeaning politeness. That was what the young ruler meant by addressing Christ as 'Good Master'; and Christ's answer to him set him, and should set us, on asking ourselves why we call very ordinary men and very ordinary actions 'good.' The scriptural notion is immensely deeper, and the scriptural employment of the word is immensely more restricted. It is more inward: it means that motives should be right before it calls any action good; it means that our central and all-influencing motive should be love to God and regard to His will. That is the Old Testament point of view as well as the New. Or to put it in other words, the 'good man' of the Bible is a man in whom outward righteousness flows from inward devotion and love to God. These two elements make up the character: godliness is an inseparable part of goodness, is the inseparable foundation of goodness, and the sole condition on which it is possible. But from this conception follows, that a man may be truly called good, although not perfect. He may be so and yet have many failures. The direction of his aspirations, not the degree to which these are fulfilled, determines his character, and his right to be reckoned a good man. Why was David called 'a man after God's own heart,' notwithstanding his frightful fall? Was it not because that sin was contrary to the main direction of his life, and because he had struggled to his feet again, and with tears and self-abasement, yet with unconquerable desire and hope, 'pressed toward the mark for the prize of his high calling'? David in the Old Testament and Peter in the New bid us be of good cheer, and warn us against the too common error of thinking that goodness means perfection. 'The new moon with a ragged edge' is even in its imperfections beautiful, and in its thinnest circlet prophesies the perfect round.

Remembering this inseparable connection between godliness and goodness we further note that—

II. Godliness brings satisfaction.

There is a grim contrast between the two halves of this verse. The former shows us the backslider in heart as filled 'with his own ways.' He gets weary with satiety; with his doings he 'will be sick of them'; and the things which at first delighted will finally disgust and be done without zest. There is nothing sadder than the gloomy faces often seen in the world's festivals. But, on the other hand, the godly man will be satisfied from within. This is no Stoical proclamation of self-sufficingness. Self by itself satisfies no man, but self, become the abiding-place of God, does satisfy. A man alone is like 'the chaff which the wind driveth away'; but, rooted in God, he is 'like a tree planted by the rivers of water, whose leaf does not wither.' He has found all that he needs. God is no longer without him but within; and he who can say, 'I live, yet not I, but Christ liveth in me,' has within him the secret of peace and the source of satisfaction which can never say 'I thirst.' Such an inward self, in which God dwells and through which His sweet presence manifests itself in the renewed nature, sets man free from all dependence for blessedness on externals. We hang on them and are in despair if we lose them, because we have not the life of God within us. He who has such an indwelling, and he only, can truly say, 'All my possessions I carry with me.' Take him and strip from him, film after film, possessions, reputation, friends; hack him limb from limb, and as long as there is body enough left to keep life in him, he can say, 'I have all and abound.' 'Ye took joyfully the spoiling of your possessions, knowing that ye have your own selves for a better possession.'

III. Godly goodness brings inward satisfaction.

No man is satisfied with himself until he has subjugated himself. What makes men restless and discontented is their tossing, anarchical desires. To live by impulse, or passion, or by anything but love to God, is to make ourselves our own tormentors. It is always true that he 'who loveth his life shall lose it,' and loses it by the very act of loving it. Most men's lives are like the troubled sea, 'which cannot rest,' and whose tossing surges, alas! 'cast up mire and dirt,' for their restless lives bring to the surface much that was meant to lie undisturbed in the depths.

But he who has subdued himself is like some still lake which 'heareth not the loud winds when they call,' and mirrors the silent heavens on its calm surface. But further, goodness brings satisfaction, because, as the Psalmist says, 'in keeping Thy commandments there is great reward.' There is a glow accompanying even partial obedience which diffuses itself with grateful warmth through the whole being of a man. And such goodness tends to the preservation of health of soul as natural, simple living to the health of the body. And that general sense of well-being brings with it a satisfaction compared with which all the feverish bliss of the voluptuary is poor indeed.

But we must not forget that satisfaction from one's self is not satisfaction *with* one's self. There will always be the imperfection which will always prevent self-righteousness. The good man after the Bible pattern most deeply knows his faults, and in that very consciousness is there a deep joy. To be ever aspiring onwards, and to know that our aspiration is no vain dream, this is joy. Still to press 'toward the mark,' still to have 'the yet untroubled world which gleams before us as we move,' and to know that we shall attain if we follow on, this is the highest bliss. Not the accomplishment of our ideal, but the cherishing of it, is the true delight of life.

Such self-satisfying goodness comes only through Christ. He makes it possible for us to love God and to trust Him. Only when we know 'the love wherewith He has loved us,' shall we love with a love which will be the motive power of our lives. He makes it possible to live outward lives of obedience, which, imperfect as it is, has 'great reward.' He makes it possible for us to attain the yet unattained, and to be sure that we 'shall be like Him, for we shall see Him as He is.' He has said, 'The water that I shall give him shall be in him a well of water springing up unto everlasting life.' Only when we can say, 'I live, yet not I, but Christ liveth in me,' will it be true of us in its fullest sense, 'A good man shall be satisfied from himself.'

WHAT I THINK OF MYSELF AND WHAT GOD THINKS OF ME

'All the ways of a man are clean in his own eyes; but the Lord weigheth the spirits.'—PROVERBS xvi. 2.

'All the ways of a man'—then there is no such thing as being conscious of having gone wrong, and having got into miry and foul ways? Of course there is; and equally of course a broad statement such as this of my text is not to be pressed into literal accuracy, but is a simple, general assertion of what we all know to be true, that we have a strange power of blinding ourselves as to what is wrong in ourselves and in our actions. Part of the cure for that lies in the thought in the second clause of the text—'But the Lord weigheth the spirits.' He weighs them in a balance, or as a man might take up something and poise it on his palm, moving his hand up and down till his muscles by their resistance gave him some inkling of its weight. But what is it that God weighs? 'The spirits.' We too often content ourselves with looking at our ways; God looks at ourselves. He takes the inner man into account, estimates actions by motives, and so very often differs from our judgment of ourselves and of one another.

Now so far the verse of my text carries me, and as a rule we have to keep ourselves within the limits of each verse in reading this Book of Proverbs, for two adjoining verses have very seldom anything to do with each other. But in the present case they have, for here is what follows: 'Commit thy works unto the Lord, and thy thoughts' (about thyself and everything else) 'shall be established.' That is to say, since we make such terrible blunders about the moral character of our own works, and since side by side with these erroneous estimates there is God's absolutely correct and all-penetrating one, common sense says: 'Put yourself into His hands, and then it will be all right.' So we consider now these very well-worn and familiar thoughts as to our strange blunders about ourselves, as to the contemporaneous divine estimate, which is absolutely correct, and as to the practical issues that come from two facts.

I. Our strange power of blinding ourselves.

It is difficult to make so threadbare a commonplace at all impressive. But yet if we would only take this thought, 'All the ways of a man'—that is me—'are right in his own eyes'—that is, my eyes—and apply it directly to our own personal experience and thoughts of ourselves, we should find that, like every other commonplace of morality and religion, the apparently toothless generality has sharp enough teeth, and that the trite truth flashes up into strange beauty, and has power to purify and guide our lives. Some one says that 'recognised truths lie bedridden in the dormitory of the soul, side by side with exploded errors.' And I am afraid that that is true of this thought, that we cannot truly estimate ourselves.

'All the ways of a man are right in his own eyes.' For to begin with, we all know that there is nothing that we so habitually neglect as the bringing of conscience to bear right through all our lives. Sometimes it is because there is a temptation that appeals very strongly, perhaps to sense, perhaps to some strong inclination which has been strengthened by indulgence. And when the craving arises, that is no time to begin asking, 'Is it right, or is it wrong to yield?' That question stands small chance of being wisely considered at a moment when, under the goading of roused desire, a man is like a mad bull when it charges. It drops its head and shuts its eyes, and goes right forward, and no matter whether it smashes its horns against an iron gate, and damages them and itself, or not, on it will go. So when great temptations rise—and we all know such times in our lives—we are in no condition to discuss that question with ourselves. Sometimes the craving is so vehement that if we could not get this thing that we want without putting our hands through the sulphurous smoke of the bottomless pit, we should thrust them out to grasp it. But in regard to the smaller commonplace matters of daily life, too, we all know that there are whole regions of our lives which seem to us to be so small that it is hardly worth while summoning the august thought of 'right or wrong?' to decide them. Yes, and a thousand smugglers that go across a frontier, each with a little package of contraband goods that does not pay any duty, make a large aggregate at the year's end. It is the trifles of life that shape life, and it is to them that we so frequently fail in applying, honestly and rigidly, the test, 'Is this right or wrong?' 'He that is faithful in that which is least,' and conscientious down to the smallest things, 'is faithful also in much.' The legal maxim has it, 'The law does not care about the very smallest matters.' What that precisely means, as a legal maxim, I do not profess to know, but it is rank heresy in regard to conduct and morality. Look after the pennies, and the pounds will look after themselves. Get the habit of bringing conscience to bear on little things, or you will never be able to bring it to bear when great temptations come and the crises emerge in your lives. Thus, by reason of that deficiency in the habitual application of conscience to bur lives, we slide through, and take for granted that all our ways are right in our eyes.

Then there is another thing: we not only neglect the rigid application of conscience to all our lives, but we have a double standard, and the notion of right and wrong which we apply to our neighbours is very different from that which we apply to ourselves. No wonder that the criminal is acquitted, and goes away from the tribunal 'without a stain on his character,' when he is his own judge and jury. 'All the ways of a man are right in his own eyes,' but the very same 'ways' that you allow to pass muster and condone in yourselves, you visit with sharp and unfailing censure in others. That strange self-complacency which we have, which is perfectly undisturbed by the most general confessions of sinfulness, and only shies when it is brought up to particular details of faults, we all know is very deep in ourselves.

Then there is another thing to be remembered, and that is—the enormous and the tragical influence of habit in dulling the mirror of our souls, on which our deeds are reflected in their true image. There are places in Europe where the peasantry have become so accustomed to minute and constantly repeated doses of arsenic that it is actually a minister of health to them, and what would poison you is food for them. We all know that we may sit in a hall like this, packed full and steaming, while the condensed breath is running down the windows, and never be aware of the foulness of the odours and the air. But when we go out and feel the sweet, pure breath of the unpolluted atmosphere, then we know how habit has dulled the lungs. And so habit dulls the conscience. According to the old saying, the man that began by carrying a calf can carry an ox at the end, and feel no burden. What we are accustomed to do we scarcely ever recognise to be wrong, and it is these things which pass because they are habitual that do more to wreck lives than occasional outbursts of far worse evils, according to the world's estimate of them. Habit dulls the eye.

Yes; and more than that, the conscience needs educating just as much as any other faculty. A man says, 'My conscience acquits me'; then the question is, 'And what sort of a conscience have you got, if it acquits you?' All that your conscience says is, 'It is right to do what is right, it is wrong to do what is wrong.' But for the explanation of what is wrong and what is right you have to go somewhere else than to your consciences. You have to go to your reason, and your judgment, and your common sense, and a hundred other sources. And then, when you have found out what is right and what is wrong, you will hear the voice saying, 'Do that, and do not do this.' Every one of us has faults that we know nothing about, and that we bring up to the tribunal of our consciences, and wipe our mouths and say, 'We have done no harm.' 'I thought within myself that I verily ought to do many things contrary to the name of Jesus of Nazareth.' 'They think that they do God service.' Many things that seem to us virtues are vices.

And as for the individual so for the community. The perception of what is right and what is wrong needs long educating. When I was a boy the whole Christian Church of America, with one voice, declared that 'slavery was a patriarchal institution appointed by God.' The Christian Church of to-day has not awakened either to the sin of war or of drink. And I have not the smallest doubt that there are hosts of things which public opinion, and Christian public opinion, regards to-day as perfectly allowable and innocent, and, perhaps, even praiseworthy, and over which it will ask God's blessing, at which, in a hundred years our descendants will hold up their hands in wonder, and say, 'How did good people—and good people they no doubt were—tolerate such a condition of things for a moment?' 'All a man's ways are right in his own eyes,' and he needs a great deal of teaching before he comes to understand what, according to God's will, really, is right and what is wrong.

Now let me turn for a moment to the contrasted picture, with which I can only deal in a sentence or two.

II. The divine estimate.

I have already pointed out the two emphatic thoughts that lie in that clause, 'God weigheth,' and 'weigheth the spirits.' I need not repeat what I said, in the introduction to these remarks, upon this subject. Just let us take with us these two thoughts, that the same actions which we sometimes test, in our very defective and loaded balances, have also to go into the infallible scales, and that the actions go with their interpretation in their motive. 'God weighs the spirits.' He reads what we do by His knowledge of what we are. We reveal to one another what we are by what we do, and, as is a commonplace, none of us can penetrate, except very superficially and often inaccurately, to the motives that actuate. But the motive is three-fourths of the action. God does not go from without, as it were, inwards; from our actions to estimate our characters; but He starts with the character and the motive—the habitual character and the occasional motive—and by these He reads the deed. He weighs, ponders, penetrates to the heart of the thing, and He weighs the spirits.

So on the one hand, 'I obtained mercy, because I did it ignorantly in unbelief,' and many a deed which the world would condemn, and in which we onlookers would see evil, God does not wholly condemn, because He, being the Inlooker as well as the Onlooker, sees the albeit mistaken yet pure motives that underlay it. So it is conceivable that the inquisitor, and the heretic that he sent to the stake, may stand side by side in God's estimate; the one if he were actuated by pure zeal for the truth, the other because he was actuated by self-sacrifice in loyalty to his Lord. And, on the other hand, many a deed that goes flaunting through the world in 'purple and fine linen' will be stripped of its gauds, and stand naked and ugly before the eyes of 'Him with whom we have to do.' He 'weighs the spirits.'

Lastly, a word about—

III. The practical issues of these thoughts.

'Commit thy works unto the Lord'—that is to say, do not be too sure that you are right because you do not think you are wrong. We should be very distrustful of our own judgments of ourselves, especially when that judgment permits us to do certain things. 'I know nothing against myself,' said the Apostle, 'yet am I not hereby justified.' And again, still more emphatically, he lays down the principle that I would have liked to have enlarged upon if I had had time. 'Happy is he that condemneth not himself in the things which he alloweth.' You may have made the glove too easy by stretching. It is possible that you may think that something is permissible and right which a wiser and more rigid and Christlike judgment of yourself would have taught you was wrong. Look under the stones for the reptiles, and remember the prayer, 'Cleanse thou me from secret faults,' and distrust a permitting and easy conscience.

Then, again, let us seek the divine strengthening and illumination. We have to seek that in some very plain ways. Seek it by prayer. There is nothing so powerful in stripping off from our besetting sins their disguises and masks as to go to God with the honest petition: 'Search me ... and try me ... and see if there be any wicked way in me, and lead me in the way everlasting.' Brethren! if we will do that, we shall get answers that will startle us, that will humble us, but that will be blessed beyond all other blessedness, and will bring to light the 'hidden things of darkness.' Then, after they are brought to light and cast out, 'then shall every man have praise of God.'

We ought to keep ourselves in very close union with Jesus Christ, because if we cling to Him in simple faith, He will come into our hearts, and we shall be saved from walking in darkness, and have the light of life shining down upon our deeds. Christ is the conscience of the Christian man's conscience, who, by His voice in the hearts that wait upon Him, says, 'Do this,' and they do it. It is when He is in our spirits that our estimate of ourselves is set right, and that we hear the voice saying, 'This is the way, walk ye in it'; and not merely do we hear the voice, but we get help to our feet in running in the way of His commandments, with enlarged and confirmed hearts. Brethren! for the discovery of our faults, which we ought all to long for, and for the conquest of these discovered faults, which, if we are Christians, we do long for, our confidence is in Him. And if you trust Him, 'the blood of Christ will cleanse'—because it comes into our life's blood—'from all sin.'

And the last thing that I would say is this. We must punctiliously obey every dictate that speaks in our own consciences, especially when it urges us to unwelcome duties or restrains us from too welcome sins. 'To him that hath shall be given'—and the sure way to condemn ourselves to utter blindness as to our true selves is to pay no attention to the glimmers of light that we have, whilst, on the other hand, the sure way to be led into fuller illumination is to follow faithfully whatsoever sparkles of light may shine upon our hearts. 'Do the duty that lies nearest thee.' Put thy trust in Jesus Christ. Distrust thine own approbation or condonation of thine actions, and ever turn to Him and say, 'Show me what to do, and make me willing and fit to do it.' Then there will be little contrariety between your estimate of your ways and God's judgments of your spirits.

A BUNDLE OF PROVERBS

'Understanding is a wellspring of life unto him that hath it: but the instruction of fools is folly. 23. The heart of the wise teacheth his mouth, and addeth learning to his lips. 24. Pleasant words are as an honeycomb, sweet to the soul, and health to the bones. 25. There is a way that seemeth right unto a man, but the end thereof are the ways of death. 26. He that laboureth laboureth for himself; for his mouth craveth it of him. 27. An ungodly man diggeth up evil: and in his lips there is as a burning fire. 28. A froward man soweth strife: and a whisperer separateth chief friends. 29. A violent man enticeth his neighbour, and leadeth him into the way that is not good. 30. He shutteth his eyes to devise froward things: moving his lips he bringeth evil to pass. 31. The hoary head is a crown of glory, if it be found in the way of righteousness. 32. He that is slow to anger is better than the mighty; and he that ruleth his spirit than he that taketh a city. 33. The lot is cast into the lap; but the whole disposing thereof is of the Lord.'—PROVERBS xvi. 22-33.

A slight thread of connection may be traced in some of the proverbs in this passage. Verse 22, with its praise of 'Wisdom,' introduces one instance of Wisdom's excellence in verse 23, and that again, with its reference to speech, leads on to verse 24 and its commendation of 'pleasant words.' Similarly, verses 27-30 give four pictures of vice, three of them beginning with 'a man.' We may note, too, that, starting with verse 26, every verse till verse 30 refers to some work of 'the mouth' or 'lips.'

The passage begins with one phase of the contrast between Wisdom and Folly, which this book is never weary of emphasising and underscoring. We shall miss the force of its most characteristic teaching unless we keep well in mind that the two opposites of Wisdom and Folly do not refer only or chiefly to intellectual distinctions. The very basis of 'Wisdom,' as this book conceives it, is the 'fear of the Lord,' without which the man of biggest, clearest brain, and most richly stored mind, is, in its judgment, 'a fool.' Such 'understanding,' which apprehends and rightly deals with the deepest fact of life, our relation to God and to His law, is a 'well-spring of life.' The figure speaks still more eloquently to Easterns than to us. In those hot lands the cool spring, bursting through the baked rocks or burning sand, makes the difference between barrenness and fertility, the death of all green things and life. So where true Wisdom is deep in a heart, it will come flashing up into sunshine, and will quicken the seeds of all good as it flows through the deeds. 'Everything liveth whithersoever the river cometh.' Productiveness, refreshment, the beauty of the sparkling wavelets, the music of their ripples against the stones, and all the other blessings and delights of a perpetual fountain, have better things corresponding to them in the life of the man who is wise with the true Wisdom which begins with the fear of God. Just as *it* is active in the life, so is Folly. But its activity is not blessing and gladdening, but punitive. For all sin automatically works its own chastisement, and the curse of Folly is that, while it corrects, it prevents the 'fool' from profiting by the correction. Since it punishes itself, one might expect that it would cure itself, but experience shows that, while it wields a rod, its subjects 'receive no correction.' That insensibility is the paradox and the Nemesis of 'Folly.'

The Old Testament ethics are remarkable for their solemn sense of the importance of words, and Proverbs shares in that sense to the full. In some aspects, speech is a more perfect self-revelation than act. So the outflow of the fountain in words comes next. Wise heart makes wise speech. That may be looked at in two ways. It may point to the utterance by word as the most precious, and incumbent on its possessor, of all the ways of manifesting Wisdom; or it may point to the only source of real 'learning,'—namely, a wise heart. In the former view, it teaches us our solemn obligation not to hide our light under a bushel, but to speak boldly and lovingly all the truth which God has taught us. A dumb Christian is a monstrosity. We are bound to give voice to our 'Wisdom.' In the other aspect, it reminds us that there is a better way of getting Wisdom than by many books,—namely, by filling our hearts, through communion with God, with His own will. Then, whether we have worldly 'learning' or no, we shall be able to instruct many, and lead them to the light which has shone on us.

There are many kinds of pleasant words, some of which are not like 'honey,' but like poison hid in jam. Insincere compliments, flatteries when rebukes would be fitting, and all the brood of civil conventionalities, are not the words meant here. Truly pleasant ones are those which come from true Wisdom, and may often have a surface of bitterness like the prophet's roll, but have a core of sweetness. It is a great thing to be able to speak necessary and unwelcome truths with lips into which grace is poured. A spoonful of honey catches more flies than a hogshead of vinegar.

Verse 25 has no connection with its context. It teaches two solemn truths, according to the possible double meaning of 'right.' If that word means ethically right, then the saying sets forth the terrible possibility of conscience being wrongly instructed, and sanctioning gross sin. If it means only *straight*, or level—that is, successful and easy—the saying enforces the not less solemn truth that sin deceives as to its results, and that the path of wrong-doing, which is flowery and smooth at first, grows rapidly thorny, and goes fast downhill, and ends at last in a *cul-de-sac*, of which death is the only outlet. We are not to trust our own consciences, except as enlightened by God's Word. We are not to listen to sin's lies, but to fix it well in our minds that there is only one way which leads to life and peace, the narrow way of faith and obedience.

The Revised Version's rendering of verse 26 gives the right idea. 'The appetite,' or hunger, 'of the labourer labours for him' (that is, the need of food is the mainspring of work), and it lightens the work to which it impels. So hunger is a blessing. That is true in regard to the body. The manifold material industries of men are, at bottom, prompted by the need to earn something to eat. The craving which drives to such results is a thing to be thankful for. It is better to live where toil is needful to sustain life than in lazy lands where an hour's work will provide food for a week. But the saying reaches to spiritual desires, and anticipates the beatitude on those who 'hunger and thirst after righteousness.' Happy they who feel that craving, and are driven by it to the labour for the bread which comes down from heaven! 'This is the work of God, that ye believe on Him whom He hath sent.'

The next three proverbs (vs. 27-29) give three pictures of different types of bad men. First, we have 'the worthless man' (Rev. Ver.), literally 'a man of Belial,' which last word probably means worthlessness. His work is 'digging evil'; his words are like scorching fire. To dig evil seems to have a wider sense than has digging a pit for others (Ps. vii. 15), which is usually taken as a parallel. The man is not merely malicious toward others, but his whole activity goes to further evil. It is the material in which he delights to work. What mistaken spade husbandry it is to spend labour on such a soil! What can it grow but thistles and poisonous plants? His words are as bad as his deeds. No honey drops from *his* lips, but scorching fire, which burns up not only reputations but tries to consume all that is good. As James says, such a tongue is 'set on fire of hell.' The picture is that of a man bad through and through. But there may be indefinitely close approximations to it, and no man can say, 'Thus far will I go in evil ways, and no further.'

The second picture is of a more specific kind. The 'froward man' here seems to be the same as the slanderer in the next clause. He utters perverse things, and so soweth strife and parts friends. There are people whose mouths are as full of malicious whispers as a sower's basket is of seed, and who have a base delight in flinging them broadcast. Sometimes they do not think of what the harvest will be, but often they chuckle to see it springing in the mistrust and alienation of former friends. A loose tongue often does as much harm as a bitter one, and delight in dwelling on people's faults is not innocent because the tattler did not think of the mischief he was setting agoing.

In verse 29 another type of evil-doer is outlined—the opposite, in some respects, of the preceding. The slanderer works secretly; this mischief-maker goes the plain way to work. He uses physical force or 'violence.' But how does that fit in with 'enticeth'? It may be that the enticement of his victim into a place suitable for robbing or murder is meant, but more probably there is here the same combination of force and craft as in chapter i. 10-14. Criminals have a wicked delight in tempting innocent people to join their gangs. A lawless desperado is a hotbed of infection.

Verse 30 draws a portrait of a bad man. It is a bit of homely physiognomical observation. A man with a trick of closing his eyes has something working in his head; and, if he is one of these types of men, one may be sure that he is brewing mischief. Compressed lips mean concentrated effort, or fixed resolve, or suppressed feeling, and in any of these cases are as a danger signal, warning that the man is at work on some evil deed.

Two sayings follow, which contrast goodness with the evils just described. The 'if' in verse 31 weakens the strong assertion of the proverb. 'The hoary head is a crown of glory; it is found in the way of righteousness.' That is but putting into picturesque form the Old Testament promise of long life to the righteous—a promise which is not repeated in the new dispensation, but which is still often realised. 'Whom the gods love, die young,' is a heathen proverb; but there is a natural tendency in the manner of life which Christianity produces to prolong a man's days. A heart at peace, because stayed on God, passions held well in hand, an avoidance of excesses which eat away strength, do tend to length of life, and the opposites of these do tend to shorten it. How many young men go home from our great cities every year, with their 'bones full of the iniquities of their youth,' to die!

If we are to tread the way of righteousness, and so come to 'reverence and the silver hair,' we must govern ourselves. So the next proverb extols the ruler of his own spirit as 'more than conquerors,' whose triumphs are won in such vulgar fields as battles and sieges, Our sorest fights and our noblest victories are within.

'Unless above himself he can
Erect himself, how poor a thing is man!'

Verse 31 takes the casting of the lot as one instance of the limitation of all human effort, in all which we can but use the appropriate means, while the whole issue must be left in God's hands. The Jewish law did not enjoin the lot, but its use seems to have been frequent. The proverb presents in the sharpest relief a principle which is true of all our activity. The old proverb-maker knew nothing of chance. To him there were but two real moving forces in the world—man and God. To the one belonged sowing the seed, doing his part, whether casting the lot or toiling at his task. His force was real, but derived and limited. Efforts and attempts are ours; results are God's. We sow; He 'gives it a body as it pleases Him.' Nothing happens by accident. Man's little province is bounded on all sides by God's, and the two touch. There is no neutral territory between, where godless chance rules.

TWO FORTRESSES

'The name of the Lord is a strong tower: the righteous runneth into it, and is safe. 11. The rich man's wealth is his strong city, and as an high wall in his own conceit'—PROVERBS xviii. 10,11.

The mere reading of these two verses shows that, contrary to the usual rule in the Book of Proverbs, they have a bearing on each other. They are intended to suggest a very strong contrast, and that contrast is even more emphatic in the original than in our translation; because, as the margin of your Bibles will tell you, the last word of the former verse might be more correctly rendered, 'the righteous runneth into it, and is *set on high*.' It is the same word which is employed in the next verse—'a high wall.'

So we have 'the strong tower' and 'the strong city'; the man lifted up above danger on the battlements of the one, and the man fancying himself to be high above it (and only fancying himself) in the imaginary safety of the other.

I. Consider then, first, the two fortresses.

One need only name them side by side to feel the full force of the intended contrast. On the one hand, the name of the Lord with all its depths and glories, with its blaze of lustrous purity, and infinitudes of inexhaustible power; and on the other, 'the rich man's wealth.' What contempt is expressed in putting the two side by side! It is as if the author had said, 'Look on this picture and on that!' Two fortresses! Yes! The one is like Gibraltar, inexpugnable on its rock, and the other is like a painted castle on the stage; flimsy canvas that you could put your foot through—solidity by the side of nothingness. For even the poor appearance of solidity is an illusion, as our text says with bitter emphasis—'a high wall *in his own conceit*.'

'The name of the Lord,' of course, is the Biblical expression for the whole character of God, as He has made it known to us, or in other words, for God

Himself, as He has been pleased to reveal Himself to mankind. The syllables of that name are all the deeds by which He has taught us what He is; every act of power, of wisdom, of tenderness, of grace that has manifested these qualities and led us to believe that they are all infinite. In the name, in its narrower sense, the name of Jehovah, there is much of 'the name' in its wider sense. For that name 'Jehovah,' both by its signification and by the circumstances under which it was originally employed, tells us a great deal about God. It tells us, for instance, by virtue of its signification, that He is self-existent, depending upon no other creature. 'I AM THAT I AM!' No other being can say that. All the rest of us have to say, 'I am that which God made me.' Circumstances and a hundred other things have made me; God finds the law of His being and the fountain of His being within Himself.

'He sits on no precarious throne,
Nor borrows leave to be.'

His name proclaims Him to be self-existent, and as self-existent, eternal; and as eternal, changeless; and as self-existent, eternal, changeless, infinite in all the qualities by which He makes Himself known. This boundless Being, all full of wisdom, power, and tenderness, with whom we can enter into relations of amity and concord, surely He is 'a strong tower into which we may run and be safe.'

But far beyond even the sweep of that great name, Jehovah, is the knowledge of God's deepest heart and character which we learn in Him who said, 'I have declared Thy name unto My brethren, and will declare it.' Christ in His life and death, in His meekness, sweetness, gentleness, calm wisdom, infinite patience, attractiveness; yearning over sinful hearts, weeping over rebels, in the graciousness of His life, in the sacredness and the power of His Cross, is the Revealer to our hearts of the heart of God. If I may so say, He has builded 'the strong tower' broader, has expanded its area and widened its gate, and lifted its summit yet nearer the heavens, and made the name of God a wider name and a mightier name, and a name of surer defence and blessing than ever it was before.

And so, dear brethren! it all comes to this, the name that is 'the strong tower' is the name 'My Father!' a Father of infinite tenderness and wisdom and power. Oh! where can the child rest more quietly than on the mother's breast, where can the child be safer than in the circle of the father's arms? 'The name of the Lord is a strong tower.'

Now turn to the other for a moment: 'The rich man's wealth is' (with great emphasis on the next little word) '*his* strong city, and as a high wall in his own conceit.' Of course we have not to deal here only with wealth in the shape of money, but all external and material goods, the whole mass of the 'things seen and temporal,' are gathered together here in this phrase.

Men use their imaginations in very strange fashion, and make, or fancy they make, for themselves out of the things of the present life a defence and a strength. Like some poor lunatic, out upon a moor, that fancies himself ensconced in a castle; like some barbarous tribes behind their stockades or crowding at the back of a little turf wall, or in some old tumble-down fort that the first shot will bring rattling down about their ears, fancying themselves perfectly secure and defended—so do men deal with these outward things that are given them for another purpose altogether: they make of them defences and fortresses.

It is difficult for a man to have them and not to trust them. So Jesus said to His disciples once: 'How hardly shall they that have riches enter into the Kingdom'; and when they were astonished at His words, He repeated them with the significant variation, 'How hard is it for them that trust in riches to enter into the Kingdom of God.' So He would teach that the misuse and not the possession of wealth is the barrier, but so, too, He would warn us that, nine times out of ten, the possession of them in more than a very modest measure, tempts a man into confidence in them.

The illusion is one that besets us all. We are all tempted to make a defence of the things that we can see and handle. Is it not strange, and is it not sad, that most of us just turn the truth round about and suppose that the real defence is the imaginary, and that the imaginary one is the real? How many men are there in this chapel who, if they spoke out of their deepest convictions, would say: 'Oh yes! the promises of God are all very well, but I would rather have the cash down. I suppose that I may trust that He will provide bread and water, and all the things that I need, but I would rather have a good solid balance at the banker's.' How many of you would rather honestly, and at the bottom of your hearts, have that than God's word for your defence? How many of you think that to trust in a living God is but grasping at a very airy and unsubstantial kind of support; and that the real solid defence is the defence made of the things that you can see?

My brother! it is exactly the opposite way. Turn it clean round, and you get the truth. The unsubstantial shadows are the material things that you can see and handle; illusory as a dream, and as little able to ward off the blows of fate as a soap bubble. The real is the unseen beyond—'the things that *are*,' and He who alone really is, and in His boundless and absolute Being is our only defence.

In one aspect or another, that false imagination with which my last text deals is the besetting sin of Manchester. Not the rich man only, but the poor man just as much, is in danger of it. The poor man who thinks that everything would be right if only he were rich, and the rich man who thinks that everything is right because he *is* rich, are exactly the same man. The circumstances differ, but the one man is but the other turned inside out. And all round about us we see the fierce fight to get more and more of these things, the tight grip of them when we have got them, the overestimate of the value of them, the contempt for the people who have less of them than ourselves. Our aristocracy is an aristocracy of wealth; in some respects, one by no means to be despised, because there often go a great many good qualities to the making and the stewardship of wealth; but still it is an evil that men should be so largely estimated by their money as they are here. It is not a sound state of opinion which has made 'what is he *worth*?' mean 'how much of *it* has he?' We are taught here to look upon the prizes of life as being mainly wealth. To win that is 'success'—'prosperity'—and it is very hard for us all not to be influenced by the prevailing tone.

I would urge you, young men, especially to lay this to heart—that of all delusions that can beset you in your course, none will work more disastrously than the notion that the *summum bonum*, the shield and stay of a man, is the 'abundance of the things that he possesses.' I fancy I see more listless, discontented, unhappy faces looking out of carriages than I see upon the pavement. And I am sure of this, at any rate, that all which is noble and sweet and good in life can be wrought out and possessed upon as much bread and water as will keep body and soul together, and as much furniture as will enable a man to sit at his meal and lie down at night. And as for the rest, it has many advantages and blessings, but oh! it is all illusory as a defence against the evils that will come, sooner or later, to every life.

II. Consider next how to get into the true Refuge.

'The righteous runneth into it and is safe,' says my text. You may get into the illusory one very easily. Imagination will take you there. There is no difficulty at all about that. And yet the way by which a man makes this world his defence may teach you a lesson as to how you can make God your defence. How *does* a man make this world his defence? By trusting to it. He that says to the fine gold, 'Thou art my confidence,' has made it his fortress— and that is how you will make God your fortress—by trusting to *Him*. The very same emotion, the very same act of mind, heart, and will, may be turned either upwards or downwards, as you can turn the beam from a lantern which way you please. Direct it earthwards, and you 'trust in the uncertainty of riches.' Flash it heavenwards, and you 'trust in the living God.'

And that same lesson is taught by the words of our text, 'The righteous runneth into it.' I do not dwell upon the word 'righteous.' That is the Old Testament point of view, which could not conceive it possible that any man could have deep and close communion with God, except on condition of a pure character. I will not speak of that at present, but point to the picturesque metaphor, which will tell us a great deal more about what faith is than many a philosophical dissertation. Many a man who would be perplexed by a theologian's talk will understand this: 'The righteous runneth into the name of the Lord.'

The metaphor brings out the idea of eager haste in betaking oneself to the shelter, as when an invading army comes into a country, and the unarmed peasants take their portable belongings and their cattle, and catch up their children in their arms, and set their wives upon their mules, and make all haste to some fortified place; or as when the manslayer in Israel fled to the city of refuge, or as when Lot hurried for his life out of Sodom. There would be no dawdling then; but with every muscle strained, men would run into the stronghold, counting every minute a year till they were inside its walls, and heard the heavy door close between them and the pursuer. No matter how rough the road, or how overpowering the heat—no time to stop to gather flowers, or even diamonds on the road, when a moment's delay might mean the enemy's sword in your heart!

Now that metaphor is frequently used to express the resolved and swift act by which, recognising in Jesus Christ, who declares the name of the Lord, our hiding-place, we shelter ourselves in Him, and rest secure. One of the picturesque words by which the Old Testament expresses 'trust' means literally 'to flee to a refuge.' The Old Testament *trust* is the New Testament *faith*, even as the Old Testament '*Name of the Lord*' answers to the New Testament '*Name of Jesus*.' And so we run into this sure hiding-place and strong fortress of the name of the Lord, when we betake ourselves to Jesus and put our trust in Him as our defence.

Such a faith—the trust of mind, heart, and will—laying hold of the name of the Lord, makes us 'righteous,' and so capable of 'dwelling with the devouring fire' of God's perfect purity. The Old Testament point of view was righteousness, in order to abiding in God. The New Testament begins, as it were, at an earlier stage in the religious life, and tells us how to get the righteousness, without which, it holds as strongly as the Old Testament, 'no man shall see the Lord.' It shows us that our faith, by which we run into that fortress, fits us to enter the fortress, because it makes us partakers of Christ's purity.

So my earnest question to you all is—Have you 'fled for refuge to lay hold' on that Saviour in whom God has set His name? Like Lot out of Sodom, like the manslayer to the city of refuge, like the unwarlike peasants to the baron's tower, before the border thieves, have you gone thither for shelter from all the sorrows and guilt and dangers that are marching terrible against you? Can you take up as yours the old grand words of exuberant trust in which the Psalmist heaps together the names of the Lord, as if walking about the city of his defence, and telling the towers thereof, 'The Lord is my rock, and my fortress, and my deliverer; my God, my strength, in whom I will trust; my buckler, and the horn of my salvation, and my high tower'? If you have, then 'because you have made the Lord your refuge, there shall no evil befall you.'

III. So we have, lastly, what comes of sheltering in these two refuges.

As to the former of them, I said at the beginning of these remarks that the words 'is safe' were more accurately as well as picturesquely rendered by 'is set aloft.' They remind us of the psalm which has many points of resemblance with this text, and which gives the very same thought when it says, 'I will set him on high, because he hath known My name.' The fugitive is taken within the safe walls of the strong tower, and is set up high on the battlements, looking down upon the baffled pursuers, and far beyond the reach of their arrows. To stand upon that tower lifts a man above the region where temptations fly, above the region where sorrow strikes; lifts him above sin and guilt and condemnation and fear, and calumny and slander, and sickness, and separation and loneliness and death; 'and all the ills that flesh is heir to.'

Or, as one of the old Puritan commentators has it: 'The tower is so deep that no pioneer can undermine it, so thick that no cannon can breach it, so high that no ladder can scale it.' 'The righteous runneth into it,' and is perched up there; and can look down like Lear from his cliff, and all the troubles that afflict the lower levels shall 'show scarce so gross as beetles' from the height where he stands, safe and high, hidden in the name of the Lord.

I say little about the other side. Brethren! the world in any of its forms, the good things of this life in any shape, whether that of money or any other, can do a great deal for us. They can keep a great many inconveniences from us, they can keep a great many cares and pains and sorrows from us. I was going to say, to carry out the metaphor, they can keep the rifle-bullets from us. But, ah! when the big siege-guns get into position and begin to play; when the great trials that every life must have, sooner or later, come to open fire at us, then the defence that anything in this outer world can give comes rattling about our ears very quickly. It is like the pasteboard helmet which looked as good as if it had been steel, and did admirably as long as no sword struck it.

There is only one thing that will keep us peaceful and unharmed, and that is to trust our poor shelterless lives and sinful souls to the Saviour who has died for us. In Him we find the hiding-place, in which secure, as beneath the shadow of a great rock, dreaded evils will pass us by, as impotent to hurt as savages before a castle fortified by modern skill. All the bitterness of outward calamities will be taken from them before they reach us. Their arrows will still wound, but He will have wiped the poison off before He lets them be shot at us. The force of temptation will be weakened, for if we live near Him we shall have other tastes and desires. The bony fingers of the skeleton Death, who drags men from all other homes, will not dislodge us from our fortress-dwelling. Hid in Him we shall neither fear going down to the grave, nor coming up from it, nor judgment, nor eternity. Then, I beseech you, make no delay. Escape! flee for your life! A growing host of evil marches swift against you. Take Christ for your defence and cry to Him,

'Lo! from sin and grief and shame,
Hide me, Jesus! in Thy name.'

A STRING OF PEARLS

'Wine is a mocker, strong drink is raging: and whosoever is deceived thereby is not wise. 2. The fear of a king is as the roaring of a lion: whoso provoketh him to anger sinneth against his own soul. 3. It is an honour for a man to cease from strife: but every fool will be meddling. 4. The sluggard will not plough by reason of the cold; therefore shall he beg in harvest, and have nothing. 5. Counsel in the heart of man is like deep water; but a man of understanding will draw it out. 6. Most men will proclaim every one his own goodness: but a faithful man who can find? 7. The just man walketh in his integrity: his children are blessed after him.'—PROVERBS xx. 1-7.

The connection between the verses of this passage is only in their common purpose to set forth some details of a righteous life, and to brand the opposite vices. A slight affinity may be doubtfully traced in one or two adjacent proverbs, but that is all.

First comes temperance, enforced by the picture of a drunkard. Wine and strong drink are, as it were, personified, and their effects on men are painted as their own characters. And an ugly picture it is, which should hang in the gallery of every young man and woman. 'Wine is a mocker.' Intemperance delights in scoffing at all pure, lofty, sacred things. It is the ally of wild profanity, which sends up its tipsy and clumsy ridicule against Heaven itself. If a man wants to lose his sense of reverence, his susceptibility for what is noble, let him take to drink, and the thing is done. If he would fain keep these fresh and quick, let him eschew what is sure to deaden them. Of course there are other roads to the same end, but there is no other end to this road. Nobody ever knew a drunkard who did not scoff at things that should be reverenced, and that because he knew that he was acting in defiance of them.

'A brawler,' or, as Delitzsch renders it, 'boisterous'—look into a liquor-store if you want to verify that, or listen to a drunken party coming back from an excursion and making night hideous with their bellowings, or go to any police court on a Monday morning. We in England are familiar with the combination on police charge-sheets, 'drunk and disorderly.' So does the old proverb-maker seem to have been. Drink takes off the brake, and every impulse has its own way, and makes as much noise as it can.

The word rendered in Authorised Version 'is deceived,' and in Revised Version 'erreth,' is literally 'staggers' or 'reels,' and it is more graphic to keep that meaning. There is a world of quiet irony in the unexpectedly gentle close of the sentence, 'is not wise.' How much stronger the assertion might have been! Look at the drunkard as he staggers along, scoffing at everything purer and higher than himself, and ready to fight with his own shadow, and incapable of self-control. He has made himself the ugly spectacle you see. Will anybody call *him* wise?

The next proverb applies directly to a state of things which most nations have outgrown. Kings who can give full scope to their anger, and who inspire mainly terror, are anomalies in civilised countries now. The proverb warns that it is no trifle to rouse the lion from his lair, and that when he begins to growl there is danger. The man who stirs him 'forfeits his own life,' or, at all events, imperils it.

The word rendered 'sins' has for its original meaning 'misses,' and seems to be so used here, as also in Proverbs viii. 36. 'Against' is a supplement. The maxim inculcates the wisdom of avoiding conduct which might rouse an anger so sure to destroy its object. And that is a good maxim for ordinary times in all lands, monarchies or republics. For there is in constitutional kingdoms and in republics an uncrowned monarch, to the full as irresponsible, as easily provoked, and as relentless in hunting its opponents to destruction, as any old-world tyrant. Its name is Public Opinion. It is not well to provoke it. If a man does, let him well understand that he takes his life, or what is sometimes dearer than life, in his hand. Not only self-preservation, which the proverb and Scripture recognise as a legitimate motive, but higher considerations, dictate compliance with the ruling forces of our times, as far as may be. Conscience only has the right to limit this precept, and to say, 'Let the brute roar, and never mind if you *do* forfeit your life. It is your duty to say "No," though all the world should be saying "Yes."'

A slight thread of connection may be established between the second and third proverbs. The latter, like the former, commends peacefulness and condemns pugnacity. Men talk of 'glory' as the warrior's meed, and the so-called Christian world has not got beyond the semi-barbarous stage which regards 'honour' as mainly secured by fighting. But this ancient proverb-maker had learned a better conception of what 'honour' or 'glory' was, and where it grew.

'Peace hath her victories
No less renowned than war,'

said Milton. But our proverb goes farther than 'no less,' and gives *greater* glory to the man who never takes up arms, or who lays them down. The saying is true, not only about warfare, but in all regions of life. Fighting is generally wasted time. Controversialists of all sorts, porcupine-like people, who go through the world all sharp quills sticking out to pierce, are less to be admired than peace-loving souls. Any fool can 'show his teeth,' as the word for 'quarrelling' means. But it takes a wise man, and a man whose spirit has been made meek by dwelling near God in Christ, to withhold the angry word, the quick retort. It is generally best to let the glove flung down lie where it is. There are better things to do than to squabble.

Verse 4 is a parable as well as a proverb. If a man sits by the fireside because the north wind is blowing, when he ought to be out in the field holding the plough with frost-nipped fingers, he will beg (or, perhaps, *seek for a crop*) in harvest, and will find nothing, when others are rejoicing in the slow result of winter showers and of their toilsome hours. So, in all life, if the fitting moments for preparation are neglected, late repentance avails nothing. The student who dawdles when he should be working, will be sure to fail when the examination comes on. It is useless to begin ploughing when your neighbours are driving their reaping machines into the fields. 'There is a time to sow, and a time to reap.' The law is inexorable for this life, and not less certainly so for the life to come. The virgins who cried in vain, 'Lord, Lord, open to us!' and were answered, 'Too late, too late, ye cannot enter now!' are sisters of the man who was hindered from ploughing because it was cold, and asked in vain for bread when harvest time had come. 'To-day, if ye will to hear His voice, harden not your hearts.'

The next proverb is a piece of shrewd common sense. It sets before us two men, one reticent, and the other skilful in worming out designs which he wishes to penetrate. The former is like a deep draw-well; the latter is like a man who lets down a bucket into it, and winds it up full. 'Still waters are deep.' The faculty of reading men may be abused to bad ends, but is worth cultivating, and may be allied to high aims, and serve to help in accomplishing these. It may aid good men in detecting evil, in knowing how to present God's truth to hearts that need it, in pouring comfort into closely shut spirits. Not only astute business men or politicians need it, but all who would help their fellows to love God and serve Him—preachers, teachers, and the like. And there would be more happy homes if parents and children tried to understand one another. We seldom dislike a man when we come to know him thoroughly. We cannot help him till we do.

The proverb in verse 6 is susceptible of different renderings in the first clause. Delitzsch and others would translate, 'Almost every man meets a man who is gracious to him.' The contrast will then be between partial 'grace' or kindness, and thoroughgoing reliableness or trustworthiness. The rendering of the Authorised and Revised Versions, on the other hand, makes the contrast between talk and reality, professions of goodwill and acts which come up to these. In either case, the saying is the bitter fruit of experience.

Even charity, which 'believeth all things,' cannot but admit that soft words are more abundant than deeds which verify them. It is no breach of the law of love to open one's eyes to facts, and so to save oneself from taking paper money for gold, except at a heavy discount. Perhaps the reticence, noted in the previous proverb, led to the thought of a loose-tongued profession of kindliness as a contrast. Neither the one nor the other is admirable. The practical conclusion from the facts in this proverb is double—do not take much heed of men's eulogiums on their own benevolence; do not trumpet your own praises. Caution and modesty are parts of Christian perfection.

The last saying points to the hereditary goodness which sometimes, for our comfort, we do see, as well as to the halo from a saintly parent which often surrounds his children. Note that there may be more than mere succession in time conveyed by the expression 'after him.' It may mean following in his footsteps. Such children are blessed, both in men's benedictions and in their own peaceful hearts. Weighty responsibilities lie upon the children of parents who have transmitted to them a revered name. A Christian's children are doubly bound to continue the parental tradition, and are doubly criminal if they depart from it. There is no sadder sight than that of a godly father wailing over an ungodly son, unless it be that of the ungodly son who makes him wail. Absalom hanging by his curls in the oak-tree, and David groaning, 'My son, my son!' touch all hearts. Alas that the tragedy should be so often repeated in our homes to-day!

THE SLUGGARD IN HARVEST

'The sluggard will not plow by reason of the cold; therefore shall he beg in harvest, and have nothing.'—PROVERBS xx. 4.

Like all the sayings of this book, this is simply a piece of plain, practical common sense, intended to inculcate the lesson that men should diligently seize the opportunity whilst it is theirs. The sluggard is one of the pet aversions of the Book of Proverbs, which, unlike most other manuals of Eastern wisdom, has a profound reverence for honest work.

He is a great drone, for he prefers the chimney-corner to the field, even although it cannot have been very cold if the weather was open enough to admit of ploughing. And he is a great fool, too, for he buys his comfort at a very dear price, as do all men who live for to-day, and let to-morrow look out for itself.

But like most of the other sayings of this book, my text contains principles which are true in the highest regions of human life, for the laws which rule up there are not different from those which regulate the motions of its lower phases. Religion recognises the same practical common-sense principles that daily business does. I venture to take this as my text now, in addressing young people, because they have special need of, and special facilities for, the wisdom which it enjoins; and because the words only want to be turned with their faces heavenwards in order to enforce the great appeal, the only one which it is worth my while to make, and worth your while to come here to listen to; the appeal to each of you, 'I beseech you, by the mercies of God, that ye yield yourselves to God' *now*.

My object, then, will be perhaps best accomplished if I simply ask you to look, first, at the principles involved in this quaint proverb; and, secondly, to apply them in one or two directions.

I. First, then, let us try to bring out the principles which are crystallised in this picturesque saying.

The first thought evidently is: present conduct determines future conditions. Life is a series of epochs, each of which has its destined work, and that being done, all is well; and that being left undone, all is ill.

Now, of course, in regard to many of the accidents of a man's condition, his conduct is only one, and by no means the most powerful, of the factors which settle them. The position which a man fills, the tasks which he has to perform, and the whole host of things which make up the externals of his life, depend upon far other conditions than any that he brings to them. But yet on the whole it is true that what a man does, and is, settles how he fares. And this is the mystical importance and awful solemnity of the most undistinguished moments and most trivial acts of this awful life of ours, that each of them has an influence on all that comes after, and may deflect our whole course into altogether different paths. It is not only the moments that we vulgarly and blindly call great which settle our condition, but it is the accumulation of the tiny ones; the small deeds, the unnoticed acts, which make up so large a portion of every man's life. It is these, after all, that are the most powerful in settling what we shall be. There come to each of us supreme moments in our lives. Yes! and if in all the subordinate and insignificant moments we have not been getting ready for them, but have been nurturing dispositions and acquiring habits, and cultivating ways of acting and thinking which condemn us to fail beneath the requirements of the supreme moment, then it passes us by, and we gain nothing from it. Tiny mica flakes have built up the Matterhorn, and the minute acts of life after all, by their multiplicity, make up life to be what it is. 'Sand is heavy,' says this wise book of Proverbs. The aggregation of the minutest grains, singly so light that they would not affect the most delicate balance, weighs upon us with a weight 'heavy as frost, and deep almost as life.' The mystic significance of the trivialities of life is that in them we largely make destiny, and that in them we wholly make character.

And now, whilst this is true about all life, it is especially true about youth. You have facilities for moulding your being which some of us older men would give a great deal to have again for a moment, with our present knowledge and bitter experience. The lava that has solidified into hard rock with us is yet molten and plastic with you. You can, I was going to say, be anything you make up your minds to; and, within reasonable limits, the bold saying is true. 'Ask what thou wilt and it shall be given to thee' is what nature and Providence, almost as really as grace and Christ, say to every young man and woman, because you are the arbiters, not wholly, indeed, of your destiny, and are the architects, altogether, of your character, which is more.

And so I desire to lay upon your hearts this threadbare old truth, because you are living in the ploughing time, and the harvest is months ahead. Whilst it is true that every day is the child of all the yesterdays, and the parent of all the to-morrows, it is also true that life has its predominant colouring, varying at different epochs, and that for you, though you are largely inheriting, even now, the results of your past, brief as it is, still more largely is the future, the plastic future, in your hands, to be shaped into such forms as you will. 'The child is father of the man,' and the youth has the blessed prerogative of standing before the mouldable to-morrow, and possessing a nature still capable of being cast into an almost infinite variety of form.

But then, not only do you stand with special advantages for making yourselves what you will, but you specially need to be reminded of the terrible importance and significance of each moment. For this is the very irony of human life, that we seldom awake to the sense of its importance till it is nearly ended, and that the period when reflection would avail the most is precisely the period when it is the least strong and habitual. What is the use of an old man like me thinking about what he could make of life if he had it to do over again, as compared with the advantage of your doing it? Yet I dare say that for once that you think thus, my contemporaries do it fifty times. So, not to abate one jot of your buoyancy, not to cast any shadow over joys and hopes, but to lift you to a sense of the blessed possibilities of your position, I want to lay this principle of my text upon your consciences, and to beseech you to try to keep it operatively in mind—you are making yourselves, and settling your destiny, by every day of your plastic youth.

There is another principle as clear in my text—viz., the easy road is generally the wrong one. The sluggard was warmer at the fireside than he would be in the field with his plough in the north wind, and so he stopped there. There are always obstacles in the way of noble life. It is always easier, as flesh judges, to live ignobly than to live as Jesus Christ would have us live. 'Endure hardness' is the commandment to all who would be soldiers of any great cause, and would not fling away their lives in low self-indulgence. If a man is going to be anything worth being, or to do anything worth doing, he must start with, and adhere to this, 'to scorn delights and live laborious days.' And only then has he a chance of rising above the fat dull weed that rots in Lethe's stream, and of living anything like the life that it becomes him to live.

Be sure of this, dear young friends, that self-denial and rigid self-control, in its two forms, of stopping your ears to the attractions of lower pleasures, and of cheerily encountering difficulties, is an indispensable condition of any life which shall at the last yield a harvest worth the gathering, and not destined to be

'Cast as rubbish to the void,
When God hath made the pile complete.'

Never allow yourselves to be turned away from the plain path of duty by any difficulties. Never allow yourselves to be guided in your choice of a road by the consideration that the turf is smooth, and the flowers by the side of it sweet. Remember, the sluggard would have been warmer, with a wholesome warmth, at the ploughtail than cowering in the chimney corner. And the things that seem to be difficulties and hardships only need to be fronted to yield, like the east wind in its season, good results in bracing and hardening. Fix it in your minds that nothing worth doing is done but at the cost of difficulty and toil.

That is a lesson that this generation wants, even more than some that have lived. I suppose it is one of the temptations of older men to look askance upon the amusements of younger ones, but I cannot help lifting up here one word of earnest appeal to the young men and women of this congregation, and beseeching them, as they value the nobleness of their own lives, and their power of doing any real good, to beware of what seems to me the altogether extravagant and excessive love, and following after, of mere amusement which characterises this day to so large an extent. Better toil than such devotion to mere relaxation.

The last principle here is that the season let slip is gone for ever. Whether my text, in its second picture, intends us to think of the sluggard when the harvest came as 'begging' from his neighbours; or whether, as is possibly the construction of the Hebrew, it simply means to describe him as going out into his field, and looking at it, and asking for the harvest and seeing nothing there but weeds, the lesson it conveys is the same—the old, old lesson, so threadbare that I should be almost ashamed of taking up your time with it unless I believed that you did not lay it to heart as you should. Opportunity is bald behind, and must be grasped by the forelock. Life is full of tragic *might-have-beens*. No regret, no remorse, no self-accusation, no clear recognition that I was a fool will avail one jot. The time for ploughing is past; you cannot stick the share into the ground when you should be wielding the sickle. 'Too late' is the saddest of human words. And, my brother, as the stages of our lives roll on, unless each is filled as it passes with the discharge of the duties, and the appropriation of the benefits which it brings, then, to all eternity, that moment will never return, and the sluggard may beg in harvest, that he may have the chance to plough once more, and have none. The student that has spent the term in indolence, perhaps dissipation, has no time to get up his subject when he is in the examination-room, with the paper before him. And life, and nature, and God's law, which is the Christian expression for the heathen one of *nature*, are stern taskmasters, and demand that the duty shall be done in its season or left undone for ever.

II. In the second place, let me, just in a few words, carry the lamp of these principles of my text and flash its rays upon one or two subjects.

Let me say a word, first, about the lowest sphere to which my text applies. I referred at the beginning of this discourse to this proverb as simply an inculcation of the duty of honest work, and of the necessity of being wide awake to opportunities in our daily work. Now, the most of you young men, and many of you young women, are destined for ordinary trades, professions, walks in commerce; and I do not suppose it to be beneath the dignity of the pulpit to say this: Do not trust to any way of getting on by dodges or speculation, or favour, or anything but downright hard work. Don't shirk difficulties, don't try to put the weight of the work upon some colleague or other, that you may have an easier life of it. Set your backs to your tasks, and remember that 'in all labour there is profit'; and whether the profit comes to you in the shape of advancement, position, promotion in your offices, partnerships perhaps, wealth, and the like, or no, the profit lies in the work. Honest toil is the key to pleasure.

Then, let me apply the text in a somewhat higher direction. Carry these principles with you in the cultivation of that important part of yourself— your intellects. What would some of us old students give if we had the flexibility, the power of assimilating new truth, the retentive memories, that you young people have? Some of you, perhaps, are students by profession; I should like all of you to make a conscience of making the best of your brains, as God has given them to you, a trust. 'The sluggard will not plough by reason of the cold.' The dawdler will read no books that tax his intellect, therefore shall he beg in harvest and have nothing. Amidst all the flood of feeble, foolish, flaccid literature with which we are afflicted at this day, I wonder how many of you young men and women ever set yourselves to some great book or subject that you cannot understand without effort. Unless you do you are not faithful stewards of the supreme gift of God to you of that great faculty which apprehends and lives upon truth. So remember the sluggard by his fireside; and do you get out with your plough.

Again I say, apply these principles to a higher work still—that of the formation of character. Nothing will come to you noble, great, elevating, in that direction, unless it is sought, and sought with toil.

'In woods, in waves, in wars, she wont to dwell,
And will be found with peril and with pain;
Before her gate high Heaven did sweat ordain,
And wakeful watches ever to abide.'

Wisdom and truth, and all their elevating effects upon human character, require absolutely for their acquirement effort and toil. You have the opportunity still. As I said a moment ago—you may mould yourselves into noble forms. But in the making of character we have to work as a painter in fresco does, with a swift brush on the plaster while it is wet. It sets and hardens in an hour. And men drift into habits which become tyrannies and dominant before they know where they are. Don't let yourselves be shaped by accident, by circumstance. Remember that you can build yourselves up into forms of beauty by the help of the grace of God, and that for such building there must be the diligent labour and the wise clutching at opportunity and understanding of the times which my text suggests.

And, lastly, let these principles applied to religion teach us the wisdom and necessity of beginning the Christian life at the earliest moment. I am by no means prepared to say that the extreme tragedy of my text can ever be wrought out in regard to the religious experience of any man here on earth, for I believe that at any moment in his career, however faultful and stained his past has been, and however long and obstinate has been his continuance in evil, a man may turn himself to Jesus Christ, and beg, and not in vain, nor ever find 'nothing' there.

But whilst all that is quite true, I want you, dear young friends, to lay this to heart, that if you do not yield yourselves to Jesus Christ now, in your early days, and take Him for your Saviour, and rest your souls upon Him, and then take Him for your Captain and Commander, for your Pattern and Example, for your Companion and your Aim, you will lose what you can never make up by any future course. You lose years of blessedness, of peaceful society with Him, of illumination and inspiration. You lose all the sweetness of the days which you spend away from Him. And if at the end you did come to Him, you would have one regret, deep and permanent, that you had not gone to Him before. If you put off, as some of you are putting off, what you know you ought to do—namely, give your hearts to Jesus Christ and become His—think of what you are laying up for yourselves thereby. You get much that it would be gain to lose—bitter memories, defiled imaginations, stings of conscience, habits that it will be very hard to break, and the sense of having wasted the best part of your lives, and having but the fag end to bring to

Him. And if you put off, as some of you are disposed to do, think of the risk you run. It is very unlikely that susceptibilities will remain if they are trifled with. You remember that Felix trembled once, and sent for Paul often; but we never hear that he trembled any more. And it is quite possible, and quite likely, more likely than not, that you will never be as near being a Christian again as you are now, if you turn away from the impressions that are made upon you at this moment, and stifle the half-formed resolution.

But there is a more solemn thought still. This life as a whole is to the future life as the ploughing time is to the harvest, and there are awful words in Scripture which seem to point in the same direction in reference to the irrevocable and irreversible issue of neglected opportunities on earth, as this proverb does in regard to the ploughing and harvests of this life.

I dare not conceal what seems to me the New Testament confirmation and deepening of the solemn words of our text, 'He shall beg in harvest and have nothing,' by the Master's words, 'Many shall say to me in that day, Lord! Lord I and I will say, I never knew you.' The five virgins who rubbed their sleepy eyes and asked for oil when the master was at hand got none, and when they besought, 'Lord! Lord! open to us,' all the answer was, 'Too late! too late! ye cannot enter now.' Now, while it is called day, harden not your hearts.

BREAD AND GRAVEL

'"Bread of deceit" is sweet to a man; but afterwards his mouth shall be filled with gravel.'—PROVERBS xx. 17.

'Bread of deceit' is a somewhat ambiguous phrase, which may mean either of two things, and perhaps means both. It may either mean any good obtained by deceit, or good which deceives in its possession. In the former signification it would appear to have reference primarily to unjustly gotten gain, while in the latter it has a wider meaning and applies to all the worthless treasures and lying delights of life. The metaphor is full of homely vigour, and the contrast between the sweet bread and the gravel that fills the mouth and breaks the teeth, carries a solemn lesson which is perpetually insisted upon in this book of Proverbs, and confirmed in every man's experience.

I. The first lesson here taught is the perpetuity of the most transient actions.

We are tempted to think that a deed done is done with, and to grasp at momentary pleasure, and ignore its abiding consequences. But of all the delusions by which men are blinded to the true solemnity of life none is more fatal than that which ignores the solemn 'afterwards' that has to be taken into account. For, whatever issues in outward life our actions may have, they have all a very real influence on their doers; each of them tends to modify character, to form habits, to drag after itself a whole trail of consequences. Each strikes inwards and works outwards. The whole of a life may be set forth in the pregnant figure, 'A sower went forth to sow,' and 'Whatsoever a man soweth, that shall he also reap.' The seed may lie long dormant, but the green shoots will appear in due time, and pass through all the stages of 'first the blade, and then the ear, and after that the full corn in the ear.' The sower has to become the reaper, and the reaper has to eat of the bread made from the product of the long past sowing. Shall *we* have to reap a harvest of poisonous tares, or of wholesome wheat? 'If 'twere done when 'tis done, 'twere well it were done quickly'; but since it begins to do when 'tis done, it were often better that it were not done at all. A momentary pause to ask ourselves when tempted to evil, 'And what then?' would burst not a few of the painted bubbles after which we often chase.

Is there any reason to suppose that these permanent consequences of our transient actions are confined in their operation to this life? Does not such a present, which is mainly the continuous result of the whole past, seem at least to prophesy and guarantee a similar future? Most of us, I suppose, believe in the life continuous through and after death retributive in a greater degree than life here. Whatever changes may be involved in the laying aside of the 'earthly house of this tabernacle,' it seems folly to suppose that in it we lay aside the consequences of our past inwrought into our very selves. Surely wisdom suggests that we try to take into view the whole scope of our actions, and to carry our vision as far as the consequences reach. We should all be wiser and better if we thought more of the 'afterwards,' whether in its partial form in the present, or in its solemn completion in the future beyond.

II. The bitterness of what is sweet and wrong.

There is no need to deny that 'bread of deceit is sweet to a man.' There is a certain pleasure in a lie, and the taste of the bread purchased by it is not embittered because it has been bought by deceit. If we succeed in getting the good which any strong desire hungers after, the gratification of the desire ministers pleasure. If a man is hungry, it matters not to his hunger how he has procured the bread which he devours. And so with all forms of good which appeal to sense. The sweetness of the thing desired and obtained is more subtle, but not less real, if it nourishes some inclination or taste of a higher nature. But such sweetness in its very essence is momentary, and even, whilst being masticated, 'bread of deceit' turns into gravel; and a mouthful of it breaks the teeth, excoriates the gums, interferes with breathing, and ministers no nourishment. The metaphor has but too familiar illustrations in the experience of us all. How often have we flattered ourselves with the thought, 'If I could but get this or that, how happy I should be'? How often when we got it have we been as happy as we expected? We had forgotten the voice of conscience, which may be overborne for a moment, but begins to speak more threateningly when its prohibitions have been neglected; we had forgotten that there is no satisfying our hungry desires with 'bread of deceit,' but that they grow much faster than it can be presented to them; we had forgotten the evil that was strengthened in us when it has been fed; we had forgotten that the remembrance of past delights often becomes a present sorrow and shame; we had forgotten avenging consequences of many sorts which follow surely in the train of sweet satisfactions which are wrong.

So, even in this life nothing keeps its sweetness which is wrong, and nothing which is sweet and wrong avoids a *tang* of intensest bitterness 'afterwards.' And all that bitterness will be increased in another world, if there is another, when God gives us to read the book of our lives which we ourselves have written. Many a page that records past sweetness will then be felt to be written, 'within and without,' with lamentation and woe.

All bitterness of what is sweet and wrong makes it certain that sin is the stupidest, as well as the wickedest, thing that a man can do.

III. The abiding sweetness of true bread.

In a subordinate sense, the true bread may be taken as meaning our own deeds inspired by love of God and approved by conscience. They may often be painful to do, but the pain merges into calm pleasure, and conscience whispers a foretaste of heaven's 'Well done! good and faithful servant.' The roll may be bitter to the lips, but, eaten, becomes sweet as honey; whereas the world's bread is sweet at first but bitter at last. The highest wisdom and the most exacting conscience absolutely coincide in that which they prescribe, and Scripture has the warrant of universal experience in proclaiming that sin in its subtler and more refined forms, as well as in its grosser, is a gigantic mistake, and the true wisdom and reasonable regard for one's own interest alike point in the same direction,—to a life based on the love of God in Christ Jesus our Lord, as being the life which yields the happiest results today and perpetual bliss hereafter. But let us not forget that in the highest sense Christ Himself is the 'true bread that cometh down from heaven.' He may be bitter at first, being eaten with tears of penitence and painful efforts at conquering sin, but even in the first bitterness there is sweetness beyond all the earth can give. He 'spreads a table before us in the presence of our enemies,' and the bread which He gives tastes as the manna of old did, like wafers made of honey. Only perverted appetites loathe this light bread and prefer the strong-favoured leeks and garlics of Egypt. They who sit at the table in the wilderness will finally sit at the table prepared in the kingdom of the heavens.

A CONDENSED GUIDE FOR LIFE

'My son, if thine heart be wise, my heart shall rejoice, even mine. 16. Yea, my reins shall rejoice, when thy lips speak right things. 17. Let not thine heart envy sinners: but be thou in the fear of the Lord all the day long. 18. For surely there is an end; and thine expectation shall not be cut off. 19. Hear thou, my son, and be wise, and guide thine heart in the way. 20. Be not among winebibbers; among riotous eaters of flesh: 21. For the drunkard and the glutton shall come to poverty: and drowsiness shall clothe a man with rags. 22. Hearken unto thy father that begat thee, and despise not thy mother when she is old. 23. Buy the truth and sell it not; also wisdom, and instruction, and understanding.'—PROVERBS xxiii. 15-23.

The precepts of this passage may be said to sum up the teaching of the whole Book of Proverbs. The essentials of moral character are substantially the same in all ages, and these ancient advices fit very close to the young lives of this generation. The gospel has, no doubt, raised the standard of morals, and, in many respects, altered the conception and perspective of virtues; but its great distinction lies, not so much in the novelty of its commandments as in the new motives and powers to obey them. Reverence for parents and teachers, the habitual 'fear of the Lord,' temperance, eager efforts to win and retain 'the truth,' have always been recognised as duties; but there is a long weary distance between recognition and practice, and he who draws inspiration from Jesus Christ will have strength to traverse it, and to do and be what he knows that he should.

The passage may be broken up into four parts, which, taken together, are a young life's directory of conduct which is certain to lead to peace.

I. There is, first, an appeal to filial affection, and an unveiling of paternal sympathy (verses 15, 16). The paternal tone characteristic of the Book of Proverbs is most probably regarded as that of a teacher addressing his disciples as his children. But the glimpse of the teacher's heart here given may well apply to parents too, and ought to be true of all who can influence other and especially young hearts. Little power attends advices which are not sweetened by manifest love. Many a son has been kept back from evil by thinking, 'What would my mother say?' and many a sound admonition has been nothing but sound, because the tone of it betrayed that the giver did not much care whether it was taken or not.

A true teacher must have his heart engaged in his lessons, and must impress his scholars with the conviction that their failure drives a knife into it, and their acceptance of them brings him purest joy. On the other hand, the disciple, and still more the child, must have a singularly cold nature who does not respond to loving solicitude and does not care whether he wounds or gladdens the heart which pours out its love and solicitude over him. May we not see shining through this loving appeal a truth in reference to the heart of the great Father and Teacher, who, in the depths of His divine blessedness, has no greater joy than that His children should walk in the truth? God's heart is glad when man's is wise.

Note, also, the wide general expression for goodness—a wise heart, lips speaking right things. The former is source, the latter stream. Only a pure fountain will send forth sweet waters. 'If thy heart become wise' is the more correct rendering, implying that there is no inborn wisdom, but that it must be made ours by effort. We *are* foolish; we *become* wise.

What the writer means by wisdom he will tell us presently. Here he lets us see that it is a good to be attained by appropriate means. It is the foundation of 'right' speech. Nothing is more remarkable than the solemn importance which Scripture attaches to words, even more, we might almost say than to deeds, therein reversing the usual estimate of their relative value. Putting aside the cases of insincerity, falsehood, and the like, a man's speech is a truer transcript of himself than his deeds, because less hindered and limited by externals. The most precious wine drips from the grapes by their own weight in the vat, without a turn of the screw. 'By thy words thou shalt be justified, and by thy words thou shalt be condemned.' 'God's great gift of speech abused' is one of the commonest, least considered, and most deadly sins.

II. We have next the one broad precept with its sure reward, which underlies all goodness (verses 17, 18). The supplement 'be thou,' in the second clause of verse 17, obscures the close connection of clauses. It is better to regard the verb of the first clause as continued in the second. Thus the one precept is set forth negatively and positively: 'Strive not after [that is, seek not to imitate or be associated with] sinners, but after the fear of the Lord.' The heart so striving becomes wise. So, then, wisdom is not the result of cultivating the intellect, but of educating the desires and aspirations. It is moral and religious, rather than simply intellectual. The magnificent personification of Wisdom at the beginning of the book influences the subsequent parts, and the key to understanding that great conception is, 'The fear of the Lord is the beginning of Wisdom.' The Greek goddess of Wisdom, noble as she is, is of the earth earthy when contrasted with that sovereign figure. Pallas Athene, with her clear eyes and shining armour, is poor beside the Wisdom of the Book of Proverbs, who dwelt with God 'or ever the earth was,' and comes to men with loving voice and hands laden with the gifts of 'durable riches and righteousness.'

He is the wise man who fears God with the fear which has no torment and is compact of love and reverence. He is on the way to become wise whose seeking heart turns away from evil and evil men, and feels after God, as the vine tendrils after a stay, or as the sunflower turns to the light. For such wholehearted desire after the one supreme good there must be resolute averting of desire from 'sinners.' In this world full of evil there will be no vigorous longing for good and God, unless there be determined abstention from the opposite. We have but a limited quantity of energy, and if it is frittered away on multifarious creatures, none will be left to consecrate to God. There are lakes which discharge their waters at both ends, sending one stream east to the Atlantic and one west to the Pacific; but the heart cannot direct its issues of life in that fashion. They must be banked up if they are to run deep and strong. 'All the current of my being' must 'set to thee' if my tiny trickle is to reach the great ocean, to be lost in which is blessedness.

And such energy of desire and direction is not to be occasional, but 'all the day long.' It is possible to make life an unbroken seeking after and communion with God, even while plunged in common tasks and small cares. It is possible to approximate indefinitely to that ideal of continually 'dwelling in the house of the Lord'; and without some such approximation there will be little realising of the Lord, sought by fits and starts, and then forgotten in the hurry of business or pleasure. A photographic plate exposed for hours will receive the picture of far-off stars which would never show on one exposed for a few minutes.

The writer is sure that such desires will be satisfied, and in verse 18 says so. The 'reward' (Rev. Ver.) of which he is sure is the outcome of the life of such seekers after God. It does not necessarily refer to the future after death, though that may be included in it. But what is meant is that no seeking after the fear of the Lord shall be in vain. There is a tacit emphasis on 'thy,' contrasting the sure fulfilment of hopes set on God with the as sure 'cutting of' of those mistakenly fixed upon creatures and vanities. Psalm xxxvii. 38, has the same word here rendered 'reward' and declares that 'the future [or reward] of the wicked shall be cut off.' The great fulfilment of this assurance is reserved for the life beyond; but even here among all disappointments and hopes of which fulfilment is so often disappointment also, it remains true that the one striving which cannot be fruitless is striving for more of God, and the one hope which is sure to be realised, and is better when realised than expected, is the hope set on Him. Surely, then, the certainty that if we delight ourselves in God He will give us the desires of our hearts, is a good argument, and should be with us an operative motive for directing desire and effort away from earth and towards Him.

III. Special precepts as to the control of the animal nature follow in verses 19-21. First, note that general one of verse 19, 'Guide thine heart in the way.' In most general terms, the necessity of self-government is laid down. There is a 'way' in which we should be content to travel. It is a definite path, and feet have to be kept from straying aside to wide wastes on either hand.

Limitation, the firm suppression of appetites, the coercing of these if they seek to draw aside, are implied in the very conception of 'the way.' And a man must take the upper hand of himself, and, after all other guidance, must be his own guide; for God guides us by enabling us to guide ourselves.

Temperance in the wider sense of the word is prominent among the virtues flowing from fear of the Lord, and is the most elementary instance of 'guiding the heart.' Other forms of self-restraint in regard to animal appetites are spoken of in the context, but here the two of drunkenness and gluttony are bracketed together. They are similarly coupled in Deuteronomy xxi. 20, in the formula of accusation which parents are to bring against a degenerate son. Allusion to that passage is probable here, especially as the other crime mentioned in it—namely, refusal to 'hear' parental reproof—is warned against in verse 22. The picture, then, here is that of a prodigal son, and we have echoes of it in the great parable which paints first riotous living, and then poverty and misery.

Drunkenness had obviously not reached the dimensions of a national curse in the date when this lesson was written. We should not put over-eating side by side with it. But its ruinous consequences were plain then, and the bitter experience of England and America repeats on a larger scale the old lesson that the most productive source of poverty, wretchedness, rags, and vice, is drink. Judges and social reformers of all sorts concur in that now, though it has taken fifty years to hammer it into the public conscience. Perhaps in another fifty or so society may have succeeded in drawing the not very obscure inference that total abstinence and prohibition are wise. At any rate, they who seek after the fear of the Lord should draw it, and act on it.

IV. The last part is in verses 22 and 23. The appeal to filial duty cannot here refer to disciple and teacher, but to child and parents. It does not stand as an isolated precept, but as underscoring the important one which follows. But a word must be spared for it. The habits of ancient days gave a place to the father and mother which modern family life woefully lacks, and suffers in many ways for want of. Many a parent in these days of slack control and precocious independence might say, 'If I be a father, where is mine honour?' There was perhaps not enough of confidence between parent and child in former days, and authority on the one hand and submission on the other too much took the place of love; but nowadays the danger is all the other way— and it is a very real danger.

But the main point here is the earnest exhortation of verse 23, which, like that to the fear of the Lord, sums up all duty in one. The 'truth' is, like 'wisdom,' moral and religious, and not merely intellectual. 'Wisdom' is subjective, the quality or characteristic of the devout soul; 'truth' is objective, and may also be defined as the declared will of God. The possession of truth is wisdom. 'The entrance of Thy words giveth light.' It makes wise the simple. There is, then, such a thing as 'the truth' accessible to us. We can know it, and are not to be for ever groping amid more or less likely guesses, but may rest in the certitude that we have hold of foundation facts. For us, the truth is incarnate in Jesus, as He has solemnly asserted. That truth we shall, if we are wise, 'buy,' by shunning no effort, sacrifice, or trouble needed to secure it.

In the lower meanings of the word, our passage should fire us all, and especially the young, to strain every muscle of the soul in order to make truth for the intellect our own. The exhortation is needed in this day of adoration of money and material good. Nobler and wiser far the young man who lays himself out to know than he who is engrossed with the hungry desire to have! But in the highest region of truth, the buying is 'without money and without price,' and all that we can give in exchange is ourselves. We buy the truth when we know that we cannot earn it, and forsaking self-trust and self-pleasing, consent to receive it as a free gift. 'Sell it not,'—let no material good or advantage, no ease, slothfulness, or worldly success, tempt you to cast it away; for its 'fruit is better than gold,' and its 'revenue than choice silver.' We shall make a bad bargain if we sell it for anything beneath the stars; for 'wisdom is better than rubies,' and he has been cheated in the transaction who has given up 'the truth' and got instead 'the whole world.'

THE AFTERWARDS AND OUR HOPE

'Be thou in the fear of the Lord all the day long. 18. For surely there is an end and thine expectation shall not be cut off.'—PROVERBS xxiii. 17, 18.

The Book of Proverbs seldom looks beyond the limits of the temporal, but now and then the mists lift and a wider horizon is disclosed. Our text is one of these exceptional instances, and is remarkable, not only as expressing confidence in the future, but as expressing it in a very striking way. 'Surely there is an end,' says our Authorised Version, substituting in the margin, for end, 'reward.' The latter word is placed in the text of the Revised Version. But neither 'end' nor 'reward' conveys the precise idea. The word so translated literally means 'something that comes after.' So it is the very opposite of 'end', it is really that which lies beyond the end—the 'sequel,' or the 'future'—as the margin of the Revised Version gives alternatively, or, more simply still, the afterwards. Surely there is an afterwards behind the end. And then the proverb goes on to specify one aspect of that afterwards: 'Thine expectation'—or, better, because more simply, thy hope—shall not be cut off. And then, upon these two convictions that there is, if I might so say, an afterclap, and that it is the time and the sphere in which the fairest hopes that a man can paint to himself shall be surpassed by the reality, it builds the plain partial exhortation: 'Be thou in the fear of the Lord all the day long.'

So then, we have three things here, the certainty of the afterwards, the immortality of hope consequent thereon, and the bearing of these facts on the present.

I. The certainty of the hereafter.

Now, this Book of Proverbs, as I have said in the great collection of popular sayings which makes the bulk of it, has no enthusiasm, no poetry, no mysticism. It has religion, and it has a very pure and lofty morality, but, for the most part, it deals with maxims of worldly prudence, and sometimes with cynical ones, and represents, on the whole, the wisdom of the market-place, and the 'man in the street.' But now and then, as I have said, we hear strains of a higher mood. My text, of course, might be watered down and narrowed so as to point only to sequels to deeds realised in this life. And then it would be teaching us simply the very much needed lessons that even in this life, 'Whatever a man soweth that shall he also reap.' But it seems to me that we are entitled to see here, as in one or two other places in the Book of Proverbs, a dim anticipation of a future life beyond the grave. I need not trouble you with quoting parallel passages which are sown thinly up and down the book, but I venture to take the words in the wider sense to which I have referred.

Now, the question comes to be, where did the coiners of Proverbs, whose main interest was in the obvious maxims of a prudential morality, get this conviction? They did not get it from any lofty experience of communion with God, like that which in the seventy-third Psalm marks the very high-water mark of Old Testament faith in regard to a future life, where the Psalmist finds himself so completely blessed and well in present fellowship with God, that he must needs postulate its eternal continuance, and just because he has made God the portion of his heart, and is holding fellowship with Him, is sure that nothing can intervene to break that sweet communion. They did not get it from any clear definite revelation, such as we have in the resurrection of Jesus Christ, which has made that future life far more than an inference for us, but they got it from thinking over the facts of this present life as they appeared to them, looked at from the standpoint of a belief in God, and in righteousness. And so they represent to us the impression that is made upon a man's mind, if he has the 'eye that hath kept watch o'er man's mortality,' that is made by the facts of this earthly life—viz. that it is so full of onward-looking, prophetic aspect, so manifestly and tragically, and yet wonderfully and hopefully. Incomplete and fragmentary in itself, that there must be something beyond in order to explain, in order to vindicate, the life that now is. And that aspect of fragmentary incompleteness is what I would insist upon for a moment now.

You sometimes see a row of houses, the end one of them has, in its outer gable wall, bricks protruding here and there, and holes for chimney-pieces that are yet to be put in. And just as surely as that external wall says that the row is half built, and there are some more tenements to be added to it, so surely does the life that we now live here, in all its aspects almost, bear upon itself the stamp that it, too, is but initial and preparatory. You sometimes see, in the bookseller's catalogue, a book put down 'volume one; all that is published.' That is our present life—volume one, all that is published. Surely there is going to be a sequel, volume two. Volume two is due, and will come, and it will be the continuation of volume one.

What is the meaning of the fact that of all the creatures on the face of the earth only you and I, and our brethren and sisters, do not find in our environment enough for our powers? What is the meaning of the fact that, whilst 'foxes have holes' where they curl themselves up, and they are at rest, 'and the birds of the air have roosting-places,' where they tuck their heads beneath their wings and sleep, the 'son of man' hath not where to lay his head, but looks round upon the earth and says, 'The earth, O Lord, is full of Thy mercy. I am a stranger on the earth.' What is the meaning of it? Here is the meaning of it: 'Surely there is a hereafter.'

What is the meaning of the fact that lodged in men's natures there lies that strange power of painting to themselves things that are not as though they were? So that minds and hearts go out wandering through Eternity, and having longings and possibilities which nothing beneath the stars can satisfy, or can develop? The meaning of it is this: Surely there is a hereafter. The man that wrote the book of Ecclesiastes, in his sceptical moment ere he had attained to his last conclusion, says, in a verse that is mistranslated in our rendering, 'He hath set Eternity in their hearts, therefore the misery of man is great upon him.' That is true, because the root of all our unrest and dissatisfaction is that we need God, and God in Eternity, in order that we may be at rest. But whilst on the one hand 'therefore the misery of man is great upon him,' on the other hand, because Eternity is in our hearts, therefore there is the answer to the longings, the adequate sphere for the capacities in that great future, and in the God that fills it. You go into the quarries left by reason of some great convulsion or disaster, by forgotten races, and you will find there half excavated and rounded pillars still adhering to the matrix of the rock from which they were being hewn. Such unfinished abortions are all human lives if, when Death drops its curtain, there is an end.

But, brethren, God does not so clumsily disproportion His creatures and their place. God does not so cruelly put into men longings that have no satisfaction, and desires which never can be filled, as that there should not be, beyond the gulf, the fair land of the hereafter. Every human life obviously has in it, up to the very end, the capacity for progress. Every human life, up to the very end, has been educated and trained, and that, surely, for something. There may be masters in workshops who take apprentices, and teach them their trade during the years that are needed, and then turn round and say, 'I have no work for you, so you must go and look for it somewhere else.' That is not how God does. When He has trained His apprentices He gives them work to do. Surely there is a hereafter,

But that is only part of what is involved in this thought. It is not only a state subsequent to the present, but it is a state consequent on the present, and the outcome of it. The analogy of our earthly life avails here. To-day is the child of all the yesterdays, and the yesterdays and to-day are the parent of tomorrow. The past, our past, has made us what we are in the present, and what we are in the present is making us what we shall be in the future. And when we pass out of this life we pass out, notwithstanding all changes, the same men as we were. There may be much on the surface changed, there will be much taken away, thank God! dropped, necessarily, by the cessation of the corporeal frame, and the connection into which it brings us with things of sense. There will be much added, God only knows how much, but the core of the man will remain untouched. 'We all are changed by still degrees,' and suddenly at last 'All but the basis of the evil.' And so we carry ourselves with us into that future life, and, 'what a man soweth, that shall he also reap.' Oh that they were wise, that they understood this, that they would consider their afterward!

II. Now, secondly, my text suggests the immortality of hope. 'Thine expectation'—or rather, as I said, 'thy hope'—'shall not be cut off.' This is a characteristic of that hereafter. What a wonderful saying that is which also occurs in this Book of Proverbs, 'The righteous hath hope in his death.' Ah! we all know how swiftly, as years increase, the things to hope for diminish, and how, as we approach the end, less and less do our imaginations go out into the possibilities of the sorrowing future. And when the end comes, if there is no afterwards, the dying man's hopes must necessarily die before he does. If when we pass into the darkness we are going into a cave with no outlet at the other end, then there is no hope, and you may write over it Dante's grim word: 'All hope abandon, ye who enter here.' But let in that thought, 'surely there is an afterwards,' and the enclosed cave becomes a rock-passage, in which one can see the arch of light at the far end of the tunnel; and as one passes through the gloom, the eye can travel on to the pale radiance beyond, and anticipate the ampler ether, the diviner air, 'the brighter constellations burning, mellow moons and happy stars,' that await us there. 'The righteous hath hope in his death.' 'Thine expectation shall not be cut off.'

But, further, that conviction of the afterward opens up for us a condition in which imagination is surpassed by the wondrous reality. Here, I suppose, nobody ever had all the satisfaction out of a fulfilled hope that he expected. The fish is always a great deal larger and heavier when we see it in the water than when it is lifted out and scaled. And I suppose that, on the whole, perhaps as much pain as pleasure comes from the hopes which are illusions far more often than they are realities. They serve their purpose in whirling us along the path of life and in stimulating effort, but they do not do much more.

But there does come a time, if you believe that there is an afterwards, when all we desired and painted to ourselves of possible good for our craving spirits shall be felt to be but a pale reflex of the reality, like the light of some unrisen sun on the snowfields, and we shall have to say 'the half was not told to us.'

And, further, if that afterwards is of the sort that we, through Jesus Christ and His resurrection and glory, know to be, then all through the timeless eternity hope will be our guide. For after each fresh influx of blessedness and knowledge we shall have to say 'it doth not yet appear what we shall be.' 'Thus now abideth'—and not only now, but then and eternally—'these three—faith, hope, and charity,' and hope will never be cut off through all the stretch of that great afterwards.

III. And now, finally, notice the bearing of all this on the daily present.

'Be thou in the fear of the Lord all the day long.' The conviction of the hereafter, and the blessed vision of hopes fulfilled, are not the only reasons for that exhortation. A great deal of harm has been done, I am afraid, by well-meaning preachers who have drawn the bulk of their strongest arguments to persuade men to Christian faith from the thought of a future life. Why, if there were no future, it would be just as wise, just as blessed, just as incumbent upon us to 'be in the fear of the Lord all the day long.' But seeing that there is that future, and seeing that only in it will hope rise to fruition, and yet subsist as longing, surely there comes to us a solemn appeal to 'be in the fear of the Lord all the day long,' which being turned into Christian language, is to live by habitual faith, in communion with, and love and obedience to, our Lord and Saviour Jesus Christ.

Surely, surely the very climax and bad eminence of folly is shutting the eyes to that future that we all have to face; and to live here, as some of you are doing, ignoring it and God, and cribbing, cabining, and confining all our thoughts within the narrow limits of the things present and visible. For to live so, as our text enjoins, is the sure way, and the only way, to make these great hopes realities for ourselves.

Brethren, that afterwards has two sides to it. The prophet Malachi, in almost his last words, has a magnificent apocalypse of what he calls 'the day of the Lord,' which he sets forth as having a double aspect. On the one hand, it is lurid as a furnace, and burns up the wicked root and branch. I saw a forest fire this last autumn, and the great pine-trees stood there for a moment pyramids of flame, and then came down with a crash. So that hereafter will be to godless men. And on the other side, that 'day of the Lord' in the prophet's vision was radiant with the freshness and dew and beauty of morning, and the Sun of Righteousness arose with healing in his wings. Which of the two is it going to be to us? We have all to face it. We cannot alter that fact, but we can settle how we shall face it. It will be to either the fulfilment of blessed hope, the 'appearance of the glory of the great God and our Saviour,' or else, as is said in this same Book of Proverbs: 'The hope of the godless' shall be like one of those water plants, the papyrus or the flag, which, when the water is taken away, 'withereth up before any other herb.' It is for us to determine whether the afterwards that we must enter upon shall be the land in which our hopes shall blossom and fruit, and blossom again immortally, or whether we shall leave behind us, with all the rest that we would fain keep, the possibility of anticipating any good. 'Surely there is an afterwards,' and if thou wilt 'be in the fear of the Lord all the day long,' then for evermore 'thy hope shall not be cut off.'

THE PORTRAIT OF A DRUNKYARD

'Who hath woe? who hath sorrow? who hath contentions? who hath babbling? who hath wounds without cause? who hath redness of eyes? 30. They that tarry long at the wine; they that go to seek mixed wine. 31. Look not thou upon the wine when it is red, when it giveth his colour in the cup, when it moveth itself aright. 32. At the last it biteth like a serpent, and stingeth like an adder. 33. Thine eyes shall behold strange women, and thine heart shall utter perverse things. 34. Yea, thou shalt be as he that lieth down in the midst of the sea, or as he that lieth upon the top of a mast. 35. They have stricken me, shalt thou say, and I was not sick; they have beaten me, and I felt it not: when shall I awake! I will seek it yet again.'—PROVERBS xxiii. 29-35.

This vivid picture of the effects of drunkenness leaves its sinfulness and its wider consequences out of sight, and fixes attention on the sorry spectacle which a man makes of himself in body and mind when he 'puts an enemy into his mouth to steal away his brains.' Disgust and ridicule are both expressed. The writer would warn his 'son' by impressing the ugliness and ludicrousness of drunkenness. The argument is legitimate, though not the highest.

The vehement questions poured out on each other's heels in verse 29 are hot with both loathing and grim laughter. The two words rendered 'woe' and 'sorrow' are unmeaning exclamations, very like each other in sound, and imitating the senseless noises of the drunkard. They express discomfort as a dog might express it. They are howls rather than words. That is one of the prerogatives won by drunkenness,—to come down to the beasts' level, and to lose the power of articulate speech. The quarrelsomeness which goes along with certain stages of intoxication, and the unmeaning maudlin misery and whimpering into which it generally passes, are next coupled together.

Then come a pair of effects on the body. The tipsy man cannot take care of himself, and reeling against obstacles, or falling over them, wounds himself, and does not know where the scratches and blood came from. 'Redness of eyes' is, perhaps, rather 'darkness,' meaning thereby dim sight, or possibly 'black eyes,' as we say,—a frequent accompaniment of drunkenness, and corresponding to the wounds in the previous clause. It is a hideous picture, and one that should be burned in on the imagination of every young man and woman. The liquor-sodden, miserable wrecks that are found in thousands in our great cities, of whom this is a picture, were, most of them, in Sunday-schools in their day. The next generation of such poor creatures are, many of them, in Sunday-schools now, and may be reading this passage to-day.

The answer to these questions has a touch of irony in it. The people who win as their possessions these six precious things have to sit up late to earn them. What a noble cause in which to sacrifice sleep, and turn night into day! And they pride themselves on being connoisseurs in the several vintages; they 'know a good glass of wine when they see it.' What a noble field for investigation! What a worthy use of the faculties of comparison and judgment! And how desirable the prizes won by such trained taste and delicate discrimination!

In verses 31 and 32 weighty warning and dehortation follow, based in part on the preceding picture. The writer thinks that the only way of sure escape from the danger is to turn away even the eyes from the temptation. He is not contented with saying 'taste not,' but he goes the whole length of 'look not'; and that because the very sparkle and colour may attract. 'When it is red' might perhaps better be rendered 'when it reddens itself,' suggesting the play of colour, as if put forth by the wine itself. The word rendered in the Authorised Version and Revised Version 'colour' is literally 'eye,' and probably means the beaded bubbles winking on the surface. 'Moveth itself aright' (Authorised Version) is not so near the meaning as 'goeth down smoothly' (Revised Version). The whole paints the attractiveness to sense of the wine-cup in colour, effervescence, and taste.

And then comes in, with startling abruptness, the end of all this fascination,—a serpent's bite and a basilisk's sting. The kind of poisonous snake meant in the last clause of verse 32 is doubtful, but certainly is one much more formidable than an adder. The serpent's lithe gracefulness and painted skin hide a fatal poison; and so the attractive wine-cup is sure to ruin those who look on it. The evil consequences are pursued in more detail in what follows.

But here we must note two points. The advice given is to keep entirely away from the temptation. 'Look not' is safe policy in regard of many of the snares for young lives that abound in our modern society. It is not at all needful to 'see life,' or to know the secrets of wickedness, in order to be wise and good. 'Simple concerning evil' is a happier state than to have eaten the fruit of the tree of knowledge. Many a young man has been ruined, body and soul, by a prurient curiosity to know what sort of life dissipated men and women led, or what sort of books they were against which he was warned, or what kind of a place a theatre was, and so on. Eyes are greedy, and there is a very quick telephone from them to the desires. 'The lust of the eye' soon fans the 'lust of the flesh' into a glow. There are plenty of depths of Satan gaping for young feet; and on the whole, it is safer and happier not to know them, and so not to have defiling memories, nor run the risk of falling into fatal sins. Whether the writer of this stern picture of a drunkard was a total abstainer or not, the spirit of his counsel not to 'look on the wine' is in full accord with that practice. It is very clear that if a man is a total abstainer, he can never be a drunkard. As much cannot be said of the moderate man.

Note too, how in all regions of life, the ultimate results of any conduct are the important ones. Consequences are hard to calculate, and they do not afford a good guidance for action. But there are many lines of conduct of which the consequences are not hard to calculate, but absolutely certain. It is childish to take a course because of a moment's gratification at the beginning, to be followed by protracted discomfort afterwards. To live for present satisfaction of desires, and to shut one's eyes tight against known and assured results of an opposite sort, cannot be the part of a sensible man, to say nothing of a religious one. So moralists have been preaching ever since there was such a thing as temptation in the world; and men have assented to the common sense of the teaching, and then have gone straight away and done the exact opposite.

'What shall the end be?' ought to be the question at every beginning. If we would cultivate the habit of holding present satisfactions in suspense, and of giving no weight to present advantages until we saw right along the road to the end of the journey, there would be fewer failures, and fewer weary, disenchanted old men and women, to lament that the harvest they had to reap and feed on was so bitter. There are other and higher reasons against any kind of fleshly indulgence than that at the last it bites like a serpent, and with a worse poison than serpent's sting ever darted; but that is a reason, and young hearts, which are by their very youth blessedly unused to look forward, will be all the happier to-day, and all the surer of to-morrow's good, if they will learn to say, 'And afterwards—what?'

The passage passes to a renewed description of the effects of intoxication, in which the disgusting and the ludicrous aspects of it are both made prominent. Verse 33 seems to describe the excited imagination of the drunkard, whose senses are no longer under his control, but play him tricks that make him a laughingstock to sober people. One might almost take the verse to be a description of delirium tremens. 'Strange things' are seen, and perverse things (that is, unreal, or ridiculous) are stammered out. The writer has a keen sense of the humiliation to a man of being thus the fool of his own bewildered senses, and as keen a one of the absurd spectacle he presents; and he warns his 'son' against coming down to such a depth of degradation.

It may be questioned whether the boasted quickening and brightening effects of alcohol are not always, in a less degree, that same beguiling of sense and exciting of imagination which, in their extreme form, make a man such a pitiable and ridiculous sight. It is better to be dull and see things as they are, than to be brilliant and see things larger, brighter, or any way other than they are, because we see them through a mist. Imagination set agoing by such stimulus, will not work to as much purpose as if aroused by truth. God's world, seen by sober eyes, is better than rosy dreams of it. If we need to draw our inspiration from alcohol, we had better remain uninspired. If we desire to know the naked truth of things, the less we have to do with strong drink the better. Clear eyesight and self-command are in some degree impaired by it always. The earlier stages are supposed to be exhilaration, increased brilliancy of fancy and imagination, expanded good-fellowship, and so on. The latter stages are these in our passage, when strange things dance before cheated eyes, and strange words speak themselves out of lips which their owner no longer controls. Is that a condition to be sought after? If not, do not get on to the road that leads to it.

Verse 34 adds another disgusting and ridiculous trait. A man who should try to lie down and go to sleep in the heart of the sea or on the masthead of a ship would be a manifest fool, and would not keep life in him for long. One has seen drunken men laying themselves down to sleep in places as exposed and as ridiculous as these; and one knows the look of the heavy lump of insensibility lying helpless on public roads, or on railway tracks, or anywhere where the fancy took him. The point of the verse seems to be the drunken man's utter loss of sense of fitness, and complete incapacity to take care of himself. He cannot estimate dangers. The very instinct of self-preservation has forsaken him. There he lies, though as sure to be drowned as if he were in the depth of the sea, though on as uncomfortable a bed as if he were rocking on a masthead, where he could not balance himself.

The torpor of verse 34 follows on the unnatural excitement of verse 33, as, in fact, the bursts of uncontrolled energy in which the man sees and says strange things, are succeeded by a collapse. One moment raging in excitement caused by imaginary sights, the next huddled together in sleep like death,—what a sight the man is! The teacher here would have his 'son' consider that he may come to that, if he looks on the wine-cup. '*Thou* shalt be' so and so. It is very impolite, but very necessary, to press home the individual application of pictures like this, and to bid bright young men and women look at the wretched creatures they may see hanging about liquor shops, and remember that they may come to be such as these.

Verse 35 finishes the picture. The tipsy man's soliloquy puts the copestone on his degradation. He has been beaten, and never felt it. Apparently he is beginning to stir in his sleep, though not fully awake; and the first thing he discovers when he begins to feel himself over is that he has been beaten and wounded, and remembers nothing about it. A degrading anaesthetic is drink. Better to bear all ills than to drown them by drowning consciousness. There is no blow which a man cannot bear better if he holds fast by God's hand and keeps himself fully exposed to the stroke, than if he sought a cowardly alleviation of it, softer the drunkard's fashion.

But the pains of his beating and the discomforts of his waking do not deter the drunkard. 'When shall I awake?' He is not fully awake yet, so as to be able to get up and go for another drink. He is in the stage of feeling sorry for himself, and examining his bruises, but he wishes he were able to shake off the remaining drowsiness, that he might 'seek yet again' for his curse. The tyranny of desire, which wakes into full activity before the rest of the man does, and the enfeebled will, which, in spite of all bruises and discomforts, yields at once to the overmastering desire, make the tragedy of a drunkard's life. There comes a point in lives of fleshly indulgence in which the craving seems to escape from the control of the will altogether. Doctors tell us that the necessity for drink becomes a physical disease. Yes; but it is a disease manufactured by the patient, and he is responsible for getting himself into such a state.

This tragic picture proves that there were many originals of it in the days when it was painted. Probably there are far more, in proportion to population, in our times. The warning it peals out was never more needed than now. Would that all preachers, parents, and children laid it to heart and took the advice not even to 'look upon the wine'!

THE CRIME OF NEGLIGENCE

'If thou forbear to deliver them that are drawn unto death, and those that are ready to be slain; 12. If thou sayest, Behold, we knew it not; doth not he that pondereth the heart consider it? and he that keepeth thy soul, doth not he render to every man according to his works?'—PROVERBS xxiv. 11, 12.

What is called the missionary spirit is nothing else than the Christian church working in a particular direction. If a man has a conviction, the health of his own soul, his reverence for the truth he has learnt to love, his necessary connection with other men, make it a duty, a necessity, and a joy to tell what he has heard, and to speak what he believes. On these common grounds rests the whole obligation of Christ's followers to speak the Gospel which they have received; only the obligation presses on them with greater force because of the higher worth of the word and the deeper misery of men without it. The text contains nothing specially bearing on Christian missions, but it deals with the fault which besets us all in our relations and in life: and the wholesome truths which it utters apply to our duties in regard to Christian missions because they apply to our duties in regard to every misery within our reach. They speak of the murderous cruelty and black sin of negligence to save any whom we can help from any sort of misery which threatens them. They appear to me to suggest four thoughts which I would now deal with:—

I. The crime of negligence.

Not to use any power is a sin; to omit to do anything that we can do is a crime: to withhold a help that we can render is to participate in the authorship of all the misery that we have failed to relieve. He who neglects to save a life, kills. There are more murderers than those who lift violent hands with malice aforethought against a hated life. Rulers or communities who leave people uncared for to die, who suffer swarming millions to live where the air is poison and the light is murky, and first the soul and then the body, are dwarfed and die; the incompetent men in high places, and the indolent ones in low, whose selfishness brings, and whose blundering blindness allows to continue, the conditions that are fatal to life—on these the guilt of blood lies. Violence slays its thousands, but supine negligence slays its tens of thousands.

And when we pass from these merely physical conditions to think of the world and of the Church in the world, where shall we find words weighty and burning enough to tell what fatal cruelty lies in the unthinking negligence so characteristic of large portions of Christ's professed followers? There is nothing which the ordinary type of Christian, so called, more needs than to be aroused to a living sense of personal responsibility for all the unalleviated misery of the world. For every one who has laid the sorrows of humanity on his heart, and has felt them in any measure as his own, there are a hundred to whom these make no appeal and give no pang. Within ear-shot of our churches and chapels there are squalid aggregations of stunted and festering manhood, of whom it is only too true that they are 'drawn unto death' and 'ready to be slain,' and yet it would be an exaggeration to say that the bulk of our congregations cast even a languid eye of compassion upon those, to say nothing of stretching out a hand to help. It needs to be dinned, far more than it is at present, into every professing Christian that each of us has an obligation which cannot be ignored or shuffled off, to acquaint ourselves with the glaring facts that force themselves upon all thoughtful men, and that the measure of our power is the measure of our obligation. The question, Has the church done its best to deliver these? needs to be sharpened to the point of 'Have I done my best?' And the vision of multitudes perishing in the slums of a great city needs to be expanded into the vision of dim millions perishing in the wide world.

II. The excuse of negligence.

The shuffling plea, 'Behold we knew it not,' is a cowardly lie. It admits the responsibility to knowledge and pretends an ignorance which it knows to be partly a false excuse, and in so far as it is true, to be our own fault. We are bound to know, and the most ignorant of us does know, and cannot help knowing, enough to condemn our negligence. How many of us have ever tried to find out how the pariahs of civilisation live who live beside us? Our ignorance so far as it is real is the result of a sinful indolence. And there is a sadder form of it in an ignorance which is the result of familiarity. We all know how custom dulls our impressions. It is well that it should be so, for a surgeon would be fit for little if he trembled and was shaken at the sight of the tumour he had to work to remove, as we should be; but his familiarity with misery does not harden him, because he seeks to remove the suffering with which he has become familiar. But that same familiarity does harden and injure the whole nature of the onlooker who does nothing to alleviate it. Then there is an ignorance of other suffering which is the result of selfish absorption in one's own concerns. The man who is caring for himself only, and whose thoughts and feelings all flow in the direction of his own success, may see spread before him the most poignant sorrows without feeling one throb of brotherly compassion and without even being aware of what his eyes see. So, in so far as the excuse 'we knew it not' is true, it is no excuse, but an indictment. It lays bare the true reason of the criminal negligence as being a yet more criminal callousness as to the woe and loss in which such crowds of men whom we ought to recognise as brethren are sunken.

III. The condemnation of negligence.

The great example of God is put forward in the text as the contrast to all this selfish negligence. Note the twofold description of Him given here, 'He that pondereth the heart,' and 'He that keepeth thy soul.' The former of these presents to us God's sedulous watching of the hearts of men, in contrast to our indolent and superficial looks; and in this divine attitude we find the awful condemnation of our disregard of our fellows. God 'takes pain,' so to speak, to see after His children. Are they not bound to look lovingly on each other? God seeks to know them. Are they not bound to know one another? Lofty disregard of human suffering is not *God's* way. Is it ours? He 'looks down from the height of His sanctuary to hear the crying of the prisoner.' Should not we stoop from our mole-hill to see it? God has not too many concerns on His hands to mark the obscurest sorrow and be ready to help it. And shall we plead that we are too busy with petty personal concerns to take interest in helping the sorrows and fighting against the sins of the world?

No less eloquently does the other name which is here applied to God rebuke our negligence. 'He preserveth thy soul.' By His divine care and communication of life, we live; and surely the soul thus preserved is thereby bound to be a minister of preservation to all that are 'ready to be slain.' The strongest motive for seeking to save others is that God has saved us. Thus this name for God touches closely upon the great Christian thought, 'Christ has given Himself for me.' And in that thought we find the true condemnation of a Christianity which has not caught from Him the enthusiasm for self-surrender, and the passion for saving the outcast and forlorn. If to be a Christian is to imitate Christ, then the name has little application to those who see 'them that are drawn to death,' and turn from them unconcerned and unconscious of responsibility.

IV. The judgment of negligence.

'Doth not He render to every man according to his works?' There is such a judgment both in the present and in the future for Christian men as for others. And not only what they do, but what they inconsistently fail to do, comes into the category of their works, and influences their position. It does so in the present, for no man can cherish such a maimed Christian life as makes such negligence possible without robbing himself of much that would tend to his own growth in grace and likeness to Jesus Christ. The unfaithful servant is poorer by the pound hidden in the napkin which might all the while have been laid out at interest with the money-changers, which would have increased the income whilst the lord was absent. We rob ourselves of blessed sympathies and of the still more blessed joy of service, and of the yet more blessed joy of successful effort, by our indolence and our negligence. Let us not forget that our works do follow us in this life as in the life to come, and that it is here as well as hereafter, that he that goeth forth with a full basket and scatters the precious seed with weeping, and yet with joy, shall doubtless come again bringing his sheaves with him. And if we stretch our view to take in the life beyond, what gladness can match that of the man who shall enter there with some who will be his joy and crown of rejoicing in that day, and of whom he shall be able to say, 'Behold I and the children whom Thou hast given me!'

I venture earnestly to appeal to all my hearers for more faithful discharge of this duty. I pray you to open your ears to hear, and your eyes to see, and your hearts to feel, and last of all, your hands to help, the miseries of the world. Solemn duties wait upon great privileges. It is an awful trust to have Christ and His gospel committed to our care. We get it because from One who lived no life of luxurious ease, but felt all the woes of humanity which He redeemed, and forbore not to deliver us from death, though at the cost of His own. We get it for no life of silken indolence or selfish disregard of the sorrows of our brethren. If there is one tear we could have dried and didn't, or one wound we could have healed and didn't, that is a sin; if we could have lightened the great heap of sorrow by one grain and didn't, that is a sin; and if there be one soul that perishes which we might have saved and didn't, the negligence is not merely the omission of a duty, but the doing of a deed which will be 'rendered to us according to our works.'

THE SLUGGARD'S GARDEN

'I went by the field of the slothful, and by the vineyard of the man void of understanding; 31. And, lo, it was all grown over with thorns, and nettles had covered the face thereof, and the stone wall thereof was broken down.'— PROVERBS xxiv. 30, 31.

This picture of the sluggard's garden seems to be intended as a parable. No doubt its direct simple meaning is full of homely wisdom in full accord with the whole tone of the Book of Proverbs; but we shall scarcely do justice to this saying of the wise if we do not see in 'the ground grown over with thorns,' and 'the stone wall thereof broken down,' an apologue of the condition of a soul whose owner has neglected to cultivate and tend it.

I. Note first who the slothful man is.

The first plain meaning of the word is to be kept in view. The whole Book of Proverbs brands laziness as the most prolific source of poverty. Honest toil is to it the law of life. It is never weary of reiterating 'In the sweat of thy brow thou shalt eat bread'; and it condemns all swift modes of getting riches without labour. No doubt the primitive simplicity of life as set forth in this book seems far behind the many ingenuities by which in our days the law is evaded. How much of Stock Exchange speculation and 'Company promoters' gambling would survive the application of the homely old law?

But it is truer in the inward life than in the outward that 'the hand of the diligent maketh rich.' After all, the differences between men who truly 'succeed' and the human failures, which are so frequent, are more moral than intellectual. It has been said that genius is, after all, 'the capacity for taking infinite pains'; and although that is an exaggerated statement, and an incomplete analysis, there is a great truth in it, and it is the homely virtue of hard work which tells in the long run, and without which the most brilliant talents effect but little. However gifted a man may be, he will be a failure if he has not learned the great secret of dogged persistence in often unwelcomed toil. No character worth building up is built without continuous effort. If a man does not labour to be good, he will surely become bad. It is an old axiom that no man attains superlative wickedness all at once, and most certainly no man leaps to the height of the goodness possible to his nature by one spring. He has laboriously, and step by step, to climb the hill. Progress in moral character is secured by long-continued walking upwards, not by a jump.

We note that in our text 'the slothful' is paralleled by 'the man void of understanding'; and the parallel suggests the stupidity in such a world as this of letting ourselves develop according to whims, or inclinations, or passions; and also teaches that 'understanding' is meant to be rigidly and continuously brought to bear on actions as director and restrainer. If the ship is not to be wrecked on the rocks or to founder at sea, Wisdom's hand must hold the helm. Diligence alone is not enough unless directed by 'understanding.'

II. What comes of sloth.

The description of the sluggard's garden brings into view two things, the abundant, because unchecked, growth of profitless weeds, and the broken down stone wall. Both of these results are but too sadly and evidently true in regard to every life where rigid and continuous control has not been exercised. It is a familiar experience known, alas! to too many of us, that evil things, of which the seeds are in us all, grow up unchecked if there be not constant supervision and self-command. If we do not carefully cultivate our little plot of garden ground, it will soon be overgrown by weeds. 'Ill weeds grow apace' as the homely wisdom of common experience crystallises into a significant proverb. And Jesus has taught the sadder truth that 'thorns spring up and choke the word and it becometh unfruitful.' In the slothful man's soul evil will drive out good as surely as in the struggle for existence the thorns and nettles will cover the face of the slothful man's garden. In country places we sometimes come across a ruined house with what was a garden round it, and here and there still springs up a flower seeking for air and light in the midst of a smothering mass of weeds. *They* needed no kindly gardener's hand to make them grow luxuriantly; can barely put out a pale petal unless cared for and guarded.

But not only is there this unchecked growth, but 'the stone wall thereof was broken down.' The soul was unfenced. The solemn imperative of duty ceases to restrain or to impel in proportion as a man yields slothfully to the baser impulses of his nature. Nothing is hindered from going out of, nor for coming into, an unfenced soul, and he that 'hath no rule over his own spirit,' but is like a 'city broken down without walls,' is certain sooner or later to let much go forth from that spirit that should have bean rigidly shut up, and to let many an enemy come in that will capture the city. It is not yet safe to let any of the fortifications fall into disrepair, and they can only be kept in their massive strength by continuous vigilance.

III. How sloth excuses itself.

Our text is followed at the distance of one verse with what seemed to be the words of the sluggard in answer to the attempt to awake him: 'Yet a little sleep, a little slumber, a little folding of the hands to sleep.' They are a quotation from an earlier chapter (ch. vi.) where 'His Laziness' is sent to 'consider the ways of the ant and be wise.' They are a drowsy petition which does not dispute the wisdom of the call to awake, but simply craves for a little more luxurious laziness from which he has unwillingly been aroused. And is it not true that we admit too late the force of the summons and yet shrink from answering it? Do we not cheat ourselves and try to deceive God with the promise that we will set about amendment soon? This indolent sleeper asks only for a *little*: 'A little sleep, a little slumber, a little folding of the hands to sleep.' Do we not all know that mood of mind which confesses our slothfulness and promises to be wide awake tomorrow but would fain bargain to be left undisturbed today? The call 'Awake thou that sleepest and arise from the dead!' rings from Christ's lips in the ears of every man, and he who answers, 'I will presently, but must sleep a little longer,' may seem to himself to have complied with the call, but has really refused it. The 'little more' generally becomes *much* more; and the answer 'presently' alas! too often becomes the answer 'never.' When a man is roused so as to be half awake, the only safety for him is *immediately* to rise and clothe himself; the head that drowsily droops back on the pillow after he has heard the morning's call, is likely to lie there long. Now, not 'by-and-by' is the time to shake off the bonds of sloth to cultivate our garden.

IV. How sloth ends.

The sleeper's slumber is dramatically represented as being awakened by armed robbers who bring a grim awakening. 'Poverty' and 'want' break in on his 'folding hands to sleep.' That is true as regards the outward life, where indulgence in literal slothfulness brings want, and the whole drift of things executes on the sluggard the sentence that if 'any man will not work, neither shall he eat.'

But the picture is more sadly and fatally true concerning the man who has made his earthly life 'a little sleep' as concerns heavenly things, and in spite of his beseechings, is roused to life and consciousness of himself and of God by death. That man's 'poverty' in his lack of all that is counted as wealth in the world of realities to which he goes will indeed come as a robber. I would press upon you all the plain question, Is this fatal slothfulness characteristic of me? It may co-exist with, and indeed is often the consequence of vehement energy and continuous work to secure wealth, or wisdom, or material good; and the contrast between a man who is all eagerness in regard to the things that don't matter, and all carelessness in regard to the things that do, is the tragedy of life amongst us. My friend! if *your* garden has been suffered by you to be overgrown with weeds, be sure of this, that one day you will be awakened from the slumber that you would fain continue, and will find yourself in a life where your 'poverty' will come as a robber and your want of all which *there* is counted treasure 'as an armed man.'

One word more. Christ's parable of the sower may be brought into relationship with this parable. He sows the true seed in our hearts, but when sown, it, too, has to be cared for and tended. If it is sown in the sluggard's garden, it will bring forth few ears, and the tares will choke the wheat.

AN UNWALLED CITY

'He that hath no rule over his own spirit is like a city that is broken down, and without walls.'—PROVERBS xxv. 28.

The text gives us a picture of a state of society when an unwalled city is no place for men to dwell in. In the Europe of today there are still fortified places, but for the most part, battlements are turned into promenades; the gateways are gateless; the sweet flowers blooming where armed feet used to tread; and men live securely without bolts and bars. But their spirits cannot yet afford to raise their defences and fling themselves open to all comers.

We may see here three points: the city defenceless, or human nature as it is; the city defended, human nature as it may be in Christ; the city needing no defence, human nature as it will be in heaven.

I. The city defenceless, or human nature as it is.

Here we are in a state of warfare which calls for constant shutting out of enemies. Temptations are everywhere; our foes compass us like bees; evils of many sorts seduce. We can picture to ourselves some little garrison holding a lonely outpost against lurking savages ready to attack if ever the defenders slacken their vigilance for a moment. And that is the truer picture of human nature as it is than the one by which most men are deluded. Life is not a playground, but an arena of grim, earnest fighting. No man does right in his sleep; no man does right without a struggle.

The need for continual vigilance and self-control comes from the very make of our souls, for our nature is not a democracy, but a kingdom. In us all there are passions, desires, affections, all of which may lead to vice or to virtue: and all of which evidently call out for direction, for cultivation, and often for repression. Then there are peculiarities of individual character which need watching lest they become excessive and sinful. Further, there are qualities which need careful cultivation and stimulus to bring them into due proportion. We each of us receive, as it were, an undeveloped self, and have entrusted to us potential germs which come to nothing, or shoot up with a luxuriance that stifles unless we exercise a controlling power. Besides all this, we all carry in us tendencies which are positively, and only, sinful. There would be no temptation if there were no such.

But the slightest inspection of our own selves clearly points out, not only what in us needs to be controlled, but that in us which is *meant* to control. The will is regal; conscience is meant to govern the will, and its voice is but the echo of God's law.

But, while all this is true, it is too sadly true that the accomplishment of this ideal is impossible in our own strength. Our own sad experience tells us that we cannot govern ourselves; and our observations of our brethren but too surely indicate that they too are the prey of rebellious, anarchical powers within, and of temptations, against the rush of which they and we are as powerless as a voyager in a bark-canoe, caught in the fatal drift of Niagara. Conscience has a voice, but no hands; it can speak, but if its voice fails, it cannot hold us back. From its chair it can bid the waves breaking at our feet roll back, as the Saxon king did, but their tossing surges are deaf. As helpless as the mud walls of some Indian hill-fort against modern artillery, is the defence, in one's own strength, of one's own self against the world. We would gladly admit that the feeblest may do much to 'keep himself unspotted from the world'; but we must, if we recognise facts, confess that the strongest cannot do all. No man can alone completely control his own nature; no man, unenlightened by God, has a clear, full view of duty, nor a clear view of himself. Always there is some unguarded place:

'Unless above himself he can
Erect himself, how mean a thing is man!'

but no man can so lift himself so as that self will not drag him down. The walls are broken down and the troops of the spoilers sack the city.

II. The defended city, or human nature as it may be in Christ.

If our previous remarks are true, they give us material for judging how far the counsels of some very popular moral teachers should be followed. It is a very old advice, 'know thyself'; and it is a very modern one that

'Self-reverence, self-knowledge, self-control
Lead life to sovereign power.'

But if these counsels are taken absolutely and without reference to Christ and His work, they are 'counsels of despair,' demanding what we cannot give, and promising what they cannot bestow. When we know Christ, we shall know ourselves; when He is the self of ourselves, then, and only then, shall we reverence and can we control the inner man. The city of Mansoul will then be defended when 'the peace of God keeps our hearts and minds in Jesus.'

He who submits himself to Christ is lord of himself as none else are. He has a light within which teaches him what is sin. He has a love within which puts out the flame of temptation, as the sun does a coal fire. He has a motive to resist; he has power for resistance; he has hope in resisting. Only thus are the walls broken down rebuilded. And as Christ builds our city on firmer foundations, He will appear in His glory, and will 'lay the windows in agates, and all thy borders in precious stones.' The sure way to bring our ruined earth, 'without form and void,' into a cosmos of light and beauty, is to open our spirit for the Spirit of God to 'brood upon the face of the waters.' Otherwise the attempts to rule over our own spirit will surely fail; but if we let Christ rule over our spirit, then it will rule itself.

But let us ever remember that he who thus submits to Christ, and can truly say, 'I live, yet not I, but Christ liveth in *me*,' still needs defence. The strife does not thereby cease; the enemies still swarm; sin is not removed. There will be war to the end, and war for ever; but He will 'keep our heads in the day of battle'; and though often we may be driven from the walls, and outposts may be lost, and gaping breaches made, yet the citadel shall be safe. If only we see to it that '*He* is the glory in the midst of us,' He will be 'a wall of fire round about us.' Our nature as it may be in Christ is a walled city as needing defence, and as possessing the defence which it needs.

III. The city defenceless, and needing no defence; that is, human nature as it will be hereafter.

'The gates shall not be shut day nor night,' for 'every thing that defileth' is without. We know but little of that future, what we know will, surely, be theirs who here have been 'guarded by the power of God, through faith, unto salvation.' That salvation will bring with it the end for the need of guardianship; though it leaves untouched the blessed dependence, we shall stand secure when it is impossible to fall. And that impossibility will be realised, partly, as we know, from change in surroundings, partly from the dropping away of flesh, partly from the entire harmony of our souls with the will of God. Our ignorance of that future is great, but our knowledge of it is greater, and our certainty of it is greatest of all.

This is what we may become. Dear friends! toil no longer at the endless, hopeless task of ruling those turbulent souls of yours; you can never rebuild the walls already fallen. Give up toiling to attain calmness, peace, self-command. Let Christ do all for you, and let Him in to dwell in you and be all to you. Builded on the true Rock, we shall stand stately and safe amid the din of war. He will watch over us and dwell in us, and we shall be as 'a city set on a hill,' impregnable, a virgin city. So may it be with each of us while strife shall last, and hereafter we may quietly hope to be as a city without walls, and needing none; for they that hated us shall be far away, for between us and them is 'a great gulf fixed,' so that they cannot cross it to disturb us any more; and we shall dwell in the city of God, of which the name is Salem, the city of peace, whose King is Himself, its Defender and its Rock, its Fortress and its high Tower.

THE WEIGHT OF SAND

'The sand is weighty.'—PROVERBS, xxvii. 3.

This Book of Proverbs has a very wholesome horror of the character which it calls 'a fool'; meaning thereby, not so much intellectual feebleness as moral and religious obliquity, which are the stupidest things that a man can be guilty of. My text comes from a very picturesque and vivid description, by way of comparison, of the fatal effects of such a man's passion. The proverb-maker compares two heavy things, stones and sand, and says that they are feathers in comparison with the immense lead-like weight of such a man's wrath.

Now I have nothing more to do with the immediate application of my text. I want to make a parable out of it. What is lighter than a grain of sand? What is heavier than a bagful of it? As the grains fall one by one, how easily they can be blown away! Let them gather, and they bury temples, and crush the solid masonry of pyramids. 'Sand is weighty.' The accumulation of light things is overwhelmingly ponderous. Are there any such things in our lives? If there are, what ought we to do? So you get the point of view from which I want to look at the words of our text.

I. The first suggestion that I make is that they remind us of the supreme importance of trifles.

If trivial acts are unimportant, what signifies the life of man? For ninety-nine and a half per cent. of every man's life is made up of these light nothings;

and unless there is potential greatness in them, and they are of importance, then life is all 'a tale told by an idiot, full of sound and fury, signifying nothing.' Small things make life; and if are small, then *it* is so too.

But remember, too, that the supreme importance of so-called trivial actions is seen in this, that there may be every bit as much of the noblest things that belong to humanity condensed in, and brought to bear upon, the veriest trifle that a man can do, as on the greatest things that he can perform. We are very poor judges of what is great and what is little. We have a very vulgar estimate that noise and notoriety and the securing of, not *great* but 'big,' results of a material kind make the deeds by which they are secured, great ones. And we think that it is the quiet things, those that do not tell outside at all, that are the small ones.

Well! here is a picture for you. Half-a-dozen shabby, travel-stained Jews, sitting by a river-side upon the grass, talking to a handful of women outside the gates of a great city. Years before that, there had been what the world calls a great event, almost on the same ground—a sanguinary fight, that had settled the emperorship of the then civilised world, for a time. I want to know whether the first preaching of the Gospel in Europe by the Apostle Paul, or the battle of Philippi, was the great event, and which of the two was the little one. I vote for the Jews on the grass, and let all the noise of the fight, though it reverberated through the world for a bit, die away, as 'a little dust that rises up, and is lightly laid again.' Not the noisy events are the great ones; and as much true greatness may be manifested in a poor woman stitching in her garret as in some of the things that have rung through the world and excited all manner of vulgar applause. Trifles may be, and often are, the great things in life.

And then remember, too, how the most trivial actions have a strange knack of all at once leading on to large results, beyond what could have been expected. A man shifts his seat in a railway carriage, from some passing whim, and five minutes afterwards there comes a collision, and the bench where he had been sitting is splintered up, and the place where he is sitting is untouched, and the accidental move has saved his life. According to the old story a boy, failing in applying for a situation, stoops down in the courtyard and picks up a pin, and the millionaire sees him through the window, and it makes his fortune. We cannot tell what may come of anything; and since we do not know the far end of our deeds, let us be quite sure that we have got the near end of them right. Whatever may be the issue, let us look after the motive, and then all will be right. Small seeds grow to be great trees, and in this strange and inexplicable network of things which men call circumstances, and Christians call Providence, the only thing certain is that 'great' and 'small' all but cease to be a tenable, and certainly altogether cease to be an important distinction.

Then another thing which I would have you remember is, that it is these trivial actions which, in their accumulated force, make character. Men are not made by crises. The crises reveal what we have made ourselves by the trifles. The way in which we do the little things forms the character according to which we shall act when the great things come. If the crew of a man-of-war were not exercised at boat and fire drill during many a calm day, when all was safe, what would become of them when tempests were raging, or flames breaking through the bulk-heads? It is no time to learn drill then. And we must make our characters by the way in which, day out and day in, we do little things, and find in them fields for the great virtues which will enable us to front the crises of our fate unblenching, and to master whatsoever difficulties come in our path. Geologists nowadays distrust, for the most part, theories which have to invoke great forces in order to mould the face of a country. They tell us that the valley, with its deep sides and wide opening to the sky, may have been made by the slow operation of a tiny brooklet that trickles now down at its base, and by erosion of the atmosphere. So we shape ourselves—and that is a great thing—by the way we do small things.

Therefore, I say to you, dear friends! think solemnly and reverently of this awful life of ours. Clear your minds of the notion that anything is small which offers to you the alternative of being done in a right way or in a wrong; and recognise this as a fact—'sand is weighty,' trifles are of supreme importance.

II. Now, secondly, let me ask you to take this saying as suggesting the overwhelming weight of small sins.

That is only an application in one direction of the general principle that I have been trying to lay down; but it is one of such great importance that I wish to deal with it separately. And my point is this, that the accumulated pressure upon a man of a multitude of perfectly trivial faults and transgressions makes up a tremendous aggregate that weighs upon him with awful ponderousness.

Let me remind you, to begin with, that, properly speaking, the words 'great' and 'small' should not be applied in reference to things about which 'right' or 'wrong' are the proper words to employ. Or, to put it into plainer language, it is as absurd to talk about the 'size' of a sin, as it is to take the superficial area of a picture as a test of its greatness. The magnitude of a transgression does not depend on the greatness of the act which transgresses—according to human standards—but on the intensity with which the sinful element is working in it. For acts make crimes, but motives make sins. If you take a bit of prussic acid, and bruise it down, every little microscopic fragment will have the poisonous principle in it; and it is very irrelevant to ask whether it is as big as a mountain or small as a grain of dust, it is poison all the same. So to talk about magnitude in regard to sins, is rather to introduce a foreign consideration. But still, recognising that there is a reality in the distinction that people make between great sins and small ones, though it is a superficial distinction, and does not go down to the bottom of things, let us deal with it now.

I say, then, that small sins, by reason of their numerousness, have a terrible accumulative power. They are like the green flies on our rose-bushes, or the microbes that our medical friends talk so much about nowadays. Like them, their power of mischief does not in the least degree depend on their magnitude, and like them, they have a tremendous capacity of reproduction. It would be easier to find a man that had not done any one sin than to find out a man that had only done it once. And it would be easier to find a man that had done no evil than a man who had not been obliged to make the second edition of his sin an enlarged one. For this is the present Nemesis of all evil, that it requires repetition, partly to still conscience, partly to satisfy excited tastes and desires; so that animal indulgence in drink and the like is a type of what goes on in the inner life of every man, in so far as the second dose has to be stronger than the first in order to produce an equivalent effect; and so on *ad infinitum*.

And then remember that all our evil doings, however insignificant they may be, have a strange affinity with one another, so that you will find that to go wrong in one direction almost inevitably leads to a whole series of consequential transgressions of one sort or another. You remember the old story about the soldier that was smuggled into a fortress concealed in a hay cart, and opened the gates of a virgin citadel to his allies outside. Every evil thing, great or small, that we admit into our lives, still more into our hearts, is charged with the same errand as he had:—' Set wide the door when you are inside, and let us all come in after you.' 'He taketh with him seven other spirits worse than himself, and they dwell there.' 'None of them,' says one of the prophets, describing the doleful creatures that haunt the ruins of a deserted city, 'shall by any means want its mate,' and the satyrs of the islands and of the woods join together! and hold high carnival in the city. And so, brethren! our little transgressions open the door for great ones, and every sin makes us more accessible to the assaults of every other.

So let me remind you how here, in these little unnumbered acts of trivial transgression which scarcely produce any effect on conscience or on memory, but make up so large a portion of so many of our lives, lies one of the most powerful instruments for making us what we are. If we indulge in slight acts of transgression be sure of this, that we shall pass from them to far greater ones. For one man that leaps or falls all at once into sin which the world calls gross, there are a thousand that slide into it. The storm only blows down the trees whose hearts have been eaten out and their roots loosened. And when you see a man having a reputation for wisdom and honour all at once coming crash down and disclosing his baseness, be sure that he began with small deflections from the path of right. The evil works underground; and if we yield to little temptations, when great ones come we shall fall their victims.

Let me remind you, too, that there is another sense in which 'sand is weighty.' You may as well be crushed under a sandhill as under a mountain of marble. It matters not which. The accumulated weight of the one is as great as that of the other. And I wish to lay upon the consciences of all that are listening to me now this thought, that an overwhelming weight of guilt results from the accumulation of little sins. Dear friends! I do not desire to preach a gospel of fear, but I cannot help feeling that, very largely, in this day, the ministration of the Christian Church is defective in that it does not give sufficient, though sad and sympathetic, prominence to the plain teaching of Christ and of the New Testament as to future retribution for present sin. We shall 'every one of us give account of himself to God'; and if the account is long enough it will foot up to an enormous sum, though each item may be only halfpence. The weight of a lifetime of little sins will be enough to crush a man down with guilt and responsibility when he stands before that Judge. That is all true, and you know it, and I beseech you, take it to your hearts, 'Sand is weighty.' Little sins have to be accounted for, and may crush.

III. And now, lastly, let me ask you to consider one or two of the plain, practical issues of such thoughts as these.

And, first, I would say that these considerations set in a very clear light the absolute necessity for all-round and ever-wakeful watchfulness over ourselves. A man in the tropics does not say, 'Mosquitoes are so small that it does not matter if two or three of them get inside my bed-curtains.' He takes care that not one is there before he lays himself down to sleep. There seems to be nothing more sad than the complacent, easy-going way in which men allow themselves to keep their higher moral principles and their more rigid self-examination for the 'great' things, as they suppose, and let the little things often take care of themselves. What would you think of the captain of a steamer who in calm weather sailed by rule of thumb, only getting out his sextant when storms began to blow? And what about a man that lets the myriad trivialities that make up a day pass in and out of his heart as they will, and never arrests any of them at the gate with a 'How camest thou in hither?' 'Look after the pence, and the pounds will look after themselves.' Look after your trivial acts, and, take my word for it, the great ones will be as they ought to be.

Again, may not this thought somehow take down our easy-going and self-complacent estimate of ourselves? I have no doubt that there are a number of people in my audience just now who have been more or less consciously saying to themselves whilst I have been going on, 'What have *I* to do with all this talk about sin, sin, sin? I am a decent kind of a man. I do all the duties of my daily life, and nobody can say that the white of my eyes is black. I have done no great transgressions. What is it all about? It has nothing to do with me.'

Well, my friend! it has this to do with you—that in your life there are a whole host of things which only a very superficial estimate hinders you from recognising to be what they are—small deeds, but great sins. Is it a small thing to go, as some of you do go on from year to year, with your conduct and your thoughts and your loves and your desires utterly unaffected by the fact that there is a God in heaven, and that Jesus Christ died for you? Is that a small thing? It manifests itself in a great many insignificant actions. That I grant you; and you are a most respectable man, and you keep the commandments as well as you can. But 'the God in whose hand thy breath is, and whose are all thy ways, hast thou not glorified.' I say that that is not a small sin.

So, dear brethren! I beseech you judge yourselves by this standard. I charge none of you with gross iniquities. I know nothing about that. But I do appeal to you all, as I do to myself, whether we must not recognise the fact that an accumulated multitude of transgressions which are only superficially small, in their aggregate weigh upon us with 'a weight heavy as frost, and deep almost as life.'

Last of all, this being the case, should we not all turn ourselves with lowly hearts, with recognition of our transgressions, acknowledging that whether it be five hundred or fifty pence that we owe, we have nothing to pay, and betake ourselves to Him who alone can deliver us from the habit and power of these small accumulated faults, and who alone can lift the burden of guilt and responsibility from off our shoulders? If you irrigate the sand it becomes fruitful soil. Christ brings to us the river of the water of life; the inspiring, the quickening, the fructifying power of the new life that He bestows, and the sand may become soil, and the wilderness blossom as the rose. A heavy burden lies on our shoulders. Ah! yes! but 'Behold the Lamb of God that beareth away the sins of the world!' What was it that crushed Him down beneath the olives of Gethsemane? What was it that made Him cry, 'My God! Why hast Thou forsaken me?' I know no answer but one, for which the world's gratitude is all too small. 'The Lord hath laid on Him the iniquity of us all.'

'Sand is weighty,' but Christ has borne the burden, 'Cast thy burden upon the Lord,' and it will drop from your emancipated shoulders, and they will henceforth bear only the light burden of His love.

PORTRAIT OF A MATRON

'Who can find a virtuous woman? for her price is far above rubies. 11. The heart of her husband doth safely trust in her, so that he shall have no need of spoil. 12. She will do him good, and not evil, all the days of her life. 13. She seeketh wool, and flax, and worketh willingly with her hands. 14. She is like the merchants' ships; she bringeth her food from afar. 15. She riseth also while it is yet night, and giveth meat to her household, and a portion to her maidens. 16. She considereth a field, and buyeth it: with the fruit of her hands she planteth a vineyard. 17. She girdeth her loins with strength, and strengtheneth her arms. 18. She perceiveth that her merchandise is good: her candle goeth not out by night. 19. She layeth her hands to the spindle, and her hands hold the distaff. 20. She stretcheth out her hand to the poor; yea, she reacheth forth her hands to the needy. 21. She is not afraid of the snow for her household: for all her household are clothed with scarlet. 22. She maketh herself coverings of tapestry; her clothing is silk and purple. 23. Her husband is known in the gates, when he sitteth among the elders of the land. 24. She maketh fine linen, and selleth it; and delivereth girdles unto the merchant. 25. Strength and honour are her clothing; and she shall rejoice in time to come. 26. She openeth her mouth with wisdom; and in her tongue is the law of kindness. 27. She looketh well to the ways of her household, and eateth not the bread of idleness. 28. Her children arise up, and call her blessed; her husband also, and he praiseth her. 29. Many daughters have done virtuously, but thou excellest them all. 30. Favour is deceitful, and beauty is vain: but a woman that feareth the Lord, she shall be praised. 31. Give her of the fruit of her hands; and let her own works praise her in the gates.'- PROVERBS xxxi 10-31.

This description of a good 'house-mother' attests the honourable position of woman in Israel. It would have been impossible in Eastern countries, where she was regarded only as a plaything and a better sort of slave. The picture is about equally far removed from old-world and from modern ideas of her place. This 'virtuous woman' is neither a doll nor a graduate nor a public character. Her kingdom is the home. Her works 'praise her in the gates'; but it is her husband, and not she, that 'sits' there among the elders. There is no sentiment or light of wedded love in the picture. It is neither the ideal woman nor wife that is painted, but the ideal head of a household, on whose management, as much as on her husband's work, its well-being depends.

There is plenty of room for modern ideals by the side of this old one, but they are very incomplete without it. If we take the 'oracle which his mother taught' King Lemuel to include this picture, the artist is a woman, and her motive may be to sketch the sort of wife her son should choose. In any case, it is significant that the book which began with the magnificent picture of Wisdom as a fair woman, and hung beside it the ugly likeness of Folly, should end with this charming portrait. It is an acrostic, and the fetters of alphabetic sequence are not favourable to progress or continuity of thought.

But I venture to suggest a certain advance in the representation which removes the apparent disjointed character and needless repetition. There are, first, three verses forming a kind of prologue or introduction (vers. 10-12). Then follows the picture proper, which is brought into unity if we suppose that it describes the growing material success of the diligent housekeeper, beginning with her own willing work, and gradually extending till she and her family are well to do and among the magnates of her town (vers. 13-29). Then follow two verses of epilogue or conclusion (vers. 30, 31).

The rendering 'virtuous' is unsatisfactory; for what is meant is not moral excellence, either in the wider sense or in the narrower to which, in reference to woman, that great word has been unfortunately narrowed. Our colloquialism 'a woman of faculty' would fairly convey the idea, which is that of ability and general capacity. We have said that there was no light of wedded love in the picture. That is true of the main body of it; but no deeper, terser expression of the inmost blessedness of happy marriage was ever spoken than in the quiet words, 'The heart of her husband trusteth in her,' with the repose of satisfaction, with the tranquillity of perfect assurance. The bond uniting husband and wife in a true marriage is not unlike that uniting us with God. Happy are they who by their trust in one another and the peaceful joys which it brings are led to united trust in a yet deeper love, mirrored to them in their own! True, the picture here is mainly that of confidence that the wife is no squanderer of her husband's goods, but the sweet thought goes far beyond the immediate application. So with the other general feature in verse 12. A true wife is a fountain of good, and good only, all the days of her life— ay, and beyond them too, when her remembrance shines like the calm west after a cloudless sunset. This being, as it were, the overture, next follows the main body of the piece.

It starts with a description of diligence in a comparatively humble sphere. Note that in verse 13 the woman is working alone. She toils 'willingly,' or, as the literal rendering is, 'with the pleasure of her hands.' There is no profit in unwilling work. Love makes toil delightful, and delighted toil is successful. Throughout its pages the Bible reverences diligence. It is the condition of prosperity in material and spiritual things. Vainly do men and women try to dodge the law which makes the 'sweat of the brow' the indispensable requisite for 'eating bread.' When commerce becomes speculation, which is the polite name for gambling, which, again, is a synonym for stealing, it may yield much more dainty fare than bread to some for a time, but is sure to bring want sooner or later to individuals and communities. The foundation of this good woman's fortune was that she worked with a will. There is no other foundation, either for fortune or any other good, or for self-respect, or for progress in knowledge or goodness or religion.

Then her horizon widened, and she saw a way of increasing her store. 'She is like the merchants' ships; she bringeth her food from afar.' She looks afield, and sees opportunities for profitable exchange. Promptly she avails herself of these, and is at work while it is yet dark. She has a household now, and does not neglect their comfort, any more than she does their employment. Their food and their tasks are both set them in the early morning, and their mistress is up as soon as they. Her toil brings in wealth, and so verse 16 shows another step in advance. 'She considereth a field, and buyeth it,' and has made money enough to stock it with vines, and so add a new source of revenue, and acquire a new position as owning land.

But prosperity does not make her relax her efforts so we are told again in verses 17-19 of her abridging the hours of sleep, and toiling with wool and flax, which would be useless tautology if there were not some new circumstances to account for the repetition. Encouraged by success, she 'girdeth her loins with strength,' and, since she sees that 'her merchandise is profitable,' she is the more induced to labour. She still works with her own hands (ver. 19). But the hands that are busy with distaff and spindle are also stretched out with alms in the open palm, and are extended in readiness to help the needy. A woman made unfeeling by wealth is a monster. Prosperity often leads men to niggardliness in charitable gifts; but if it does the same for a woman, it is doubly cursed. Pity and charity have their home in women's hearts. If they are so busy holding the distaff or the pen that they become hard and insensible to the cry of misery, they have lost their glory.

Then follow a series of verses describing how increased wealth brings good to her household and herself. The advantages are of a purely material sort, Her children are 'clothed with scarlet,' which was not only the name of the dye, but of the stuff. Evidently thick material only was dyed of that hue, and so was fit for winter clothing, even if the weather was so severe for Palestine that snow fell. Her house was furnished with 'carpets,' or rather 'cushions' or 'pillows,' which are more important pieces of furniture where people recline on divans than where they sit on chairs. Her own costume is that of a rich woman. 'Purple and fine linen' are tokens of wealth, and she is woman enough to like to wear these. There is nothing unbecoming in assuming the style of living appropriate to one's position. Her children and herself thus share in the advantages of her industry; and the husband, who does not appear to have much business of his own, gets his share in that he sits among the wealthy and honoured inhabitants of the town, 'in the gates,' the chief place of meeting for business and gossip.

Verse 24 recurs to the subject of the woman's diligence. She has got into a 'shipping business,' making for the export trade with the 'merchants'— literally, 'Canaanites' or Phoenicians, the great traders of the East, from whom, no doubt, she got the 'purple' of her clothing in exchange for her manufacture. But she had a better dress than any woven in looms or bought with goods. 'Strength and dignity' clothe her. 'She laugheth at the time to come'; that is, she is able to look forward without dread of poverty, because she has realised a competent sum. Such looking forward may be like that of the rich man in the parable, a piece of presumption, but it may also be compatible with devout recognition of God's providence. As in verse 20, beneficence was coupled with diligence, so in verse 26 gentler qualities are blended with strength and dignity, and calm anticipation of the future.

A glimpse into 'the very pulse' of the woman's nature is given. A true woman's strength is always gentle, and her dignity attractive and gracious. Prosperity has not turned her head. 'Wisdom,' the heaven-descended virgin, the deep music of whose call we heard sounding in the earlier chapters of Proverbs, dwells with this very practical woman. The collocation points the lesson that heavenly Wisdom has a field for its display in the common duties of a busy life, does not dwell in hermitages, or cloisters, or studies, but may guide and inspire a careful housekeeper in her task of wisely keeping her husband's goods together. The old legend of the descending deity who took service as a goat-herd, is true of the heavenly Wisdom, which will come and live in kitchens and shops.

But the ideal woman has not only wisdom in act and word, but 'the law of kindness is on her tongue.' Prosperity should not rob her of her gracious demeanour. Her words should be glowing with the calm flame of love which stoops to lowly and undeserving objects. If wealth leads to presumptuous reckoning on the future, and because we have 'much goods laid up for many years,' we see no other use of leisure than to eat and drink and be merry, we fatally mistake our happiness and our duty. But if gentle compassion and helpfulness are on our lips and in our hearts and deeds, prosperity will be blessed.

Nor does this ideal woman relax in her diligence, though she has prospered. Verse 27 seems very needless repetition of what has been abundantly said already, unless we suppose, as before, new circumstances to account for the reintroduction of a former characteristic. These are, as it seems to me, the increased wealth of the heroine, which might have led her to relax her watchfulness. Some slacking off might have been expected and excused; but at the end, as at the beginning, she looks after her household and is herself diligent. The picture refers only to outward things. But we may remember that the same law applies to all, and that any good, either of worldly wealth or of intellectual, moral, or religious kind, is only preserved by the continuous exercise of the same energies which won it at first.

Verses 28 and 29 give the eulogium pronounced by children and husband. The former 'rise up' as in reverence; the latter declares her superiority to all women, with the hyperbolical language natural to love. Happy the man who, after long years of wedded life, can repeat the estimate of his early love with the calm certitude born of experience!

The epilogue in verses 30 and 31 is not the continuation of the husband's speech. It at once points the lesson from the whole picture for King Lemuel, and unveils the root of the excellences described. Beauty is skin deep. Let young men look deeper than a fair face. Let young women seek for that beauty which does not fade. The fear of the Lord lies at the bottom of all goodness that will last through the tear and wear of wedded life, and of all domestic diligence which is not mere sordid selfishness or slavish toil. The narrow arena of domestic life affords a fit theatre for the exercise of the highest gifts and graces; and the woman who has made a home bright, and has won and kept a husband's love and children's reverence, may let who will grasp at the more conspicuous prizes which women are so eager after nowadays. She has chosen the better part, which shall not be taken from her. She shall receive 'of the fruit of her hands' both now and hereafter, if the fear of the Lord has been the root from which that fruit has grown; and 'her works shall praise her in the gate,' though she sits quietly in her home. It is well when our deeds are the trumpeters of our fame, and when to tell them is to praise us.

The whole passage is the hallowing of domestic life, a directory for wives and mothers, a beautiful ideal of how noble a thing a busy mother's life may be, an exhibition to young men of what they should seek, and of young women of what they should aim at. It were well for the next generation if the young women of this one were as solicitous to make cages as nets, to cultivate qualities which would keep love in the home as to cultivate attractions which lure him to their feet.

ECCLESIASTES; OR, THE PREACHER

WHAT PASSES AND WHAT ABIDES

'One generation passeth away, and another generation cometh: but the earth abideth for ever.'—ECCLES. i. 4.

'And the world passeth away, and the lust thereof; but he that doeth the will of God abideth for ever.'—1 JOHN ii. 17.

A great river may run through more than one kingdom, and bear more than one name, but its flow is unbroken. The river of time runs continuously, taking no heed of dates and calendars. The importance that we attach to the beginnings or endings of years and centuries is a sentimental illusion, but even an illusion that rouses us to a consciousness of the stealthy gliding of the river may do us good, and we need all the helps we can find to wise retrospect and sober anticipation. So we must let the season colour our thoughts, even whilst we feel that in yielding to that impulse we are imagining what has no reality in the passing from the last day of one century to the first day of another.

I do not mean to discuss in this sermon either the old century or the new in their wider social and other aspects. That has been done abundantly. We shall best do our parts in making the days, and the years, and the century what they should be, if we let the truths that come from these combined texts sink into and influence our individual lives. I have put them together, because they are so strikingly antithetical, both true, and yet looking at the same facts from opposite points of view, But the antithesis is not really so complete as it sounds at first hearing, because what the Preacher means by 'the earth' that 'abideth for ever' is not quite the same as what the Apostle means by the 'world' that 'passes' and the 'generations' that come and go are not exactly the same as the men that 'abide for ever.' But still the antithesis is real and impressive. The bitter melancholy of the Preacher saw but the surface; the joyous faith of the Apostle went a great deal deeper, and putting the two sets of thoughts and ways of looking at man and his dwelling-place together, we get lessons that may well shape our individual lives.

So let me ask you to look, in the first place, at—

I. The sad and superficial teaching of the Preacher.

Now in reading this Book of Ecclesiastes—which I am afraid a great many people do not read at all—we have always to remember that the wild things and the bitter things which the Preacher is saying so abundantly through its course do not represent his ultimate convictions, but thoughts that he took up in his progress from error to truth. His first word is: 'All is vanity!' That

- 428 -

conviction had been set vibrating in his heart, as it is set vibrating in the heart of every man who does as he did, viz., seeks for solid good away from God. That is his starting-point. It is not true. All is not vanity, except to some *blasé* cynic, made cynical by the failure of his voluptuousness, and to whom 'all things here are out of joint,' and everything looks yellow because his own biliary system is out of order. That is the beginning of the book, and there are hosts of other things in the course of it as one-sided, as cynically bitter, and therefore superficial. But the end of it is: 'Let us hear the conclusion of the whole matter; fear God, and keep His commandments: for this is the whole duty of man.' In his journey from the one point to the other my text is the first step, 'One generation goeth, and another cometh: the earth abideth for ever.'

He looks out upon humanity, and sees that in one aspect the world is full of births, and in another full of deaths. Coffins and cradles seem the main furniture, and he hears the tramp, tramp, tramp of the generations passing over a soil honeycombed with tombs, and therefore ringing hollow to their tread. All depends on the point of view. The strange history of humanity is like a piece of shot silk; hold it at one angle, and you see dark purple, hold at another, and you see bright golden tints. Look from one point of view, and it seems a long history of vanishing generations. Look to the rear of the procession, and it seems a buoyant spectacle of eager, young faces pressing forwards on the march, and of strong feet treading the new road. But yet the total effect of that endless procession is to impress on the observer the transiency of humanity. And that wholesome thought is made more poignant still by the comparison which the writer here draws between the fleeting generations and the abiding earth. Man is the lord of earth, and can mould it to his purpose, but it remains and he passes. He is but a lodger in an old house that has had generations of tenants, each of whom has said for a while, 'It is mine'; and they all have drifted away, and the house stands. The Alps, over which Hannibal stormed, over which the Goths poured down on the fertile plains of Lombardy, through whose passes mediaeval emperors led their forces, over whose summits Napoleon brought his men, through whose bowels this generation has burrowed its tunnels, stand the same, and smile the same amid their snows, at the transient creatures that have crawled across them. The primrose on the rock blooms in the same place year after year, and nature and it are faithful to their covenant, but the poet's eyes that fell upon them are sealed with dust. Generations have gone, the transient flower remains. 'One generation cometh and another goeth,' and the tragedy is made more tragical because the stage stands unaltered, and 'the earth abides for ever.' That is what sense has to say—'the foolish senses'—and that is all that sense has to say. Is it all that can be said? If it is, then the Preacher's bitter conclusion is true, and 'all is vanity and chasing after wind.'

He immediately proceeds to draw from this undeniable, but, as I maintain, partial fact, the broad conclusion which cannot be rebutted, if you accept what he has said in my text as being the sufficient and complete account of man and his dwelling-place. If, says he, it is true that one generation comes and another goes, and the earth abides for ever, and if that is all that has to be said, then all things are full of labour. There is immense activity, and there is no progress; it is all rotary motion round and round and round, and the same objects reappear duly and punctually as the wheel revolves, and life is futile. Yes; so it is unless there is something more to be said, and the life that is thus futile is also, as it seems to me, inexplicable if you believe in God at all. If man, being what he is, is wholly subject to that law of mutation and decay, then not only is he made 'a little lower than the angels for the suffering of death,' but he is also inferior to that persistent, old mother-earth from whose bosom he has come. If all that you have to say of him is, 'Dust thou art, and unto dust shalt thou return,' then life is futile, and God is not vindicated for having produced it.

And there is another consequence that follows, if this is all that we have got to say. If the cynical wisdom of Ecclesiastes is the ultimate word, then I do not assert that morality is destroyed, because right and wrong are not dependent either upon the belief in a God, or on the belief in immortality. But I do say that to declare that the fleeting, transient life of earth is all does strike a staggering blow at all noble ethics and paralyses a great deal of the highest forms of human activity, and that, as has historically been the case, so on the large scale, and, speaking generally, it will be the case, that the man whose creed is only 'To-morrow we die' will very speedily draw the conclusion, 'Let us eat and drink,' and sensuous delights and the lower side of his nature will become dominant.

So, then, the Preacher had not got at the bottom of all things, either in his initial conviction that all was vanity, or in that which he laid down as the first step towards establishing that, that man passes and the earth abides. There is more to be said; the sad, superficial teaching of the Preacher needs to be supplemented.

Now turn for a moment to what does supplement it.

II. The joyous and profounder teaching of the Apostle.

The cynic never sees the depths; that is reserved for the mystical eye of the lover. So John says: 'No, no; that is not all. Here is the true state of affairs: "The world passeth away, and the lust thereof: but he that doeth the will of God abideth for ever."' The doctrine of the passing generations and the abiding earth is fronted squarely in my second text by the not contradictory, but complementary doctrine of the passing world and the abiding men. I do not suppose that John had this verse of Ecclesiastes in his mind, for the word 'abide' is one of his favourite expressions, and is always cropping up. But even though he had not, we find in his utterance the necessary correction to the first text. As I have said, and now need not do more than repeat in a sentence, the antithesis is not so complete as it seems. John's 'world' is not the Preacher's 'earth,' but he means thereby, as we all know, the aggregate of created things, including men, considered apart from God, and in so far as it includes voluntary agents set in opposition to God and the will of God. He means the earth rent away from God, and turned to be what it was not meant to be, a minister of evil, and he means men, in so far as they have parted themselves from God and make up an alien, if not a positively antagonistic company.

Perhaps he was referring, in the words of our text, to the break-up of the existing order of things which he discerned as impending and already begun to take effect in consequence of the coming of Jesus Christ, the shining of the true Light. For you may remember that in a previous part of the epistle he uses precisely the same expression, with a significant variation. Here, in our text, he says, 'The world passeth away'; there he says, 'The darkness has passed and the true light now shineth.' He sees a process installed and going on, in which the whole solid-seeming fabric of a godless society is being dissolved and melted away. And says he, in the midst of all this change there is one who stands unchanged, the man that does God's will.

But just for a moment we may take the lower point of view, and see here a flat contradiction of the Preacher. He said, 'Men go, and the world abides.' 'No,' says John; 'your own psalmists might have taught you better: "As a vesture shalt Thou change them, and they shall be changed."' The world, the earth, which seems so solid and permanent, is all the while in perpetual flux, as our later science has taught us, in a sense of which neither Preacher nor Apostle could dream. For just as from the beginning forces were at work which out of the fire-mist shaped sun and planets, so the same forces, continuing in operation, are tending towards the end of the system which they began; and a contracting sun and a diminished light and a lowered temperature and the narrower orbits in which the planets shall revolve, prophesy that 'the elements shall melt with fervent heat,' and that all things which have been made must one day cease to be. Nature is the true Penelope's web, ever being woven and ever being unravelled, and in the most purely physical and scientific sense the world is passing away. But then, because you and I belong, in a segment of our being, to that which thus is passing away, we come under the same laws, and all that has been born must die. So the generations come, and in their very coming bear the prophecy of their going. But, on the other hand, there is an inner nucleus of our being, of which the material is but the transient envelope and periphery, which holds nought of the material, but of the spiritual, and that 'abides for ever.'

But let us lift the thought rather into the region of the true antithesis which John was contemplating, which is not so much the crumbling away of the material, and the endurance of the spiritual, as the essential transiency of everything that is antagonism to the will of God, and the essential eternity of everything which is in conformity with that will. And so, says he, 'The world is passing, and the lust thereof.' The desires that grasp it perish with it, or perhaps, more truly still, the object of the desire perishes, and with it the possibility of their gratification ceases, but the desire itself remains. But what of the man whose life has been devoted to the things seen and temporal, when he finds himself in a condition of being where none of these have accompanied him? Nothing to slake his lusts, if he be a sensualist. No money-bags, ledgers, or cheque-books if he be a plutocrat or a capitalist or a miser. No books or dictionaries if he be a mere student. Nothing of his vocations if he lived for 'the world.' But yet the appetite is abiding. Will that not be a thirst that cannot be slaked?

'The world is passing and the lust thereof,' and all that is antagonistic to God, or separated from Him, is essentially as 'a vapour that appeareth for a little time, and then vanishes away,' whereas the man who does the will of God abideth for ever, in that he is steadfast in the midst of change.

'His hand the good man fastens on the skies,
And lets earth roll, nor heeds its idle whirl.'

He shall 'abide for ever,' in the sense that his work is perpetual. In one very deep and solemn sense, nothing human ever dies, but in another all that is not running in the same direction as, and borne along by the impulse of, the will of God, is destined to be neutralised and brought to nothing at last. There may be a row of figures as long as to reach from here to the fixed stars, but if there is not in front of them the significant digit, which comes from obedience to the will of God, all is but a string of ciphers, and their net result is nothing. And he 'abideth for ever,' in the most blessed and profound sense, in that through his faith, which has kindled his love, and his love which has set in motion his practical obedience, he becomes participant of the very eternity of the living God. 'This is eternal life,' not merely to know, but 'to do the will' of our Father. Nothing else will last, and nothing else will prosper, any more than a bit of driftwood can stem Niagara. Unite yourself with the will of God, and you abide.

And now let me, as briefly as I can, throw together—

III. The plain, practical lessons that come from both these texts.

May I say, without seeming to be morbid or unpractical, one lesson is that we should cultivate a sense of the transiency of this outward life? One of our old authors says somewhere, that it is wholesome to smell at a piece of turf from a churchyard. I know that much harm has been done by representing Christianity as mainly a scheme which is to secure man a peaceful death, and that many morbid forms of piety have given far too large a place to the contemplation of skulls and cross-bones. But for all that, the remembrance of death present in our lives will often lay a cool hand upon a throbbing brow; and, like a bit of ice used by a skilful physician, will bring down the temperature, and stay the too tumultuous beating of the heart. 'So teach us to number our days that we may apply our hearts to wisdom.' It will minister energy, and lead us to say, like our Lord, 'We must work the works of Him that sent Me while it is day; the night cometh.'

Let me say again—a very plain, practical lesson is to dig deep down for our foundations below the rubbish that has accumulated. If a man wishes to build a house in Rome or in Jerusalem he has to go fifty or sixty feet down, through potsherds and broken tiles and triturated marbles, and the dust of ancient palaces and temples. We have to drive a shaft clear down through all the superficial strata, and to lay the first stones on the Rock of Ages. Do not build on that which quivers and shakes beneath you. Do not try to make your life's path across the weeds, or as they call it in Egypt, the 'sudd,' that floats on the surface of the Nile, compacted for many a mile, and yet only a film on the surface of the river, to be swept away some day. Build on God.

And the last lesson is, let us see to it that our wills are in harmony with His, and the work of our hands His work. We can do that will in all the secularities of our daily life. The difference between the work that shrivels up and disappears and the work that abides is not so much in its external character, or in the materials on which it is expended, as in the motive from which it comes. So that, if I might so say, if two women are sitting at the same millstone face to face, and turning round the same handle, one of them for one half the circumference, and the other for the other, and grinding out the same corn, the one's work may be 'gold, silver, precious stones,' which shall abide the trying fire; and the other's may be 'wood, hay, stubble,' which shall be burnt up. 'He that doeth the will of God abideth for ever.'

So let us set ourselves, dear friends! to our several tasks for this coming year. Never mind about the century, it will take care of itself. Do your little work in your little corner, and be sure of this, that amidst changes you will stand unchanged, amidst tumults you may stand calm, in death you will be entering on a fuller life, and that what to others is the end will be to you the beginning. 'If any man's work abide, he shall receive a reward,' and he himself shall abide with the abiding God.

The bitter cynic said half the truth when he said, 'One generation goeth, and another cometh; but the earth abides.' The mystic Apostle saw the truth steadily, and saw it whole when he said, 'Lo! the world passeth away, and the lust thereof; but he that doeth the will of God abideth for ever.'

THE PAST AND THE FUTURE

'The thing that hath been, it is that which shall be; and that which is done is that which shall be done: and there is no new thing under the sun.'—ECCLES. i. 9.

'That he no longer should live the rest of his time in the flesh to the lusts of men, but to the will of God. 3. For the time past of our life may suffice us to have wrought the will of the Gentiles.'—1 PETER iv. 2, 3.

If you will look at these two passages carefully you will, I think, see that they imply two different, and in some respects contradictory, thoughts about the future in its relation to the past. The first of them is the somewhat exaggerated utterance of a dreary and depressing philosophy, which tells us that, as in the outer world, so in regard to man's life, there is an enormous activity and no advance, that it is all moving round like the scenes in some circular panorama, that after it has gone the round back it comes again, that it is the same thing over and over again, that life is a treadmill, so to speak, with an immense deal of working of muscles; but it all comes to nothing over again. 'The rivers run into the sea and the sea is not full, and where the rivers come from they go back to; and the wind goes to the south, turns to the north, and whirls about continually. Everything is full of labour, and it has all been done before, and there is nothing fresh; everything is flat, stale, and unprofitable.'

Well that is not true altogether, but though it be not true altogether—though it be an exaggeration, and though the inference that is built upon it is not altogether satisfactory and profound—yet the thought itself is one that has a great deal in it that is true and important, and may be very helpful and profitable to us now; for there is a religious way, as well as an irreligious way, of saying there is nothing new under the sun. It may be the utterance of a material, *blasé*, unprofitable, spurious philosophy, or it may be the utterance of the profoundest, and the happiest, and the most peaceful religious trust and confidence.

The other passage implies the opposite notion of man's life, that however much in my future may be just the same as what my past has been, there is a region in which it is quite possible to make to-morrow unlike to-day, and so to resolve and so to work as that 'the time past of our lives' may be different from 'the rest of our time in the flesh'; that a great revolution may come upon a man, and that whilst the outward life is continuous and the same, and the tasks to be done are the same, and the joys the same, there may be such a profound and radical difference in the spirit and motive in which they are done as that the thing that has been is *not* that which shall be, and for us there *may* be a new thing under the sun.

And so just now I think we may take these two passages in their connection—their opposition, and in their parallelism—as suggesting to us two very helpful, mutually completing thoughts about the unknown future that stretches before us—first, the substantial identity of the future with the past; second, the possible total unlikeness of the future and the past.

First then, let us try to get the impress from the first phrase of that conviction, so far as it is true, as to the sameness of the things that are going to be with the things that have been. The immediate connection in which the words are spoken is in regard, mainly, to the outer world, the physical universe, and only secondarily and subordinately in regard to man's life. And I need not remind you how that thought of the absolute sameness and continuous repetition of the past and the future has gained by the advance of physical science in modern times. It seems to be contradicted no doubt by the continual emergence of new things here and there, but they tell us that the novelty is only a matter of arrangement, that the atoms have never had an addition to them since the beginning of things, that all stand just as they were from the very commencement and foundation of all things, and that all that seems new is only a new arrangement, so that the thing which has been is that which shall be. And then there comes up the other thought, upon which I need not dwell for a moment, that the present condition of things round about us is the result of the uniform forces that have been working straight on from the very beginning. And yet, whilst all that is quite true, we come to our own human lives, and we find there the true application of such words as these: to-morrow is to be like yesterday. There is one very important sense in which the opposite of that is true, and no to-morrow can ever be like any yesterday for however much the events may be the same, we are so different that, in regard even to the most well trodden and beaten of our paths of daily life, we may all say, 'We have not passed this way before!' We cannot bring back that which is gone—that which is gone is gone for good or evil, irrevocable as the snow or the perfume of last year's flowers. I dare say there are many here before me who are saying to themselves, 'No! life can never again be what life has been for me, and the only thing that I am quite sure about in regard to to-morrow is that it is utterly impossible that it should ever be as yesterday was!' Notwithstanding, the word of my text is a true word, the thing that hath been is that which shall be. I need not dwell on the grounds upon which the certainty rests, such, for instance, as that the powers which shape to-morrow are the same as the powers which shaped yesterday; that you and I, in our nature, are the same, and that the mighty Hand up there that is moulding it is the same; that every to-morrow is the child of all the yesterdays; that the same general impression will pervade the future as has pervaded the past. Though events may be different the general stamp and characteristics of them will be the same, and when we pass into a new region of human life we shall find that we are not walking in a place where no footprints have been before us, but that all about us the ground is trodden down smooth.

'That which hath been is that which shall be.' Thus, while this is proximately true in regard to the future, let me just for a moment or two give you one or two of the plain, simple pieces of well-worn wisdom which are built upon such a thought. And first of all let me give you this, 'Well, then, let us learn to tone down our expectations of what may be coming to us.' Especially I speak now to the younger portion of my congregation, to whom life is beginning, and to whom it is naturally tinted with roseate hue, and who have a great deal stretching before them which is new to them, new duties, new relationships, new joys. But whilst that is especially true for them it is true for all. It is a strange illusion under which we all live to the very end of our lives, unless by reflection and effort we become masters of it and see things in the plain daylight of common sense, that the future is going somehow or other to be brighter, better, fuller of resources, fuller of blessings, freer from sorrow than the past has been. We turn over each new leaf that marks a new year, and we cannot help thinking: 'Well! perhaps hidden away in its storehouses there may be something brighter and better in store for me.' It is well, perhaps, that we should have that thought, for if we were not so drawn on, even though it be by an illusion, I do not know that we should be able to live on as we do. But don't let us forget in the hours of quiet that there is no reason at all to expect that any of these arbitrary, and conventional, and unreal distinctions of calendars and dates make any difference in that uniform strand of our life which just runs the same, which is reeled off the great drum of the future and on to the great drum of the past, and that is all spun out of one fibre and is one gauge, and one sort of stuff from the beginning to the end. And so let us be contented where we are, and not fancy that when I get that thing that I am looking forward to, when I get into that position I am waiting for, things will be much different from what they are to-day. Life is all one piece, the future and the past, the pattern runs right through from the beginning to the end, and the stuff is the same stuff. So don't you be too enthusiastic, you people who have an eager ambition for social and political advancement. Things will be very much as they are used to be, with perhaps some slow, gradual, infinitesimal approximation to a higher ideal and a nobler standard; but there will be no jump, no breaks, no spasmodic advance. We must be contented to accept the law, that there is no new thing under the sun. As you would lay a piece of healing ice upon the heated forehead, lay that law upon the feverish anticipations some of you have in regard to the future, and let the heart beat more quietly, and with the more contentment for the recognition of that law.

And then I may say, at the same time, though I won't dwell upon it for more than a moment, let us take the same thought to teach us to moderate our fears. Don't be afraid that anything whatever may come that will destroy the substantial likeness between the past and the future; and so leave all those jarring and terrifying thoughts that mingle with all our anticipations of the time to come, leave them very quietly on one side and say, 'Thou hast been my Help leave me not, neither forsake me, O God of my salvation.'

And then there are one or two other points I mean to touch upon, and let me just name them. Do not let us so exaggerate that thought of the substantial sameness of the future and the past as to flatten life and make it dreary and profitless and insignificant. Let us rather feel, as I shall have to say presently, that whilst the framework remains the same, whilst the general characteristics will not be much different, there is room within that uniformity for all possible play of variety and interest, and earnestness and enthusiasm, and hope. They make the worst possible use of this fixity and steadfastness of things who say, as the dreary man at the beginning of the Book of Ecclesiastes is represented as saying, that because things are the same as they will and have been, all is vanity. It is not true. Don't let the uniformity of life flatten your interest in the great miracle of every fresh day, with its fresh continuation of ancient blessings and the steadfast mercies of our Lord.

And let us hold firmly to the far deeper truth that the future will be the same as the past, because God is the same. God's yesterday is God's to-morrow—the same love, the same resources, the same wisdom, the same power, the same sustaining Hand, the same encompassing Presence. 'A thousand years are as one day, and one day as a thousand years'; and when we say there is no new thing under the sun let us feel that the deepest way of expressing that thought is, 'Thou art the same, and Thy steadfast purposes know no alteration.'

Turn to the other side of the thought suggested by the second passage of the text. It speaks to us, as I have said, of the possible entire unlikeness between the future and the past. To-morrow is the child of yesterday—granted; 'whatsoever a man soweth, that shall he reap'—certainly; there is a persistent uniformity of nature, and the same causes working make the future much of the same general structure as all the past has been—be it so; and yet within the limits of that identity there may be breathed into the self-sameness of to-morrow such an entire difference of disposition, temper, motive, direction of life, that my whole life may be revolutionised, my whole being, I was going to say, cleft in twain, my old life buried and forgotten, and a new life may emerge from chaos and from the dead. Of course, the question, Is such an alteration possible? rises up very solemnly to men, to most of them, for I suppose we all of us know what it is to have been beaten time after time in the attempt to shake off the dominion of some habit or evil, and to alter the bearing and the direction of the whole life, and we have to say, 'It is no good trying any longer my life must run on in the channel which I have carved for it; I have made my bed and I must lie on it; I cannot get rid of these things.' And, no doubt, in certain aspects, change is impossible. There are certain limitations of natural disposition which I never can overcome. For instance, if I have no musical ear I cannot turn myself into a musician. If I have no mathematical faculty it is no good poring over Euclid, for, with the best intentions in the world, I shall make nothing of it. We must work within the limits of our natural disposition, and cut our coat according to our cloth. In that respect to-morrow will be as yesterday, and there cannot be any change. And it is quite true that character, which is the great precipitate from the waters of conduct, gets rocky, that habits become persistent, and man's will gets feeble by long indulgence in any course of life. But for all that, admitting to the full all that, I am here now to say to every man and woman in this place, 'Friend, you may make your life from this moment so unlike the blotted, stained, faultful, imperfect, sinful past that no words other than the words of the New Testament will be large enough to express the fact. "If any man be in Christ he is a new creature, old things are passed away."' For we all know how into any life the coming of some large conviction not believed in or perceived before, may alter the whole bias, current, and direction of it; how into any life the coming of a new love not cherished and entertained before, may ennoble and transfigure the whole of its nature; how into any life the coming of new motives, not yielded to and recognised before, may make all things new and different. These three plain principles, the power of conviction, the power of affection, the power of motive, are broad enough to admit of building upon them this great and helpful and hopeful promise to us all—'The time past of our life may suffice us to have wrought the will of the Gentiles,' that 'henceforth we may live the rest of our time in the flesh according to the will of God.'

To you who have been living in the past with little regard to the supreme powers and principles of Christ's love and God's Gospel in Him, I bring the offer of a radical revolution; and I tell you that if you like you may this day begin a life which, though it shall be like yesterday in outward things, in the continuity of some habits, in the continuance of character, shall be all under the influence of an entirely new, and innovating, and renovating power. I ask you whether you don't think that you have had enough, to use the language of my text, in the part of obeying the will of the flesh; and I beseech you that you will let these great principles, these grand convictions which cluster round and explain the cross of Jesus Christ, influence your mind, character, habits, desires, thoughts, actions; that you will yield yourself to the new power of the Spirit of life in Christ, which is granted to us if only we submit ourselves to it and humbly desire it. And to you who have in some measure lived by this mighty influence I come with the message for you and for myself that the time to come may, if we will, be filled very much fuller than it is; 'To-morrow may be as this day, and much more abundant.' I believe in a patient, reflecting, abundant examination of the past. The old proverb says that 'Every man by the time he is forty is either a fool or a physician'; and any man or woman by the time they get ten years short of that age, ought to know where they are weakest, and ought to be able to guard against the weak places in their character. I do not believe in self-examination for the purpose of finding in a man's own character reasons for answering the question, 'Am I a Christian?' But I do believe that no people will avail themselves fully of the power God has given them for making the future brighter and better than the past who have not a very clear, accurate, comprehensive, and penetrating knowledge of their faults and their failures in the past. I suppose if the Tay Bridge is to be built again, it won't be built of the same pattern as that which was blown into the water last week; and you and I ought to learn by experience the places in our souls that give in the tempests, where there is most need for strengthening the bulwarks and defending our natures. And so I say, begin with the abundant recognition of the past, and then a brave confidence in the possibilities of the future. Let us put ourselves under that great renovating Power which is conviction and affection and motive all in one. 'He loved me and gave Himself for me.' And so while we front the future we can feel that, God being in us, and Christ being in us, we shall make it a far brighter and fairer thing than the blurred and blotted past which to-day is buried, and life may go on with grand blessedness and power until we shall hear the great voice from the Throne say, 'There shall be no more death, no more sorrow, no more crying, no more pain, for the former things are passed away, 'Behold! I make all things new.'

TWO VIEWS OF LIFE

'This sore travail hath God given to the sons of man, to be exercised therewith.—ECCLES. i. 13.

'He for our profit, that we might be partakers of His holiness.'—HEBREWS xii. 10.

These two texts set before us human life as it looks to two observers. The former admits that God shapes it; but to him it seems sore travail, the expenditure of much trouble and efforts; the results of which seem to be nothing beyond profitless exercise. There is an immense activity and nothing to show for it at the end but wearied limbs. The other observer sees, at least, as much of sorrow and trouble as the former, but he believes in the 'Father of spirits,' and in a hereafter; and these, of course, bring a meaning and a wider purpose into the 'sore travail,' and make it, not futile but, profitable to our highest good.

I. Note first the Preacher's gloomy half-truth.

The word rendered in our text 'travail' is a favourite one with the writer. It means occupation which costs effort and causes trouble. The phrase 'to be exercised therewith,' rather means to *fatigue themselves*, so that life as looked upon by the Preacher consists of effort without result but weariness.

If he knew it at all, it was very imperfectly and dimly; and whatever may be thought of teaching on that subject which appears in the formal conclusion of the book, the belief in a future state certainly exercises no influence on its earlier portions. These represent phases through which the writer passes on his way to his conclusion. He does believe in 'God,' but, very significantly, he never uses the sacred name 'Lord.' He has shaken himself free, or he wishes to represent a character who has shaken himself free from Revelation, and is fighting the problem of life, its meaning and worth, without any help from Law, or Prophet, or Psalm. He does retain belief in what he calls 'God,' but his pure Theism, with little, if any, faith in a future life, is a creed which has no power of unravelling the perplexed mysteries of life, and of answering the question, 'What does it all mean?' With keen and cynical vision he looks out not only over men, as in this first chapter, but over nature; and what mainly strikes him is the enormous amount of work that is being done, and the tragical poverty of its results. The question with which he begins his book is, 'What profit hath a man of all his labour wherein he laboureth under the sun?' And for answer he looks at the sun rising and going down, and being in the same place after its journey through the heavens; and he hears the wind continually howling and yet returning again to its circuits; and the waters now running as rivers into the sea and again drawn up in vapours, and once more falling in rain and running as waters. This wearisome monotony of intense activity in nature is paralleled by all that is done by man under heaven, and the net result of all is 'Vanity and a strife after wind.'

The writer proceeds to confirm his dreary conclusion by a piece of autobiography put into the mouth of Solomon. He is represented as flinging himself into mirth and pleasure, into luxury and debauchery, and as satisfying every hunger for any joy, and as being pulled up short in the midst of his rioting by the conviction, like a funeral bell, tolling in his mind that all was vanity. 'He gave himself to wisdom, and madness, and folly'; and in all he found but one result—enormous effort and no profit. There seemed to be a time for everything, and a kind of demonic power in men compelling them to toil as with equal energy, now at building up, and now at destroying. But to every purpose he saw that there was 'time and judgment,' and therefore, 'the misery of man was great upon him.' To his jaundiced eye the effort of life appeared like the play of the wind in the desert, always busy, but sometime busy in heaping the sands in hillocks, and sometimes as busy in levelling them to a plain.

We may regard such a view of humanity as grotesquely pessimistic; but there is no doubt that many of us do make of life little more than what the Preacher thought it. It is not only the victims of civilisation who are forced to wearisome monotony of toil which barely yields daily bread; but we see all around us men and women wearing out their lives in the race after a false happiness, gaining nothing by the race but weariness. What shall we say of the man who, in the desire to win wealth, or reputation, lives laborious days of cramping effort in one direction, and allows all the better part of his nature to be atrophied, and die, and passes, untasted, brooks by the way, the modest joys and delights that run through the dustiest lives. What is the difference between a squirrel in the cage who only makes his prison go round the faster by his swift race, and the man who lives toilsome days for transitory objects which he may never attain? In the old days every prison was furnished with a tread-mill, on which the prisoner being set was bound to step up on each tread of the revolving wheel, not in order to rise, but in order to prevent him from breaking his legs. How many men around us are on such a mill, and how many of them have fastened themselves on it, and by their own misreading and misuse of life have turned it into a dreary monotony of resultless toil. The Preacher may be more ingenious than sound in his pessimism, but let us not forget that every godless man does make of life 'Vanity and strife after wind.'

II. The higher truth which completes the Preacher's.

Of course the fragmentary sentence in our second text needs to be completed from the context, and so completed will stand, 'God chastens us for our profit, that we should be partakers of His holiness.' Now let us consider for a moment the thought that the true meaning of life is *discipline*. I say discipline rather than 'chastening,' for chastening simply implies the fact of pain, whereas discipline includes the wholesome *purpose* of pain. The true meaning of life is not to be found by estimating its sorrows or its joys, but by trying to estimate the effects of either upon us. The true value of life, and the meaning of all its tears and of all its joys, is what it makes us. If the enormous effort which struck the Preacher issues in strengthened muscles and braced limbs, it is not 'vanity.' He who carries away with him out of life a character moulded as God would have it, does not go in all points 'naked as he came.' He bears a developed self, and that is the greatest treasure that a man can carry out of multitudinous toils of the busiest life. If we would think less of our hard work and of our heavy sorrows, and more of the loving purpose which appoints them all, we should find life less difficult, less toilsome, less mysterious. That one thought taken to our hearts, and honestly applied to everything that befalls us, would untie many a riddle, would wipe away many a tear, would bring peace and patience into many a heart, and would make still brighter many a gladness. Without it our lives are a chaos; with it they would become an ordered world.

But the recognition of the hand that ministers the discipline is needed to complete the peacefulness of faith. It would be a dreary world if we could only think of some inscrutable or impersonal power that inflicted the discipline; but if in its sharpest pangs we give 'reverence to the Father of spirits,' we shall 'live.' Of course, a loving father sees to his children's education, and a loving child cannot but believe that the father's single purpose in all his discipline is his good. The good that is sought to be attained by the sharpest chastisement is better than the good that is given by weak indulgence. When the father's hand wields the rod, and a loving child receives the strokes, they may sting, but they do not wound. The 'fathers of our flesh chasten us after their own pleasure,' and there may be error and arbitrariness in their action; and the child may sometimes nourish a right sense of injustice, but 'the Father of spirits' makes no mistakes, and never strikes too hard. 'He for our profit' carries with it the declaration that the deep heart of God doth not willingly afflict, and seeks in afflicting for nothing but His children's good.

Nor are these all the truths by which the New Testament completes and supersedes the Preacher's pessimism, for our text closes by unveiling the highest profit which discipline is meant to secure to us as being that we should be 'partakers of His holiness.' The Biblical conception of holiness in God is that of separation from and elevation above the creature. Man's holiness is separation from the world and dedication to God. He is separated from the world by moral perfection yet more than by His other attributes, and men who have yielded themselves to Him will share in that characteristic. This assimilation to His nature is the highest 'profit' to which we can attain, and all the purpose of His chastening is to make us more completely like Himself. 'The fathers of our flesh' chasten with a view to the brief earthly life, but His chastening looks onwards beyond the days of 'strife and vanity' to a calm eternity.

Thus, then, the immortality which glimmered doubtfully in the end of his book before the eyes of the Preacher is the natural inference for the Christian thought of moral discipline as the great purpose of life. No doubt it might be possible for a man to believe in the supreme importance of character, and in all the discipline of life as subsidiary to its development, and yet not believe in another world, where all that was tendency, often thwarted, should be accomplished result, and the schooling ended the rod should be broken. But such a position will be very rare and very absurd. To recognise moral discipline as the greatest purpose of life, gives quite overwhelming probability to a future. Surely God does not take such pains with us in order to make no more of us than He makes of us in this world. Surely human life becomes 'confusion worse confounded' if it is carefully, sedulously, continuously tended, checked, inspired, developed by all the various experiences of sorrow and joy, and then, at death, broken short off, as a man might break a stick across his knee, and the fragments tossed aside and forgotten. If we can say, 'He for our profit that we might be partakers of His holiness,' we have the right to say 'We shall be like Him, for we shall see Him as He is.'

'A TIME TO PLANT'

'A time to plant.'—Eccles. iii. 2.

The writer enumerates in this context a number of opposite courses of conduct arranged in pairs, each of which is right at the right time. The view thus presented seems to him to be depressing, and to make life difficult to understand, and aimless. We always appear to be building up with one hand and pulling down with the other. The ship never heads for two miles together in the same direction. The history of human affairs appears to be as purposeless as the play of the wind on the desert sands, which it sometimes piles into huge mounds and then scatters.

So he concludes that only God, who appoints the seasons that demand opposite courses of conduct, can understand what it all means. The engine-driver knows why he reverses his engine, and not the wheels that are running in opposite directions in consecutive moments according to his will.

Now that is a one-sided view, of course, for it is to be remembered that the Book of Ecclesiastes is the logbook of a voyager after truth, and tells us all the wanderings and errors of his thinking until he has arrived at the haven of the conclusion that he announces in the final word: 'Hear the sum of the whole matter: Fear God, and keep His commandments, for this is the whole duty of man.'

I have nothing to do just now with the conclusion which he arrives at, but the facts from which he starts are significant and important. There are things in life, God has so arranged it, which can only be done fittingly, and for the most part of all, at certain seasons; and the secret of success is the discernment of present duty, and the prompt performance of it.

And this is especially true about your time of life, my young friends. There are things, very important things, which, unless you do them now, the overwhelming probability is that you will never do at all; and the certainty is that you will not do them half as well. And so I want to ask you to look at these words, which, by a legitimate extension of the writer's meaning, and taking them in a kind of parabolic way, may sum up for us the whole of the special duties of youth. 'A time to plant.'

I. Now, my first remark is this: that you are now in the planting time of your lives.

No wise forester will try to shift shrubs or to put them into his gardens or woods, except in late autumn or early spring. And our lives are as really under the dominion of the law of seasons as the green world of the forest and the fields. Speaking generally, and admitting the existence of many exceptions, the years between childhood and, say, two or three-and-twenty, for a young man or woman, for the most part settle the main outline of their character, and thereby determine their history, which, after all, is mainly the outcome of their character.

You have wide possibilities before you, of moulding your characters into beauty, and purity, holiness, and strength.

For one thing, you have got no past, or next to none written all over, which it is hard to erase. You have substantially a clean sheet on which to write what you like. Your stage of life predisposes you in favour of novelty. New things are glad things to you, whereas to us older people a new thought coming into some of our brains is like a new bit of furniture coming into a crowded room. All the other pieces need to be arranged, and it is more of a trouble than anything else. You are flexible and plastic as yet, like the iron running out of the blast furnace in a molten stream, which in half an hour's time will be a rigid bar that no man can bend.

You have all these things in your favour, and so, dear young friends, whether you think of it or not, whether voluntarily or not, I want you to remember that this awful process is going on inevitably and constantly in every one of you. You are planting, whether you recognise the fact or no. What are you planting?

Well, for one thing, you are making *habits*, which are but actions hardened, like the juice that exudes from the pine-tree, liquid, or all but liquid, when it comes out, and when exposed to the air, is solidified and tenacious. The old legend of the man in the tower who got a slim thread up to his window, to which was attached one thicker and then thicker, and so on ever increasing until he hauled in a cable, is a true parable of what goes on in every human life. Some one deed, a thin film like a spider's thread, draws after it a thicker, by that inevitable law that a thing done once tends to be done twice, and that the second time it is easier than the first time. A man makes a track with great difficulty across the snow in a morning, but every time that he travels it, it is a little harder, and the track is a little broader, and it is easier walking. You play with the tiger's whelp of some pleasant, questionable enjoyment, and you think that it will always keep so innocent, with its budding claws not able to draw blood, but it grows—*it grows.* And it grows according to its kind, and what was a plaything one day is a full-grown and ravening wild beast in a while. You are making habits, whatever else you are making, and you are planting in your hearts seeds that will spring and bear fruit according to their kind.

Then remember, you are planting *belief.*—Most of us, I am afraid, get our opinions by haphazard; like the child in the well-known story, whose only account of herself was that 'she expected she growed.' That is the way by which most of you come to what you dignify by the name of your opinions. They come in upon you, you do not know how. Youth is receptive of anything new. You can learn a vast deal more easily than many of us older people can. Set down a man who has never learned the alphabet, to learn his letters, and see what a task it is for him. Or if he takes a pen in his hand for the first time, look how difficult the stiff wrist and thick knuckles find it to bend. Yours is the time for forming your opinions, for forming some rational and intelligent account of yourself and the world about you. See to it, that you plant truth in your hearts, under which you may live sheltered for many days.

Then again, you are planting character, which is not only habit, but something more. You are making *yourselves*, whatever else you are making. You begin with almost boundless possibilities, and these narrow and narrow and narrow, according to your actions, until you have laid the rails on which you travel—one narrow line that you cannot get off. A man's character is, if I may use a chemical term, a 'precipitate' from his actions. Why, it takes acres of roses to make a flask of perfume; and all the long life of a man is represented in his ultimate character. Character is formed like those chalk cliffs in the south, built up eight hundred feet, beetling above the stormy sea; and all made up of the relics of microscopic animals. So you build up a great solid structure—yourself—out of all your deeds. You are making your character, your habits, your opinions.—And you are making your reputation too. And you will not be able to get rid of that. This is the time for you to make a good record or a bad one, in other people's opinions.

And so, young men and women, boys and girls, I want you to remember the permanent effects of your most fleeting acts. Nothing ever dies that a man does. Nothing! You go into a museum, and you will see standing there a slab of red sandstone, and little dints and dimples upon it. What are they? Marks made by a flying shower that lasted for five minutes, nobody knows how many millenniums ago. And there they are, and there they will be until the world is burned up. So our fleeting deeds are all recorded here, in our permanent character. Everything that we have done is laid up there in the testimony of the rocks:—

   'Through our soul the echoes roll,
And grow for ever and for ever.'

You are now living in 'a time to plant.'

II. Notice, in the next place, that as surely as *now* is the time to plant, *then* will be a time to reap.

I do not know whether the writer of my text meant the harvest, when he put in antithesis to my text the other clause, 'and a time to pluck up that which is planted.' Probably, as most of the other pairs are opposites, here, too, we are to see an opposite rather than a result; the destructive action of plucking up, and not the preservative action of gathering a harvest. But, however that may be, let me remind you that there stands, irrefragable, for every human soul and every human deed, this great solemn law of retribution.

Now what lies in that law? Two things—that the results are similar in kind, and more in number. The law of likeness, and the law of increase, both of them belong to the working of the law of retribution. And so, be sure that you will find out that all your past lives on into your present; and that the present, in fact, is very little more than the outcome of the past. What you plant as a youth you will reap as a man. This mysterious life of ours is all sowing and reaping intermingled, right away on to the very end. Each action is in turn the child of all the preceding and the parent of all that follows. But still, though that be true, your time of life is predominantly the time of sowing; and my time of life, for instance, is predominantly the time of reaping. There are a great many things that I could not do now if I wished. There are a great many things in our past that I, and men of my age, would fain alter; but there they stand, and nothing can do away the marks of that which once has been. We have to reap, and so will you some day.

And I will tell you what you will have to reap, as sure as you are sitting in those pews. You will have the enlarged growth of your present characteristics. A man takes a photograph upon a sensitive plate, half the size of the palm of my hand; and then he enlarges it to any size he pleases. And that is what life does for all of us. The pictures, drawn small on the young man's imagination, on the young woman's dreaming heart, be they of angels or of beasts, are permanent; and they will get bigger and bigger and bigger, as get older. You do not reap only as much as you sowed, but 'some sixty fold, and some an hundred fold.'

And you will reap the increased dominion of your early habits. There is a grim verse in the Book of Proverbs that speaks about a man being tied and bound by the chains of his sins. And that is just saying that the things which you chose to do when you were a boy, many of them you will have to do when you are a man; because you have lost the power, though sometimes not the will, of doing anything else. There be men that sow the wind, and they do not reap the wind, but the law of increase comes in and they reap the whirlwind. There be men who, according to the old Greek legend, sow dragon's teeth and they reap armed soldiers. There are some of you that are sowing to the flesh, and as sure as God lives, you will 'of the flesh reap corruption.' 'Whatsoever a man soweth, that,' even here, 'shall he also reap.'

And let me remind you that that law of inheriting the fruit of our doings is by no means exhausted by the experience of life. Whenever conscience is awakened it at once testifies not only of a broken law, but of a living Law-giver; and not only of retribution here, but of retribution hereafter. And I for my part believe that the modern form of Christianity and the tendencies of the modern pulpit, influenced by some theological discussions, about details in the notion of retribution that have been going on of late years, have operated to make ministers of the Gospel too chary of preaching, and hearers indisposed to accept, the message of 'the terror of the Lord.' My dear friends! retribution cannot stop on this side of the grave, and if you are going yonder you are carrying with you the necessity in yourself for inheriting the results of your life here. I beseech you, do not put away such thoughts as this, with the notion that I am brandishing before you some antiquated doctrine, fit only to frighten old women and children. The writer of the Book of Ecclesiastes was no weak-minded, superstitious fanatic. He was far more disposed to scepticism than to fanaticism. But for all that, with all his sympathy for young men's breadth and liberality, with his tolerance for all sorts and ways of living, with all his doubts and questionings, he came to this, and this was his teaching to the young men whom in idea he had gathered round his chair,—'Rejoice, oh young man, in thy youth. And let thy heart cheer thee in the days of thy youth, and walk in the ways of thine heart, and in the sight of thine eyes.' By all means, God has put you into a fair world, and meant you to get all the good out of it. 'But,' and that not as a kill-joy, 'know thou, that for all these things God will bring thee into judgment,' and shape your characters accordingly.

III. Still further, let me say, these things being so, you especially need to ponder them.

That is so, because you especially are in danger of forgetting them. It is meant that young people should live by impulse much more than by reflection.

'If nature put not forth her power
About the opening of the flower,
Who is there that could live an hour?'

The days of calculation will come soon enough; and I do not want to hurry them. I do not want to put old heads upon young shoulders. I would rather see the young ones, a great deal. But I want you not to go down to the level of the beast, living only by instinct and by impulse. You have got brains, you are meant to use them. You have the great divine gift of reason, that looks before and after, and though you have not much experience yet, you can, if you will, reflect upon such things as I have just been saying to you, and take them into your hearts, and live accordingly. My dear young friend! enjoy yourself, live buoyantly, yield to your impulses, be glad for the beautiful life that is unfolding around you, and the strong nature that is blossoming within you. And then take this other lesson, 'Ponder the path of thy feet,' and remember that all the while you dance along the flowery path, you are planting what you will have to reap.

Then, still further, it is especially needful for you that you should ponder these things, because unless you do you will certainly go wrong. If you do not plant good, somebody else will plant evil. An untilled field is not a field that nothing grows in, but it is a field full of weeds; and the world and the flesh and the devil, the temptations round about you and the evil tendencies in you, unless they are well kept down and kept off, are sure to fill your souls full of all manner of seeds that will spring up to bitterness, and poison, and death. Oh! think, think! for it is the only chance of keeping your hearts from being full of wickedness—think what you are sowing, and think what will the harvest be. There are some of you, as I said, sowing to the flesh, young men living impure and wicked lives, and 'their bones are full of the sins of their youth.' There are some of you letting every wind bring the thistledown of vanities, and scatter them all across your hearts, that they may spring up prickly, and gifted with a fatal power of self-multiplication. There are some of you, young men, and young women too, whose lives are divided between Manchester business and that ignoble thirst for mere amusement which is eating all the dignity and the earnestness out of the young men of this city. I beseech you, do not slide into habits of frivolity, licentiousness, and sin, for want of looking after yourselves. Remember, if you do not ponder the path of your feet, you are sure to take the turn to the left.

Again, it is needful for you to ponder these things, for if you waste this time, it will never come back to you any more. It is useless to sow corn in August. There are things in this world that a man can only get when he is young, such as sound education, for instance; business habits, habits of industry, of application, of concentration, of self-control, a reputation which may avail in the future. If you do not begin to get these before you are five-and-twenty, you will never get them.

And although the certainty is not so absolute in regard to spiritual and religious things, the dice are frightfully weighted, and the chances are terribly small that a young man who, like some of you, has passed his early years in church or chapel, in weekly contact with earnest preaching, and has not accepted the Saviour, will do it when he grows old. He may; he may. But it is a great deal more likely that he will not.

IV. The conclusion of the whole matter is, Begin on the spot, to trust and to serve Jesus Christ.

These are the best things to plant—simple reliance upon His death for your forgiveness, upon His power to make you pure and clean; simple submission to His commandment. Oh! dear young friend; if you have these in your hearts everything will come right. You will get habit on your side, and that is much; and you will be saved from a great deal of misery which would be yours if you went wrong first, and then came right.

If you will plant a cutting of the tree of life in your heart it will yield everything to you when it grows. The people in the South Seas, if they have a palm-tree, can get out of it bread and drink, food, clothing, shelter, light, materials for books, cordage for their boats, needles to sew with, and everything. If you will take Jesus Christ, and plant Him in your hearts, everything will come out of that. That Tree 'bears twelve manners of fruits, and yields His fruit every month.' With Christ in your heart all other fair things will be planted there; and with Him in your heart, all evil things which you may already have planted there, will be rooted out. Just as when some strong exotic is carried to some distant land and there takes root, it exterminates the feebler vegetation of the place to which it comes; so with Christ in my heart the sins, the evil habits, the passions, the lusts, and all other foul spawn and offspring, will die and disappear. Take Him, then, dear friend! by simple faith, for your Saviour. He will plant the good seed in your spirit, and 'instead of the briar shall come up the myrtle.' Your lives will become fruitful of goodness and of joy, according to that ancient promise: 'The righteous shall flourish like the palm-tree; he shall grow like a cedar in Lebanon. Those that be planted in the house of the Lord shall flourish in the courts of our God. They shall still bring forth fruit in old age.'

ETERNITY IN THE HEART

'He hath made every thing beautiful in his time: also He hath set the world in their heart.'—ECCLES. iii. 11.

There is considerable difficulty in understanding what precise meaning is to be attached to these words, and what precise bearing they have on the general course of the writer's thoughts; but one or two things are, at any rate, quite clear.

The Preacher has been enumerating all the various vicissitudes of prosperity and adversity, of construction and destruction, of society and solitude, of love and hate, for which there is scope and verge enough in one short human life; and his conclusion is, as it always is in the earlier part of this book, that because there is such an endless diversity of possible occupation, and each of them lasts but for a little time, and its opposite has as good a right of existence as itself; therefore, perhaps, it might be as well that a man should do nothing as do all these opposite things which neutralise each other, and the net result of which is nothing. If there be a time to be born and a time to die, nonentity would be the same when all is over. If there be a time to plant and a time to pluck, what is the good of planting? If there be a time for love and a time for hate, why cherish affections which are transient and may be succeeded by their opposites?

And then another current of thought passes through his mind, and he gets another glimpse somewhat different, and says in effect, 'No! that is not all true—God has made all these different changes, and although each of them seems contradictory of the other, in its own place and at its own time each is beautiful and has a right to exist.' The contexture of life, and even the perplexities and darknesses of human society, and the varieties of earthly condition—if they be confined within their own proper limits, and regarded as parts of a whole—they are all co-operant to an end. As from wheels turning different ways in some great complicated machine, and yet fitting by their cogs into one another, there may be a resultant direct motion produced even by these apparently antagonistic forces.

But the second clause of our text adds a thought which is in some sense contrasted with this.

The word rendered 'world' is a very frequent one in the Old Testament, and has never but one meaning, and that meaning is *eternity*. 'He hath set *eternity* in their heart.'

Here, then, are two antagonistic facts. They are transient things, a vicissitude which moves within natural limits, temporary events which are beautiful in their season. But there is also the contrasted fact, that the man who is thus tossed about, as by some great battledore wielded by giant powers in mockery, from one changing thing to another, has relations to something more lasting than the transient. He lives in a world of fleeting change, but he has 'eternity' in 'his heart.' So between him and his dwelling-place, between him and his occupations, there is a gulf of disproportion. He is subjected to these alternations, and yet bears within him a repressed but immortal consciousness that he belongs to another order of things, which knows no vicissitude and fears no decay. He possesses stifled and misinterpreted longings which, however starved, do yet survive, after unchanging Being and eternal Rest, And thus endowed, and by contrast thus situated, his soul is full of the 'blank misgiving of a creature moving about in worlds not realised.' Out of these two facts—says our text—man's *where* and man's *what*, his nature and his position, there rises a mist of perplexity and darkness that wraps the whole course of the divine actions—unless, indeed, we have reached that central height of vision above the mists, which this Book of Ecclesiastes puts forth at last as the conclusion of the whole matter—'Fear God, and keep His commandments.' If transitory things with their multitudinous and successive waves toss us to solid safety on the Rock of Ages, then all is well, and many mysteries will be clear. But if not, if we have not found, or rather followed, the one God-given way of harmonising these two sets of experiences—life in the transient, and longings for the eternal—then their antagonism darkens our thoughts of a wise and loving Providence, and we have lost the key to the confused riddle which the world then presents. 'He hath made everything beautiful in his time: also He hath set Eternity in their heart, so that no man can find out the work that God maketh from the beginning to the end.'

Such, then, being a partial but, perhaps, not entirely inadequate view of the course of thought in the words before us, I may now proceed to expand the considerations thus brought under our notice in them. These may be gathered up in three principal ones: the consciousness of Eternity in every heart; the disproportion thence resulting between this nature of ours and the order of things in which we dwell; and finally, the possible satisfying of that longing in men's hearts—a possibility not indeed referred to in our text, but unveiled as the final word of this Book of Ecclesiastes, and made clear to us in Jesus Christ.

I. Consider that eternity is set in every human heart.

The expression is, of course, somewhat difficult, even if we accept generally the explanation which I have given. It may be either a declaration of the actual immortality of the soul, or it may mean, as I rather suppose it to do, the consciousness of eternity which is part of human nature.

The former idea is no doubt closely connected with the latter, and would here yield an appropriate sense. We should then have the contrast between man's undying existence and the transient trifles on which he is tempted to fix his love and hopes. We belong to one set of existences by our bodies, and to another by our souls. Though we are parts of the passing material world, yet in that outward frame is lodged a personality that has nothing in common with decay and death. A spark of eternity dwells in these fleeting frames. The laws of physical growth and accretion and maturity and decay, which rule over all things material, do not apply to my true self. 'In our embers is something that doth live.' Whatsoever befalls the hairs that get grey and thin, and the hands that become wrinkled and palsied, and the heart that is worn out by much beating, and the blood that clogs and clots at last, and the filmy eye, and all the corruptible frame; yet, as the heathen said, 'I shall not *all* die,' but deep within this transient clay house, that must crack and fall and be resolved into the elements out of which it was built up, there dwells an immortal guest, an undying personal self. In the heart, the inmost spiritual being of every man, eternity, in this sense of the word, does dwell.

'Commonplaces,' you say. Yes; commonplaces, which word means two things—truths that affect us all, and also truths which, because they are so universal and so entirely believed, are all but powerless. Surely it is not time to stop preaching such truths as long as they are forgotten by the overwhelming majority of the people who acknowledge them. Thank God! the staple of the work of us preachers is the reiteration of commonplaces, which His goodness has made familiar, and our indolence and sin have made stale and powerless.

My brother! you would be a wiser man if, instead of turning the edge of statements which you know to be true, and which, if true, are infinitely solemn and important, by commonplace sarcasm about pulpit commonplaces, you would honestly try to drive the familiar neglected truth home to your mind and heart. Strip it of its generality and think, 'It is true about *me*. *I* live for ever. My outward life will cease, and *my* dust will return to dust—but *I* shall last undying.' And ask yourselves—What then? 'Am I making "provision for the flesh, to fulfil the lusts thereof," in more or less refined fashion, and forgetting to provide for that which lives for evermore? Eternity is in *my* heart. What a madness it is to go on, as if either I were to continue for ever among the shows of time, or when I leave them all, to die wholly and be done with altogether!'

But, probably, the other interpretation of these words is the truer. The doctrine of immortality does not seem to be stated in this Book of Ecclesiastes, except in one or two very doubtful expressions. And it is more in accordance with its whole tone to suppose the Preacher here to be asserting, not that the heart or spirit is immortal, but that, whether it is or no, in the heart is planted the *thought*, the *consciousness* of eternity—and the longing after it.

Let me put that into other words. We, brethren, are the only beings on this earth who can think the thought and speak the word—Eternity. Other creatures are happy while immersed in time; we have another nature, and are disturbed by a thought which shines high above the roaring sea of circumstance in which we float.

I do not care at present about the metaphysical puzzles that have been gathered round that conception, nor care to ask whether it is positive or negative, adequate or inadequate. Enough that the word has a meaning, that it corresponds to a thought which dwells in men's minds. It is of no consequence at all for our purpose, whether it is a positive conception, or simply the thinking away of all limitations. 'I know what God is, when you do not ask me.' I know what eternity is, though I cannot define the word to satisfy a metaphysician. The little child taught by some grandmother Lois, in a cottage, knows what she means when she tells him 'you will live for ever,' though both scholar and teacher would be puzzled to put it into other words. When we say eternity flows round this bank and shoal of time, men know what we mean. Heart answers to heart; and in each heart lies that solemn thought—for ever!

Like all other of the primal thoughts of men's souls, it may be increased in force and clearness, or it may be neglected and opposed, and all but crushed. The thought of God is natural to man, the thought of right and wrong is natural to man—and yet there may be atheists who have blinded their eyes, and there may be degraded and almost animal natures who have seared their consciences and called sweet bitter and evil good. Thus men may so plunge themselves into the present as to lose the consciousness of the eternal—as a man swept over Niagara, blinded by the spray and deafened by the rush, would see or hear nothing outside the green walls of the death that encompassed him. And yet the blue sky with its peaceful spaces stretches above the hell of waters.

So the thought is in us all—a presentiment and a consciousness; and that universal presentiment itself goes far to establish the reality of the unseen order of things to which it is directed. The great planet that moves on the outmost circle of our system was discovered because that next it wavered in its course in a fashion which was inexplicable, unless some unknown mass was attracting it from across millions of miles of darkling space. And there are 'perturbations' in our spirits which cannot be understood, unless from them we may divine that far-off and unseen world, that has power from afar to sway in their orbits the little lives of mortal men. It draws us to itself—but, alas! the attraction may be resisted and thwarted. The dead mass of the planet bends to the drawing, but we can repel the constraint which the eternal world would exercise upon us—and so that consciousness which ought to be our nobleness, as it is our prerogative, may become our shame, our misery, and our sin.

That Eternity which is set in our hearts is not merely the thought of ever-during Being, or of an everlasting order of things to which we are in some way related. But there are connected with it other ideas besides those of mere duration. Men know what perfection means. They understand the meaning of perfect goodness; they have the notion of infinite Wisdom and boundless Love. These thoughts are the material of all poetry, the thread from which the imagination creates all her wondrous tapestries. This 'capacity for the

Infinite,' as people call it—which is only a fine way of putting the same thought as that in our text—which is the prerogative of human spirits, is likewise the curse of many spirits. By their misuse of it they make it a fatal gift, and turn it into an unsatisfied desire which gnaws their souls, a famished yearning which 'roars, and suffers hunger.' Knowing what perfection is, they turn to limited natures and created hearts for their rest. Having the haunting thought of an absolute Goodness, a perfect Wisdom, an endless Love, an eternal Life—they try to find the being that corresponds to their thought here on earth, and so they are plagued with endless disappointment.

My brother! God has put eternity in *your* heart. Not only will you live for ever, but also in your present life you have a consciousness of that eternal and infinite and all-sufficient Being that lives above. You have need of Him, and whether you know it or not, the tendrils of your spirits, like some climbing plant not fostered by a careful hand but growing wild, are feeling out into the vacancy in order to grasp the stay which they need for their fruitage and their strength.

By the make of our spirits, by the possibilities that dawn dim before us, by the thoughts 'whose very sweetness yieldeth proof that they were born for immortality,'—by all these and a thousand other signs and facts in every human life we say, 'God has set eternity in their hearts!'

II. And then turn to the second idea that is here. The disproportion between this our nature, and the world in which we dwell.

The writer of this book (whether Solomon or no we need not stay to discuss) looks out upon the world; and in accordance with the prevailing tone of all the earlier parts of his contemplations, finds in this prerogative of man but another reason for saying, 'All is vanity and vexation of spirit.'

Two facts meet him antagonistic to one another: the place that man occupies, and the nature that man bears. This creature with eternity in his heart, where is he set? what has he got to work upon? what has he to love and hold by, to trust to, and anchor his life on? A crowd of things, each well enough, but each having a *time*—and though they be beautiful in their time, yet fading and vanishing when it has elapsed. No multiplication of *times* will make *eternity*. And so with that thought in his heart, man is driven out among objects perfectly insufficient to meet it.

Christ said, 'Foxes have holes, and birds of the air have nests, but the Son of man hath not where to lay His head'—and while the words have their proper and most pathetic meaning in the history of His own earthly life of travail and toil for our sakes, we may also venture to give them the further application, that all the lower creatures are at rest here, and that the more truly a man is man, the less can he find, among all the shadows of the present, a pillow for his head, a place of repose for his heart. The animal nature is at home in the material world, the human nature is not.

Every other creature presents the most accurate correspondence between nature and circumstances, powers and occupations. Man alone is like some poor land-bird blown out to sea, and floating half-drowned with clinging plumage on an ocean where the dove 'finds no rest for the sole of her foot,' or like some creature that loves to glance in the sunlight, but is plunged into the deepest recesses of a dark mine. In the midst of a universe marked by the nicest adaptations of creatures to their habitation, man alone, the head of them all, presents the unheard-of anomaly that he is surrounded by conditions which do *not* fit his whole nature, which are not adequate for all his powers, on which he cannot feed and nurture his whole being. 'To what purpose is this waste?' 'Hast thou made all men in vain?'

Everything is 'beautiful in its time.' Yes, and for that very reason, as this Book of Ecclesiastes says in another verse, 'Because to every purpose there is time and judgment, therefore the misery of man is great upon him.' It was happy when we loved; but the day of indifference and alienation and separation comes. Our spirits were glad when we were planting; but the time for plucking up that which was planted is sure to draw near. It was blessed to pour out our souls in the effluence of love, or in the fullness of thought, and the time to speak was joyous; but the dark day of silence comes on. When we twined hearts and clasped hands together it was glad, and the time when we embraced was blessed; but the time to refrain from embracing is as sure to draw near. It is good for the eyes to behold the sun, but so certainly as it rolls to its bed in the west, and 'leaves the world to darkness' and to us, do all earthly occupations wane and fade, and all possessions shrivel and dwindle, and all associations snap and drop and end, and the whirligig of time works round and takes away everything which it once brought us.

And so man, with eternity in his heart, with the hunger in his spirit after an unchanging whole, an absolute good, an ideal perfectness, an immortal being—is condemned to the treadmill of transitory revolution. Nothing continueth in one stay, 'For all that *is* in the world, the lust of the flesh, and the lust of the eyes, and the pride of life, is not of the Father, but is of the world. And the world passeth away, and the lust thereof.' It is limited, it is changeful, it slips from under us as we stand upon it, and therefore, mystery and perplexity stoop down upon the providence of God, and misery and loneliness enter into the heart of man. These changeful things, they do not meet our ideal, they do not satisfy our wants, they do not last even our duration.

'The misery of man is great upon him,' said the text quoted a moment ago. And is it not? Is this present life enough for you? Sometimes you fancy it is.

Many of us habitually act on the understanding that it is, and treat all that I have been saying about the disproportion between our nature and our circumstances as not true about them. 'This world not enough for me!' you say—'Yes! it is; only let me get a little more of it, and keep what I get, and I shall be all right.' So then—'a little more' is wanted, is it? And that 'little more' will always be wanted, and besides it, the guarantee of permanence will always be wanted, and failing these, there will be a hunger that nothing can fill which belongs to earth. Do you remember the bitter experience of the poor prodigal, 'he would fain have filled his belly with the husks'? He tried his best to live upon the horny, innutritious pods, but he could not; and after them he still was 'perishing with hunger.' So it is with us all when we try to fill the soul and satisfy the spirit with earth or aught that holds of it. It is as impossible to still the hunger of the heart with that, as to stay the hunger of the body with wise sayings or noble sentiments.

I appeal to your real selves, to your own past experience. Is it not true that, deep below the surface contentment with the world and the things of the world, a dormant but slightly slumbering sense of want and unsatisfied need lies in your souls? Is it not true that it wakes sometimes at a touch; that the tender, dying light of sunset, or the calm abysses of the mighty heavens, or some strain of music, or a line in a book, or a sorrow in your heart, or the solemnity of a great joy, or close contact with sickness and death, or the more direct appeals of Scripture and of Christ, stir a wistful yearning and a painful sense of emptiness in your hearts, and of insufficiency in all the ordinary pursuits of your lives? It cannot but be so; for though it be true that our natures are in some measure subdued to what we work in, and although it is possible to atrophy the deepest parts of our being by long neglect or starvation, yet you will never do that so thoroughly but that the deep-seated longing will break forth at intervals, and the cry of its hunger echo through the soul. Many of us do our best to silence it. But I, for my part, believe that, however you have crushed and hardened your souls by indifference, by ambition, by worldly cares, by frivolous or coarse pleasures, or by any of the thousand other ways in which you can do it—yet there is some response in your truest self to my poor words when I declare that a soul without God is an empty and an aching soul!

These things which, even in their time of beauty, are not enough for a man's soul—have all but a time to be beautiful in, and then they fade and die. A great botanist made what he called 'a floral clock' to mark the hours of the day by the opening and closing of flowers. It was a graceful and yet a pathetic thought. One after another they spread their petals, and their varying colours glow in the light. But one after another they wearily shut their cups, and the night falls, and the latest of them folds itself together, and all are hidden away in the dark. So our joys and treasures, were they sufficient did they last, cannot last. After a summer's day comes a summer's night, and after a brief space of them comes winter, when all are killed and the leafless trees stand silent.

'Bare, ruined choirs, where late the sweet birds sang.'

We cleave to these temporal possessions and joys, and the natural law of change sweeps them away from us one by one. Most of them do not last so long as we do, and they pain us when *they* pass away from us. Some of them last longer than we do, and *they* pain us when we pass away from them. Either way our hold of them is a transient hold, and one knows not whether is the sadder—the bare garden beds where all have done blowing, and nothing remains but a tangle of decay, or the blooming beauty from which a man is summoned away, leaving others to reap what he has sown. Tragic enough are both at the best—and certain to befall us all. We live and they fade; we die and they remain. We live again and they are far away. The facts are *so*. We may make them a joy or a sorrow as we will. Transiency is stamped on all our possessions, occupations, and delights. We have the hunger for eternity in our souls, the thought of eternity in our hearts, the destination for eternity written on our inmost being, and the need to ally ourselves with eternity proclaimed even by the most short-lived trifles of time. Either these things will be the blessing or the curse of our lives. Which do you mean that they shall be for you?

III. These thoughts lead us to consider the possible satisfying of our souls.

This Book of Ecclesiastes is rather meant to enforce the truth of the weariness and emptiness of a godless life, than of the blessedness of a godly one. It is the record of the struggles of a soul—'the confessions of an inquiring spirit'—feeling and fighting its way through many errors, and many partial and unsatisfactory solutions of the great problem of life, till he reaches the one in which he can rest. When he has touched that goal his work is done. And so the devious way is told in the book at full length, while a sentence sets forth the conclusion to which he was working, even when he was most bewildered. 'The conclusion of the whole matter' is 'Fear God and keep His commandments.' That is all that a man needs. It is 'the whole of man.' 'All is' *not* 'vanity and vexation of spirit' *then*—but 'all things work together for good to them that love God.'

The Preacher in his day learned that it was possible to satisfy the hunger for eternity, which had once seemed to him a questionable blessing. He learned that it was a loving Providence which had made man's home so little fit for him, that he might seek the 'city which hath foundations.' He learned that all the pain of passing beauty, and the fading flowers of man's goodliness, were capable of being turned into a solemn joy. Standing at the centre, he saw order instead of chaos, and when he had come back, after all his search, to the old simple faith of peasants and children in Judah, to fear God and keep His commandments, he understood why God had set eternity in man's heart, and then flung him out, as if in mockery, amidst the stormy waves of the changeful ocean of time.

And we, who have a further word from God, may have a fuller and yet more blessed conviction, built upon our own happy experience, if we choose, that it *is* possible for us to have that deep thirst slaked, that longing appeased. We have Christ to trust to and to love. He has given Himself for us that all our many sins against the eternal love and our guilty squandering of our hearts upon transitory treasures may be forgiven. He has come amongst us, the Word in human flesh, that our poor eyes may see the Eternal walking amidst the things of time and sense, and may discern a beauty in Him beyond 'whatsoever things are lovely.' He has come that we through Him may lay hold on God, even as in Him God lays hold on us. As in mysterious and transcendent union the divine takes into itself the human in that person of Jesus, and Eternity is blended with Time; we, trusting Him and yielding our hearts to Him, receive into our poor lives an incorruptible seed, and for us the soul-satisfying realities that abide for ever mingle with and are reached through the shadows that pass away.

Brethren, yield yourselves to Him! In conscious unworthiness, in lowly penitence, let us cast ourselves on Jesus Christ, our Sacrifice, for pardon and peace! Trust Him and love Him! Live by Him and for Him! And then, the loftiest thoughts of our hearts, as they seek after absolute perfection and changeless love, shall be more than fulfilled in Him who is more than all that man ever dreamed, because He is the perfection of man, and the Son of God.

Love Christ and live in Him, taking Him for the motive, the spring, and the very atmosphere of your lives, and then no capacities will languish for lack of either stimulus or field, and no weariness will come over you, as if you were a stranger from your home. For if Christ be near us, all things go well with us. If we live for Him, the power of that motive will make all our nature blossom like the vernal woods, and dry branches break into leafage. If we dwell in Him, we shall be at home wherever we are, like the patriarch who pitched his tent in many lands, but always had the same tent wherever he went. So we shall have the one abode, though its place in the desert may vary—and we shall not need to care whether the encampment be beneath the palm-trees and beside the wells of Elim, or amidst the drought of Marah, so long as the same covering protects us, and the same pillar of fire burns above us.

Love Christ, and then the eternity in the heart will not be a great aching void, but will be filled with the everlasting life which Christ gives, and is. The vicissitude will really become the source of freshness and progress which

God meant it to be. Everything which, when made our all-sufficient portion, becomes stale and unprofitable, even in its time, will be apparelled in celestial light. It shall all be lovely and pleasant while it lasts, and its beauty will not be saddened by the certainty of its decay, nor its empty place a pain when it has passed away.

Take Christ for Saviour and Friend, your Guide and Support through time, and Himself, your Eternity and Joy, then all discords are reconciled—and 'all things are yours—whether the world, or life, or death, or things present, or things to come; all are yours, and ye are Christ's, and Christ is God's.'

LESSONS FOR WORSHIP AND FOR WORK

'Keep thy foot when thou goest to the house of God, and be more ready to hear, than to give the sacrifice of fools: for they consider not that they do evil. 2. Be not rash with thy mouth, and let not thine heart be hasty to utter anything before God: for God is in heaven, and thou upon earth; therefore let thy words be few. 3. For a dream cometh through the multitude of business; and a fool's voice is known by multitude of words. 4. When thou vowest a vow unto God, defer not to pay it; for He hath no pleasure in fools: pay that which thou hast vowed. 5. Better is it that thou shouldest not vow, than that thou shouldest vow and not pay. 6. Suffer not thy mouth to cause thy flesh to sin; neither say thou before the angel, that it was an error: wherefore should God be angry at thy voice, and destroy the work of thine hands? 7. For in the multitude of dreams and many words there are also divers vanities: but fear thou God. 8. If thou seest the oppression of the poor, and violent perverting of judgment and justice in a province, marvel not at the matter: for he that is higher than the highest regardeth; and there be higher than they. 9. Moreover, the profit of the earth is for all: the king himself is served by the field. 10. He that loveth silver shall not be satisfied with silver; nor he that loveth abundance with increase. This is also vanity. 11. When goods increase, they are increased that eat them: and what good is there to the owners thereof, saving the beholding of them with their eyes? 12. The sleep of a labouring man is sweet, whether he eat little or much: but the abundance of the rich will not suffer him to sleep.'—ECCLES. v. 1-12.

This passage is composed of two or perhaps three apparently disconnected sections. The faults in worship referred to in verses 1-7 have nothing to do with the legalised robbery of verse 8, nor has the demonstration of the folly of covetousness in verses 10-12 any connection with either of the preceding subjects. But they are brought into unity, if they are taken as applications in different directions of the bitter truth which the writer sets himself to prove runs through all life. 'All is vanity.' That principle may even be exemplified in worship, and the obscure verse 7 which closes the section about the faults of worship seems to be equivalent to the more familiar close which rings the knell of so many of men's pursuits in this book, 'This also is vanity.' It stands in the usual form in verse 10.

We have in verses 1-7 a warning against the faults in worship which make even it to be 'vanity,' unreal and empty and fruitless. These are of three sorts, arranged, as it were, chronologically. The worshipper is first regarded as going to the house of God, then as presenting his prayers in it, and then as having left it and returned to his ordinary life. The writer has cautions to give concerning conduct before, during, and after public worship.

Note that, in all three parts of his warnings, his favourite word of condemnation appears as describing the vain worship to which he opposes the right manner. They who fall into the faults condemned are 'fools.' If that class includes all who mar their worship by such errors, the church which holds them had need to be of huge dimensions; for the faults held up in these ancient words flourish in full luxuriance to-day, and seem to haunt long-established Christianity quite as mischievously as they did long-established Judaism. If we could banish them from our religious assemblies, there would be fewer complaints of the poor results of so much apparently Christian prayer and preaching.

Fruitful and acceptable worship begins before it begins. So our passage commences with the demeanour of the worshipper on his way to the house of God. He is to keep his foot; that is, to go deliberately, thoughtfully, with realisation of what he is about to do. He is to 'draw near to hear' and to bethink himself, while drawing near, of what his purpose should be. Our forefathers Sunday began on Saturday night, and partly for that reason the hallowing influence of it ran over into Monday, at all events. What likelihood is there that much good will come of worship to people who talk politics or scandal right up to the church door? Is reading newspapers in the pews, which they tell us in England is not unknown in America, a good preparation for worshipping God? The heaviest rain runs off parched ground, unless it has been first softened by a gentle fall of moisture. Hearts that have no dew of previous meditation to make them receptive are not likely to drink in much of the showers of blessing which may be falling round them. The formal worshipper who goes to the house of God because it is the hour when he has always gone; the curious worshipper (?) who draws near to hear indeed, but to hear a man, not God; and all the other sorts of mere outward worshippers who make so large a proportion of every Christian congregation—get the lesson they need, to begin with, in this precept.

Note, that right preparation for worship is better than worship itself, if it is that of 'fools.' Drawing near with the true purpose is better than being near with the wrong one. Note, too, the reason for the vanity of the 'sacrifice of fools' is that 'they know not'; and why do they not know, but because they did not draw near with the purpose of hearing? Therefore, as the last clause of the verse says, rightly rendered, 'they do evil.' All hangs together. No matter how much we frequent the house of God, if we go with unprepared minds and hearts we shall remain ignorant, and because we are so, our sacrifices will be 'evil.' If the winnowing fan of this principle were applied to our decorous congregations, who dress their bodies for church much more carefully than they do their souls, what a cloud of chaff would fly off!

Then comes the direction for conduct in the act of worship. The same thoughtfulness which kept the foot in coming to, should keep the heart when in, the house of God. His exaltation and our lowliness should check hasty words, blurting out uppermost wishes, or in any way outrunning the sentiments and emotions of prepared hearts. Not that the lesson would check the fervid flow of real desire. There is a type of calm worship which keeps itself calm because it is cold. Propriety and sobriety are its watchwords— both admirable things, and both dear to tepid Christians. Other people besides the crowds on Pentecost think that men whose lips are fired by the Spirit of God are 'drunken,' if not with wine, at all events with unwholesome enthusiasm. But the outpourings of a soul filled, not only with the sense that God is in heaven and we on earth, but also with the assurance that He is near to it, and it to Him, are not rash and hasty, however fervid. What is condemned is words which travel faster than thoughts or feelings, or which proceed from hearts that have not been brought into patient submission, or from such as lack reverent realisation of God's majesty; and such faults may attach to the most calm worship, and need not infect the most fervent. Those prayers are not hasty which keep step with the suppliant's desires, when these take the time from God's promises. That mouth is not rash which waits to speak until the ear has heard.

'Let thy words be few.' The heathen 'think that they shall be heard for much speaking.' It needs not to tell our wants in many words to One who knows them altogether, any more than a child needs many when speaking to a father or mother. But 'few' must be measured by the number of needs and desires. The shortest prayer, which is not animated by a consciousness of need and a throb of desire, is too long; the longest, which is vitalised by these, is short enough. What becomes of the enormous percentage of public and private prayers, which are mere repetitions, said because they are the right thing to say, because everybody always has said them, and not because the man praying really wants the things he asks for, or expects to get them any the more for asking?

Verse 3 gives a reason for the exhortation, 'A dream comes through a multitude of business'—when a man is much occupied with any matter, it is apt to haunt his sleeping as well as his waking thoughts. 'A fool's voice comes through a multitude of words.' The dream is the consequence of the pressure of business, but the fool's voice is the cause, not the consequence, of the gush of words. What, then, is the meaning? Probably that such a gush of words turns, as it were, the voice of the utterer, for the time being, into that of a fool. Voluble prayers, more abundant than devout sentiments or emotions, make the offerer as a 'fool' and his prayer unacceptable.

The third direction refers to conduct after worship. It lays down the general principle that vows should be paid, and that swiftly. A keen insight into human nature suggests the importance of prompt fulfilment of the vows; for in carrying out resolutions formed under the impulse of the sanctuary, even more than in other departments, delays are dangerous. Many a young heart touched by the truth has resolved to live a Christian life, and has gone out from the house of God and put off and put off till days have thickened into months and years, and the intention has remained unfulfilled for ever. Nothing hardens hearts, stiffens wills, and sears consciences so much as to be brought to the point of melting, and then to cool down into the old shape. All good resolutions and spiritual convictions may be included under the name of vows; and of all it is true that it is better not to have formed them, than to have formed and not performed them.

Verses 6 and 7 are obscure. The former seems to refer to the case of a man who vows and then asks that he may be absolved from his vow by the priest or other ecclesiastical authority. His mouth—that is, his spoken promise—leads him into sin, if he does not fulfil it (comp. Deut. xxiii, 21, 22). He asks release from his promise on the ground that it is a sin of weakness. The 'angel' is best understood as the priest (messenger), as in Malachi ii.7. Such a wriggling out of a vow will bring God's anger; for the 'voice' which promised what the hand will not perform, sins.

Verse 7 is variously rendered. The Revised Version supplies at the beginning, 'This comes to pass,' and goes on 'through the multitude of dreams and vanities and many words.' But this scarcely bears upon the context, which requires here a reason against rash speech and vows. The meaning seems better given, either by the rearranged text which Delitzsch suggests, 'In many dreams and many words there are also many vanities' (so, substantially, the Auth. Ver.), or as Wright, following Hitzig, etc., has it, 'In the multitude of dreams are also vanities, and [in] many words [as well].' The simile of verse 3 is recurred to, and the whirling visions of unsubstantial dreams are likened to the rash words of voluble prayers in that both are vanity. Thus the writer reaches his favourite thought, and shows how vanity infects even devotion. The closing injunction to 'fear God' sets in sharp contrast with faulty outward worship the inner surrender and devotion, which will protect against such empty hypocrisy. If the heart is right, the lips will not be far wrong.

Verses 8 and 9 have no direct connection with the preceding, and their connection with the following (vs. 10-12) is slight. Their meaning is dubious. According to the prevailing view now, the abuses of government in verse 8 are those of the period of the writer; and the last clauses do not, as might appear at first reading, console sufferers by the thought that God is above rapacious dignitaries, but bids the readers not be surprised if small officials plunder, since the same corruption goes upwards through all grades of functionaries. With such rotten condition of things is contrasted, in verse 9, the happy state of a people living under a patriarchal government, where the king draws his revenues, not from oppression, but from agriculture. The Revised Version gives in its margin this rendering. The connection of these verses with the following may be that they teach the vanity of riches under such a state of society as they describe. What is the use of scraping wealth together when hungry officials are 'watching' to pounce on it? How much better to be contented with the modest prosperity of a quiet country life! If the translation of verse 9 in the Authorised Version and the Revised Version is retained, there is a striking contrast between the rapine of the city, where men live by preying on each other (as they do still to a large extent, for 'commerce' is often nothing better), and the wholesome natural life of the country, where the kindly earth yields fruit, and one man's gain is not another's loss.

Thus the verses may be connected with the wise depreciation of money which follows. That low estimate is based on three grounds, which great trading nations like England and the United States need to have dinned into their ears. First, no man ever gets enough of worldly wealth. The appetite grows faster than the balance at the banker's. That is so because the desire that is turned to outward wealth really needs something else, and has mistaken its object. God, not money or money's worth, is the satisfying possession. It is so because all appetites, fed on earthly things, increase by gratification, and demand ever larger draughts. The jaded palate needs stronger stimulants. The seasoned opium-eater has to increase his doses to produce the same effects. Second, the race after riches is a race after a phantom, because the more one has of them the more people there spring up to share them. The poor man does with one servant; the rich man has fifty; and his own portion of his wealth is a very small item. His own meal is but a small slice off the immense provisions for which he has the trouble of paying. It is so, thirdly, because in the chase he deranges his physical nature; and when he has got his wealth, it only keeps him awake at night thinking how he shall guard it and keep it safe.

That which costs so much to get, which has so little power to satisfy, which must always be less than the wish of the covetous man, which costs so much to keep, which stuffs pillows with thorns, is surely vanity. Honest work is rewarded by sweet sleep. The old legend told of unslumbering guards who kept the treasure of the golden fruit. The millionaire has to live in a barred house, and to be always on the lookout lest some combination of speculators should pull down his stocks, or some change in the current of population should make his city lots worthless. Black care rides behind the successful man of business. Better to have done a day's work which has earned a night's repose than to be the slave of one's wealth, as all men are who make it their aim and their supreme good. Would that these lessons were printed deep on the hearts of young Englishmen and Americans!

NAKED OR CLOTHED?

'As he came forth of his mother's womb, naked shall he return to go as he came, and shall take nothing of his labour, which he may carry away in his hand.'—ECCLES. v. 15.

'... Their works do follow them.'—REV. xiv. 13.

It is to be observed that these two sharply contrasted texts do not refer to the same persons. The former is spoken of a rich worldling, the latter of 'the dead who die in the Lord.' The unrelieved gloom of the one is as a dark background against which the triumphant assurance of the other shines out the more brightly, and deepens the gloom which heightens it. The end of the man who has to go away from earth naked and empty-handed acquires new tragic force when set against the lot of those 'whose works do follow them.' Well-worn and commonplace as both sets of thought may be, they may perhaps be flashed up into new vividness by juxtaposition; and if in this sermon we have nothing new to say, old truth is not out of place till it has been wrought into and influenced our daily practice. We shall best gather the lessons of our text if we consider what we must leave, what we must take, and what we may take.

I. What we must leave.

The Preacher in the context presses home a formidable array of the limitations and insufficiencies of wealth. Possessed, it cannot satisfy, for the appetite grows with indulgence. Its increase barely keeps pace with the increase of its consumers. It contributes nothing to the advantage of its so-called owner except 'the beholding of it with his eyes,' and the need of watching it keeps them open when he would fain sleep. It is often kept to the owner's hurt, it often disappears in unfortunate speculation, and the possessor's heirs are paupers. But, even if all these possibilities are safely weathered, the man has to die and leave it all behind. 'He shall take nothing of his labour which he can carry away in his hand'; that is to say, death separates from all with whom the life of the body brings us into connection.

The things which are no parts of our true selves are ours in a very modified sense even whilst we seem to possess them, and the term of possession has a definite close. 'Shrouds have no pockets,' as the stern old proverb says. How many men have lived in the houses which we call ours, sat on our seats, walked over our lands, carried in their purses the money that is in ours! Is 'the game worth the candle' when we give our labour for so imperfect and brief a possession as at the fullest and the longest we enjoy of all earthly good? Surely a wise man will set little store by possessions of all which a cold, irresistible hand will come to strip him. Surely the life is wasted which spends its energy in robing itself in garments which will all be stripped from it when the naked self 'returns to go as he came.'

But there are other things than these earthly possessions from which death separates us. It carries us far away from the sound of human voices and isolates us from living men. Honour and reputation cease to be audible. When a prominent man dies, what a clatter of conflicting judgments contends over his grave! and how utterly he is beyond them all! Praise or blame, blessing or banning are equally powerless to reach the unhearing ear or to agitate the unbeating heart. And when one of our small selves passes out of life, we hear no more the voice of censure or of praise, of love or of hate. Is it worth while to toil for the 'hollow wraith of dying fame,' or even for the clasp of loving hands which have to be loosened so surely and so soon?

Then again, there are other things which must be left behind as belonging only to the present order, and connected with bodily life. There will be no scope for material work, and much of all our knowledge will be antiquated when the light beyond shines in. As we shall have occasion to see presently, there is a permanent element in the most material work, and if in handling the transient we have been living for the eternal, such work will abide; but if we think of the spirit in which a sad majority do their daily tasks, whether of a more material or of a more intellectual sort, we must recognise that a very large proportion of all the business of life must come to an end here. There is nothing in it that will stand the voyage across the great deep, or that can survive in the order of things to which we go. What is a man to do in another world, supposing there is another world, where ledgers and mills are out of date? Or what has a scholar or scientist to do in a state of things where there is no place for dictionaries and grammars, for acute criticism, or for a careful scientific research?

Physical science, linguistic knowledge, political wisdom, will be antiquated. The poetry which glorifies afresh and interprets the present will have lost its meaning. Half the problems that torture us here will cease to have existence, and most of the other half will have been solved by simple change of position. 'Whether there be tongues, they shall cease; whether there be knowledge, it shall vanish away'; and it becomes us all to bethink ourselves whether there is anything in our lives that we can carry away when all that is 'of the earth earthy' has sunk into nothingness.

II. What we must take.

We must take *ourselves*. It is the same 'he' who goes 'naked as he came'; it is the same 'he' who 'came from his mother's womb,' and is 'born again' as it were into a new life, only 'he' has by his earthly life been developed and revealed. The plant has flowered and fruited. What was mere potentiality has become fact. There is now fixed character. The transient possessions, relationships, and occupations of the earthly life are gone, but the man that they have made is there. And in the character there are predominant habits which insist upon having their sway, and a memory of which, as we may believe, there is written indelibly all the past. Whatever death may strip from us, there is no reason to suppose that it touches the consciousness and personal identity, or the prevailing set and inclination of our characters. And if we do indeed pass into another life 'not in entire forgetfulness, and not in utter nakedness,' but carrying a perfected memory and clothed in a garment woven of all our past actions, there needs no more to bring about a solemn and continuous act of judgment.

III. What we may take.

'Their works do follow them.' These are the words of the Spirit concerning 'the dead who die in the Lord.' We need not fear marring the great truth that 'not by works of righteousness but by His mercy He saved us,' if we firmly grasp the large assurance which this text blessedly contains. A Christian man's works are perpetual in the measure in which they harmonise with the divine will, in the measure they have eternal consequences in himself whatever they may have on others. If we live opening our minds and hearts to the influx of the divine power 'that worketh in us both to will and to do of His good pleasure,' then we may be humbly sure that these 'works' are eternal; and though they will never constitute the ground of our acceptance, they will never fail to secure 'a great recompence of reward.' To many a humble saint there will be a moment of wondering thankfulness when he sees these his 'children whom God hath given him' clustered round him, and has to say, 'Lord, when saw I Thee naked, or in prison, and visited Thee?' There will be many an apocalypse of grateful surprise in the revelations of the heavens. We remember Milton's noble explanation of these great words which may well silence our feeble attempts to enforce them—

'Thy works and alms and all thy good endeavour
Stood not behind, nor in the grave were trod,
But as faith pointed with her golden rod,
Followed them up to joy and bliss for ever.'

So then, life here and yonder will for the Christian soul be one continuous whole, only that there, while 'their works do follow them,' 'they rest from their labours.'

FINIS CORONAT OPUS

'Better is the end of a thing than the beginning.'—ECCLES. vii. 8.

This Book of Ecclesiastes is the record of a quest after the chief good. The Preacher tries one thing after another, and tells his experiences. Amongst these are many blunders. It is the final lesson which he would have us learn, not the errors through which he reached it. 'The conclusion of the whole matter' is what he would commend to us, and to it he cleaves his way through a number of bitter exaggerations and of partial truths and of unmingled errors. The text is one of a string of paradoxical sayings, some of them very true and beautiful, some of them doubtful, but all of them the kind of things which used-up men are wont to say—the salt which is left in the pool when the tide is gone down. The text is the utterance of a wearied man who has had so many disappointments, and seen so many fair beginnings overclouded, and so many ships going out of port with flying flags and foundering at sea, that he thinks nothing good till it is ended; little worth beginning—rest and freedom from all external cares and duties best; and, best of all, to be dead, and have done with the whole coil. Obviously, 'the end of a thing' here is the parallel to 'the day of death' in verse 1, which is there preferred to 'the day of one's birth.' That is the godless, worn-out worldling's view of the matter, which is infinitely sad, and absolutely untrue.

But from another point of view there is a truth in these words. The life which is lived for God, which is rooted in Christ, a life of self-denial, of love, of purity, of strenuous 'pressing towards the mark,' is better in its 'end' than in its 'beginning.' To such a life we are all called, and it is possible for each. May my poor words help some of us to make it ours.

I. Then our life has an end.

It is hard for any of us to realise this in the midst of the rush and pressure of daily duty; and it is not altogether wholesome to think much about it; but it is still more harmful to put it out of our sight, as so many of us do, and to go on habitually as if there would never come a time when we shall cease to be where we have been so long, and when there will no more arise the daily calls to transitory occupations. The thought of the certainty and nearness of that end has often become a stimulus to wild, sensuous living, as the history of the relaxation of morality in pestilences, and in times when war stalked through the land, has abundantly shown. 'Let us eat and drink, for tomorrow we die,' is plainly a way of reasoning that appeals to the average man. But the entire forgetfulness that there is an end is no less harmful, and is apt to lead to over-indulgence in sensuous desires as the other extreme. Perhaps the young need more especially to be recalled to the thought of the 'end' because they are more especially likely to forget it, and because it is specially worth their while to remember it. They have still the long stretch before the 'end' before them, to make of it what they will. Whereas for us who are further on in the course, there is less time and opportunity to shape our path with a view to its close, and to those of us in old age, there is but little need to preach remembrance of what has come so close to us. It is to the young man that the Preacher proffers his final advice, to 'rejoice in his health, and to walk in the ways of his heart, and in the sight of his eyes,' but withal to know that 'for these God will bring him into judgment.'

And in that counsel is involved the thought that 'the end which is better than the beginning' is neither old age, with its limitations and compulsory abstinences, nor death, which is, as the dreary creed of the book in its central portions believes it to be, the close of all things, but, beyond these, the state in which men will reap as they have sown, and inherit what they have earned. It is that condition which gives all its importance to death—the porter who opens the door into a future life of recompence.

II. The end will, in many respects, not be better than the beginning.

Put side by side the infant and the old man. Think of the undeveloped strength, the smooth cheek, the ruddy complexion, the rejoicing in physical well-being, of the one, with the failing senses, the tottering limbs, the lowered vitality, the many pains and aches, of the other. In these respects the end is worse than the beginning. Or go a step further onwards in life, and think of youth, with its unworn energy, and the wearied longing for rest which comes at the end; of youth, with its quick, open receptiveness for all impressions, and the horny surface of callousness which has overgrown the mind of the old; of youth, with its undeveloped powers and endless possibilities, which in the old have become rigid and fixed; of youth, with the rich gift before it of a continent of time, which in the old has been washed away by the ocean, till there is but a crumbling bank still to stand on; of youth, with its wealth of hopes, and of the hopes of the old, which are solemn ventures, few and scanty—and then say if the end is not worse than the beginning.

And if we go further, and think of death as the end, is it not in a very real and terrible sense, loss, loss? It is loss to be taken out of the world, to 'leave the warm precincts and the cheerful day,' to lose friends and lovers, and to be banned into a dreary land. Yet, further, the thought of the end as being a state of retribution strikes upon all hearts as being solemn and terrible.

III. Yet the end may be better.

The sensuous indulgence which Ecclesiastes preaches in its earlier portions will never lead to such an end. It breeds disgust of life, as the examples of in all ages, and today, abundantly shows. Epicurean selfishness leads to weariness of all effort and work. If we are unwise enough to make either of these our guides in life, the only desirable end will be the utter cessation of being and consciousness.

But there is a better sense in which this paradoxical saying is simple truth, and that sense is one which it is possible for us all to realise. What sort of end would that be, the brightness of which would far outshine the joy when a man-child is born into the world? Would it not be a birth into a better life than that which fills and often disturbs the 'threescore years and ten' here? Would it not be an end to a course in which all our nature would be fully developed and all opportunities of growth and activity had been used to the full? which had secured all that we could possess? which had happy memories and calm hopes? Would it not be an end which brought with it communion with the Highest—joys that could never fade, activities that could never weary? Surely the Christian heaven is better than earth; and that heaven may be ours.

That supreme and perfect end will be reached by us through faith in Christ, and through union by faith with Him. If we are joined to the Lord and are one with Him, our end in glory will be as much better than this our beginning on earth as the full glory of a summer's day transcends the fogs and frosts of dreary winter. 'The path of the just is as the shining light, which shineth more and more unto the perfect day.'

If the end is not better than the beginning, it will be infinitely worse. Golden opportunities will be gone; wasted years will be irrevocable. Bright lights will be burnt out; sin will be graven on the memory; remorse will be bitter; evil habits which cannot be gratified will torment; a wearied soul, a darkened understanding, a rebellious heart, will make the end awfully, infinitely, always worse than the beginning. From all these Jesus Christ can save us; and, full as He fills the cup of life as we travel along the road, He keeps the best wine till the last, and makes 'the end of a thing better than the beginning.'

MISUSED RESPITE

'Because sentence against an evil work is not executed speedily, therefore the heart of the sons of men is fully set in them to do evil'—ECCLES. viii. 11.

When the Pharaoh of the Exodus saw there was respite, he hardened his heart. Abject in his fear before Moses, he was ready to promise anything;

insolent in his pride, he swallows down his promises as soon as fear is eased, his repentance and his retractation of it combined to add new weights about his neck. He was but a conspicuous example of a universal fault. Every nation, I suppose, has its proverb scoffing at the contrast between the sick man's vow and the recovered man's sins. The bitter moralist of the Old Testament was sure not to let such an instance of man's inconceivable levity pass unnoticed. His settled habit of dragging to light the seamy side of human nature was sure to fall on this illustration of it as congenial food. He has wrapped up here in these curt, bitter words a whole theory of man's condition, of God's providence, of its abuse, and of the end to which it all tends.

I. Note the delay in executing sentence.

Every 'evil work' is already sentenced. 'He that believeth not,' said Christ, 'is condemned already'; and that is one case of a general truth. The text writes the sentence as passed, though the execution is for a time suspended. What is the underlying fact expressed by this metaphor? God's thorough knowledge of, and displeasure at, every evil. When one sees vile things done on earth, and no bolt coming out of the clear sky, it is not easy to believe that all the foulness is known to God; but His eye reaches further than He wills to stretch His arm. He sits a silent Onlooker and beholds; the silence does not argue indifference. The sentence is pronounced, but the execution is delayed. It is not wholly delayed, for there are consequences which immediately dog our evil deeds, and are, as it were, premonitions of a yet more complete penalty. But in the present order of things the connection between a man's evil-doing and suffering is, on the whole, slight, obscure, and partial. Evil triumphs; goodness not seldom suffers. If one thinks for a moment of the manifold evils of the world, which swathe it, as it were, in an atmosphere of woe—the wars, the slavery, the oppressions, the private sorrows—and then thinks that there is a God who lets all these go on from generation to generation, we seem to be in the presence of a mystery of mysteries. The Psalmist of old exclaimed in adoring wonder, 'Thy judgments are a great deep'; but the absence of His judgments seems to open a profounder abyss into which even the great mountains of His righteousness appear in danger of falling.

II. The reasons for this delay.

It is not only a mystery, but it is a 'mystery of love.' We can see but a little way into it, but we can see so far as to be sure that the apparent passivity of God, which looks like leaving evil to work its unhindered will, is the silence of a God who 'doth not willingly afflict,' and is 'slow to anger,' because He is perfect love.

The ground of necessity for the delay in executing the sentence lies, partly, in the probationary character of this present life. If evil-doing was always followed by swift retribution, obedience would be only the obedience of fear, and God does not desire such obedience. It would be impossible that testing could go on at all if at every instant the whole of the consequences of our actions were being realised. Such a condition of things is unthinkable, and would be as confusing, in the moral sphere, as if harvest weather and spring weather were going on together. Again, the great reason why sentence against an evil work is not executed speedily lies in God's own heart, and His desire to win us to Himself by benefits. He does not seek enforced obedience; He neither desires our being wedded to evil, nor our being weighed upon by the consequences of our sin, and so He holds back His hand. It is to be remembered that He not merely does thus restrain the forthcoming of His hand of judgment, but, instead of it, puts forth a hand of blessing. He moves around us wooing us to Himself, and, in patience possessing His spirit, marks all our sins, but loves and blesses still. He gives us the vineyard, though we do not give Him the fruit. Still He is not angry, but sends His messengers, and we stone them. Still He waits: we go on heaping year upon year of rebellious forgetfulness, and no lightning flashes from His eye, no exclamation of wearied-out patience, comes from His lips, no rush of the sudden arrow from His long-stretched bow. The endless patience of God has no explanation but only this, that He loves us too well to leave any means untried to bring us to Him, and that He lingers round us to win our hearts. O rare and unspeakable love, the patient love of the patient God!

III. The abuse of this delay.

We have the knack of turning God's pure gifts into poison, and practise a devilish chemistry by which we distil venom from the flowers of Eden and the roses of the garden of God. I don't suppose that to many men the respite which marks God's dealing with them actually tends to doubts of His righteousness, or of His power, or of His being. We have evidence enough of these; and the apparently counter evidence, arising from the impunity of evil-doers, is fairly enough laid aside by our moral instincts and consciousness, and by the consideration that the mighty sweep of God's providence is too great for us to decide on the whole circle by the small portion of the circumference which we have seen. But what most men do is simply that they permit impunity to deaden their sense of right and wrong, and go on in their course without any serious thought of God's blessings, to jostle Him out of their mind; they *despise the riches of His long-suffering goodness,* and never suffer it to *lead them to repentance.* To the unthinking minds of most of us, the long continuance of impunity lulls us into a dream of its perpetuity. Man's godless ingratitude is as deep a mystery as is God's loving patience. It is strange that, with such constant failure of His love to win, God should still persevere in it. For more than seventy times seven He persists in forgiving the rebellious child who sins against Him, and for more than seventy times seven the child persists in the abuse of the Father's love, which still remains- an abuse of sin above all sins.

IV. The end of the delay.

The sentence is passed. It is impossible that it should not be executed. When God has done all, and sees that the point of hopelessness is reached, or when the time has for other reasons come, then He lets the sentence take effect. He kept back the destroying angels from Sodom, but He sent them forth at last. There is a point in the history of nations and of men when iniquity is 'full,' and when God sees that it is best, on world-wide grounds or personal ones, to end it. So there come for nations and for individuals crises; and the law for the divine working is, 'A short work will the Lord make on the earth.' For long years Noah was building the ark, and exposed to the scoffs of a generation whose sentence had been pronounced and not yet executed; but the day came when he entered into its covert, and 'the flood came and destroyed them all.' For generations He would fain have gathered the people of Jerusalem to His bosom 'as a hen gathereth her chickens under her wings, and they would not'; but the day came when the Roman soldiers cast their torches into the beautiful house where their fathers had praised Him, and sinned against Him, and it was left unto them desolate. Let us not be high-minded nor victims of our levity and inconsiderateness, but fear.

Let us remember too that the intensity of the execution is aggravated by all the sins committed during the delay. By them we 'treasure wrath against the day of wrath.' He says to His angels at last 'Now,' and the sword falls, and justice is done. 'The mills of God grind slowly, but they grind exceeding small.' The sum of the whole matter is, every evil of ours is sentenced already; the punishment is delayed for our sins, and because Christ has died. God is wooing our hearts, and trying to win us to love Him by the holding back of the sentence which we are daily abusing. Shall we not accept His forbearance and take His gifts as tokens of the patient tenderness of His heart? Or are we to be like 'the brutes that perish,' knowing neither the hand that feeds them, nor the hand that kills them. The delay in rendering 'the just recompence of reward' only aggravates its weight when it falls. As in some levers, the slower the motion, the greater the force of the lift.

FENCES AND SERPENTS

'... Whoso breaketh an hedge, a serpent shall bite him.'—ECCLES. x. 8.

What is meant here is, probably, not such a hedge as we are accustomed to see, but a dry-stone wall, or, perhaps, an earthen embankment, in the crevices of which might lurk a snake to sting the careless hand. The connection and purpose of the text are somewhat obscure. It is one of a string of proverb-like sayings which all seem to be illustrations of the one thought that every kind of work has its own appropriate and peculiar peril. So, says the Preacher, if a man is digging a pit, the sides of it may cave in and he may go down. If he is pulling down a wall he may get stung. If he is working in a quarry there may be a fall of rock. If he is a woodman the tree he is felling may crush him. What then? Is the inference to be, Sit still and do nothing, because you may get hurt whatever you do? By no means. The writer of this book hates idleness very nearly as much as he does what he calls 'folly,' and his inference is stated in the next verse—'Wisdom is profitable to direct.' That is to say, since all work has its own dangers, work warily, and with your brains as well as your muscles, and do not put your hand into the hollow in the wall, until you have looked to see whether there are any snakes in it. Is that very wholesome maxim of prudence all that is meant to be learned? I think not. The previous clause, at all events, embodies a well-known metaphor of the Old Testament. 'He that diggeth a pit shall fall into it,' often occurs as expressing the retribution in kind that comes down on the cunning plotter against other men's prosperity, and the conclusion that wisdom suggests in that application of the sentence is, 'Dig judiciously,' but 'Do not dig at all.' And so in my text the 'wall' may stand for the limitations and boundary-lines of our lives, and the inference that wisdom suggests in that application of the saying is not 'Pull down judiciously,' but 'Keep the fence up, and be sure you keep on the right side of it.' For any attempt to pull it down—which being interpreted is, to transgress the laws of life which God has enjoined—is sure to bring out the hissing snake with its poison.

Now it is in that aspect that I want to look at the words before us.

I. First of all, let us take that thought which underlies my text—that all life is given us rigidly walled up.

The first thing that the child learns is, that it must not do what it likes. The last lesson that the old man has to learn is, you must do what you ought. And between these two extremes of life we are always making attempts to treat the world as an open common, on which we may wander at our will. And before we have gone many steps, some sort of keeper or other meets us and says to us, 'Trespassers, back again to the road!' Life is rigidly hedged in and limited. To live as you like is the prerogative of a brute. To live as you ought, and to recognise and command by obeying the laws and limitations stamped upon our very nature and enjoined by our circumstances, is the freedom and the glory of a man. There are limitations, I say—fences on all sides. Men put up their fences; and they are often like the wretched wooden hoardings that you sometimes see limiting the breadth of a road. But in regard to these conventional limitations and regulations, which own no higher authority or lawgiver than society and custom, you must make up your mind even more certainly than in regard of loftier laws, that if you meddle with them, there will be plenty of serpents coming out to hiss and bite. No man that defies the narrow maxims and petty restrictions of conventional ways, and sets at nought the opinions of the people round about him, but must make up his mind for backbiting and slander and opposition of all sorts. It is the price that we pay for obeying at first hand the laws of God and caring nothing for the conventionalities of men.

But apart from that altogether, let me just remind you, in half a dozen sentences, of the various limitations or fences which hedge up our lives on every side. There are the obligations which we owe, and the relations in which we stand, to the outer world, the laws of physical life, and all that touches the external and the material. There are the relations in which we stand, and the obligations which we owe, to ourselves. And God has so made us as that obviously large tracts of every man's nature are given to him on purpose to be restrained, curbed, coerced, and sometimes utterly crushed and extirpated. God gives us our impulses under lock and key. All our animal desires, all our natural tendencies, are held on condition that we exercise control over them, and keep them well within the rigidly marked limits which He has laid down, and which we can easily find out. There are, further, the relations in which we stand, and the obligations and limitations, therefore, under which we come, to the people round about us. High above them all, and in some sense including them all, but loftier than these, there is the all-comprehending relation in which we stand to God, who is the fountain of all obligations, the source and aim of all duty, who encompasses us on every side, and whose will makes the boundary walls within which alone it is safe for a man to live.

We sometimes foolishly feel that a life thus hedged up, limited by these high boundaries on either side, must be uninteresting, monotonous, or unfree. It is not so. The walls are blessings, like the parapet on a mountain road, that keeps the travellers from toppling over the face of the cliff. They are training-walls, as our hydro-graphical engineers talk about, which, built in the bed of a river, wholesomely confine its waters and make a good scour which gives life, instead of letting them vaguely wander and stagnate across great fields of mud. Freedom consists in keeping willingly within the limits which God has traced, and anything else is not freedom but licence and rebellion, and at bottom servitude of the most abject type.

II. So, secondly, note that every attempt to break down the limitations brings poison into the life.

We live in a great automatic system which, by its own operation, largely avenges every breach of law. I need not remind you, except in a word, of the way in which the transgression of the plain physical laws stamped upon our constitutions avenges itself; but the certainty with which disease dogs all breaches of the laws of health is but a type in the lower and material universe of the far higher and more solemn certainty with which 'the soul that sinneth, it shall die.' Wherever a man sets himself against any of the laws of this material universe, they make short work of him. We command them, as I said, by obeying them; and the difference between the obedience and the breach of them is the difference between the engineer standing on his engine and the wretch that is caught by it as it rushes over the rails. But that is but a parable of the higher thing which I want to speak to you about.

The grosser forms of transgression of the plain laws of temperance, abstinence, purity, bring with them, in like manner, a visible and palpable punishment in the majority of cases. Whoso pulls down the wall of temperance, a serpent will bite him. Trembling hands, broken constitutions, ruined reputations, vanished ambitions, wasted lives, poverty, shame, and enfeebled will, death—these are the serpents that bite, in many cases, the transgressor. I have a man in my eye at this moment that used to sit in one of these pews, who came into Manchester a promising young man, a child of many prayers, with the ball at his foot, in one of your great warehouses, the only hope of his house, professedly a Christian. He began to tamper with the wall. First a tiny little bit of stone taken out that did not show the daylight through; then a little bigger, and a bigger. And the serpent struck its fangs into him, and if you saw him now, he is a shambling wreck, outside of society, and, as we sometimes tremblingly think, beyond hope. Young men! 'whoso breaketh an hedge, a serpent shall bite him.'

In like manner there are other forms of 'sins of the flesh avenged in kind,' which I dare not speak about more plainly here. I see many young men in my congregation, many strangers in this great city, living, I suppose, in lodgings, and therefore without many restraints. If you were to take a pair of compasses and place one leg of them down at the Free Trade Hall, and take a circle of half a mile round there, you would get a cavern of rattlesnakes. You know what I mean. Low theatres, low music-halls, casinos, haunts of yet viler sorts—there the snakes are, hissing and writhing and ready to bite. Do not 'put your hand on the hole of the asp.' Take care of books, pictures, songs, companions that would lead you astray. Oh for a voice to stand at some doors that I know in Manchester, and peal this text into the ears of the fools, men and women, that go in there!

I heard only this week of one once in a good position in this city, and in early days, I believe, a member of my own congregation, begging in rags from door to door. And the reason was, simply, the wall had been pulled down and the serpent had struck. It always does; not with such fatal external effects always, but be ye sure of this, 'God is not mocked; "whatsoever a man," or a woman either, "soweth, that shall he also reap."' For remember that there are other ways of pulling down walls than these gross and palpable transgressions with the body; and there are other sorts of retributions which come with unerring certainty besides those that can be taken notice of by others. I do not want to dwell upon these at any length, but let me just remind you of one or two of them.

Some serpents' bites inflame, some paralyse; and one or other of these two things—either an inflamed conscience or a palsied conscience—is the result of all wrongdoing. I do not know which is the worst. There are men and women now in this chapel, sitting listening to me, perhaps half interested, without the smallest suspicion that I am talking about them. The serpent's bite has led to the torpor of their consciences. Which is the worse—to loathe my sin and yet to find its slimy coils round about me, so that I cannot break it, or to have got to like it and to be perfectly comfortable in it, and to have no remonstrance within when I do it? Be sure of this, that every transgression and disobedience acts immediately upon the conscience of the doer, sometimes to stir that conscience into agonies of gnawing remorse, more often to lull it into a fatal slumber.

I do not speak of the retributions which we heap upon ourselves in loading our memories with errors and faults, in polluting them often with vile imaginations, or in laying up there a lifelong series of actions, none of which have ever had a trace of reference to God in them. I do not speak, except in a sentence, of the retribution which comes from the habit of evil which weighs upon men, and makes it all but impossible for them ever to shake off their sin. I do not speak, except in a sentence, of the perverted relations to God, the incapacity of knowing Him, the disregard, and even sometimes the dislike, of the thought of Him which steal across the heart of the man that lives in evil and sin; but I put all into two words—every sin that I do tells upon myself, inasmuch as its virus passes into my blood as *guilt* and as *habit*. And then I remind you of what you say you believe, that beyond this world there lies the solemn judgment-seat of God, where you and I have to give account of our deeds. O brother, be sure of this, 'whoso breaketh an hedge'—here and now, and yonder also—'a serpent shall bite him'!

That is as far as my text carries me. It has nothing more to say. Am I to shut the book and have done? There is only one system that has anything more to say, and that is the gospel of Jesus Christ.

III. And so, passing from my text, I have to say, lastly, All the poison may be got out of your veins if you like.

Our Lord used this very same metaphor under a different aspect, and with a different historical application, when He said, 'As Moses lifted up the serpent in the wilderness, so must the Son of Man be lifted up, that whosoever believeth in Him should not perish, but have eternal life.'

There is Christ's idea of the condition of this world of ours—a camp of men lying bitten by serpents and drawing near to death. What I have been speaking about, in perhaps too abstract terms, is the condition of each one of us. It is hard to get people, when they are gathered by the hundred to listen to a sermon flung out in generalities, to realise it. If I could get you one by one, and 'buttonhole' you; and instead of the plural 'you' use the singular 'thou,' perhaps I could reach you. But let me ask you to try and realise each for himself that this serpent bite, as the issue of pulling down the wall, is true about each soul in this place, and that Christ endorsed the representation. How are we to get this poison out of the blood? Reform your ways? Yes; I say that too; but reforming the life will deliver from the poison in the character, when you cure hydrophobia by washing the patient's skin, and not till then. It is all very well to repaper your dining-rooms, but it is very little good doing that if the drainage is wrong. It *is* the drainage that is wrong with us all. A man cannot reform himself down to the bottom of his sinful being. If he could, it does not touch the past. That remains the same. If he could, it does not affect his relation to God. Repentance—if it were possible apart from the softening influence of faith in Jesus Christ—repentance alone would not solve the problem. So far as men can see, and so far as all human systems have declared, 'What I have written I have written.' There is no erasing it. The irrevocable past stands stereotyped for ever. Then comes in this message of forgiveness and cleansing, which is the very heart of all that we preachers have to say, and has been spoken to most of you so often that it is almost impossible to invest it with any kind of freshness or power. But once more I have to preach to you that Christ has received into His own inmost life and self the whole gathered consequences of a world's sin; and by the mystery of His sympathy, and the reality of His mysterious union with us men, He, the sinless Son of God, has been made sin for us, that we might be made the righteousness of God in Him. The brazen serpent lifted on the pole was in the likeness of the serpent whose poison slew, but there was no poison in it. Christ has come, the sinless Son of God, for you and me. He has died on the Cross, the Sacrifice for every man's sin, that every man's wound might be healed, and the poison cast out of his veins. He has bruised the malignant, black head of the snake with His wounded heel; and because He has been wounded, we are healed of our wounds. For sin and death launched their last dart at Him, and, like some venomous insect that can sting once and then must die, they left their sting in His wounded heart, and have none for them that put their trust in Him.

So, dear brother, here is the simple condition—namely, faith. One look of the languid eye of the poisoned man, howsoever bloodshot and dim it might be, and howsoever nearly veiled with the film of death, was enough to make him whole. The look of our consciously sinful souls to that dear Christ that has died for us will take away the guilt, the power, the habit, the love of evil;

and, instead of blood saturated with the venom of sin, there will be in our veins the Spirit of life in Christ, which will 'make us free from the law of sin and death.' 'Look unto Him and be ye saved, all the ends of the earth!'

THE WAY TO THE CITY

'The labour of the foolish wearieth every one of them, because he knoweth not how to go to the city.'—ECCLES. x. 15.

On the surface this seems to be merely a piece of homely, practical sagacity, conjoined with one of the bitter things which Ecclesiastes is fond of saying about those whom he calls 'fools.' It seems to repeat, under another metaphor, the same idea which has been presented in a previous verse, where we read: 'If the iron be blunt, and he do not whet the edge, then must he put to more strength; but wisdom is profitable to direct.' That is to say, skill is better than strength; brain saves muscle; better sharpen your axe than put yourself into a perspiration, hitting fierce blows with a blunt one. The prerogative of wisdom is to guide brute force. And so in my text the same general idea comes under another figure. Immense effort may end in nothing but tired feet if the traveller does not know his road. A man lost in the woods may run till he drops, and find himself at night in the place from which he started in the morning. The path must be known, and the aim clear, if any good is to come of effort.

That phrase, 'how to go to the city,' seems to be a kind of proverbial comparison for anything that is very plain and conspicuous, just as our forefathers used to say about any obvious truth, that it was 'as plain as the road to London town.' The road to the capital is sure to be a well-marked one, and he must be a fool indeed who cannot see that. So our text, though on the surface, as I say, is simply a sarcasm and a piece of homely, practical sagacity, yet, like almost all the sayings in this Book of Ecclesiastes, it has a deeper meaning than appears on the surface; and may be applied in higher and more important directions. It carries with it large truths, and enshrines in a vivid metaphor bitter experiences which, I suppose, we can all confirm.

I. We consider, first, the toil that tires.

'The labour wearies every one of them.' The word translated 'labour' seems to carry with it both the idea of effort and of trouble. Or to recur to a familiar distinction in modern English, the word really covers both the ground of work and of worry. And it is a sad and solemn thought that a word with that double element in it should be the one which is most truly applicable to the efforts of a large majority of men. I suppose there never was a time in the world's history when life went so fast as it does in these great centres of civilisation and commerce in which you and I live. And it is awful to have to think that the great mass of it all ends in nothing else but tired limbs and exhaustion. That is a truth to be verified by experience, and I am bold to believe that every man and woman in this chapel now can say more or less distinctly 'Amen!' to the assertion that every life, except a distinctly and supremely religious one, is worry and work without adequate satisfying result, and with no lasting issue but exhaustion.

Let us begin at the bottom. For instance, take a man who has avowedly flung aside the restraints of right and wrong and conscience, and does things habitually that he knows to be wrong. Every sin is a blunder as well as a crime. No man who aims at an end through the smoke of hell gets the end that he aims at. Or if he does, he gets something that takes all the gilt off the gingerbread, and all the sweetness out of the success. They put a very evil-tasting ingredient into spirits of wine to prevent its being drunk. The cup that sin reaches to a man, though the wine moveth itself aright and is very pleasant to look at before being tasted, cheats with *methylated* spirits. Men and women take more pains and trouble to damn themselves than ever they do to have their souls saved. The end of all work, which begins with tossing conscience on one side, is simply this—'The labour of the foolish wearieth every one of them.'

Take a step higher—a respectable, well-to-do Manchester man, successful in business. He has made it his aim to build up a large concern, and has succeeded. He has a fine house, carriages, greenhouses; he has 'J.P.' to his name; he stands high in credit and on Change. His name is one that gives respectability to anything that it is connected with. Has he 'come to the city'? Has he got what he thought he would get when he began his career? He has succeeded in his immediate and smaller purpose; has that immediate and smaller purpose succeeded in bringing him what he thought it would bring him? Or has he fallen a victim to those—

'juggling fiends ...
That palter with us in a double sense;
That keep the word of promise to the ear,
And break it to the hope?'

They tell us that if you put down in one column the value of the ore that has been extracted from all the Australian gold-mines, and in another the amount that it has cost to get it, the latter sum will exceed the former. There are plenty of people in Manchester who have put more down into the pit from which they dig their wealth than ever they will get out of it. And their labour, too, leaves a very dark and empty aching centre in their lives, 'and wearieth every one of them.' And so I might go the whole round. We students, so long as our pursuit of knowledge has not in it as supreme, directing motive, and ultimate aim and issue, the glory and the service of

God, come under the lash of the same condemnation as those grosser and lower forms of life of which I have been speaking. But wherever we look, if there be not in the heart and in the life a supreme regard to God and a communion with Him, then this characteristic is common to all the courses, that, whilst they may each meet some immediate and partial necessity of our natures, none of them is adequate for the whole circumference of a man's being, nor any of them able, during the whole duration of that being, to be his satisfaction and his rest. Therefore, I say, all toil, however successful to the view of a shorter range of vision, and however noble—excluding the noblest of all—all toil that ends only in securing that which perishes with the using, or that which we leave behind us here when we pass hence, is condemned for folly and labour that wearies the men who are fools enough to surrender themselves to it.

I need not remind you of the wonderful variety of metaphor under which that threadbare thought, which yet it is so hard for us to believe and make operative in our lives, is represented to us in Scripture. Just let me recall one or two of them in the briefest way. 'Why do ye spend your money for that which is not bread, and your labour for that which profiteth not?' 'They have hewn for themselves cisterns, broken cisterns that can hold no water.' 'Their webs shall not become garments.' That may want a word of explanation. The metaphor is this. You are all like spiders spinning carefully and diligently your web. There is not substance enough in it to make a coat out of. You will never cover yourselves with the product of your own brains or your own efforts. There is no clothing in the spider's webs of a godless life.

Ah! brother, all these earthly aims which some of my friends listening to me now have for the *sole* aims of their lives, are as foolish and as inadequate to accomplish that which is sought for by them, as it would be to seek to quench raging thirst by lifting to the lips a golden cup that is empty. Some of us have a whole sideboard full of such, and vary our pursuits according to inclination and task. Some of us have only one such, but they are all empty, and the lip is parched after the cup has been lifted to it as it was before.

II. And so, consider now, secondly, the foolish ignorance that makes the toil tiresome.

The metaphor of my text says that the reason why the 'fool' is so wearied after the day's march is that he does not in the morning settle where he is going, and how he is to get there; and so, having started to go nowhither, he has got where he started for. He 'does not know how to go to the city'— which, being translated into plain and unmetaphorical English, is just this, that many men wreck their lives for want of a clear sight of their true aim, and of the way to secure it.

There is nothing more tragical than the absence, in the great bulk of men, of anything like deliberate, definite views as to their aim in life, and the course to be taken to secure it. There are two things obviously necessary for success in any enterprise. One is, that there shall be the most definite and clear conception of what is aimed at; and the other, that there shall be a wisely considered plan to get at it. Unless there be these, if you go at random, running a little way for a moment in this direction, and then heading about and going in the other, you cannot expect to get to the goal.

Now, what I want to ask some of my friends here is, Did you ever give ten deliberate minutes to try to face for yourselves, and put into plain words, what you are living for, and how you mean to secure it? Of course I know that you have given thought and planning in plenty to the nearer aims, without which material life cannot be lived at all. I do not suppose that anybody here is chargeable with not having thought enough about how to get on in business, or in their chosen walk of life. It is not that kind of aim which I mean at all; but it is a point beyond it that I want to press upon you. You are like men who would carefully victual a ship and take the best information for their guide as to what course to lie, and had never thought what they were going to do when they got to the port. So you say, 'I am going to be such-and-such a thing.' Well, what then? 'Well, I am going to lay myself out for success.' Be it commercial, be it intellectual, be it social, be it in the sphere of the affections, or whatever it may be. Well, what then? 'Well, then I am going to advance in material prosperity, I hope, or in wisdom, or to be surrounded by loving faces of children and those that are dear to me.' What then? 'Then I am going to die.' What then?

It is not till you get to that last question, and have faced it and answered it, that you can be said to have taken the whole sweep of the circumstances into view, and regulated your course according to the dictates of common sense and right reason. And a terribly large number of us live with careful adaptation of means to ends in regard of all the smaller and more immediately to be realised aims of life, but have never faced the larger question which reduces all these smaller aims to insignificance. The simple child's interrogation which in the well-known ballad ripped the tinsel off the skeleton, and showed war in its hideousness, strips many of your lives of all pretence to be reasonable. 'What good came of it at the last?' Can you answer the question that the infant lips asked, and say, 'This good will come of it at last. That I shall have God for my own, and Jesus Christ in my heart'?

Brother! if I could only get you to this point, that you would take half an hour now to think over what you ought to be, and to ask yourself whether your aims in life correspond to what your aims should be, I should have done more than I am afraid I shall do with some of you. The naturalist can tell when he picks up a skeleton something of the habits and the element of the creature to which it belonged. If it has a hollow *sternum* he knows it is meant to fly. On your nature is impressed unmistakably that your destiny is not to creep, but to soar. Not in vain does the Westminster Catechism lay the foundation of everything in this, the prime question for all men, 'What is the chief end of man?' Ask that, and do not rest till you have answered it.

Then there is another idea connected with this ignorance of my text—viz. that it is the result of folly. Now the words 'folly' and 'foolish' and 'foolishness,' and their opposites, 'wisdom' and 'wise,' in this Book of Ecclesiastes, as in the Book of Proverbs, do not mean merely dull stupidity intellectually, which is a thing for which a man is to be pitied rather than to be blamed, but they always carry besides the idea of intellectual defect, also the idea of moral obliquity. 'The fear of the Lord is the beginning of wisdom'; and, conversely, the absence of that fear is the foundation of that which this writer stigmatises as 'folly' He is not merely sneering at men with small brains and little judgments. There may be plenty of us who are so, and yet are wise unto salvation and possessed of a far higher wisdom than that of this world. But he tells us that so strangely intertwined are the intellectual and moral parts of our nature, that wheresoever there is the obscuration of the latter there is sure to be the perversion of the former, and the man knows not 'how to go to the city' because he is 'foolish.'

That is to say, you go wrong in your judgment about your conduct because you have gone wrong morally. And your blunders about life, and your ignorance of its true end and aim, and your mistakes as to how to secure happiness and blessedness, are your own faults, and are owing to the aversion of your nature from that which is highest and noblest, even God and His service. Therefore you are not only to be pitied because you are out of the road, but to be blamed because you have darkened the eyes of your mind by loving the darkness rather than the light. And you 'do not know how to go to the city,' because you do not want to go to the city, and would rather huddle here in the wilderness, and live upon its poor supplies, than pass within the golden gates. My brethren! the folly which blinds a man to his true aim and mission in life is a folly which has in it the darker aspect of sin, and is punishable as such.

III. Lastly, note the plain path which the foolish miss.

He 'does not know how to go to the city.' What on earth will he be able to see if he cannot see that broad highway, beaten and white, stretching straight before him, over hill and dale, and going right to the gates? A man must be a fool who cannot find the way to London.

The principles of moral conduct are trite and obvious. It is plain that it is better to be good than bad. It is better to be unselfish than selfish. It is better not to live for things that perish, seeing that we are going to last for ever. It is better not to make the flesh our master here, seeing that the spirit will have to live without the flesh some day. It is better to get into training for the world to coma, seeing that we are all drifting thither. All these things are plain and obvious.

Man's destiny for God is unmistakable. 'Whose image and superscription hath it?' said Christ about the coin. 'Caesar's!' 'Then give it to Caesar.' Whose image and superscription hath my heart, this restless heart of mine, this spirit that wanders on through space and time, homeless and comfortless, until it can grasp the Eternal? Who are you meant for? God! And every fibre of your nature has a voice to say so to you if you listen to it. So, then, a godless life such as some of you, my hearers, are contentedly living, ignores facts that are most patent to every man's experience. And while before you, huge 'as a mountain, open, palpable,' are the commonplaces and undeniable verities which declare that every man who is not a God-fearing man is a fool, you admit them all, and, bowing your heads in reverence, let them all go over you and produce no effect.

The road is clearer than ever since Jesus Christ came. He has shown us the city, for He has brought life and immortality to light by the Gospel. He has shown us the road, for His life is the pattern of all that men ought to aim at and to be. The motto of the eternal Son of God, if I may venture upon such a metaphor, is like the motto of the heir-apparent of the English throne, 'I serve.' Lo! 'I come to do Thy will'—and that is the only word which will make a human life peaceful and strong and beautiful. In the presence of His radiant and solitary perfection, men no longer need to wonder, What is the ideal to which conduct and character should be conformed? And Jesus Christ has come to make it possible to go to the city, by that cross on which He bore the burden of all sin, and takes away the sin of the world, and by that Spirit of life which He will impart to our weakness, and which makes our sluggish feet run in the way of His commandments, and not be weary, and walk and not faint.

Take that dear Lord for your revelation of duty, for your Pattern of conduct, for the forgiveness of your sins, for the Inspirer with power to do His will, and then you will see stretching before you, high up above the surrounding desert, so that no lion nor ravenous beast shall go up there, the highway on which the ransomed of the Lord shall walk, 'and the wayfaring man, though a fool, shall not err therein.' 'Blessed are they that wash their robes, that they may enter in through the gates into the City.'

A NEW YEARS SERMON TO THE YOUNG

'Rejoice, O young man, in thy youth, and let thy heart cheer thee in the days of thy youth, and walk in the ways of thine heart, and in the sight of thine eyes: but know thou, that for all these things God will bring thee into judgment.... Remember now thy Creator in the days of thy youth, while the evil days come not, nor the years draw nigh, when thou shalt say, I have no pleasure in them.'—ECCLES. xi. 9; xii. 1.

This strange, and in some places perplexing Book of Ecclesiastes, is intended to be the picture of a man fighting his way through perplexities and half-truths to a clear conviction in which he can rest. What he says in his process of coming to that conviction is not always to be taken as true. Much that is spoken in the earlier portion of the Book is spoken in order to be confuted, and its insufficiency, its exaggerations, its onesidedness, and its half-truths, to be manifest in the light of the ultimate conclusion to which he comes. Through all these perplexities he goes on 'sounding his dim and perilous way,' with pitfalls on this side of him and bogs on that, till he comes out at last upon the open way, with firm ground under foot and a clear sky overhead. These phrases which I have taken are the opening sentences and the final conclusion on which he rests. How then are they meant to be understood? Is that saying, 'Rejoice, O young man! in the days of thy youth, and let thy heart cheer thee in the days of thy youth, and walk in the ways of thine heart and in the sight of thine eyes,' to be taken as a bit of fierce irony? Is this a man taking the maxims of the foolish world about him and seeming to approve of them in order that he may face round at the end with a quick turn and a cynical face and hand them back their maxims along with that which will shatter them to pieces—as if he said, 'Oh, yes! go on, talk your fill about making the best of this world, and rejoicing and doing as you like, dancing on the edge of a precipice, and fiddling, like Nero, whilst a worse fire than that of Rome is burning'? Well, I do not think that is the meaning of it. Though there is irony to be found in the Bible, I do not think that fierce irony like that which might do for the like of Dean Swift, is the intention of the Preacher. So I take these words to be said in good faith, as a frank recognition of the fact that, after all we have been hearing about vanity and vexation of spirit, life is worth living for, and that God means young people to be glad and to make the best of the fleeting years that will never come back with the same buoyancy and elasticity all their lives long. And then I take it that the words added are not meant to destroy or neutralise the concession of the first sentence, but only to purify and ennoble a gladness which, without them, would be apt to be stained by many a corruption, and to make permanent a joy which, without them, would be sure to die down into the miserable, peevish, and feeble old age of which the grim picture follows, and to be quenched at last in death. So there are three words that I take out of this text of mine, and that I want to bring before my young friends as exhortations which it is wise to follow. These are Rejoice, Reflect, Remember. Rejoice—the fitting gladness of youth; reflect—the solemn thought that will guard the gladness from stain; remember—the religion which will make these things ever last.

First of all 'Rejoice.' Do as you like, for that is the English translation of the words, 'Walk in the ways of thine heart and in the sight of thine eyes.' Buoyantly and cheerfully follow the inclinations and the desires which are stamped upon your nature and belong to your time of life. All young things are joyful, from the lamb in the pastures upwards, and are meant to be so. The mere bounding sense of physical strength which leads so many of you young men astray is a good thing and a blessed thing—a blessing to be thankful for and to cherish. Your smooth cheeks, so unlike those of old age, are only an emblem of the comparative freedom from care which belongs to your happy condition. Your memories are not yet like some—a book written within and without with the records of mourning and disappointment and crosses. There are in all probability long years stretching before you, instead of a narrow strip of barren sand, before you come to the great salt sea that is going to swallow you up, as is the case with some of us. Christianity looks with complacency on your gladness, and does not mean to clip the wing of one white-winged pleasure, or to breathe one glimmer of blackness on your atmosphere. You are meant to be glad, but it is gladness in a far higher sense that I want to secure for you, or rather to make you secure for yourselves. God delights in the prosperity and light-hearted buoyancy of His children, especially of His young children. Ah! but I know there are young lives over which poverty or ill-health or sorrows of one kind or another have cast a gloom as incongruous to your time of life as snow in the garden in the spring, that pinches the crocuses and weighs down young green beech-leaves, would be. And if I am speaking to any young man or young woman at this time who by reason of painful outward circumstances has had but a chilling spring and youth, I would say to them, 'don't lose heart'; a cloudy morning often breaks into a perfect day. It is good for a man to have to 'bear the yoke in his youth,' and if you miss joy, you may get grace and strength and patience, which will be a blessing to you all your days. For all that, the ordinary course of things is that the young should be glad, and that the young life should be as the rippling brook in the sunshine. I want to leave upon your minds this impression, that it is all right and all in the order of God's providence, who means every one of you to rejoice in the days of your youth. The text says further, 'Walk in the ways of thine heart.' That sounds very like the unwholesome teaching, 'Follow nature; do as you like; let passions and tastes and inclinations be your guides.'

Well, that needs to be set round with a good many guards to prevent it becoming a doctrine of devils. But for all that, I wish you to notice that that has a great and a religious side to it. You have come into possession of this mystical life of yours, a possession which requires that you must choose what kind of life you will follow. Every one has this awful prerogative of being able to walk in the way of their heart. You have to answer for the kind of way that is, and the kind of heart out of which it has come. But I want to go to more important things, and so with a clear understanding that the joy of youth is all right and legitimate, that you are intended to be glad, and to feel the physical and intellectual spring and buoyancy of early days, let us go on to the next thing. 'Rejoice,' says my text, and it adds, 'Reflect.' It is one of the blessings of your time of life, my young friends, that you do not do much of that. It is one of your happy immunities that you are not yet in the habit of looking at life as a whole, and considering actions and consequences. Keep that spontaneity as long as you can; it is a good thing to keep. But for all that, do not forget this awful thing, that it may turn to exaggeration and excess, and that it needs, like all other good things, to be guarded and rightly used. And so, 'Rejoice,' and 'walk in the sight of thine eyes'; *but*—'know that for all these things God will bring thee to judgment.' Well, now, is that thought to come in (I was going to say, like a mourning-coach driven through a wedding procession) to kill the joys we have been seeming to receive from the former words? Are we taking back all that we have been giving, and giving out instead something that will make them all cower and be quiet, like the singing birds that stop their singing and hide in the leaves when they see the kite in the sky? No, there is no need for anything of the sort. 'For all these things God will bring thee to judgment': that is not the thought that kills, but that purifies and ennobles. Regard being had to the opinions expressed at various points in the earlier portion of this Book, we may be allowed to think of this testimony as having reference to the perpetual judgment that is going on in this world always over every man's life. A great German thinker has it, in reference to the history of nations, that the history of the world is the judgment of the world, and although that is not true if it is a denial of a physical day of judgment, it is true in a very profound and solemn sense with regard to the daily life of every man, that whether there be a judgment-seat beyond the grave or not, and whether this Preacher knew anything about that or no, there is going on through the whole of a man's life, and evolving itself, this solemn conviction, that we are to pass away from this present life. All our days are knit together as one whole. Yesterday is the parent of today, and today is the parent of all the tomorrows. The meaning and the deepest consequence of man's life is that no feeling, no thought that flits across the mirror of his life and heart dies utterly, leaving nothing behind it. But rather the metaphor of the Apostle is the true one, 'That which thou sowest, that shalt thou also reap.' All your life a seed-time, all your life a harvest-time too, for the seed which I sow today is the seed which I have reaped from all my former sowings, and so cause and consequence go rolling on in life in extricable entanglement, issuing out in this, that whatever a man does lives on in him, and that each moment inherits the whole consequence of his former life. And now, you young men and women, you boys and girls, mind! this seed-time is the one that will be most powerful in your lives, and there is a judgment you do not need to die to meet. If you are idle at school, you will never learn Latin when you go to business. If you are frivolous in your youth, if you stain your souls and soil your lives by outward coarse sin here in Manchester in your young days, there will be a taint about you all your lives. You cannot get rid of that brave law that 'Whatever a man sows, that, thirtyfold, sixtyfold, an hundredfold, that shall he also reap'—the same kind, but infinitely multiplied in quantity. Let me therefore name some of the ways in which your joys or pleasures, as lads, as boys and girls, as growing young men and women, will bring you to judgment. Health, that is one; position, that is two; reputation, that is three; character, that is four. Did you ever see them build one of those houses they make in some parts of the country, with concrete instead of stones? Take a spadeful of the mud, and put it into a frame on the wall. When it is dry, take away the frame and the supports, and it hardens into rock. You take your single deeds—the mud sometimes, young men!—pop them on the wall, and think no more about it. Ay, but they stop there and harden there, and lo! a character—a house for your soul to live in—health, position, memory, capacity, and all that. If you have not done certain things which you ought to have done, you will never be able to do them, and there are the materials for a judgment. That is going on every moment, and especially is it going on in the region of your pleasures. If they are unworthy, you are unworthy; if they are gross, and coarse, and low, and animal, they are dragging you down; if they are frivolous and foolish, they are making you a poor butterfly of a creature that is worth nothing and will be of no good to anybody; if they are pure, and chaste, and lofty, and virginal and white, they will make your souls good and gracious and tender with the tenderness and beauty of God.

But that is not all. I am not going to travel beyond the limits of this present life with any words of mine, but as I read this final conclusion in this Book of Ecclesiastes, I think I can perceive that the doubts and the scepticisms about a future life, and the difference between a man and a beast which are spoken of in the earlier chapters, have all been overcome, and the clear conviction of the writer is expressed in these twofold great sayings: 'The spirit shall return unto God who gave it, and the words with which He stamps all His message upon our hearts, the final words of His book'; 'God shall bring every work into judgment with every secret thing.' And I come to you and say, 'I suppose you believe in a state of retribution beyond?' I suppose that most of the young folk I am speaking to now at all events believe that 'Thou wilt come to be our judge,' as the *Te Deum* has it; and that it is this same personal self of mine that is to stand there who is sitting here? God shall bring *thee* into judgment. Never mind what is to come of the body, the quivering, palpitating, personal centre. The very same self that I know myself to be will be carried there. Now, take that with you and lay it to heart, and let it have a bearing on your pleasure. It will kill nothing that deserves to live, it will take no real joy out of a man's life. It will only strain out the poison that would kill you. You turn that thought upon your heart, my friends. Is it like a policeman's bull's-eye turned upon a lot of bad characters hiding under a railway arch in the corner there? If so, the sooner you get rid of the pleasures and inclinations that slink away when that beam of light strikes their ugly faces, the better for yourselves and for your lives. 'Rejoice in the way of thine heart and, that thy joy may be pure, know that for all this God will bring thee into judgment.'

And now my last word, 'Remember God,' says my text. The former two sayings, if taken by themselves, would make a very imperfect guide to life. Self-indulgence regulated by the thought of retribution is a very low kind of life after all. There is something better in this world, and that is work; something higher, and that is duty; something nobler than self-indulgence, and that is self-sacrifice. And so no religion worthy the name contents itself by saying to a man, 'Be good and you will be glad'; but, 'Never mind whether you are glad; be good at any rate, and such gladness as is good for you will come to you, and you can want the rest.' 'Remember thy Creator in the days of thy youth.' Recall God to your thoughts, and keep Him in your mind all the day long. That is wonderfully unlike your life, is it not? Remember thy Creator; shift the centre of your life. What I have been saying might be true of a man, the centre of whose life was himself, and such a man is next door to a devil, for, I suppose, the definition of devil is 'self-engrossed still,' and whosoever lives for himself is dead. Don't let the earth be the centre of your system, but the sun. Do not live to yourselves, or your pleasures will all be ignoble and creeping, but live to God. 'Remember.' Well, then, you and I know a good deal more about God than the writer of the Book of Ecclesiastes did—both about what He is and how to remember Him. I am not going to content myself by taking his point of view, but I must take a far higher and a far better one. If he had been here he would have said 'Remember God.' He would have said, 'Look at God in Jesus Christ, and trust Him and love Him; go to Him as your Saviour, and take all the burden of your past sin and lay it upon His merciful shoulders, and for His dear sake look for forgiveness and cleansing; and then for His dear sake live to serve and bless Him. Never mind about yourself, and do not think much about your gladness. Follow in the footsteps of Him who has shown us that the highest joy is to give oneself utterly away. Love Jesus Christ and trust Him and serve Him, and that will make all your gladness permanent.' There is one

- 488 -

thing I want to teach you. Look at that description, or rather read when you go home the description which follows my text, of that wretched old man who has got no hope in God and no joy, feeble in body, going down to the grave, and dying out at last. That is what rejoicing in the days of thy youth, and walking in the ways of thine own heart, come to when you do not remember God. There is nothing more miserable on the face of this earth than an ill-conditioned old man, who is ill-conditioned because he has lost his early joys and early strength, and has got nothing to make up for them. How many of your joys, my dear young friends, will last when old age comes to you? How many of them will survive when your eye is no longer bright, and your hand no longer strong, and your foot no longer fleet? How many of them, young woman! when the light is out of your eye, and the beauty and freshness out of your face and figure, when you are no longer able for parties, when it is no longer a pastime to read novels, and when the ballroom is not exactly the place for you,—how many of your pleasures will survive? Young man! how many of yours will last when you can no longer go into dissipation, and stomach and system will no longer stand fast living, nor athletics, and the like? Oh! let me beseech thee, go to the ant and consider her ways, who in the summer layeth up for the winter; and do ye likewise in the days of your youth, store up for yourselves that which knows no change and laughs at the decay of flesh and sense. A thousand motives coincide and press on my memory if I had words and time to speak them. Let me beseech you— especially you young men and women of this congregation, of some of whom I may venture to speak as a father to his children, whom I have seen growing up, as it were, from your mothers' arms, and the rest of you whom I do not know so well—Oh! carry away with you this beseeching entreaty of mine at the end. Love Jesus Christ and trust to Him as your Saviour; serve Him as your Captain and your King in the days of your youth. Do not offer Him the fag end of a life—the last inch of the candle that is burning down into the socket. Do it now, for the moments are flying, and you may never have Him offered to you any more. If there is any softening, any touch of conscience in your heart, yield to the impulse and do not stifle it. Take Christ for your Saviour, take Him now—'Now is the accepted time, now is the day of salvation.'

THE CONCLUSION OF THE MATTER

'Remember now thy Creator in the days of thy youth, while the evil days come not, nor the years draw nigh, when thou shalt say, I have no pleasure in them; 2. While the sun, or the light, or the moon, or the stars, be not darkened, nor the clouds return after the rain; 3. In the day when the keepers of the house shall tremble, and the strong men shall bow themselves, and the grinders cease because they are few, and those that look out of the windows be darkened, 4. And the doors shall be shut in the streets, when the sound of the grinding is low, and he shall rise up at the voice of the bird, and all the daughters of musick shall be brought low; 5. Also when they shall be afraid of that which is high, and fears shall be in the way, and the almond tree shall flourish, and the grasshopper shall be a burden, and desire shall fail: because man goeth to his long home, and the mourners go about the streets: 6. Or ever the silver cord be loosed, or the golden bowl be broken, or the pitcher be broken at the fountain, or the wheel broken at the cistern. 7. Then shall the dust return to the earth as it was: and the spirit shall return unto God who gave it.... 13. Let us hear the conclusion of the whole matter: Fear God, and keep His commandments: for this is the whole duty of man. 14. For God shall bring every work into judgment, with every secret thing, whether it be good, or whether it be evil.'—ECCLES. xii. 1-7,13,14.

The Preacher has passed in review 'all the works that are done under the sun,' and has now reached the end of his long investigation. It has been a devious path. He has announced many provisional conclusions, which are not intended for ultimate truths, but rather represent the progress of the soul towards the final, sufficient ground and object of belief and aim of all life, even God Himself. 'Vanity of vanities' is a cheerless creed and a half-truth. Its completion lies in being driven, by recognising vanity as stamped on all creatures, to clasp the one reality. 'All is vanity' apart from God, but He is fullness, and possessed and enjoyed and endured in Him, life is not 'a striving after wind.' Leave out this last section, and this book of so-called 'Wisdom' is one-sided and therefore error, as is modern pessimism, which only says more feebly what the Preacher had said long ago. Take the rest of the book as the autobiography of a seeker after reality, and this last section as his declaration of where he had found it, and all the previous parts fall into their right places.

Our passage omits the first portion of the closing section, which is needed in order to set the counsel to remember the Creator in its right relation. Observe that, properly rendered, the advice in verse 1 is 'remember also,' and that takes us back to the end of the preceding chapter. There the young are exhorted to enjoy the bright, brief blossom-time of their youth, withal keeping the consciousness of responsibility for its employment. In earlier parts of the book similar advice had been given, but based on different grounds. Here religion and full enjoyment of youthful buoyancy and delight in fresh, unhackneyed, homely pleasures are proclaimed to be perfectly compatible. The Preacher had no idea that a devout young man or woman was to avoid pleasures natural to their age. Only he wished their joy to be pure, and the stern law that 'whatsoever a man soweth that shall he also reap' to be kept in mind. Subject to that limitation, or rather that guiding principle, it is not only allowable, but commanded, to 'put away sorrow and evil.' Young people are often liable to despondent moods, which come over them like morning mists, and these have to be fought against. The duty of joy is the more imperative on the young because youth flies so fast, or, as the Preacher says,' is vanity.'

Now these advices sound very like the base incitements to sensual and unworthy delight which poets of the meaner sort, and some, alas! of the nobler in their meaner moments, have presented. But this writer is no teacher of 'Gather ye rosebuds while ye may,' and wicked trash of that sort. Therefore he brings side by side with these advices the other of our passage. That 'also' saves the former from being misused, just as the thought of judgment did.

That possible combination of hearty, youthful glee and true religion is the all-important lesson of this passage. The word for Creator is in the plural number, according to the Hebrew idiom, which thereby expresses supremacy or excellence. The name of 'Creator' carries us back to Genesis, and suggests one great reason for the injunction. It is folly to forget Him on whom we depend for being; it is ingratitude to forget, in the midst of the enjoyments of our bright, early days, Him to whom we owe them all. The advice is specially needed; for youth has so much, that is delightful in its novelty, to think about, and the world, on both its innocent and its sinful side, appeals to it so strongly, that the Creator is only too apt to be crowded out of view by His works. The temptation of the young is to live in the present. Reflection belongs to older heads; spontaneous action is more characteristic of youth. Therefore, they specially need to make efforts to bring clearly to their thoughts both the unseen future and Him who is invisible. The advice is specially suitable for them; for what is begun early is likely to last and be strong.

It is hard for older men, stiffened into habits, and with less power and love of taking to new courses, to turn to God, if they have forgotten Him in early days. Conversion is possible at any age, but it is less likely as life goes on. The most of men who are Christians have become so in the formative period between boyhood and thirty. After that age, the probabilities of radical change diminish rapidly. So, 'Remember ... in the days of thy youth,' or the likelihood is that you will never remember. To say, 'I mean to have my fling, and I shall turn over a new leaf when I am older,' is to run dreadful risk. Perhaps you will never be older. Probably, if you are, you will not want to turn the leaf. If you do, what a shame it is to plan to give God only the dregs of life! You need Him, quite as much, if not more, now in the flush of youth as in old age. Why should you rob yourself of years of blessing, and lay up bitter memories of wasted and polluted moments? If ever you turn to God in your older days, nothing will be so painful as the remembrance that you forgot Him so long.

The advice is further important, because it presents the only means of delivering life from the 'vanity' which the Preacher found in it all. Therefore he sets it at the close of his meditations. This is the practical outcome of them all. Forget God, and life is a desert. Remember Him, and 'the desert will rejoice and blossom as the rose.'

The verses from the middle of verse 1 to the end of verse 7 enforce the exhortation by the consideration of what will certainly follow youth, and advise remembrance of the Creator before that future comes. So much is clear, but the question of the precise meaning of these verses is much too large for discussion here. The older explanation takes them for an allegory representing the decay of bodily and mental powers in old age, whilst others think that in them the advance of death is presented under the image of an approaching storm. Wright, in his valuable commentary, regards the description of the gradual waning away of life in old age, in the first verses, as being set forth under images drawn from the closing days of the Palestinian winter, which are dreaded as peculiarly unhealthy, while verse 4_b_ and verse 5 present the advent of spring, and contrast the new life in animals and plants with the feebleness of the man dying in his chamber and unable to eat. Still another explanation is that the whole is part of a dirge, to be taken literally, and describing the mourners in house and garden. I venture, though with some hesitation, to prefer, on the whole, the old allegorical theory, for reasons which it would be impossible to condense here. It is by no means free from difficulty, but is, as I think, less difficult than any of its rivals.

Interpreters who adopt it differ somewhat in the explanation of particular details, but, on the whole, one can see in most of the similes sufficient correspondence for a poet, however foreign to modern taste such a long-drawn and minute allegory may be. 'The keepers of the house' are naturally the arms; the 'strong men,' the legs; the 'grinding women,' the teeth; the 'women who look out at the windows,' the eyes; 'the doors shut towards the street,' either the lips or, more probably, the ears. 'The sound of the grinding,' which is 'low,' is by some taken to mean the feeble mastication of toothless gums, in which case the 'doors' are the lips, and the figure of the mill is continued. 'Arising at the voice of the bird' may describe the light sleep or insomnia of old age; but, according to some, with an alteration of rendering ('The voice riseth into a sparrow's'), it is the 'childish treble' of Shakespeare. The former is the more probable rendering and reference. The allegory is dropped in verse 5a, which describes the timid walk of the old, but is resumed in 'the almond trees shall flourish'; that is, the hair is blanched, as the almond blossom, which is at first delicate pink, but fades into white. The next clause has an appropriate meaning in the common translation, as vividly expressing the loss of strength, but it is doubtful whether the verb here used ever means 'to be a burden.' The other explanations of the clause are all strained. The next clause is best taken, as in the Revised Version, as describing the failure of appetite, which the stimulating caper-berry is unable to rouse. All this slow decay is accounted for, 'because the man is going to his long home,' and already the poet sees the mourners gathering for the funeral procession.

The connection of the long-drawn-out picture of senile decay with the advice to remember the Creator needs no elucidation. That period of failing powers is no time to begin remembering God. How dreary, too, it will be, if God is not the 'strength of the heart,' when 'heart and flesh fail'! Therefore it is plain common sense, in view of the future, not to put off to old age what will bless youth, and keep the advent of old age from being wretched.

Verses 6 and 7 still more stringently enforce the precept by pointing, not to the slow approach, but to the actual arrival of death. If a future of possible weakness and gradual creeping in on us of death is reason for the exhortation, much more is the certainty that the crash of dissolution will come. The allegory is partially resumed in these verses. The 'golden bowl' is possibly the head, and, according to some, the 'silver cord' is the spinal marrow, while others think rather of the bowl or lamp as meaning the body, and the cord the soul which, as it were, holds it up. The 'pitcher' is the heart, and the 'wheel' the organs of respiration. Be this as it may, the general thought is that death comes, shivering the precious reservoir of light, and putting an end to drawing of life from the Fountain of bodily life. Surely these are weighty reasons for the Preacher's advice. Surely it is well for young hearts sometimes to remember the end, and to ask, 'What will ye do in the end?' and to do before the end what is so hard to begin doing at the end, and so needful to have done if the end is not to be worse than 'vanity.'

The collapse of the body is not the end of the man, else the whole force of the argument in the preceding verses would disappear. If death is annihilation, what reason is there for seeking God before it comes? Therefore verse 7 is no interpolation to bring a sceptical book into harmony with orthodox Jewish belief, as some commentators affirm. The 'contradiction' between it and Ecclesiastes iii. 21 is alleged as proof of its having been thus added. But there is no contradiction. The former passage is interrogative, and, like all the earlier part of the book, sets forth, not the Preacher's ultimate convictions, but a phase through which he passed on his way to these. It is because man is twofold, and at death the spirit returns to its divine Giver, that the exhortation of verse 1 is pressed home with such earnestness.

The closing verses are confidently asserted to be, like verse 7, additions in the interests of Jewish 'orthodoxy.' But Ecclesiastes is made out to be a 'sceptical book' by expelling these from the text, and then the character thus established is taken to prove that they are not genuine. It is a remarkably easy but not very logical process.

'The end of the matter' when all is heard, is, to 'fear God and keep His commandments.' The inward feeling of reverent awe which does not exclude love, and the outward life of conformity to His will, is 'the whole duty of man,' or 'the duty of every man.' And that plain summary of all that men need to know for practical guidance is enforced by the consideration of future judgment, which, by its universal sweep and all-revealing light, must mean the judgment in another life.

Happy they who, through devious mazes of thought and act, have wandered seeking for the vision of any good, and having found all to be vanity, have been led at last to rest, like the dove in the ark, in the broad simplicity of the truth that all which any man needs for blessedness in the buoyancy of fresh youthful strength and in the feebleness of decaying age, in the stress of life, in the darkness of death, and in the day of judgment, is to 'fear God and keep His commandments'!